Strategic Marketing and Management

Strategic Marketing and Management

Edited by

Howard Thomas

and

David Gardner

Department of Business Administration
University of Illinois at Urbana-Champaign

JOHN WILEY & SONS
Chichester · New York · Brisbane · Toronto · Singapore

Library of Congress Cataloging in Publication Data:
Main entry under title:

Strategic marketing and management.

   Papers presented at a conference co-sponsored by the Marketing Education Division of the
American Marketing Association and the Dept. of Business Administration, College of
Commerce and Business Administration at the University of Illinois at Urbana-Champaign, held
May 10–11, 1982 at the university.
   1. Marketing—Congresses. 2. Marketing—Management—Congresses. I. Thomas, H.
(Howard) II. Gardner, David Morgan, 1936–   . III. American Marketing Association.
Marketing Education Division. IV. University of Illinois at Urbana-Champaign. Dept. of
Business Administration.
HF5411.S87   1984   658.8   83-25902

ISBN 0 471 90423 6

British Library Cataloguing in Publication Data:
Strategic marketing and management.
   1. Marketing
   I. Thomas, Howard   II. Gardner, David
   658.8   HF5415

ISBN 0 471 90423 6

Typeset by Activity Ltd., Salisbury, Wilts.
Printed at St Edmundsbury Press Ltd., Suffolk.

Contents

Preface

This volume has developed from a conference organized by the editors of this book and held at the Illini Union, University of Illinois at Urbana-Champaign on 10–11 May, 1982. It was co-sponsored through grants from the Marketing Education Division of the American Marketing Association and the Department of Business Administration and College of Commerce and Business Administration at the University of Illinois at Urbana-Champaign. The original papers were revised, following a referred reviewing process, during the remainder of 1982, and in some cases were subject to futher revision during the first half of 1983.

The aims of the conference set by David Gardner, a Professor of Marketing and Howard Thomas, a Professor of Strategic Management, were to provide a forum for research in strategic marketing and to examine the linkages between strategic marketing and strategic management. In particular, we wished to define the boundaries of the strategic marketing field, to indicate many of the research questions and issues requiring attention and to establish worthwhile linkages between the fields of strategic marketing and strategic management. It is clear from a careful review of the twenty-five papers presented at the Conference that those aims appear to have been achieved. While many of the authors are marketing academics, there is solid evidence of useful cross-fertilization with leading scholars from the strategic management field. Indeed, strategic management experts contributed about one-third of the papers and provided many useful insights during the conference discussion.

It should be emphasized that the final volume is not solely a record of the conference proceedings. Indeed, it is now an integrated volume with some additional textual material, Chapters 1 through 7, and section introductions written by the editors specifically to link the various papers and themes together, and to show the interrelationships between concepts developed in both the fields of strategic marketing and management.

We owe a great intellectual debt to both Lou Pondy, the Head of the Department of Business Administration, and Vern Zimmerman, Dean of the College of Commerce and Business Administration. They have provided a warm and creative atmosphere in which to carry out our work. Their constant personal encouragement and organizational support has also enabled us to bring this volume to a worthwhile and publishable conclusion.

Finally, Tami Meyers has provided administrative and typing support from the conference's inception through to this final volume. We wish to acknowledge her help and professionalism.

Champaign, Illinois, 1983   HOWARD THOMAS
                                                               DAVID GARDNER

Strategic Marketing and Management
Edited by H. Thomas and D. Gardner
© 1985 John Wiley & Sons Ltd

CHAPTER 1
What is Strategic Marketing?

INTRODUCTION

Although marketing as a recognized economic activity certainly dates back to the industrial revolution or even earlier, the formal study of marketing is a rather recent phenomenon. In the somewhat short history of marketing thought, approaches to the study of marketing have focused on the commodity, institutional, functional and managerial approaches. Each approach increased our understanding of marketing and affected its practice.

Both marketing thought and practice are being heavily influenced by the application of a planning oriented philosophy that has the potential not only to clarify what marketing is and does, but to significantly alter and hopefully improve the theory and practice of marketing. This planning oriented philosophy is what has come to be known variously as strategic marketing or marketing strategy.

To appreciate and understand this stage in the development of marketing thought it is necessary to explore briefly the basic premises of the managerial approach to marketing.

The first basic premise of the managerial approach to marketing is that it is necessary for organizations to make conscious, integrated decisions to obtain an appropriate marketing mix for a given target market. The second premise, organized around the rubric of the marketing concept, is that the customer is central and that the organization must identify the needs and wants of its chosen target market in order to provide a product or service to achieve a unique competitive advantage.

While it could be argued that the marketing concept is not widely practiced or that organizations are only customer-oriented under special circumstances, many organizations do seem to subscribe to the marketing concept. The disagreements, however, are most likely the result of perspective. At the functional, or operating level, the marketing concept, out of necessity, is prominent. However, as the distance from the operating level increases, the less likely customers are to be the central issue. Rather, the survival of the organization is seen as most critical. Consequently, decisions may be made to discontinue serving some target groups, reduce levels of service, raise price and/or enter entirely new markets. Under the marketing concept this approach is handled in two ways. First, there is almost always the caveat, 'at a profit' which emphasizes the need to make a profit in serving any particular target market. Second, it has been assumed that new products and services must constantly be introduced to offset the decline of existing products and services for the organization to be viable in the future.

DEFINITIONS OF STRATEGY AND STRATEGIC MARKETING

Strategy and its definitions vary by organizational level. Strategic thinking and the resultant strategy formulation occurs at three levels in the organization (Vancil and Lorange, 1975). These three levels are corporate, business, and functional.

It is argued here that strategic marketing provides an organized and cohesive framework for understanding and improving the managerial approach to marketing and the total practice of marketing. Note that this view implies that the central focus of the marketing concept should be directed primarily to the functional level, leaving the broader issues of what markets are to be served to be determined at the business unit level. Therefore, if a decision is made to serve a particular target market, that decision is based both on demand and on the organization's ability to supply that demand. Given that decision, the marketing concept becomes central to implementing the market entry.

It appears that marketing management and strategic marketing have similar aims—survival at a 'profit' for the organization. However, the current interest in strategic marketing compared to marketing management has been fostered by at least the following four factors.

(1) As corporations adopted a more external, future oriented planning approach, the corporate culture demanded a planning emphasis from all functional areas in the organization, but especially marketing. Except for natural monopolies, organizations prosper or fail by satisfying customers. Therefore, marketing is being forced to give guidance on markets to be entered and exited, as well as to become even more expert at determining the types of products, services, and the implementation of plans necessary for future competitive advantage.

(2) Implicit or explicit realizations that the present age is one of discontinuity. Peter Drucker formally announced this almost 15 years ago (Drucker, 1969). The implications for marketing are that the past is no longer a reliable guide for the future. Trends can be destroyed overnight. Entire markets can emerge or disappear in very short time periods. In particular, three things are apparent. Technology is altering dramatically not only

the products and services offered, but the very manner in which they are distributed. Second, competition is more likely to emerge outside traditionally defined industries. Third, the shift towards a global economy and global competition is apparent (Drucker, 1980).

(3) Increasing managerial familiarity with such strategy concepts as the product life cycle and the growth share matrix.

(4) The corporation, in its dual role of determining the appropriate portfolio of businesses and allocating resources to these businesses, out of necessity, often focused primarily on markets. This emphasis inevitably led to the realization that market potential depends not only on the stage in the product life cycle and the amount of resources devoted to a particular market, but also to how resources were managed or deployed. Consequently, marketing has been 'rediscovered' in many organizations. One of the principal rediscoveries has been market segmentation.

It is not uncommon for a departure or new thrust to proceed for some time with an often confusing variety of definitions. As different people approach this new area they bring their own backgrounds, biases, and reasons for interest. Consequently, some early definitions tend to be very global, others very specific. This seems to be the present situation with regard to strategic marketing and marketing strategy.

Clearly the different perspectives and viewpoints adopted by marketing practitioners, corporate strategists and academics must be reviewed for clues about the nature of strategic marketing. For example, marketing practitioners describe their activities. Textbook writers define marketing. Corporate strategists make assumptions about marketing. Various studies at both the academic and practice level explore various aspects of marketing. However, these different contributions must be synthesised. It is essential that the boundaries of strategic marketing (or marketing strategy) are firmly established. Only then is it possible to ensure that it is our understanding and practice of strategic marketing which is being improved and not something else. Otherwise, everything in marketing becomes strategy-related, and as a result an integrated and bounded set of assumptions, theory, and practice may be lost.

An interesting integrative attempt has been made by Biggadike (1981) who hypothesizes that marketing has made five major contributions to the discipline of strategic management. They are:

(1) the marketing concept;
(2) market segmentation;
(3) positioning;
(4) segmentation/positioning and market/business definition;
(5) product life cycle

While this checklist is extremely useful, we believe that marketing should also be concerned with the broader strategy issues which we believe are so important. In particular, it is necessary to lay out the concepts, propositions, and theories that allow us to differentiate this particular thrust of marketing thought from others, and to identify relevant overlapping concepts, (see Zaltman *et al.*, 1982).

One of the potentially confusing issues in defining strategic marketing and marketing strategy is the presence of the diversified corporate structure of most large firms who usually serve as a prime point of reference. It is important to recognize this structure, but not to be bound by it, even though it often seems all-pervasive. The logical starting point for a definition of strategic marketing and marketing strategy, is the diversified corporate structure. It presents a logical starting point because much of what has been called strategic planning and management has come from attempts to better manage these diversified organizations.

Vancil and Lorange state that in diversified organizations, taken as given are that strategy formulation, implementation and control takes place at three levels; namely, the corporate, business, and functional organizational levels (Vancil and Lorange, 1975, p. 82).

If it is assumed that corporate strategic planning deals with the basic questions of what types of businesses to be in, and how resources are to be allocated between businesses*, then it is logical to assume that corporate strategic planning also is heavily involved in setting objectives for those businesses.

Fortunately, or unfortunately, in most diversified organizations the most prominent factor influencing decisions about the type of business to be undertaken, as well as resource allocation, is not marketing but financial. That is, corporate level decisions tend to be 'business'-oriented—not 'market'-oriented. Of course, businesses exist because they serve markets. Consequently, any assessment of a business at corporate level requires an assessment of both market potential and the capacity to be competitive in that market.

Decisions to allocate resources in a particular fashion within a diversified organization are generally not thought to be marketing decisions, although many of the inputs to this decision are marketing-related. These decisions are primarily related to overall corporate goals. Therefore, a business that one corporation may decide is not consistent with its mission may be very consistent with another organization's mission. Much of the literature dealing with corporate portfolio strategy addresses this issue (Wind and Mahajan, 1981). The interface between corporate strategy and marketing is most apparent as objectives are determined for the various businesses.

At the business unit level management attempts to secure, organize and control resources needed to accomplish specific objectives in designated

*For not-for-profit organizations activities is substituted for businesses.

markets. This is in contrast to the functional levels where action programs designed to maximize resource productivity are implemented to achieve objectives.

Unfortunately, defining strategic marketing and/or marketing strategy has been confused by the seemingly endless use of the terms strategy and strategic. Not only are there numerous references to distribution strategy, price strategy, promotion strategy, and product strategy, but some books have appeared that contain the words strategy in their marketing-related titles. That is not necessarily bad, except that everyone seems to have his or her own definition, or worse yet, ignores all definitions and uses the term very loosely. For instance, one textbook, entitled *Marketing Strategy and Structure*, defines marketing, has a chapter on planning, and two chapters have the word strategy in their title (Rachman, 1974). But nowhere in the book is strategy defined; not even in the planning chapter.

A review of the definitions of strategic marketing and marketing strategy combined with the use of these terms is confusing. Obviously, these definitions are directed at different aspects, and in several cases appear to have minimal or no overlap with other definitions. But even more unfortunate is the seeming lack of meaningful definitions. Consequently, without boundaries, these terms could easily become vacuous and, thereby, useless. Moreover, an opportunity to expand our knowledge of marketing and to improve the practice of marketing may slide away.

SUMMARY

This discussion is not the first attempt to review definitions of strategic marketing and marketing strategy. Nor will it be the last because as areas develop, boundaries need to be continually examined and redefined.

One cannot discuss and define strategic marketing and marketing strategy without first realizing that these terms are somehow necessarily linked to corporate strategy, strategic business units, product/market units, and the functional activities of marketing (Day, 1981). While this may seem obvious, it is necessary to consciously make this link; otherwise an incomplete definition may be offered.

Strategic marketing is concerned with the issues of defining the broad structure of the marketing 'mix' in the context of the long-term competitive position of the organization and its constituent businesses. This is a process, whether implicit or explicit, whereby the organization arrives at its basic approach to its market. Strategic marketing, therefore, has a long-term future orientation that guides the organization in the more traditional implementation actions to achieve a particular competitive position.

Strategic marketing should be viewed, in our opinion, as a subset of strategic management. If the premise is accepted that strategic management is acquiring a strategic planning (or thinking) perspective at all levels of the organization, then strategic marketing is the specific application of the strategic planning perspective to that area of the firm identified as marketing (A definition of marketing is left to others).

On the other hand, several definitions seem to point to a general agreement that the term marketing strategy is related to the marketing mix. For instance:

> A marketing strategy focuses on some target customers, with a view to developing a more satisfying and profitable marketing mix—one that will give the firm differential advantage over its competitors (McCarthy, 1975: 35).
>
> [Marketing strategy is] the blending of the marketing mix to satisfy the needs of target buyers best, subject to the constraints of the marketing environment (Robin, 1978: 6)

It is suggested here too that the term marketing strategy involves the design and implementation of a plan that combines the elements of the marketing mix to accomplish the shorter-term objectives of the organization consistent with the strategic marketing plan. These definitions, then, are tied to organizational level. They should apply to organizations of all sizes. Strategic marketing is associated with marketing planning issues at the business level, while marketing strategy deals with the planning issues at the functional level. Thus, what has been called marketing management is closely related to marketing strategy. Strategic marketing deals with broader marketing issues particularly at the level of the individual business. Sometimes, in organizations where marketing is the key strategic 'driving force', strategic marketing's influence extends to corporate level strategy.

REFERENCES

Biggadike, E. Ralph (1981). 'The contributions of marketing to strategic management', *Academy of Management Review*, **6** (4), 621–632.

Day, George S. (1981). 'Strategic market analysis and definition: an integrated approach', *Strategic Management Journal*, **2** (3; July/Sept.), 281–301.

Drucker, Peter F. (1969). *The Age of Discontinuity*. Harper & Row, New York.

Drucker, Peter F. (1980). *Managing in Turbulent Times*. Harper & Row, New York.

McCarthy, E. Jerome (1975). *Basic Marketing*, 5th edn, Richard D. Irwin, Inc., Homewood.

Rachman, David J. (1974). *Marketing Strategy and Structure*. Prentice-Hall, Englewood-Cliffs.

Robin, Donald P. (1978). *Marketing: Basic Concepts for Decision Making*. Harper & Row, New York.

Vancil, Richard F., and Peter Lorange (1975). 'Strategic planning in diversified companies', *Harvard Business Review*, **53** (Jan.–Feb.), 81–90.

Wind, Jerry, and Vijay Mahajan (1981). 'Designing product and business portfolios', *Harvard Business Review*, **59** (Jan.–Feb.), 155–165.

Zaltman, Gerald, Karen LeMastters, and Michael Heffring (1982). *Theory Construction in Marketing: Some Thoughts on Thinking*. John Wiley & Sons, New York.

Strategic Marketing and Management
Edited by H. Thomas and D. Gardner
© 1985 John Wiley & Sons Ltd

Introduction to Conference Papers on Strategic Marketing and Management

The term strategic marketing is of relatively recent origin. As a separate field of study it is at a fairly young and relatively evolutionary stage. As a result many definitions of strategic marketing abound and terms such as 'strategic marketing' and 'marketing strategy' often mean precisely the same thing to different authors. Whilst conflict about definitions, confusion, and an abundance of jargon characterize scientific endeavor in emerging fields, it is useful to summarize and synthesize the alternative viewpoints. The three papers in this section all address the issue of the subject-matter and content of the field.

Claycamp, who possesses a unique blend of senior academic and corporate experience, states that the corporate and marketing strategy field should concentrate more on fundamentals and less on minutia. He believes that clearer and more focused understanding of the roles of marketing and strategic management and planning in the organizational context should lead to more effective and successful implementation of strategic concepts. He also provides the reader with five criteria for effective strategic planning:

(1) Make sure the process is focused on objectives and resource allocation decisions.
(2) The need for appropriate quantification.
(3) The presence of the attributes of flexibility, efficiency, and responsiveness in converting data to relevant information for specific decisions.
(4) The need for involvement and commitment of operating management in the implementation of strategic management.
(5) The need for pre- and post-linkage to operating plans and results.

Gardner and Thomas present a wide-ranging review of the development of marketing strategy to provide an early sensitization to the current scope of work in the field. They point to the dominant themes in existing research; namely, conceptual building blocks (such as segmentation research and the product life cycle) and the range of analytic models (which include market and competitive analysis and portfolio analysis). They conclude with the theme that

7

strategic marketing and planning involves a process of insightfully combining the various planning models and theories into a program of strategic inquiry. This program should lead to more effective strategy development through a process of debate and dialogue.

Schendel, one of the pioneers of modern strategic management, provides a thorough review of the strategic management field and its constituent parts. He then addresses the role of marketing in the strategic management process. He argues (p. 62) that

> In general, marketing has much to contribute to creating and maintaining competitive advantage at the business unit level. Marketing has a lesser role to play in creating and maintaining competitive advantage at the corporate strategy level.

In summary, these papers raise some of the following issues:

(1) The need to avoid endless debate about definitions in the field. There is a clear requirement for a precise language and vocabulary in order to avoid purely semantic confusion.
(2) The need to clear up problems in existing literature:
      (a) What should the basic unit of analysis be? For example, the product-market unit or the business unit or some other level.
      (b) What is really meant in operational organizational terms by the concept of competitive advantage?
      (c) What do we mean by market share given that its value can be considerably changed by amending the market definition?
      (d) How should linkages between marketing and overall corporate strategy be defined in the organizational context? Should marketing's role be limited to one of the functional areas or should its corporate role in competitive and market analysis be given greater emphasis?

The definitive article which addresses these and a range of other issues has probably yet to be written. However, continued discussion about these papers, and a number of the papers in the Spring 1983 issue of the *Journal of Marketing*, should bring that goal nearer to fruition.

Strategic Marketing and Management
Edited by H. Thomas and D. Gardner
© 1985 John Wiley & Sons Ltd

1.1
Strategic Management Fundamentals

H. J. CLAYCAMP
Visiting Professor of Management,
Krannert Graduate School of Management, Purdue University.
Formerly, Vice-President for Corporate Planning,
International Harvester Company

I am pleased to have this opportunity to speak to the Strategic Marketing Conference since it will give me the opportunity to talk about two of my favorite topics—marketing and strategic management.

In this chapter I would like to share some of the things I think I have learned about the requirements for effective corporate and market strategy from nearly 12 years of being responsible for planning and marketing functions. Since most of you are experts in the field of marketing, I would like to begin by discussing some of the similarities I see between the stages marketing went through in the 1960s and 1970s and recent developments in strategic management and planning.

In the 1960s marketing was a field undergoing rapid change. At the center of the turmoil was a new realization of the importance of customer satisfaction as a driving force in business and a catch-phrase called 'the marketing concept'. Enthusiasm for the Marketing Concept and the desire to become a 'marketing oriented-company' grew steadily until the high-demand, shortage economy of the early 1970s abruptly gave way to the steepest recession since the 1930s. Suddenly the 'death of the marketing concept' and the failure of marketing were the topics of many business and academic meetings such as this.

As I look back on that period, it seems that much of the disenchantment with marketing occurred because people lost sight of important fundamentals. Academics were so busy with sophisticated refinements of the marketing concept, and practitioners were so obsessed with 'satisfying customer needs and wants' that both seemed to forget the ultimate goal of the entire activity is to make a profit.

Corporate strategy and planning seem to be approaching a similar state today. The new catch-phrases are 'strategic management' and 'strategic planning'. For example, nearly every major business publication now has a section devoted to corporate strategy stories, and hardly a day passes when I do not receive one or more mailings about conferences on strategic management or the formation of a new consulting firm concentrating in the area.

Enthusiasm also abounds in the academic community. Most major business schools have already created, or are considering creation of, a research center or curriculum concentration in strategic management; and two new journals have been formed in the past few years to provide an outlet for academic publications on the subject.

Unfortunately, as I try to assess much of what I read and hear, I am often reminded of the commentary accompanying pro-football games on TV. There is so much talk about hang time of punts, time of possession, turnovers, and pass completion percentages, that it is hard to remember what Vince Lombardi demonstrated so well—the objective of the game is to score more points than your opponent, and the team that employs a strategy that emphasizes blocking and tackling better than the competition usually wins.

In my discussion I would like to focus on fundamentals—such as blocking and tackling—more than on abstract theory or specific company examples of strategy applications. For example, I would like to start with a very simple definition of strategic management and strategic planning. I believe that 'strategic management' is to a large extent a new catch-phrase coined to describe what CEOs have always been paid to do, and that strategic planning is, or should be, the process and tools they use to get their job done. These definitions make it necessary to think carefully about the fundamental responsibilities of the top management of an organization. In my opinion there are three basic aspects of the job:

(1) making decisions about objectives and major resource allocations;
(2) motivating the organization to implement them; and
(3) making sure desired results are achieved.

I am also convinced that strategy acquires real meaning only when it is embodied in the commitment of resources to a specific course of action. Hence these definitions, though admittedly simplistic, serve to position strategic management and strategic planning in the domain of top management, and focus attention on critical decisions involved in managing organizational objectives, allocating resources, and achieving results.

In stressing basic decisions I do not want to leave the impression that little value has been created by the immense amount of attention focused on corporate strategy in recent years. For example, one of the more significant developments is the growing acceptance of the idea that the overriding objective of the firm should be the creation of value for its shareholders. This idea is, of course, not new to economists who have long regarded maximization of stockholder wealth as a fundamental purpose of business activity. What is new is the development of better techniques for making the concept operationally useful. For example, two rapidly growing strategy consulting firms have developed useful techniques for evaluating the contribution of individual strategies and business units to company value and for relating a firm's expected return and cost of capital to the market/book ratio of its stock.

A second major contribution is the development of the 'business unit' or 'product portfolio' approach to corporate strategy. Although there is no single, unified 'portfolio' theory, virtually every approach advocated today has in common the idea that a competitively defined business—usually called a strategic business unit or SBU—is an appropriate unit for strategy formulation and resource allocation. This concept recognizes that most companies are made up of a complement of businesses with unique strategic characteristics. Consequently, when management makes a decision to 'invest and grow', or 'hold', or 'shrink', a business, it determines to a large extent the kind of competition it will face as well as financial and non-financial resources required for success.

For example, as a result of strategic planning efforts a number of years ago in my company the decision was made to emphasize selected segments of the capital goods industry with common strategic characteristics and to de-emphasize other businesses. This basic decision, and the accompanying resource allocations, committed the company to competition in businesses characterized by high capital intensity, sensitivity to technological innovation in product performance and manufacturing processes, dependence on franchised distribution systems, and a trend toward global sourcing of componentry. As a result of these decisions, the company now has nearly all-new product lines and leading or strong second place market shares in its core businesses and little or no resources committed to non-core businesses.

Before discussing strategic planning, I would like to make one additional point about the management of organization objectives. Although it may seem to be a fine distinction, I want to stress that I have been using the phrase 'management of objectives', not 'management by objective'. 'Management by objective' strikes me as an operating concept that emphasizes achievement of agreed-upon goals; whereas, I regard 'management of objectives' as a strategic concept involving management's responsibility to make sure that the 'right' objectives are selected and that they provide continuity of direction to the organization.

Management must do more than set an overall financial objective for the total company. Explicit strategic objectives for individual businesses are essential. They must also be supported by internally consistent performance objectives stated in readily measurable terms. Both types of objectives are needed to stimulate the creation of sound strategy and effective implementation.

It is hard to overemphasize this fundamental prerequisite for effective strategy, Without decisiveness in determining what businesses you want to be in, and discipline in applying specific performance measurement criteria, only sheer luck can prevent strategic drift and wasted resources.

One of the most frequently observed symptoms of poor objective management is what many people jokingly call the 'hockey stick' plan. Unfortunately, hockey sticks are not a joke. They are, in fact, deadly serious when they are based on wishful thinking and become excuses for management delay of strategic decisions about problem businesses.

The second problem with hockey sticks is that even temporary delays and relatively minor shortfalls in near-term results greatly magnify the rate of improvement needed to close the gap between current performance and long-range objectives. The first step in overcoming this difficulty is to recognize that the fundamental purpose of long-term objectives is to promote decisiveness *today* in strategy formulation and resource commitment. I will say more about a way to avoid 'hockey stick' plans later.

Up to this point I have presented a simplified view of strategic management in terms of fundamental top management decisions. I would now like to discuss why this 'simple' concept frequently seems difficult to implement in practice.

Earlier, I stated that strategic planning should be the process and tools used by top management to get the strategic management task done. Unfortunately, strategic planning is frequently regarded as something people called 'planners' do, that has little relevance to *real* decision-making or to 'running the business'. Although it is currently 'in' to have a strategic planning department and to talk about all of the esoteric things being done, when the activity is divorced from implementation the only tangible output usually created is a set of books marked 'confidential' that no-one reads.

I find it very useful to think of strategic planning as a decision support system designed to provide top management with the information and analytics necessary to make sound strategic decisions, and the control information necessary to insure that short-term performance is consistent with long-term objectives. The work of Michael Scott-Morton and other pioneers in the DSS field has shown that most successful decision support systems have three characteristics in common:

(1) design to meet the user's needs;
(2) flexibility and ease of use;
(3) responsiveness and efficiency in converting large quantities of data into critical information needed for specific decisions.

These basic ideas can be easily translated into five criteria for effective strategic planning. Not surprisingly, the first criterion is to make sure the process is focused on *objectives and resource allocation decisions*. One of the most important functions of this process is to provide unambiguous top-down communication of corporate objectives and internally consistent business unit objectives. I have found that one of the best ways to accomplish this in practice is to segment SBU objectives into broad strategic objectives and specify performance objectives in terms of variables such as profitability, market share, productivity, and cash yield. I have also found that it is extremely useful to use a 'best competitor' standard for selected performance variables and to specify the time path for reaching long-term goals as a 'reverse hockey stick'.

The primary benefit of the reverse hockey stick goal achievement path (GAP) is that it forces management to address problem businesses early in the strategy generation process since relatively greater improvement is required in the near-term than in later years. This technique also provides top management with a disciplined way to screen alternative strategic plans and investment programs. It also can be used to set and communicate incentive programs that are compatible with long-term objectives.

It is important to note that the reverse GAP technique does not imply that management should accept only those strategies that promise immediate financial returns, or that they should expect immediate improvement on all measures of performance. For example, if a SBU has an invest and grow strategic objective, realistic GAPs for performance measures such as market share and cash yield investment will show divergent paths as investments are made to increase market position. Ultimately, the specific time path for the primary and subsidiary performance measures needs to be set by negotiation between operating and top management.

The result of this process can be summarized and communicated to the organization as a resource priority matrix which positions each business in terms of its strategic objective and priority for funds. Given this kind of top-down guidance, operating management can develop strategies for management review with minimal wasted effort and greater assurance that action will result from the planning activity. For example, nearly all of the businesses designated as 'harvest' or 'divest' in our 1978 planning cycle have now been eliminated from the company's business portfolio, and the businesses designated as 'invest/grow' now have improved market shares and more competitive product lines.

From DSS point of view, implementation of this process requires an appropriate data base and tools for using it efficiently. At my company it required an entirely new perspective of the organization as well as a totally new data base. For example, during 1977–78 extensive efforts were devoted to defining strategic business units and developing data bases that would provide management with appropriate information for decision-making. This effort resulted in the definition of approximately 38 SBUs composed of approximtely 150 segments. This structure encompassed the company's world-wide operations and departed substantially from the existing profit center organization

The second essential criterion for effective strategic planning is the need for *appropriate quantification*.

By its very nature, strategic planning deals with quantitative variables such as cash flow, return on equity, capital expenditures, and so on. Hence, numeric representation of plans and results is absolutely essential to understanding and communication. It should also be quite clear that one does not need accounting accuracy to deal with major strategy decisions and that most financial reporting systems are inadequate support systems. What is needed is a simple, easy-to-use data base that provides appropriate information on markets, competition, revenues, costs, resource requirements, and returns. For example, with 15 variables collected on business segments, management can assess growth potentials, competitive position, and resource allocation for individual businesses and the overall company. By analyzing historical versus projected results on four simple charts showing market attractiveness versus competitive strength, profitability versus competitive strength, market growth versus sales growth, and share change versus change in the return on assets (or equity); and a limited amount of qualitative information; it is possible to tell a great deal about the internal consistency of a strategy, as well as whether projected hockey sticks are supported by more than wishful thinking.

The third criterion I want to stress is *flexibility*, *efficiency*, and *responsiveness* in converting data to relevant information for specific decisions.

During the past few years, I have become convinced that it is virtually impossible to be truly responsive to top management's needs without the use of computerized DSS systems designed specifically for this purpose.

In fact, lack of simplicity, flexibility, and responsiveness in the planning process is, in my opinion, a major cause of executive frustration with typical strategic planning processes. The sources of the frustration are easy to identify. First of all, one must recognize that a basic conflict exists between the typical planning cycle calendar and the real-time needs of the CEO. Because of the need to coordinate many functions in strategic planning, a fixed calendar for the submission, analysis, and review of plans is absolutely essential. However, the opportunities and threats that are the substance of the CEO's decision-making task do not occur according to a fixed timetable. To effectively meet his needs the planning system must be capable of providing rapid response to requests for the implications of alternative strategic objectives or resource allocations for specific businesses and the overall company.

The second problem is the paperwork morass usually created by planning processes. Unless care is taken to simplify input *and* output, the process frequently becomes one of completing countless forms and producing lengthy documents that confuse more than clarify basic issues and decisions to be made.

Practical, cost-effective solutions to these problems have been available for some time using computerized decision support systems. For example, several years ago we developed an interactive system for storing, analyzing, and displaying—upon demand—critical strategic management information for any segment of the company. Plans developed by operating units were stored in computer files and mechanically transferred to the corporate data file to minimize paper handling. Once the individual plans were present in corporate data files, they could be consolidated quickly and used in simulation models to analyze strategy alternatives and the compatibility of bottom-up plans with top-down corporate objectives.

A major payoff from these tools is the increased capability they provide for the analysis of alternatives. It is difficult to overemphasize this aspect of strategic management. In fact, I firmly believe that the analysis of options is the key to creative strategy.

Unfortunately, in-depth analysis of alternatives is rarely done. Quite often a major reason for this deficiency in planning is the intimidation of manual data manipulation. The amount of number-crunching necessary to look at even a small number of options and the limited time available, mean that usually only one well-documented strategy is presented for top management review. When this happens, management is faced with the undesirable choice of accepting the plan as presented, or delaying the process by sending business unit managers back to the drawing board. With the current state of the art in computer software, hardware and DSS concepts this is clearly not necessary.

Few people would question the need for *involvement and commitment* of *operating management* in all aspects of business, and it is especially critical in the implementation of strategic management. While it is top management's responsibility to provide strategic direction, the responsibility for results falls upon operations managers. If strategic planning is to function well as a decision support system, it must be seen as a useful tool by both levels of management. Although there is no single best way to obtain operating management commitment to a strategy—especially when faced with an objective of shrinking or exiting from businesses—the chances for success are far greater when operating managers understand why the decision makes sense and are given the chance to design the strategy and be rewarded for accomplishing it. It is no surprise to me that operating managers often exhibit confusion, indifference, or outright resistance when faced with poorly communicated objectives and strategies developed by planners and/or well-meaning task forces.

The last criterion I want to discuss is the need for *pre- and post-linkage to operating plans and results*. I have already covered the importance of making sure that corporate and business unit objectives are internally consistent and the need for interim goal achievement paths for performance criteria.

I also stressed at the outset that one of the fundamental tasks of top management is to monitor and control progress. The importance of completing the loop from objective to resource allocation, to performance measurement, to adjustments of objectives and resource commitments, is so basic it hardly seems necessary to mention it. Yet the lack of this connection ranks with the factors I mentioned earlier as a major cause of poorly executed strategy. A common mistake seems to be the belief that traditional financial accounting and reporting systems can meet this need. What is required is a much more concise and flexible support system that provides only that information necessary to thoroughly understand the dynamics of the plan and to monitor critical performance measures.

One way to meet this need is a concise approach called a 'causal factor' model which can be easily programmed in a computerized DSS. This model can be designed to analyze the causes of change in any variable of interest to management. For example, a causal analysis of planned sales segregates annual differences in company sales into effects of changes in industry sales, market share, selling price, and dealer inventories; whereas a causal analysis of income includes these factors, plus effects of changes in variable and fixed costs.

With this simple analytical tool and a limited amount of qualitative information, top management can quickly assess whether a projected dramatic improvement in profits is due to optimistic forecasts of industry sales and/or market penetration, or to overly aggressive pricing and cost improvement assumptions. When this kind of information is linked to the business units' strategic objective, strategy review discussions between top executives and operating management rapidly focus on the real issues and risks inherent in a plan.

Closing the loop requires, of course, that accounting and/or ancillary information systems capture actual performance data and near-term forecasts of critical variables so that the planning data base can be kept current. If the interface is well designed the end result should be an integrated management support system with the accounting system providing information for day-to-day control of operations; and selected inputs which, when combined with data in the planning support system, give management the information necessary to assess progress toward long-term goals and make sound decisions about required strategic and tactical adjustments.

In closing, I would like to re-emphasize my belief that many of the barriers to effective strategic management arise because people lose sight of fundamentals—like blocking and tackling—that must be done well to achieve success. Although I am well aware of the fact that business is more complex than football, I have a strong conviction that a company that focuses its top executive's attention on the management of organization objectives and resource allocation decisions, and has sound process for surfacing relevant information and obtaining organizational commitment to explicit actions, is more likely to have a winning strategy than one that does not.

Strategic Marketing and Management
Edited by H. Thomas and D. Gardner
© 1985 John Wiley & Sons Ltd

1.2

Strategic Marketing: History, Issues, and Emergent Themes

DAVID M. GARDNER AND HOWARD THOMAS
University of Illinois at Urbana-Champaign

INTRODUCTION

The purpose of this paper is to examine the development of the concept of strategic marketing. The issues raised include marketing strategy and its definition; marketing and its role in achieving the aims of corporate strategy and objectives; those areas of research including organisational behavior and economics, which have provided stimuli for the emergence of strategic marketing; and, finally, those emergent themes in the strategy and strategic marketing field which require further examination and resolution.

No attempt is made therefore to provide an exhaustive survey of either the field of strategic marketing, or of the strategic management literature. In the former area contributions by Boyd and Larreche (1978), Kerin and Peterson (1980), Abell and Hammond (1979), Biggadike (1981), and Day (1977) are particularly useful. In the latter area Schendel and Hofer (1979), Bracker (1980), Gluck *et al.* (1980), Greenwood and Thomas (1981), and Porter (1980, 1981) provide useful frameworks and reviews.

DEFINING THE ORGANIZATIONAL–MARKETING STRATEGY LINKS

Separating marketing strategy from organization or corporate strategy and various other functional area strategies is important, but difficult. It is important in the sense that it is assumed that the strategic problem differs by level and function. It is difficult because of the overlapping boundaries of organizations that are striving to avoid sub-optimization.

Hofer and Schendel (ch. 2, 1978) provide a wide-ranging discussion of the strategy concept and its evolution. They present alternative definitions of strategy given by several authors and demonstrate that there is a major problem involved in defining the breadth and scope of the strategy concept in the emerging field of strategic management.

They also stress how difficult it is to set boundaries which define the content and legitimate areas of interest in this field.

Bracker (1980) also attempts to synthesize some recent definitions of strategy and concludes:

> business strategy has the following characteristics: an *environmental* and *situational* analysis is used to determine a firm's posture in its field, and then the firm's *resources* are utilized in an appropriate manner to attain its major goals.
>
> Strategic management is the direct organizational application of the concepts of business strategy that have been developed in the academic realm. That is, strategic management entails the analysis of internal and external environments of a firm to maximize the utilization of *resources* in relation to *objectives*.

In this paper, the Hofer/Schendel (1978) definition of strategy is adopted as follows:

> An organization's strategy is the fundamental pattern of present and planned resource deployments and environmental interactions that indicates how the organization will achieve its objectives.

They elaborate this definition in two important ways. First, by indicating that there are four components to any organization's strategy, namely *scope* (or organizational *domain*), *resource deployments* (or *distinctive competences*), *competitive advantages*, and *synergy*. Second, by pointing out that there are hierarchies of strategies: (1) corporate strategy, (2) business strategy, and (3) functional area strategy. Thus, at the corporate level, strategy is mainly concerned with defining the set of businesses that should form the company's overall profile. However, at the business level, strategy focuses on the definition of the manner of competition in a given industry or product/market segment. Finally, at the functional area (e.g. marketing) level, strategy focuses around the issue of the maximization of resource productivity.

While Hofer and Schendel's decomposition of strategy in terms of content and level provides an extremely useful approach for viewing strategy, the authors recognize nevertheless the importance of achieving a coherent and consistent fit between the various levels of strategy. This may not always be easy to achieve and may require the adoption of concepts from the systems approach (see for example, Ackoff (1970), Churchman (1968)), to ensure that there is an understanding of how, for example, marketing subsystems are constrained by and operate within the organizational system as a whole. Day (1981: 293) discusses how business units (often labelled strategic business units (SBUs)) and product-market units (PMUs) should be linked, and concludes that an SBU should be composed of PMUs similar on strategically relevant factors. Some of these might be cost, technology, capital require-ments, and a series of customer-oriented factors. Day also stresses the difficulties inherent in defining strategic relevance in relation to a given market. Such difficulties are seen to occur because the market is ever-changing, and particularly so in relation to the major strategic market dimensions. As a result, aggregation from the PMU level to either the SBU level or the industry level is likely to be a complex problem. In addition, Biggadike (1981) feels that many marketers may not want to change their strategy focus from the PMU level, and will choose to concentrate on further refinement of marketing concepts and methods at that level. This will be examined later in the paper.

WHAT IS MARKETING STRATEGY?

Are terms such as strategic marketing and marketing strategy indicative of new substantive trends in marketing thought, or are they merely passing fads? Are they ubiquitous adjectives which describe what marketing does and what good marketing has always been about, or do the terms represent something more permanent?

One thing is certain—the term 'marketing strategy' is not a new term in the marketing literature. Although it is difficult to determine exactly when the concept was introduced, Leverett S. Lyon (1926: 3) is generally accredited with being the first person to use the concept in a comprehensive manner.

> Observation of the social conditions which influence the activities of a business unit, and of the factors within a trade and a business which limit the work of the marketing manager, leads toward the view of marketing strategy which it is desired to present. The conditioning environment of marketing management is ever re-arranging itself. As a result, a constant readjustment of policies and methods to meet an ever-changing situation is necessary. Marketing management, therefore, may be conceived of as the continuous task of re-planning the marketing activities of a business to meet the constantly changing conditions within and without the enterprise. Inasmuch as the adjustment to a given situation may be made for a period of greater or less duration, there arise sets of plans which may be called marketing programs or campaigns. These are, however, but parts of a greater whole. In each of these programs or campaigns one or more objectives must be set up and certain instruments must be used to attain the purposes desired. The plan, the combination of ends and instruments, is the strategy in each program.

These concepts are very familiar to present-day marketing scholars and practitioners. While there are obvious differences, Lyon's understanding of marketing strategy is remarkably similar to views held by some writers about what marketing strategy encompasses in the 1980s. It is interesting to note, however, how Lyon (1926: 3) saw marketing strategy.

> The similarity between marketing strategy for a given period and military strategy is sufficiently great to allow of a worthwhile comparison. In each, the aim is to achieve certain ends by the means available. In marketing strategy, therefore, as in military strategy, a first step is the determination of objectives.

The military usage is still prominent today, with strategy implicitly being the 'grand' plan and the exact deployment of the 4 Ps—product, price, pace, and promotion—being tactics (Hughes, 1978: 9). This theme, stated or not, seems to run through much of the marketing literature. Henderson (1981: 8) also draws upon a military analogy in the following excerpt:

> Successful market strategies in effect segment the total market in a way that minimizes competitors' strengths while maximizing yours. The parallel in military strategy is 'isolating the battlefield'.

Marketing strategy has been defined in many ways. For example, Alderson and Green (1964: 356) define it as 'a core idea from which a marketing plan is evolved'. Simon and Freimer (1970) believe that a marketing strategy has two principal components:

(1) selection of a market target group toward whom the effort of the firm will be devoted, and
(2) development of a marketing mix.

This evidently relates directly to the marketing concept which emphasizes the crucial role of the customer in strategy formulation, and implicitly to the constraints set upon the firm by the market. However, it begs the question of what criteria should be used to select a particular strategy which, in turn, entails the existence of a set of objectives or decision criteria. Further, the process by which a marketing strategy fits into the overall corporate strategy and criteria for marketing strategy selection related to these are not discussed.

Henderson (1981: 8) stresses the role of segmentation in market strategies as follows:

> Market strategies are all based upon segmentation and concentration of resources.

He also emphasizes the relevance of understanding competition and competitive strength (1981: 4):

> A market can be viewed in many different ways, and a product can be used in many different ways. Each time the product-market pairing is varied, the relative competitive strength is varied too. Many businessmen do not recognize that a key element in strategy is choosing the competitor whom you wish to challenge, as well as choosing the market segment and product characteristics with which you will compete.

A review of the marketing literature led Boyd and Larreche (1978) to conclude that not only has the word 'strategy' been used in a variety of ways, but that a hierarchy of strategies could be defined. They identified the three levels of strategies as: marketing strategies, marketing element strategies, and product-market entry strategies.

Our review of the literature leads us to believe that much potential confusion exists, mainly because of the current emphasis on corporate strategic planning. This type of planning has a clear environmental and future-based orientation and it leads to the examination of longer-term issues such as what set of businesses a firm should be involved in, and the allocation of resources between business units. In other words, marketing strategy is viewed not so much as a process, as in corporate strategic planning, but as a specific set of 'how to' plans. Therefore, it often appears that what corporate planners hope will emerge as strategic marketing planning (a process) at the SBU level, is thought of *not* as a process, but as a plan (marketing strategy). Often overlooked is Ansoff's (1965: 5) statement that 'strategic decisions are primarily concerned with external, rather than internal, problems of the firm and specifically with selection of the product-mix which the firm will produce and the market to which it will sell'.

Kotler (1980: 64–65) addresses this issue with a clear demarkation between the strategic management process and the strategic marketing process. His strategic management process is very similar to Hofer and Schendel's paradigm presented earlier. It describes the steps taken to develop long-run strategies for the continued existence and growth of the corporation at the corporate and divisional levels. The strategic marketing process is then defined as taking place within the context of the strategic management process, and as being concerned with the development of marketing positions and programs at product and market levels.

Abell and Hammond (1979: 9–10) take a rather similar position. They define a strategic market plan as involving four sets of related decisions: *defining the business*, *determining the mission of the business*, *formulating functional strategies* and *budgeting*. They continue as follows:

> A strategic market plan *is not* the same, therefore, as a marketing plan; it is a plan of *all* aspects of an organization's strategy in the market place. A marketing plan, in contrast, deals primarily with the delineation of target segments and the product, communication, channel, and pricing policies for reaching and servicing those segments—the so-called marketing mix.

There seems little doubt, therefore, that the strategic emphasis and orientation in marketing thought is here to stay. There are perhaps two main reasons for this. First, the business environment is the second half of the 1970s, and for all of the 1980s, is less predictable. For example, economic and competitive conditions are far less stable, leading to a redefinition of the roles, functions and strategic driving forces which the marketing area can provide for the organization. Second, there is increasing recognition that marketing problems are not well-structured and tactical in orientation. They are typically ill-structured, difficult to formulate, and involve such factors as behavioral and creative elements. Further, marketing processes are in a continual state of movement and suffer from severe measurement difficulties. All of this suggests that strategic thinking needs to be given as much emphasis as the accepted operational and tactical orientation in marketing decision-making.

But, there still is a pressing need to distinguish between the process (and hence the necessary definition of linkages to organization and functional areas) and the resultant statement of how marketing objectives are to be achieved. It is imperative that references to marketing strategy be clearly divided into process and plan. Otherwise, marketing strategy is likely to be treated as not much more than a new name for organizing the implementation of the marketing mix. The process focuses on environmental trends, gap analysis, *and* implementation. The plan is the resulting program with its focus on implementation.

In subsequent sections of this paper the important themes and forces involved in the development of strategic marketing concepts are reviewed and discussed. Particular attention is directed towards the design of inquiry systems which can integrate analytical techniques and conceptual approaches for strategic marketing. Such inquiry systems can provide palatable information which may improve processes of dialogue and debate about options and strategic choices.

THEMES IN EXISTING RESEARCH

Introduction

One of the main themes in the development of the literature in strategic market planning has been the use of analytical model building and conceptual schema to develop planning systems of various forms (Abell and Hammond, 1979: 11–12).

The main conceptual schema and analytical building blocks include the following:

Environmental analysis (see Utterback, 1979; Clelland and King, 1974)
   What are the appropriate and relevant environmental variables?
   What approaches, such as econometric analysis and technological forecasting, may be used for forecasting economic, social, political, legal, regulatory and technological change?
Industry and competitive analysis (see Porter, 1979)
   The problem of industry definition.
   Structural analysis of the industry.
   Industry life cycle.
   Cost and investment analysis.
   Impact of technology.
   Analysis of suppliers.
   Barriers to entry and exit.
Market analysis (Porter, 1980; Wind, 1978; Montgomery and Weinberg, 1977)
   The problem of market definition.

Market structure.

Product life cycles.

Customer analysis and segmentation methods.

Competitive analysis.

Market research and strategic intelligence systems.

Firm capability and resource analysis (Stevenson, 1976)

Analysis of strengths and weaknesses to identify areas of potential competitive advantage.

Transferability of skills and resources to other situations.

The main planning approaches developed have included PIMS, strategic boxes, and portfolio planning models. The PIMS (*Profit Impact on Market Share*) model of the Strategic Planning Institute examines the relationship between profitability and market share across industries. (Schoeffler, *et al.*, 1974). The matrix or strategic box approaches seek to examine the character of the businesses which form the firm's portfolio. These have been developed by such organizations as the Boston Consulting Group (Hedley, 1977), GE, McKinsey and Shell (Hussey, 1978). Portfolio planning approaches (Wind and Mahajan, 1981) are based around the adaptation of such financial theories as risk/return portfolio efficient sets (Markowitz, 1959) and capital asset pricing models (Copeland and Weston, 1979) to business portfolio planning.

As has already been noted, planning approaches have taken a variety of forms over the last 20 years. Earlier models were discarded when they were unable to cope with either the added complexity of the planning situations or changing conditions in the underlying business environment. Generally, however, the newer models used the basic building blocks developed in the earlier stages. Gluck *et al.* (1980) identify four phases in the development of approaches for strategic planning and management. They label these phases as *meet the budget* (Phase 1), *predict the future* (Phase 2), *think strategically* (Phase 3) and *create the future* (Phase 4). In other words, planning has moved from an initial deterministic orientation through a probabilistic forecasting phase to a current requirement for flexible, creative systems which encourage effective strategic thinking. Strategic thinking is considered essential for the development of successful competitive strategies which stress the need to identify, create, and exploit sustainable competitive advantage and anticipate potential competitive responses. What then are the important analytic models and planning approaches for identifying competitive strength and competitive advantage?

Important analytic models

The fields of economics and marketing provide the main analytic frameworks for strategic marketing. In *economics* models of *industry and competitive analysis* and *resource and capability analysis* deserve particular emphasis. On the other hand in the field of marketing such approaches as *customer segmentation*, *marketing positioning*, and the role of *product life cycles* have an important bearing on strategy formulation.

In the following paragraphs the main economic and marketing analysis models are reviewed.

Economic analysis models

Porter (1981) and Caves (1980) summarize the contribution of industrial organization paradigms and research to corporate strategy and its formulation. Porter's conceptual model (reproduced as Figure 1.2.1) has had much recent

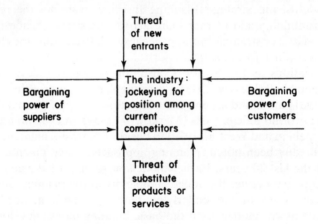

Figure 1.2.1 Forces governing competition in an industry (*Source*: Porter, 1979)

influence upon the conduct of industry analysis. Horsky and Sen (1980) also point to the increased cross-fertilization of ideas and efforts between economics and marketing. After reviewing more recent research by economists, they state their position (1980: 58) as follows:

> Apparently, economists are realizing the importance of the problems that have traditionally interested marketing researchers. It is also becoming clear that the basic analyses done in economics can be applied to such problems. However, the complexity of the problems in the marketing area seems also to call for an expansion of economic theory for their solution.

This latter point is echoed by Biggadike (1981), who points to the need to develop a theory of market evolution:

> The common premise behind this work is that we can understand and predict market evolution only after an analysis of the drivers and market characteristics:

customer needs, problems or functions (of both end-users and channels); competitor strategies; substitute and complementary products; technology and cost/price characteristics.

It should be stressed that the concept of 'drivers' referred to in the above quote is an important one. Biggadike argues that in developing theories of market evolution, it is imperative to identify what he calls 'environmental drivers' which influence the characteristics of a market. Such 'environmental drivers' may be an experience curve effect, the existence of significant economics of scale, or considerable potential for product differentiation through the identification of heterogeneity in customer demand.

Tregoe and Zimmerman (1981) use a very similar term, namely 'strategic driving force'. They identify nine strategic areas that impact and influence the nature and direction of any organization. They argue that these driving forces relate to such factors as product/market characteristics, organizational strengths, and financial targets, and that they can determine the organization's future strategy path.

The basic focus of the economic analysis approach is, therefore, the identification of competitive strategy. Strategy involves the irrevocable commitment of resources in a competitive environment, characterised by differing degrees of concentration on the supply side and different demand patterns leading to the potential for product differentiation. The basic frame of reference is the determination of whether there are persistent or transient differences in performance between firms operating in similar competitive environments. If persistent differences exist then the strategic management question involves the identification and control of the underlying competitive edge. Thus, for the single business, strategy analysis involves an understanding of such factors as *business economics*, the *competitive position* faced by the business, the *future growth* potential of that business, and the set of *competitive strategies* currently existing in the marketplace.

In addressing business economics, the Boston Consulting Group (Henderson, 1981) postulated that experience curves could explain cost differentials and relative costs in the following terms:

> Total value-added costs net of inflation involved in making, distributing, marketing a product can be made to decline by a constant percentage each time accumulated production experience doubles.

This leads to the proposition that each competitor's profit margin is a function of his relative accumulated experience (or market share). This proposition is qualified by a number of important caveats. First, it can only be applied straightforwardly to a single business. Second, even then there may be transfers of experience and different factor costs. Third, businesses based upon technological or patent monopoly, or having differential access to low-cost resources, will not exhibit the 'experience effect'. Fourth, there should be recognition that total costs consist of several elements which are of differing importance and which 'behave' differently. This means that the cost structure may vary across the product range and the different customer groups.

The implication of the above is that the experience effect is not a generalizable phenomenon in every market. When it does exist it will pose a barrier to entering that market. In most cases, therefore, both the supply and demand side of the market must be examined closely. For example, if the market is concentrated on the supply side and produces a relatively undifferentiated product, then an organizational 'drive' down the 'experience curve' for the lowest cost position in association with a marketing-driven share-building strategy is the most viable competitive strategy. However, if a competitor cannot achieve overall share and is not satisfied with 'follower' performance, then it may be able to adopt a *strategic segmentation* focus. The minimum economic conditions for this to exist are not only the ability to differentiate customers, but also a 'production technology' which makes any one competitor high-cost if it serves several segments. In other words, a form of cost/benefit judgement has to be made by the low-cost supplier. This judgement would be stated in terms such as that the benefits of scale may be overwhelmed by the costs of complexity which exist in the market place.

Michael Porter (1979, 1980, 1981) is certainly the most influential of the researchers addressing the central role of industry and firm economics in strategy formulation. Quite apart from identification of cost economics and competitive positioning at the firm level, much work is now being carried out at the industry level. The notions of such strategic influences as *mobility barriers* (e.g. entry, exit, strategic posture), *strategic groups* (i.e. that clusters of firms exist within industries according to their strategic postures), industry *structural characteristics*, and *strategic positioning* have enabled the development of theory concerning firm profitability in the strategic group and industry contexts. Other industry studies such as Hatten and Schendel (1977) and Schendel and Patton (1978) have examined and tested similar notions.

Porter believes that through an understanding of industry structure and competitive economics, the company can identify certain generic strategies. For example, *overall cost leadership* is possible in a concentrated industry setting with a homogeneous product offering. *Differentiation* is possible if there is heterogeneity in demand which will allow high quality to be offered at a relatively high price level whilst *focused strategies* can allow firms to address specific customer needs in geographic, product, or distribution dimensions.

In simple terms the thrust behind the work of Porter (1980), Abell (1980), Biggadike (1981), and Henderson (1981) is the identification, measurement, achievement, and retention of sustainable competitive advantage for the firm. Their pioneering efforts are leading to theories, approaches, and empirical studies which address the nature of competition in several different industries and also examine the benefits of alternative diversification strategies and multi-business forms of organizational structure (Harrigan, 1979; Rumelt, 1974; Newman, 1978).

Marketing analysis models

Many of the currently popular marketing planning approaches, such as PIMS, strategic boxes and portfolio planning models, were developed in the period before the middle 1970s when the competitive structures of most major industries were relatively more stable and when corporations adopted more focused, concentric strategies.

With the change in the rules of the competitive game and the environment of slower, less predictable economic growth, much criticism has been aimed recently at the relevance of such approaches. This has led to a shift toward the search for selective growth opportunities and the generation of innovative strategies for securing and sustaining competitive advantage. In the following section a brief critique of PIMS and portfolio models is presented. The purpose of this critique is not to provide a detailed review of those methods, but rather to point out that they are more useful for the tactical, operational, well-structured types of marketing situations. It is further argued that segmentation to seek competitive advantage may be the most important strategic analytic tool because it seeks to identify the characteristics of customer groups with common product or service needs.

PIMS research

PIMS models, which according to Springer (1973), received developmental impetus in 1973/74 from the planning work at GE, have been subject to extensive review by such writers as Anderson and Paine (1978); Zeithaml, *et al.* (1981); Wensley (1982); Woo (1981) and Rumelt and Wensley (1981).

While these authors agree, for example, with the generalized PIMS finding that there is a statistically significant global relationship between profitability (as measured by pre-tax ROI) and market share, they also point to significant 'scatter' or variation about this average relationship. Since strategy problems exist at the firm level (or occasionally at strategic group level), it is argued that allowance should be made for the more strategically significant firm-to-firm variations that underlie 'average' relationships. To highlight this point Schendel and Patton's (1978) model of the brewery industry found a statistically significant relationship between profitability and market share for the industry as a whole. However, when they stratified the industry into three *strategic groups*—namely, national brewers, large regional brewers, and small regional brewers, the same profit–market share relationship was found to be much weaker and non-significant.

Zeithaml, *et al.* (1981) divided their PIMS sample into three groups, according
to the level of environmental uncertainty, and found that differences existed in
the relationships between strategic variables and ROI performance measures in
those three groups. They suggested that there may be a trade-off between
market share and profitability depending upon market conditions and levels of
market uncertainty. They also argued for a more contingency-based use of this
data base for strategy formulation in strategic management research. Rumelt
and Wensley (1981), Abell (1977), and Capon (1978) have also suggested that
market share is an outcome measure and a performance variable, but probably
not a strategic variable. The possible exception is in the context of relatively
simple market structures and stable marketing channels and segments, where
there may be value in market share leadership. Otherwise, market-share/ROI
relationships cannot determine appropriate business strategies unless the
groundwork of market analysis and product market segmentation has been
carried out beforehand to identify more clearly the range of strategic variables in
the given problem situation.

It could be argued, therefore, that PIMS prescriptions can only be translated
directly into market-share-based strategies with relatively well-structured
strategic market problems and situations. The term 'well-structured' would be
used where such factors as the market, business units, competition, and
product-market units are clearly and unambiguously defined. With more
complex, ill-structured situations there would appear to be no alternative than to
test the robustness of the strategic prescriptions on an individual basis taking
account of the underlying market and situational factors.

Portfolio research

Followers of strategic portfolio matrices, such as BCG, categorize business
strategies and resource allocation decisions according to the position of strategic
business units in the matrix. For example, a commonly held prescription, at least
in the popular management media (Kiechel, 1981), is that low relative-market
share, low market growth businesses ('dogs') should be divested.

The status of these models has been thoroughly examined by writers such as
Day (1977, 1981), Haspelagh (1982), Kiechel (1981), Wensley (1981), and
Wind and Mahajan (1981). Numerous application pitfalls have been identified
which focus around the fundamental criticism that simple taxonomies fail to
represent the richness and multi-dimensional nature of marketing strategy
problems. In short, it is argued that such approaches tend to over-simplify the
strategy problem, and encourage mechanistic market and competitive analyses
from which rather rigid strategic prescriptions are routinely obtained.

Researchers have pointed out that portfolio approaches are flawed because
viable strategic prescriptions need to be based upon sound market and business
definitions. Often businesses are misclassified in product portfolios because

important shared experience and synergistic effects between product-market units are not recognized. Market definitions are sometimes too restricted, and this then hinders prompt recognition of changing products, competitive, and marketing innovations. In addition, these simple matrices ignore the effects of market structure, competitive strategies, and market stability on the nature of strategic options. For example, it has been demonstrated that dominant market share businesses in stable, oligopolistic mature markets may not be able to operate so-called 'cash cows' as cash generators because of the nature of competition in those contexts.

Since the above criticisms imply that simple taxonomies are too rigid, later portfolio researchers (Wind and Mahajan, 1981; Larreche and Srinavasan, 1981) have argued that more flexible, tailor-made portfolio models should be developed as aids and not hindrances to strategic thinking. Thus it is suggested that they should incorporate such important factors as financial (risk-return) and market-oriented relationships so that a richer type of model can be used as a basis for identifying and discussing strategic options. Models, such as STRATPORT (Larreche and Srinavasan (1981)), can therefore be categorized as decision-support or strategic intelligence systems (Montgomery and Weinberg, 1977) because they provide intelligence information for strategic thinking and dialogue.

Segmentation research

The principle of segmenting markets to seek competitive advantage is widely understood, and is increasingly being applied to industrial as well as consumer markets. It is perhaps the most valuable strategic tool in competitive analysis. Biggadike's (1981) statement illustrates this view:

> I think market segmentation and its counterpart, positioning, must rank as marketing's most important contribution to strategic management. . . . Thus, these two concepts deal directly with analyzing a firm's environment so as to make a strategic decision about the extent of the firm's domain in that environment.

Henderson's (1981) comments are also extremely relevant in this context, particularly his articulation of the concept of strategic sectors. He argues, (1981: 8), that:

> Most dramatically successful business strategies are based on market segmentation and concentration of resources in that segment.

He develops this theme (1981: 13) by delineating how resources should be concentrated, as follows:

> Concentration of resources can be achieved in several ways:

Choose the most vulnerable segment.

Choose products or markets which require response rates beyond a competitor's ability.

Choose products or markets which require capital that a competitor is unwilling to commit.

Recognize the commercial potential of new technology early.

Exploit managerial differences in style, method, or system, such as overhead rate, distribution channels, market image, or flexibility.

His notion of segmentation is intimately related to his strategic sector concept (1981: 36, 37).

> A strategic sector is one in which you can obtain a competitive advantage and exploit it. . . . Strategic sectors are the key to strategy because each sector's frame of reference is competition. The largest competitor in an industry can be unprofitable if the individual strategic sectors are dominated by smaller competitors.

Henderson's more strategic concept of segmentation is broader than the product-market focus dominant in marketing research, which seeks to partition consumers into groups in terms of primarily marketing-mix types of variables. Wind (1978) and Winter (1979) provide useful summaries of marketing segmentation research issues and trends.

From a strategic marketing viewpoint it may be useful to recognize a wider definition of business segmentation. That is, as the identification of customer groups which currently or potentially provide sustainable economic advantage to a competitor who focuses on serving them. Thus, the segmentation process involves defining *strategic segments* on the basis not only of product-market variables but also of analyses of such factors as defensible barriers, experience effects by major businesses, markets and distribution channels, technology, financing requirements, and corporate risk attitude. The key question for strategic managers is 'what do I have to dominate in this business in order to have a profitable and defensible position?' This may require recognition that organizational belief systems and structures may lead to an implicit segmentation structure, and a consequent focusing of effort and investment in the business. This 'corporate mythology' of strategic sectors may, in fact, turn out to be counterproductive and may not reinforce any competitive strengths or cost advantages.

The design of strategic segmentation schemas to maximize competitive advantage and recognize the dynamic nature of shifting segments ultimately requires answers to questions about the relevant bases for specialization (e.g. customer, product line, technology), the relevant markets in which to offer and sell the product line, and the nature of products to be offered. In other words, there is no substitute for basic groundwork and research to isolate the key variables by which the firm can secure and maintain a significant competitive advantage.

Product life cycle

It is important to recognize the value of the product life cycle model as a conceptual schema for thinking about the nature of strategy development and market positioning through time. Despite its lack of precision and operationalization (Polli and Cook, 1969; Dhalla and Yuspeh, 1976; Rink and Swan, 1979) the concept has descriptive validity and intuitive appeal. It has provided one of the main building blocks for the newer theories of market evolution discussed earlier in this paper.

Where do analytic models and approaches lead?

This review of analytic planning and strategy models has focused upon the most appropriate and popular economic and marketing analysis models.

One general conclusion is that some analytic models, notably experience curves, BCG, and portfolio approaches, can most usefully be applied to well-structured, tactical or operational situations. This is because while the underlying model assumptions may fit simpler situations, it is clear that they do not fit the realities of complex, ill-structured marketing strategy problems where there is often considerable uncertainty about the problem situation, its structure, and the nature of the key underlying variables.

Perhaps the major role of the analytic models is to provide some potential insights about problem situations for further problem debate and dialogue in the process of formulating marketing strategies. Clearly, analytic models cannot provide easily formulated strategic alternatives for marketing strategy problems. Analytical models also make strong implicit underlying assumptions about the nature of a problem, and often focus on one part of a business system instead of on the system as a whole. As Mason and Mitroff (1981: 287) say: 'What does it mean to classify a business as a cow? What does it do for the organization as a whole?'

The fundamental point is that analytic models adopt a rationalistic perspective which may be more appropriate for relatively well-structured situations. Such models require good problem definition, and this may be difficult to achieve with strategy problems of a more complex nature. In other words, there may be much more uncertainty about problem structure than about the nature of underlying strategic variables. Further, problem structuring relies heavily on the ability of individuals to judge and creatively evaluate options in the light not only of information and analytic input, but also hunch and intuition.

Challenges and emergent themes

A number of the emergent research directions discussed earlier should gain increasing emphasis in the research literature. In particular, the development of theories of market evolution, of the more focused use off PIMS and other data bases, and of improved concepts of strategic segmentation, will provide useful structuring and thinking frameworks for strategic management. This should also lead to the development of a more contingency-based set of generic strategies which will, therefore, overcome the rather rigid strategies currently suggested.

While further simple planning tools may well be proposed, they should be treated with caution and healthy skepticism. This is because the main challenge for strategic marketing is the development of a problem-solving process, a strategic inquiry system which will identify and clarify the differential roles of analytic models, conceptual frameworks, dialogue, and debate in defining and attacking those strategic problems. The key objective for such a system should be to identify the basis on which to achieve and sustain competitive advantage in the market place.

Perhaps the main challenge in developing flexible problem-solving approaches is to avoid 'analysis-paralysis' (Livingston, 1971) in the process of generating strategic options. That is, strategy development should not rely solely upon standard programs of market and competitive analyses. If analysis dominates, then considerable energy will be focused on developing 'optimal' strategies rather than on challenging problem structures, assumptions, and the characterization of the underlying strategic variables. In the development of many planning systems there has been a recognition that they have become a rigid, bureaucratic ritual which has hindered the development of strategic thinking. A recent Boston Consulting Group research note (1981) illustrates this viewpoint.

> No simple, monolithic set of rules or strategy imperatives will point automatically to the right course. No planning system guarantees the development of successful strategies. Nor does any technique. The Business Portfolio (The Growth/Share Matrix) made a major contribution to strategic thought. Today it is misused and overexposed. It can be a helpful tool, but it can also be misleading or, worse, a strait-jacket.

In subsequent paragraphs a number of important challenges for further work in this area will be identified. These include the challenging of static assumptions, the recognition of human and organizational barriers to strategic thinking, and the importance of problem structuring in strategy formulation.

Challenging static strategic planning assumptions

Most organizations are vulnerable to competition, and sometimes do not adequately monitor the competitive environment. Unforeseen changes in the crucial competitive factors, environmental variables, or existing product-market segments generally provide both strategic opportunities and challenges for the organization. There is therefore a continual need to re-examine current definitions of market segmentation and competitors. However, there is a real concern about whether they can be successfully attacked by the use of standardized approaches and existing planning methodologies. It is felt that such methodologies produce a rather arid set of strategic options.

Springer (1973: 1180), while discussing strategic management in General Electric, calls this problem of adaptation to change in the underlying competitive environment the missing link in most strategic planning efforts.

> But mere technique is not sufficient here. . . . The analysis must be based on what we call 'wide-spectrum' knowledge, i.e., knowledge that remains valid under a wide-spectrum of environmental, objective, and strategic changes. This is the missing link in most strategic planning efforts. The local experience of local management is not sufficient, because, even though it often produces a very deep knowledge of a specific business situation, it is not wide-spectrum. So an evaluation based on an analysis of a single business, even a deep and sophisticated analysis, can become unreliable when the competitive environment, the strategy of the business or its competitors, or the economic climate, undergo a major change.

Indeed, this missing link has been recognized by those writers (Porter, 1980, 1981; Biggadike, 1981; Abell, 1980) working to develop theories of market evolution. It is argued that such theories will provide bases for identifying competitive advantage for both single and multi-business firms. Similar arguments are also emerging from such eminent consultancies as BCG. To quote from one of their recent notes:

> Two factors in particular give one a sense of the nature of that (competitive) environment. The first is the size of the advantage that can be created over other competitors. The second is the number of unique ways in which that advantage can be created. The combination of these two factors both gives a sense of the long-term value of a business and dictates the strategy requirements.

However, business strategy formulation may not necessarily be facilitated by extensive analyses of the size and extent of competitive advantage. It may still require those rare managerial abilities of perception and articulation of a strategy for competitive positioning and for adapting to business movements through time. Strategy probably starts as an idea or an intended pattern in the mind of the strategic decision-maker. This idea can be aided and refined by the existence of strategic intelligence and competitive analysis. However, it is unlikely that such ideas can emerge solely through the use of strategic planning tools. As Hunsicker (1980: 9) puts it:

> Such bold strategic moves as General Electric's recent acquisition of Utah International are not arrived at by formula. Rather they require the wit to perceive and the ingenuity to exploit and shape significant change, in the 'givens' underlying a business.

Individual and organizational influences on strategic thinking and strategy development

Since strategy formulation is heavily dependent on the judgement of strategic decision-makers, it is appropriate to ask what is known about judgemental biases and their potential effects on strategy formulation.

Research in such areas as cognitive psychology, behavioral decision theory and organizational behavior (Schwenk and Thomas, 1981; Taylor, 1975; Hogarth and Makradakis, 1981) has uncovered a number of biases which can afflict decision-makers in their decision-making processes.

For example, decision-makers may try to simplify their decision process and reduce uncertainty and stress associated with strategic decision-making. Simon (1976) introduces the 'satisficing' notion of bounded rationality which implies that strategic decision-makers will apply limited strategy searches. Steinbruner (1974) develops the notion of *single outcome* calculations, in which decision-makers may focus on a single goal and a single alternative course of action for achieving it. They will then ignore other alternatives, and justify their own choice in terms of a multi-dimensional set of organizational goals. Lindblom's (1959) concept of 'muddling through' and Quinn's concept of 'logical incrementalism' can also be regarded as decision simplification mechanisms.

Tversky and Kahneman (1974), in a now classic article, identified a number of biases and heuristics associated with judgements under uncertainty. A discussion about the strategic implications of two of their heuristics, *availability* and *anchoring*, follows.

Availability biases can arise through the judgement of events (such as success of a business or marketing strategy) by the ease with which instances of the events are retrieved by decision-makers. Thus, decision-makers may adopt a particular marketing strategy simply because they remember its success in a recent instance, or because they perceive retrievable cues relevant to the strategy in the current problem situation. This bias can set up a cognitive path in which complacency may occur, and attitudes such as 'what you don't know, you don't worry about' may be fostered.

Studies by Alpert and Raiffa (1969), Moore and Thomas (1975), and Selvidge (1976) have shown that decision-makers assess 'too tight' predictions about uncertain outcomes. This is because they 'anchor' on a particular outcome value which they believe will occur, and do not make adequate adjustments about this 'anchored' value to reflect their uncertainty about outcomes. *Anchoring and inadequate adjustment* biases may, therefore, lead to overconfidence in judgement about strategic outcomes.

Langer (1975) catalogues a bias 'illusion of control' which leads decision-makers to believe that they have control over outcomes. Planning activities are often undertaken to give strategic decision-makers the illusion of mastering and controlling their environment. Indeed, the individual strategist who may have had a string of successes with a particular marketing strategy, may hold on to such a strategy rigidly, even if confronted with compelling evidence of its failure.

How then can such potential strategic decision-making biases be overcome in the context of organizational decision-making? First, organizational structures and organizational objectives must emphasize and stress the value of strategic thinking directed toward achieving competitive advantage. Second, organizations must encourage constructive dialogue and debate about strategy amongst members of the decision-making group. Planning systems must encourage criticism and reduce the resistance to debate about strategy which often exists in organizational contexts. This is because managers identify with their formulation of the strategy problem, and see criticism as a challenge to their competence. Therefore, there should be a planning and strategy dialogue which is viewed as a negotiation process, and not a threat. In this process, alternative problem assumptions should be identified and differing strategy viewpoints should be presented in a positive manner. This should involve both extensive critiques of existing plans and formulation of newer alternative strategic positions. If implemented successfully, such debate processes can help managers to share experiences and identify those underlying assumptions which are likely to pose real threats both to the organization and its competitive strategy.

CONCLUSION: PROCESS DESIGN AND PROBLEM UNCERTAINTY

Perhaps the key issue stressed in this paper is that strategy problems are ill-structured (i.e. they are 'wicked problems of organized complexity') (Mason and Mitroff, 1981) and therefore require more effort for their resolution than the routine application of quantitative analysis or rigid planning tools.

There is a need to recognize that strategy problems are characterized not only by stochastic uncertainty about variables and outcomes but, more importantly, by considerable uncertainty about problem structure. Lippman and Rumelt (1981) have advanced an additional proposition about 'option uncertainty' in the context of strategy problems. They are interested in the notion of 'uncertain imitability', which means that firms in a competitive environment may face uncertainty about their ability to imitate (or replicate) the strategy of, say, the initial entrant in the market.

Given this uncertainty about problem structure, options, variables, and outcomes, there is a need to devise richer planning and strategy processes. Essential features would be the encouragement of a dialogue and debate process about options and the provision of quantitative analyses acting as decision support and information systems for strategic decision-making. It is argued here that approaches such as strategic assumptions analysis (Mason and Mitroff, 1981), which rely on dialectical inquiry systems, can improve the quality of strategy options and solutions. In a recent study, Schwenk and Thomas (1982) confirm that a combined devil's advocate/dialectical inquiry process can improve solution quality when compared against so-called 'expert' or analytic modelling processes.

In conclusion, we would argue as Mason and Mitroff (1981: 302) do that planning and strategy processes must incorporate analytic models, information gathering and structured debate processes.

> the real world of policy, planning and strategy is inherently complex. . . . As a result, dialectical methods, structured debate and argumentation analysis are necessary to cope with this complexity. However, these methods are not necessarily sufficient. Other methods, such as the systems approach, analytical modelling, the case approach, PIMS, and product portfolio analysis are necessary as well in a program of strategic inquiry. The focus should be on 'program' and 'inquiry' not on any single method that pretends to answer all problems. Whatever methods are used they should always aid in challenging strategic planning assumptions.

The key issue in strategy formulation is thus the design of a strategic inquiry system for generating and resolving strategic options. New developments in quantitative analytic models should take the focus of strategic intelligence systems, since quantitative analyses can *only* test or confirm hypotheses about strategies already conceived judgementally—they cannot meaningfully generate strategies.

REFERENCES

Abell, Derek F., 'Using PIMS and portfolio analysis in strategic market planning: a comparative analysis', *Harvard, ICCH Note*, 9-578-017 (1977).

Abell, Derek F., *Defining the Business*. Prentice-Hall, Englewood Cliffs, N.J., 1980.

Abell, D. F., and J. S. Hammond, *Strategic Market Planning*. Prentice-Hall, Englewood Cliffs, N.J., 1979.

Ackoff, Russell L., *A Concept of Corporate Planning* John Wiley, New York, 1970.

Alderson, W., and P. E. Green, *Planning and Problem Solving in Marketing*, Richard D. Irwin Inc., Homewood, Ill., 1964.

Alpert, M., and H. Raiffa, 'A progress report on the training of probability assessors'. Unpublished working paper, Harvard Business School, 1969.

Anderson, Carl R., and Frank T. Paine, 'PIMS: a re-examination', *Academy of Management Review*, July 1978, pp. 602–612.

Ansoff, H. Igor, *Corporate Strategy*. Penguin Books, London, 1965.

Biggadike, E. Ralph, 'The contributions of marketing to strategic management', *Academy of Management Review*, 6(4) (Oct. 1981), 621–633.

Boston Consulting Group, 'Competition in the 1980s' *Consulting Perspectives*, Boston, Mass. 1981.

Boyd, H. W. Jr, and J. C. Larreche, 'Foundations of marketing strategy', in *Review of Marketing* (eds. G. Zaltman and T. Bonoma). American Marketing Association, 1978.

Bracker, Jeffrey, 'The historical development of the strategic management concept', *Academy of Management Review*, 5(2) (1980), 219–224.

Capon, N., and J. R. Spogli, 'A comparison and critical examination of the PIMS and BCG approaches to strategic market planning', *Harvard, ICCH Note*, 9-578-148 (1978).

Caves, R. E., 'Industrial organization, corporate strategy and structure', *Journal of Economic Literature*, Mar. 1980, pp. 64–92.

Churchman, C. W., *The Systems Approach*. Dell Publishing, New York, 1968.

Clelland, D. I., and W. R. King, 'Environmental information systems for strategic marketing planning', *Journal of Marketing*, **38**(4) (Oct. 1974), 35–40.

Copeland, T. S., and J. F. Weston, *Financial Theory and Corporate Policy*. Addison-Wesley, Reading, Mass., 1979.

Day, G. S. 'Diagnosing the product portfolio', *Journal of Marketing*, **41** (Apr. 1977), 29–38.

Day, G. S. 'Strategic market analysis and definition: an integrated approach', *Strategic Management Journal*, **2**(3), (July/Sept. 1981), 281–301.

Dhalla, N. R., and S. Yuspeh, 'Forget the product life cycle concept', *Harvard Business Review*, Jan./Feb. 1976, pp. 102–112.

Gluck, F. W., S. P. Kaufman, and A. S. Walleck, 'Strategic management for competitive advantage', *Harvard Business Review*, July/Aug. 1980, pp. 154–161.

Greenwood, Paul, and Howard Thomas, 'A review of analytical models in strategic planning', *Omega*, **9**(4) (1981), 397–417.

Harrigan, K. R., 'Strategies for Declining Business'. Unpublished doctoral dissertation, Harvard University, 1979.

Haspelagh, P., 'Portfolio planning: uses and limits', *Harvard Business Review*. Jan./Feb. 1982, pp. 58–74.

Hatten, K. J., and D. E. Schendel, 'Heterogeneity within an industry: firm conduct in the U.S. brewing industry, 1952–71', *Journal of Industrial Economics*, Dec. 1977, pp. 97–113.

Hedley, B., 'Strategy and the business portfolio', *Long Range Planning*,**10**, Feb. 1977.

Henderson, Bruce D., *Henderson on Coporate Strategy*. Abt Books, Cambridge, Mass., 1981.

Hofer, C. W., and D. E. Schendel, *Strategy Formulation: Analytical Concepts*. West Publishing Co., St. Paul, MN, 1978.

Hogarth, R. N., and S. Makradakis, 'Forecasting and planning: an evaluation', *Management Science*, **27**(2), (Feb. 1981), 115–138.

Horsky, Dan, and Subrata, K. Sen, 'Interfaces between marketing and economics: an overview', *Journal of Business*, **53**(3) (1980), 55–58.

Hughes, G. David, *Marketing Management: A Planning Approach*. Addison-Wesley, Reading, Mass., 1978.

Hunsicker, J. Q., 'The malaise of strategic planning', *McKinsey Quarterly*, Spring 1980, pp. 2–13.

Hussey, D. E., 'Portfolio analysis: practical experience with the directional policy matrix', *Long Range Planning*, **11** (Aug. 1978), 2–8.

Kerin, R. A., and R. A. Peterson, *Perspectives on Strategic Marketing Management*. Allyn and Bacon, Inc., Boston, Mass., 1980.

Kiechel, III, Walter, 'Oh where, oh where has my little dog gone? or my cash cow? or my star?' *Fortune*, Nov. 2, 1981, pp. 148–154.

Kotler, Philip, *Marketing Management: Analysis, Planning and Control*. Prentice-Hall, Englewood Cliffs, N.J., 1980.

Langer, E. J., 'The illusion of control', *Journal of Personality and Social Psychology*, **32**(2) (1975), 311–328.

Larreche, J. C., and V. Srinavasan, 'Stratport: a decision support system for strategic planning', *Journal of Marketing*, **45** (Fall 1981), 39–52.

38   Strategic Marketing and Management

Lindblom, C. E., 'The science of muddling through', *Public Administration Review*, 1959.
Lippman, S. A., and R. P. Rumelt, 'Efficiency differentials under competition: a stochastic approach to industrial organization', Working Paper, UCLA Graduate School of Management, 1981.
Livingston, J. Sterling, 'The myth of the well educated manager', *Harvard Business Review*, 1971.
Lyon, Leverett, S., *Salesmen in Marketing Strategy*, Macmillan, New York, 1926.
Markowitz, H., *Portfolio Selection*. John Wiley & Sons, New York, 1959.
Mason, R. O., and I. I. Mitroff, *Challenging Strategic Planning Assumptions*, John Wiley & Sons, New York, 1981.
Montgomery, D. B., and C. B. Weinberg, 'Toward strategic intelligence systems', *Journal of Marketing*, **43**(4), 1979, 41–52.
Moore, P. G., and H. Thomas, 'Measuring uncertainty', *Omega*, **3**(6) (1975), 657–672.
Newman, H. H. 'Strategic groups and the structural/performance relationship', *Review of Economics and Statistics*, **60** (1978), 417–427.
Polli, R., and V. J. Cook, 'Validity of the product life cycle', *Journal of Business*, **42**(4) (Oct. 1969), 385–400.
Porter, Michael E., 'The contributions of industrial organization to strategic management', *Academy of Management Review*, **6**(4) (Oct. 1981), 609–621.
Porter, Michael E., 'How competitive forces shape strategy', *Harvard Business Review*, **57** (Mar./Apr. 1979), 137–156.
Porter, Michael E., *Competitive Strategy*. Free Press, New York, 1980.
Rink, D. R., and J. E. Swan, 'Product life cycle research: a literature review', *Journal of Business Research*, 1979, pp. 219–242.
Rumelt, R. P., *Strategy, Structure and Economic Performance*. Division of Research, Harvard Business School, 1974.
Rumelt, R. P., and J. R. C. Wensley, 'In search of the market share effect', *Academy of Management Proceedings*, 1981, pp. 1–6.
Schendel, D. E., and C. W. Hofer, *Strategic Management*. Little, Brown, Boston, Mass., 1979.
Schendel, Dan, and G. Richard Patton, 'A simultaneous equation model of corporate strategy', *Management Science*, **24**(15) (Nov. 1978), 1161–1621.
Schoeffler, S., R. D. Buzzell, and D. F. Heany, 'Impact of strategic planning of profit performance', *Harvard Business Review*, Mar./Apr. 1974, pp. 137–145.
Schwenk, C. R., and H. Thomas, 'Formulating the mess: the role of decision analysis and other decision aids in problem formulation'. Working Paper, Department of Business Administration, University of Illinois, 1981. (Published in *Omega*, **11**(3), 1983, 239–252).
Schwenk, C. R., and H. Thomas, 'Effects of decision aids on problem structuring and solutions quality'. Working Paper, Department of Business Administration, University of Illinois, 1982 (and in *Decision Sciences*, 1984 (in press).
Selvidge, J., 'Rapid screening of decision options', Tech. Report, 76–12. Decisions and Designs Inc., Mclean, Va., 1976.
Simon, H. A. *Administrative Behavior* (3rd ed.) Free Press, New York, 1976.
Simon, L. S., and M. Freimer, *Analytical Marketing*. Harcourt, Brace & World, New York, 1970.
Springer, C. H., 'Strategic management in General Electric, *Operations Research*, Nov./Dec. 1973, pp. 1177–1182.
Steinbruner, J. D., *The Cybernetic Theory of Decision*. Princeton University Press, Princeton, N.J., 1974.

Stevenson, Howard H., 'Defining corporate strengths and weaknesses', *Sloan Management Review*, **17**(3) (Spring 1976), 51–58.

Taylor, R. N., 'Psychological determinants of bounded rationality: implications for decision-making', *Decisions Sciences*, **6** (1975), 409–429.

Tregoe, B. B., and J. W. Zimmerman, *Top Management Strategy*. New York: Simon & Schuster, New York, 1981.

Tversky, A., and D. Kahneman, 'Judgement under uncertainty: heuristics and biases', *Science*, **185** (1974), 1124–1131.

Utterback, James M., 'Environmental analysis and forecasting', in D. E. Schendel and C. W. Hofer (eds), *Strategic Management*, pp. 134–144. Little, Brown, Boston, 1979.

Wensley, Robin, 'Strategic marketing: betas, boxes or basics', *Journal of Marketing*, **45** (Summer 1981), 173–182.

Wensley, J. R. C., 'PIMS and BCG: new horizons or false dawn', *Strategic Management Journal*, **3**, April/June 1982, 147–158.

Wind, Y., 'Issues and advances in segmentation research', *Journal of Marketing Research*, **15** (Aug. 1978), 317–337.

Wind, Yoram, and Vijay Mahajan, 'Designing product and business portfolios', *Harvard Business Review*, Jan./Feb. 1981, pp. 155–165.

Winter, F. W., 'A cost benefit approach to market segmentation', *Journal of Marketing*, **43** (Fall 1979), 103–111.

Woo, C. Y., 'Market share leadership, does it always pay off', *Academy of Management Proceedings*, 1981, pp. 7–11.

Zeithaml, C. P., C. R. Anderson, and F. T. Paine, 'An empirical reexamination of selected PIMS findings', *Academy of Management Proceedings*, 1981, pp. 12–16.

1.3

Strategic Management and Strategic Marketing: What's Strategic About Either One?

DAN E. SCHENDEL

Purdue University, Krannert Graduate School of Management, West Lafayette, Indiana 47907

INTRODUCTION

An increasingly popular term in the marketing literature is 'strategic management'. Equally popular in the policy literature is the term 'strategic management'. An interesting question is whether there is a meaningful distinction to be drawn between management or marketing that is strategic, and that which is not? Indeed, what's strategic about either marketing or management? In this paper, these questions will be examined in terms of some basic constructs now developing in the strategy field.

We begin the search for answers by examining some constructs of value. The first construct involves identifying the difference between operating the firm and making strategy for it. There is a significant and useful difference to be noted. Because of its central role (some might say its over-use) the term strategy is examined in detail, including the useful distinctions to be made between strategies developed at the three basic levels of organization structure in today's modern firm. Then, three elements central to strategic management, goals, strategy, and environment, are briefly examined, along with a look at the generic strategic management tasks. We will then be able to consider what is strategic about marketing and how it relates to strategic management.

OPERATIONS AND STRATEGY

In his classic book, *The Functions of the Executive*, Chester Barnard (1938) made a useful distinction between efficiency and effectiveness. Peter Drucker (1973) writing much later, and without reference to Barnard, made the same distinction, as is his gift, in far clearer language, when he remarked that there is a difference between '. . . doing things right' and '. . . doing the right things'. To any firm, there is a significant difference between being efficient and being effective, between doing things right (efficiency) and doing the right things (effectiveness). A firm must be both efficient and effective to survive, and it must understand the difference between them. We can develop this distinction using the terms 'operations management' to mean managing for efficiency, a concern with doing things right, and 'strategic management' to mean managing for effectiveness, a concern with doing the right things. The latter deals with enhancing success and sometimes just with mere survival. Both operations and strategic management must be done well to survive in a competitive system.

The difference between operations and strategic management can be illustrated by examining the early history of the automobile industry and the two most prominent survivors of that early history, General Motors and Ford. Perhaps the most celebrated entrepreneur in American economic history is Henry Ford, who proved to be a notable strategist, first by success and second by failure, or at least relative failure.

About 1908 there were two landmark events in the auto industry, Ford introduced the Model T, and the General Motors Company (the forerunner of the corporation) was formed. Ford soared to success, while General Motors was undistinguished, and in fact remained so until it was reorganized in 1914 to form the corporation. GM underwent still further financial difficulties under Durant's attempts to pull together a variety of companies that were to be the backbone of GM.

For nearly 20 years the Model T set the low cost standard and gave Ford the sales and market share leadership in the auto industry. In 1928, using what was essentially a strategy of segmenting the market and matching to it manufacturing scale economies, GM took over leadership in the American auto industry and has never been headed since. So, after 20 years Ford lost its leading position and with it gave up the fruits of leadership. What went wrong for Ford, and what went right for GM? The answer lies in the difference between effectiveness and efficiency, in the difference between operations and strategy.

The genius of Henry Ford was in seeing the necessity for driving the cost of an automobile so low that more people could afford to buy one (strategic insight) *and* in seeing how those low cost levels could be attained through such innovations as the moving assembly line (operating insight). Such entrepreneurial actions are usually simple and brilliant in hindsight. And it worked, for 20 years. But the strength of Ford proved his downfall. His obsession with efficiency caused him to overlook the changing affluence in the marketplace, changes which Sloan and others at GM not only saw, but did something about. GM devised a strategy, including an organization structure and process, and it served an evolving market that Henry Ford could not or would not see. So, while Henry Ford's company was very efficient, it proved ineffective in the late

1920s. His concentration on operations, and an unwillingness to alter his formerly winning strategy, relegated Ford to second position, and for a time even to third position in the auto industry behind Chrysler.

There are many examples of companies that started with a brilliant strategy and ended obsessed with efficiency and a lack of understanding as to why an entrepreneur's original strategy was made obsolete by a change in the marketplace, a change in technology, changes in government regulation, or some other significant change in the firm's environment. There is a difference between operations and strategy and this difference is worth exploring if we are to understand what it is that is strategic about management or marketing, and what the relationship is between strategic management and strategic marketing.

Operations management

Efficiency, and operations management, are concerned with input and output, more output for the same input, or the same output for less input. It is concerned with cost, revenue, and profit, with a net benefit gain. It is not concerned with changing direction, it is concerned with maintaining direction, in our terms, direction established by a basic strategy. Operations management, by which I do not mean the narrow connotation of manufacturing management now associated with that term in many business schools, is concerned with the day-to-day maintenance of direction, under some existing strategy.

Strategic management

Strategic management is concerned with direction, with basic choices of actions that will achieve goals, subject to the constraints offered by the set of environmental, non-controllable forces facing the firm. Strategic management is concerned with creating a strategy, with choosing a strategy that can be used efficiently, and with assuring the future viability of the firm. While strategic management does not dominate operations management, it supplies the cues for the directions operations management must take.

STRATEGY

A fundamental definition of strategy is at the core of this distinction, and it is worth further examination. In his seminal work, Chandler (1962) defined strategy as, '. . . the determination of the basic long-term goals and objectives of an enterprise, and adoption of courses of action and the allocation of resources necessary for carrying out these goals'. Chandler's interest was in relating organizational structure and strategy. He defined strategy as though it was a managerial process. It is not. It is a concept that guides managerial actions, or operations management, in our terms.

Others have since developed other notions of strategy, among them Ansoff (1965) and Andrews (1971). The evolution of the strategy concept has been well documented and developed by Hofer and Schendel (1978), and Schendel and Hofer (1979). All of the strategy notions advanced deal basically with establishing or meeting goals through a set of actions related to resource allocating decisions and with establishing a set of guidelines, sometimes called policies, which are intended to guide and constrain the day-to-day decisions needed to operate any complex organization.

COMPONENTS OF STRATEGY

For our purposes strategy can be viewed in terms of components, or areas, in which key decisions are needed to give life to the notion of strategy. There are five components to be considered: (1) scope of operations, (2) resource availability and deployment, (3) competitive advantage, (4) operating policies, and (5) administrative structure. Note that this 'component' definition of strategy excludes goals, although clearly, like all other definitions of strategy, it assumes a given set of goals. Moreover, strategy–goal sets can only be generated and chosen in the light of environmental opportunities and threats.

The first three components can be labeled the 'entrepreneurial components' of strategy. These represent the three decision areas at the heart of the choices made by the entrepreneur, such as Henry Ford, in starting a business, and they are at the heart of strategic management as it struggles with the task of choosing viable directions for the firm. Above everything else, strategic management deals with entrepreneurial activities, albeit more frequently in the on-going firm than in new business start-ups.

The third and fourth components of strategy can be labeled the 'integrating components' of strategy. These represent the decision areas which fulfill another major role of strategy, that of coordinating the activities of the organization and assuring the strategy is properly implemented or used. It was Chandler (1962) who advanced the thesis that strategy and structure were related, in fact, related sequentially according to him, with structure following strategy. He argued, for example, that GM was not able to effect the strategy used to overcome Ford in the 1920s until it was able to devise an administrative structure capable of implementing the strategy. The integrating components of strategy deal with operations management more directly than do the entrepreneurial components.

Both the entrepreneurial and integrating components of strategy are of central importance to strategic management. The three entrepreneurial components are of more recent origin in the strategy construct; indeed, as important as the role is in a capitalistic economy, it has been only in recent times that the study of entrepreneurship has taken a serious turn away from its anecdotal origins. The original view of the emerging area of strategic management was that it was simply a matter of coordinating, through policy directives, the actions of functional areas of the business, meaning marketing, finance, manufacturing, and such-like. In other words, strategy was seen essentially as a matter of policy-making, a tag by which it is much better known even today. But there is much more to it, as we can see from an examination of the five strategy components in greater detail.

Scope

The scope of General Electric can be said to be greater than the scope of General Motors. GE is involved in many more businesses than is GM. Not size, but the range of different businesses in which a firm competes, is a measure of its scope. This aspect of scope, the choice of in which product/markets to compete, is an important dimension of corporate-level strategy we shall examine below. While ordinarily a matter of diversification and divestment, this aspect of scope includes both related diversification and vertical integration, as well as the matter of unrelated diversification.

There are scope decisions of interest at another level of strategy, which will interest us below; those of business-level strategy. Business-level strategy is concerned with how a single product/market competes or positions itself in the competitive arena. Two important aspects of scope at this level of interest are the geographic (and other segmentation) choices made and the product line choices, matched to these segments. Will the business (sometimes labeled a division, or strategic business unit) be a full-line competitor or will it restrict its activity? How will it position itself among its competitors?

Scope decisions are difficult to make, but once made, define the business in many important respects. For our purposes, one of the major reasons why scope is so important is that it defines the environment in which the firm competes, and the environment is the major source of change in the balance sought between goals, strategy, and environment. Scope decisions are a significant aspect of strategy often taken for granted because they are not made very often.

Resource availability and deployment

There are two aspects to the resource component of strategy. First, the ability of the overall firm and/or business unit to generate resources must be understood. Resources here are defined in the widest sense to include the strengths of the firm, including people, cash, patents, favored raw materials sources, site locations, consumer franchises, etc. What is the nature of the firm's resources, the strengths, the distinctive competences, and in what levels and amount are they capable of being generated and regenerated by the firm in the future?

The second aspect of resources is at the very heart of the entrepreneurial side of strategy: 'How should the available resources be deployed?' Resource allocation is made to initiate and sustain actions which in turn will achieve goals. Resource allocation can be made rationally only in light of the firm's goals and environmental assumptions the strategist is willing to make about the future.

Competitive advantage

The choice of scope and the resource deployments made will determine the competitive advantage achieved in the competitive arena. Indeed, the measure of the quality of any strategy, proposed or in use, is the competitive advantage it is expected to deliver or has delivered to the firm. Competitive advantage, differential advantage, whatever it is called, is in fact what is sought, for without it there is no protection for the firm, no guarantee of its survival. A common measure of competitive advantage is return from investment, in the most global sense, the amount of cash that is returned compared to the amount of cash put at risk. If a strategy cannot produce a competitive advantage it is a poor strategy. For any firm to survive it must produce some competitive advantage that at least equals that of its fellow competitors.

Summary of entrepreneurial components

The three entrepreneurial components of strategy—scope, resource availability and deployment, and competitive advantage—are at the center of strategic management, and yet choices in these areas cannot be made without knowledge of the goals sought by the firm and without some definite assumptions about the environment in which the firm will compete. The challenge to the strategist lies not so much in the nature of the decisions themselves, although they are difficult, but in the process by which the decisions are, or better still, should be made. This decision-making process involves the simultaneous determination of goals and strategy, in balance with the environment, and three different levels of the organization structure. There is a Catch-22, a circularity, that must be overcome in practice, which while beyond the scope of this paper is real nevertheless, and is perhaps the most difficult aspect of strategic management.

Operating policies

A policy can be defined as a decision rule, to be used in recognizable, repetitive structured problem-solving situations. If certain specific conditions are encounterd, then certain specific responses are to be given. For example, policies governing working hours, vacations, retirement, and granting of credit are common operating policies. Such decision rules are cast up by the thousands in large organizations, and are often referred to as Standard Operating Procedures. Our interest in these is in the guidance such policies provide for coordinating the activities of the organization in implementing or using the entrepreneurial choices we have just discussed. In a very small business, a single business, operating policies are about the only strategy component that needs to be made explicit; the remainder can reside in the head of the entrepreneur/manager/strategist. Such policies coordinate and guide operations and represent the decisions of owner–managers. The entrepreneurial components of strategy are embedded in the original entrepreneurial decisions to enter and operate the business in the first place. One of the reasons why it is difficult for many managers to understand the importance of strategy and strategy-making lies in this embedding of strategy components in operating practice.

Administrative structure

Administrative structure includes the reporting relationships, authority distributions, personnel choices, measurement and reward systems, decision-making processes, information systems, and such other managerial processes used to administer an organization through managerial labor specialization (Galbraith and Nathanson, 1978). The entrepreneurial components of strategy imply the work tasks that must be accomplished by the organization in meeting its operating management responsibilities. For example the strategy of Revlon requires different marketing tasks than does the strategy of Avon.

The administrative structure must also address those managerial activities needed to formulate and use strategy as well. In other words, both the work of operating management and strategic management must be accomplished through the administrative structure devised for the organization. This dual-level assignment is a very difficult one, for the structure devised to operate an organization does not need to be like the one needed to manage it strategically, although few organization structures are differentiated in these terms.

Inclusion of the administrative structure component in the integrating role of strategy is prompted by the work of Chandler (1962), and others, which have shown that strategy and structure are intimately linked. In an on-going organization it is not clear whether structure always follows strategy as Chandler suggested, or whether structure does not place constraints on what strategies are possible. To be successful a strategy must deliver a competitive advantage, and to do that requires use of a chosen strategy in an efficient way, in the way intended.

Summary of integrating components

Our interest in the two integrating components is clearly one of using the strategy and insuring that the strategy can be used. While essential to sound strategic management practice, our interest in these two components in the remainder of the paper will be much less than in the three entrepreneurial components.

STRATEGY HIERARCHY

The administrative structure that permitted General Motors to implement a new strategy of multiple models in the 1920s was essentially the use of a divisional organization structure, along with a variety of new information systems and decision processes. By about 1950 some one-third of the *Fortune* 500 used a divisional structure, or more importantly, some one-third of those major firms were operating multiple businesses. The birth of the diversified (multiple-business) organization gave rise to a different, and additional, strategy question than faces the single business. Not only must a strategy be devised for every business, but so presumably must there be a strategy for the multiple-business grouping. Figure 1.3.1 depicts the classic three-level organization so common today, and shows there the three levels of strategy needed: (1) corporate level strategy, (2) business level strategy, and (3) functional area strategy.

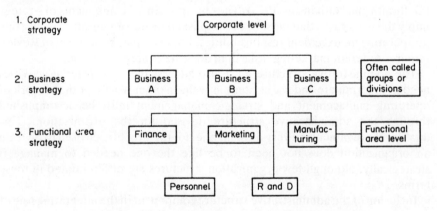

Figure 1.3.1   Organization and strategy hierarchy

Corporate level strategy

As indicated, the major concern at the corporate strategy level is what businesses to enter, which to hold, and which to divest. The central issue is like that facing the banker: what should be the portfolio of businesses held by the firm at any given time? There is an essential difference in the manager's portfolio problem, however. Unlike the banker, the manager must manage the portfolio of businesses after an investment is made. There is a social welfare question embedded in this issue, which need not concern us, about whether it makes sense for society to permit multiple businesses to be held by one legal entity. The argument goes that no value is created in the firm holding multiple businesses that could not be created by an independent investor diversifying his portfolio through stock purchases in the market. Yet, such multiple-business organizations have arisen and must be managed and whether they create social gain is a matter better left to another discussion. For our purposes a corporate level strategy decision is required concerning which businesses to enter and hold, and which to divest. The same entrepreneurial and integrating components cited earlier are central to the corporate level strategy decision.

Business level strategy

At this level, the essential question to be dealt with is what competitive advantage can be achieved and maintained by the given business? If the business is part of a larger portfolio, another question, which will be essential to business level strategy-making, is what kind of return and what level of risk can be shown by the business relative to all others in the portfolio. Resources made available to the business are determined by the answer to this question and, in this respect, are influenced by the nature of the portfolio-mates and not just by the characteristics of the business alone. Resource needs of the business will be determined by the inherent rate of growth in the markets served and the degree of competition for the demand.

Functional area strategy

To this point no attention has been given to this important level of strategy, but it does not differ from the other levels in the sense of components, although it does in the nature of its contributions. By functional level strategy is meant marketing strategy, financial strategy, manufacturing strategy, manpower strategy, R and D strategy, and so on. Functional areas result from the first form of managerial labor specialization that occurs when volume grows to a point where the owner–manager can no longer do the entire management job alone. Functional area managers are selected on the basis of a different kind of expertise than managers who are chosen at the other two levels. At the functional area level, the expertise is based on knowledge of a discipline. At the other two higher levels expertise is based on skills needed by a general manager, one charged with integrating the activities of many functional areas, and one who must keep not one but all functional balls in the air at one time.

One of the original concepts of strategic management, the one held under the earlier policy construct mentioned, is that all that is required of the general manager's position is to initiate policy directives which would coordinate the functional areas as they pursued operations management tasks. Under this construct the need for strategy changes comes so infrequently as to permit the policy view to suffice. Such a view overlooks the synergy gains that come not from the contribution of a single functional area, but the combination of the functional areas, and their integration through business and corporate level strategy.

All of this brings us to the relationship between strategic management and marketing. Marketing is a functional area, of course, and in this respect it is similar to the finance, manufacturing, and other areas. Marketing has both a strategic and an operating role to play, and it needs to play its strategic and operating roles in the larger context of business units and the corporate whole. To see what is strategic about marketing, and how strategic marketing relates to strategic management, we need to recognize the essential nature of the strategic management process.

GOALS, STRATEGY, AND ENVIRONMENT

Strategic management is concerned with the processes and techniques for developing, implementing, and maintaining a balance among the means, called *strategies*, that help achieve ends, called *goals*, subject to the opportunities and threats offered by the *environment* in which the firm competes. This definition outlines the three basic elements of strategic management. Taken together these three elements, shown in Figure 1.3.2, define the basic characteristics of the firm, indeed, can be used to define any organization, whether for profit or not-for-profit. These three elements always seek a balance; a change in any one of them leads to a change in the other two elements. For reasons we shall examine, the environment element is most likely to be the source of change.

A brief look at each of the elements will help illustrate the work facing the strategic manager. We have already examined the strategy element in some detail, so let us look at goals and environment.

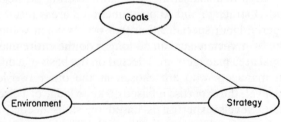

Figure 1.3.2   Elements of the strategic management
process

Goals

Goals motivate actions, or strategies. In a business firm the capital markets set the ultimate goal of the firm, return on capital employed, or in reality, net cash flow and the ability to return the cash invested at risk. However, there must be some further definition of goals if they are to be of managerial value in motivating action. There must be some hierarchy of goals to match the hierarchical levels of the organization and, in turn, strategies need to be devised to achieve these goals, notably business level goals and functional area goals. This hierarchical notion of goals is an essential counterpart of corporate, business, and functional level strategies already described. Indeed, it is through this hierarchical notion that functional area goals such as marketing goals arise, for example.

Except in cases of crises—for example, danger of bankruptcy—goal structures normally do not change in any strategic sense. In other words changes in goals are not a likely source of change in the balance between the three elements we are examining. Crises, and their corollary, changes in senior management, are the major conditions under which changes in goal structures can be expected. Of course, as the organizational hierarchy is descended toward the business units and functional areas, changes in goals are more likely to occur.

Environment

The environment is by definition all of those variables that affect the firm, but which cannot be chosen or fixed, as management would select strategy or establish the goals of the firm. The environment is composed of non-controllable variables. In contrast, goals and strategy are controllable. In this concept of the environment, management can only influence its environment, it cannot manage it. In this sense it is like the weather; man can influence the weather, but in no practical sense can the weather be managed. We forecast the weather, we react to the weather, but we do not manage the weather, we do plan for the weather. We adapt to it, and so must the firm adapt to its environment, if it can. In effect, the firm must make assumptions about what the environment will be like and act as though the assumptions were correct. In no sense is the environment a managerial variable.

Changes in the environment are the most common cause of alterations in the dynamic balance sought among goals, strategy, and environment. It is important to understand the components comprising the environment because they must be forecast and evaluated for their potential to change strategy and goals. Figure 1.3.3 suggests the four major classes of environmental variables that need to be monitored and evaluated. The specific variables to be monitored must be selected with care because there are literally thousands to

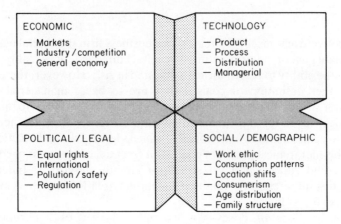

Figure 1.3.3   Enviromental components

be considered in any specific situation. The scope of the strategy in general will determine what the variables will be. However, all of these environmental variables can be categorized usefully into the four categories shown in Figure 1.3.3.

STRATEGIC MANAGEMENT PROCESS

To this point we have developed a series of constructs that are central to understanding what is strategic about strategic management, and where marketing as a function fits into the scheme. The major constructs are these: (1) there is a difference between operations and strategic management; (2) the concept of strategy can be viewed in terms of its entrepreneurial and integrating components; (3) matching the modern-day complex organization structure is a strategy (and a goal and environmental) hierarchy of corporate level, business level, and functional level and these three strategy levels differ, not in terms of entrepreneurial and integrating components, but in terms of issues of central interest; (4) that there are three basic elements in the strategic management construct: goals, strategy and environment; and finally (5) that there exists a strategic management process that can be viewed in terms of generic work tasks.

The constructs we have been discussing imply managerial work, strategic work that can be accomplished in a variety of ways. Whatever the processes used to do this strategic work, all must accomplish a similar set of tasks and, not surprisingly, these tasks all relate to one of the three elements: strategy, goals, or environment. These generic tasks must be incorporated into any strategic planning process used. A schematic depiction of these tasks and how they relate to one another is presented in Figure 1.3.4. Any strategic planning

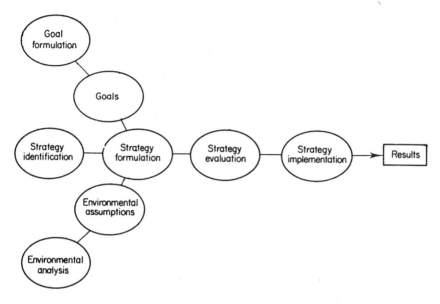

Figure 1.3.4   Generic tasks in the strategic management process

process can be cataloged in terms of these tasks in the strategic management process.

MARKETING: STRATEGY AND OPERATIONS

We are now in a position to examine just what it is that is strategic about strategic marketing, and how strategic management and marketing are related. First, marketing, as with any of the other functional areas, is related to business level strategy, and in fact, can be coordinated with all of the other functional areas to insure consistency among them. Under such a view it is difficult to suggest that any of the functional areas have any priority over any other. If a priority exists for any functional area it exists only in terms of the relatively higher contribution to competitive advantage it can make to the business strategy proposed, or that in use.

In considering the relative roles of the various functional areas, there are perhaps only two basic competitive advantages that can be gained. One is being the lowest-cost producer among those competitors offering the product or service; the other is offering a differentiated product or service for which ready and immediate substitutes do not exist and for which, therefore, some consuming segment is willing to pay a premium for what is a relatively higher-cost product or service.

As with any of the functional areas, there is an operating side, usually as important and often more important than the strategic side. Only those aspects of the marketing function that contribute to development of strategy, especially to the competitive advantage component, and finally to the use of strategy in the achievement of strategic goals, can be called strategic in nature. To better see the relationship of marketing as a functional area to the constructs developed here Table 1.3.1 arrays goals and strategy against the organizational hierarchy of corporate, business, and functional levels to identify the essential nature of each organizational level. Marketing is used as an example of the relationship of a functional area in Table 1.3.1. Note that only the three entrepreneurial components of strategy—scope, resource availability and deployment, and competitive advantage—are used in the matrix presented in Table 1.3.1. There are several points that can made from this comparison.

Goals and marketing

The strategic goals for the marketing function are derivatives of the business goals, which in turn are derivatives of the corporate goals. Note we are speaking here not of goals used in operations management, which may arise from other sources. For marketing these operating goals arise internally within the marketing function itself, for the most part as it seeks to manage its activities efficiently. Strategic goals, while not necessarily formulated on a strictly top-down basis, in fact must act that way, if the hierarchy of strategic goals is to be consistent among vertical organization levels and horizontally across functional areas. It would be confusing for the finance function to be working toward different growth goals than those set for the marketing function, or for manufacturing to be working toward one capacity level while marketing works toward a different one. Hence, only where the marketing function is assigned a strategic goal, as for example in the extension of geographic scope, would there exist the need for strategic action on the part of marketing.

Strategy and marketing

From a strategic viewpoint, marketing or any other function must develop a strategy that works toward the strategic goals established for it. Because the marketing literature has long used the term 'marketing strategy' as a means of otherwise describing the marketing mix, we need to make a distinction between our usage and the conventional usage of the term. Here, marketing strategy means something else, and does not refer to the marketing mix as that term is used in an operating sense, the context which represents the normal usage of the term.

It should also be noted in this strategic context that marketing as a function really has little to do with corporate level strategy formulation. Corporate level strategy deals with portfolio issues and is more centrally concerned with financial and managerial synergy as sources of competitive advantage than it is with

Table 1.3.1 Goals, strategy, and organizational level

Components	Corporate level	Business level	Functional area level (marketing)
Goal structure	Institutional role Purpose/mission Capital markets Return. Cash flow	Business goals Portfolio position Cash usage and growth rates Strategic group/positioning	Derivatives of business goals Marketing goals: sales level Volume (growth and share)
Entrepreneurial strategy components			
Scope	What businesses to be in? Risk/return/growth balance Acquire/divest? Diversification	Geographic market segments Breadth of product line Vertical integration Product/process life cycle	Broaden geographic markets Product design and development
Resource availability	Capital market valuation Past performance results Operating efficiency Strategic productivity Capital structure	Bank with corporation Cash generation/usage Non-cash resources	No separate cash generation Consumer franchise Personnel skills
Resource deployment	Portfolio issues Risk/return Growth/maintain/harvest Acquire/divest	Product/market segments growth Functional areas budgets Working capital	Further allocation of budget Marketing mix allocation Strategic information
Competitive advantage	Financial synergy Risk/cost of capital Managerial synergy Scale economies	Strategic group position Cost-based Technology/market-based	Marketing contribution Lowest cost (share) Differentiation contributions

market position, competitors, market share, growth rates, position in the life cycle, and other such matters of central concern to business level strategy. Marketing as a function can help develop managerial synergy at the corporate level in the sense that scale economies accrue from centralized marketing research, a common sales force, jointly used distribution outlets, etc. and in this sense marketing participates at the corporate level. While decisions about which business to have and to hold will depend upon a thorough assessment of the potential of each business, it is only in this more indirect sense that marketing deals with corporate strategy formulation.

Hence, marketing strategy needs to be viewed primarily in the context of business level strategy, and as a set of actions to be undertaken in consort with the other functional areas, all of which are ultimately contributing to the entrepreneurial components of business level strategy. Table 1.3.1 suggests how marketing is involved in each of the entrepreneurial components of strategy. These activities are of two basic kinds: one is in strategic information-generation necessary to business level and marketing level strategic decisions, and the other is in the implementation of the marketing strategy devised to support the business strategy.

It is worth noting that the marketing function does not generate its own resources in the sense that a business does. Rather, marketing is dependent upon a budget allocation, which in turn is in part dependent, insofar as its strategic component is concerned, upon decisions made at the corporate and business level. This hierarchical budget allocation decision, incidentally, is interesting because of its simultaneous nature, i.e. the corporate decision cannot be made without a knowledge of the business level which, in turn, requires functional level input. The circle cannot be broken, but the budget value at each level can be simultaneously determined, an interesting challenge for strategic planning process design, but beyond the scope of this paper.

Also worth noting is the special matter of competitive advantage. No single functional area is the sole source of that competitive advantage, including marketing. All functional activities must act in a coordinated and consistent manner to create competitive advantage, whether the low-cost alternative or the differentiation alternative is chosen.

Environment and marketing

The scope decisions made as a part of strategy formulation define the environmental variables that will influence the dynamic balance between goals, strategy, and environment. In assessing the environment and determining the assumptions to be made about the values and impact of the relevant environmental variables, the marketing function has a very special role to play because of the essentially external focus of marketing. By its very nature, marketing deals essentially with the environment, and is perhaps the strongest boundary-spanning function of any business.

The capabilities developed in marketing for consumer research, sales forecasting, determining competitor response, etc. make it a natural place in which to develop strategic information necessary to environmental forecasting and assumption making. Figure 1.3.3 outlines the four categories of environmental assumptions necessary to strategy formulation. Table 1.3.2 indicates areas where marketing should have special expertise in helping to develop environmental assumptions necessary to strategy formulation. While it depends in major part upon the source of competitive advantage sought, probably no other functional area plays as strong a role as does marketing in environmental analysis.

WHAT IS STRATEGIC MARKETING?

As developed here, marketing activities can be either strategic or operations-oriented, depending upon the nature of the issue faced. For the most part marketing work, as is true of functional work in general, is operations-oriented, involves what is often called tactics, and is concerned mainly with implementing marketing-related aspects of business strategy and goals. The contributions that marketing can make to strategic management, the contributions that make marketing strategic, arise from the work involved in the strategy-making process, as outlined in Figure 1.3.4.

There is in some marketing literature the notion that marketing is the starting point of the strategic planning process. In this view, nothing can really happen until marketing, working from the mandate of the marketing concept, initiates the strategy. While such a notion may have appeal to some, it oversimplifies what is a very complex undertaking, which may or may not proceed from a bottom-up view as implied by the idea of marketing as the center of the planning universe. The viewpoint against which we are arguing is characterized by statements such as this one:

> Nobody has the right to put market opportunities into their plan except the marketing people because of their franchise. The market opportunities provide the central focus for the total strategic plan. . . . The market opportunities are contained in the strategic marketing plan. Therefore, strategic marketing has to be the lead function in strategic planning (Zabriskie and Huellmantel, 1981).

Anyone experienced with strategic planning work realizes there is no reason why 'strategic marketing' has to be the lead function in strategic planning. In fact, an argument can be made against such a starting point.

The basis for strategic marketing as a participant in strategy-making and strategy usage is much more like that suggested by Kotler (1980):

> Management is the entrepreneurial agent that interprets market needs and translates them into satisfactory products and services. To do this, management

Table 1.3.2 Environmental forecasting and assumptions—a role for marketing

Environmental category	Examples of assumptions needed	Importance of marketing's role*
1. Economic		
General economy	GNP, growth rates, inflation rate, unemployment, interest rates and capital costs, risk levels	2
Market demand	Sales forecast, market share, promotion response, life cycle position	1
Competitor/industry	Competitor capabilities and vulnerabilities, structural evolution, capacity, strategic groups	1
Supplier analysis	Buying power and processes, vertical integration potential	1
Distributor/consumer analysis	Buying power and processes, vertical integration potential	1
2. Technology		
Product development	Product design, product line, market development	1
Process development	Manufacturing scale economics, productivity changes, new technological processes	3
Distribution	New distribution methods, credit, distributor channels	2
Managerial	New administrative processes, decision processes, information systems, decision support systems, office productivity, organizational forms	3
3. Political/legal/regulatory		
Domestic	FTC, justice, other governmental, equal rights, EPA, safety	2
International		2
4. Social/cultural		
Demographic	Shifts in population age, locations, family formation	1
Social norms	Consumerism, consumption patterns, work ethic	1

* (1 = highest)

goes through a strategic planning process and a marketing process. The strategic planning process describes the steps taken at the corporate and divisional levels to develop long-run strategies for survival and growth. This provides the context for the marketing process, which describes the steps taken at the product and market levels to develop viable marketing positions and programs (p. 9).

While he does not use the distinction drawn here between 'operations' and 'strategic' management, the sequencing activities suggested by Kotler recognizes the broader challenge of strategic planning and strategy-making. It is only in its relationship to the strategic management process that marketing activity takes on its strategic nature and becomes strategic marketing.

CONTRIBUTIONS OF MARKETING TO STRATEGIC MANAGEMENT

The remarks above notwithstanding, marketing as a function has been an important contributor to the strategy field. While other functional areas have made significant contributions as well, marketing's orientation to the environment gives it a special place to deal with problems of forecasting and adapting to change.

Biggadike (1981) has examined the contributions of marketing to strategic management in terms of the 64 new marketing knowledge examples identified by Myers *et al.* (1979) in their study of research results in marketing over the period 1952–77. In comparing the 64 areas to his own strategic management paradigm[1] he concludes that nearly 60 percent of the new marketing knowledge reported makes no contribution to strategic management, either because the knowledge is relevant to the operating level of marketing, it was derived from a [too?] narrow unit of analysis, or some of it is still what he termed undiffused, which one must assume means unclear as to its application. Biggadike suggests:

> Overall, I judge that marketing has made a number of conceptual contributions but few theoretical ones. The contributions occur most frequently at the environmental analysis stage and at the business unit level. Also, marketing has contributed more to the choice of strategy than to the choice of [organizational] structure. . . . Essentially, marketing sees strategic management as being market driven, and provides aids for hypothesizing about customer needs and competitor behavior (p. 621).

Of course, marketing does not become involved in many issues central to strategy-making, such as choice of manufacturing technology, manufacturing processes used, financial structure and the use of debt, manpower issues, and

---

[1] The paradigm is offered in summary form as: environment + organization capabilities + current competitive position = strategy.

the like. Many times these other issues are at the heart of competitive advantage and the central role of the customer is of lesser importance. In language current today in political and economic circles, supply-side considerations are often of greater importance to strategy and competitive advantage determination than are demand-side considerations.

Overall, Biggadike sees five areas of knowledge development in marketing with considerable relevance to strategy-making: (1) the marketing concept, (2) market segmentation, (3) positioning, (4) mapping, and (5) the product life cycle. Points (2), (3), and (4) are related, in his view.

There is no question that the marketing concept has highlighted the concern with the external environment and probably had more to do with shifting managerial focus away from internal concerns and what we have labeled an operations management focus than any other single idea. To the extent that the marketing concept has fostered the kind of view offered by Zabriskie and Huellmantel cited earlier, however, it only serves to replace one form of parochialism with another. There is more to strategy-making for a business than consideration of the customer alone. There are other claims that must be satisfied before any business can be viable; among them, the issue of earning a return that equals or exceeds capital costs. No amount of understanding the customer can replace the inability to cover capital costs. Hence, a central concern with the marketplace and the consumer, while a necessary condition, is not in itself a sufficient condition for success, as zealous proponents of the marketing concept would believe.

Biggadike believes, and there is considerable merit in his belief, that market segmentation—and what he labels its counterpart, positioning—ranks as marketing's most important contribution to strategic management. Perceptual mapping is an important tool, really the entire kitbag of tools in the multi-dimensional scaling and clustering areas represent significant tools, of great potential in strategic management. But the emphasis must be on potential rather than reality, if only because usage thus far has been limited essentially to the brand level. There is a developing literature in dealing with strategic groups within industries that goes beyond the product level and extends to positioning within an industry (Hatten *et al.*, 1978; Porter, 1976). The matter of strategic positioning is central to competitive advantage determination at the business strategy level. What marketers have learned about market segmentation, brand positioning, mapping, etc. should apply to strategic group determination and participation. More work is needed in adapting these techniques to strategic planning work, however.

The life cycle concept rivals the segmentation area for its value to strategy-making at the business level. Developing in the strategy field is an understanding of the dynamics of strategy in terms of stage in the life cycle and in particular the expectation of growth in the business. Certain strategies seem to have greater potential for contributing to strategic goals in certain stages ιλan do others. Moreover, the stage of life cycle seems to matter in terms of non-marketing strategy variables, such as manufacturing process, investment levels, where to attempt market share gains, experience curve theory, and other variables involved in lowest-cost positioning for the business unit.

Both the demand and supply sides of the life cycle seem to be important, i.e. life cycle needs to be considered in terms of product/market life cycles. Products (technologies) and markets (needs) often develop together and both need to considered jointly (Galbraith and Schendel, 1983). The expectation, not the fact of, growth, appears to explain both why empirical evidence supporting the life cycle is mixed, and why the notion of life cycle is important to understanding the dynamics of business strategy. Whether a differentiation-based business strategy is sought, or a lowest-cost strategy, the life cycle evolutionary position needs to be understood, and research in marketing has made strong contributions in this area.

CONCLUSIONS

Perhaps in the position marketing held in the early 1960s in terms of relative development, the strategy field is now developing at a very rapid rate. Much of that development is taking place in better practice and even in consulting rather than academics. In this respect it differs from marketing in the 1960s, where changes appeared to be of academic origin. In terms of consulting practice, it appears that the high growth management consultants will be those with a strong strategic management offering. Certainly the greatest growth for consultants has come out of the strategy field over the last decade. Such a trend, whether in consulting or in business practice, compares to the happenings in market research in the late 1950s and early 1960s.

Whatever its source, and whatever the rate of development, there is little question that there is a field building now called Strategic Management. The major constructs of that field have been outlined in this paper, albeit in abstract terms. No attempt was made to review the substance of strategy, what we know about strategies that work, why they work, and the individual and specific techniques and organizational practices for making them work. What was attempted was to develop the constructs to provide a backdrop against which the question 'What is strategic about strategic marketing?' could be examined.

These constructs define a role for the so-called functional areas of a business unit, including marketing. What goes unrecognized in the literature of most functional areas, especially marketing (but finance and manufacturing can be included) is that modern-day, complex organization structures have evolved well past the notion of the President with Vice Presidents of function X type—what is called a Stage II type of organization structure—and have gone on to variations of a corporate/multiple-business/functional area, or Stage III type. These forms of organization have risen for a variety of reasons, some argue because of information economies (Williamson, 1975), others because of the need for uncertainty reduction (Thompson, 1967), and others for reasons of power, social and economic power. Whatever their origin, such complex organizations exist and have extended themselves into so-called multinational firms.

Many functional areas have not caught up with these developments, primarily because their focus is, and must be, on the single business unit of which they are a part. Such parochialism is perhaps more true of academic people than of practitioners or consultants. Nevertheless, a narrow view of the marketing field leads to conclusions that strategy-making is essentially the realm of marketing staff. Similar views can be found among those laboring in finance, accounting, and other fields.

What is needed is the recognition that administrative structures are changing and becoming much more complex than the simple view of Stage II type organizations. Not just the form of the organization in the sense of levels is changing, but so also is the complexity of the decision and information processes and systems being used. Increasingly, we are seeing distinctions made between how the matter of strategy-making is approached and how strategy usage is conducted. In other words we are seeing an increasing distinction between strategic management and operations management. No longer are the organization and administrative processes used to formulate strategy necessarily the same as those used to operate the business. The literature in marketing is beginning to make these distinctions, but it needs to see the distinction much more clearly if it is to make the contributions of which it is capable, and it needs to see its relationship to the other functional areas more clearly.

In terms of the constructs developed here, marketing can make strong contributions in the area of environmental analysis, especially understanding demand, the consumer, and what changes to expect in competition and growth rates. In general, marketing has much to contribute to creating and maintaining competitive advantage at the business unit level. Marketing has a lesser role to play in creating and maintaining competitive advantage at the corporate strategy level.

What is strategic about marketing, or finance, or for that matter management in general, depends upon whether it involves strategy-making and strategy use and whether it involves the three elements of goals, strategy, and environment. In this view there is an aspect of marketing that is oriented to operations, maintaining existing directions at ever more efficient levels, and there is an aspect that is strategic that contributes toward changing the direction of the business. It is a simple distinction, but an important one to make, and one complex in its implications. Much activity is oriented to operations and efficiency as it should be, and probably some lesser amount is directed toward strategy-making and use. The strategy part is less obvious, and about it we need to know a great deal more, whether the viewpoint is strategic marketing or strategic managment.

REFERENCES

Andrews, Kenneth R., *The Concept of Corporate Strategy*. Dow Jones-Irwin, Homewood, Ill., 1971.

Ansoff, H. Igor, *Corporate Strategy*. McGraw-Hill, New York, 1965.

Barnard, Chester, *The Functions of the Executive*. Harvard University Press, Cambridge, Mass., 1938.

Biggadike, Ralph, 'The contributions of marketing to strategic management', *Academy of Management Review*, **6**(4) (1981), pp. 621–632.

Chandler, Alfred D., *Strategy and Structure*. MIT Press, Cambridge, Mass., 1962.

Drucker, Peter F., *Management*. Harper & Row, New York, 1973.

Galbraith, Craig, and Dan Schendel, 'An empirical analysis of strategy types', *Strategic Management Journal*, **4**(2) 1983, pp. 153–173.

Galbraith, Jay, R., and Daniel A. Nathanson, *Strategy Implementation: The Role of Structure and Process*. West Publishing Co., St Paul, 1978.

Hatten, Kenneth, Dan Schendel and Arnold C. Cooper, 'A strategic model of the U.S. brewing industry, 1952–1971', *Academy of Management Journal*, Dec. 1978, pp. 592–610.

Hofer, Charles W. and Dan Schendel, *Strategy Formulation: Analytical Concepts*. West Publishing Co., St Paul, 1978.

Kotler, Philip, 'Strategic planning and the marketing process', *Business*, May-June 1980, pp. 2–9.

Myers, John G., Stephen A. Greyser, and William F. Massy, 'The effectiveness of marketing's "R&D" for marketing management: an assessment', *Journal of Marketing*, **43**(1) (1979), pp. 17–29.

Porter, Michael E., *Interbrand Choice, Strategy and Bilateral Market Power*. Harvard Economic Studies, Vol. 146. Harvard University Press, Cambridge, Mass., 1976.

Schendel, Dan, and Charles W. Hofer, (eds.) *Strategic Management: A New View of Business Policy and Planning*. Little, Brown & Co., Boston, 1979.

Thompson, James D., *Organizations in Action*. McGraw-Hill, New York, 1967.

Williamson, Oliver, *Markets and Hierarchies*. The Free Press, New York, 1975.

Zabriskie, Noel B., and A. B. Huellmantel, 'Strategic marketing's four basic tasks', *Marketing News*, 26 June 1981, section 2, pp. 4–5.

Strategic Marketing and Management
Edited by H. Thomas and D. Gardner
© 1985 John Wiley & Sons Ltd

CHAPTER 2

Concepts of Planning in Strategic Management

INTRODUCTION

During the last two decades in particular, a substantial body of literature has been developed in the fields of strategic management, strategic planning, corporate and business policy, and related topics. As a result, many definitions of strategic planning exist and it is important to discuss and review the alternative modes and perspectives for planning.

Steiner and Miner (1977: 150) define formal, comprehensive managerial planning 'in at least four ways':

(1) dealing 'with the futurity of current decisions', i.e. 'the choice of cause-and-effect over time of an actual or intended decision that a manager is going to make' together with 'the alternative courses of action that are open in the future, and, when choices are made, they become the basis for current decisions. The essence of long-range planning is the systematic identification of opportunites and threats that lie in the future which, in combination with other relevant data, provide a basis for management to make better current decisions to exploit the opportunities and avoid the threats' (1977: 150).

(2) 'Comprehensive corporate planning is a process that begins with the development of objectives, defines strategies and policies to achieve objectives, and develops detailed plans to make sure that the strategies are carried out to achieve the objectives' (1977: 151).

(3) 'It is a philosophy'—i.e. 'an assurance of the proper climate in [the] enterprise to do the most effective corporate planning' (1977: 151)—i.e. implying organizational structure aspects.

(4) It is a 'structure of plans . . . that integrates strategic with short-range operational plans. In this structure are integrated, at all levels, major objectives, strategies, policies, and functions of an enterprise' (1977: 151).

Thus, Steiner and Miner emphasize the relationships between planning and strategy formulation. In particular, they point out the dynamics of longer-term strategy formulation, its linkage with shorter-term operational planning, and, by inference, to the fact that strategy formulation is an ongoing process continually reaching toward longer time horizons and anticipating both opportunities and problems related to the future of the business enterprise.

Ackoff (1970: Chapter 1) in alluding to the nature of planning states that

> Planning is clearly a decision-making process, but equally clearly, not all decision-making is planning. Not so clear, however, are the characteristics that make it a special kind of decision-making. It is special in three ways.

Ackoff's three ways can be summarized as:

(1) Planning is anticipatory decision making. That is planning is something we do in advance of taking action.
(2) Planning involves making and evaluating a series of interrelated decisions (a system of decisions) before action is required.
(3) Planning is a process that is directed towards producing one or more future states which are desired and which are not expected to occur unless something is done.

Further review of the planning literature would demonstrate that many additional styles and techniques of planning have been advanced as being suitable for given sets of circumstances. Concepts have progressed from 'forecast and respond' to 'design of a desired future and of the means of achieving it'.

In subsequent paragraphs the criticisms made against the more common planning styles are addressed, as are some of the circumstances affecting the choice of a particular planning approach.

RATIONAL–ANALYTIC PLANNING MODES

A dominant theme in much of the literature on planning has been the purposeful, rational–analytic planning mode. Typically, it involves steps such as goal-setting for the organization, methods for the identification of strategic options and programs, evaluation of such options, and programs and mechanisms for implementation and 'on-going' monitoring of plans.

Many critiques of the rational planning model exist. A common critique arises from growing dissatisfaction with its narrowly construed problem-solving emphasis. Much of the criticism has been derived from work on the nature of ill-structured problems (Mason and Mitroff, 1981; Mintzberg *et al.*, 1976); work on cognitive styles (McKenney and Keen 1974; Mitroff *et al.*, 1977), work on right-brain function (Mintzberg, 1976) and usable knowledge (Lindblom and Cohen, 1979).

Writers such as Mason and Mitroff (1981), stress the complexity of planning problems and the consequent need for a free and open inquiry process. They further advance the proposition that it is in the problem-formulation and problem-finding process that the essence of good planning and problem-solving is to be found.

OTHER POSSIBLE PLANNING MODES

Some writers, including McCaskey (1982), Mintzberg (1981), Quinn (1980) and Mason and Mitroff (1981), have argued that it is only by studying what managers do with ambiguous, ill-structured problems that we can identify what planning means. That is, it is essential to focus upon what planning processes achieve for strategic managers in their day-to-day activities.

For example, through an intensive field study of a small number of organizations (Quinn, 1980) modifies the concept of purposeful planning and identifies planning as an interactive process involving a series of incremental steps or probes of the environment. He postulates a process in which managers formulate a series of partial, incremental views of the problem, and through learning and dialogue devise a solution of the logical incremental type. However, managers rarely seem to resolve the critical issue of goal formulation and its definition (Quinn, 1980: 179) which is central to the philosophy of purposeful planning.

Kotter (1982) undertook painstaking field research and diary approaches in his study of effective general managers, and showed them to be more informal, less systematic, and more adaptive than a proponent of rational models or formal planning systems would assume.

Thus, Kotter, Quinn and other writers draw attention to the appropriate role of planning in an organization. Mintzberg (1981: 323), in an insightful and engagingly titled article, 'What is planning anyway?', concludes

> that planners and planning find their roles more on either side of the strategy making process than at its center. At the front end, planners feed in ad hoc analysis to managers who develop the broad visions or strategies. And then at the back, or output, end, where necessary the planners program the consequences of these strategies turning them into systematic plans. But the heart of the process is reserved for managers using less formal procedures.

Planning, in Mintzberg's perspective, is an input to a strategic inquiry system led and directed by senior managers. Therefore, if planning is recognized as a tool, technique, or approach, it can provide a range of inputs (or 'lenses') about the strategic problem. First, planners can carry out specific analyses (financial, marketing, corporate, etc.) as requested by managers. These analytic inputs then form part of the evidence for the decision-making and policy dialogue processes of senior management. Second, planners can be directed to formally elaborate upon the consequences of a strategy well-formulated by senior managers in the organization. In this sense, planning seeks to develop sub-strategies and implementation processes for senior managers, and thus makes them more aware of the consequences of their desired actions. Third, planners may be directed to use their armory of approaches both to encourage and stimulate strategic thinking and, more importantly, managerial views and thinking about the future. Mason and Mitroff's (1981) book echoes this latter theme. They argue for the development of procedures and processes to expose and challenge assumptions underlying strategic planning models. They believe that effective managerial debate about planning assumptions may improve the quality of planning solutions simply because unchallenged assumptions are exposed for thorough scrutiny by members of the management team.

CONCLUSIONS

In this section some conclusions about planning concepts and their application are proposed.

First, the literature review shows that the comprehensive, formal, purposeful strategic planning systems devised in the 1960s have limited appeal in terms of practical application. More than anything else planning is not seen now as a panacea for all ills but more as a partial diagnostic process for helping to improve the quality of management decisions. Second, planning is viewed as a means of coordination in situations of interdependence and structural uncertainty (Ackoff, 1970). Various planning styles are available which inevitably affect perceptions about outcomes. Therefore, the relationship between problem circumstances and planning styles and techniques is important in designing approaches for strategic planning. Third, planning has several possible outcomes. For example, a formal and well-documented strategic long-range plan may emerge from the planning activity (Lorange and Vancil, 1977). Alternatively, planning may be viewed as producing benefits from the introduction of a coherent long-term thinking process or from the greater managerial understanding of uncertainty and its impacts upon strategic problems. Mintzberg's (1981) view of the general manager(s) as the driving forces in strategy formulation suggests that the output of a planning processes will be closely related to the different roles required of planning by the organizational leaders—i.e. whether planning is seen as a central control system, or as a framework for innovation, or as a process involving value differences and other conflict processes in the context of strategic decision-making.

Therefore, it seems clear that there is no form of planning which is sensible for every problem, situation, or set of organizational circumstances. However, some of the important factors in designing planning approaches are as follows:

(1)   The nature of uncertainty in the strategic problems. Is the crucial factor uncertainty about the effects of particular actions (UE), or is it

uncertainty about values to be placed on alternative outcomes (UV), or is it uncertainty about the relationship (UR) with other (present or future) decisions, or is it structural uncertainty (US) involving concerns about whether certain options were ignored? Notice that these sources of uncertainty reflect the strategic character of planning problems and are much broader than probabilistic concepts of uncertainty.

Clearly, if UE, UV, UR, and US are small then planning is a technical calculation amenable to solution using rational–analytic models. Planning problems, and their solutions, become more difficult as uncertainty increases. For example, if UV is high then planning problems probably become very political in nature.

(2)   The degree of complexity in the situation. That is, it may be the case that the solution to strategic problem A will strongly affect the values and outcomes attached to strategic options in problem situation B. Therefore, strategic planning involves situations of interconnectedness, interdependence, and problems which often have wide-ranging implications.

(3)   The degree of consensus or conflict about the problem situation. The more closely the values of relevant actors agree, the more likely it is that planning will be a more technical, analytic process.

(4)   The extent of involvement in the problem. If the strategic problem involves a range of agencies, organizations, and actors the more likely it becomes that the planning mode will involve organizational and inter-organizational bargaining processes.

(5)   The scope and time horizon of the problem. Clearly the wider the scope of the problem and the longer-run the time horizon, the more likely it is that the planning processes will seek to encourage and stimulate strategic thinking and understanding.

No review of this type can provide a comprehensive treatment of corporate planning. However it can suggest frameworks and possible procedures for implementing planning within organizations. Finally, in devising planning procedures certain features must be stressed. First, the need to devise a system for problem formulation which identifies the 'mess' (Schwenk and Thomas, 1983) in the planning problem. Second, the preference for a focus around the planning of desirable futures and of ways to make the future happen. Third, the identification of resource requirements and planning constraints which may impede the process of strategy implementation. Fourth, the ever-present need to design and modify organizational structures so that proper management systems to implement and control strategic plans are in place at the appropriate time. That is, the linkage between strategy and structure (Chandler, 1962) may strongly influence corporate performance.

REFERENCES

Ackoff, R. L., *A Concept of Corporate Planning*. Wiley-Interscience, New York, 1970.

Chandler, A. D., *Strategy and Structure*. MIT Press, Cambridge, Mass., 1962.

Kotter, J. P., *The General Managers*. Free Press, New York, 1982.

Lindblom, C. E., and D. K. Cohen, *Usable Knowledge*. Yale University Press, New Haven, 1979.

Lorange, P., and R. F. Vancil, *Strategic Planning Systems*. Prentice-Hall, Englewood Cliffs, N.J., 1977.

Mason, R. O., and I. I. Mitroff, *Challenging Strategic Planning Assumptions*. John Wiley and Sons, New York, 1981.

McCaskey, M. B., *The Executive Challenge*. Pitman, Marshfield, Mass., 1982.

McKenney, J. L., and P. G. W. Keen, 'How managers' minds work', *Harvard Business Review*, May/June 1974, p. 80.

Mintzberg, H., 'Planning on the left side and managing on the right', *Harvard Business Review*, July/Aug. 1976.

Mintzberg, H., 'What is planning anyway', *Strategic Management Journal*, **2**(3) (July-Sept. 1981), 319–325.

Mintzberg, H., D. Raisinghani, and A. Theoret, 'The structure of "unstructured" decision processes', *Administrative Science Quarterly*, **21** (1976), 246–275.

Mitroff, I. I., V. P. Barbabba, and R. Kilmann, 'The application of behavioral and philosophical technologies to strategic planning: a case study of a large federal agency', *Management Science*, **24** (1977), 44–58.

Quinn, J. B., *Strategies for Change*. Irwin, Homewood, Ill., 1980.

Schwenk, C. R., and H. Thomas, 'Formulating the mess: the role of decision aids in problem formulation', *Omega*, **10**(2) (1983), 1–14.

Steiner, G. A., and J. B. Miner, *Management Policy and Strategy*, MacMillan & Co., New York, 1977.

Strategic Marketing and Management
Edited by H. Thomas and D. Gardner
© 1985 John Wiley & Sons Ltd

Introduction to Conference Papers on Planning Concepts

The papers in this section reflect three important concerns in the implementation of strategic planning, namely:

(1) evidence on the value of formal strategic planning in marketing;
(2) the definition of appropriate units of analysis for strategic planning;
(3) the connections between decision support systems and the strategic planning process.

Armstrong and Reibstein describe the formal planning process as consisting of five explicit and separate steps: specifying objectives, generating strategies, evaluating alternatives, monitoring results, and gaining commitment. In their study they examined three types of evidence on the value of this formal planning process and in each case found little support for the use of formal planning for marketing strategy. First, the formal process was not accepted by marketing planners; second, experts in marketing planning ignored some of the formal steps; and third, they were unable to find a single study on the value of formal planning in marketing. However, they argue that evidence from corporate planning and from organizational behavior provides support for the use of formal planning processes. They recommend further research on the value of formal approaches to marketing planning involving surveys of planners, experimental studies using cases, and laboratory experiments.

Cravens and Lamb focus upon the important issue of the definition of the appropriate unit for strategic analysis in a given strategic problem situation. They illustrate how the choice of inappropriate planning units has sometimes led to poor strategic planning outcomes. They argue that good definition should be an important element for success of the planning process and subsequent strategy formulation.

Montgomery quotes Little's (1979) views about marketing decision support systems:

> In the past 10 years, a new technology has emerged for assisting and improving marketing decision making. We define a marketing decision support system as a coordinated collection of data, models, analytic tools, and computing power by

71

which an organization gathers information from the environment and turns it into a basis for action. Where such systems have taken root, they have grown and become increasingly productive for their organizations.

Montgomery argues that strategic marketing planning has evolved as the latest, 'highest level' of marketing planning. Its development has paralleled similar developments in corporate planning. During the same period Decision Support Systems (DSS) have evolved as the most recent 'highest level' application of computers in the modern organization. He then explores and illustrates the way in which DSS are increasingly being developed to support strategic marketing decisions.

REFERENCE

Little, J. D. C. (1979). 'Decision support systems for marketing managers', *Journal of Marketing*, **43**(3) (Summer), 9–27.

Strategic Marketing and Management
Edited by H. Thomas and D. Gardner
© 1985 John Wiley & Sons Ltd

2.1
Evidence on the Value of Strategic Planning in Marketing: How Much Planning Should a Marketing Planner Plan?

J. SCOTT ARMSTRONG AND DAVID J. REIBSTEIN

Department of Marketing, Wharton School, University of Pennsylvania, Philadelphia, Pa. 19104

What evidence exists on the value of formal planning for strategic decision-making in marketing? This paper reviews the evidence. This includes two tests of face validity. First, we use the market test: *Are formal procedures used for marketing planning?* Next, we examine expert prescriptions: *What do they say is the best way to plan?* More important than face validity, however, are tests of construct or predictive validity: *What empirical evidence exists on the relative value of formal and informal approaches to marketing planning?* The paper concludes with suggestions on the types of research that would be most useful for measuring the value of formal marketing planning.

Before reviewing the evidence, we present a framework for the formal planning process.

THE FORMAL PLANNING PROCESS

Although various formulations differ slightly, the basic framework for corporate strategic planning can be described by five steps: specify objectives, generate alternative strategies, evaluate strategies, monitor results, and seek commitment. Many corporate planners argue that each of these steps should be carried out in a formal manner (that is with operational guidelines and presumably with each step written out). The relationships among the various steps are shown in Figure 2.1.1. A detailed description of each of these steps is provided in Armstrong (1983).

The various steps in the planning process have been studied by researchers in organizational behavior. This research, summarized in Armstrong (1982),

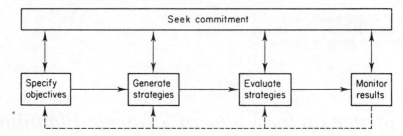

Figure 2.1.1   Formal strategic planning process

suggests that explicit objective setting and monitoring of results are especially important to the success of planning. In addition, research on group problem-solving has implied that the development of *alternative* strategies should be helpful (Janis and Mann, 1977).

Field research on the value of corporate strategic planning has been of limited value in identifying which of these steps are more important. The one exception was that explicit attempts to involve key stakeholders (commitment seeking) did tend to be related to the profitability of firms (Armstrong, 1982).

Formal strategic planning is not expected to be useful in all situations. With the exception that formal planning tends to be useful in situations involving large changes (Armstrong, 1982), the research has been of little help in identifying the situations in which formal strategic planning is most useful. Various authors have suggested aspects of situations where planning should be valuable. For example, planning should be useful in situations that are complex and where uncertainty is high (e.g. the introduction of a new technical product). It should also be useful where a cooperative effort is required.

THE MARKET TEST

To what extent do marketing planners follow the formal five-step procedure described above? To examine this, we reanalyzed data from Hopkins (1981), who had surveyed 267 manufacturing and service firms that prepare formal marketing plans. Almost all of the respondents were senior marketing managers who were responsible for the preparation of their company's marketing plan.

Hopkins (1981) summarized the 'features' included by the companies in their marketing plans in his Tables 12, 13, and 14. We reclassified these features according to our five-step procedure. This gave us a rough indication of the extent to which formal processes were used. The setting of objectives and the generation of strategies were the features appearing most often in company plans. Only one-third of the firms discussed the evaluation of strategies, one-fifth monitored results, and a negligible percentage included a discussion of commitment. These results are summarized in the first row of Table 2.1.1.

As an alternative to the examination of marketing plans, we considered surveys on planning practices. Unfortunately, we found no prior studies that would lend themselves to analysis. Coe (1981) used a survey to assess usage of formal strategic planning techniques, but this was limited to techniques for the generation and evaluation of strategies; she did not examine the complete planning process.

To gain additional information on the use of formal planning, we surveyed 50 participants in a marketing planning seminar for executives. The program was sponsored by the Wharton School Marketing faculty in January 1982. About two-thirds of these participants were from marketing functions. They had substantial experience with planning as 54 percent reported planning to be 'a major part of my job' and another 32 percent said it was 'some aspect of my job'. Over 90 percent reported planning to be 'useful' or 'very useful' (the top two categories on a five-point scale) for strategic decision-making in their organizations.

A closer examination of the Wharton survey revealed a different picture of the use of formal planning, however. This survey, self-administered in a group setting, asked: 'What are the different steps involved in your company's procedure for developing its marketing strategy?' Of the 42 respondents to this question, 12 described only data that they collected, and two described administrative steps. The remaining 28 described something resembling a planning process. Of these, 19 (38 percent of total sample) said they examined objectives, and five (10 percent) said they looked at overall corporate objectives. Eleven respondents (22 percent) mentioned that explicit strategies should be developed, but none suggested the need to look at alternative strategies. Two (4 percent) said strategies were evaluated, none mentioned monitoring, and two (4 percent) mentioned implementation. In short, their stated procedures for formal planning did not follow the entire five-step process of Figure 2.1.1, nor did they describe formal procedures that fell outside of our five-step process. A summary of the procedures is provided in the second row of Table 2.1.1.

EXPERT PRESCRIPTIONS

Two types of sources were used to examine expert prescriptions. The first, 'published sources', represents the writing of experts. To be included, the source had to be published (book, paper in journal, or monograph); it had to relate to marketing; and it had to be a source where the reader would expect to find a comprehensive treatment of the planning process. The second, 'company sources', was based on procedural manuals for marketing planning used by large corporations. Presumably, these were written by experts who are involved with actual marketing problems. These sources frequently covered

Table 2.1.1   Use of formal planning process for strategic marketing: the market test

Sources	Identify objectives		Generate strategies			Evaluate strategies	Monitor results	Gain commitment
	Marketing	Corporate	Explicit	Multiple	Contingency			
Hopkins (1981) (267 firms): 'Spelled out in detail'	80	n.a.	100*	30	24	36	20	0
Wharton School, Marketing Planning Seminar (50 Planners): 'Procedures'	38	10	22	0	0	4	0	4

n.a. information not available.
* Presumably, only those procedures that asked for an explicit strategy were included in this sample.

topics other than the planning process. For example, some would devote much consideration to the situation in which planning was to be used, and some would go into detail on techniques that could be used in a particular phase of the planning process. We were not selective; we used all sources that we could obtain that met the above criteria.

Each source was coded according to how closely it followed the five-step process summarized in Figure 2.1.1. This coding was not simple. Few of the sources drew upon the corporate strategy literature. Thus the format and the jargon varied considerably from that used in corporate strategy.

In speaking of 'objectives', some sources restricted themselves solely to *marketing objectives*, apparently under the assumption that these objectives would be consistent with the organization's overall objectives. Other sources stressed the need to view marketing strategy as part of a larger system. The latter viewpoint is more consistent with the corporate strategy literature, which states that one benefit of explicit planning is to ensure that the various components of the system are consistent with one another. Formal techniques in this area would include checklists, non-directive interviews of key stakeholders, and survey research.

The 'generation of strategies' in corporate planning has stressed three aspects. First there is a need for an *explicit* strategy. Second, it is desirable to examine *alternative* strategies. Third, *contingency* strategies should be developed in case the organization's environment or capabilities change. Formal approaches here would draw upon such techniques as checklists, brainstorming, PIMS (Anderson and Paine, 1978), experience curves, and structured group meetings.

The 'evaluation of strategies' refers to formal procedures for rating the possible outcomes against the stated objectives. At the simplest level this might involve checklists with subjective ratings. It would also include such techniques as cost accounting, survey research, regression analysis, decision trees, Delphi, mathematical programming, or the devil's advocate.

To 'monitor results' in an explicit way, one would look for procedures outlining how to track inputs and outputs (e.g. surveys, cost accounting), what results would lead to change to a contingency plan, when to schedule periodic reviews, and when the plan should be revised. PERT charts would be relevant to monitor the implementation of the strategy.

Finally, explicit approaches for 'gaining commitment' would include procedures for identifying who should be involved in the planning process (i.e. which stakeholder groups), when they should be involved (e.g. in which phases of the planning process), and how should they be involved (e.g. receive information, provide information, or participate in decision-making).

This coding procedure was then applied to both published and company sources as described in the following sections.

Published sources

Our intent was to provide a complete listing since 1970 of all published sources where the reader might expect to find a comprehensive approach to marketing planning. Of course, the reader's expectations may not have been matched by the author's intent. For example, Boyd and Larreche (1980), Day (1975) and Wilson *et al.* (1978) said that they did not intend their papers to be comprehensive (personal communication).

Many sources were suggested to us by experts in marketing planning.* Among these was the anthology by Guiltinan and Paul (1982). References in these sources led to additional sources. Finally, we circulated various drafts of this paper during a 6-month period in an attempt to find additional sources.

Initially, we coded each source independently. A source was coded as 'brief mention' when the topic was mentioned but was not discussed in any substantive manner. If it then went on to describe operational procedures it was labelled as a 'discussion'. Next we met to discuss our codings. We also sent copies of this paper to the authors of each source to determine how they would code their own work. Our ratings are provided in Table 2.1.2 (ratings by the authors are also provided if they differed from ours).

Concerning objectives, few sources took a systems viewpoint. That is, rather than looking at all who are affected by the marketing plan, they looked only at 'marketing objectives'. Further, this viewpoint was narrowly defined, with the emphasis upon subgoals, such as market share. This conclusion was reached independently in a review by Anderson (1982).

Although all of the sources saw a need for generating explicit strategies, it was not so common for them to recommend the generation of multiple strategies, and it was even less common to recommend the creation of contingency plans. Evaluation of strategies, however, received much attention.

The monitoring of the plan and commitment were given modest consideration. However, as with the other phases, the experts were recommending much more formality in these areas than currently exists. (Compare their prescriptions with the estimated use of formal planning in Table 2.1.1.)

Company sources

Hopkins' (1981) survey also described the planning processes recommended by each of 38 selected firms. These 38 had been selected in an attempt to provide a wide range of approaches. This sample included most of the procedures considered to be exemplary (personal communication with Hopkins). We discarded three firms (Exhibits 21, 29 and 36 in Hopkins) as the documentation seemed incomplete.

---

* Vijay Mahajan was especially helpful in our search for relevant sources.

Table 2.1.2 Expert recommendations on planning process

Sources	Identify objectives		Generate strategies			Evaluate strategies	Monitor results	Gain commitment
	Marketing	Corporate	Explicit	Multiple	Contingency			
Published by experts								
Abell[a] and Hammond (1979)	*a+	a++	**	*a+		**		*a+
Boyd[a] and Larreche (1980)			**					
Buijs (1979)	*		**	*		a++		
Day[a] (1975)	*	*	*	*	*	*	*	
Hopkins (1981)	**		**			*	*	
Jain (1981)	**	**	**			*		
Kollat et al. (1972)	*a+	a+	**			*	*	
Luck[a] and Ferrell (1979)	*a+	a+	**	*	*	**	**	
Murray (1979)	*	*	*					
Schanck (1979)	*							**
Stasch[a] and Lanktree (1980)	*	a+				a+	*	**
Webster[a] (1979)	*	a+	**a−					
Wilson, George[a], and Solomon (1978)	*		*a+	a+	a+	*		**
Percentage of experts recommending	85	54	92	46	23	77	38	31
Company prescriptions Hopkins (1981): '35 Firms'								
Percentage of firms recommending	94	11	89	9	9	20	11	9

* Brief mention; ** discussion.

[a] These authors responded to our request for feedback on the ratings. An a+ means that the authors coded their publication as more comprehensive than we did, while an a− means their rating was towards 'less comprehensive'.

The planning guidelines from Hopkins, summarized at the bottom of Table 2.1.2, suggest an even more narrow viewpoint than that provided in the published sources. Within the scope of these planning guidelines, little attention was given to marketing as part of a system; alternative and contingency strategies were seldom requested; little attention was given to evaluation; and even less attention was given to procedures for monitoring results and gaining commitment. It was interesting to note that *none* of the firms in Hopkins' sample is known to have included the complete five-step procedure in their set of guidelines for preparing marketing plans. (Hopkins said that the procedures for some firms were considerably more extensive than reported in his exhibits, so our summary may understate the prescriptions for formal planning.)

Although expert prescriptions are more favorable to the use of formal planning than the market test, the experts also ignored steps in the planning process. These omissions were more common by those experts who are closest to the planning process. Academic experts ignored fewer steps. In particular, they were more likely than the company experts to recommend an explicit evaluation of strategies.

EMPIRICAL EVIDENCE

If one argues that marketing planning is a unique activity, and that tests on the value of formal planning must be carried out in a marketing context, the situation is bleak. *We were unable to find a single published study that presented an empirical test on the value of formal planning for marketing.* In other words, there were no studies that compared formal and informal processes to determine which led to the more successful performance by a firm.

Possibly our search has not been adequate. We were, however, aided by experts in the field, we made a library search at the University of Pennsylvania, early versions of this paper were circulated to the people cited in Table 2.1.2, and, a version of this paper was presented at the University of Illinois conference on marketing planning in April 1982. Numerous leads were provided but few of them contained empirical evidence on the value of formal planning. Furthermore, Stasch and Lanktree (1980) reached a similar conclusion when they studied the process used to develop the annual marketing plan.

An alternative position, one that seems reasonable to us, is that marketing merely represents a subset to the decisions examined by corporate planners. (This viewpoint is shared by many practitioners; see Hopkins, 1981, Tables 1 and 3.) The research on planning provides no reason to expect that the process for formal strategic planning should differ if one examines only that subset of decisions involving marketing strategy.

To assess the extent to which authors drew upon the research on planning from corporate strategy and organizational behavior, we used the review in Armstrong (1982) and asked what percentage of the 26 field studies in corporate strategy and the 24 studies in organizational behavior were cited by each author advocating formal planning for marketing. The results were striking: None of the sources in Table 2.1.2 cited a single study containing empirical validation!

RESEARCH NEEDS: THE ARROWSMITH DILEMMA

Consider an analogy to medicine. Doctors are preparing a treatment that they claim will cure the plague. Although they have not tested it, the treatment sells well, especially when the plague is rampant.

Martin Arrowsmith (Lewis, 1925) was a doctor who proposed that research be conducted to test the value of a medical treatment. Arrowsmith became unpopular. The beliefs were: 'The drug either works or it doesn't work. If people buy it, it must work. Arrowsmith is being negative'. The choice faced by Arrowsmith was whether to abandon his research on the value of the treatment, or to continue his research and become ostracized from the establishment.

Does this analogy fit the field of marketing planning? Is it possible that strategic marketers are preparing ever more complex treatments without bothering to test them for efficacy?

We are hesitant to suggest that formal planning has no value for marketing because much of the advice on formal marketing planning has face validity. More importantly, some of it is consistent with the research from corporate strategy and organizational behavior. However, one can also suggest plausible hypotheses *against* the use of formal planning for marketing strategy. For example, it might hamper creativity, reduce flexibility, or lead to apathy among those excluded from the planning process. It seems desirable, then, to obtain evidence on the value of planning.

Validation research is needed to determine whether formal planning is useful for strategic decision-making in marketing. If it is useful, then additional questions are relevant:

(1) Which stakeholders benefit from such planning (and which lose)?
(2) Which steps in planning are most useful (and how should effort be allocated among these steps)?
(3) Which stakeholders should be involved in each step of the planning process?
(4) In what situations is formal planning most useful?
(5) What are the costs of the various planning methods?

A variety of approaches might be used to study these issues. These include surveys of planning practices, observation of the processes, or experimentation with different planning processes. Based on our review of the previous research in corporate strategy and in organizational behavior, we offer opinions here on the relative merits of each research method. First, we describe some criteria by which to judge the various research methods. Then we examine each of the methods against the criteria.

Criteria

We propose nine criteria for evaluating the approaches to research. Some of these criteria may be more important than others and this will undoubtedly depend upon the situation. The criteria are as follows:

(A) *'Feasibility.'* Will organizations permit the research? In some cases the firm may believe that the data, procedures, or strategies are confidential. In other cases it may be difficult to locate the people who have relevant information about the planning process or planning outcomes.

(B) *'Realism.'* Is the situation realistic? Evidence is preferred from situations that closely approximate actual situations faced by firms. Realism would add to the validity of the findings.

(C) *'Relevance.'* Is the test situation one where formal planning might be expected to be worthwhile? Are the subjects representative of the different types of decision-makers?

(D) *'Variation in the planning process.'* Does the planning process vary substantially among firms (i.e. are some highly formal and others highly intuitive)? Does it vary over time (i.e. do some firms adopt a more formal approach at some point)? Comparisons are easier to make when comparing highly formal planners with intuitive planners.

(E) *'Measurement error: process.'* Can the planning process be accurately described? In other words, good measures are required for each step in the process that was actually used.

(F) *'Measurement error: outcomes.'* Can the costs and benefits of the planning process be measured? For example, what was the impact of the planning process on profits, customer satisfaction, or employee welfare? It is important to be able to measure the impact of planning on each element in the system.

(G) *'Control group.'* Is there an equivalent control group to serve as a basis for the study of the impact of planning? Ideally, the control group would be selected by probability sampling.

(H) *'Cost.'* How much does it cost to use each of the research methods?

(I) *'Time.'* How long will it take to complete the research study (i.e. calendar time)?

Research methods

This section examines three major approaches: surveys, observation, and experimentation. Within each of these we examine specific research methods.

Surveys of experts might seem attractive because they are feasible and inexpensive. But the shortcomings of the expert survey are serious. This approach lacks a control group and it provides inadequate information on the process and the outcomes. It is not likely that we can learn much about the value of formal planning by surveying experts. Expert surveys have not been used by those doing research on the value of corporate planning, nor should they have been used, in our opinion.

Surveys of planners can be helpful in identifying which firms plan and which do not. Results can be contrasted between formal and informal planners. This approach has been a popular one in studies on the value of formal corporate planning (Armstrong, 1982). It was used effectively in the study by Ansoff *et al.* (1970) as they examined a situation, major acquisitions, where formal planning should be helpful. But most of the surveys of corporate planners failed to obtain adequate information on the planning process, the situation, or the effects of planning on the whole system. As a result, these studies were of much less value than they might have been.

Observation provides another approach to research on planning. One could observe the prescribed process, the actual plans, or the planning process. The major difficulty in observing the *prescribed process* (as done in Hopkins, 1981) is that one cannot be sure whether the actual process corresponds with the prescribed process. Furthermore, as was found with the Hopkins sample, it is difficult to obtain a sample of firms in which the prescribed process differs significantly in the degree of formality.

Observation of the *plans* themselves offers advantages beyond merely looking at prescriptions because prescriptions are often ignored. One can try to infer the degree of formality by looking at these plans. For example, coders might be used to classify the various plans according to the formality in each step of planning.

Alternatively, one can observe the *actual planning process*. With this approach, substantially more time would be required, as it would be years before the results were available. We are not aware of any validation studies that were based on observation of the planning process but we see some promise in this approach. It would make the most sense in a situation where formal planning would be expected to be important, such as for the introduction of a major new product. Cases must then be found to allow for a comparison of formal and informal planning.

Experimental studies offer substantial promise. Although *laboratory experiments* suffer from a lack of realism, they offer the best way to assess the relative contributions of the various steps in planning. Research in this area has been growing rapidly since 1970, as summarized in Armstrong (1982). An example was provided by Montanari *et al.* (1980) with the 'Space Tower Exercise'. Management games might be used as a basis for such experiments.

Experimental studies of cases have not been used as far as we can tell. Here, the success of experimental groups, trained in formal planning, would be contrasted with the success of untrained control groups who solve the same case. Coders who are blind to the hypotheses would be asked to rate the extent to which each subject (or group) actually used the formal planning guidelines. A number of expert coders, also blind to the hypotheses, but knowing the outcome, would rate the degree of success that each plan might have achieved. This approach might be used during courses in marketing strategy. Cases should be selected for situations where formal planning would seem relevant (e.g. large and complex changes, such as with new product introductions). Also the cases should have known outcomes. The study that comes closest to this experimental case study is Nutt (1977), except that there was no known outcome.

The field experiment would provide the most valid and reliable results. These should be long-term studies involving pre- and post-measures, as well as comparisons between formal and informal planners. The field experiment is also appealing because of its realism. The study in corporate planning that comes closest to this ideal is Van de Ven (1980), which used a quasi-experimental design to study the value of formal planning for the introduction of community child care programs.

Table 2.1.3 summarizes each of the research methods and provides our subjective ratings of each method against each of the nine criteria. Of the methods examined, the experimental study of cases has the fewest shortcomings; no criteria scored lower than 3.0. Laboratory experiments, which also scored well, would serve as a complement to case experimentation. As a start, surveys of planners offer an inexpensive and realistic approach. The most serious shortcomings occurred with surveys of experts and with field experiments.

Obviously the ratings are subject to question. To improve the reliability, each of us did the coding independently at two different times, approximately 2 months apart in each case. Test–retest reliability was high, as the two ratings by each author were within one point of each other for 87 percent of the items. Interrater reliability was also high as 83 percent of the composite ratings for each author were within one point of the other author's ratings. (By chance alone, one would expect agreement for only 29 percent of the ratings.) The four ratings for each item were then averaged and rounded. (If the rating ended in 0.5 it was rounded toward 3.0.)

CONCLUSIONS

The formal planning process consists of five steps: specify objectives, generate strategies, evaluate strategies, monitor results, and gain commitment.

Table 2.1.3 Methods to study formal planning of marketing strategy (1 = unfavorable to 5 = favorable)

Research method	Feasibility A	Realism B	Relevance C	Variation in Process D	Measurement Error: in Process E	Measurement Error: in Outcomes F	Control Group G	Cost H	Time I
Surveys									
Experts	5	4	3	2	2	2	1	5	5
Planners	5	5	3	2	3	2	2	5	5
Observation									
Prescriptions	4	3	3	2	2	3	2	3	4
Plans	3	4	3	2	3	3	2	3	4
Process	2	4	3	2	3	3	2	3	2
Experimentation									
Laboratory	5	2	5	5	4	4	5	3	3
Cases	5	3	5	4	4	3	5	4	3
Field	1	5	4	4	4	4	4	2	2

Marketing planners frequently ignore steps in the formal planning process. One cannot argue, then, that 'the market' accepts formal planning. In particular, marketing planning frequently lacks formal linkages to corporate planning, it is narrow in its generation and evaluation of strategies, it lacks formal schemes for monitoring the success of the plan, and formal approaches are not used to implement the plan.

Experts in marketing planning also ignore key steps in formal planning. This was more true for experts in companies than for academic experts. In general experts recommended an increase in formality for some steps, especially for the evaluation of strategies.

By far the most conclusive type of evidence is that drawn from research studies. We found *no* empirical evidence on the value of formal planning for marketing strategy. Nor did any of the planning advocates draw upon the existing evidence from research in corporate planning or in organizational behavior.

We suggest the following approaches to research on strategic planning for marketing:

(1) *Surveys of planners* have proven to be a useful and low-cost approach in the study of corporate planning; it seems logical to extend this for research on marketing strategy. Such studies are most useful when they obtain detailed information on the planning process, the situation, and the impact of planning on all key interest groups.

(2) *Observation* of the prescriptions, the planning process and of the plans might be useful for organizations facing large changes, if it is possible to also obtain a control (informal planning) group.

(3) *Experimental studies of cases* would be desirable. Groups trained in formal planning procedures would be matched against informal planners on cases where the outcomes are known to the experimenters.

(4) *Laboratory experiments* are especially useful in studying which aspects of the planning process are most useful.

Hopefully, a variety of these approaches will be used in an effort to rule out alternative explanations of the results and to determine how much formality should be introduced for given situations. These could add significantly to our knowledge on how much planning a marketing planner should plan—if a planner could plan plans.

REFERENCES

Abell, Derek K., and John S. Hammond, *Strategic Market Planning*. Prentice Hall, Englewood Cliffs, N.J., 1979.

Anderson, Carl R. and Frank T. Paine, 'PIMS: a reexamination', *Academy of Management Review*, 3 (1978), 602–612.

Anderson, Paul F., 'Marketing, strategic planning and the theory of the firm', *Journal of Marketing*, **46** (Spring 1982), 15–26.

Ansoff, Igor *et al.*, 'Does planning pay? The effect of planning on success of acquisitions in American firms', *Long-Range Planning*, **3** (Dec. 1970), 2–7.

Armstrong, J. Scott, 'The value of formal planning for strategic decisions: review of empirical research', *Strategic Management Journal*, **3** (1982), 197–211.

Armstrong, J. Scott, 'Strategic planning and forecasting fundamentals', in Kenneth Albert (ed.), *The Strategic Management Handbook*. McGraw-Hill, New York, 1983, pp. 2-1 to 2-32.

Boyd, Harper, and Jean-Claude Larreche, 'The foundations of marketing strategy', in Roger A. Kerin and Robert A. Peterson (eds), *Perspectives on Strategic Marketing Management*. Allyn & Bacon, Boston, 1980, pp. 84–103.

Buijs, Jan, 'Strategic planning and product innovation—some systematic approaches', *Long-Range Planning*, **12** (Oct. 1979), 23–34.

Coe, Barbara J., 'Use of strategic planning concepts by industrial marketers', in Kenneth Bernhardt *et al.* (eds), *The Changing Marketing Environment: New Theories and Applications*. American Marketing Association, Chicago, 1981, pp. 13–16.

Day, George S., 'A strategic perspective on product planning', *Journal of Contemporary Business*, **4** (Spring 1975), 1–34.

Guiltinan, Joseph P., and Gordon W. Paul, *Readings in Marketing Strategies and Programs*. McGraw-Hill, New York, 1982.

Hopkins, David S., *The Marketing Plan*. The Conference Board, New York, 1981.

Jain, Subhash C., *Marketing Decision Making*. Free Press, New York, 1977.

Janis, Irving L. and Leon Mann, *Decision Making*. Free Press, N.Y. 1977.

Kollat, David T., R. D. Blackwell, and J. F. Robeson, *Strategic Marketing*. Holt, Rinehart & Winston, New York, 1972.

Lewis, Sinclair, *Arrowsmith*. Harcourt, Brace & World, New York, 1925.

Luck, David J. and O. C. Ferrell, *Marketing Strategy and Plans*. Prentice Hall, Englewood Cliffs, N.J., 1979.

Montanari, John R., G. Moorhead, and E. O. Montanari, 'A laboratory study of a strategic decision making methodology', *Proceedings of the American Institute for Decision Sciences*, Nov. 1980, pp. 472–474.

Murray, John A., 'Strategic Marketing', *Long Range Planning*, **12** (Apr. 1979), 76–83.

Nutt, Paul C., 'An experimental comparison of the effectiveness of three planning methods', *Management Science*, **23** (1977), 499–511.

Schanck, J. Thomas, 'Strategic planning for industrial markets', *Industrial Marketing Management*, **8** (Spring 1979), 257–263.

Stasch, Stanley F., and Patricia Lanktree, 'Can your marketing planning procedures be improved?' *Journal of Marketing*, **44** (Summer 1980), 79–90.

Van de Ven, Andrew H., 'Problem solving, planning, and innovation, Part I. Test of the program planning model', *Human Relations*, **33** (1980), 711–740.

Webster, Frederick W., Jr, *Industrial Marketing Strategy*. John Wiley, New York, 1979.

Wilson, Ian H., William R. George, and Paul J. Solomon, 'Strategic planning for marketers', *Business Horizons*, **21** (1978), 65–73.

Strategic Marketing and Management
Edited by H. Thomas and D. Gardner
© 1985 John Wiley & Sons Ltd

2.2
Defining and Selecting Strategic Marketing Planning and Control Units

DAVID W. CRAVENS AND CHARLES W. LAMB, JR.

M. J. Neeley School of Business, Texas Christian University, Fort Worth, Texas 76129

Choosing a planning unit is an essential step in the strategic marketing planning process (Cravens, 1981: 12–19). Surprisingly, defining and selecting strategic planning units has received limited attention from strategic planners. Strategic analysis and the interpretations underlying the analysis can be influenced by the unit that is used. For example, analysis of an industry can lead to a different strategic interpretation than analysis of a particular market niche. Consider the following illustration. Nucor Corp. is a small steel producer whose 1982 sales should exceed $600 million. Nucor, if analyzed using the Boston Consulting Group's market attractiveness/business strength grid, is clearly a dog compared to the rest of the steel industry. Nucor is tiny by size comparison and the overall attractiveness of this troubled industry is low. If the comparison is changed to the steel joist product-market, Nucor fares much better. With the leading market share in this product-market and a market attractiveness that is higher than the entire steel industry, Nucor falls into the high–high corner of the grid. Thus, the definition and choice of appropriate planning and control units (PCUs) for strategic analysis and planning are important decisions at both the corporate and marketing level.

Since there are alternative approaches to establishing PCU boundaries, and a hierarchy of planning levels, the choice of an appropriate unit of analysis in a given situation is far from obvious (Day, 1981: 89–105). There is a clear need for operational methods and guidelines for use in defining strategic planning and control units. Once defined, criteria are needed to evaluate the usefulness of alternative planning units. Prevailing approaches to defining and selecting planning units rely heavily upon managerial judgement, with limited analytical support for the choices that are made. Most strategic planning methods assume the existence of a unit of analysis. In some cases the unit selected may be so aggregate in scope that analysis does not uncover important underlying strategic marketing implications. There are dangers in defining PCUs either too narrowly or broadly. If the PCU is too aggregate it may hide key strategic issues such as how to position the unit against competition, the financial performance of sub-units, and the opportunity present in specific market niches. At the other extreme, too much fragmentation can lead to high costs of analysis and unnecessary complexity in strategy development.

We begin with an examination of alternative PCUs. These range from an entire corporation to specific product-market niches. In fact, individual customers may be appropriate marketing planning units for some firms. After identifying the hierarchy of planning levels and the critical issues associated with each planning unit category, available approaches to forming planning units will be examined. Criteria for selecting planning units appropriate in a given situation are identified and analyzed. Finally, high-priority research areas are considered.

APPROACHES TO FORMING PCUs

Since both market-centered and organizational-centered factors are often relevant in PCU definition, the possibilities can be large and the needs of corporate and marketing planners often vary. Nevertheless, since the planning levels are clearly interrelated, the choice of a PCU that can serve as a common denominator between the two levels can greatly facilitate information gathering and analysis. The selection of an appropriate PCU also affects the availability and costs of information for strategic analysis. Illustrative units for strategic analysis and planning are shown in Figure 2.2.1.

Three central issues are relevant in PCU definition: (1) should the PCU definition be market-centered or organization-centered? (2) should the unit be formed by disaggregation or built up from smaller units of analysis? and (3) should PCU definition be determined by end-users or management? These issues are discussed, followed by a critical assessment of the available approaches for defining PCUs.

Issues in PCU definition

First, should the PCU definition be market-centered or organization centered? From an organizational perspective, a PCU definition based upon products and/or organizational units is useful in resource allocation decisions and for management and control of business operations. A market-centered definition is useful in targeting marketing strategy and competitive positioning. Since both internal (organizational) and external (market) considerations are important in strategic analysis and planning, incorporating both organizational and market perspectives into the definition of PCUs seems appropriate. Dimensions that are often useful in defining PCUs include: identification of the

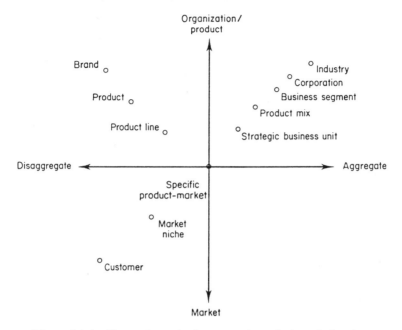

Figure 2.2.1   Illustrative units for strategic analysis and planning

need or want that the firm (business unit) is attempting to satisfy; description of the end-user customers management wants to serve; and determination of the product or service that will be used to meet the needs of end-user customers (Abell and Hammond, 1979: 392). An important question in using these dimensions to guide PCU definition is selecting an approach which will incorporate the dimensions into an operational definition. We shall return to an examination of the available methods for doing this shortly.

The second issue is whether to form the PCU by disaggregation of an organization and/or market, to build the PCU from a smaller unit of analysis such as customers, or to use a combination approach. In organizational planning, disaggregation has been the prevailing approach. Consider, for example, the following description of SBU formation by the General Foods Corporation:

> We started out with four divisions: Kool-Aid, Bird's Eye, Jello, and Post. Among the products in those four divisions, we saw five basic menu segments in addition to coffee: dessert, main meal, breakfast, beverage, and pet food. We combined these five strategic business units—SBUs—into three new divisions: main meal and dessert SBUs became the food products division; beverage and breakfast SBUs were combined into one division, and pet foods—which we considered a major growth opportunity—was put into a third division (Ferguson, 1980: 6).

Marketing strategists have used both the breakdown and build-up approaches in market niche formation. One key question is deciding whether to start with an SBU and decompose it into specific product-markets, to build a market structure using the three-factor classification scheme, or to start by defining a generic product-market and then determine the specific product-market categories that are competitive with each other? It may, in fact, be appropriate to use all of these viewpoints depending upon the purpose of the product-market analysis (Cravens, 1982: 130–131).

The third issue is whether PCU definition should be end-user or management determined. There are several considerations that may affect this issue, including available information, management's insights, end-user ability to participate in PCU definition, and costs. We turn now to an examination of the three prevailing approaches to forming PCUs: judgement and experience, classification/structured, and research-based approaches. This will be helpful in illustrating the advantages and limitations of managment versus end-user PCU definition.

Judgement and experience

The earlier discussion of SBU formation by the General Foods Corporation is an example of the use of judgement and experience in forming PCUs. Assuming that product and market considerations will always be involved in defining planning units, a major issue is whether management's judgement and experience will be sufficient in establishing PCU boundaries. At the more disaggregate levels, such as market niches, customer-oriented research may be needed in identifying product-markets (Day *et al.* 1979: 8–19). Alternatively, at more aggregate levels such as the SBU, judgement and experience may be adequate for establishing broad organizational planning categories.

An illustration will be useful in demonstrating the strengths and limitations of judgemental determination of PCUs. Consider the illustration shown in Figure 2.2.2. Suppose four strategic business units have been formed as shown. Note that both product and market categories serve as a basis for SBU formation. Assuming the objective is to form SBUs from two or more product-markets, judgement and experience are essential in establishing the SBU boundaries shown in Figure 2.2.2. Of course, another issue is how to define the product-market cells (Xs) that are used to make up each SBU. For example, should the analyst work with a product line, specific product, or brand? Will total markets be used or niches within one or more markets (A–G)? Should the SBU serve as the PCU or should each product-market category be designated as a PCU? At this disaggregate level (product-market), judgement and experience may not be adequate for establishing PCU boundaries. In particular product-markets in which there are substantial variations in customer needs and wants and ways (product/services) of

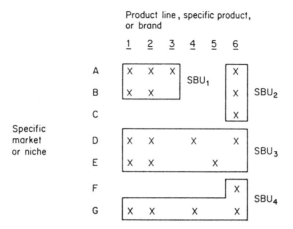

Figure 2.2.2 Illustrative definition of strategic business units

meeting these needs, research may be necessary to identify market niches (segments).

Classification/structured approaches

There are several classification-based approaches that can be used to assist in the formation of PCUs. The basis of classification may be by product or by product-market. While these approaches rely heavily upon management judgement and experience, they differ from purely intuitive approaches in two respects. First, the basis of classification can be generalized across firms and thus is not unique to a particular firm. Second, there are often rules for establishing the classification scheme.

Product-type classification

Industry-based classification approaches are widely used as a basis for PCU determination. The portfolio and screening grid approaches and PIMS frequently use an industry-type PCU for analysis. For example, the standard industrial classification (SIC) code system provides detailed subcategories within major industry categories. Using product-type classifications such as the SIC code, government and industry trade groups provide a wide range of information useful in strategic analysis and planning. A major limitation is that the classification categories are rather large and they may not define competitive arenas in any specific way. Consider, for example, the difference between industry shipments and product shipments.

Industry shipments refer to the total value of all products made by one industry. . . . Variations between industry and product shipments vary by the particular industry. For the majority of industries, the difference tends to be relatively small, i.e. less than 10 percent, but for some the divergence is much more substantial (US Department of Commerce, 1981: x–xi).

This problem illustrates the importance of understanding how the data base is formed in product-type classifications such as the *US Industrial Outlook*. Since the results of strategic analysis may be affected by the composition of the classification categories, the strategist must evaluate the impact of composition of the data base on his/her specific situation.

Porter (1979: 137–145; 1980) has developed a promising approach to industry and competitive analysis, focusing on assessment of the threat of new entrants, bargaining power of customers, bargaining power of suppliers, threat of substitute products or services, and jockeying for position among current competitors. Inclusion of these factors into industry definition expands the perspective to include market and competitive influences that, for example, SIC code classification does not consider.

Product-market structure

Another structured approach to product-market definition described by Cravens (1982: 137–145) starts with a generic need that can be met by a group of products/services. The approach is structured, yet judgement and experience can be used in the formation of product-market boundaries. This method incorporates both industry/product and end-users into determination of product-market structure.

Research-based approaches

These methods have one common characteristic—product-market definition is based largely upon customers' needs and requirements as described below:

(1) People want the benefits that products provide rather than the products *per se*. Specific products or brands represent the available combinations of benefits and costs.
(2) Consumers consider the available alternatives from the vantage point of the usage contexts with which they have experience or the specific applications they are considering (Day *et al.*, 1979: 10).

There are various research-based methods to building product-market boundaries. One promising method is called substitution-in-use analysis. It starts with a specific product and then expands uses and products so that one or more generic product-markets is defined and its composition determined. First, it is necessary to identify what uses or applications exist for the product. Does it satisfy multiple needs and wants? For example, a tape recorder may be used in various ways. When used to record music it meets a generic need for home entertainment. When an executive uses the product to dictate a letter, it fulfills a generic office service function. At the same time uses and applications are identified, other specific products that satisfy these same uses and applications should be indicated. By starting with the product the objective is to position it along with other products that meet a common generic need (e.g. office information processing). Next, specific product-markets are broken out. Finally, the brands that compete are identified. A major characteristic of the research-based approaches is that end-user research is used to determine product uses and generic, specific, and brand product-markets of interest to the firm.

Critique of approaches

A comparison of approaches to forming PCUs is shown in Table 2.2.1. In general the more aggregate the PCU (e.g. strategic business unit), the less likely research-based approaches will be needed in defining the PCU. Of course, if an SBU is built from smaller PCUs such as product-market niches, then research may be needed to define the niches. In any event, the use of more formal guidelines than judgement and experience should be considered by the strategist. The product-market structure approach offers some distinct advantages over both the judgement and research approaches (Cravens, 1982: 153–154). It provides the strategist a framework to define product-market levels, draws upon management judgement and experience and available information on products and markets, and links families of product-markets into a hierarchy that can be systematically examined at increasingly more specific levels. The structured approach also enables the analyst to draw from common types of information regardless of the product-market under study.

Research approaches, on the other hand, are intended to form arenas of competing products and brands from pools of many products and uses. They are particularly useful when a firm is trying to locate promising brand niches or gaps in product-markets that can be filled with new products. In some cases, however, end-users may not be able to answer the questions necessary to develop a product-market definition.

Research and structured approaches are best viewed as complementary rather than as substitutes. They both start from a large generic product category and move toward defining the set of brands that compete for a particular set of customer needs. In some situations consumer research is not needed. In other complex or changing product-market situations a consumer orientation is needed to identify relevant product categories.

A problem that compounds the difficulty of defining PCUs is the wide variation in the use of terms such as market, segment, niche, and product-market between strategists and researchers. The widespread coining of new buzz

Table 2.2.1 Comparison of approaches to forming PCUs

Approaches	Features	Limitations
Judgement and experience approaches	Incorporates management's intuitive understanding of product and market factors and organizational factors	In complex product-markets, important competitive and customer factors may not be identified or considered in strategy formulation
	Corresponds to management's strategic perspective of how the business is viewed and operated	Often internal considerations weigh heavily in PCU determination, thus excluding customers' perspectives
Classification/data-based approaches	Conform to categories familiar to management	Some of the approaches have a strong product and industry orientation rather than a customer orientation
	Substantial amount of published information available from government and private organizations	Categories tend to be too aggregate for comprehensive competitive analysis and strategy development
	Boundaries between categories are established based on specific guidelines	Disaggregation of categories (e.g. specific product-market into niches or segments) may require a research-based approach
Research-based approaches	Product-market boundaries are established based upon product functions and user needs and wants	Customer-based research and analysis is expensive and may not be justified in well-defined product markets
	Considerable flexibility is provided in defining product-market boundaries	Approaches tend to result in a scrambled rather than structured product-market
	PCUs can be defined at very disaggregate levels (e.g. product-market niche)	

words by marketing authors further complicates the problem. Fennell (1982: 10) comments upon the problem:

> Unfortunately, there is more to the problem than the mere misalignment of terms and levels of analysis. Missing from the 'market segmentation variables' exhibit is the notion of the nesting of one set of tasks (market segmentation) within another (market definition) and the corresponding distinction between the groups of variables appropriate to each set of tasks. To the extent, however, that levels of analysis is a contributing factor I am hopeful that work which addresses the distinction among the corporate, business, and program levels (e.g., Abell, 1980) may sensitize authors to this potential source of confusion.

CRITERIA FOR SELECTING PCUs

The direction provided to the strategist in selecting an appropriate PCU is limited. Two approaches, a 'divide up' and a 'build up', have been advocated. Day (1981: 91–92) describes the approaches in some detail and suggests a series of tests to assess the strategic relevance and administrative feasibility of resulting PCUs.

Several criteria may be important in selecting PCUs. These include the strategic relevance of the PCU, administrative requirements, information availability, applicability of the PCU to strategic analysis using available methods, flexibility, and the costs and benefits associated with the use of the PCU for strategic analysis and planning. Following is a brief discussion of these issues.

Strategic relevance

How the PCU is to be used has an important influence upon the choice of an appropriate unit. Two aspects of strategic relevance are important in choosing the right PCU(s). First, at least three different organizational levels may be involved. These include top management, business unit management, and marketing management. There may be differences in the PCU needed by each type of executive. Top management is primarily concerned with the company, business segment, and SBU levels. Business unit management is primarily interested in the business segment and SBU levels, whereas marketing executives concentrate much of their attention at the SBU level and below.

Second, there are several aspects of analysis that may be relevant to the strategist. These include: (1) consideration of entry into a new business, product, or market area; (2) strategy formulation for strategic business units, product-markets and niches; (3) diagnosis and control of existing PCUs; and (4) consideration of exit from a business, product, or market area.

Together, the two considerations (management level and strategic need) have an important influence upon PCU selection.

Administrative requirements

This issue was discussed earlier in terms of the use of the PCU as a feasible administrative unit. Both internal and external factors may be important from an administrative point of view. Internally, financial management and control factors can affect the usefulness of one PCU versus another. Financial reporting is another consideration. The external focus of marketing strategy argues strongly for a market-centered perspective as opposed to functional-, product-, or manufacturing-centered PCUs. The ideal solution to the PCU decision should attempt to satisfy both internal and external influences upon adminstrative processes.

Information availability

While not a controlling factor, the availability of information for use in strategic analysis may make one PCU desirable over another. An important issue is whether a particular PCU under consideration corresponds to information that can be obtained at acceptable cost/benefit levels. For example, one of the major features of industry- and product-based PCUs is the extensive amount of published information available.

In general, the more specific and disaggregate the PCU, the more difficult it is to obtain market and competitor information. Use of PCUs based on product-market niches will require greater use of primary data collection to supplement published information. Yet it is at these more disaggregate levels where competitive positioning is often critical to successful performance.

Strategic analysis methods

The PIMS, portfolio, and screening methods tend to use relatively aggregate units, PIMS operating at the most aggregate level of all:

> The PIMS data do not break down market volume into segments or submarkets. Yet most markets include several—sometimes many—distinct subdivisions of customer groups, product variations, price versus quality levels, or distribution methods. We are confident that if data on segments within markets were available, they would show that most of the businesses achieving major share gains did so by focusing their efforts on selected segments—often ones that were relatively small at first (Buzzell and Wiersema, 1981: 144).

The portfolio and screening methods have also been largely used at industry and total market levels, although there is no apparent reason why they cannot be used with more disaggregate PCUs. Also, specific products have been used as the unit of analysis. The lack of information for disaggregate analysis is one reason why more aggregate PCUs have been used in strategic analysis. There is a clear need for the development of strategic analysis methods for use at market niche levels. Customer research offers a potentially promising method for product-market structure analysis and positioning (Srivastava *et al.*, 1981: 38–48).

The developers of a new strategic analysis model called STRATPORT acknowledge that they have assumed the firm has appropriately defined its business units (Larreche and Srinivasan, 1981: 39–52). Nevertheless, they recognize the importance of PCU definition. Interestingly, the STRATPORT model can be used to test the robustness of a given portfolio strategy compared to alternative definitions of business units. Thus, it may be helpful in examining the usefulness of alternative PCUs.

Flexibility

It seems clear that one PCU is unlikely to meet the needs of all of the strategists in the organization. Because of this, selection of a unit of analysis that can be aggregated or broken down to serve executives at various strategic levels is certainly desirable. Building up from product-market niches into SBUs is often more feasible than breaking up an aggregate PCU. American Hospital Supply Corporation's vice president—planning and development—comments on the firm's choice of a PCU as follows:

> We plan by market segment. We do not plan the $2.5 billion corporation from the top down. Rather, we plan from the bottom up, one market segment of product line at a time. That goes for every element of the process—including plans for new business development, strategy, capital spending, and operations (Bailey, 1982: 64).

Suppose the product-market niche is used as the basic PCU. What rules should be used to form composite units? Should this task be situation-specific to the firm or general across all firms? A related issue is selecting the basis of aggregation. Should it be market-centered, product-centered, or a combination of the two?

Cost/benefits

Finally, the costs of PCU definition and analysis must be compared to the estimated benefits. Defining and analyzing very disaggregate units of analysis is costly, and compounds administrative requirements. Management's options range from major business units to individual customers. The objective is to select a PCU that is large enough to represent a meaningful unit in strategy development and performance tracking, while being small enough to facilitate planning and management.

RESEARCH ISSUES

The need for research into PCU definition and analysis should be apparent from our discussion so far. The following examination of research issues is not intended to be exhaustive. Instead, our objective is to illustrate the nature and scope of needed research.

Conceptual development

A critical research need is the conceptualization of variables and relationships associated with strategic marketing planning. While we have some general managerial frameworks, additional work is needed. For example, what are the critical variables and relationships linking business strategy and marketing strategy? Even less attention has been given to conceptualization of the relevant variables in a product-market structure.

A more immediate need is reaching an agreement upon definitions of terms such as strategic business unit, product-market, and market segment. A classification scheme for linking PCUs at various levels of aggregation is also needed. Work on definition, classification, and elimination of multiple designations for the same item may be appropriate as a project sponsored by the American Marketing Association or a joint effort between marketing and management professional organizations.

Methodology for defining PCUs

A comprehensive investigation is needed of alternative ways of defining PCUs. The objective should be the development of a methodology for forming PCUs. Both break-down and build-up approaches should be critically evaluated to determine the strengths and limitations of each approach. For example, is a single approach for product-market definition feasible, and, if so, is it desirable. Product-market definition represents a major research need and opportunity. Such research will undoubtedly contribute to the development of one or perhaps alternative methodologies for defining planning and control units.

Closely associated with methodological development is the issue of a common denominator for use in forming PCUs at various levels of aggregation. Is the determination of a common denominator a desirable objective? Our position is that it is desirable to determine a basic unit of analysis that can be aggregated to form higher-level PCUs. Nevertheless, this issue requires further study.

Role of PCU in strategy determination

Many of the questions concerning the definition and selecting of PCUs are linked to how the PCU will be used in strategic analysis, planning and control at corporate, business unit, and marketing levels. Below are some illustrative research questions:

(1)   How important is the choice of a PCU in strategy determination? For example, will loosely defined PCUs lead to the same strategic interpretations as will more rigorous methods?

(2)   What will be the effect of choosing a PCU upon the results of strategic analysis using portfolio, screening, PIMS, and other methods? For example, is there consistency in diagnosis regardless of the type of PCU used?

(3)   What modifications are needed in the strategic analysis methods to make them usable at any level of aggregation? Alternatively, what constraints should be specified regarding the application of each method?

Marketing professionals are uniquely equipped to meet this research challenge. Unlike strategic planners and financial analysts, we have conceptual and analytical capabilities in product-market definition and analysis. It is clear that product-market units must somehow be tied into the choice of PCUs. While the selection of specific directions of research require further study, both the need and opportunity are clear.

CONCLUDING NOTE

The excitement and glamour of strategic marketing planning have overshadowed two basic and critical issues: (1) How should strategic planning and control units be defined; and (2) What should be the appropriate unit of analysis in a given strategic situation? The unit of analysis in strategic marketing planning can be an important determinant of the success of the planning process. Research attention should be directed to investigating methodologies for defining PCUs and to developing criteria and approaches for selecting the appropriate PCU(s) for a given strategic situation.

REFERENCES

Abell, Derek F. *Defining the Business*. Prentice-Hall, Inc., Englewood Cliffs, N.J., 1980.

Abell, Derek F., and John S. Hammond, *Strategic Market Planning*. Prentice-Hall, Inc., Englewood Cliffs, N.J., 1979, p. 392.

Bailey, Earl L., *Product-Line Strategies*. The Conference Board, 1982.

Buzzell, Robert D., and Frederick D. Wiersema, 'Successful Share-Building Strategies,' *Harvard Business Review*. Jan.–Feb. 1981, p. 144.

Cravens, David W., 'How to match marketing strategies with overall corporate planning', *Management Review*, Dec. 1981, pp. 12–19.

Cravens, David W., *Strategic Marketing*. Richard D. Irwin, Inc., Homewood, Ill., 1982.

Day, George S. 'Analytic approaches to strategic market planning', in *Review of Marketing 1981*, B. M. Enis and K. J. Roering (eds.), American Marketing Association, 1981, pp. 89–105.

Day, George S., Allan Shocker and Rajendra K. Srivastava, 'Customer-oriented approaches to identifying product-markets', *Journal of Marketing*. Fall 1979, pp. 8–19.

Fennell, Geraldine, 'Terms v. concepts: markets segmentation, brand positioning and other aspects of the academic–practitioner gap'. Paper presented at the AMA Special Educators Conference, Marketing Theory: Philosophy of Science Perspectives, San Antonio, Texas, February 1982.

Ferguson, James L., 'General Foods' super-marketer', *MBA Executive*. Mar.–Apr. 1980.

Larreche, Jean-Claude, and V. Srinivasan, 'STRATPORT: a decision support system for strategic planning', *Journal of Marketing*, Fall 1981, pp. 39–52.

Porter, Michael, 'How competitive forces shape strategy', *Harvard Business Review*. Mar.–Apr. 1979, pp. 137–145.

Porter, Michael, *Competitive Strategy*. The Free Press, New York, 1980.

Srivastava, Rajendra K., Robert P. Leone, and Allan D. Shocker, 'Market structure analysis: hierarchial clustering of products based on substitution-in-use', *Journal of Marketing*, Summer 1981, pp. 38–48.

US Department of Commerce, Bureau of Industrial Economics. *1981 US Industrial Outlook*. US Government Printing Office, 1981.

Strategic Marketing and Management
Edited by H. Thomas and D. Gardner
© 1985 John Wiley & Sons Ltd

2.3
Toward Decision Support Systems for Strategic Marketing

DAVID B. MONTGOMERY*
Robert A. Magowan Professor of Marketing, Graduate School of Business, Stanford University.

DECISION SUPPORT SYSTEMS

Accounting and elementary operations control dominated the early applications of computers. Simple sales analysis was the most prevalent in marketing. Most applications were cost-justified and the relatively simple tasks were well matched to the limited capacity of the hardware and software which were available. A second generation concerned marketing information systems and management science applications, the latter being primarily addressed to operating and tactical decisions (e.g. media selection models). These second-generation applications involved more sophisticated tasks such as report generation and solutions to carefully defined and structured decision problems.

Decision support systems represent a third generation of computer applications to management problems. Keen and Scott Morton (1978) characterize DSS as follows:

> The impact is on *decisions* in which there is sufficient structure for computer and analytic aids to be of value, but where manager's judgment is essential.
> The payoff is in extending the range and analysis capability of managers' decision processes to assist them in improving their *effectiveness*.
> The relevance for managers is in the creation of a *decision support tool*, which remains *under their control* in that it does not attempt to automate the decision process, impose solutions, or predefine objectives.

The development of DSS has been supported by significant improvements in hardware and software, as well as improved data and methods of analysis. Continuing developments on these fronts should continue to fuel progress in the development of DSS.

* The author acknowledges the helpful inputs of Rajev Batra, Ph.D. candidate at Stanford to the section on Strategic Marketing.

Table 2.3.1 Evolution of strategic marketing planning*

	Sales plan	Marketing plan	Strategic market plan (+ annual marketing plan)
I. *Type of plan*			
(a) Scope	Sales and distribution function	Product and market segments	SBU
(b) Decisions involved	Sales	Marketing mix	Business definition Business scope Objectives Product-market selection Positioning Strategic aspects of marketing mix
II. *Corporate planning activity*	*Financial plan* Extended budgeting	*Long-range plan* (a) Extrapolative (b) Rigid format (c) Focus on financial variables	*Strategic plan* (a) Systematic generation and evaluation of alternatives (b) Opportunity/competence match (c) Portfolio logic (d) Centralized resource allocation (e) Competitor analysis (f) Contingency plans
III. *Organization*	Functional	Profit center or division with common objective	SBU with differentiated objectives

* Adapted from personal communication from George S. Day

Managers take action with respect to a competitive environment in order to achieve organizational objectives. To do this they must perceive, interpret, and predict how customers and competitors will respond to their actions as well as to environmental events such as recession and recovery. They must sift through the plethora of factors varying in the environment in order to focus upon key considerations and relationships. Managers then must develop and evaluate alternative strategies and finally choose one to implement. The inanimate part of the process, which is designed to *assist* the manager in these tasks, is what will be termed the DSS.

The components of a DSS are illustrated in Figure 2.3.1 within the dotted lines. The manager addresses questions to the system and receives responses.

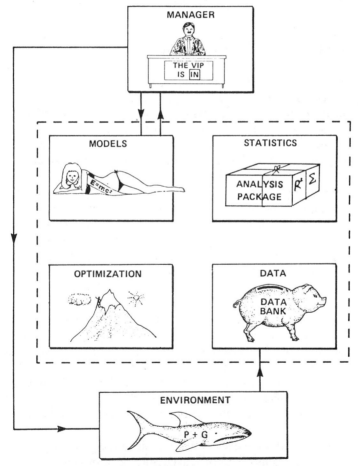

Figure 2.3.1   The Manager and the Components of a Decision Support System (DSS) Adapted from Little's (1979) adaptation of Montgomery and Urban (1969)

The manager will also supply judgemental inputs to many of the analyses. The environment consists of customers, potential customers, competitors, and other environmental factors (e.g. political, economic, social, technological, regulatory, and legal) which may provide opportunities and threats as well as constraints on managerial decisions. Systematic analysis needs to be given to how to structure the monitoring of the environment as input to both the manager and the data bank. For an approach to this strategic intelligence activity see Montgomery and Weinberg (1979). The individual components will be discussed in later sections relative to applications in strategic marketing.

STRATEGIC MARKETING

Before turning to a discussion of the four components of a DSS in relation to strategic marketing, it is well to consider briefly the nature of strategic marketing. A decision may be called *strategic*, rather than *tactical*, if it serves not only to shape the action at issue but also, by its very nature, delimits the range, scope or direction of other—tactical—decisions.

Strategic *marketing* decisions obviously have to do with marketing, in the sense that they relate either to marketing variables or to decisions that impact on other corporate effort variables, but are based on assessments of product-markets. Such strategic marketing decisions, thus defined, can be made at all corporate decision-making levels.

At the corporate 'entity' level, decisions—such as SBU entry strategies, resource allocation among SBUs, etc.—are strategic marketing decisions to the extent that they are based on features of the markets and consumers relevant to the decision. Such decisions also form part of what has been studied as 'corporate strategic planning'; however, corporate strategic marketing decisions need not always be strategic *marketing* decisions if, for instance, they deal with issues of debt vs. equity capitalization, choice of manufacturing process, etc.

Similar logic holds good at the SBU level. Resource allocation and other decisions made at the SBU or divisional level will sometimes, but not always, be strategic decisions. Thus a decision to back one product-line rather than another because of market trends is a strategic marketing decision. A decision to reduce the total advertising budget in favor of R and D outlays is a SBU strategic decision, which entails a strategic marketing component. A decision to adopt a Japanese 'just in time' inventory approach would often not relate closely to marketing strategy.

Most strategic marketing decisions are made at the product-line level when they involve comparisons *across* products. Such decisions include:

(1)   the allocation of resources between new products (as a group) and current products (as a group);

(2) the allocation of resources among new products, and among current products;
(3) product elimination decisions;
(4) decisions to launch new products aimed at certain market segments, rather than others;
(5) decisions dealing with overall, across-marketing-mix aspects of a product's (or brand's) marketing strategy, such as the choice between 'low price, few features, market penetration' vs. 'high price, many features, market skimming'. Such decisions would accompany segmentation decisions.

A few marketing strategy decisions made at the individual product level also qualify for strategic marketing decision status, if they 'pre-empt' the range or locus of other 'tactical' decisions. Examples are positioning decisions: a market positioning decision constrains product pricing, distribution, advertising (both creative and media), and product feature decisions to a strategically consistent, synergistic range. Most other single-product marketing decisions are usually tactical: which ad media do we use? do we spend in pulses, or in a long stretch? do we price at $1.30 per unit or $1.45?

In sum, strategic marketing decisions are made at all organizational levels, but most frequently at the Group Brand Manager or Marketing VP level, when they deal not with *product* management but with *product line* management, when they involve resource allocation between products, or between the mix elements of one product, or between marketing and other corporate functions. See Table 2.3.1 for a view of the evolution of strategic marketing planning.

Strategic marketing issues

This paper examines some of the major strategic marketing issues which interface with DSS. Cady (personal communication) has provided an interesting perspective on the differences between strategic and conventional marketing (see Table 2.3.2). Especially salient features of this comparison relate to portfolio analysis, market scope as a strategic choice, the concern for competitive advantage which requires knowledge of competitors as well as customers, and marketing's integrated role in business strategy.

Ohmae (1982) has suggested that three interrelated factors are of key strategic significance in formulating strategy: knowledge of customers and how to create value in the customer's eyes, understanding of the company's capabilities and weaknesses in relation to customers and competitive offerings, and knowledge of competitors' capabilities and weaknesses as well as likely actions. Rothschild (1979) reinforces the strategic analysis of competitors as perhaps the most important element. The substantial recent focus upon competitive analysis in the strategy literature reflects the fairly recent realization that strategy should entail a search for sustainable competitive

Table 2.3.2   Differences in perspective*

	Conventional marketing	Strategic marketing
Planning unit	Individual product	Product line (portfolio) SBU
Market scope	Treated as a given	Strategic choice
Goals, performance measures	Sales market share	Profit, cash flow of SBU, market share
Competition	Satisfy customer via marketing mix	Beat competition via total capabilities
Time horizon	Annual plan	Long-term
Role of marketing	One of several functions	Part of integrated business planning

* Personal communication from John Cady, Graduate School of Business, Harvard.

advantage. Merely satisfying customers with readily duplicated strategies may lead to delighted customers, but disappointed shareholders. Consequently, one would expect to see competitive analysis emerge as an important aspect of DSS to support strategic marketing.

Other issues of importance in strategic marketing are the interrelated issues of market and business definition and scope, market opportunity identification, and the selection of product/market targets. Another is the development of methods for forecasting and evaluating outcomes of alternative strategic scenarios. The development of positioning strategies for companies and products is yet another area of substantial importance in strategic marketing. Clearly, more work needs to be done to generate a comprehensive theory of strategic marketing issues; however, it is hoped this short list will be suggestive.

MODELS

A key element in the generation, evaluation, and selection of strategic marketing options is construction of conditional sales forecasts. Such forecasts project revenues, units, and market shares given a set of marketing actions by the firm and given certain assumptions concerning competitive actions and the state of the environment (e.g. recession or recovery, tight money, etc.). While such conditional forecasts may be constructed directly, the use of models generally facilitates this process. See Figure 2.3.2 for a conceptual schema.

The impact of models for such purposes has been reviewed and summarized by Montgomery and Weinberg (1973). Their summary conclusions are presented in Table 2.3.3. As a structuring element in the development of

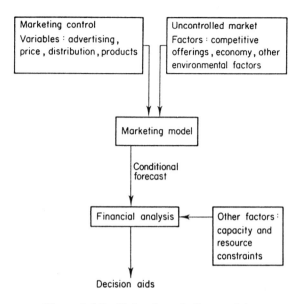

Figure 2.3.2   Role of marketing models

Table 2.3.3   Functions models can perform*

Help to better utilize a manager's judgement
Limit a manager's tendency to overreact to pressures of the immediate and recent situation
Require an explicit listing of input assumptions which leads to more informed discussion
Provide a method for quick and convenient evaluation of the consequences of alternative plans
Search for improved plans or better solutions to problems
Allow the emergence of politically unmentionable solutions
Expand the range of questions which can be answered by use of the notion of derived judgement
Distill from available data relevant information as in new product forecasting
Provide a basis for relating marketing inputs to market results and, hence, serves as basis for marketing planning
Diagnose, based on early data, the adequacy of a market plan and locate areas needing improvement

---

* From Montgomery and Weinberg (1973).

conditional sales forecasts for strategic marketing decision support systems, models provide assistance in a variety of ways including:

(1)   Helping managers focus upon areas of agreement and disagreement in the

construction of conditional sales forecasts. The specificity of model-based analysis facilitates this process.

(2) Facilitating the conduct of sensitivity analysis to determine which factors (firm actions, competitor actions, or environmental events) are crucial in determining outcomes and which are of secondary importance.

(3) Identifying what measures should be obtained via marketing research. The construction of a model-based conditional sales forecast will suggest what factors should be measured in order to make such a forecast. Further, sensitivity analysis of a model may suggest that a few factors are vital in determining outcomes. Measurement attention should focus upon vital factors about which there is disagreement in terms of their market impact. However, care should also be given to avoiding erroneous 'conventional wisdom'.

(4) Providing a basis for analyzing and projecting market measurements.

Several examples are given below of model-based strategic marketing analysis.

Xerox's introduction of the 9700 Electronic Printing System, a computer-controlled laser scanning computer printer, provides an excellent illustration of the role of models in developing conditional sales forecasts (Oren *et al.*, 1980). At the time the 9700 was Xerox's largest development project outside its main business. The project was nearly killed when IBM announced its own high-speed laser scanning system. In what has been described as a controversial decision, Xerox decided to keep the project alive for one more year by allocating just enough funds to keep the key elements of the technical team together. This core team was told to use the year to generate a credible market forecast.

In order to generate a credible market forecast the study team first developed a model of the process whereby customers would choose among computer printing options. For a given computer site, the model predicts the customer's product choices and his usage levels of the selected products. The forecasting system was composed of three interrelated models—value model, choice model, and market dynamics model (see Figure 2.3.3). The value model has two submodels. The cost throughput model determines the minimum cost configuration of impact and non-impact computer printers given the existing hardware on the site, the site's workload, paper costs, and printer availability. The output of this submodel is an optimal printer configuration for the site as well as the direct costs, throughput, availability, and usage of computer printers at the site. The value-added model establishes a dollar value for intangible product attributes such as brand name, reliability, and copy quality. Direct costs and value-added then become inputs to the choice model. The latter produces customer product choice assuming all alternative products are fully available and each customer is fully aware of all of the alternatives. The market dynamics model then modifies choice to reflect differences in product availability, awareness, and penetration rates. Further, it accounts for customer resistance to

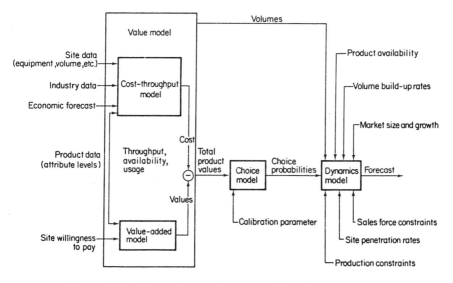

Figure 2.3.3 Xerox forecasting system (from Oren *et al.*, 1980)

change. The ultimate output is a detailed forecast of product populations and usage over time.

The model was constructed prior to any field marketing research. It dictated ahead of time the measures which would be needed to construct the forecast. Telephone and two site interviews were conducted at a stratified sample of about 100 installations from International Data Corporation's computer site files. These interviews provided the data to parameterize the value and choice models. When the field data, which cost $250,000 to generate, came in, the existence of the model facilitated its timely analysis. Interestingly, previous, non-model-based market research had failed to establish a clear case regarding market potential for the 9700.

The forecasting system was run under a wide variety of competitive product scenarios. A product scenario consisted of products and their associated attributes, product introduction dates, product launch strategies (e.g., timing of city openings), sales force sizes, and production constraints. In one set of scenarios top management wanted to see what would happen to the 9700 unit forecasts if a major competitor were to introduce a very low-cost, high-speed computer printer using a new technology. To their surprise, a series of forecasts based upon successively lower prices for this competitor's potential product were found not to decrease significantly the demand forecast for the 9700 until the hypothetical printer had greatly reduced the forecast for other non-impact printers. The latter implied that the competitor would cannibalize a great deal of its own demand if it were to choose such a strategy. Through use of the model-generated forecasts under a variety of scenarios, Xerox management were convinced that the 9700 product should be launched.

In addition to the fundamental 'GO' decision on the 9700, the model also impacted other elements of the pre-launch strategy. The model assured management that the timing of introduction and the planned geographically constrained product introduction were appropriate. However, examination of alternative pricing strategies suggested an unusual pricing plan that would effectively eliminate the incremental pricing charge between 1 million and 1.4 million impressions per month. This model-suggested pricing plan was still in effect in 1982, 5 years after product launch. Management continued to utilize the forecasting system after launch as a basis for evaluating the market impact of proposed product enhancements—e.g. two-sided printing. These evaluations were used to allocate resources and set priorities for enhancements.

The model-driven forecasting system turned Xerox around on the 9700. As of June 1981 the thousandth 9700 was installed, which translates into a revenue base of approximately $10 million per month. The forecasts have tracked well over time. A fundamental impact of the model-structured forecasting system was that debate focused on assumptions. The process changed from a negotiated forecast to negotiated assumptions.

RCA's entry strategy into the satellite communications business provides another example of a model-based analysis impacting in a significant manner upon a major management strategy. The model was a probabilistic simulation which modeled the interactions and relationships among a collection of important variables (Nigam, 1975). The variables included the size and mix of potential markets, competitive actions from both terrestrial and other satellite carriers, and combinations of satellite characteristics with launch vehicles. After evaluating approximately 300 strategy alternatives using the model, the model development team recommended an immediate and independent RCA market entry using a particular satellite. The investment requirement was on the order of $125 million over the first 5 years. Although this recommendation was at variance with management's initial expectations and plans, it was adopted in only slightly modified form within 6 months of the original recommendation. The model enabled the managers and the model developers to assess the efficacy of many more potential strategy combinations than could ever have been done without the structure and the rapid manipulation power provided by the model. RCA has subsequently used this approach in assessing other new business opportunities.

Conditional forecasting models such as those at Xerox and RCA have also been useful for developing brand strategies for frequently purchased consumer products. Figure 2.3.4 presents a schematic of the brand strategy model developed and used at a major consumer products company. The model is calibrated by a combination of historical data analysis and management judgement. It starts by developing a momentum forecast of sales and contribution by package conditional upon market trends, assumed competitor

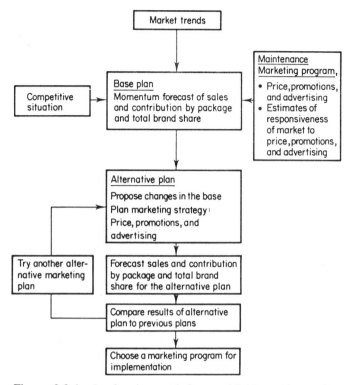

Figure 2.3.4   A planning tool for establishing price, price promotion, and advertising strategy

actions, and its own marketing program which will be required to support the momentum forecast. In addition, estimates of the sensitivity of the market to price, price promotions, and advertising are made. These provide the basis for assessing the impact of changing the company's marketing program from the levels established for the momentum forecast. The product manager may then use the model to estimate the sales and contribution results which would be expected to occur should either the competitors or the company (or both) operate under strategies different from the ones postulated in the momentum forecast. In many instances the company has used the model to discover marketing strategies which have enabled them to improve simultaneously market share and return on the marketing investment. Subsequent implementation has found the model to be reasonably accurate in its forecast levels and very accurate in indicating beneficial directions for change in marketing strategy. A similar model has been in use at another consumer products company since the mid-1960s. An early version of this model is described in the Concorn Kitchens case in Day *et al.* (1973).

Little (1975) has formulated a comprehensive brand strategy model called BRANDAID. The model structure is modular, which enables a product manager to consider or ignore phenomena at his/her discretion. As in the previous two consumer product models a reference or momentum conditional forecast is made, market response to changes from reference conditions are assessed, and the model is used to assess market response and the profit impact of alterations in the reference marketing strategy or conditions. Although initially intended for annual brand strategy formulation, Little reports that implementation has shown that it is important to have the model readily available at all times, to enable the product manager to develop rapidly tactical response to changed conditions. He cites a case where a product manager heard a rumor that his advertising budget was going to be cut in half. Using BRANDAID, by 5 o'clock that evening he was able to develop a comprehensive analysis of what he felt the impact would be on sales and profits for this brand over the next 2 years.

Dutta and King (1980a,b) have proposed a meta-game theoretic model for assessing competitive scenarios. The model structure explicitly models competitor reactions to a firm's moves, and may be used to identify robust market strategies based upon anticipated strategies of major competitors. Although their reported case study did not demonstrate the potential of their model to help in strategy formulation, their approach seems promising and merits further research.

The benefits of model-based marketing analysis have been illustrated by Montgomery and Weinberg (1973) and are summarized in Table 2.3.3. Although certain of the illustrations derive from more tactical applications, the general benefits would seem to apply to strategic marketing as well.

OPTIMIZATION

Optimization models seek to identify the best strategy to achieve management's objectives, generally under conditions of resource scarcity. In this section two prototypical strategic marketing optimization models will be considered. The first deals with the question of defining market scope in the context of a firm selecting target end-user markets. The second develops an explicit cash flow and profit model suitable for conducting product portfolio analysis.

Zoltners and Dodson (1983) have developed a market selection model (MSM) to assist companies in choosing which, among multiple-user markets, to target so as to achieve company goals and establish certain standards for aggregate company markets. In the model an end-use market is defined to be any customer or customer group which can be characterized by a single attribute profile. Each end-use market is described by a set of attributes such as growth, revenue, net income, ROI, cash flow, and cyclicality. Timing of production demand may also be an attribute of interest to a firm seeking to balance production so as to avoid capacity constraints. A key aspect of the

MSM is the specification of functions which aggregate across end-use markets attributes which are in the profile. While these functions are arbitrary, the authors report thatt linear aggregation functions are often most useful as, for example, in aggregating revenue across end-use markets to obtain total company revenues. Of course, demand synergies between end-use markets would invalidate the simple linear form.

Given a set of end-use markets each described in terms of the attribute profile, MSM will enable management to address any of the following problems:

(1) Choose end-use markets so as to match best a specified profile on the aggregate market attributes.
(2) Identify a set of end-use markets so that certain minimum and maximum constraints on the aggregate attributes are satisfied.
(3) Find a set of end-use markets which maximize (or minimize) some aggregate attribute subject to all other aggregate attributes being within some specified ranges.

The authors report implementing MSM at a division of a large commercial bank with the following results:

(1) The division's profits rose 5 percent as a result of the alteration in market emphasis suggested by the model.
(2) The profit increase was achieved by reducing the division's staff size.
(3) The analysis indicated that for the 12 end-use markets, one should be dropped, one cut back, and several others should receive more emphasis.
(4) The division's prospect conversion rates were found to be too low to support the current level of effort.

One of the most widespread strategic marketing tools has been product portfolio analysis, which was popularized by the Boston Consulting Group. Haspeslagh (1982) estimates that, as of 1979, 45 percent of the *Fortune* '500' industrial companies were using some variant of portfolio planning. Larreche and Srinivasan (1981, 1982) have developed a model, STRATPORT, which is designed to suggest an optimal allocation of marketing resources across strategic business units. The key relationships in the model for each business unit are:

(1) *Market response function*. Market share at the end of the planning period (usually 2–5 years) is taken as a function of aggregate market investment by the business unit. The relationship may be S-shaped or concave depending upon the inputs.
(2) *Maintenance marketing function*. In order to avoid myopic optimization results, STRATPORT models a post-planning period (usually 5–15 years). Marketing expenditures (as a percentage of sales) needed to

maintain market share over the post-planning period are modeled as a linear function of the total SBU sales.

(3) *Capacity expenditures.* Capacity is expanded or contracted to meet SBU demand. The cash flow requirements to increase capacity (or the cash flow generated by asset liquidation) are explicitly modeled.

(4) *Working capital requirements.* Working capital for accounts receivable and inventory are modeled as a diminishing returns function of sales.

(5) *Experience curves.* Both cost and industry price are subject to experience curves; however, industry price may have kinks in the relationship reflecting margins which are increasing or decreasing.

Using data and/or management judgement, these relationships must be calibrated for each current and potential business unit. The objective in STRATPORT is to allocate marketing resources across the SBUs (current and potential) so as to maximize the discounted present value of the profit stream over the planning and post-planning periods subject to a cash flow constraint. STRATPORT explicitly allows for different discount rates to be used for each business unit thereby linking the strategic perspective of portfolio analysis to the risk considerations of financial portfolio theory.

STRATPORT repeats the profit-maximizing allocation at several levels of the cash flow constraint. This provides an optimal profit vs. cash flow envelope as illustrated in Figure 2.3.5. From the figure the status quo strategy is seen to be far from optimal. Nearly twice as much cash could be extracted from those SBUs with no loss in profits, if the marketing expenditures were to be redeveloped in the manner suggested by STRATPORT. Alternatively, several options are available for obtaining a substantial increase in profitability with a more modest level of cash extraction.

Both the STRATPORT and the MSM may also be used to evaluate a proposed management strategy. However, it is their optimization capability which makes them of greatest interest from the standpoint of developing marketing strategy.

DATA

Decision support systems for strategic marketing need to provide for environmental monitoring, especially the competitive and customer environments. For example, a firm will want to monitor a competitor's capacity (both current and intended), its product announcements, its market share by product/market, speeches by its key executives, its financial performance and capabilities, its personnel activities (especially in technical areas), and even the consultants they are using. The objective is to identify and evaluate the competitor's strategy; assess its capabilities; and understand its goals, objectives, and assumptions about its environment. The end-product of all this

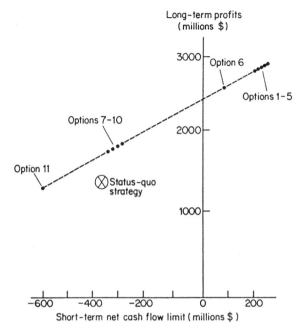

Figure 2.3.5   STRATPORT optimum profit cash flow
envelope

is hopefully an enhanced ability to predict a competitor's likely actions or reactions in the marketplace. Further, a firm must attend to potential sources of new competition—technical substitutes, new entrants (especially foreign), forward integration by suppliers, and backward integration by buyers. Porter (1980) presents an extensive analysis of this area.

In developing environmental data, a firm must establish priorities. The importance of identifying an environmental event which may impact the firm's marketing strategy is a positive function of the importance of the event to the firm, of the speed with which the event may impact the firm, of the likelihood the event will occur, and of the time it will take the firm to respond successfully to the event. Montgomery and Weinberg (1979) have suggested a structure for a strategic intelligence system to monitor the customer, competitor, technical, economic, political and regulatory, and social environments. Much of the data emanating from such a system should interface with, and become part of, the data base for a strategic marketing DSS.

Historical data often provide the basis for analysis that yields significant strategic insights. Two well-known and large-scale historical studies—PIMS and Advisor—have collected multi-firm information which may be used to analyze the impact of strategic choices, forecast ROI and cash flow, and develop norms for marketing expenditures as a percentage of sales.

The structure of the data portion of a DSS should provide for flexible, easy, and rapid use. Historical data should be retained so as to provide a basis for subsequent analysis using the statistics and models modules of the DSS. Ideally, data should be maintained in their most elemental, disaggregated form in order to maximize flexibility in their future use. Little (1979) suggests that successful applications of marketing DSS nearly always have a closely coupled and strong data support system. He further advocates on-line computer access via powerful manipulative commands designed to provide easy application of a wide variety of statistical packages. The incredible current and projected advances in the price/performance features of computer data storage and retrieval hardware and software will support substantial developments on this front over the next few years.

Studies are also beginning to emerge which provide some guidance as to how such systems should be designed to interface with users. Using a dynamic competitive simulation, Chorba and New (1980) conducted an experiment which indicated that decision-makers who have the opportunity to select the data reported to them progress faster in identifying a successful strategy than do those that receive an externally prescribed report, independent of the amount of information in the external report. This suggests the need to provide a very flexible, user-controlled data retrieval and generation system.

STATISTICS

The statistics module should contain a wide variety of analytical methods, from simple tabulation to sophisticated econometric and multivariate statistical techniques. It should encompass experimental analysis as well as the perceptual and preference techniques embodied in multidimensional scaling (MDS) and conjoint analysis. Use of these tools will be facilitated by data availability in the data module as well as software systems to enable their rapid and easy use. The later criteria are intended to encourage more systematic and thorough analysis of strategic marketing issues. Examples of the strategic use of statistical analysis of historical data, experimental data, and customer judgement and preference data are given below.

Historical data

To illustrate the use of statistical analysis of historical data, an example presented by Montgomery and Silk (1972) which assessed market response to the communications mix of an ethical pharmaceutical will be used. The dependent variable in this analysis was a brand's market share of new prescriptions, while the independent variables were variously lagged values of direct mail, samples and literature, and journal advertising expenditures. Econometric analysis of 5 years of monthly data suggested that in this time frame the brand had been quite responsive to journal advertising, somewhat responsive to samples and literature, and scarcely responsive to direct mail. Yet over this same period the company had made the following average monthly allocation of marketing expenditures: direct mail $1630, samples and literature, $1355, and journal advertising $1209. That is, the company had allocated its marketing communication budget precisely in inverse relation to measured market response. Montgomery and Silk suggest that the reason was not stupidity on the part of the product manager, but rather a failure on the part of the information system to provide relevant feedback to enable the product manager to learn systematically and correctly from experience. In the absence of information concerning how responsive the market was to journal advertising, the product manager tended to over-allo-cate to direct mail, which generates a very tangible and measurable response in the form of reply cards. The measurement of advertising response calls for more sophisticated data analysis, which a properly designed DSS should provide. Once an imbalance in the communications mix is identified, the communications strategy may be changed to balance the mix by increasing the budget for the most responsive elements or reallocating a given budget to reflect market response. It should be noted that this analysis was possible only because a far-sighted manager had retained the necessary historical data. Too often firms destroy their history by destroying data without realizing its potential to yield strategic insights or to calibrate strategy models such as BRANDAID.

The PAR reports based upon the PIMS data base represent an example of analysis of a multi-firm historical data base. Using data from over 2500 SBUs, the PAR reports use cross-sectional regression to suggest what ROI or cash flow might be expected from an SBU having certain strategic parameters such as relative market share, relative price, relative quality, investment intensity, etc. The full-scale PAR model contains over 30 variables and has an $R^2 = 0.80$. A firm may compare its actual performance with those given by the PAR equations as one basis for assessing its strategic performance and for determining remedial action where required. It should be noted that Wensley (1982) has criticized the PIMS method for confounding differences in SBU risk with strategic performance.

Statistical analyses of the PIMS data have spawned many studies in strategic marketing. These are illustrated by the Farris and Buzzell (1979) study of how advertising and promotional costs vary across firms. They found an encouraging amount of consistency in their descriptive models of consumer and industrial businesses.

A key strategic marketing issue is the identification of product/market boundaries. Day *et al.* (1979) suggest several forms of analysis based upon customer purchase or usage behavior which might be used to identify product-markets. These methods include econometric measurement of demand cross-elasticities, measurement of similarities in usage behavior, and analysis of brand switching using stochastic models.

Experimentation

A classic example of the use of controlled market experimentation on marketing strategy is the Anheuser–Busch experiments on advertising budgets. A series of experiments in the mid-1960s enabled the analysis team to convince management that the advertising budget could be reduced substantially without eroding the company's market position. It is reported that the budget was reduced from just under $15 million to about $10 million as a result of these experiments, without damaging the firm's position.* Some of the freed-up resources were invested in strengthening distribution with the remainder falling down to the bottom line. Hence a substantial shift in advertising strategy was the result of the advertising budget experiments.

Another example is provided by the introduction of a new food product, described in the Newfood cases in Eskin and Montgomery (1975). Prior to product introduction, management believed it should introduce the product with a high price coupled with high advertising or at a low price with low advertising. A preposterior decision analysis indicated a high expected value of sample information. Consequently, the company conducted an experiment in four test market cities. Using multiple stores per city, the company designed a full factorial experiment with high and low advertising, three prices, and two different in-stores locations for the new product. Surprisingly, the experiment demonstrated that the new product was substantially more price-elastic under high advertising than under low advertising. Further profit analysis demonstrated that the original plan of high price and high advertising or low price and low advertising were both inferior to a strategy of high advertising coupled with low price or low advertising with high price. The test market experiment thus dramatically changed the firm's introduction strategy for the new product.

Judgement and preference

There are a wide variety of data collection and analysis techniques which may be used to analyze customer judgement and preferences. Many of these rely upon perceptions of overall product/service similarity or dissimilarity. From these perceptions a geometric representation is developed of the customer's perceptions of the qualities possessed by the product/service. The geometric representation is developed so that products/services which are close together are seen as similar, and those which are far apart as dissimilar. These

---

* Personal communication from T. Newall, late director of the Stanford Alumni Association and an executive at the Anheuser–Busch advertising agency at the time of the experiments.

techniques are also capable of identtifying a customer's ideal or most preferred product/service location in the space. The theory suggests that, other things being equal, a customer is more likely to choose a product/service closer to his/her ideal than one which is farther away. Segments are formed by customers who have similar ideal points.

Such geometric configurations provide an analytic tool for identifying and monitoring the positioning of products and services. The popular MARKSTRAT strategic marketing game makes extensive use of such techniques in the formulation of dynamic competitive strategy (Larréché and Gatignon, 1977). These tools indicate which products/services are competitive for which segments, and further suggest market opportunities by indicating which segments are as yet not well satisfied by market offerings.

A measurement and estimation methodology which allows a firm to estimate the choice share of a product/service which does not even exist has gained wide acceptance (Cattin and Wittink, 1982). Termed conjoint analysis, the method views products/services as bundles of attributes and calibrates the extent to which a customer may be willing to give up some level of performance on one attribute to increase performance on another (Green and Wind, 1975). From this calibration the method produces a utility function which represents the utility to the customer of each level of each attribute. Once these measures have been obtained from a number of customers (100 to 1000), different product scenarios (both company and competitive products) may be analyzed based upon these customer utility functions. In this case the theory states that the customer will choose the product for which he/she has the highest utility. In this way one may estimate the choice share for a product defined by a combination of attribute levels which currently does not exist. In a recent case a company used this technique to estimate customer response to an improved service offering, as well as the customers' willingness to pay for the improved service. The analysis was an important input to a multimillion dollar investment to implement the new offering. Conjoint analysis may also be used to help set strategic priorities. In this case the attributes might be such things as market share, cash flow, profits, etc.

SUMMARY

After a brief overview of DSS, attention was given to issues in strategic marketing. Illustrative examples of currently available technology to support strategic marketing in each of the DSS modules were then presented. With the rapid advances in computer hardware and software which are anticipated, and with further refinement of strategic concepts in marketing, the next decade is bright with promise for the emergence of significant, integrated decision support systems for strategic marketing.

REFERENCES

Cattin, P., and D. R. Wittink (1982). 'Commercial use of conjoint analysis: a survey', *Journal of Marketing*, **46**(3) (Summer), 44–53.

Chorba, R. W., and J. L. New (1980). 'Information support for decision-maker learning in a competitive environment: an experimental study', *Decision Sciences*, **11**, 603–15.

Day, G. S., G. J. Eskin, D. B. Montgomery, and C. B. Weinberg (1973). *Planning: Computer and Model Assisted Cases in Marketing*. Scientific Press, Palo Alto, California.

Day, G. S., A. D. Shocker, and R. Srivastava (1979). 'Customer-oriented approaches to identifying product markets', *Journal of Marketing*, **43**(4) (Fall), 8–19.

Dutta, B. K., and W. R. King (1980a). 'A competitive scenario modeling system', *Management Science*, **26**(3) (March), 261–273.

Dutta, R. K., and W. R. King (1980b) 'Metagame analysis of competitive strategy', *Strategic Management Journal*, **1**(4) (Oct.–Dec.), 357–370.

Eskin, G. J., and D. B. Montgomery (1975). *Data Analysis: Cases in Computer and Model Assisted Marketing*. Scientific Press, Palo Alto, California.

Farris, P. W., and R. D. Buzzell (1979). 'Why advertising and promotional costs vary: some cross sectional analyses', *Journal of Marketing*, **43**(4) (Fall), 112–122.

Green, P., and Y. Wind (1975). 'New way to measure consumers' judgments', *Harvard Business Review*, **53**(4) (July–Aug.), 107–117.

Haspeslagh, Philippe (1982). 'Portfolio planning: uses and limits', *Harvard Business Review*, **60**(1) (Jan.–Feb.), 58–73.

Johnson, R. M. (1971). 'Market segmentation: a strategic management tool', *Journal of Marketing Research*, **8**(1) (Feb.), 13–18.

Keen, P. G. W., and M. S. Scott Morton (1978). *Decision Support Systems: An Organizational Perspective*. Addison-Wesley, Reading, Massachusetts.

Larreche, J. C., and H. Gatignon (1977). *MARKSTRAT: A Marketing Strategy Game*. Scientific Press, Palo Alto, California.

Larreche, J. C., and V. Srinivasan (1981). 'STRATPORT: a decision support system for strategic planning', *Journal of Marketing*, **45**(4) (Fall), 39–52.

Larreche, J. C., and V. Srinivasan (1982). 'STRATPORT: a model for the evaluation and formulation of business portfolio strategies', *Management Science*, **28**(9) (Sept.), 979–1001.

Little, J. D. C. (1975). 'BRANDAID: a marketing-mix model. Part 1: Structure; Part 2: Implementation, calibration, and case study', *Operations Research*, **23**(4) (July–Aug.), 628–673.

Little, J. D. C. (1979). 'Decision support systems for marketing managers', *Journal of Marketing*, **43**(3) (Summer), 9–27.

Montgomery, D. B., and A. J. Silk (1972). 'Estimating dynamic effects of market communications expenditures', *Management Science*, **18**(10) (June), 485–501.

Montgomery, D. B., and G. L. Urban (1969). *Management Science in Marketing* Prentice-Hall, Englewood Cliffs, N.J.

Montgomery, D. B., and C. B. Weinberg (1973). 'Modeling marketing phenomena: a managerial perspective', *Journal of Contemporary Business* (Autumn), 17–43.

Montgomery, D. B., and C. B. Weinberg (1979). 'Toward strategic intelligence systems', *Journal of Marketing*, **43**(4) (Fall), 41–52.

Montgomery, D. B., and D. R. Wittink (1980), in D. B. Montgomery and D. R. Wittink (eds), *Market Measurement and Analysis*. Marketing Science Institute, Cambridge, Mass., pp. 298–309.

Nigam, A. K. (1975). 'Analysis for a satellite communications system', *Interfaces*, **5**(2) (Feb.), 37–47.

Ohmae, K. (1982). *The Mind of the Strategist*. McGraw-Hill, New York, N.Y.

Oren, S. S., M. H. Rothhopf, and R. D. Smallwood (1980). 'A causal market forecasting system: theory and application', in D. B. Montgomery and D. R. Wittink (eds), *Market Measurement and Analysis*. Marketing Science Institute: Cambridge, Mass., pp. 9–21.

Porter, M. E. (1980). *Competitive Strategy*. Free Press, New York, N.Y.

Rothschild, W. E. (1979). 'Comment', *Journal of Marketing*, **43**(4) (Fall), 53–54.

Wensley, R. (1982). 'PIMS and BCG: new horizons or false dawn?' *Strategic Measurement Journal*, **3**(2) (Apr.–June), 147–158.

Zoltners, A., and J. Dodson (1983). 'A market selection model for multiple end-use products', *Journal of Marketing*, **47**(2) (Spring), 76–88.

Strategic Marketing and Management
Edited by H. Thomas and D. Gardner
© 1985 John Wiley & Sons Ltd

CHAPTER 3

Planning Techniques and Their Role as Strategic Inquiry Systems

INTRODUCTION

The most visible aspect of strategic marketing has been the various planning techniques (Abell and Hammond, 1980; Larreche and Strong, 1982). Unfortunately, misunderstanding and hence misapplication of these techniques has been far too frequent (Kiechel, 1981; Wensley, 1982).

It is somewhat surprising that so few planning techniques exist for a functional area of the importance of marketing. Even more surprising is the general lack of prescriptive planning techniques for strategic marketing.

The best-known planning techniques, such as portfolio matrices and the PIMS research tools, came about to address management issues raised by the increased complexity of managing multi-division, multi-product organizations in the 1960s and 1970s. Not only were the 1960s the age of the conglomerate, but growth, mergers, and diversification often produced large diversified organizations.

The problems created for managers of these large diversified organizations were complex, not only due to size and diversity, but due to rapidly changing technical and environmental factors. In particular, the resource allocation problem between divisions and products was troublesome. To meet this need, several techniques have emerged.

A partial list of more popular approaches is given below.

Arthur D. Little approach
PIMS
Market attractiveness
BCG
Shell Chemical
Future scenarios

Each of these techniques has application at both the corporate level and at the strategic marketing level.

The clear attractiveness, logic, and relative simplicity of these various planning methods led many multi-divisional and conglomerate companies to apply them to their strategic problems. More recently, a spate of articles (see, for example, Kiechel, 1981; Wensley, 1982) have emerged which have sought to question the value of these planning approaches. Criticisms have ranged from the view that such models lead to the inappropriate specification of simplistic strategies to the view that naive planning methods can never replace the creative strategic thinking of the able chief executive officer.

The role of planning methods in strategy formulation is examined in this chapter. It is argued that no single planning approach can provide a clear-cut answer to a strategy problem. Indeed, it is suggested that the various planning methods can provide different insights for the development of strategic thinking within the organization. It is also argued that strategic choice should emerge from a debate process in which various viewpoints, analyses, and assumptions are examined and reconciled through constructive and open dialogue. Such dialogue may need to be facilitated by approaches such as the Nominal Group Technique (Van de Ven and Delbecq, 1974) and dialectical inquiry (Mason and Mitroff, 1981).

PLANNING METHODS AND STRATEGIC INQUIRY SYSTEMS

The roles and functions of alternative planning methods can be conceptualized in terms of Churchman's (1971) development of inquiry systems. Churchman's inquiry systems are derived from the writings of such philosophers as Leibnitz, Locke, Kant, Hegel, and Singer. Mason and Mitroff (1981) and Mitroff and Mason (1982) have also explained how these philosophical stances can be used to provide frameworks for understanding problem formulation and solving processes in the policy field.

Leibnitzian systems are characterized by the development of a single, near-optimal problem formulation, generally based upon some underlying theories and problem structures. This formulation of an analytic model of rational logical form is followed by data collection to support it and the generation of results, namely, deductive conclusions, which are consistent with the model. Lockean inquiry systems, however, have a much more empirical focus. Data are collected relevant to the decision problem, and the Lockean aim is to infer patterns from the data through inductive reasoning to support a single problem structure. Both Leibnitzian and Lockean systems are regarded as being suited to resolving well-structured problems.

Kantian and Hegelian systems are more appropriate for resolving ill-structured policy and planning problems. Kantian inquiry systems are characterized by the existence of multiple frameworks for viewing problems, and by the presence of alternative conceptual viewpoints. These viewpoints are based upon the differing assumption bases of the members of the decision-making group. Efforts are made to combine these views and to achieve consensus by presenting each set of underlying assumptions. Hegelian inquiry systems also involve multiple frameworks and viewpoints, but they require the introduction of conflict—challenging and questioning assumptions—to achieve a sound problem formulation process. A synthesis emerges through conflict, structured debate, and dialectical inquiry. (Mason, 1969).

Such strategic inquiry systems can explain the logic underlying many planning processes in organizations. In practice, in many planning situations, one planning model is suggested initially and data are collected to support this single 'view of the world' (note that this is a simple, somewhat naive form of a Leibnitzian inquiry system).

This initial view of the problem is often discussed by the management team and alternative assumptions, scenarios, and product-market concepts are suggested. Often managers begin to advocate alternative extreme scenarios and wildly differing 'views of the world'. Thus, the questioning and debate process indicates a significant change in the character of the strategic inquiry system. The problem formulation system is now more complex and multidimensional, and is much closer to Kantian and Hegelian form. This occurs because several views about the problem are held, and it is believed that consensus and synthesis about problem formulation should be achieved through a process of group debate and dialogue. That is, alternative planning models and approaches should be examined and their outputs should aid strategic dialogue by generating additional information about the possible consequences of alternative assumptions, problem formulations and future scenarios.

PLANNING MODELS AS ALTERNATIVE PROBLEM SCANS

If the premise that most planning processes can be cast as strategic inquiry systems is accepted, it seems sensible to ask whether confusion or clarity is generated by advocating the use of combinations of planning approaches to develop alternative problem viewpoints for policy dialogue.

A number of planning approaches have been identified in the literature. For market and competitive analysis, the most frequently mentioned tools are Steiner and Miner's (1977) WOTS-UP analysis for assessing a firm's strengths and weaknesses, BCG's (Boston Consulting Group's) experience curve approach for cost dynamics and the Strategic Planning Institute's PIMS, PAR, and market share analyses for estimating competitive position.

Portfolio models, such as the BCG growth/share matrix (Henderson, 1979), the Shell directional policy matrix (Hussey, 1978), the ADL (Arthur D. Little) matrix of business strength and the GE/McKinsey business screen (Hofer and Schendel, 1978), are most often used to examine corporate portfolio balance and the strengths and weaknesses of individual strategic business units in the light of overall corporate objectives.

Each of these models, which are really cognitive simplification mechanisms for corporate strategic thinking, probably highlight only a small part of the strategic problem. For example, PIMS can clearly assess a business's ROI and cash flow relative to the "PAR-ROI" and cash flow of businesses in somewhat similar strategic situations. However, it cannot analyze competitive cost economics and industry structural differences in the manner of tools such as the experience curve and others drawn from the literature on industrial organization.

Different portfolio models also throw different perspectives upon strategic problems. Financially-based approaches such as the capital asset pricing model (CAPM), (Mullins, 1982), and risk analysis approaches (Hertz and Thomas, 1983) assess the viability of strategic alternatives by examining the fit between strategic options and the risk/return characteristics of the corporate portfolio. Growth/share matrices essentially examine the corporate portfolio as a closed financial system and highlight the cash generation and cash use characteristics of the elements of the corporate portfolio. The target goal is directed toward the achievement of a corporate portfolio with a healthy cash balance and the recommendation that businesses should be examined not only for their present and future cash generation potential, but also for their cash interrelationships with other businesses. GE screens and the Shell matrix are approaches adopted most often to categorize the attractiveness or quality of businesses by using a finer screen than the market growth/relative market share screen adopted in the BCG approach. Arthur D. Little refine the portfolio concept even further by merging it with the product life cycle in an attempt to identify the dynamics of market evolution and the necessary adaptation of strategies to fit the stages of market evolution.

It is clear that each planning method discussed here has a unique set of underlying assumptions and aims. Therefore, much can be gained from using a range of planning tools and approaches commensurate with the needs and organization structure present in each company situation. The aim must be to ensure that such methods supplement creative strategic thinking by enabling managers to debate the alternative positions, viewpoints, and insights advanced by each method.

CONCLUSIONS

Strategy formulation involves a program of strategic inquiry in which alternative viewpoints and frameworks about policy and planning should be encouraged in the process of arriving at strategic choice. Analytic modeling, BCG, PIMS, GE screens, and others provide different perspectives from which to examine messy strategic problems. Those working within a given perspective sometimes suggest that they are developing universal guidelines for practice, without recognizing the assumptions underlying their guidelines or the inherent limitations of their approach.

Criticisms of planning approaches are not new. No single approach is a panacea. Multiple approaches may facilitate the art of strategic decision-making by providing a basis for policy dialogue amongst the decision-making group. By exercising judgement, managers can assess which approaches are most useful in given circumstances and make strategic decisions based upon consideration of a number of different problem perspectives.

Finally, in an extremely useful summary chapter of their book, Mason and Mitroff (1981) review a wide range of approaches which have been developed for strategic planning. They conclude that no one approach by itself is best for all organizations and problems. Indeed their final paragraph is important and is reproduced below (Mason and Mitroff, 1981: 302).

> Therefore, any program of strategic inquiry using planning approaches should aim to improve problem understanding and the effectiveness of the entire planning process. It is incorrect to reject certain planning approaches on the basis of criticisms which fail to recognize their contribution to the overall effectiveness of the strategic planning process.

REFERENCES

Abell, D. F., and J. A. Hammond, *Strategic Market Planning*. Prentice-Hall, Englewood-Cliffs, N.J., 1979.

Churchman, C. W. *The Design of Inquiring Systems*. Basic Books, New York, 1971.

Henderson, B., *Henderson on Corporate Strategy*, Abt Books, Cambridge, Mass., 1979.

Hertz, D. B., and H. Thomas, *Risk Analysis and Its Applications*, John Wiley & Sons, Ltd, Chichester, 1983.

Hofer, C. W., and D. E. Schendel, *Strategy Formulation: Analytical Concepts*. West Publishing, St Paul, MN, 1978.

Hussey, D. E., 'Portfolio analysis: practical experience with the directional policy matrix', *Long Range Planning*, **11** (Aug. 1978), 2–8.

Kiechel, III, Walter, 'Oh where, oh where has my little dog gone? or my cash cow? or my star?' *Fortune*, 2 November 1981, pp. 148–154.

Larreche, J. C., and E. Strong, *Readings in Marketing Strategy*. Scientific Press, Palo Alto, CA, 1982.

Mason, R. O , 'A dialectical approach to strategic planning', *Management Science*, **15** (1969), B403–B414.

Mason, R. O., and I. I. Mitroff, *Challenging Strategic Planning Assumptions*, John Wiley & Sons, Ltd, New York, 1981.

Mitroff, I. I., and R. O. Mason, 'Business policy and metaphysics: some philosophical considerations', *Academy of Management Review*, **7**(3) (1982), 361–371.

Mullins, D. W. Jr., 'Does the capital asset pricing model work?' *Harvard Business Review*, Jan./Feb. 1982, pp. 105–114.

Steiner, G. A., and J. B. Miner, *Management Strategy and Policy*, Macmillan, New York, 1977.

Van de Ven, A. H., and A. L. Delbecq, 'The effectiveness of NGT, Delphi and group decision making processes', *Academy of Management Journal*, **17**(4) (1974), 605–621.

Wensley, J. R. C., 'PIMS or BCG: new horizons or false dawn', *Strategic Management Journal*, **3**, (April/June 1982), 147–158.

Strategic Marketing and Management
Edited by H. Thomas and D. Gardner
© 1985 John Wiley & Sons Ltd

Introduction to Conference Papers on Planning Techniques

Several papers, including the Gardner and Thomas review in chapter 1.2 and the material in chapter 3, describe the range of planning techniques developed for strategic planning and management. The papers in this section provide evidence about problems and research issues in relation to the application and implementation of such planning approaches in strategic decision-making contexts. In subsequent paragraphs the aims of the various authors are briefly discussed.

Cady and Hunker argue that strategic prescriptions based on the portfolio models used in strategic marketing frequently deal with the issue of diversification. Managers who wish to diversify their firm's portfolio of businesses may choose to do so internally or through acquisition. Although there may be substantial benefits from acquisition, there are numerous risks: business, financial, and legal. Their paper discusses the issue of legal risks involved in market extension mergers. Two forms of legal risk are identified: case selection by the Antitrust Division of the Department of Justice or the Federal Trade Commission; and the litigation process. Guidelines for financial and non-financial mergers are proposed that may allow managers to anticipate and reduce the legal risk of related diversification acquisitions.

Fitzroy's study uses the PIMS data base of the Strategic Planning Institute to examine the effects of the bargaining power of suppliers and buyers upon firm profitability. His initial results show that a firm's gross margins are strongly influenced by the degree of buyer and seller power. He qualifies his findings by concluding that the influence of other characteristics, including firm-specific parameters such as market share and the importance of the purchase to the customer, must be examined in further research.

Frazier and Howell's objective is to discuss the data aggregation problem inherent in data collection procedures and empirical analysis for strategic market planning. They provide recommendations for the proper analysis of cross-sectional and/or time-series data composed of business firm performance, strategy, and operating variables. They recommend the use of the joint time-series, cross-sectional model for strategic market planning purposes.

Lillis, Cook, Best, and Hawkins discuss a set of strategic planning models that have been developed by General Electric Corporate Consulting Services to aid GE managers in more effectively adjusting their marketing mix efforts to the business situation in order to achieve a desired market share. They review the validity and usefulness of these 'market share change' models in the context of application to GE.

The focus of Mahajan and Wind's paper is on the integration of finance-oriented portfolio models and product portfolio models. Financial portfolio approaches are based on the two conceptually desirable dimensions of return and risk, which are typically not considered by most standardized portfolio models. On the other hand, the optimal allocation of resources among products suggested by the financial portfolio approaches exclude relevant considerations related to the product strength and market attractiveness. Mahajan and Wind demonstrate the application of their integrated portfolio approach by analyzing the product portfolio of a Fortune 500 firm.

Montgomery and Day provide a thorough and extremely useful review of the experience curve concept and its areas of application in marketing modeling and policy. They focus upon certain practical issues which require analytic examination mainly from an econometric viewpoint. They also discuss how such experience curve-based models have been, and can be, fruitfully applied in the strategy field.

Urban, Carter, and Mucha examine the strategy of being the first entrant in a market. They investigate empirically the market share effects of being a pioneering brand, and discuss the strategic managerial implications of their research. It appears that there are considerable benefits to be reaped from being a pioneer in a given market. However, these benefits may be quickly eroded unless the product is carefully designed and positioned, and is also protected by aggressive defensive tactics centered around the use of advertising and other marketing tools.

Winter and Thomas take one of the more intuitively appealing aspects of marketing, the concept of market segmentation, and try to position its role within the strategic framework of the firm. They argue that strategic segmentation requires a focus upon a whole range of cost, demand, and competitive factors—that is, the entire gamut of competitive strategy. It should also indicate not only why market segments currently exist, but predict how segments might shift and change in composition through time.

Strategic Marketing and Management
Edited by H. Thomas and D. Gardner
© 1985 John Wiley & Sons Ltd

3.1

The Legal Risks in Related Diversification Through Acquisition*

JOHN F. CADY
Associate Professor of Business Administration, Harvard Business School

AND

JEFFREY A. HUNKER
Consultant, Boston Consulting Group

INTRODUCTION

The proliferation of portfolio tools to guide the allocation of resources to business or products has subsided. There is an abundance of standardized and customized planning matrices available for corporate, divisional, SBU, and product line managers to choose from. Concern in practice, and in the strategy-oriented literature, has begun to shift from the generation of new planning tools to their implementation in practice. The process of implementation is difficult; the problems many. Business units must be defined, reorganizations orchestrated, incentive systems adjusted to accommodate differences in performance criteria, management selection and succession systems evaluated, and an appropriate strategic planning process instituted. Despite these problems of implementation, numerous large and financially successful corporations now use some form of portfolio planning as a principal aid in allocating resources to existing and new businesses (Haspeslagh, 1982). The use of portfolio models for allocating resources relies on certain prescriptive generalizations, many of which relate to the attractiveness of various diversification moves. Such moves, within the framework of the general portfolio model, are meant to increase the firm's position in attractive markets and to reduce the firm's commitment in relatively unattractive markets.

A principal means by which such moves are accomplished is through the acquisition or sale of businesses. Acquisition is clearly not without some

* The authors gratefully acknowledge the financial support of the Division of Research, Harvard Business School, for this research.

financial and business risk. The evidence of over a decade of major conglomerate merger activity indicates that, in general, companies that diversify through acquisition earn lower returns than those that follow a strategy of developing strong positions in their core businesses (Salter and Weinhold, 1979). In addition, empirical evidence suggests that the more unrelated an acquisition, the lower the expected returns.

There are other sources of risk as well. A major one is the risk that an acquisition will trigger an investigation and complaint by either the Antitrust Division of the Department of Justice or the Federal Trade Commission. Such a complaint can easily lead to protracted legal proceedings, enjoinment from further acquisitions in specific industries, or the divestiture of firms already acquired. These costs can be non-trivial, and an important question for managers is whether they can be avoided. Under what circumstances is it rational not to avoid legal risk in the pursuit of a desired acquisition? In this article, these questions are addressed. The first section reviews the stimuli to acquire and divest that are central to the more frequently used portfolio models. The second section briefly reviews the economic and institutional underpinnings that support contemporary antitrust policy with respect to diversification. The third and fourth sections provide an empirical perspective on the issue of legal risk. First, we address the extent to which legal risk of case selection for challenge under the antitrust laws is systematic, predictable, and capable of being explicitly incorporated into the firm's acquisition screening process. Second, we address the issue of outcome. If an acquisition is selected for a complaint, under what circumstances, if any, is the expected legal outcome favorable to the acquirer? Under what circumstances is a strategy of litigation preferable to abandoning a merger and selecting a new merger partner? Finally, we offer several management guidelines for handling the legal dimensions of acquisition risk.

PORTFOLIO MODELS FOR STRATEGIC MARKET PLANNING

Business/product portfolios of all varieties are generally designed to facilitate the allocation of corporate or SBU resources in a manner designed to optimize some specific criterion such as cash flow, ROI, or future profitability. Regardless of the criterion or the dimensions along which business units or products are arrayed, most portfolio models offer prescriptions for appropriate strategies based primarily on the location of the business units in the portfolio. Some of the most difficult managerial problems concern those businesses that participate in attractive markets but which have relatively unattractive current market positions. These are the 'question marks' or 'problem children' of the share/growth portfolio adherents. Such businesses provide a stimulus for a great deal of merger activity.

On the one hand, managers who decide to commit resources to these businesses may try to improve their relative market position through acquisition.

On the other hand, managers who decide not to commit resources to a particular 'problem child' may sell the business to a firm seeking to invest in that market. Timing is important. An acquisition must be made while the industry is attractive in order to optimize the potential returns to the acquisition. A decision to sell is equally affected by time. If the selling firm waits until industry growth slows, or becomes otherwise unattractive, the business will not only generate suboptimal returns, but will be viewed as relatively unattractive to buyers who will adjust their offer price accordingly.

HOW PORTFOLIO PLANNING AFFECTS ACQUISITION/ DIVESTITURE DECISIONS

Portfolio planning affects acquisition decisions in two specific ways. The first is by focusing management's attention on the creation of a financially balanced portfolio of current and future earnings contributors. Portfolio planning encourages management to continually assess internal opportunities for selling businesses and external opportunities for acquiring businesses. During the 1960s, for example, General Electric sold its computer business in order to concentrate on alternative businesses in nuclear power and jet aircraft engines. Acquisitions made for the purpose of adding to the corporate portfolio will frequently be unrelated diversification mergers of the pure conglomerate variety. For example, the management of a company in a high-growth industry may perceive the need to acquire a cash-flow source to maintain growth and improve its market share position. Tyco Labs, a manufacturer of high-technology products, acquired Grinnel from ITT in the mid-1970s. Grinnel was a major force in the low-growth fire protection business and Grinnel's cash flow fueled Tyco's internal growth and subsequent growth through acquisition (Salter and Weinhold, 1979).

The second way portfolio planning influences acquisition decisions is by focusing management's attention on appropriate strategies for current businesses within the portfolio. Decisions must be made regarding the means to enhance current business position or current competitive capability. In some cases management may conclude that the need to capitalize quickly on an opportunity favors acquisition over internal business development. These acquisitions are primarily related diversification acquisitions since they are related to the products or markets of the existing business and are undertaken to enhance either market position or competitive capabilities, or both. For example, beginning in the mid-1950s and through the mid-1960s, Foremost Dairies acquired a number of dairy producers across the country during a time when the market structures of the dairy industry were undergoing considerable concentration. The FTC, which challenged the mergers, determined that Foremost's economic power and competitive strengths overall provided it with a 'substantial economic advantage' in the markets it had entered by acquisition.

Portfolio planning may also influence the pattern of unrelated and related acquisitions that a firm undertakes. Consider entry into an attractive high-growth business. Management may initially make a diversifying acquisition in order to enter an attractive growing business. To improve or maintain the competitive position of this acquired business, management may subsequently make one or more related acquisitions. In the late 1970s, for example, Pillsbury acquired the privately owned Totino's in order to enter the fast-growing frozen pizza business. Having entered the business (its initial venture into any frozen food line), and faced with substantial and numerous competitors, Pillsbury became capacity constrained. Management perceived that the lead time to build a new plant would put Totino at a severe competitive disadvantage and the company acquired a small, regional frozen pizza manufacturer in order to expand capacity.

ANTITRUST INVOLVEMENT IN THE DIVERSIFICATION DECISIONS

The basic economic philosophy of antitrust is to maintain sufficiently competitive market structures and market conduct to insure that firms perform in a socially acceptable manner. Rather than direct involvement, as in the so-called 'regulated' industries, antitrust is directed at maintaining sufficient competition in the market so that market forces result in desirable economic performance. The purpose of Section 7 of the Clayton Antitrust Act is consistent with this basic philosophy. Its purpose, in the words of a former FTC Bureau of Economics Director, is to 'prevent the emergence of anticompetitive market structures by preventing certain kinds of mergers' (*Economic Papers, 1966–69*).

Since the passage of the Cellar–Kefauver Act, merger enforcement has been a cornerstone of antitrust activity, consuming many of the resources of its two enforcement agencies, the Federal Trade Commission and the Antitrust Division of the Department of Justice. By 1978, for example, merger enforcement accounted for a significant portion of the entire Department of Justice's available personnel time (Shenefield, 1978).

The merger guidelines

In 1968 the Department of Justice published merger guidelines outlining that agency's approach to merger enforcement. The general enforcement policy articulated in the guidelines focused on market structure:

> Market structure is the focus of the Department's merger policy chiefly because the conduct of the individual firms in a market tends to be controlled by the structure of that market. Not only does emphasis on market structure generally produce economic predictions that are fully adequate for the purposes of a statute . . . but

an enforcement policy emphasizing a limited number of structural factors also facilitates both enforcement decision-making and business planning which involves anticipation of the Department's enforcement intent (*Merger Guidelines*, 1968).

The Antitrust Division's indicia for competitive market structures are clearly articulated in terms of market share and market concentration for horizontal and vertical mergers. However, the criteria are vague for all types of conglomerate mergers. The Antitrust Division considers three classes of conglomerate mergers—those involving potential entrants, those creating a danger of reciprocal buying, and those threatening to entrench the market power of the acquired firm—to be understood well enough to issue specific guidelines. Of these categories, those involving potential entrants and those dealing with entrenchment are the most relevant for market extension mergers.

The guidelines also anticipate that conglomerate mergers may involve 'novel' problems that are not well understood. As a result, the Division '. . . considers it necessary . . . to carry on a continuous analysis and study of the ways in which mergers may have significant anticompetitive consequences in circumstances beyond those covered by the guidelines' (*Merger Guidelines*, 1968).

INSTITUTIONAL PROVISIONS AND AGENCY ENFORCEMENT PRACTICES

The enforcement of Section 7 resides jointly with the Antitrust Division and the Federal Trade Commission. Recently various writers have closely examined these agencies' enforcement practices in order to determine what factors influence case selection and what factors motivate the decision to prosecute particular cases (Katzman, 1980; Weaver, 1977). These studies indicate that the Antitrust Division and the FTC employ numerous economic and non-economic criteria in case selection and somewhat different approaches to case litigation.

Suzanne Weaver made a detailed study of the case selection, management, and litigation process at the Antitrust Division and found that the process reflects not only the structural economics and the legal grounding of the case, but the perceived litigability of the case as well. This 'litigability' factor reflects the overall attractiveness of the case to the attorneys with respect to numerous criteria including the external visibility of the case, the quality of the evidence, and whether or not the case breaks new legal ground.

But the single factor that seems to spark an investigation and motivate the Division staff more than any other is size. Although there is no consensus among attorneys on this factor, Weaver provides the following as an example of prevailing staff attitude:

Usually, we look at market concentration more than at absolute size. For instance, in the —— merger I was telling you about [Firm A] was the number-two firm in a market where the top two firms had 85%. And [Firm B] was third in the market.

But I would say we are more concerned about larger firms. For instance, in banking we won't look at acquisitions under ten million dollars, though we'll lower it some if the market is very small and localized. But with smaller firms, you always have to pay attention to the size of the market. Not with the bigger companies so much. For instance, you take the conglomerates. Absolute size is why we've been so innovative there . . . If I had to name an absolute level where I'm really going to go all out to get them, I'd say that the Fortune 500 is the trigger (Weaver, 1977).

Robert Katzman has concluded that the FTC case selection is largely the product of interaction between two bureaus and the five FTC Commissioners. These two bureaus are the Bureau of Competition (the lawyers' unit) and the Bureau of Economics (the economists' unit). Each bureau, according to Katzman, has its own conception of antitrust goals and cases that the agency should pursue. The interaction of these two bureaus and the contentious nature of their relationship has given rise to an inconsistency in the enforcement of Section 7 by the FTC over time. It has been argued, for example, that the Commission's cases have focused less on 'hard' economic criteria and more on 'soft' legal theories with unsupportable assertions of consumer benefit. As a result, 'conglomerate mergers have been attacked by the FTC on the basis of a number of questionable theories' (Meyer, 1977).

THE PRESENT STUDY

In order to assess the legal risks facing firms that are considering related diversification, the present study examined all market extension mergers that took place over an 11-year period, mid-1963 through mid-1973. This period accounts for approximately one-third of the total merger enforcement experience since the passage of the Cellar–Kefauver Amendment. A second reason for selecting this time period is that it provides a representative sample of all mergers that have taken place since the passage of Cellar–Kefauver. The mergers that took place during the study period mirror the mergers of the entire 1950–80 period on measures such as mergers involving large firms, percentage of assets acquired through the various categories of merger types. Finally, the study period covers one of the most discussed periods in merger history—the so-called third merger wave; the conglomerate merger movement of the late 1960s. This period witnessed an unprecedented number of conglomerate mergers of all types: pure conglomerate, product extension, and market extension.

Risk in case selection

For managers contemplating diversification through mergers, legal risk takes two forms: first, the risk that the merger will be challenged under Clayton 7 provisions; second, the risk inherent in the litigation following a complaint. This section will examine the first of these issue, while the second will be addressed subsequently.

To determine what differences, if any, existed between mergers challenged under the Clayton Act and those mergers which escaped challenge, a sample of challenged and non-challenged mergers was analyzed. Significant differences between the two populations were hypothesized to provide insight into the policies of enforcement agencies. From each of the years 1963–73, all challenged market extension mergers were selected. In addition, from each year, a sample of non-challenged mergers was randomly selected from the FTC's 'Large Merger Series'.

Market extension mergers were pooled with horizontal mergers for the purpose of contrasting challenged and non-challenged mergers. This pooling was necessitated by the small number of challenged market extension mergers in the Large Merger Series over the study period. It was believed that this pooling should not introduce a serious bias into the analysis since the structural standards for market extension and horizontal mergers are similar.

The initial results displayed in Table 3.1.1 indicate that all of the measures of size, with one exception, display significant time trends. This result, which indicates that the average size of acquiring and acquired firms has increased over time, might be expected simply due to the effects of inflation. All but one of the acquisitions' size measures display a significant effect. Thus, acquisitions that are challenged tend to be significantly larger than those that are unchallenged. All of the size interaction terms are significant, indicating that the challenged mergers were larger than unchallenged even after accounting for the effects of inflation on size.

Acquiring firm market shares increased over the time period. However, the market shares of acquired firms showed no such trend. This result indicates that over time acquisitions were undertaken by firms in relatively stronger market positions. In fact, the average market share of acquiring firms is slightly larger than the merger guidelines criteria for challenging potential entrants. The significant interaction indicates that when time effects are considered, challenged acquirers have stronger market positions than non-challenged acquirers.

By contrast, for acquired firms the effects of market position with respect to enforcement are insignificant in all cases. The market position of the typical acquired firm neither changed over time, nor was there any significant difference in enforcement activity with respect to acquired firm market positions.

Dollar profits of acquiring and acquired firms show expected significant time trends. In addition, the results indicate that challenged mergers have higher dollar profits even when the effects of inflation are factored in.

Concentration in the acquiring firm's market shows no time trend, and the average four-firm concentration of both acquiring and acquired firms' markets is classified by the merger guidelines as 'less highly concentrated'. The concentration trends in acquiring firms' markets also show no historical trends. The average four-firm concentration in a firm's market during the year of the

Table 3.1.1 Analysis of variance (ANOVA): time and enforcement effects for market extension and horizontal mergers

Measures of size	Mean	Significance of time effect	Beta	Enforcement effect	Beta	Significance of interaction
Industry sales	5367×10^6	0.013	0.62	n.s		0.001
Acquiring firm sales	584×10^6	0.003	0.93	0.001	0.59	0.008
Acquired firm sales	124×10^6	0.001	0.63	0.001	0.32	0.001
Acquiring firm assets	471×10^6	0.022	0.79	0.010	0.47	0.004
Acquired firm assets	136×10^6	0.001	0.64	0.001	0.30	0.001
Acquiring firm equity	228×10^6	n.s.		0.022	0.51	0.002
Measures of market position						
Acquiring firm market share	28%	0.008	0.97	n.s.		0.015
Acquired firm market share	3%	n.s.		n.s.		n.s.
Performance measures						
Acquiring firm profits	26.3×10^6	0.029	0.73	0.004	0.57	0.003
Acquired firm profits	6.3×10^6	0.001	0.64	0.001	0.29	0.001
Acquiring firm ROA	6%	n.s.		n.s.		n.s.
Acquired firm ROA	5%	n.s.		n.s.		n.s.
Acquiring firm ROE	9%	n.s.		n.s.		n.s.
Industry concentration measures						
Four-firm concentration—acquiring firm's market	38%	n.s.		n.s.		n.s.
Four-firm concentration—acquired firm's market	37%	0.015	0.75	0.066	0.25	n.s.
Past concentration—acquiring firm's market	38%	n.s.		n.s.		n.s.
Past concentration—acquired firm's market	36%	0.078	0.74	n.s.		n.s.

n.s. = not significant.

acquisition is the same as the concentration 4 years prior to the acquisition. Concentration in the acquired firms' markets show both significant time and enforcement trends but, with one exception, the results are weak. In addition, the growth in concentration in acquired firms' markets was slight, averaging only 1 percent over the 4-year period prior to the acquisition.

These results suggest that absolute size, however measured, is a more significant predictor of enforcement activity than are measures of relative market position, financial performance, industry concentration, or trends in concentration.

Additional analysis indicated some differences between the FTC and the Antitrust Division with respect to case selection. The average size of acquiring firms challenged by the Antitrust Division was larger than the average size of those challenged by the FTC, whether or not the effects of time were accounted for. In addition, the acquiring firms of the Antitrust Division's challenged mergers were in larger industries than those challenged by the FTC.

In order to examine case selection and consider the influence of several variables simultaneously, a simple dummy variable regression model was specified where the dependent variable was a dichotomous measure of challenge and the independent variables included multiple measures of size, profits, and so forth.* Rather than estimating various combinations of variables, a step-wise regression procedure was used. The results are presented in Table 3.1.2. These results suggest that the typical challenged merger is one

Table 3.1.2 Dummy variable regression of case selection criteria

Variable	Beta*	Standard error	'T'
Sales 2	9.0312	0.002	8.36
Profit 2	−7.9792	0.035	7.99
Assets 1	−1.2057	0.000	6.68
ROA 1	0.3686	1.803	3.88
C42 year 3	0.1918	0.000	1.97

$\bar{R}^2 = 0.87$; $p < 0.01$
Sales 2   = Sales of acquired firm
Profit 2   = Profits of acquired firm
Assets 1   = Assets of acquiring firm
ROA 1   = Return on assets of acquiring firm
C42 year 3 = Four-firm concentration/year interaction, cubed.
* Standardized regression coefficient.

* Multiple measures of these constructs were necessitated due to the fact that there is no standard format for presenting economic or legal arguments in merger complaints. As a result, some complaints referred to return on assets or return on equity. This variation necessitated the calculations of multiple measures of the economic factors in each case since there was no way to determine *a priori* which measure was a superior measure of the underlying construct.

in which a relatively small, but profitable, acquirer looks to improve its competitive position or leverage its competitive capabilities by acquiring a large, but relatively unprofitable, firm in a market which is rapidly becoming concentrated. The conditions clearly seem to fall into a classification of mergers which could be viewed as 'disruptive' and which might contribute significantly to a trend toward increasing concentration in the acquired firm's market.

Risks in litigation

Between 1964 and 1973 there were 24 market extension mergers litigated by the Antitrust Division or the FTC. In some instances multiple product or geographic markets were specified in the allegations; complaints which specified multiple markets were split into separate 'cases' with each case containing the information relevant to one line of commerce mentioned in the complaint. These cases were treated in the analysis as though they were separate mergers.* The outcomes for challenged mergers range from 'merger abandoned' through 'defendant won', or 'consent decree' and 'plaintiff won' as their outcome. The consent decrees contained requirements and proscriptions which ranged from prohibitions on future mergers for a period of years to very specific proscriptions on future acquisitions. In general, consent decrees represent at least a partial victory for the enforcing agency; however, the scope of that victory varies considerably. The variation within the consent decree outcome category may explain why more 'plaintiff won' or 'merger abandoned' outcomes were not observed. Only two cases fell into these two categories.

The approach used to examine litigation risk was to develop models that would allow managers (or enforcement officers) to predict the eventual outcome of a merger litigation on the basis of observable data, and to test these models on the sample data. The three general models considered are the economic model, the legal model, and the mixed model. The economic model contained all available information describing the economic characteristics of the merger. The assumption underlying the use of the economic model is that enforcement agencies and the courts rely primarily on economic theory in determining the legal standing of merger cases.

The legal model contained all of the legal arguments and allegations presented by the complainant and the legal arguments presented by the respondent. The assumptions underlying the use of the legal model are two. The first assumption is that a primary motive of the litigators in the Antitrust

---

* The treatment of the cases in this manner is justified on the grounds that Section 7 proscribes a merger, 'where in any line of commerce in any section of the country, the effect of such acquisition may be substantially to lessen competition, or tend to create a monopoly' (15 USC 1914, as amended).

Division and the Bureau of Competition is to find 'interesting' legal cases in which legal theory can be extended, or 'cutting-edge' legal theories applied. Such cases may be viewed by trial attorneys as both intellectually challenging and highly visible. The second assumption is that, as stated in the *Merger Guidelines*, economic theory with respect to conglomerate mergers is not well understood. Conglomerate cases may, therefore, require 'novel' approaches and arguments to successfully litigate.

The mixed model contains both economic and legal variables describing the cases. The rationale for employing the mixed model is that merger litigation reflects elements of economic and legal theory; neither one alone may be sufficient to predict the eventual outcome of a case.

Discriminant analysis was used in an attempt to determine the ability of each of the models to predict classification outcome. The discriminating variables, together with existing theory, enforcement policy, and practice were then used to gain insight into the determinants of successful litigation strategies for both managers and enforcement officers. Due to the predominance of outcomes in the two categories of 'defendant won' and 'consent decree', the discussion will focus on these outcomes.

THE ECONOMIC MODEL: AGGREGATE RESULTS

Pure market extension financial mergers were strongly associated with a 'defendant won' outcome; whereas financial mergers with alleged horizontal components tended toward consent decrees. Apart from these results, an acquiring firm with a relatively large market share in a concentrated industry attempting a large merger tends to enter into a consent decree. A high industry rank resulting from the acquisition without either the market share or concentration characteristics is associated with a 'defendant won' outcome. Resulting industry rank *per se* in a market extension merger is probably not a significant factor in estimating the competitive effects of a merger. Thus, the economic model applied to litigation outcome appears consistent with the view that the enforcement process actually follows the underlying economic rationale expressed in the merger guidelines.

THE LEGAL MODEL

Using as the set of discriminating variables only the case allegation characteristics, two points stand out. First, the ability to mount a very specific defense is associated with a favorable outcome for the defendant. On the other hand, a weak defense consisting of a general denial of charges or the assertion that the merger is in the public interest results in an unfavorable outcome for defendants. This finding is most evident when such a defense is coupled with specific and focused complaint allegations such as the existence of capital barriers to entry. This pattern of challenge and response is associated with a consent decree. In other words, a weak defense coupled with a strong complaint leads to an outcome favorable to the complainant. The second point that stands out is that the agency which issues the complaint has a discernible impact on the eventual outcome. FTC cases are strongly associated with consent decrees. These results raise several additional questions.

In order to gain further insight into these issues, a second analysis was made removing the 'agency' variable and the 'elimination of actual competition' allegation variable. Comparing the results of this analysis with the previous one, it is evident that a unique, specific defense is associated with a 'defendant won' outcome. Allegations of the existence of 'other' non-specific entry barriers or barriers based on such notions as 'special technical knowledge' or 'distribution channel barriers' appear to be counter-productive to the complainant since the presence of these variables is associated with a 'defendant won' outcome. Symmetrical with the previous results, a strong specific defense coupled with a weak, general challenge results in a successful case for the defendant.

Financial market extension mergers that do not have a horizontal component show a strong association with a 'defendant won' outcome. If the merger has a horizontal component, however, the merger challenge tends to result in a consent decree. The underlying basis for the importance of the agency variable remains unclear. It may be that the agency variable is principally reflecting the mix of financial and non-financial mergers. On the other hand, there do appear to be some agency-related differences in the outcome of a challenge for non-financial mergers as well. Among non-financial FTC market extension mergers, there were no 'defendant won' outcomes. Of the five non-financial Justice Department mergers, two resulted in 'defendant won' outcomes.

Financial mergers

All financial merger challenges were undertaken by the Antitrust Division. In total, there were 10 mergers and 11 cases. The outcome of one merger was pending.

The economic model

The results from the application of the economic model are similar to those describing the aggregated cases. There is a clear distinction between pure market extension mergers and those with an alleged horizontal component. A second insight with respect to the financial mergers is the importance of market position. Challenges of mergers involving financial institutions that are relatively large in their markets are associated with consent decrees. On the other hand, firms that are large in terms of revenue, but small relative to their competitors, are more likely to win a challenge. A somewhat speculative interpretation of these results may be that large banks may have the sophistication or legal resources to effectively rebut the challenging agency, whereas banks that are small (although relatively large in their own market) may lack these resources and suffer less favorable outcomes.

Non-financial mergers—economic model

The results of this analysis clearly suggest that a merger between two firms with large market shares, in concentrated industries, and where the absolute size of the firms is large, tends toward a consent decree. In contrast, mergers between firms in concentrated markets which are small both in absolute and relative terms tend to result in a favorable outcome for the defendants. This analysis provided one surprising result. Non-financial market extension mergers with an alleged horizontal component are associated with a 'defendant won' outcome. This is in contrast to the earlier analyses and is puzzling since the antitrust standards for horizontal mergers are generally stricter than for conglomerate mergers.

Legal model results

The application of the legal model to both financial and non-financial mergers provided results very consistent with those described earlier. For both financial and non-financial mergers, the party that is able to put forward a specific argument against either a general allegation or defense is likely to obtain a more favorable outcome.

MIXED MODEL RESULTS

The only mixed model results that provided any additional insights were for the non-financial mergers. These results indicated that a challenge based on weak potential competition arguments is favorable to the defendant. However, if the merger is a large one for the acquiring firm and there are allegations of entry barriers, a consent decree tends to result. The absence of an alleged horizontal component is also associated with a consent decree.

Differences between mergers challenged by the FTC and the Antitrust Division were also apparent based on a discriminant analysis using both the economic and legal characteristics of the cases. These results suggest that the Antitrust Division cases are characterized by higher levels of acquiring firm industry concentration, larger acquiring firm market shares, and higher levels of acquired firm industry concentration. In an economic sense these cases might represent the more significant mergers, In contrast, the economic basis for FTC challenge is a relatively high industry rank resulting from the merger and unspecified entry barriers. Legal arguments characterizing the FTC cases are the general charges 'encouragement of further acquisitions' and 'establishment or enhancement of entry barriers'. These general allegations tend to lead to a 'defendant won' outcome when responded to with a specific defense. On the other hand, FTC cases are more likely than Antitrust Division cases to end in consent decrees. The implication of these results is that the cases challenged by the FTC cannot be, or for other reasons are not, met by specific legal responses.

CONCLUSIONS AND IMPLICATIONS

The degree of risk facing managers who seek to undertake related diversification market extension mergers is predictable. Furthermore, the ability to manage the degree of risk inherent in a challenge to this type of merger is significant due to the fact that challenged mergers appear to fall closely along the merger guidelines. Over time, the Antitrust Division and the FTC have tended to challenge relatively larger, more profitable, and more significant mergers. Both agencies have focused on relatively large acquisitions, by acquirers with relatively strong market positions. The Antitrust Division seems, in particular, to focus on size as a primary factor stimulating challenge. Its challenges are of larger, more profitable acquirers in larger industries than the FTC challenges.

However, enforcement officers in both agencies tend to challenge acquisitions in markets that are not highly concentrated. This may reflect either the fact that firms in highly concentrated industries do not undertake market extension mergers or the fact that firm characteristics are viewed by enforcement officers as more important than market characteristics. Over time, however, challenges have focused on mergers in markets with higher levels of concentration.

All things considered, challenged mergers can be characterized as involving a large acquisition in a market undergoing rapid concentration by a likely potential entrant, or at least one which is profitable enough to undertake entry. To the acquirer who views the merger as a means of leveraging the skills it possesses through a large firm which is in need of those skills, the attractiveness of such an acquisition is apparent. The rapid rate of concentration in the acquired firm's market serves to increase the immediacy of the merger for both parties. The acquirer may wish to move quickly rather than be foreclosed from the market or face stronger competition in the future. The acquisition candidate may perceive a need for greater competitive skills and profits in order to succeed against larger competitors.

It is also possible to understand the challenge to such a merger based on the structuralist criteria employed by antitrust enforcers. With concentration increasing rapidly, the profitability of the firms in the market would be anticipated to increase. The merger involves a large current participant with a profitable acquirer; one who could prove to be a likely potential entrant, and provide meaningful competition in the market.

The ability to predict the risk inherent in litigation is also possible. The analyses presented here suggest that management can, at the time a complaint is issued, identify with some certainty the likelihood that fighting the challenge in litigation will end in a favorable outcome. This ability to identify the characteristics of a merger that will have a good chance of success in litigation is valuable. An immediate decision can be made whether or not to abandon the merger and seek a new acquisition, or litigate the challenge.

The results of this investigation suggest that economic criteria alone cannot always successfully distinguish between cases which are likely to be concluded favorably for management. It is equally important for managers to focus on the legal arguments that are proposed by enforcement officers and the quality of the legal defenses that can be presented. In general, if a respondent firm is able to effectively argue a very specific defense to a potential (rather than actual) competition claim, its chance of a successful defense is significantly improved. The effect of a very specific defense is particularly strong when the agency challenge is broad and general in nature. These findings do not suggest that legal arguments are determinative, however. Market extension mergers among non-financial firms, for example, indicate that a weak potential competition challenge tends to result in an outcome favorable to management unless the acquisition is a relatively large one and the complainant alleges specific entry barriers.

Financial and non-financial mergers are treated differently. First, all financial mergers are enforced by the Antitrust Division as a result of the Bank Merger Act provisions. Second, challenges to financial mergers have outcomes that differ significantly from non-financial mergers. Financial market extension mergers that have an alleged horizontal component are associated with a consent decree, whereas similar non-financial mergers tend to result in an outcome favorable to management. The reason for this result may have to do with the market or markets defined in the non-financial merger complaints. Enforcement officers in both agencies tend to define the geographic boundaries of the market very broadly for non-financial mergers. Presumably, this is done in order to provide a basis for a challenge to the merger which includes a horizontal component. For example, one merger involving two retail chains became the subject of an FTC investigation. In the proposed complaint, staff attorneys alleged city, SMSA, state, ADI, and regional geographic markets. The smaller of these market areas resulted in no overlap between the merging parties, whereas the larger (region) market definition resulted in significant overlap. However, it was successfully argued that such a large relevant market area was probably not appropriate for measuring the impact of the merger on competition. Even if it had been relevant to examine a regional geographic market, the resulting 'market' shares of the merging firms were inconsequential and far below the *Merger Guidelines* standards.

It appears, therefore, that the FTC and the Antitrust Division attorneys have a tendency to stretch and assert the boundaries of the market beyond the ability to prove those boundaries. This tendency provides an opportunity for the responding firms to offset the challenge with specific evidence as to geographic boundary, and propose a case based on a more favorable set of economic factors. Table 3.1.3 provides a summary of the legal risk factors that impact on the potential attractiveness of an acquisition after an initial challenge is made.

Several guidelines emerge from this study that may facilitate managers' ability to deal with the legal risks inherent in related diversification acquisitions.

(1) The risk of case selection can be significantly reduced by acquiring a relatively small 'follower' firm or firms rather than a market leader. This is particularly important if the market in which the acquisition is made is undergoing rapid concentration through acquisition.

(2) Avoid 'following the crowd'. If a market is becoming concentrated and acquisitions becoming frequent, it may be preferable to find merger partners in another market rather than make a late acquisition and trigger an antitrust challenge.

(3) The risks inherent in litigation are significantly increased when the acquisition involves firms with large market shares. Size *per se*, however, is less important in litigation than in case selection. This, once again, indicates the acquisition of a 'follower' to reduce legal risk.

(4) Challenges based primarily on the basis of firm size tend to be general, non-specific legal broadsides. The ability to counter such a challenge with a very specific defense (for example, in one successful case the defense showed that the acquisition was necessary to settle an estate) is critical.

(5) Financial mergers that are challenged with an allegation of a horizontal component to the merger should probably be abandoned and a new merger partner sought.

(6) Non-financial mergers with a horizontal component generally will require substantial efforts toward market re-definition. In general, such efforts are rewarded with an outcome favorable to the defendant.

REFERENCES

Alan, Meyer, *Economic Regulation and the Public Interest*. Cornell University Press, Ithaca, N.Y., 1977.
Economic Papers 1966–69, U.S. Government Printing Office, Washington, D.C.
Haspeslagh, Philippe, 'Portfolio planning: uses and limits', *Harvard Business Review*, Jan.–Feb. 1982, p. 58.

Table 3.1.3 Degree of legal risk associated with market extension merger characteristics

| | Legal risk | | | |
| | High risk | | Low risk | |
Merger type	Economic characteristics	Legal characteristics	Economic characteristics	Legal characteristics
Non-financial	Large market share participants High industry concentration	Specific 'actual competition' allegations General denial of charges	High industry rank Small share Large firm size	Specific defense available Non-specific allegations Broad market definition
Financial	Large market share participants	Horizontal component Specific 'actual competition' allegations General denial of charges	Large firm size	Non-specific allegations Specific defense available

150   *Strategic Marketing and Management*

Katzman, Robert, *Regulatory Bureaucracy: The Federal Trade Commission and Antitrust Policy*. MIT Press, Cambridge, Mass., 1980.
Merger Guidelines of the Department of Justice, 30 May, 1968.
Meyer (1977)
Salter, Malcolm S., and Wolf Weinhold, *Diversification Through Acquisition*, Free Press, New York, 1979.
Shenefield, John, Statement before the Committee on the Judiciary, US Senate, 5 April, 1978.
Steiner, Peter O., *Mergers: Motives, Effects, Policies*. University of Michigan Press, Ann Arbor, Mi., 1975.
Weaver, Suzanne. *Decision to Prosecute: Organization and Public Policy in the Antitrust Division*. MIT Press, Cambridge, Mass., 1977.

Strategic Marketing and Management
Edited by H. Thomas and D. Gardner
© 1985 John Wiley & Sons Ltd

3.2
Effects of Buyer/Seller Concentration on Profitability

P. T. FitzRoy
Monash University, Clayton, Victoria 3168, Australia

The study of strategic management and business policy has experienced the continuing dialectic between a conceptual and an empirical approach. The early literature in business policy had a purely conceptual and descriptive framework. Concepts such as the product life cycle, the evolution of strategy over the life cycle, and growth alternatives were descriptive and conceptual in nature. This was also true of the early paradigm of strategy where strategy was seen as involving choices about goals, products, markets, facilities, and so on. Success in strategy was seen as being determined by the interplay between company strengths and weaknesses and environmental threats and opportunities (Learned *et al.*, 1969). This framework specified the general process to follow, but little in the way of general principles of strategy or how these could be applied in a given situation. More recently the PIMS program has provided a rich data base and the possibility of substantive empirical research in business policy. Analysis of the data base indicates such general principles of strategy as the value of market share and how these principles can be applied by a specific business.

Paralleling this evolution in business policy another discipline, industrial organization, has seen major developments and the opportunity now exists for positive fertilization between these two previously unrelated areas. Industrial organization has a strong conceptual and methodological tradition which should be of interest to practitioners and researchers in the strategy area. Economists have developed a number of concepts such as entry barriers, exit barriers, and concentration levels, which are finding increasing application by policy researchers. The fundamental industrial organization paradigm holds that performance is dependent on the characteristics of the industry and market environment in which it competes. So we have the familiar paradigm in Figure 3.2.1.

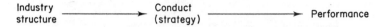

Figure 3.2.1   The industrial orgainization paradigm

Structure refers to the economic and technical characteristics of the industry including such measures as the size distribution of competitors, barriers to entry, and so on. Conduct—or in policy terms, strategy—represents the choice by individual firms of such key decision variables as: price, research and development, and product quality. Performance is defined primarily in a social sense representing the economists' concern with allocative efficiency, and thus involves such measures as profitability and innovativeness. In a recent article, Porter (1981) has recently examined the contribution of industrial organization to strategy, and has suggested some reasons for the lack of synthesis and understanding between these two disciplines. While it is apparent that they are growing closer together it is also clear that these can learn from each other since each has made significant contributions.

One key problem has been the unit of analysis. Students of policy are primarily interested in strategy at the level of the individual firm or, for a diversified firm, the strategic business unit level. Industrial organization students have adopted the industry as the unit of analysis. They have been relatively unconcerned with differences in structure, strategy, and performance of different firms within the same industry. To a large degree this difference in the unit of analysis reflects different objectives of the two bodies and is also partly explained by the lack of publicly available data at the firm level. Economists in industrial organizations, with their strong empirical tradition, have typically used publicly available data and this is generally available at the industry level rather than at the level of the specific firm or business unit within that industry.

This historic paradigm was recently extended by Porter (1980) who conceptualized business success as shown in Figure 3.2.2. This conceptualization postulates that performance of a given firm is influenced by two sets of structural characteristics. Firstly those characteristics which are external to the industry, such as the bargaining power of buyers or the threat of substitute products, and secondly the pattern and form of competition that exists within a given industry. Rivalry occurs since, in most industries, competitive moves by one firm elicit a reaction by others. Rivalry is likely to be high when there are a large number of firms, or where they are relatively equal in terms of resources. Intra-industry competition is further influenced by such factors as industry growth, levels of differentiation, rate of innovation, and so on.

This paradigm reinforces what is readily apparent from even the most casual observation, namely that while average profitability varies across industries there is also wide variability of profitability within a given industry. These intra-industry forces and intra-industry patterns of competition do not affect all

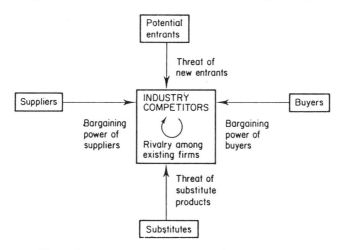

Figure 3.2.2   Forces driving industry competition

competitors equally. With this paradigm the essence of strategy for a given company is to recognize its resources, its strategic position in the industry, the interaction of the numerous external and inter-industry structural characteristics and ultimately to choose a strategy for dealing with these changes.

This paper examines two of the parameters of the above model. Our objective is to explore two structural characteristics—the bargaining power of buyers and sellers and their effect on seller profitability.

LITERATURE REVIEW

A number of studies in industrial organization have investigated the relationship between industry concentration (one structural characteristic) and profitability. Economic theory suggests that high levels of industry concentration should be associated with higher profitability, where profitability is measured by the price/cost margin. The empirical studies which have explored this relationship (see Collins and Preston, 1969; Eckstein and Wyss, 1972; Straszheim and Straszheim, 1976; van Lommel and de Brabander, 1979) typically use industry price/cost margin as a proxy for profit, and have explored its association with a variety of structural variables. These included concentration, type of good, capital/output ratio, growth rate, and geographic dispersion. The general conclusion is that price/cost margins are positively related to concentration, although the strength of the relationship varies.

These empirical results have been criticized on both conceptual and methodological grounds (Ornstein, 1975; Phillips, 1976). Industry averages have generally been used as the dependent variable, despite the fact that the theoretical under-pinnings are based on a single firm. Potential biases from aggregation are ignored. With a few exceptions (see, for example Collins and Preston, 1969), most studies have ignored within-industry variability in margin.

A strict relationship between any concentration measure and the distribution of firm size also seems tenuous. Concentration is generally measured by C_4, the share of industry output accounted for by the four largest firms. But a concentration measure of, say, 0.6 can exist with widely differing configurations of competitors and relative sizes. One extension is to use C_8–C_4, the share of industry output accounted for by the fifth to the eighth largest firms, as a measure of the likelihood of collusion (van Lommel and de Brabander, 1979). Size distribution of firms has also been represented by the Herfindahl index and the market shares of the two largest competitors (Kwoka, 1979).

Porter (1979) has extended the study of concentration with the recognition of the distinction between industry-wide factors and firm-specific factors. Certain characteristics, such as barriers to entry, protect all firms, and thus market power is an asset shared by all firms. But all firms are clearly not alike and follow different strategies with respect to degree of vertical integration and so forth. He examined structure within industry, as well as industry-wide characteristics, and utilized the concept of strategic groups to explain differences in performance and conduct both between and within an industry. He defined strategic groups as groups of firms that are pursuing broadly similar strategies in terms of the key decision variables for that particular market. He further postulated mobility barriers whereby different strategic groups are relatively isolated or insulated from competition with each other. His results show clearly that the profit levels for firms which are differently situated in an industry can be explained by the structural features that exist, in particular the characteristics of these strategic subgroups, for example, where they are seen as a leader or a follower in industry or whether they are adopting a niching type strategy.

These studies above report essentially one characteristic, namely the effect of the size distribution of sellers on measures of both conduct and performance, particularly profitability. Few studies have looked at the concentration of buyers and the effect that buyer structure, using such characteristics as concentration, size, or purchase quantity, may have on profitability. Where there are few buyers one would anticipate that they have substantial power over a particular supplier with an ability to force down price. This is not inconsistent with the countervailing power proposition first proposed by Galbraith, who suggested that large suppliers induces buyers to grow large to neutralize the power of suppliers. Lustgarten examined the effect of buyer and seller concentration on price–cost margins. In this he found buyer concentration was positively correlated with seller concentration and at the same time negatively correlated with seller price–cost margin. In other words high seller concentration tended to be associated with low price–cost margins for sellers (Lustgarten, 1975).

Summarizing, there is a voluminious literature in industrial organization on the effect of seller concentration on profitability. These studies suggest that profitability is influenced positively by concentration although the magnitude of the effect depends on which other structural characteristics are considered. One explanation for the lack of precision is the unit of analysis. This has been the industry, ignoring inter-firm variability in performance. The use of the price–cost margin as a performance measure can be argued on both theoretical and practical grounds.

RESEARCH DESIGN

The objective of the research is to examine the extent to which powerful customers and sellers in a market can exercise control over that market. Control may be exercised in a number of ways. In this study we adopt as our focus the effect on price as reflected in the gross margin. In a given marketplace how power is exercised will depend on the parameters of competition for that marketplace, and other competitive variables that may be effected such as innovation, quality, and service will not be examined here. To a large measure these are derivatives of profitability. If margins in an industry are forced to be artificially low due to powerful customers the funds available for product development and innovation are reduced and the industry will have a lower level of new product introductions. The proposition is that if a business faces powerful customers with a strong bargaining power they will act to force down the market price. Powerful sellers, on the other hand, act to raise market price.

The research reported on here uses the PIMS data base to explore the interaction of buyer power and seller power on seller profitability. The data base consists of 1499 PIMS businesses which are drawn primarily from the US, although about 15 percent operate in other geographic regions. They include a broad array of types of businesses, consumer durable and non-durable, industrial durable and non-durable. For each of these 1499 businesses a variety of measures are available in the study, both financial and market. Some of the variables, such as market share, are measured continuously while others are categorical in nature. When a continuous measure such as market share is utilized the value used for each individual business is an average of the last 4 years of operation.

PERFORMANCE MEASURE

Of concern in the research is how to measure the effect of power on market prices. Since we do not have a model of a 'fair' price the effect of such a phenomenon must be ascertained in other ways. If prices are forced down then margins must behave in the same way, and consequently the primary performance measure selected was the price–cost margin defined as the ratio of gross margin to sales. Gross margin of a business is defined as (sales) less (purchases, manufacturing expenses, distribution expenses, and depreciation).

Looking at this measure another way gross margin is defined as (profit) plus (marketing expenses, R&D expenses, and other expenses). So gross margin is profit plus discretionary expenses after an allowance for depreciation.

This measure is, as has been shown, widely used in the literature. It also has one other characteristic in that in a negotiating situation between a buyer and a seller the gross margin is the 'figure on the table'. Under conditions of extreme duress sellers may be prepared to except a very small gross margin; in other words to cover basically just their variable costs and may even bargain away depreciation.

As shown in Figure 3.2.3, businesses in the data base show considerable variability in gross margin, from less than 10 percent to a high of over 70 percent, with a mean of 26.6 percent.

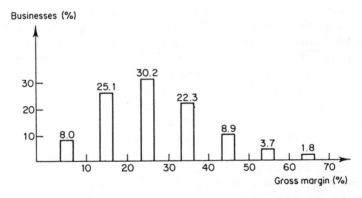

Figure 3.2.3   Variability of gross margin

SELLER POWER

Suppliers in industries with powerful sellers are generally considered to act in ways to raise industry prices. The typical measure of industry power is some measure of concentration which includes both the number of competitors and the size distribution of those competitors.

Market-specific power is that component of power which can be attributed to any competitor in the marketplace, i.e. to all sellers. This is related to the number and size distribution of sellers and the measure chosen is specified below:

Seller power $s = \dfrac{1}{H}$

$H = Herfindahl\ index$

$\quad = \sum m_i^2$

(m_i = market share of *i*th supplier)

An interpretation of seller power s is the equivalent number of equal-sized competitors in the marketplace. If the marketplace consists of n equal-sized competitors each with a market share of $1/n$ then s is equal to n. In the data base shares are not available for all businesses but only for the PIMS business plus its three largest competitors. The PIMS business may not be one of the largest four competitors in the marketplace but it generally is, since the average market share for all PIMS businesses is about 25 percent. So H and consequently s are defined as the sum of the market shares of the four businesses reported by the PIMS business; that is, its market share plus the market share of its three largest competitors. While this may introduce some bias in the results it is unlikely to be very serious since the contribution from other businesses is likely to be small. The industry or the market measure of seller power is then s and if s is large then the average seller power in the industry is low. Figure 3.2.4 shows the relationship between gross margin and net margin with seller power. As seller power increases, or as the number of equivalently equal-sized competitors is reduced, both gross margin and net margin are increased.

Another possible industry-specific measure which could be used is industry capacity utilization. As industry capacity utilization approaches 100 percent demand and supply are more finely balanced, which will increase the power of suppliers. Alternatively if industry capacity utilization is low prices will soften. Unfortunately no measure of industry capacity utilization exists in the data

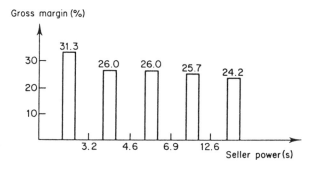

Figure 3.2.4   Gross margin vs. seller power

Strategic Marketing and Management

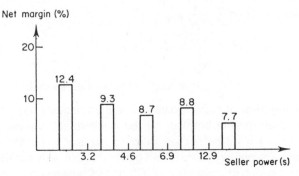

Figure 3.2.5   Net margin vs. seller power

base. Although the capacity utilization of the PIMS business is reported by subscribers it was not considered an adequate surrogate for industry capacity utilization by this researcher.

We draw a distinction between seller power as a structural characteristic of an industry and the seller power of a specific business within that industry. The seller power s defined above is interpreted as a measure of seller power for all competitors in an industry since the same value would be calculated for all competitors. The other component of seller power is a firm-specific measure. Different competitors in a given market are likely to have different relative powers within that market. The measures included were market share and capacity utilization of the supplier. A high market share or a high capacity utilization for a given supplier should result in higher seller power for that supplier with less susceptibility to margin degradation.

BUYER POWER

Buyers in any industry attempt to force down prices and thus reduce margins. Conceptually, buyers will be powerful if they have large purchases or if there is a small number of potential customers. If we sell to only one customer, that customer obviously has substantial influence over our selling prices and other elements of product and service strategy. Again a distinction is made between (a) market level customer power and (b) the power of a specific customer.

Buyers in a market are powerful when they purchase in large volume relative to the sales of the seller. In the PIMS data base market-wide customer power is measured in two ways: (a) the average purchase amount in dollars and (b) the number of customers accounting for 50 percent of sales.

In the PIMS data base these parameters are measured for the PIMS business not for the industry, and consequently the PIMS business figure is taken as surrogate of the industry value. The second measure, the number of customer accounting for 50 percent of sales for the business, is obtained by multiplica

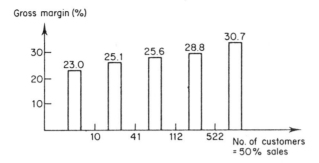

Figure 3.2.6   Gross margin vs. buyer power

tion—the number of customers multiplied by the percentage of customers accounting for 50 percent of sales. Figure 3.2.6 shows for the entire data base the relationship between gross margin and buyer power, indicating that as buyer power increases then so does the gross margin of suppliers reduce.

A buyer group is powerful not only when purchases are large relative to seller sales but also if (a) the products he purchases from the industry represent a significant amount of the buyer's purchases; (b) if the products are undifferentiated; (c) if buyers face few switching costs; (d) if the industry earns low profits; (e) buyers can vertically integrate backwards; (f) the industry's products are unimportant to the quality of the buyer's product or service (Porter, 1980). In this research only the first of these parameters are measurable.

A customer-specific measure of buyer power which exists in the data base is the percentage of purchases by the customer accounted for by products of this type. Consider a supermarket and the power that that particular customer may exercise over a supplier of two products, one of pet food and one of soy sauce. Pet foods account for a high proportion of purchases by that supermarket whereas soy sauce is a relatively minor product. The total purchases of all brands of soy sauce from all suppliers will be a very small proportion of total purchases by the supermarket. We would expect that the supermarket will negotiate more strongly with these important products since they represent a large proportion of their own costs and ultimate profitability.

We may expect some intercorrelation between independent variables, and this is the case here. Gross margin includes a component of marketing expenditures and it would be expected that with large purchase quantities or a small number of customers the ratio of marketing to sales would decline. If a supplier is only marketing to one or two customers their marketing expenses, measured in terms of marketing to sales, would be expected to be low and consequently their gross margin to be higher. Net margins, however, behave in a similar fashion with purchase amount or number of customers, so if we were to measure performance by net margins we would observe the same effect of buyer power on profitability.

JOINT EFFECT OF BUYER POWER AND SELLER POWER

Table 3.2.1 shows the effect of buyer power and seller power on seller margins. For this table the data base was split into nine cells on the basis of buyer power or seller power in the market and an average margin for each cell computed, where each cell contains approximately 160 businesses. As can be seen average margins vary from a low of 22.6 percent to a high of 35.7 percent, showing monotonic relationships with the buyer power and seller power.

Table 3.2.1   Joint effect of buyer power and seller power

		Lo		Hi
Buyer power	Lo $1,000	28.6	30.1	35.7
(typical purchase amount)	$10,000	24.1	26.3	30.5
	Hi	22.6	22.8	26.6
		7.8		4.1

Seller power (*s*)

It does appear, however, that this relationship is not linear; the ability of sellers to exercise their power has to be considered relative to the level of buyer power that exists. In industries where there is low buyer power sellers find it easier to exercise the power that they possess. On the other hand, if buyer power is higher, sellers find it difficult to exercise their power. Not only is there an industry- and a firm-specific component of power but power itself needs to be measured in a relative way rather than an absolute way, i.e. relative to the other negotiating party. This provides some methodological problems since it indicates we need a measure of power which is consistent for both buyers and sellers but the two measures adopted to date do not possess this property.

BUSINESS-SPECIFIC MEASURES OF POWER

Importance of the purchase

To obtain a preliminary insight into the effect of firm-specific measures a series of three-way cost tables were produced. Consider for example the buyer-specific measure: importance. Businesses in the data base are asked to indicate the proportion of the typical immediate customer's total annual purchases accounted for by purchases of the type of product sold by the business. This is a categorical measure, with five categories ranging from less than 0.25 percent to greater than 25 percent. If a given product class represents a high proportion of total purchases by the immediate customer, purchases will have a significant effect on their profitability and these customers can be expected to adopt a tougher bargaining stance.

To investigate this, the data base was split into three groups. The first group were those businesses for whom purchases of products of this type by buyers represented less than 1 percent of total purchases, the second group were purchases between 1 and 5 percent and the third group were those businesses for whom purchases of products of this type represented more than 5 percent of total purchases by the customer. Table 3.2.2 indicates the joint effect of buyer power and seller power at the market level coupled with this buyer-specific measure of importance. Table 3.2.2 only shows the results for the two extreme groups; low importance (<1 percent of purchases) and high importance (>5 percent of purchases).

Table 3.2.2   Effect of importance of the purchase on margins

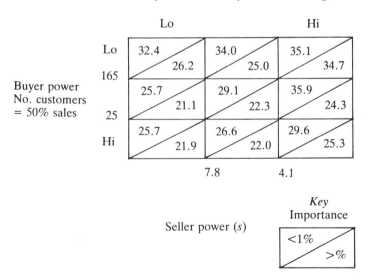

As is apparent, importance of the purchase to the customer has a consistent negative impact on seller margins, for any combination of market seller and buyer power. The average difference in margins is 5.7 points. Where the product group has a significant effect on customer profitability, customers bargain more tenaciously, forcing down the selling price and seller margins. Generally, as buyer power increases, the differential in margin reduces, suggesting more than an additive relationship between market power and customer-specific power.

INVESTMENT INTENSITY

Industrial organization studies suggest that investment intensity is an important structural characteristic influencing price–cost margins. Generally, investment intensity is measured at the industry level by the capital/output ratio which introduces possible problems of multicollinearity. To eliminate this, investment intensity was defined as gross current value of plant and equipment plus working capital divided by total costs. Gross current value is the current cost of replacing plant and equipment. Total costs comprise manufacturing, distribution, R&D, and marketing costs.

We also note from Table 3.2.3 that sellers who are characterized by high levels of investment intensity have difficulty exercising their supposed power. Margins increase with increasing seller power but at a much reduced rate when the seller is investment intensive.

Table 3.2.3   Effect of investment intensity on margins

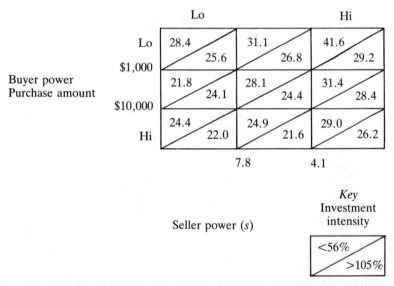

As Table 3.2.3 demonstrates, those businesses with high investment intensity (or a high ratio of fixed to variable costs) consistently earned lower margins for any combination of buyer and seller power than those businesses with investment intensity—with one exception. The average difference in margins is 3.6 points. Yet if businesses were all aiming for a uniform return on investment we would expect higher margins for these high investment-intensive businesses, not lower. Again it is difficult to separate out the effect of all the independent variables. As the ratio of fixed to variable costs increases then so do depreciation expenses, and consequently gross margins as defined in this study would be reduced. However not only should depreciation be increased with these high investment-intensive businesses but variable costs should be reduced. What the data suggest is that the higher depreciation charges are not being offset by lower variable costs, or alternatively that high investment-intensive businesses cannot sustain adequate margins to compensate for their higher depreciation charges. They will tend to cover variable costs and be prepared under conditions of high buyer power to negotiate away the depreciation component of gross margin.

CAPACITY UTILIZATION

One other firm-specific measure of seller power is capacity utilization. If the capacity utilization of a supplier is low we would anticipate a greater concern with attempts to load the plant with consequent effect on prices. A business is less likely to resist price pressure when its current level of capacity utilization is low. If capacity utilization is high a business finds it unnecessary to engage in contribution pricing and price discounts. Table 3.2.4, in the same format as previously, indicates the effect of seller capacity utilization. Notice here the

Table 3.2.4   Effect of capacity utilization on margins

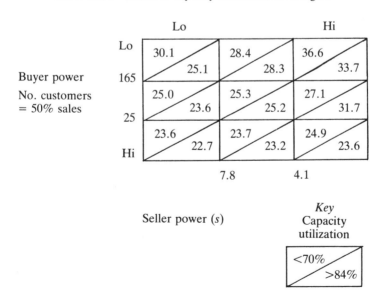

effect is not as strong as had been initially thought; in fact the gross margin is lower for businesses with high capacity utilization in the majority of cases. This is quite different from *a priori* reasoning, which would have suggested that if capacity utilization is high gross margin should be high.

MARKET SHARE

Market share is widely recognized as an important variable in business strategy. Its relationship with profitability has been well documented, and consequently it is considered a crucial element in any strategy statement. Table 3.2.5 shows the relation between gross margin and power, where market share is used as an additional measure of seller-specific power. High market share competitors always have higher margins than low market share competitors, the average difference being 5.9 points.

Table 3.2.5   Effect of market share on margins

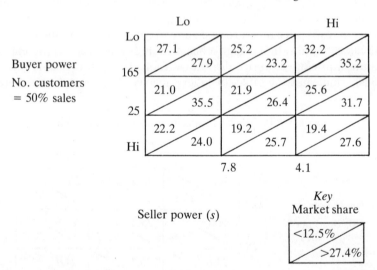

Seller power (*s*)

Key
Market share

Table 3.2.5 indicates possible interaction between market level and firm-specific seller power. As a general rule we have noted that higher seller power is accompanied by higher margins. But consider markets characterized by high buyer power, a small number of customers. Further, consider the situation for two suppliers to that market, one with a small share and one with a large share. As seller power increases, as the number of suppliers to the market decreases, margins increase for the large-share businesses from 24.0 to 27.6 percent, and reduce for the small-share businesses from 22.2 to 19.4 percent.

The implication is that small-share competitors are disadvantaged when there are strong buyers if the market is characterized by a high seller power. Small competitors must supply to powerful buyers in competition with other large powerful suppliers and they cannot take advantage of the apparent market power of these larger competitors. So while seller power as a market parameter typically helps the margins of suppliers it does not necessarily help all competitors in the marketplace equally. Small competitors cannot take advantage of this seemingly higher concentrated market.

CONCLUSIONS

This study has analyzed the effect of buyer power and seller power on the margins of sellers. It has shown that the gross margins are strongly influenced by each of these parameters. In addition, the study has highlighted the distinction between structural characteristics at the market level and the business level. Firm-specific parameters, such as market share and importance of the purchase to the customer, must also be considered.

The next steps in the research are to investigate the effect of other characteristics, explore the use of other performance variables, look for ways of measuring power on a single dimension, and utilize more powerful methodological approaches such as AID and multiple regression.

REFERENCES

Collins, N. R., and L. E. Preston, 'Price–cost margins and industry structure', *Review of Economics and Statistics*, **51** (1969), 271–286.

Eckstein, O., and D. Wyss, 'Industry price equations', in O. Eckstein (ed.), *The Econometrics of Price Determination*. Federal Reserve Board, Washington, D.C., 1972, pp. 133–165.

Kwoka, J. E., 'The effect of market share distribution on industry performance', *Review of Economics and Statistics*, **61**(1) (1979), 101–109.

Learned, E. P., C. R. Christenson, K. R. Andrews, and W. Guth, *Business Policy*. Irwin, Homewood, Ill., 1969.

Van Lommel, E., and B. de Brabander, 'Price–cost margins and market structure: a contingency approach', *Journal of Industrial Economics*, **28**(1) (Sept. 1979), 1–22.

Lustgarten, S. H., 'The impact of buyer concentration in manufacturing industries', *Review of Economics and Statistics*, **62**(2) (1975), 125–132.

Ornstein, S. I., 'Empirical uses of the price–cost margin', *Journal of Industrial Economics*, **24**(2) (Dec. 1975), 105–117.

Phillips, A., 'A critique of empirical studies of relations between market structure and profitability', *Journal of Industrial Economics*, **24**(4) (June 1976), 241–249.

Porter, M. E., 'The structure within industries and companies' performance', *Review of Economics and Statistics*, **61**(2) (1979), 214–227.

Porter, M. E., *Competitive Strategy*. Free Press, New York, 1980.

Porter, M. E., 'The contributions of industrial organization to strategic management', *Academy of Management Review*, **C**(4), (1981), 609–620.

Straszheim, D. H., and M. R. Straszheim, 'An econometric analysis of the determination of prices in manufacturing industries', *Review of Economics and Statistics*, **58** (1976), 191–201.

Strategic Marketing and Management
Edited by H. Thomas and D. Gardner
© 1985 John Wiley & Sons Ltd

3.3

The Data Aggregation Issue in Empirical Analysis For Strategic Market Planning

GARY L. FRAZIER

Assistant Professor of Business Administration (Marketing), School of Commerce and Business Administration, University of Illinois

AND

ROY D. HOWELL

Associate Professor of Marketing, College of Business Administration, Texas Tech. University

INTRODUCTION

Strategic market planners face a difficult situation. On the one hand they see the complexity inherent in the strategic market planning process, the need to consider a wide variety of organizational, strategic, competitive, technological, and general environmental variables in formulating their plans and policies. On the other hand, due to time constraints, lack of appropriate data, and limited processing capabilities, they realize that a thorough analysis of all relevant variables is a seemingly insurmountable task. The question often asked is: 'Based on our firm's present business situation, what should we consider in developing our strategic market plan and in what manner?'

Clearly, empirical analyses of relationships between firm performance measures and strategic and operational variables over which managers have control (e.g. between sales volume and price) should play an important role in answering the above question. While some managers bypass empirical analysis and rely on available planning models such as the market-share growth matrix or the industry attractiveness–business strength screen, these models have considerable problems and rely on assumptions concerning variable relationships (e.g. between profitability and market share) that require additional empirical testing in a variety of industry settings.* Other managers rely merely

---

* For a more complete discussion and evaluation of these models, see Day (1977), Abell and Hammond (1979), Porter (1980), Wensley (1981), and Sheth and Frazier (1982).

on 'seat of the pants' strategic market planning (the entrepreneurial approach) or a reactive strategy, both having obvious weaknesses.

Empirical analysis implies the need for data. The firm's management is faced with the options of collecting and developing an appropriate data base internally or relying on an existing data base gathered by another organization. For example, many Fortune 500 firms have joined the PIMS (Profit Impact of Marketing Strategies) project. Unfortunately, PIMS is apparently burdened with a number of methodological problems dealing with (1) the lack of theory in guiding the data collection and analyses, (2) the representativeness of the firms in the data base, (3) the means of collecting the data, (4) the reliability and validity of the measures, (5) the methods of analysis, and (6) the meaning and implications of the results for the strategic planner (cf. Anderson and Paine, 1978; Abell and Hammond, 1979; Porter, 1980; Sheth and Frazier, 1982). The inter-industry, cross-sectional nature of the data base also presents difficulties, as discussed later in the paper. Many of these same problems are usually present in trade association data collection and analyses. Therefore, together with the problems inherent in present planning models and frameworks for strategic market planning, in many situations, managers must consider gathering and analyzing their own data to aid in developing strategic plans.

In order to perform empirical analyses for strategic market planning purposes, the model to be estimated, including the dependent and independent variables, must be specified. Then, multiple observations on each variable must be gathered; data can be collected or assembled (1) across firms in one time period; (2) across organizational subdivisions and/or territories in one time period; (3) across time periods for one firm; or (4) some combination of the above.

This paper centers on one issue pertaining to the collection and analysis of data for strategic planning purposes, the data aggregation problem. This concerns the biases that can occur in estimating parameters of a firm performance model when data are aggregated across dissimilar business firms or strategic business units, dissimilar territories or divisions of a business, or dissimilar time periods. Each data collection unit will be discussed in light of the data aggregation problem, including recommendations for appropriate collection and analysis techniques. The joint time-series, cross-sectional model appears the most appropriate and useful for strategic market planning purposes.

CROSS-SECTIONAL ANALYSIS

Across firms or strategic business units

The collection of data across business firms or strategic business units in one time period has been a popular method in addressing the firm performance issue. Industrial economists have long attempted to explain performance by estimating variable relationships based on data assembled from firms across a variety of industries (cf. Gort, 1963; Grether, 1970; Scherer, 1970; Bain, 1972). In the 1960s General Electric gathered and analyzed data from a cross-section of its strategic business units. The ongoing PIMS program attempts to explain ROI and cash flow by analyzing data collected from more than 150 companies operating more than 1000 businesses in a variety of industries (cf. Schoeffler *et al.*, 1974; Buzzell, *et al.*, 1975). The general form of the cross-sectional equation is

$$y_i = \sum_{j=1}^{J} \beta X_{ji} + \varepsilon_i \qquad (1)$$

where the *i* represent cross-sectional observations.

To date, a major assumption generally made by programs or studies dealing with a cross-section of firms across industries is that 'natural business laws' and general variable relationships exist throughout the business community, that certain regularities exist across industries. This homogeneity assumption appears highly questionable with regard to strategic planning and marketing strategy. Porter (1976) and Bass *et al.* (1977, 1978) show that aggregation of firms across industries can bias parameter estimates; variable relationships can and do vary in strength, significance, and sign across industries or grouping of industries. As Porter (1980: 3) explains:

> Although the relevant environment is very broad, encompassing social as well as economic forces, the key aspect of the firm's environment is the industry or industries in which it competes. Industry structure has a strong influence in determining the competitive rules of the game as well as strategies potentially available to the firm.

What is important for a consumer products manufacturer to consider in developing its strategic market plan can be very different from that of a capital equipment manufacturer; consumers' customs, needs, and values and their reactions to varying strategies differ across cultures, countries, industries, and product areas. The impact of major environmental forces will vary by industry.

Perhaps recognizing the existence of such problems, 'sector' models are being developed for the PIMS data to control for variations in relationships across industries. For example, Farris and Buzzell (1979) report results for the entire sample as well as individually for capital goods, raw materials and components, supply, and consumer businesses. Unfortunately, although disaggregating the data one step further, this procedure may still be inadequate.

The homogeneity assumption will also be inappropriate *within* an industry if the firms therein are highly dissimilar in nature. Frazier and Howell (1982a) contend that a firm's market segmentation strategy can effectively differentiate it from firms following alternative segmentation strategies in the same industry. In a study in the medical supply and equipment channel, they divided wholesalers into three different groups based on their segmentation strategy: (1) hospital-concentrated; (2) physician-concentrated; and (3) mixed firms serving hospitals and physicians as well as other customer groups. Empirical results indicated that the ability of a group of sales force management, financial management, asset management, and firm size variables to explain wholesaler net profit varied significantly across the groups. Beta coefficients varied in significance, sign, and direction.

In an extension of their previous work, Frazier and Howell (1982b) provide a systematic basis for determining the proper level of data aggregation in an intra-industry study by merging Porter's (1980) concept of strategic groups with Abell's (1980) dimensions for defining a business. Porter (1980) suggests that the relevant level of analysis in attempts to explain firm performance and develop strategic market plans is the *strategic group*, composed of firms within an industry following a similar strategy. However, he gives little direction in how to define and identify 'similar strategies'. In this regard the dimensions organized by Abell (1980) for *defining the business* appear to be very useful in identifying firms with a similar focus; firms serving the same *customer groups* and *customer functions* (needs with the same *technology* (ways used to satisfy the needs) would appear to comprise a strategic group in that a variation on any of the above dimensions will significantly affect a firm's structural position in its industry.

This discussion suggests that one way to properly address the firm performance issue in an intra-industry study would be to specify the model and analyze data separately for each strategic group in the industry. Each group would be composed of firms serving similar customers and functions with a similar technology. In situations where such measures are unavailable (e.g. the Compustat data base), an empiricist rather than a conceptual approach could be used in identifying varying strategic groups.

The problem with the above approach is that the number of firms comprising any group may be very small, especially for the manufacturing sector. This will constrain the number of independent variables used to explain firm performance; specification error may be a serious problem. A second approach involves analyzing the entire group of firms as one, but specifying, measuring, and including in the analysis primary moderating variables which cause a shift in the significance, level, and sign of parameters in the firm performance model. The customer group(s) served, the function(s) served, and the technology or technologies used in performing the function(s) appear to be the *major* moderator variables that may mitigate general dependent and independent variable relationships within an industry, although other important moderator variables could certainly exist. Dummy variables could be created on the customer group, function, and technology dimensions and included in the equation. Additionally, each independent variable would be multiplied by each of the dummy variables and included as interaction terms in analyzing structural shifts in general variable relationships; three- and four-way interaction terms could also be studied. Of course, theory could be used in determining which independent variables are influenced by each moderator variable in possibly reducing the number of terms in the equation. The main effect of each independent variable would also be analyzed.

In many situations, looking at firms on one level within one industry can still constrain the size of the model to be estimated. An analysis of a cross-section of firms across industries may be necessary. An appropriate analysis procedure becomes relatively complex here because the effect of major environmental forces (e.g. the national economy, social and life style trends) can vary across industries. Additionally, researchers in the organizational behavior literature have identified a variety of environmental dimensions on which to compare the properties of organizations belonging to alternative task environments or industries. For example, Aldrich (1979) indicates that industries can vary in their (1) environmental capacity (the relative level of resources available to the organizations in the task environment), (2) concentration (the degree to which resources, including the population served and other elements, are evenly distributed over the range of the environment or concentrated in particular locations); and (3) stability (the length of time organizations are a member of the network and the degree of turnover of the parties). Van de Ven *et al.* (1975) discuss domain consensus, the degree to which the organizations' goals are disputed, and homogeneity, the functional and structural similarity of the organizations.*

Therefore, aside from the customer group, function, and technology dimensions, including (1) estimates of the degree of impact general environmental forces have on each industry and (2) evaluations of environmental dimensions (e.g. environmental capacity, domain consensus, turbulence) present in each industry appears to be a necessity in an inter-industry analysis to explain variations in firm performance. These variables would be included by themselves as well as in interaction terms with the independent variables (e.g. price, advertising). Again, some discretion can be used, based on *a priori* theory, concerning which independent variables are likely to be influenced by each moderating variable, although such assumptions can and should be tested.

Across territories, divisions, distributors, and retailing establishments

Another method for collecting cross-sectional data is within a company across territories, divisions, distributors, and/or retailing establishments. Most of

---

* Some of these dimensions, as well as others, are also discussed in Levine and White (1961), Emery and Trist (1965), Evan (1966), Thompson (1967), and Child (1972).

the empirical research in the sales force management literature is based on data collected within one company across salespeople located in alternative sales territories. Within the distribution channel, data are often available on distributors and associated retail firms. For example, within a franchise system the franchisor usually has access to data on each franchisee's operations.

Here again, to pool data across territories, divisions, distributors, or retailing establishments without proper controls may lead to biased parameter estimates. Similar to the earlier discussion, one way to ensure confidence in the analysis results would be to assemble territories or divisions or distributors or retailers/dealers into homogeneous groups. This classification could be based on either conceptual notions or an empiricist approach. Alternatively, dissimilar units could be pooled if primary moderator variables are included in the analyses, individually as well as in interaction terms with each independent variable.

'Customers served' again appears to be a worthy dimension to consider in classifying units, or to include as a primary moderating variable in an aggregate analysis. For example, if alternative sales territories have very different distributions of customers (e.g. relative percentage of department stores versus hardware stores), it would not be appropriate to ignore this fact in the data analysis. 'Functions served' can also have a bearing. For example, a Holiday Inn is not a Holiday Inn. Some are extravagant, high-priced resort hotels that have a dining room, a bar, nightly entertainment, recreation facilities, and offer a wide variety of services. Others are more a motel, located in smaller towns and having very few facilities other than a room to spend the night. Obviously, the functions served by each group are very different and therefore they should not be straightforwardly pooled prior to data analysis. Finally, the 'technology employed' in serving the customers and functions can distinguish different territories, divisions, distributors, and retailers. For example, if some wholesalers have generally computerized their operations and others have not, each group is not serving customers and functions from the same basis.

A variety of other moderator variables may also exist here. For example, the geographic location of territories, divisions, distributors, and retailers could have an important bearing as environmental forces may have differential impacts across regions. The set of moderating variables to be included here appears more situation-specific compared to analysis involving a cross-section of business firms.

TIME-SERIES ANALYSIS

The preceding discussion has illustrated some of the potential problems inherent in using cross-sectional data in the estimation of variable relationships for use in strategy formulation. Another alternative available for estimating variable relationships is to use time-series data generated by the firm itself over time. This approach has the potential for solving some of the problems inherent in cross-sectional analysis, but has problems of its own. Among the advantages of this approach is the relatively high degree of accessibility of data of this type. While the data base requirements of the strategic planning model utilized may be beyond the scope of historical accounting and operating records as they currently exist, the firm need not face problems of confidentiality, comparability, or ambiguous measurement since the data are its own. Most internally focused management information/decision support systems will be able to generate longitudinal data for this type of analysis, although unless a model of firm performance formed the basis of the data gathering, one may find that only limited (and probably mis-specified) models can be estimated. However, the SBU or firm can begin appropriate data collection without having to seek external cooperation. Specifically, the time series model would be

$$y_\tau = \sum_{j=1}^{J} \beta X_{j\tau} + \varepsilon_\tau. \tag{2}$$

The critical problem with using intra-firm or intra-unit time-series data is the potential lack of variation on key predictors. This may result in part from the consistent use of a set of decision rules for resource allocation, leading to the modeling of the decision rule in use rather than the variable relationships in their true causal direction. Since firms might find experimenting with the allocation of critical resources in order to infer their impact on revenue or profitability undesirable, they may allocate resources based on some 'rule of thumb' or implied response elasticity. Thus, intra-firm time-series data sets may contain little variation on key variables of interest, making inference difficult or impossible, especially so outside a very narrow range of values. Similarly, strategic variables such as plant capacity, capital intensity ratios, product quality, etc. are very unlikely to change or to take on more than 2 or 3 values over any but the longest time-series.

Thus, in order to capture enough variation in some variables to estimate their covariation with outcome variables, long time-series would have to be employed if anything other than simple (probably mis-specified) models are to be estimated. By 'long', a time-series of 30 or more observations is implied. If yearly data are used this implies that parameters of relationship are to be estimated on data beginning in at least the mid-1950s. The same problem experienced in cross-sectional analysis becomes apparent here. Just as with cross-sectional analysis, time-series analysis implies that the relationships between the predictor variables and the dependent variable be homogeneous across the observations if biased parameter estimates are to be avoided. The question then becomes whether the variable relationships that hold for the 1950s can be expected to hold for the 1980s. It is expected that this question can be answered affirmatively in only the rarest of instances. Just as the nature of the firm, its customers, and its products has changed over the last 30 years, so has the environment in which the firm operates. For example, the efficiency of advertising and the media allocation process has almost certainly changed over this period; such changes can be expected to substantially affect the value of the parameter relating advertising expenditures to sales or profitability. Nor does one have to go back 30 years to find non-homogeneous time periods within the observation set. Changes in customer groups, functions, and technologies occur with sufficient rapidity that parameter estimates remaining stable for more than 10 years would be expected to be the exception rather than the rule.

Where specific events can be identified which are expected to affect parameters, such events can be accounted for through the use of a dummy variable in the appropriate time period in interaction with selected predictors. However, when changes are evolutionary and brought about by a complex of changing internal and external factors, such an approach may prove difficult to implement.

Note that more observations can be generated over a shorter time period through the use of monthly or quarterly data. This may lead to a false sense of abundance in degrees of freedom, however, if many of these shorter-interval observations contain identical unchanging values on several variables, as each new observation has not contributed any unique or new information to the model estimation process.

An alternative approach would be to treat the β parameters in model (2) as random, time-varying parameters. This approach implies the model

$$y_\tau = \sum_{j=1}^{J} \beta X_{j\tau} + \varepsilon_\tau \tag{3}$$

$$\varepsilon_\tau = U_\tau + e_\tau$$

where U_τ is the time varying component of the error term, and e_τ is the true random error. This is a model of 'specific ignorance' which explicitly recognizes that even the dummy variable approach implies ignorance. This model formulation simply differentiates the specific ignorance of time from the general ignorance represented by e_τ. While this approach could be expected to yield more consistent parameter estimates with lower bias, it does not solve all of the problems with intra-firm time-series observations.

Cross-sectional time-series data

The foregoing discussion has raised questions as to the value of either cross-sectional *or* time-series observations in estimating models of perform-ance. Since the homogeneity of observations is the overriding problem with both cross-sectional and time-series analysis, leading to the potential problem of too few similar cross-sectional or time-series entities for estimation, the pooling of observations across firms, or units within firms, over time may provide a data base of sufficient size without the sacrifice of homogeneity. The problem is thus to specify a model that allows for differences in behavior over such cross-sectional units as firms, divisions within a firm, geographic areas, etc., as well as differences in behavior over time for a given cross-sectional unit.

The most general form of this type of model is

$$y_{i\tau} = \sum_{k=1}^{k} B_{ki\tau} X_{ki\tau} + e_{i\tau} \qquad (4)$$

where $i = 1, \ldots, N$ refers to the cross-sectional units, $\tau = 1, \ldots, T$ represents time periods, $y_{i\tau}$ is the dependent variable of the ith unit in the τth time period, $X_{ki\tau}$ is the value of the kth explanatory variable for the ith unit at time τ, and $B_{ki\tau}$ is the response parameter to be estimated (Raj and Ullah, 1981). By convention, the data set is assumed ordered by time-period observations *within* cross-section observations. Thus, if there are N cross-sectional observations with T time-series observations on each, the result will be an NT by K data matrix.

The model in (4) is the natural result of the collection of cross-sectional data on the same set of entities over several time periods, and is, therefore, the logical result of an ongoing cross-sectional approach as it is continued from year to year. Models for the analysis of data sets of this type are generally discussed in the econometric literature under the rubric of 'panel data'; this is appropriate since the ongoing process of collecting data from firms can easily be thought of as the establishment of a 'panel'.

The model in (4) presents unique analytical opportunities, since the information across time can be used to empirically assess homogeneity across entities, and vice-versa. Hatten and Schendel (1977) present an innovative analysis of data of this type from the US brewing industry, finding *both* cross-sectional and time-period heterogeneity to exist in that data set.

Several types of estimates are available for the parameters of (4). One obvious approach would be to apply OLS to the data set as a whole. This may lead to biased and inconsistent estimates of the parameters if heterogeneous firms or time periods are present. For example, Lodish (1982) uses a data base composed of observations on 151 stores over 14 monthly time periods to parameterize a model of price and advertising effects for a retail decision support system. In addition to confronting the seasonality problem which often accompanies the use of monthly data, as well as potential autocorrelation and biased error estimates which may result from time series models, Lodish notes (1982: 55):

> Issues of pooling and store segmentation should be more carefully considered. It may be inappropriate to assume the same model parameters for different store types or regions of the country. The present national planning model considers the average response over the country. However, data analysis at the store level may show that different response models are appropriate for different regions or store

types. Presently, the data analysis has pooled both cross-sectional and time series data. This may be inappropriate.

A traditional approach to analyzing such data has been the use of dummy variables to represent each of the cross-sectional entities. This is possible, of course, only when there are several time-series observations on each. This approach can be refined through the examination of the statistical significance of the coefficients associated with the 'firm' dummies, with those not statistically significant dropped and pooled into the overall intercept term.

Alternatively, a dummy variable could be included in model (4) to represent each time period, or a combination of cross-sectional dummies and time-series dummies could be employed. Of course, the latter approach requires some degree of subjective judgement with regard to which dummies to employ, since a dummy variable for each time period and each cross-section would clearly use up all available degrees of freedom.

Therefore, the use of selected dummy variables to represent time periods of substantial change and/or, as discussed previously under cross-sectional analysis, dummy variables to represent cross-sectional entities with shared strategically important characteristics, could be used. In all of the above cases, however, it must be remembered that dummy variables affect only the intercept, while changes in coefficients associated with managerial decision variables are of primary interest. If a dummy variable type of analysis is used, it is imperative that the dummies be included in interaction with the decision variables in order to assess slope as well as intercept differences. This will be quite costly in terms of degrees of freedom in all but the simplest models. Thus, both OLS applied to the aggregate data set and OLS in conjunction with dummy variables appear to present serious problems.

However, other transformations of the data are possible, which render OLS useful in some cases. For example, the error term in the model in equation (4) can be decomposed as:

$$\varepsilon_{i\tau} = m_i + s_\tau + \mu_{i\tau} \qquad (5)$$

where m_i is the systematic component, or effect, associated with the ith cross-sectional unit, and s_τ is the effect associated with the τth time period. As noted by Mundlak (1978), the critical issue in the analysis of cross-sectional or time-series data is not the decomposition of the error term in (4) into its components, but is rather what effect this method of decomposition should have on the method of estimation of the remaining parameters in the model.

Two alternative approaches have been suggested, the fixed effects and the random effects models. The fixed effects model is analogous to the analysis of covariance, and is often designated the '*within-groups*' estimator. Estimation is accomplished by eliminating the firm effect in the sample by transforming the data into deviations from cross-sectional means. That is, the mean, across time periods, is calculated for each cross-sectional observation, with the data across time for that firm being transformed into deviations from the firm average.

Unfortunately, as noted by Hausman and Taylor (1981), OLS coefficient estimates from the transformed data have three major problems: (1) errors in the variables are exacerbated by this type of transformation; (2) any variables in the data set which do not change over the time period measured are eliminated by the transformation, such that cross-sectional coefficients for these variables cannot be estimated; and (3) within-groups estimators cannot be fully efficient since they ignore across-firm variation in the sample.

The first two, and especially the second, problems appear to be most critical in estimating models for use in strategic market planning. It is quite likely that many of our predictors will be difficult to measure directly, thus resulting in an error-in-the-variables problem exacerbated by the transformation. Additionally, the manager may be interested in the effect of variables that either structurally, or due to consistent decision rules, do not vary over the time-series for the cross-section. Investment in plant and equipment may be an example of this, as might relative product quality.

Another approach to analyzing cross-sectional time-series data involves the use of the so-called '*between-groups*' estimator, calculated from the data averaged over time for each cross-sectional entity. This is the approach reported by the PIMS project after four periods of data gathering. Within-firm variations which could be used to identify between-firm differences are lost in this approach. A third approach, yielding what are known as Gauss–Markov or *Balestra–Nerlove* estimators, is essentially an optimally weighted average of the within- and between-group estimators.

Earlier econometric work on variance-components models and much current work in econometrics focuses on the analysis of models of this type. While it is beyond the scope of this paper to provide a detailed examination of procedures for estimating these models, one approach in particular seems to offer distinct advantages.

Hausman and Taylor (1981) consider a model

$$y_{i\tau} = X_{i\tau}\beta + Z_i\Gamma + \alpha_i + \eta_{i\tau} \quad (i = 1, N; \tau = 1, T) \tag{5}$$

where β and Γ are k and g vectors of coefficients associated with time-varying and time-invariant observable variables, respectively. The model allows for a latent (unobservable) individual firm effect (α_i) which is assumed to be a time-invariant random variable. In the cost and production function literature, α_i has been used to denote the managerial efficiency of the ith firm, and the use of the within-group estimator to obtain unbiased estimates of the remaining parameters has been suggested. However, if α_i is correlated with X and Z, these estimates, and as a result Balestra–Nerlove estimates, are biased (Hausman and Taylor, 1981). It would seem that the α_i parameter would be of interest to the strategic market planner, as would estimates of the Γ coefficients associated with variables that do not change, or change slowly, for firms over time (which was one of the major drawbacks to intra-firm time-series observations).

It is suggested, then, that the analysis of time-series of homogeneous cross-sections, as defined previously, represents the appropriate direction for data base construction and analysis in this area, using models such as (5) above. Although estimation procedures for such models are considerably more involved and complex than OLS models, it is suggested that the better conceptual integrity and resultant parameter estimates will be worth the price.

CONCLUSIONS

Relationships among variables provide the basis for virtually all logic in strategic planning, and if empirical estimates of variable relationships are to be obtained, multiple observations are required. This paper has discussed several methods for obtaining multiple observations and noted the potential for aggregation bias in parameter estimates stemming from each of the approaches. In the light of potential problems which may be encountered in finding enough strategically equivalent firms for cross-sectional analysis or enough strategically equivalent years for time-series analysis, a joint cross-sectional, time-series data base composed of homogeneous firms over homogeneous time periods appears to be the logical mode for data collection and analysis in this area. Additionally, guidelines for assessing similarity have been discussed.

A model which allows for the estimation of firm effects and cross-sectional effects for variables which are time-invariant (under the periods of observation), as well as time-varying effects within firms is presented. The overriding concern of this paper is to discuss the bias which may result from using poorly conceptualized aggregate data; the observatiosn—whether firms, firm subdivisions, time periods, or a combination—*must* reflect the same underlying process driving the parameter relationships. In general, it will be difficult to determine the appropriateness of a data set in a strictly empirical manner; a combination of sound theory and empirical estimates must be employed.

REFERENCES

Abell, Derek (1980). *Defining the Business*. Prentice-Hall, Inc., Englewood Cliffs, N.J.
Abell, Derek and John Hammond (1979). *Strategic Marketing Planning*. Prentice-Hall, Inc., Englewood Cliffs, N.J.
Aldrich, Howard (1979). *Organizations and Environments*. Prentice-Hall, Inc., Englewood Cliffs, N.J.
Anderson, Carl and Frank Paine (1978). 'PIMS: a reexamination', *Academy of Management Review*, **3**, 602–12.

Bain, J. (1972). *Essays on Price Theory and Industrial Organization*. Little-Brown, Boston.

Bass, Frank, Phillippe Cattin, and Dick Wiltink (1977). 'Market structure and industry influence on profitability', in Hans Thorelli (ed.), *Strategy and Structure Equals Performance*. Indiana University Press, Bloomington, IN.

Bass, Frank, Phillippe Cattin, and Dick Wiltink (1978). 'Firm effects and industry effects in the analysis of market structure and profitability', *Journal of Marketing Research*, **15** (Feb.), 3–10.

Buzzell, Robert, B. Gale, and R. Sultan (1975). 'Market share—a key to profitability', *Harvard Business Review* (Jan.–Feb.), pp. 97–106.

Child, John (1972). 'Organization structure, environment, and performance—the role of strategic choice', *Sociology*, **6** (Jan.), 1–22.

Day, George (1977). 'Diagnosing the product portfolio', *Journal of Marketing*, **41** (Apr.), 29–38.

Emery, F. and E. Trist (1965). 'The causal texture of organizational environments', *Human Relations*, **18** (Feb.), 21–32.

Evan, William (1966). 'The organization-set: toward a theory of interorganizational relations', in James Thompson (ed.), *Approaches to Organizational Design*. University of Pittsburgh Press, Pittsburgh, pp. 175–190.

Farris, Paul, and Robert Buzzell (1979). 'Why advertising and promotional costs vary: some cross sectional analyses', *Journal of Marketing*, **43** (Fall), 112-22.

Frazier, Gary L., and Roy D. Howell (1982a). 'Effects of intraindustry marketing strategy on the analysis of profitability', forthcoming in *Journal of Business Research*.

Frazier, Gary L., and Roy D. Howell (1982b). 'Business definition, intra-industry heterogeneity, and strategic market planning'. Working paper, University of Illinois, Urbana, IL.

Gort, Michael (1963). 'Analysis of stability and change in market shares', *Journal of Political Economy* (Feb.), pp. 58–69.

Grether, E. T. (1970). 'Industrial organization: retrospect and prospect', *American Economic Review*, **60** (May), 83–89.

Hatten, Kenneth, and Dan Schendel (1977). 'Heterogeneity within an industry: firm conduct in the U.S. brewing industry, 1952–71', *Journal of Industrial Economics* (Dec.), 97–113.

Hausman, Jerry, and William Taylor (1981). 'Panel data and unobservable individual effects', *Econometrica*, **49**(6) (Nov.), 1377–1398.

Heckman, J., and B. Singer (1980) (eds). *Longitudinal Labor Market Studies: Theory, Methods and Empirical Results*. Academic Press, New York.

Levine, S., and P. White (1961). 'Exchange as a conceptual framework for the study of interorganizational relationships', *Administrative Science Quarterly*, **5** (Mar.), 583–610.

Lodish, L. (1982). 'A marketing decision support system for retailers', *Marketing Science*, **1**(1), 31–56.

Mundlak, Yair (1978). 'On the pooling of time series and cross section data', *Econometrica*, **46**(1), 69–85.

Porter, Michael (1976). *Interbrand Choice, Strategy, and Bilateral Market Power*. Harvard Uuniversity Press, Cambridge.

Porter, Michael (1980). *Competitive Strategy*. Free Press, New York.

Raj, Balder, and A. Ullah (1981). *Econometrics: A Varying Coefficients Approach*. St Martins Press, New York.

Scherer, Frederick (1970). *Industrial Market Structure and Economic Performance*. Rand McNally, Chicago.

Schoeffler, Sidney, Robert Buzzell, and Donald Heany (1974). 'Impact of strategic planning on profit performance', *Harvard Business Review* (Mar.–Apr.), pp. 137–45.
Sheth, Jagdish, and Gary L. Frazier (1982). 'An earnings-return model for strategic market planning'. Working paper, University of Illinois, Urbana, IL.
Thompson, James (1967). *Organizations in Action*. McGraw-Hill, New York.
Van de Ven, Andrew, Dennis Emmett, and Richard Koenig (1975). 'Frameworks for interorganizational analysis', in Anant Negandhi (ed.), *Interorganization Theory*, Kent State University Press, Oxford, Ohio; pp. 19–35.
Wensley, Robin (1981). 'Strategic marketing: betas, boxes or basics', *Journal of Marketing*, **45** (Summer), 173–82.

Strategic Marketing and Management
Edited by H. Thomas and D. Gardner
© 1985 John Wiley & Sons Ltd

3.4
Marketing Strategy to Achieve Market Share Goals

CHARLES LILLIS
Manager, Marketing and Business Strategy Consulting, General Electric Company

JAMES COOK ˙
Consultant, Marketing and Business Strategy Consulting, General Electric Company

ROGER BEST
Associate Professor of Marketing, University of Oregon

AND

DEL HAWKINS
Professor of Marketing, University of Oregon

Market share goals and the process of generating strategies to attain new share goals is an ongoing business activity of great importance (Skov and Spetzler, 1979; Royce, 1979). For example, once Owens-Illinois decided to harvest its share of the glass container market (1981) a specific marketing strategy needed to be put in place to accomplish that goal in a profit-efficient manner. Likewise, marketing strategies pursued by Xerox to grow share in the low-priced copier market (1981) and Perrier to hold its leader position (Wheatley, 1980) each required a certain level of marketing effort to accomplish their share goal in a particular business situation. Because each business situation is different in terms of market environment, the strategic path and marketing effort needed to achieve a particular share goal is also different.

Market share goals are generally set with financial performance in mind. A hold, grow, or harvest strategy each is directly or indirectly linked to expected revenues, cash flows, and net incomes (Schoeffler *et al.*, 1977). Share goals, however, are often easier to state than actually achieve. That is, share goals are often set without full consideration of the market environment and the resources needed to attain a desired share goal. As a result, some businesses fall short of their share goal while others exceed their target with relative ease.

Thus, there is a need to better reconcile share goals with the expected share that is likely to result given a particular market environment and the marketing mix plan being implemented to attain a particular level of market share.

The purpose of this paper is to discuss a set of strategic planning models that have been developed by General Electric Corporate Consulting Services to aid GE managers in more effectively adjusting their marketing mix efforts to the business situation in order to achieve a desired market share. In this paper we will present a planning system for managing market share change and a set of models used to aid managers in evaluating the reasonableness of their share goal in light of the environment they face and the marketing effort they plan. The validity and usefulness of these share change models is also examined in this paper.

MANAGING THE MIX FOR SHARE CHANGE

In an attempt to better align share goals with share outcomes, General Electric developed the planning system shown in Figure 3.4.1. As shown, at the top of this system, a share goal and current share position are compared to determine the rate of share growth needed to achieve a desired share position. At the center of this system a comparison is made between the rate of share change that is *needed* and the rate of share change that is *expected* (estimated) to occur given a particular set of share impacts created by the business situation and the business's marketing effort. If these rates of share change are approximately equal, the share goal has a reasonable chance of being achieved. However, a major differential in *what is needed* vs. *what is expected*, requires a reworking of the marketing mix effort, or revising the share goal, or both.

Our objective in developing this system was to help managers detect problems in managing changes in their marketing mix when given the challenge of a particular market share objective. As shown in the equation below, in this system discernible changes in the sales force, media and promotional spending, product quality, customer service, and level of new products each contribute to share change. Significant increases in these marketing mix variables should contribute to gains in share while discernible decreases in these variables should result in share decline.

$$MSC = \underbrace{b_1 SF + b_2 ASP + b_3 PQ + b_4 CS + b_5 NP}_{\text{controllable mix variables}}$$

$$\underbrace{- b_6 MSB - b_7 SMG - b_8 CI + b_9 CE + b_{10} NPB}_{\text{uncontrolled influences}}$$

Where:

MSC = change in market share

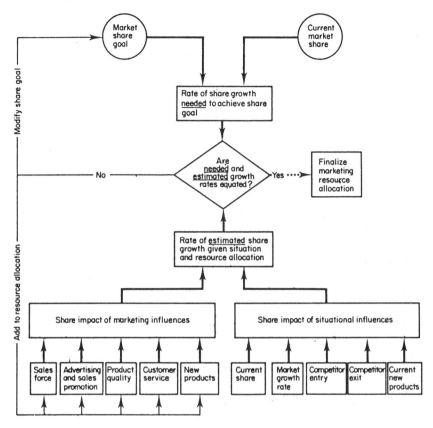

Figure 3.4.1   Managing for market share goals

SF   = change in sales force
ASP = change in media advertising and sales promotion
PQ   = change in product quality
CS   = change in customer service
NP   = change in level of new products
MSB = current market share
SMG = growth rate of served market
CI   = competitor entry
CE   = competitor exit
NPB = current level of new products

Uncontrollable factors such as a business's current level of market share, rate of growth of a business's served market, and competitor entry each have an inverse effect on market share. A large share is much more difficult to increase 25 percent than a small share. Likewise, the faster a market is expanding in size, the more difficult it is to grow sales at a rate faster than the market is growing. And the entry of a competitor generally results in some level of share erosion. On the positive side, a competitor exiting the market is likely to produce some level of share gain. The more new products a business has in place at the start of a marketing effort to affect share, the better position it is in to accomplish that task.

Combining the share impacts created by the situational influences with the share impacts created by changes in the marketing mix yields a net expected (estimated) rate of share change. As shown in Figure 3.4.1, when *expected* rate of share change is equated with a *needed* rate of share change to achieve a particular share goal, the manager has put together a marketing mix effort that has a reasonable chance of succeeding. When this is the case, the mix strategy has enough impacts in it to counter the environment to reasonably reach a desired share target. Of course, just because the level of effort seems reasonable for a given situation and share goal, poor performance in that effort will certainly lessen the likelihood of achieving the share goal.

MARKET SHARE CHANGE MODELS

The share change model we have proposed is very similar to the share change model proposed by Buzzell and Wiersema, 1981; Buzzell, 1981), the work presented by Lillien (1979) and comments by Wind and Mahajan (1981) and Farris and Buzzell (1980). To evaluate the proposed share change system, the specified variables were operationally defined and measured as they are represented in the Strategic Planning Institute's (SPI) research data base. Table 3.4.1 provides an operational definition of each variable along with measures of each variable's mean and standard deviation. The SPI research data base contain 1377 strategic business units and it is from the base of information that the hypothesized share change model was constructed.

This particular data analysis examined changes in market share over a 4-year period. The dependent variable described in Table 3.4.1 is the rate of change in market share over a 4-year period. Therefore, a business with a 10 percent beginning share that grew at a rate of 12 percent per year would reach a share of 15.73 percent in 4 years. In this model it is important to keep in mind that the dependent variable is the rate of change over a 4-year period and not a change in share points.

Changes in expenditures on the sales force, and advertising and promotion, were measured the same way that share change was measured. Thus, each of these mix variables also represents rates of change in these variables over a 4-year period. As shown in Table 3.4.1, the average SBU grew its sales force expense at the rate of 11.3 percent per year while spending on media advertising and promotion grew at an annual rate of 9.53 percent.

Changes in relative product quality, relative customer services, and relative new products are measured as points changes over the 4-year period. In this case the average point change in each of these marketing variables was very small. In the case of new products, there was a slight decrease. This may in fact signal the difficulty a business faces in attempting to outperform its competitors in the areas of product quality, customer service, and new products. That is, while substantial improvements may have been made by a business in each of these marketing variables, competitors may have kept pace with these changes. Hence, no relative advantage was captured by the average SBU in the research data base for each of these three marketing mix variables.

The average SBU had a beginning market share of 23.11 percent and was participating in a served market growing at a rate of 11.4 percent per year. Twenty-nine percent of the SBUs saw new competitors enter their served markets during this 4-year period while 20 percent of the SBUs saw competitors exit their markets. At the beginning of this 4-year period the average SBU had a slight advantage in new products with approximately 1 percent more new product sales than competitors.

Utilizing these variable definitions, all 1377 businesses were used to estimate a single share change equation. Standardized estimates of the estimated parameters are shown in the MSC equation below. In each case the estimated coefficient was found to be statistically significant ($p \leq 0.10$) and its effect on share change in the hypothesized direction. The variance in market share change explained by this share change equation was 37 percent. Trimming the dependent variable of 2.5 percent of its outliers (1.96 standard deviations above and below the average rate of share change) increased the explained variance to 46 percent without changing the relative size of the standardized coefficients shown in the equation above.

$$MSC = 0.375SF + 0.134ASP + 0.108PQ + 0.055CS + 0.043NP$$

controllable mix variables

$$- 0.168MSB - 0.156SMG - 0.048CI + 0.049EX + 0.12NPB$$

uncontrollable influences

Because this data base is made up of a very diverse set of businesses, separated regression models were constructed for each of eight major sectors of business. In Table 3.4.2 are the standardized coefficients that were found to be significant ($p \leq 0.10$) and also uncorrelated with other variables in each of the respective equations. Three important observations can be made from the results presented in Table 3.4.2. First, not all variables were significant in each of the eight sectors of business examined. Second, variables that were significant in one sector of business had very similar levels of impact in other sectors where this variable was significant. And third, the explained variance of

Table 3.4.1 Operational measures of the share change variables

Variable name	Symbol	Mean	Standard deviation	Operational measure
Percentage change in market share	MSC	2.39	9.06	Percentage rate of change in market share over a 4-year period
Percentage change in sales force	SF	11.3	14.92	Percentage rate of change in sales force expenditures (as a percentage of sales) over a 4-year period
Percentage change in advertising & sales promotion	ASP	9.53	20.37	Percentage rate of change in spending on media advertising and sales promotion (as a percentage of sales) over a 4-year period
Change in relative product quality	PQ	0.80	5.1	Point change in relative product quality over a 4-year period where relative product quality is measured as the percentage of products sold by the business that are superior to competitors in quality minus the percentage of products sold that are inferior to competition products
Change in relative quality of customer services	CS	0.03	0.22	Point change in relative customer services over a 4-year period where the quality of customer services is rated relative to competition on a five-point scale

Change in percentage relative new products	NP	−0.12	4.03	Point change in relative new products over a 4-year period where relative new product is measured as the percentage of sales that are new products minus the percentage of sales that are new products for competitors
Market share beginning	MSB	23.11	17.89	Average market share for the first 2 years of the 4-year period
Growth rate of served market	SMG	11.40	10.42	Percentage rate of change in the size of the served market over the 4-year period
Competitor entry	CI	0.46	0.29	Dummy variable set equal to one when a competitor enters the served market
Competitor exit	CE	0.20	0.40	Dummy variable set equal to one when a competitor exits the served market
Relative percentage new products beginning	NPB	1.06	8.31	Average of relative percentage new products for the first 2 years of the 4-year period

Table 3.4.2 Standardized regression coefficients by industry category

Variable name	Consumer non-durables	Consumer durables	Capital equipment	Raw materials	Component products	Supplies	Services	Distribution	All businesses
Marketing Mix (Controllable)									
Percentage change in sales force	0.468	0.582	0.317	0.193	0.401	0.337	0.309	0.639	0.375
Percentage change in advertising and sales promotion	0.134	0.167	0.146	0.201	0.140	0.125	0.134	0.293	0.134
Percentage change in product quality	0.107	0.146	0.113	0.153	0.183	0.113		0.196	0.108
Percentage change in customer services	0.077		0.072	0.259					0.055
Percentage change in new products	0.097		0.111						0.043
Situational influences (uncontrollable)									
Beginning market share	-0.183		-0.261	-0.180	-0.188	-0.186			-0.168
Served market growth	-0.112	-0.128	-0.213	-0.189	-0.127	-0.153	-0.360		-0.156
Competitor entry	-0.093	-0.095	-0.060		-0.084				-0.048
Competitor exit	0.091					0.106			0.049
Beginning new product	0.131		0.112			0.270	0.204		0.120
Explained variance (R^2)	0.51	0.39	0.45	0.31	0.41	0.35	0.46	0.67	0.37
Sample size (N)	210	146	279	133	346	195	34	33	1377

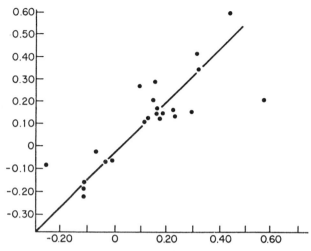

Figure 3.4.2   Pairs of randomly matched variable coefficients

sector-derived change models was considerably larger than the explained variance of the aggregate model constructred from all 1377 businesses.

The fact that the coefficients for a given variable were fairly similar in magnitude across the eight sectors of business warrants further discussion of this result. Therefore, to better illustrate the consistency of these results, Figure 3.4.2 was constructed. This figure represents a plot of pairs of coefficients for a given variable selected at random. For example, since the change in sales force was significant in all eight sectors of business, four pairs of coefficients were selected using a table of random numbers. This was done for each variable to produce the graphic shown in Figure 3.4.2. In this case the correlation between pairs of randomly matched coefficients was 0.82. This level of consistency adds to the credibility of these factors as meaningful correlates of market share change. Furthermore, if we view each sector of business as a dissimilar measure of a business trait that contributes to share change, then there is some value in arguing that there is convergent validity in terms of each variable's sign and relative impact. While it is not the intent of this paper to argue the generic nature of these effects on market share change, it is worth recognizing the consistency in these results across eight diverse categories of business.

VALIDATING ESTIMATED MARKET SHARE CHANGES

While the results are statistically meaningful and managerially useful, before putting this type of planning aid into practice, an evaluation of the share change models was performed. In this evaluation 21 General Electric Company businesses *not* in the SPI research data base were used to evaluate the accuracy of predictions made using the share change models.

The 21 businesses provided information on each of the 10 variables used in the share change equation. Using this information, values for these variables were computed according to the definitions presented in Table 3.4.1. These values were then used respectively to estimate the rate of share change for each of the 21 GE businesses. The estimated rates of share change were then compounded over four periods and multiplied by beginning market shares in order to make a 1980 estimate of market share for each business. The results are presented in Figure 3.4.3.

The average business changed three share points while point change ranged from 0.05 to 12.5 share points. The most accurate share estimate was for business that grew its share from 19 to 21.3. The predicted 1980 share was 21.2. The worst share prediction was for a business that had a 30 percent share that gained 11.5 share points over the 4-year period while the share change model predicted a 3.5 point gain in share. Overall, the results were encouraging as the correlation between predicted shares in 1980 and actual shares was approximately 0.95.

USING THE SHARE CHANGE MODELS

While no single planning model could ever account for the many factors that influence the market share of a business over a 4-year period, the share change models presented in this paper make a reasonable contribution to managing at least some aspects of this process. These models are being used not for predictive purposes, but for evaluative planning purposes. For example, in one application a business with a very large share in a growing market believed it could hold that position over a 4-year period without making any additions to marketing effort. Using the appropriate share change model, we inferred that they would lose five share points if they were to pursue a 'no change' marketing mix strategy. Our comment to the business was not that you can expect to lose five share points in 4 years pursuing a 'no change' strategy, but other OEM businesses in a similar situation have lost this amount of share with a 'no change' strategy.

Recognizing that there are differences in the quality of marketing efforts between businesses, and a great many other influences that we cannot account for in a share change model, we feel most comfortable in using these models as planning aids rather than predictive models. At best, they take into account in a mathematical manner the impact of several key environmental and marketing mix influences. In a planning framework such as the one presented in Figure 3.4.1, we simply want the manager to rethink his strategy when a needed rate of share growth is severely out of line with an expected rate of share growth derived from the share change models we have developed and tested. Used in

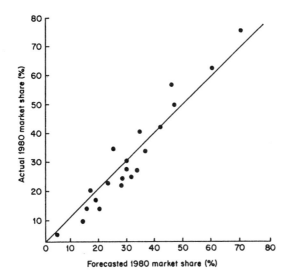

Figure 3.4.3   Actual vs. predicted market share

this manner, we feel we can contribute in a positive way to shaping realistic share goals and assist managers with the level of marketing effort needed to attain a particular market share goal.

REFERENCES

Buzzell, R. D., and F. D. Wiersema (1981). 'Successful share building strategies', *Harvard Business Review*, **59** (Jan.–Feb.), 135–144.

Buzzell, R. D. (1981). 'Modeling changes in market share: a cross-sectional analysis', *Strategic Management Journal*, **2** (Jan.–Feb.), 27–42.

Farris, P., and R. D. Buzzell (1980). 'A comment on "modeling the marketing mix decision for industrial products" ', *Management Science*, **25** (Jan.), 97–100.

Lillien, G. L. (1979). 'ADVISOR 2: modeling the marketing mix decision for industrial planning', *Management Science*, **25** (Feb.), 191–204.

Owens-Illinois, (1981). 'Owens-Illinois: giving up market share to improve profits', *Business Week*, (11 May 1981), pp. 81–82.

Royce, N. S. (1979). 'Generating strategic alternatives'. Business Intelligence Program, Research Report No. 620, SRI International, pp. 1–25.

Schoeffler, S., R. D. Buzzell, and D. F. Heany (1977). 'Impact of strategic planning on profit performance', *Harvard Business Review*, **52** (Mar.–Apr.), 137–145.

Skov, P. B., and C. S. Spetzler (1979). 'Strategic management process'. Business Intelligence Program, Research Report No. 617, SRI International, pp. 1–25.

Wheatley, R. (1980). 'How Perrier found the source of their poster campaign', *Advertising*, **65** (Autumn), 24–26.

Wind, Y., and V. Mahajan (1981). 'Market share: concepts, findings, and directions for future research', *Review of Marketing*, Volume 2.

Xerox, (1981). 'Xerox gets tough on small copiers', *Business Week*, (16 February), p. 82.

3.5

Integrating Financial Portfolio Analysis with Product Portfolio Models*

VIJAY MAHAJAN
Herman W. Lay Professor of Marketing, Southern Methodist University, Dallas

AND

JERRY WIND
The Lauder Professor, The Wharton School, University of Pennsylvania

INTRODUCTION

Over the past few years a number of product/business portfolio models have been proposed. The portfolio perspective requires a company to view itself as offering a variety of product lines, each requiring a certain investment and promising a certain return on that investment. Top management's role is to determine the products or businesses that will comprise the portfolio and to allot funds to them on some rational basis.

In a recent article, Wind and Mahajan (1981) have classified product portfolio models into three broad categories: standardized models, customized models, and finance-oriented models. Examples of standardized models include the Boston Consulting Group's growth/share matrix, the McKinsey/GE business assessment array, the A. D. Little business profile matrix, and the Shell International directional policy matrix. Customized product portfolio models, as compared to the standardized models, allow management greater freedom in selecting the portfolio dimensions and include both a conjoint analysis-based approach with a resource allocation simulator (Wind, 1982) and the analytic hierarchy process (Wind and Saaty, 1980).

The application of financial portfolio models such as the Markowitz risk/return or mean/variance (EV) model to the product mix decisions was originally suggested by Wind (1974), and more recently Cardozo and Wind

* This research was supported by the Center for Marketing Strategy Research of the Wharton School.

(1982) have suggested a modification of the risk/return model which overcomes some of the difficulties involved in applying the conventional risk/return model to the product portfolio decisions. The financial portfolio models have the unique ability to identify an efficient frontier of products or portfolios from which management can select their preferred target portfolio by specifying the desired trade-off between risk and return. That is, the financial portfolio analysis classifies products and portfolios into those dominated by others and those not dominated by others. The undominated or admissible set of product options provides a smaller set from which the optimal choice can be determined.

It has been argued in the financial economics literature (see, for example, Whitmore and Findlay, 1978) that the mean-variance approach is the optimal efficient rule only if the utility function is quadratic and the probability distributions of returns are normal. It has been further pointed out that both assumptions are implausible since the first assumption implies increasing absolute risk aversion and the second excludes consideration of asymmetry or skewness in the probability distributions of returns. These criticisms have led to the development of the stochastic dominance (SD) rules. The SD rules identify the efficient frontier under specific stated assumptions on the nature of the underlying utility functions without the need for subjective estimation of the utility functions. In addition, the SD rules (a) require no prior assumptions concerning the shape of the probability distribution of returns and (b) utilize every point in the probability distribution. Three types of stochastic dominance rules have been generally presented for decision-making under uncertainty: first-order stochastic dominance (FSD), second-order stochastic dominance (SSD), and third-order dominance (TSD).

An application of the SD approach to diagnose the product portfolio of an insurance company (State Farm Fire and Casualty Company) has been provided by Mahajan *et al.* (1982). The approach is also briefly discussed in Appendix A.

The SD approach, although theoretically and empirically superior to the mean-variance approach, has a major drawback when applied to the product portfolio decisions—its sole dependence on the analysis of return distributions. In contrast, standardized and customized product portfolio models suggest other relevant product- and market-related factors (such as share, growth, market attractiveness, business strength, etc.) but tend to ignore the risk and return factors. Since exclusion of such factors in the application of financial portfolio models and the exclusion of risk/return factors from the standardized portfolio models may lead to improper allocation of resources, the objective of this paper is to propose the integration of both approaches.

An approach integrating financial portfolio analysis with product portfolio models is proposed and illustrated. A modified stochastic dominance approach is presented and its results compared and augmented by those of the

GE/McKinsey type product portfolio model. The integrated approach is illustrated next by applying it to the product portfolio of an industrial firm.

AN APPLICATION OF INTEGRATED APPROACH

The potential use of the integrated approach for evaluating and selecting a product portfolio is illustrated for an industrial firm. More specifically, the reported analysis is restricted to six major product lines offered by one of the SBUs of a Fortune 500 company. To maintain confidentiality, products are identified only by numbers.

A conventional stochastic dominance approach

Table 3.5.1 presents the return characteristics of the six product lines for the period 1972–81. This table also includes projected return characteristics for the years 1977–86. The use of projected return characteristics will be discussed later.

Table 3.5.1   Return characteristics of product lines

| | Time period covered | | | |
| | 1972–1981 | | 1977–1986* | |
Product	Mean rate of return	Variance	Mean rate of return	Variance
1	1.683	0.3025	1.741	0.8617
2	3.063	0.1821	2.907	0.0358
3	2.021	1.0452	3.121	0.3242
4	1.017	0.0629	1.182	0.0562
5	0.695	0.1035	0.474	0.0298
6	0.078	0.0564	0.275	0.0010

* Projected data are developed by assuming that the product sales would grow at the market growth rate.

Before constructing the efficient portfolios, the SD and EV rules were used to test the efficiency of the six product lines. These results are summarized in Table 3.5.2. Examination of this table suggests:

(1)   product 2 was identified as an efficient product by all four rules;
(2)   products 4 and 6 were identified as efficient products by the EV rule but were clearly inefficient even by the FSD rule—the least restrictive SD rule;

Table 3.5.2   Results of EV and SD rules for product lines (1972–81)

Product line	EV	Dominated product lines		
		FSD	SSD	TSD
1	—	5,6	5,6	5,6
2	1,3	1,4,5,6	1,3,4,5,6	1,3,4,5,6
3	—	4,5,6	4,5,6	4,5,6
4	5	5,6	5,6	5,6
5	—	6	6	6
6	—	—	—	—
Undominated product lines	2,4,6	2,3	2	2

(3)   product 3 was identified as an efficient product only by the FSD rule.

The results of SSD dominance pattern are presented in Table 3.5.3 indicating the relative dominance of one product over others.

Table 3.5.3   SSD dominance pattern

Product line	1	2	3	4	5	6
1					X	X
2	X		X	X	X	X
3				X	X	X
4					X	X
5						X
6						
Total number of times a product is dominated	1	0	1	2	4	5

Note: Row dominates column.

In order to develop portfolio allocations, it is first necessary to generate all feasible portfolios. This requires generation of different sets of weights by considering combinatorial solutions to the following equation:

$$\sum_{i=1}^{6} w_i = 100$$

where w_i represents the percentage of funds allocation to product i. In order to evaluate manageable number of feasible portfolios only the solutions in increments of 10 percent were considered. In addition, a constraint was imposed to restrict the maximum allocation to any product by 50 percent. This required evaluation of 120 feasible portfolios.

Table 3.2.5 summarizes the results for the EV, SSD, and TSD rules. The application of the SSD and the TSD rules eliminated all but three portfolios. That is, by this rule, these portfolios represent the 'best' portfolios from which the optimal choice can be determined. The EV rule yielded 10 efficient portfolios including the three identified by the SSD and TSD rules. The efficient portfolios identified by the various rules are depicted in Figure 3.5.1. This figure also presents the return characteristics of the present portfolio identified by the current resource allocations to the various products given in the last row of Table 3.5.4. These results suggest that:

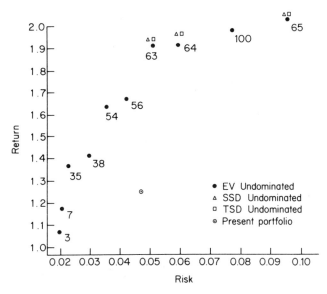

Figure 3.5.1   Portfolio analysis: efficient frontier

(1)   the company's present portfolio is not optimal since the company can get higher return for the same level of risk, or lower risk for the same level of return;

(2)   all three of the SSD and TSD efficient portfolios (Nos. 63, 64, and 65) suggest that maximum resources should be allocated to product 2 (40 percent) and minimum (10 percent) to product 1 and 6;

(3)   for the remaining products—3, 4, and 5—the three SSD/TSD efficient portfolios suggest different allocations.

Based on these results, it can be suggested that, as compared to current allocations, management should increase resource commitment to product 2,

Table 3.5.4 Portfolio analysis: results of EV, SSD, and TSD rules (1972–81)

Portfolio			Undominated set			Portfolio weights					
No.	Mean return	Variance	EV	SSD	TSD	1	2	3	4	5	6
3	1.072	0.02233	X			0.1	0.1	0.1	0.1	0.4	0.2
7	1.166	0.02248	X			0.1	0.1	0.1	0.2	0.4	0.1
35	1.370	0.02396	X			0.1	0.2	0.1	0.1	0.4	0.1
38	1.403	0.02943	X			0.1	0.2	0.1	0.2	0.3	0.1
54	1.607	0.03482	X			0.1	0.3	0.1	0.2	0.3	0.1
56	1.639	0.04354	X			0.1	0.3	0.1	0.2	0.2	0.1
63	1.844	0.05284	X	X	X	0.1	0.4	0.1	0.1	0.2	0.1
64	1.876	0.06482	X	X	X	0.1	0.4	0.1	0.2	0.1	0.1
100	1.943	0.08170	X			0.2	0.4	0.1	0.1	0.1	0.1
65	1.977	0.09592	X	X	X	0.1	0.4	0.2	0.1	0.1	0.1
Present	1.222	0.04629				0.268	0.087	0.125	0.185	0.157	0.178

decrease resource allocations to products 1 and 6, and maintain or slightly increase resource allocations to products 3, 4, and 5.

A modified stochastic dominance approach

The traditional SD approach does suffer, however, from two major limitations: (a) it is based on historical data and not projected data based on a conditional forecast, which takes into account the expected market response function to the planned marketing strategy of the firm and its competitors under a variety of environmental conditions (Wind, 1982); and (b) it assumes that the allocation of resources among the portfolio components can easily be changed ignoring the constraints on management's ability to change the current mix of operations.

Incorporating projected data

Additional SD analyses were conducted using projected data, based on the growth rates for each of the six products. The products were assessed to grow at their respective product class growth rates. A desired modification would be to project the returns based on a conditional forecast model (and simulation). Such an analysis is currently under way but was not completed in time for inclusion in this paper. The right-hand panel of Table 3.5.1 gives the projected return characteristics and the efficient portfolio allocations are presented in Table 3.5.5. The SSD and TSD rules identify three efficient portfolios which are also included in the EV efficient set. Unlike the allocations based on the historical data (Table 3.5.4), all three SSD/TSD efficient portfolios based on the projected data suggest allocating more resources to products 2 and 3.

Adding constraints on management ability to change the current portfolio

Stochastic dominance allows a user (management) to determine the magnitude of resources allocated to each product, including the option of no allocation (zero resources). Yet, in most applications more limited input has been obtained from management focusing on the increment of resources (typically 5 or 10 percent) to be considered as the building blocks of the resource allocation plan. Consistent with this practice the application described in the two earlier sections involved a constraint that the portfolio be based on allocated resources in increments of 10 percent.

Such an overall allocation rule ignores the idiosyncratic characteristics of each of the products and, in particular, the likely market response pattern for each. This information was obtained as part of the management sessions and resulted in the following rules.

Table 3.5.5 Portfolio analysis: results of EV, SSD, and TSD rules for projected data (1977–86)

Portfolio No.	Mean return	Variance	Undominated set EV	SSD	TSD	Portfolio weights 1	2	3	4	5	6
101	1.373	0.01155	X			0.3	0.1	0.1	0.1	0.1	0.3
104	1.464	0.01330	X			0.3	0.1	0.1	0.2	0.1	0.2
86	1.490	0.01355	X			0.2	0.2	0.1	0.1	0.1	0.3
116	1.520	0.01388	X			0.4	0.1	0.1	0.1	0.1	0.2
111	1.636	0.01406	X			0.3	0.2	0.1	0.1	0.1	0.2
96	1.753	0.01608	X			0.2	0.3	0.1	0.1	0.1	0.2
119	1.804	0.01654	X			0.4	0.1	0.1	0.1	0.1	0.1
115	1.900	0.01730	X			0.3	0.3	0.2	0.1	0.1	0.1
114	1.921	0.01922	X			0.3	0.2	0.1	0.1	0.1	0.1
100	2.016	0.01933	X			0.2	0.4	0.2	0.1	0.1	0.1
99	2.038	0.02375	X			0.2	0.3	0.2	0.1	0.1	0.1
65	2.154	0.03011	X	X	X	0.1	0.4	0.2	0.1	0.1	0.1
61	2.176	0.04326	X	X	X	0.1	0.3	0.3	0.1	0.1	0.1
51	2.197	0.06266	X	X	X	0.1	0.2	0.4	0.1	0.1	0.1
Present portfolio	1.452	0.01450				0.268	0.087	0.125	0.185	0.157	0.178

(1)   Do not reduce the allocation of resources to any product by more than 20 percent of current allocation. (This reflects management's assessment of the maximum change they can implement in any given year.)
(2)   Do not change the allocation to product 2 since the market response function suggests that any incremental marketing investment in this product will not result in increased sales, and a decrease in investment will result in decreased sales.
(3)   Do not increase the allocation to the products by more than 25 percent of current allocation.

Incorporating these decision rules with the projected returns for the six products resulted in the SD portfolios given in Table 3.5.6.

The application of the EV rule yielded 13 efficient portfolios and only two of these portfolios (Nos. 196 and 170) are included in the SSD set and one in the TSD set (No. 170). Keeping the resource commitment to product 2 at the current level, the two SSD portfolios suggest the following increase (or decrease) in resource commitments:

| Portfolio | Products | | | | | |
No.	1	3	4	5	6
196	20%	10%	same	−20%	−20%
170	10%	20%	10%	−20%	−20%

That is:

(1)   increase resource commitment to products 1 and 3;
(2)   decrease resource commitment to products 5 and 6;
(3)   increase or keep the resource commitment to product 4 at the current level.

It is interesting to point out that the portfolio based on the current allocation of resources (bottom row in Table 3.5.6) was identified inefficient by all the efficiency rules.

Adding a market attractiveness–product strength model

The SD-based allocations do not take into consideration other relevant product- and market-related factors. To obtain further insights into the attractiveness of these products, a McKinsey/GE type portfolio matrix was developed. Top management identified 21 variables as measures of market attractiveness and 12 variables as measures of product strength. These

Table 3.5.6 Constrained portfolio analysis results of EV, SSD, and TSD rules projected data (1977–86)

Portfolio No.	Mean return	Variance	Undominated set EV	SSD	TSD	Portfolio weights* 1	2	3	4	5	6
171	1.424	0.01272	X			0.322	0.087	0.101	0.149	0.126	0.214
172	1.440	0.01300	X			0.322	0.087	0.101	0.167	0.126	0.196
173	1.456	0.01330	X			0.322	0.087	0.101	0.186	0.126	0.179
183	1.487	0.01348	X			0.321	0.087	0.124	0.147	0.125	0.195
184	1.493	0.01375	X			0.321	0.087	0.125	0.148	0.141	0.178
187	1.503	0.01381	X			0.321	0.087	0.124	0.166	0.125	0.177
188	1.509	0.01407	X			0.321	0.087	0.125	0.166	0.141	0.160
192	1.528	0.01411	X			0.322	0.087	0.138	0.148	0.126	0.178
193	1.534	0.01435	X			0.322	0.087	0.138	0.149	0.142	0.161
194	1.545	0.01447	X			0.322	0.087	0.138	0.167	0.126	0.161
195	1.550	0.01470	X			0.322	0.087	0.138	0.167	0.142	0.143
196	1.561	0.01485	X	X		0.322	0.087	0.138	0.185	0.126	0.143
170	1.569	0.01605	X	X	X	0.294	0.087	0.149	0.203	0.125	0.142
Current portfolio	1.452	0.01450				0.268	0.087	0.125	0.185	0.157	0.178

* Weights do not exactly add up to one because of rounding errors.

variables are listed in Appendix B. The management team was also asked to rate the importance of the various factors, and evaluate the six products on each of the factors using a nine-point scale. This evaluation was done separately for each relevant market segment. Once all these evaluations were completed, the team was asked to agree on an overall evaluation of each product on the two dimensions. The final position of each product on the two portfolio dimensions was obtained after presenting the group with the calculated position of each product (on the weighted factors by segment) and discussing the results. The resulting consensus position of the six products on the two-dimensional matrix are depicted in Figure 3.5.2. The results suggest the following:

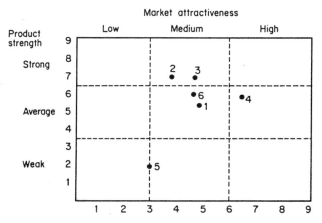

Figure 3.5.2   Overall perceived product strength and market attractiveness of the current drugs

(1) The company does not have any products in the high market attractive-ness and high product strength cell.
(2) Products 2 and 3 are the only 'best' products in the portfolio having strong product strength and medium market attractiveness. Note that these are the only two products identified as the efficient products by FSD (see Table 3.5.2).
(3) Products 1 and 6 fall into average product strength and medium market attractiveness cell.
(4) Product 4 is of average strength but in a highly attractive market.
(5) Product 5 is a weak product possessing weak product strength and low market attractiveness.

Following the resource allocation guidelines suggested by the traditional McKinsey/GE type portfolio analysis, the following recommendations can be offered for the six products:

(1)   invest or increase resource allocations to products 2, 3 and 4;
(2)   maintain resource commitments to products 1 and 6;
(3)   divest or decrease resource allocation to product 5.

Given the results of modified stochastic dominance (Table 3.5.6) and the market attractiveness/product strength model (Figure 3.5.2), it is now possible to integrate these two models to develop resource allocations. (Note that resource allocation to product 2 is kept at the current level in Table 3.5.6).

(1)   The modified SD, as well as the market attractiveness/product strength analysis, suggests decreasing resource commitment to product 5.
(2)   Both the analyses suggest increasing resource allocations to products 3 and 4.
(3)   The two analyses differ in terms of their recommendations for products 1 and 6. The SD analysis suggests that the resource commitment to product 1 should be increased and the resource commitment to product 6 should be decreased. Although both of these products fall into average product strength and medium market attractiveness cell in the portfolio matrix, it is clear that the SD analysis of returns indicate supporting product 1 but not product 6.

The above analysis suggests that the integration of financial portfolio analysis results with product portfolio models generates better insights in determining the relative potential of the various product lines and provides better guidelines for resource allocation.

CONCLUSIONS

Increased recognition of the importance of product portfolio analysis and decisions as an integral part of a firm's market planning efforts has led to an emergence of a number of portfolio models. As demonstrated by Wind *et al.* (1983), depending upon the measures used to operationalize portfolio dimensions, various standardized models can classify the same products differently, leading to different product designations and resource allocation guidelines. However, the various portfolio models tend to emphasize different portfolio objectives (e.g. management of cash flows in the case of the BCG approach and return on investment in the case of the McKinsey/GE business assessment array) and offer different levels of flexibility to conduct portfolio analysis. Given the proliferation of portfolio models, it is imperative that attempts be made to integrate the various models to take advantage of their unique capabilities to develop reliable portfolio analysis. This paper has proposed the integration of the basic concepts of financial portfolio analysis, particularly those of the stochastic dominance rules, with the GE/McKinsey type portfolio approaches. Such a hybrid approach offers several advantages:

(1) Through the SD approach, a focus on two conceptually desirable dimensions of return and risk. These are especially relevant since most standardized portfolio models do not include them explicitly.
(2) Whereas the standardized portfolio models focus on *individual* product (product line or business) evaluation, financial portfolio analysis focuses on *portfolios* of products (product lines or businesses) and allows for an allocation of resources reflecting projected data and various management constraints.
(3) The financial portfolio analysis clearly classifies products and portfolios into those dominated by others and those not dominated by others. The undominated or admissible set of product options provides a smaller set from which the optimal choice can be determined. In this respect, the stochastic dominance approach (as compared with the traditional risk/return (EV) approach) requires fewer restrictions on the nature of the underlying utility functions or return distributions. It thus provides an effective analytical tool to screen the available alternatives without the subjective estimation of the utility function.
(4) The SD approach allows the evaluation of alternative resource allocation plans. As shown in Tables 3.5.4–3.5.6 each of the portfolios is defined in terms of specific products, the specific percentage of the total portfolio allocated to each product, and the return and risk (variance) of each portfolio.
(5) The determination of the target portfolio reflects not only the expected risk and return of each product but also management's judgement concerning the market attractiveness and product strength of each product (across its relevant market segments).

Integration of financial portfolio analysis approaches with product portfolio models results in a target portfolio which is quite different from the one generated by either of the approaches separately. This is clearly highlighted in Table 3.5.7.

The major implications of this study are: (a) whenever possible, it is advisable to use more than a single portfolio approach; (b) a hybrid approach based on a modified stochastic dominance and the GE/McKinsey type approach is especially attractive.

Further integration of this hybrid approach with a more comprehensive customized portfolio approach has been recently designed and implemented (Wind and Mahajan, 1982). This approach is similar in spirit to the hybrid approach described here but differs from it in a number of significant ways. It not only incorporates the modified stochastic dominance with the GE/

Table 3.5.7 A comparison of the recommendations of the various approaches

Product No.	Conventional stochastic dominance (Table 3.5.4)	Modified stochastic dominance (Table 3.5.6)	Market attractiveness/product strength matrix (Figure 3.5.2)	Integrated approach (Table 3.5.6 and Figure 3.5.2)
1	Decrease resources	Increase resources	Maintain	Increase resources
2	Increase resources	No change	Increase resources	No change
3	Maintain	Increase resources	Increase resources	Increase resources
4	Maintain	Maintain/Increase resources	Increase resources	Increase resources
5	Maintain	Decrease resources	Decrease resources/divest	Decrease resources/divest
6	Decrease resources	Decrease resources	Maintain	Decrease resources

McKinsey approach but also includes a synergy analysis (note that approaches such as the GE/McKinsey classify products and ignore any positive or negative synergy among them), and a functional requirement analysis (what are the support functions required to deliver the desired portfolio?) and incorporates all these approaches using the analytic hierarchy framework which provides the methodology for generation and evaluation of portfolio strategies.

APPENDIX A: STOCHASTIC DOMINANCE*

The financial approach to the portfolio selection problem assumes that the profits from portfolio items (such as product lines, stocks, bonds, etc.) are random variables, and estimates concerning their distribution (subjective or objective) are known. Furthermore, the rates of profit for different items may be correlated and hence the need to examine the portfolio items collectively. The expected rate of return on a portfolio is simply the weighted average of the expected rates of return of the items contained in that portfolio, i.e.:

$$\bar{R}_p = \sum_{i=1}^{m} w_i R_i \quad \text{and} \quad \sum_{i=1}^{m} w_i = 1 \tag{1}$$

where w_i is the portion of funds invested in item i, R_i is the expected value of return for item i, m is the total number of items in the portfolio, and $\bar{R}_p$ is the expected rate of return for the portfolio. If variance is used as the measure of risk associated with a portfolio, it may be obtained by

$$V_p = \sum_{i=1}^{m} \sum_{j=1}^{m} w_i w_j \sigma_{ij} \tag{2}$$

where V_p is the portfolio variance, w_i and w_j are the portion of funds invested in items i and j, respectively, and σ_{ij} is the covariance between returns of items i and j.

The systematic steps which characterize the portfolio selection decision may be stated:

(1) *Determine all possible items to be considered in the portfolio and generate all feasible portfolios.* The major objective of this step is to specify a finite number (m) of items and generate a set of feasible portfolios. The number of feasible portfolios can be determined by generating combinational solutions to the equation $\sum_{i=1} w_i = 1$ within the constraints imposed on the values of w_i.

(2) *Generate the admissible (efficient or undominated) portfolios.* The objective here is to reduce the large number of feasible portfolios to a smaller number using certain 'efficient' rules. These rules are derived by

* The appendix is adopted from Mahajan *et al.* (1982).

making certain stated assumptions on the nature of the investor's underlying utility function. The reduced number of portfolios are termed as efficient, admissible, or undominated portfolios. Although a number of effficient rules have been proposed in the financial literature, this paper concentrated on mean-variance (EV) and stochastic dominance (SD) rules for generating efficient product portfolios.

(3) *Determine the optimal portfolio from the admissible portfolios.* The efficient rules provide a mechanism to divide the feasible portfolios into two groups: those dominated by others and those not dominated by others. The undominated or admissible portfolios provide a smaller set of alternatives from which the optimal choice can be made by obtaining further information on the investor's utility function (risk/return trade-off).

The most widely used efficiency criterion for portfolio selection is the mean–variance (EV) rule suggested by Markowitz. Since the decisions about investment may be viewed as choices among alternative probability distributions of returns, the EV rule suggests that, for risk-averse individuals, the admissible set may be obtained by discarding those investments with a lower mean and a higher variance. That is, in a choice between two investments, designated by return distributions F and G, respectively, a risk-averse investor is presumed to prefer F to G, or to be indifferent between the two if the mean of F is as large as the mean of G and the variance of F (reflecting the associated risk) is not greater than the variance of G, i.e., if $\mu_F \geq \mu_G$ and $\sigma_F \leq \sigma_G$. Furthermore, if at least one of these inequalities is strict, then some investors prefer F to G in the strict sense, and F is said to dominate G in the sense of EV. In this case, G can be eliminated from the admissible set. If only one of the inequalities holds, the selection depends on the individual's personal mean–variance trade-off, and neither F nor G can be eliminated under the EV dominance rule. The rule can be applied easily to the portfolio selection problem by ordering all portfolios by increasing means and excluding any portfolio i such that the variance of portfolio i is greater than or equal to the variance of portfolio j where $i < j$.

In spite of its popularity, the mean–variance approach has been subject to serious criticisms. It has been argued that the EV rule is the optimal efficient rule only if the utility function is quadratic and the probability distributions of returns are normal. It has been further pointed out that both assumptions are implausible since the first assumption implies increasing absolute risk aversion and the second excludes consideration of asymmetry or skewness in the probability distributions of returns. An important result of these criticisms of the EV approach has been the development of stochastic dominance rules. (For a state-of-the-art review, see Whitmore and Findlay, 1978).

Stochastic dominance is a relationship between pairs of probability distributions; in particular, it involves comparison of the relative positions of the cumulative distribution functions. Three types of stochastic dominance rules have been generally presented for decision-making under uncertainty: first-order stochastic dominance (FSD), second-order stochastic dominance (SSD), and third-order stochastic dominance (TSD). These rules have been derived by considering certain stated assumptions on the form of the utility function U. If U', U'', and U''' stand for the first, second, and third derivatives of the utility function, the FSD rule assumes that $U' \geqslant 0$; the SSD rule assumes that $U' \geqslant 0$ and $U'' \leqslant 0$, and the TSD rule assumes that $U' \geqslant 0$, $U'' \leqslant 0$, and $U''' \geqslant 0$. That is, the FSD rule requires only that the first derivative of the utility function be positive throughout; therefore, it allows risk preference, risk indifference, or risk aversion. The SSD rule eliminates risk preference by adding the restriction that the second derivative be everywhere non-positive. Finally, the TSD rule requires that the third derivative be everywhere non-positive. Finally, the TSD rule requires that the third derivative of the utility function be everywhere non-negative. These assumptions are clearly more reasonable than the assumptions of a quadratic utility function with increasing absolute risk aversion implied by the EV rule. To summarize, the admissible set of portfolios generated by:

(1)   the FSD rule provides the efficient set for all decision-makers with utility functions increasing in wealth;
(2)   the SSD rule provides the efficient set for the subset of decision-makers having increasing utility functions and risk-aversion;
(3)   the TSD rule provides the efficient set for the subset of risk-averse decision-makers with decreasing absolute risk.

The optimal portfolio for the investor can then be determined, based on his/her risk–return trade-off, from among the relevant smaller set of admissible choices.

The three specific stochastic dominance rules were developed originally for continuous probability functions. Yet, since the true form of the probability distributions is rarely known with complete certainty, to apply the three SD rules to portfolio selection it is often necessary to estimate the underlying structures of the distributions using discrete sets of sample observations. These discrete sets may be determined by sampling various points from the continuous distributions. The first-, second-, and third-order stochastic dominance rules for discrete observations are defined as:

FSD

The discrete distribution, $f(x)$, is said to dominate the discrete distribution, $g(x)$, by FSD if and only if $F_1(x_n) \leqslant G_1(x_n)$ for all $n \leqslant N$ with at least one strict inequality, and N is the total number of discrete observations in both distributions, where:

$$F_1(x_n) = \sum_{i=1}^{n} f(x_i), \quad n = 2, 3, \ldots, N \tag{3}$$

$G_1(x_n)$ is similarly defined.

SSD

The discrete distribution, $f(x)$, is said to dominate the discrete distribution, $g(x)$, by SSD if and only if $F_2(x_n) \leq G_2(x_n)$ for all $n \leq N$ with at least one strict inequality, where:

$$F_2(x_n) = \sum_{i=2}^{n} F_1(x_{i-1})(x_i - x_{i-1}), \quad n = 2, 3, \ldots, N \tag{4}$$

$F_2(x_i) = 0$. $G_2(x_n)$ is similarly defined.

TSD

The discrete distribution, $f(x)$, is said to dominate the discrete distribution, $g(x)$, by TSD if and only if $F_3(x_n) \leq G_3(x_n)$ for all $n \leq N$ with at least one strict inequality, where

$$F_3(x_n) = 1/2 \sum_{i=2}^{n} [F_2(x_i) + F_2(x_{i-1})](x_i - x_{i-1}), \quad n = 2, 3, \ldots, N \tag{5}$$

and $F_3(x_i) = 0$. $G_3(x_n)$ is similarly defined.

Stochastic dominance provides a powerful tool for portfolio analysis since (a) no prior assumptions concerning the shape of the probability function are required, and (b) every point in the probability distribution is utilized. The SD approach, however, is not without its limitations. The estimation of each probability function for each portfolio for a practical application may be very time-consuming in comparison to the EV approach, which requires estimation of only two parameters—mean and variance. For example, consider the computational requirements of generating the EV and SSD admissible set for 50 portfolios, each having 25 observations. To calculate either requires that each portfolio be compared with every other portfolio; thus there would be 1225 comparisons. For the EV efficient set each comparison involves two parameters (mean and variance) or a total of 2450 paired comparisons. For the SSD comparison each test requires 50 data points (25 from each portfolio) or a total of 61,250 paired comparisons. Since the FSD probabilities must be calculated prior to the calculation of the SSD probabilities the total number of paired comparisons would be 122,500. As the number of portfolios and/or the number of sample data points increases, the number of calculations may become prohibitive.

Furthermore, the EV approach has been formulated as a quadratic programming problem. This implies that it is not necessary to generate all the feasible portfolios since the algorithms determine the optimal allocation of resources across the product lines and hence the efficient portfolios. The SD approach, on the other hand, does not utilize an optimizing algorithm to determine the allocation of resources. This necessitates the determination and examination of all feasible portfolios to identify the efficient ones. In the presence of a large number of portfolios the implementation of SD again may be computationally prohibitive.

Appendix B: The factors used to assess the market attractiveness and business strength

Market attractiveness factors	Product strength factors
The market	*Positioning (differentiation)*
Expected market size-$	Uniqueness (me-too vs.
Expected market size-Units	innovation)
Expected growth rate-$	Positioning
Expected growth rate-Units	Life cycle stage
Demand cyclicality/seasonality	Customer loyalty
Loyalty-switching pattern	One time vs. continued usage
Market has a need	
One time vs. continued usage	
Competition	*Market Response Functions*
Availability of substitutes	Pricing
Number of current competitors	Advertising
Strength of current competitors	Sampling
Potential competition	Other promotions
Current level and growth of generic	Sales force
Private label competition	
Marketing activities	*Expected profitability*
Price level (elasticity)	Price levels
Total promotion expenditures	Cost of goods
Total sales force effectiveness	Marketing/promotional expenditure
Promotional effectiveness	Synergistic effects
New product activities and acceptance	*Susceptability to envirnomental forces*
Level of new product entry	Legal/regulatory problems/
Market responsiveness to new products	opportunities
	Entry of generic
Environment	
Legal/regulatory problems/opportunities	
Likely development of new technology	

REFERENCES

Cardozo, R., and Y. Wind (1982). 'Applying a risk–return approach to product portfolio analysis and strategy'. Wharton School Working Paper.

Mahajan, V., Y. Wind, and J. W. Bradford (1982). 'Stochastic dominance rules for product portfolio models', *Special Studies in Management Science, Marketing Planning Models*, Andy Zoltners (ed.) North-Holland, New York.

Saaty, T. L. (1980). *The Analytic Hierarchy Process: Planning, Priority Setting and Resource Allocation*. McGraw-Hill, New York.

Whitmore, G. A., and M. C. Findlay (1978). *Stochastic Dominance*. Lexington Books, Lexington, MA.

Wind, Y. (1974). 'Product portfolio analysis: a new approach to the product mix decisions', *Combined Proceedings*, Curhan, R. C. (ed.). American Marketing Association, Chicago, pp. 460–464.

Wind, Y. (1982). *Product Policy: Concepts, Methods and Strategy*. Addison-Wesley, Reading, MA.

Wind, Y., and V. Mahajan (1981). 'Designing product and business portfolios', *Harvard Business Review*, **59** (Jan.–Feb.), 155–165.

Wind, Y., and V. Mahajan (1982), 'Toward a marketing oriented integrated portfolio system'. Wharton School Working Paper.

Wind, Y., V. Mahajan, and D. Swire (1983). 'An empirical comparison of standardized portfolio models', *Journal of Marketing*, **47** (Spring), 89–99.

Wind, Y., and T. L. Saaty (1980). 'Marketing applications of the analytic hierarchy process', *Management Science*, **26** (July), 641–658.

Strategic Marketing and Management
Edited by H. Thomas and D. Gardner
© 1985 John Wiley & Sons Ltd

3.6

Experience Curves: Evidence, Empirical Issues, and Applications

DAVID B. MONTGOMERY
Robert A. Magowan Professor of Marketing, Graduate School of Business, Stanford University

AND

GEORGE S. DAY
Professor of Marketing, University of Toronto

The notion that unit costs and prices decline systematically in real terms as cumulative volume increases has been one of the most widely discussed and utilized concepts in the evolution of strategic management during the past two decades. Labeled the experience effect by the Boston Consulting Group (BCG) this phenomenon has had major impact upon corporate strategy, marketing strategy, and the strategy literature. Further, the experience effect often plays a substantial role in determining the outcome of competition in both domestic and international markets as it did in the world motorcycle industry (BCG, 1975).

Nevertheless, application of the experience effect presents a bewildering array of practical problems, whose solution is at best only partially understood. Further, the strategic implications of the phenomenon have been the subject of growing controversy (Kiechel, 1981). Day and Montgomery (1983) diagnose certain practical issues which need to be considered in applying the experience curve, and explore some of the strategic implications and delusions which have emerged. The purpose of the present paper is to analyze certain of these empirical issues in greater depth and to discuss further the application of experience curves in strategy, policy, and marketing models. Before turning to these issues, attention will be given to an overview of the experience phenomenon and some of the empirical evidence relating to it.

THE EXPERIENCE CURVE

The experience curve has as its antecedent the learning curve, first observed in connection with man-hours required to produce an aircraft. The learning curve (see Yelle, 1979 for an extensive review) reflects the general observation that factor input requirements, such as man-hours per unit, tend to decline systematically as the cumulative number of units produced increases. For example, Hirshman (1964) reports that man-hours required per barrel of refined petroleum decreased by 30 percent each time the cumulative number of barrels produced doubled between 1860 and 1962. Similarly for steel, man-hours per ton declined 30 percent for each doubling of cumulative tons of steel produced between 1867 and 1956. Factor output productivity has also been found to be associated with cumulative output. Fusfeld (1973) shows such a relation between pounds of rice produced per acre and cumulative rice production in Japan over the past 1200 years. Interestingly, the Japanese experience has witnessed accelerated productivity gains in modern times, beginning with the 'opening of Japan' in 1854–68. The exposure to Western influence led to accelerated productivity gains due to the use of better fertilizer, better credit facilities, double cropping, and more intensive methods of farming.

In the mid-1960s BCG (1972) generalized the notion of the learning curve to apply to all costs (e.g. marketing, distribution, administrative), not just production costs, as well as to price. Thus, the experience curve postulates that all value-added costs and prices will decline systematically in real terms as cumulative experience or volume increases. In cost terms, the usual form of the experience curve is

$$C_n = C_1 n^{-\lambda} \tag{1}$$

where: C_n = real cost of the nth unit
C_1 = real cost of the first unit
n = cumulative number of units
λ = elasticity of unit costs with respect to cumulative volume.

A similar form, albeit with a different elasticity, is generally posited for price which is substituted for cost in equation (1). This model is linear in the logarithm and may be estimated using regression analysis when data are available. Each time cumulative experience doubles, cost (price) will decline to

$$k = 2^{-\lambda} \tag{2}$$

percent of its previous level. Thus if cost (price) declines to 80 percent of its previous level, the experience curve is said to be an 80 percent experience curve or have an 80 percent slope.

Difficulties in empirical application may arise in measuring costs and prices, and are discussed in the empirical issues section. Confusion and inappropriate strategy conclusions may result if a firm simplistically tries to place its competitors on its own experience curve. For reasons discussed in the applications section, cross-sectional or competitive cost comparison curves will often have a higher slope than a firm's own cost experience curve.

Several caveats should be noted with respect to an experience curve. Firstly, the curves are postulated to apply to real costs and prices. This means that in applications an index must be used which will render costs and price at different points in time on a comparable basis. Ideally one would want an index that reflects the changing value of money. The GNP deflator is often used for this purpose. If an index is used which relates too closely to the industry, the experience effect may be washed out due to the index itself capturing a substantial portion of the productivity gains in the industry. Secondly, it should be noted that the curves apply to cumulative experience and not to calendar time. While cumulative experience and calendar time-related cost and price declines will tend to be positively associated, the experience curve is postulated to apply to cumulative experience. Of course, experience will tend to cumulate faster in calendar time during periods of rapid growth and relatively early in a product's life cycle. Thirdly, the curve is usually intended to apply to the value-added component of a product or service. To be sure, raw material input costs may also follow an experience curve, but these may be expected to follow a curve having a different elasticity since the experience progress will depend upon suppliers' performance and is not under the direct control of the firm. Fourthly, the real cost declines reflected in the experience curve are not automatic. Rather, they may be realized by creative and intelligent management operating in a competitive milieu. Finally, there are other caveats relative to product-market definition, the appropriate units of experience, and joint product economies. They are discussed in Day and Montgomery (1983) and are noted below as appropriate.

EVIDENCE OF EXPERIENCE CURVES

A variety of evidence supports the concept of the experience curve. Most of the evidence is graphical, with a substantial proportion prepared by BCG in client assignments (BCG, 1972). These examples illustrate that the experience curve is international in scope, applies to services as well as manufacturing, applies to marketing costs as well as manufacturing costs, and may be found for a wide variety of consumer and industrial products.

While the graphical evidence is impressive, it does not support a more scientific assessment of experience curves. Fortunately, several studies which are more carefully presented do lend credence to the experience phenomenon. Although this review is by no means exhaustive, several studies of cost and price experience curves will be examined to illustrate the nature of the results and the typical values of experience slopes.

Using data from BCG case files which had never before been assembled for statistical analysis, Wooley (1972) developed cost experience curves for 18 products from 10 companies. Although he did not test alternative specifications of the cost functions, and no check was made for autocorrelation (both of which are nearly universal defects in experience curve studies), he did select his sample carefully to avoid many of the difficult application issues discussed below and in Day and Montgomery (1973). The GNP deflator was used to relate costs to a common base. His results, which are presented in Table 3.6.1, are strongly consistent with the existence of cost experience effects in all of these cases. Over 80 percent of the adjusted R^2s were above 0.8 and all of the experience elasticities, λ's, were significant at the 0.05 level. In fact, 23 of the 25 λ's are significant at the more stringent 0.01 level. The median experience curve slope, k, was 77.5 percent and over three quarters of the estimated slopes

Table 3.6.1   Wooley (1972) cost experience curves

Equation number	Product name	No. of observations	λ	$\bar{R}^2$	k
1	Chem Film	8	0.330	0.92	79.6
1a	Chem Film (less resin cost)	8	0.301	0.72	81.2
2	Chem Treated Paper	6	0.225	0.99	85.6
3	Fab. Knit	5	0.256	0.97	83.7
4	Knit	5	0.451	0.96	73.2
5	Finishing and Dye	5	0.453	0.92	73.0
6	Facial Tissue (1933–1945)	13	0.249	0.96	84.1
6a	Facial Tissue (1946–1966)	14	0.253	0.94	83.9
7	Steel	13	0.952	0.92	51.6
8	Lawnmower # 1	4	0.309	0.78	80.7
9	Lawnnmower # 2	4	0.460	0.96	72.7
10	Complex Elec. Tube	11	0.557	0.92	67.9
11	Plastic Film	11	0.492	0.96	71.1
12	Electronic Sensor	6	0.569	0.95	67.4
13	Elec. Record Instr.	10	1.17	0.89	44.4
14	Elec. Meas. Instr. # 1	7	0.165	0.89	89.1
14a	Elec. Meas. Instr. # 1 (less joint costs)	7	0.261	0.96	83.4
15	Elec. Meas. Instr. # 2	9	0.119	0.55	92.0
15a	Elec. Meas. Instr. # 2 (less joint costs)	9	0.236	0.83	84.8
16	Elec. Meas. Instr. # 3	9	0.113	0.34	92.5
16a	Elec. Meas. Instr. # 3 (less joint costs)	9	0.255	0.63	83.8
17	Elec. Comp. Assem. # 1	7	0.282	0.92	82.2
17a	Elec. Comp. Assem. # 1 (less joint costs)	7	0.345	0.95	78.7
18	Elec. Comp. Assem. # 2	7	0.326	0.96	79.7
18a	Elec. Comp. Assem. # 2 (less joint costs))	7	0.512	0.96	70.1

Notes: $\bar{R}^2$ is adjusted R^2.
λ is the experience curve elasticity.
k is the experience curve slope.

were between 70 and 90 percent, the usual range suggested by BCG based upon their client studies.

Further statistical evidence consistent with a cost experience curve was found by Preston and Keachie (1964). Pooling data from five pieces of radar equipment to yield a total of 22 observations, they found significant experience curves for both unit labor costs and unit total costs. Although no formal pooling test was made, the authors argued that the pooling of data was appropriate given the similarity in the technologies of the five products. The λ's were significant at the 0.01 level in both cases and the R^2 values were 0.9 for both equations. Cumulative experience was found to have a more powerful effect on unit labor costs, where the slope was 78.7 percent, than upon unit total costs, where the slope was 86.9 percent.

Evidence to support the existence of price experience curves comes from studies by Stobaugh and Townsend (1975) and Lieberman (1981). Stobaugh and Townsend studied price changes over intervals of 1, 3, 5, and 7 years for 82 petrochemicals. In addition to cumulative industry experience their model included competition (number of producers), the degree of product standardization, and static scale economies (average production per producer). Their results indicate that cumulative industry experience is a statistically significant predictor of price changes over each of the time intervals. However, the models explained only a modest proportion of the variation in price with R^2s ranging from 0.03 for 1-year price changes to 0.27 for 7-year price changes. The price experience slopes ranged from 88.9 percent for 1-year to 92.7 percent for 7 years. Lieberman's (1981) study of 3-year price changes for 37 products in the chemical processing industry also found significant effects of cumulative experience on price changes. He found a much steeper slope of 77 percent and a better fit with R^2's above 0.5. Together, these studies confirm the existence of price experience curves, but indicate that the price curves promise less forecasting leverage than the cost experience curves discussed above.

Sources of the experience effect

Given that there is evidence to support the existence of an experience effect, the question arises as to why this effect appears. There are three major sources of the effect: learning, technological advances, and scale effects.

Learning

Learning encompasses the increasing efficiency of all aspects of labor input (production, maintenance, supervision, marketing, sales, administration) as the people involved gain experience in the activity in question. This might be termed the 'practice effect', a phenomenon familiar to any parent who has attempted to assemble Christmas toys. It also entails the discovery of better ways to organize work via improved methods and work specialization (doing one-half as much two times as often). It also entails getting better performance from production equipment as personnel become better acquainted with it. For example, Abell and Hammond (1979) note that the capacity of a fluid catalytic cracking unit typically 'grows' about 50 percent over a 10-year period as operators, engineers, and managers gain experience in operating the unit. Similarly, Joskow and Rozanski (1979) found that learning by doing increases the effective capacity or output of a particular piece of nuclear equipment by approximately 5 percent per year. The reason is that with experience workers were more effective in using and maintaining the equipment and various technical 'bugs' were identified and corrected. These latter two examples show how learning by doing even impacts upon scale in certain cases.

A novel view of learning is presented by Rosenberg (1982) who develops a concept of learning by using. Learning by using produces gains which result from subsequent use of a product, in contrast to learning by doing where the gains result from improvements made internal to the production process. Arguing that learning by using will become increasingly important in a high-technology economy, Rosenberg illustrates his case by examples from aviation. He writes:

> the maintenance history of particular engines, especially the turbojet generation, reflects a very strong learning by using dimension, where prior knowledge based upon reciprocating propeller engines was largely inadequate to anticipate the durability and reliability of the gas turbine engines (indeed, that earlier experience turned out to be positively misleading).

Technological improvements

These also contribute to the experience effect. New production processes, especially in capital-intensive industries, often contribute substantial economies. For example, Golden Wonder's introduction of continuous-flow potato chip manufacture versus the traditional batch frying mode enabled them to achieve substantial economies in heating and quality control and played an important part in Golden Wonder's achievement of market share parity with the formerly dominant firm (Beevan, 1974). Changes in the resource mix, such as automation replacing labor, also provide a technology-driven basis for the experience effect. Process and product changes which produce yield improvements are yet another source of experience effects. Product standardization and redesign are also sources of the effect, as in the economies achieved in the automobile industry by modularization of the engine, chassis, and transmission production and the substitution of plastic, synthetic fiber, and rubber for leather in ski boots.

Scale effects

Scale effects may also be a source of experience gains. Plant-level scale economies result from capital cost savings (as the scale of a plant increases, the capital costs increase less fast), an increased potential for division of labor, and better utilization of indivisible resources. Firm level scale economies derive from overhead economies (e.g. R&D and top management), economies in bulk handling (e.g. volume discounts), inventory economies, and marketing and financial economies.

Decomposing the experience curve

There are a few empirical results suggestive of the relative importance of the three main effects of learning, technology, and scale. These are suggestive only and do not reflect a scientific sampling of circumstances. Perhaps the most that can be said is that they appear likely to apply to chemical and related industries, which provide the main source of the results. Hollander (1965) in a study of the sources of efficiency increases at DuPont rayon plants concluded that only 10–15 percent of the efficiency gains were due to scale effects, whereas the remainder was accounted for by technology and learning. Of the remainder due to technology and learning, between 32 and 75 percent (depending on the plant) were ascribed to learning. Hence scale seems relatively less important while technology and learning have major impact. Interestingly, Hollander found that the largest proportion of the technology-driven cost reductions were due to minor technical changes, suggesting a dynamic process of small incremental change akin to Quinn's (1981) 'logical incrementalism'.

In their study of unit labor and total costs for five pieces of radar equipment, Preston and Keachie (1964) also found that cumulative experience (learning) was a far more powerful predictor of cost declines than was scale of production (measured as lot size). Here again learning appears to play a substantial role.

Similar results for price experience were found by Stobough and Townsend (1975) and Lieberman (1981). The former report that static scale economies did not account for price changes to the same extent that the confounded experience variables of learning, technology, and dynamic scale did. The latter found a 71 percent experience curve when scale, new plant introductions, and new competitive entry were implicity confounded with cumulative volume while the slope rose to 77 percent when these variables were separately analyzed. Thus, while scale plays an obvious role, it does not, in these instances, appear to be a dominant component of the experience effect.

For strategic application of the experience curve it is important to understand the basis for experience gains. For example, if experience gains are vested in the current management and employees, care must be taken that personnel and compensation policies take account of the need to maintain this human capital. Further, as Porter (1979) has noted, if costs are falling due to economies of scale via more efficient, automated facilities and/or vertical integration, then cumulative volume may be unimportant to relative cost position. The key issue is that it is vital to understand the reasons behind cost declines in any given situation.

EMPIRICAL ISSUES

This section will consider a variety of issues of importance in developing empirical estimates of experience curves. These issues concern aggregation, errors in the variables, the functional specification of the experience relation, and measurement.

Aggregation

The aggregation issue deals with the level at which the usual experience curve represented by equation (1) should be specified. Consider a product which is produced by a two-step process, each step of which may be characterized by equation (1), albeit with different λs. The total unit cost for the product would then be given by

$$C_n = C_1 n^{-\lambda_1} + C_2 n^{-\lambda_2} \qquad (3)$$

which clearly has a different form from equation (1) and further is no longer linear in the logarithm. Consequently, if each cost component follows equation (1), the total unit cost logically cannot. Although this aggregation issue was recognized by Conway and Schultz (1959), it seems to have been quite generally ignored in practice. As experience accumulates, the total unit cost will tend to be dominated by the component which experiences the slowest cost decline with experience.

Yet ignoring the aggregation issue may lull the analyst into a false sense of statistical security under conditions which may lead to poor forecasting performance of the estimated experience curve. To illustrate, suppose cost data are available for the various levels of cumulative experience given in Table 3.6.2. Now suppose an analyst runs regressions of the form

$$\ln C_n = A + B \ln n \qquad (4)$$

and obtains the results presented in the top half of Table 3.6.3. At this point the analyst is likely to be quite pleased with himself. After all, the adjusted R^2s are all above 0.99, indicating outstanding fit of the model, and the estimates of A and B are all very much larger than their standard errors with t ratios above 70. The only small cause for concern is the very low Durbin–Watson statistic, which seems to indicate positive autocorrelation.

Table 3.6.2 Experience and doublings for cost components and prior experience models

No. of observations	Cumulative experience (n)	No. of doublings	No. of observations	Cumulative experience (n)	No. of doublings
1	100		16	2400	
2	200	1	17	2800	
3	300		18	3200	5
4	400	2	19	4000	
5	500		20	4800	
6	600		21	5600	
7	700		22	6400	6
8	800	3	23	8000	
9	900		24	9600	
10	1000		25	11200	
11	1200		26	12800	7
12	1400		27	16000	
13	1600	4 ·	28	19200	
14	1800		29	22400	
15	2000		30	25600	8

It turns out that the true unit costs used in estimating equation (4) and presented in Table 3.6.3 were based upon a general cost model of the form

$$C_n = C_0 + C_1 n^{-\lambda_1} + C_2 n^{-\lambda_2} \qquad (5)$$

where total unit costs are composed of two cost components subject to experience effects and an irreducible component, C_0. Hence, regressing the log of total unit costs on the log of experience entailed using a mis-specified model. That the problem is not a trivial one may be seen by examining the forecasting results presented at the bottom of Table 3.6.3. At the top of each column is the cumulative volume n and the corresponding true cost from equation (5). This figure may be contrasted to $\hat{C}_n$, which represents the forecasted value of unit cost based upon the mis-specified regression model. For example, consider the first row, where the regression equation was based upon the first eight observations. In this case the regression forecast for unit cost when $n = 12800$ (4 doublings) would be 230.46, whereas the true cost is known to be 278.41. Hence, the forecast based upon the mis-specified model predicts much lower future costs than will actually occur, in this case about 20 percent lower. For runs with $C_0 = 100$, the corresponding result is 25 percent lower. In many cases such large forecasting errors will prove to be unacceptably high.

Fortunately, the data analysis itself contained a warning that the level of aggregation chosen was inappropriate. The analyst should pay attention to the significant positive autocorrelation indicated by the Durbin–Watson statistic. Kenkel (1974) recommends using the d_u statistic, and Savin and White (1977) provide extended tables. For all cases considered here positive autocorrelation would be indicated at the 0.01 level for any d statistic less than one. In all cases

Table 3.6.3 Cost components model

$C_0 = 0$
$K_1 = 0.9$
$L_1 = 0.152003$

$C_1 = 1000$
$K_2 = 0.7$
$L_2 = 0.514573$

$C_2 = 5310.56$

Fitting period

Max n in fitting period	No. of observations	DW (Durbin-Watson)	$\bar{R}^2$	A	S.E.A. (Standard Error of A)	B	S.E.B. (Standard Error of B)
800	8	0.94	0.999	8.27	0.024	−0.299	0.004
1600	13	0.55	0.998	8.20	0.025	−0.287	0.004
3200	18	0.37	0.997	8.13	0.027	−0.275	0.004
6400	22	0.27	0.995	8.06	0.028	−0.265	0.004

Forecast

Max n in fitting period	No. of observations		n			
		1600	3200	6400	12,800	25,600
		C_n				
		445.04	376.69	322.33	278.41	242.39
800	8	$\hat{C}_n$ 429.16	348.83	283.53	230.46	187.32
		$\hat{C}_n/C_n$ 1.037	1.080	1.137	1.208	1.294
1600	13	$\hat{C}_n$	359.16	294.35	241.24	197.70
		$\hat{C}_n/C_n$	1.049	1.095	1.154	1.226
3200	18	$\hat{C}_n$		304.17	251.33	207.67
		$\hat{C}_n/C_n$		1.060	1.108	1.167
6400	22	$\hat{C}_n$			259.95	216.39
		$\hat{C}_n/\hat{C}$			1.071	1.120

the statistic was less than one, thereby indicating positive autocorrelation. For further examples, see Montgomery (1984).

Given the utility of the Durbin–Watson statistic in this context, it is remarkably absent in virtually all applications. Only Hirsch (1952) presents information on the autocorrelation of the residuals, from which the statistic may be computed. In this case, the Durbin–Watson test suggests that positive autocorrelation is indeed rampant throughout his results.

The results on the forecasting problems of using the wrong level of aggregation when different components of cost are subject to widely varying experience slopes, further suggest that care be given to proper model specification and testing. In particular, it implies that Yelle's (1976) procedure for estimating an aggregate cost curve for a new product is inappropriate and may lead to poor cost projection.

Errors in variables

Shared experience, whether prior or concurrent, may create errors in variables problems for empirically determined experience curves. This is readily seen for prior experience if the true total unit cost relationship is specified as

$$C_{n_2} = C_0 + C_1(n_1 + n_2)^{-\lambda} \tag{6}$$

where: C_{n_2} = total unit cost when the n_2th unit is produced
n_1 = cumulative volume of prior experience
n_2 = cumulative volume of current experience.

If the analyst ignores (or is ignorant of) the prior experience and estimates (assuming $C_0 = 0$).

$$\ln C_{n_2} = A + B \ln n_2 \tag{7}$$

ln n_2 will be a noisy predictor variable. One again finds that the usual regression statistics appear excellent except for the Durbin–Watson statistic which again indicates positive autocorrelation (see Table 3.6.4). The usual errors in variables bias creates a tendency to estimate B near zero. Consequently, k is substantially over-estimated and forecasts of $\hat{C}$ based upon the regression will substantially over-estimate actual costs. For further cases, see Montgomery (1984).

Errors in variables other than experience may occur in models where experience is but one of several variables in the relation. Rapping (1965), in his study of learning and production functions for World War II Liberty vessels, notes that his capital measure overstates the capital employed in producing the Liberty vessels.

Table 3.6.4 Prior experience model

$C_0 = 0$ $C_1 = 1000$
$K = 0.7$ $L = 0.514573$
Prior experience 800

Fitting period

Max n in fitting period	No. of observations	DW (Durbin-Watson)	$\bar{R}^2$	A	S.E.A. (Standard Error of A)	B	S.E.B. (Standard Error of B)	Est. K
800	8	0.85	0.949	4.10	0.075	−0.144	0.013	0.905
1600	13	0.47	0.936	4.35	0.091	−0.188	0.014	0.878
3200	18	0.31	0.934	4.63	0.103	−0.235	0.015	0.850
6400	22	0.23	0.937	4.90	0.113	−0.278	0.016	0.825

Forecast

Max n in fitting period	No. of observations		n			
		1600	3200	6400	12,800	25,600
	C_n	18.2	14.0	10.4	7.5	5.3
800	8					
	$\hat{C}_n$	20.9	18.9	17.1	15.5	14.0
	$C_n/\hat{C}_n$	0.872	0.741	0.605	0.481	0.378
1600	13					
	$\hat{C}_n$		17.0	14.9	13.1	11.5
	$C_n/\hat{C}_n$		0.825	0.694	0.570	0.461
3200	18					
	$\hat{C}_n$			13.1	11.1	9.4
	$C_n/\hat{C}_n$			0.792	0.672	0.562
6400	22					
	$\hat{C}_n$				9.7	8.0
	$C_n/\hat{C}_n$				0.770	0.663

Functional form

While the usual form of the experience curve is given by equation (1), others have been postulated. Spence (1981) posits

$$C_n = C_1 e^{-\lambda n} \tag{8}$$

which may be estimated as

$$\ln C_n = A + Bn \tag{9}$$

This curve implies a constant proportional decline in unit costs every time n units are produced. The usual curve implies a constant proportional decline in costs each time experience doubles. Thus the Spence curve produces more rapid experience-based cost declines. Empirical evidence is lacking as to which form might dominate, but it is readily testable by comparing the goodness of fit for $\ln C_n$ regressed first on n and then on $\ln n$.

Yelle (1979) in his extensive review of the learning curve notes that four alternatives to the log-linear model of equation (1) have been proposed. One of these, the Stanford-B model, was found by Boeing to best describe its actual experience with the Boeing 707, and was used to incorporate design changes in this aircraft (Garg and Milliman, 1961). This function uses a factor b added to n to reflect prior experience.

Omitted variables may distort results. Rapping (1965) found that omitting raw material inventory would tend to bias downward his estimates of capital and labor elasticities. Lieberman (1981) found that the price experience slope rose from 71 percent to 77 percent when scale, new plants, and entry were incorporated into the model.

Dolan and Jeuland (1981) argue for including current scale of output in the cost function. Preston and Keachie (1964) did so in their analysis of five types of radar equipment. They found that cumulative output was a more powerful predictor of unit labor and unit total cost than was current scale. Further, they found that current scale was relatively more important for total unit costs than for labor unit costs. These studies would suggest using more general and complete cost and price models, with experience being only one component.

Rutenberg (1976) suggests several generalizations of the Rapping (1965) model. His ultimate version is

$$X_{iT} = A M_{iT}^{\beta_1} K_{iT}^{\beta_2} \left(\sum_{t=0}^{T} X_{iT} \right)^{\beta_3} \left(\sum_{\text{YARDS}} \sum_{t=0}^{T} X_{iT} \right)^{\beta_4} \tag{10}$$

$$e^{\beta_5 T} (X_{it} - X_{i,T-1})^{\beta_6}$$

where: X_{iT} = output of yard i in year T
  M_{iT} = manpower in year T
  K_{iT} = capital employed in year T
  β_1 = manpower elasticity

β_2 = capital elasticity
β_3 = usual experience elasticity
β_4 = elasticity of cross-fertilization between shipyards
β_5 = elasticity of time reflecting flow of experience from outside the shipyard environment
β_6 = elasticity which may reflect the inefficiency of rapid experience gain.

Unfortunately, this specification has not been subjected empirical test.

Measurement

Empirical application of experience curves requires the analyst to deal with several difficult measurement issues. The relevant product (service) market must be defined, a measure of experience selected, and costs (or prices) measured. Problems which arise in each of these areas are discussed below. To date, no totally satisfactory approach to addressing these issues has been identified. Nevertheless empirical applications require that choices be made.

Defining the boundaries of the product market for experience analysis creates substantial uncertainty. This may be especially problematical for companies which manufacture products which are closely related in both their physical features and their manufacturing processes. For example, companies in the industrial roller chain business tend to manufacture many models and sizes. The production process for each model and size has many similar, yet some dissimilar, features. Should the experience curve be specified in terms of pounds of chain, links of chain, or pounds and links of a specific chain? Products also change over time in terms of both technology and market functions. For example, calculators have changed technically in going from mechanical to electronic and in terms of market functions as they have evolved from desk-top to pocket and/or briefcase models. The question is when a product has changed sufficiently that a new experience curve should be specified. Day and Montgomery (1983) suggest that if the consequence of a new technology is primarily to reduce production costs without a major change in functions provided to the market, then a new curve is unnecessary. Given the uncertainties inherent in defining product markets, it may be well to repeat the experience curve analysis using several product-market definitions. Wooley (1972) solved this problem in the cases reported in Table 3.6.1 by selecting products which had undergone only slight technological change.

A second measurement issue relates to the choice of the measure of experience. Candidate measures are cumulative units of output, cumulative gross investment, and time. Most industrial applications have used cumulative output. Practice among economists has varied. Arrow (1962) used cumulative investment, Rapping (1965) used cumulative output and time, while Sheshinski (1967) used all three. Rapping (1965) found that cumulated output was both statistically and economically significant in explaining output variation given labor and capital inputs. However, its precise effect was sensitive to the particular definition of cumulative output used. Further, cumulative output dominated time as an explanatory variable. Sheshinski's (1967) results suggest that either cumulative output or investment are important, and both dominate time empirically.

The measurement of unit costs or prices will be impacted by the definition of the product-market boundaries and the definition of the proper unit. For example, the cost per unit for commercial aircraft has risen over time as the airplane evolved from the single-engine piston to the modern wide-bodied jet. Yet the cost per seat mile has gone down a 75 percent experience curve. It has been suggested that industry-wide experience curves are most evident when rather broad product-market definitions—e.g. gallons of beer, pounds of viscose rayon, or kilowatt hours of electricity—are used, because these broad definitions encompass most sources of shared experience. For further discussion, see Day and Montgomery (1983).

Even if the analyst has successfully dealt with all the thorny definitional issues involved, measurement of unit cost and price remains difficult. Considerable time and effort must be invested in measuring C_n for several values of n so that the curve may be estimated. Few, if any, accounting systems are organized to supply this data readily. Sallenave (1976) has provided an interesting perspective on unit cost measurement. As the nth unit is produced, the following sequence of investments has been made

$$S_n = C_1 + C_2 + \ldots + C_{n-1} + C_n \tag{11}$$

where S_n = accumulated spending at the nth unit.

Sallenave (1976) shows that if C_n follows equation (1), accumulated spending will be

$$S_n = \frac{C_1 n^{1-\lambda}}{1 - \lambda} \tag{12}$$

which may be estimated by

$$\ln S_n = \ln \left(\frac{C_1}{1 - \lambda} \right) + (1 - \lambda) \ln n \tag{13}$$

It would seem that S_n would be more readily available than C_n from the usual accounting system and thus less subject to measurement error. Consequently, equation (13) may be a preferred empirical specification for estimating λ. Models of this form have yet to be used. In any case, the time seems ripe for applications-oriented strategists to join forces with managerial accountants to seek better data bases for experience curve analysis.

Unit price also presents measurement problems. List prices are notoriously inaccurate given the fluctuating, often hidden discount structures designed to cope with changes in the industry supply picture (Burck, 1972). Further, a single industry price may be misleading if it requires averaging across disparate models, features, and accessories or when competitors use markedly different strategies such as full service vs. bare-bones product offerings.

USE OF EXPERIENCE EFFECTS

Strategy consultants early pointed to several potential business effects of the experience curve. Business growth was seen as a key strategic variable. Based upon the experience effect relative costs should improve if a company were able to grow faster than competitors, thereby descending its experience curve at a faster rate. A corollary was that costs tend to vary inversely with market share, which was often interpreted as indicating market share as a vital competitive objective.

Predictable experience-based cost declines were prescribed as the basis for cost control and managment evaluation. At one time TI, in anticipation of a rapid cost decline as it captured the market, announced a $20 digital watch when its current unit costs were $40. It was also suggested that product design choices should be influenced by differentials in initial experience and experience slopes among the elements of each design alternative. Further, make-or-buy decisions should be impacted by the relative experience between the company and its vendors. In general, it was suggested that for purposes of procurement negotiations, the value to a supplier of a large-scale procurement could be calculated, if the rate of normal cost decline for the supplier could be estimated.

The application issues discussed earlier in this paper suggest that these business uses of experience curves, while often correct in principle, may be very difficult to implement properly.

Strategy uses

Porter's (1980) presentation of generic business strategies identifies cost leadership as one of the three generic strategies. Experience-based cost advantages represent one important way to achieve a cost leadership position.

Hall's (1980) analysis of 64 companies in eight industries subject to adverse environments lends credence to the Porter generic strategies. Hall defined adverse environments as ones in which the industry is mature and experiencing slower, erratic growth. Further, intensifying regulatory pressure and domestic and foreign competition, when added to inflationary pressures, renders the environments of these industries hostile to the participants. Yet the eight leaders in these hostile environments averaged better ROE and ROI than the leading companies in other more advantaged industries. They achieved these results by establishing and maintaining a leadership position in terms of relative delivered product cost or relative product differentiation. A couple of companies were able to achieve leadership positions in both, but most found it necessary to achieve pre-eminence in one or the other. Interestingly, four of the eight low-cost producers were able to achieve their low-cost position without benefit of high relative market shares. All four of these companies focused their plants by emphasizing modern, automated process technology and made heavy investments in distribution to gain scale-based cost reductions in their distribution systems. Instead of fully integrating they generally have invested to have the most efficient process technology in at least one stage of the vertical chain. In contrast, the losers in these adverse industries were all high-cost with largely undifferentiated products which were usually below average in quality and performance. Many of these also-rans had at one time enjoyed a cost or a product leadership position which they had allowed to erode over time.

Hammermesh and Silk (1979), in a somewhat more anecdotal analysis, suggest that successful companies in stagnant industries pay constant attention to cost reduction. They cite the increasing automation of production in the cigar industry as it has declined and consolidated as an illustration of their basic point. Continuing pursuit of quality differentiation is also important in such industries, as evidenced by the fact that the PIMS studies show that high quality has greater leverage on ROI in low-growth environments.

Experience curves have been incorporated in models for analyzing dynamic pricing strategy. An interesting example done at RCA by Robinson and Lakhani (1975) demonstrated dramatic impact upon the selection of a pricing strategy. Their model considers a planning horizon of 5 years for a monopolist. The monopolist faces demand modeled by the Bass (1969) innovator/imitator model modified by price elasticity. Unit costs were taken to decline on a 75 percent experience curve. Future profits were discounted at 40 percent in order to penalize severely future returns.

The discounted profit implications of four pricing strategies were then compared. The pricing strategies were:

(1) *Marginal pricing.* The firm sets prices each quarter such that marginal revenue equals marginal cost. This is the myopic (or non-dynamic) economic strategy.

(2) *Optimum constant return on sales.* Each quarter price is adjusted to yield a 26 percent margin on sales. The margin of 26 percent was found to yield the optimum discounted profits over the planning horizon.

(3) *Optimum constant price.* Price was set at a constant level for the entire planning horizon of 5 years. The level was chosen to maximize the discounted present value of the profits from each period.

(4) *Optimum dynamic price.* Using dynamic programming, the optimal price was found for each quarter in order to maximize the discounted present value of the profits from each period.

The results of their analysis of these four pricing stategies are presented in Table 3.6.5. Notice that although the discounted present value of the profits is virtually identical for the marginal pricing and the constant return on sales strategies, the price the monopolist would set in the fourth quarter of each year is dramatically different for these strategies. More significant, however, is the profit advantage which acrues to either the optimum constant price or the optimum dynamic price policies, the latter having a six-fold advantage over the marginal pricing and constant returns on sales strategies. Further, the optimum dynamic price enjoys about a 20 percent discounted profit advantage over the optimum constant price. An interesting aspect of these results is that a monopolist, using severe (40 percent) discounting of future profits, would find a low initial price or penetration price strategy to be far more profitable than the two myopic strategies which suggest an initial skimming pricing strategy. Considerations of competitive entry potential or more modest discount rates would only serve to enhance the advantage of the optimum dynamic strategy. The combination of demand acceleration via imitation, price elasticity of unit volume, and experience-based cost declines thus creates an incentive for even a high discount rate monopolist to opt for a market penetration price.

The often observed market share/profitability association (Buzzell *et al.*, 1975) and the experience curve rationale for this association, have sometimes led to misguided strategies. Experience curves could lead to this association since market shares often tend to change slowly over time and consequently the firms having larger market shares should have greater accumulated experience and therefore should enjoy the lowest costs. The problem in deriving strategic implications from this relates to the role of price in capturing market share and to the nature of cross-sectional or inter-firm application of the experience curve.

In a study of six types of PIMS business—consumer durables, consumer non-durables, capital goods, materials, components, and supplies—Phillips *et al.* (1983) have shed light on the first of these issues. Using a causal modeling approach, they found that high relative price had a statistically significant and positive influence on relative market share for all businesses except materials and components, where the impact was insignificant. Consequently, a strategy of lowest price did not appear to be a general formula for success in capturing market share for the PIMS businesses.

Their results indicated that lower direct costs tended to increase ROI significantly for all businesses except consumer durables. Further, both relative quality and relative direct costs were found to increase relative price significantly. The authors conclude that:

Table 3.6.5 Price strategy results for RCA new durable model*

Price strategy	Year	Unit[a] price ($)	Unit[b] cost ($)	Accumulated volume (10^3)	Discounted[c] accumulated $ (10^3)
Marginal	0	12.86	10.00	10	0
	1	9.13	6.73	32	56
	2	6.73	3.87	107	181
	3	5.44	2.58	295	386
	4	4.68	1.82	703	684
	5	4.29	1.34	1546	1100
Optimum constant return on sales (26%)	0	13.89	10.00	10	0
	1	9.42	6.78	26	47
	2	5.17	3.73	118	161
	3	2.73	1.96	586	379
	4	1.47	1.06	2730	741
	5	1.02	0.69	8239	1114
Optimum constant price	0	3.25	10.00	10	0
	1	3.25	2.06	522	−14
	2	3.25	1.27	1739	1062
	3	3.25	0.90	4066	2917
	4	3.25	0.73	6955	4700
	5	3.25	0.66	8915	5582
Optimum dynamic price	0	2.82	10.00	10	0
	1	2.96	1.42	1322	−793
	2	4.15	1.00	3180	1482
	3	4.57	0.83	5108	3932
	4	4.42	0.73	6883	5652
	5	3.55	0.67	8508	6602

*From Robinson and Lakhani (1975)
[a] Unit price in fourth quarter of year.
[b] Unit cost is for last unit produced.
[c] Discount rate of 40%.

> The finding that both higher relative quality and costs lead to increased prices . . ., combined with the finding that quality does not significantly influence direct costs across most businesses, suggests that pursuit of a quality strategy enables a company to command profit margins superior to lower-quality competitors. . . . However, the higher prices that emerge from a high quality strategy apparently do not deter market penetration. . . . These findings refute the inverse price-share relationship predicted by economic models and market niche theories of product quality. We must conclude that no lawlike connection exists between price and share in mature markets and that, instead, these two variables covary positively as a function of some common cause such as product differentiation.

Finally, it should be noted that relative market share was found to have a positive, significant relationship to ROI for all businesses except consumer non-durables and materials, where the relationship was insignificant. Except for the materials business, high relative market share was associated with lower relative costs, consistent with experience effects. When coupled with the positive ROI impact of lower relative costs, this suggests that the market share/profitability relation via relative costs has empirical support. The strategy error often occurs when price is the focus of attempted share gains.

While the Phillips *et al.* (1983) results affirm that the relative cost-mediated relation between relative market share and ROI appears empirically valid, simplistic experience curve interpretations may be misleading in assessing competitors' costs. In the first place, a company will need to assess carefully the issues of prior and shared experience for each significant competitor. Although imprecise and judgemental, one large chemical company reports success in understanding competitors' relative cost positions in textiles, an industry with high levels of shared experience between types of fibers. It claims that such analyses have provided insights into the company's position which otherwise would have eluded them.

Second, cross-sectional or competitive cost comparison curves are generally more difficult to determine than the company's own experience curve. The prior discussion has indicated that there are substantial difficulties in measuring the company's own cost experience curve. Even if a firm has a good idea of its own curve, a competitor's costs cannot simply be estimated by placing that competitor on the company's own experience curve according to the competitor's cumulative experience. Doing so is highly likely to overstate cost differences between competitors. Day and Montgomery (1983) cite several reasons why the cross-sectional competitive cost comparison curve is likely to be shallower than a company experience curve:

(1) followers may have lower initial costs due to learning from the leader's mistakes, personnel, or product, or by leapfrogging the earlier entrant via product or process innovation;
(2) shared cost reductions by common suppliers of components or production equipment;

(3) some competitors may have lower costs due to location advantages, government subsidies, etc.;
(4) smaller firms may have lower overhead rates than large multi-divisional companies; and
(5) if market share positions have been volatile, current market shares may not be a good measure of relative cumulative output.

Policy use

The experience curve relates to public policy considerations when issues of economic performance are considered. Industry concentration, entry barriers, market performance, and predatory pricing are all part of the broad governmental and legal interest in industry structure and performance.

In an interesting discussion of predatory pricing, Thompson (1979) suggests the possibility that the experience effect may often prove to be a persuasive and reasonable defense to charges of predatory pricing, even though current law does not explicitly recognize such a defense. To date, the courts have used concepts such as 'below cost pricing' or 'predatory intent' in attempting to set a standard against which predatory pricing behavior could be assessed. Thompson notes that 'a necessary condition for predation is the sacrifice of short-run profits which occurs in all the experience curve cases'. This was graphically illustrated earlier in the Robinson and Lakhani (1975) example where even a monopolist might have strong motivation to price below marginal costs in order to penetrate a market. Thompson suggests that firms might do well to anticipate an experience cost-based defense by beforehand choosing a proper unit of analysis, developing relevant historical information on cost components, and using an estimated experience relationship to project future cost components, allowing for shared experience. Given the earlier analysis of cost component projections, his suggestion to develop this analysis by component is certainly well founded. He further notes that an experience curve-based defense for below marginal cost pricing would seem most justifiable for rapid growth situations since experience will double more rapidly than at later, more mature stages. Even so, a smaller rival might be able to justify it even during slower growth on the basis of rapid relative experience increases.

Spence (1981) has developed a model which he used to explore the implications of the presence of experience effects in terms of entry barriers and market performance. Competitors were assumed to have their own, perhaps idiosyncratic, experience curve; demand was modeled by a constant elasticity formulation; and an open loop equilibrium concept was employed. The latter implies that each firm will select its optimal path, given the paths chosen by competitors, and that competitors' paths will be optimal and correctly anticipated by each firm. Spence studied market entry and performance under a fairly wide variety of parameter specifications. His conclusions were:

(1) Experience curves can create substantial barriers to entry.
(2) Moderate rates of learning create the greatest entry barriers. Where learning is rapid, new entrants may catch up quickly with the market leaders. For very low learning rates, only small cost advantages acrue to the early entrants.
(3) With moderately rapid learning, and over a reasonable range of time horizons, entry usually ceases after three or four firms have entered.
(4) Examination of consumer surplus suggests that market performance increases sharply from one to two to three firms, but relatively slowly thereafter.

The last point suggests that market performance may be acceptable as long as there are three or four (non-colluding) firms. Spence suggests that any attempt to enforce deconcentration by explicit or implicit limits on market share, risks reducing the technical efficiency of the industry. Spence cautions that his model does not consider aggressive pricing to deter competition, but rather simply assumes that prices are responsive to true marginal costs which are subject to experience-based improvements. Nevertheless, Spence's results do indicate a very interesting relation between experience curves and regulatory policy in a dynamic environment.

Finally, Smiley (1982) developed and analyzed an economic simulation model to ascertain whether or not it is possible for learning, or experience, effects to cause a positive association between industry profits and concentration, a result often observed and of concern in the economics literature. Further, he was interested in whether learning was sufficient to generate this profits/concentration association. The industry modeled postulated that all firms face the same learning curve, but that all learning is proprietary to each firm. Proprietary learning implies that Firm A's costs will not benefit from Firm B's cumulative production experience. Thus hiring a competitor's knowledgeable production personnel, and industrial espionage, are specifically precluded. Each industry in the simulation began with 20 firms competing and with both entry and exit possible. Prices were set at competitive levels. Firms are assumed to grow at different rates chosen randomly from an underlying normal distribution for each year in the simulation.

Smiley's results show that in an economy with experience effects, industries which are more concentrated will also be more profitable, even though price is established competitively, and not collusively. Industries in which learning is more important (i.e. a higher percentage of costs affected by learning) will also be more profitable. Smiley performed a sensitivity analysis which indicated that the results are not sensitive to the particular parameters chosen, or to the assumed forms of the relationships.

The policy implication of Smiley's result is that antitrust economists and politicians may be ill-advised to use industry profits as an indication of implicit collusion, and thereby an invitation to dismantle concentrated industries. If the breaking up of large firms in concentrated industries results in a loss of the experience achievements, such a policy may have deleterious effects on efficiency and even upon international competitiveness of the industry. Clearly, these results suggest caution in applying such a policy.

Marketing models

The experience curve has increasingly become an important element in the formulation of many marketing models. This has been especially true for dynamic pricing models and models of new product diffusion. Virtually all of these models utilize the equation (1) form of the experience curve. Examples may be found in Robinson and Lakhani (1975), Davis (1974), Davis and Simmons (1976), Bass (1980), Larreche and Srinivasan (1981), Dolan and Jeuland (1981), Clarke *et al.* (1982), Clarke and Dolan (1982), and Erickson (1982). Experience curves also play a prominent role in the widely used MARKSTRAT strategic marketing game (Larreche and Gatignon, 1977).

As in the Robinson and Lakhani (1975) model discussed in an earlier section, Clarke and Dolan (1982) found that in the presence of both cost (i.e. experience effects) and demand dynamics, penetration pricing strategies may quite significantly improve discounted profits in comparison to myopic profit maximizing. Improvements of 25 percent were routine in their simulations with some profit improvements as high as 75 percent. They found that skimming strategies would similarly improve profits over the myopic case. Their studies thus far suggest that the relative performance of penetration versus skimming pricing strategies depends upon a complex interaction of cost and demand dynamics. While it did not hold in all cases, they found that mid-range values of experience slopes had greater impact than more extreme values, as was found by Spence (1981). However, Erickson's (1982) recent study found that the optimal price path was impacted more by market price sensitivity and competitive market entry than by the presence of experience effects for the case he studied. In view of the Spence (1981) and Clarke and Dolan (1982) results, it may well be that Erickson's use of a very moderate 8 percent experience curve diminished its relative impact in his study.

Experience curves of the usual form have also been incorporated into product mix optimization models (Reeves and Sweigart, 1981) and cost–volume–profit analysis (McIntyre, 1977). In sum, experience curves are coming to play a significant role in modeling for analyzing marketing and management decision problems. Consequently, research to improve the specification and empirical estimation of experience curves seems badly needed.

SUMMARY

Empirical application of the experience curve requires attention to several issues—aggregation, errors in variables, functional form, and measurement. In particular, autocorrelation was shown to be an indicator of serious model mis-specification which could disrupt forecasts. Clearly, substantial research remains in order to resolve all the issues raised. The results in this paper suggest that this research effort is important, and the answers may have far-reaching consequences for the empirical application of experience curves.

REFERENCES

Abell, D. F., and J. S. Hammond (1979). *Strategic Market Planning: Problems and Analytical Approaches*. Prentice-Hall, Englewood Cliffs, N.J.

Arrow, K. J. (1962). 'The economic implications of learning by doing', *Review of Economic Studies*, 155–173.

Barkai, H., and D. Levhari (1973). 'The impact of experience in kibbutz farming', *Review of Economics and Statistics*, Feb., 56–63.

Bass, F. M. (1969). 'A new product model for consumer durables', *Management Science*, 15(5) (Jan.), 215–227.

Bass, F. M. (1980). 'The relationship between diffusion rates, experience curves, and demand elasticity for consumer durable technological innovations', *Journal of Business*, 53(3), Part 2, S51–S67.

Beevan, A. (1974). 'The U.K. potato crisp industry, 1960–1972: a study of new entry competition', *Journal of Industrial Economics*, 22 (June), 281–297.

Boston Consulting Group (1972). *Perspectives on Experience*. Boston.

Boston Consulting Group (1975). *Strategy Alternatives for the British Motorcycle Industry*. Her Majesty's Stationery Office, London.

Burck, G. (1972). 'The myths and realities of corporate pricing', *Fortune* (April).

Buzzell, R. D., B. T. Gale, and R. G. M. Sultan (1975). 'Market share—a key to profitability', *Harvard Business Review*, Jan.–Feb., 97–106.

Clarke, D. G., and R. J. Dolan, (1982). 'A simulation model for the evaluation of pricing strategies in a dynamic environment'. Harvard Business School Research Paper.

Clarke, F. H., M. N. Darrough, and J. M. Heincke (1982). 'Optimal pricing policy in the presence of experience effects', *Journal of Business*, 55(4), 517–530.

Conway, R., and A. Schultz (1959). 'The manufacturing progress function', *Journal of Industrial Engineering*, 10, 39–53.

Davis, K. R. (1974). 'Some aspects of price strategy', *Omega*, 2(4), 515–522.

Davis, K. R., and L. F. Simmons (1976). 'Exploring market pricing strategies via dynamic programming', *Decision Sciences*, 7, 281–293.

Day, G. S., and D. B. Montgomery (1983). 'Diagnosing the experience curve', *Journal of Marketing*, 47 (Winter).

Dolan, R. J., and A. P. Jeuland (1981). 'Experience curves and dynamic demand models: implications for optimal pricing strategies', *Journal of Marketing*, **45** (Winter), 52–62.

Erickson, G. M. (1982). 'The separate effects of competitive entry, price sensitivity, and the learning curve on the dynamic pricing of new durable products'. University of Washington Research Paper.

Fusfeld, A. R. (1973). 'The technological progress function', *Technology Review*, Feb., 29–38.

Garg, A., and P. Milliman (1961). 'The aircraft progress curve—modified for design changes', *Journal of Industrial Engineering*, **12**(1) (Jan.–Feb.), 23–28.

Hall, W. K. (1980). 'Survival strategies in a hostile environment', *Harvard Business Review*, **58**(5) (Sept.–Oct.), 75–85.

Hammermesh, R. G., and S. B. Silk (1979). 'How to compete in stagnant industries', *Harvard Business Review*, **57**(5) (Sept.–Oct.), 161–168.

Hirsch, W. Z. (1952). 'Manufacturing progress functions', *Review of Economics and Statistics*, **34**(2) (May), 143–155.

Hirsch, W. Z. (1956). 'Firm progress ratios', *Econometrica*, **24**, 136–143.

Hirschmann, W. B. (1964). 'Profit from the learning curve', *Harvard Business Review*, **42** (Jan.–Feb.).

Hollander, S. (1965). *The Sources of Increased Efficiency: A Study of DuPont Rayon Manufacturing Plants*. MIT Press, Cambridge, MA.

Joskow, P. L., and G. A. Rozanski (1979). 'The effect of learning by doing on nuclear plant operating reliability', *Review of Economics and Statistics*, **61** (May), 161–168.

Kenkel, J. L. (1974). 'Some small sample properties of Durbin's tests for serial correlation in regression models containing lagged dependent variables', *Econometrica*, **42**(4) (July), 763–769.

Kiechel, W. (1981). 'The decline of the experience curve', *Fortune*, 5 Oct., 139–146.

Larreche, J. C., and H. Gatignon (1977). *MARKSTRAT: A Marketing Strategy Game* Scientific Press, Palo Alto, CA.

Larreche, J. C., and V. Srinivasan (1981). 'STRATPORT: a decision support system for strategic planning', *Journal of Marketing*, **45** (Fall), 39–52.

Lieberman, M. B. (1981). 'The experience curve, pricing and market structure in the chemical processing industries'. Working paper, Harvard University.

McIntyre, E. V. (1977). 'Cost–volume–profit analysis adjusted for learning', *Management Science*, **24**(2) (Oct.), 149–160.

Montgomery, D. B. (1984). 'Some empirical issues relating to cost component and prior experience models of experience curves'. Technical Report 73, Graduate School of Business, Stanford University.

Phillips, L. W., D. R. Chang, and R. D. Buzzell (1983). 'Product quality, cost position, and business performance: a test of some key hypotheses', *Journal of Marketing*, **47** (Winter).

Porter, M. E. (1979). 'How competitive forces shape strategy', *Harvard Business Review*, **57** (Mar.–Apr.), 137–145.

Porter, M. E. (1980). *Competitive Strategy*. The Free Press, New York.

Preston, L. E., and E. C. Keachie (1964). 'Cost functions and progress functions: an integration', *American Economic Review*, **54**(1) (March), Part I, 100–107.

Quinn, J. B. (1981). 'Formulating strategy one step at a time', *Journal of Business Strategy*, 42–63 (Winter).

Rapping, L. (1965). 'Learning and World War II production functions', *Review of Economics and Statistics*, 81–86 (Feb.).

Reeves, G. R., and J. R. Sweigart (1981). 'Product mix models when learning effects are present', *Management Science*, **27**(2) (Feb.), 204–211.

Robinson, B., and C. Lakhani (1975). 'Dynamic price models for new product planning', *Management Science*, **21**(10) (June), 1113–1122.

Rosenberg, N. (1982). 'Learning by using', Chapter 6 in N. Rosenberg (ed.), *Inside the Black Box*, Cambridge University Press, Cambridge, England.

Rutenberg, D. (1976). 'What strategic planning expects from management science'. Working Paper 89-75-76, Carnegie-Mellon University (Dec.).

Sallenave, J. P. (1976). *Experience Analysis for Industrial Planning*, Lexington Books, Lexington, MA.

Savin, N. E., and K. J. White (1977). 'The Durbin–Watson test for serial correlation with extreme sample sizes or many regressors', *Econometrica*, **45**(8) (Nov.), 1989–1996.

Sheshinski, E. (1967). 'Tests of the learning by doing hypothesis', *Review of Economics and Statistics*, **49**(4), 568–578.

Smiley, R. (1982). 'Learning and the concentration–profitability relationship', *Quarterly Review of Economics and Business*, **22**(2) (Summer).

Spence, A. M. (1981). 'The learning curve and competition', *Bell Journal of Economics*, **12**(1) (Spring), 49–70.

Stobaugh, R. B., and P. L. Townsend (1975). 'Price forecasting and strategic planning: the case of petro chemicals', *Journal of Marketing Research*, **12** (Feb.), 19–29.

Thompson, D. N. (1979). 'Pricing and the experience curve'. Presented at the Third Triennial Canadian Marketing Workshop.

Wooley, K. M. (1972). "Experience curves and their use in planning'. Unpublished Ph.D. dissertation, Stanford University.

Yelle, L. E. (1976). 'Estimating learning curves for potential products, *Industrial Marketing Management*, **5**, 147–154.

Yelle, L. E. (1979). 'The learning curve: historical review and comprehensive survey', *Decision Sciences*, **10**, 302–328.

3.7
Market Share Rewards to Pioneering Brands: An Exploratory Empirical Analysis

GLEN L. URBAN, THERESA CARTER, AND ZOFIA MUCHA
Sloan School of Management, Massachusetts Institute of Technology, Cambridge, Mass., USA

INTRODUCTION

One strategy for new product development is based on innovation and the creation of new markets. It is expensive and risky (Urban and Hauser, 1980). The costs of development are often large and the first firm in a market must allocate funds to make consumers aware of its product and convince them to buy it. The risk of failure is high because the potential demand is not known with certainty. An alternative strategy is based on being the second (or later) entrant into the market. The costs may be lower since the innovator has created the primary demand and the basic product design exists; the risk also may be less because a proven demand is evident. If an equal market share can be gained this strategy could be more profitable. If, on the other hand, as a result of being the first entrant in a market, a dominant market share is achieved and maintained, the innovation strategy may be superior. The purpose of this paper is to investigate empirically the market share effects of being a pioneering brand.

If the market grants a long-run market share reward to early entrants, this would encourage innovation. From a public policy point of view this would serve a similar function to that of patents by providing an additional reward to innovators. Although patents sometimes provide protection, in many cases they are ineffective because of difficulties of establishing and protecting the rights and the ability of other firms to invent around the patent as technology advances (von Hippel, 1982). This difficulty of protecting an innovation is compounded by the fact that imitators generally take less time and require fewer funds to copy the innovation (Mansfield *et al.*, 1981). If pioneering brands earn a long-run market share advantage, the effectiveness of patent

239

protection may be less critical in providing incentives for innovation and firms may be more willing to innovate without patent protection.

Several authors have argued on theoretical grounds that such long-lived advantages can exist. Early ideas by Bain (1956) indicated that existing products can have an advantage accruing from fundamental consumer traits that lead to stable preference patterns. Schmalensee's (1982) theoretical model is based on the fundamental notion that once buyers use the first entrant's product, they will be willing to pay more for it, if it works, because they are not certain the second product will work. Based on a number of assumptions (e.g. products either work or do not work, second entrant objectively equal to first, no response by pioneer to new entrant, and no advertising effects) he shows that a long-run price advantage can persist for the pioneering brand. In this model the second entrant must offer a price reduction to persuade consumers to try and learn about the product. This can imply higher profits for the pioneer. Lane and Wiggins (1981) similarly assume that consumers only know the exact quality of the products they have used. Their model is similar to Schmalensee's but includes advertising and some response by the pioneer to later entrants. After examining profit-maximizing strategies they find 'even with entry, the first entrant's advantage persists in the form of higher demand and profitability' (p. 3).

Hauser and Shugan (1983) have formulated a defensive strategy model which uses the product positioning of the new entrant to determine share. In this model the persistence of the sales levels of pioneering brands depends on how well the pioneer designed the product attributes to meet heterogeneous consumer preferences. If the 'best' positioning was chosen by the first firm, later entrants may have lower market shares because if they want to differentiate they must adopt an inferior position. However, if the first brand to enter did not fully understand consumer preferences, the second entrant could get a preferential positioning advantage and earn a greater share.

These theoretical models show the possibility of long-run market share rewards for pioneering brands and indicate these rewards will be a function of the product positioning and pricing strategies of the new and old products.

A limited amount of empirical analysis on the benefits of early entry has been reported. Biggadike (1976), studied 40 product entries into new markets conducted by large firms in the PIMS project. He found that after 4 years the average share of these entrants was 15 percent and the share of the largest existing competitor in each of the 40 businesses decreased from 47 percent to 28 percent after the new entrant came on the market. These data suggest that the share of the pioneering brand decreases as the results of subsequent entry, but a share advantage persists.

Two industry studies have been conducted which have information relevant to entry effects. The first is by Bond and Lean (1977), and reflects a study of two related prescription drugs (diuretics and antianginals). A historical review and time-series regression analysis of the sales, entry, and promotion in each of these led the authors to conclude for these prescription drugs that 'the first firm to offer and promote a new type of product received a substantial and enduring sales advantage' (p. vi). Neither heavy promotional outlays nor low price dislodged the pioneers. However, later entrants that offered therapeutic novelty did achieve substantial sales volumes when backed by heavy promotional expenditures. They found that 'large scale promotion of brands that offer nothing new is likely to go unrewarded' (p. vi).

An interpretative study of trends in seven cigarette submarkets by Whitten (1979) led to the finding that the 'first entry brand received a substantial and enduring sales advantage' in six of the seven cigarette market segments (p. 41). She found, however, that later entry brands which were early in a growing market or which were significantly differentiated could gain a substantial share in the market or even dislodge the first entry brand from its dominant position.

These theoretical and empirical analyses suggest order of entry may affect the market share potential of later entries, and that this effect is mediated by the entrant's positioning, pricing, and advertising strategy. The purpose of this paper is to enlarge the body of empirical analysis of testing these theoretical propositions on the effects of order of entry on market share. In contrast to the two industry studies, our work reflects a cross-product analysis over many (15) categories of frequently purchased brands of consumer goods. It includes effects of entry as well as advertising and positioning variables. We begin by describing the data base. We next specify the statistical model and describe its fit to an initial data base of 38 brands. We consider the strategic implications of our findings and close with a discussion of future research needs.

DATA

Pre-test market assessment procedures have been widely used in the markets for frequently purchased brands of consumer products. One such system, called ASSESSOR (Silk and Urban, 1978) provides a rich data base for the study of order of entry effects. In this procedure, data on existing products are collected first and then new product response is measured. We are concerned here with only the data on existing products (all brands that had been on the market at least 3 years). In each category studied, 300 (or more) respondents are interviewed to determine their evoked set of brands,* their preferences for these brands (constant sum paired comparisons across each consumer's evoked set), the last brand they purchased, and ratings of the evoked brands on products attribute scales. These data allow market shares to be estimated by the fraction of the sample which last purchased the brand. The preference and

---

* Based on positive unaided response to one of the following conditions: now using, ever used, on hand, would consider using, or would not consider using. Over 90 percent of evoking is associated with use experience.

ratings data are the basis of determining product position and differentiation. An initial sample of 15 categories was selected for exploratory analysis; 38 major brands existed across these categories. The sample represents tightly defined categories of frequently purchased goods (e.g. liquid detergent, instant freeze-dried coffee, fabric softener, anti-dandruff shampoo), and has three or fewer major brands in each category. These data were supplemented by advertising expenditures obtained from the *Leading National Advertisers* (LNA) published media audits. Although these audits may not report 100 percent of each brand's spending, they are useful in comparing relative advertising expenditures if we assume any biases are systematic across brands. Since all brands considered had been on the market at least 3 years, these spending levels represent sustaining expenditures.

The order of entry was determined by identifying the time of national introduction for each brand. This was done by personally calling the firms who market each of these products and determining when it was introduced. In the few cases where the firms were not willing to provide these data, at least two competitors were asked to provide an estimate of the entry time.

These data provide a cross-sectional data base for the investigation of order effects. At the time of each study the shares for the existing brands, the time of each product's entry into the market, the brand's recent advertising spending, and the relative product preferences are known.

STATISTICAL MODEL

The dependent variable in this study is the ratio of the market share of the nth (second, third, fourth . . .) brand to enter the market to that of the first product to enter. Since the number of brands in each category varies the absolute shares also vary; the ratio allows a meaningful comparison of relative relationships of brands within and across categories. Brands are included in the analysis if they were advertised at a significant level (greater than $1 million per year in *LNA*) and a reasonable share estimate could be obtained (at least 30 respondents reporting them as last brand purchased).

The order of entry (first, second, third . . .) is used as an independent variable. This variable can empirically reflect the theoretical long-lived share advantages of pioneering brands argued for by Schmalensee, and by Lane and Wiggins. If, as theorized, the early entrant becomes the standard of comparison and subsequent brands require consumers to make additional investments in learning, the order of entry variable will be negatively correlated to the share index. This variable is supplemented by another which is defined as the number of years between the nth entry and the one which immediately preceded it. Being the second brand in the category is likely to have a different share effect if the lag between the pioneer is 1 year rather than 2, 3, or 4 years. Whitten stressed the importance of a firm being early after a new trend is established. Advertising is represented by the total advertising expenditure over the last 3 years by the nth brand to enter the category divided by that of the pioneering brand. This variable reflects the sustaining level of advertising spending, and allows the order of entry effect to be mediated by the application of marketing resources.

Differential product positioning has been identified as another mediator of the effect of order of entry. The Bond and Lean and the Whitten studies stress its significance. Hauser and Shugan also argue for its importance. One method of constructing a positioning variable is by combining the product attribute ratings to estimate the utility for a brand. (See Urban and Hauser, 1980, or Shocker and Srinivasan, 1979, for a review). Many procedures exist and they usually reproduce stated preferences or choices well. Another method is to use stated preferences directly. This has the advantage of avoiding variance due to lack of fits between the attributes and preferences, but has the disadvantage of not linking the attributes to preference. Because our primary purpose is to use the positioning variable as a covariate of order of entry in explaining share rather than supporting the design of new products, we choose to use preference to construct the positioning variable. The constant sum preferences supplied by each respondent over their evoked set reflect their overall evaluations of the brand's price and features. After scaling the preferences by least-square procedures, we obtain a preference value for each evoked brand j, respondent i, and category c (V_{ijc}). We define a relative preference for each consumer and average over all individuals:

$$R_{jc} = \frac{1}{I_c} \sum_i \left[\frac{V_{ijc}^{\beta_c}}{\sum_j V_{ijc}^{\beta_c}} \right] \tag{1}$$

where: V_{ijc} = preference value for respondent i and brand j in category c
I_c = number of respondents in category c
β_c = scale parameter for category c
R_{jc} = relative preference of brand j in category c.

The value of R_{jc} reflects the consumers' evaluation of the products given that it is evoked. In most cases this means after having used the brand. If it performs well and price is low, R_{jc} will be high; if it does not perform well and price is high R_{jc} will be low. The scale parameter β_c is estimated by logit procedures (see Silk and Urban, 1978, for details) and it has values in the range of 1 to 3 with a median of about 2. This scaling of preferences results in R_{jc} approximating the probability of purchase of the brand given that it is evoked. The driving forces behind R_{jc} are the measured preferences across the evoked set, but this scaling must be remembered when the statistical analysis is interpreted (see below).

Another aspect to emphasize is that R_{jc} is conditioned by evoking. The same market share (e.g. 10 percent) for a brand could be due to high preference given evoking and low evoking (e.g. 50 percent preference given evoking and 20 percent evoking), low conditioned preference and high evoking (e.g. 20 percent preference and 50 percent evoking) or moderate levels of both (e.g. 33 percent preference and 33 percent evoking). The variable R_{jc} is not necessarily correlated to share. Before 1974, Tylenol had a low share, but pre-test market evaluations indicated high preference by those who had used it. After Tylenol advertised and promoted its product, its share increased dramatically as the fraction of the population evoking it increased.

The positioning variable R_{jc} reflects consumers' preference for their evoked brand. It is scaled to approximate the probability of purchase conditioned by the fact that the brand is evoked. In our model we are interested in the positioning quality of later entrants relative to the pioneer, so we define ratio of R_{jc} for the nth brand to R_{jc} for the first brand to enter as the variable to represent the relative preference given evoking. If the later entrant is superior, the ratio is greater than one, and if less desirable, the ratio is less than one.

The form of the model is non-linear to reflect the hypothesis that the impact of the second brand to enter on the pioneer will be greater than the third or fourth brand. Considerable precedent exists for modeling a non-linear response to advertising (Little, 1979). Since Bond and Lean's work indicates an interaction between order, position, and marketing promotion, we choose a log-linear form to reflect interactions and non-linearities.

Formally for brand n ($n > 1$) in category c:

$$S_{nc} = \alpha_0 + \alpha_1 E_{nc} + \alpha_2 P_{nc} + \alpha_3 A_{nc} + \alpha_4 L_{nc} \qquad (2)$$

where: S_{nc} = log of ratio of the market shares of the nth brand to enter category c to the market share of the first brand to enter the category

E_{nc} = log of order to entry of nth brand in category c ($n = 1, 2, 3, 4$ . . .)

P_{nc} = log of ratio of preference for given evoking for nth brand to preference for first brand given evoking

$$P_{nc} = \frac{R_{nc}}{R_{1c}}$$

where R_{jc} = preference for jth brand in category c conditioned by evoking—see eqn (1)

A_{nc} = log of the ratio of the last 3 years advertising for nth brand to enter to 3-year advertising for first brand

L_{nc} = log of number of years between n and $n - 1$ brand entry.

This model captures the major theoretical phenomena. If α_1 is negative and significant it supports the notion of an enduring share advantage for early entrants. If α_2 is positive and significant it confirms the notion that the order of entry effect can be moderated by a product which is perceived as superior in price and features by those who have it in their evoked set. If α_3 is positive and significant it suggests advertising may mediate the order effect. If α_4 is negative and significant it would indicate a larger penalty for the nth entrant the later it arrives on the market.

FITTING

The model is applied to an initial sample of 38 brands across 15 categories. Regression is used to estimate the parameters in eqn (2). These regression procedures are based on 23 data points because the first brand is not appropriate for inclusion in relative share formulation given in eqn (2). The $F(4,18)$ is 52.1 and the fit is very good. The t and F values are all significant at the 1 percent level (see Table 3.7.1). The order coefficient (α_1) is negative as hypothesized, indicating that subsequent entrants are associated with reduced

Table 3.7.1   Statistical results

Parameter	Value	Statistic*
α_0	1.31	3.28
α_1	−1.30	−3.04
α_2	1.62	9.07
α_3	−0.34	6.28
α_4	−0.20	3.19

* All values significant at 1% level. Critical value with 18 degrees of freedom and two-tail test is $t = 2.88$.

shares relative to the pioneering brand. The positioning effect (α_2) is positive and indicates good positioning is associated with larger shares. In this multiplicative model the position effect increases share proportionately at each entry point. Therefore share for the nth entrant is reduced by the order effect (α_1) and mediated by the positioning effect (α_2). If the positioning index is greater than one (superior price and quality), share will not decrease as much as if it is low (less than one or inferior positioning). It is possible for the nth entrant to earn a dominant share when its positioning is sufficiently superior to overcome the order effect penalty. The relative advertising coefficient (α_3) is also positive and reflects another correlate to increased share when a brand is a late entrant. Superior positioning and aggressive advertising spending would be the most likely correlates of dominance in a category by a later entrant. The parameter reflecting the time between entry (α_4) is negative and indicates if one is a later entrant ($E = n$), it is better to be only 1 year behind ($L = 1$) the previous entrant ($E = n - 1$) than 2 or 3 years ($L = 2$ or $L = 3$).

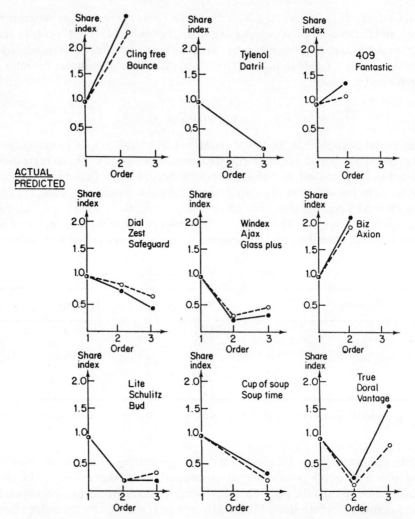

Figure 3.7.1   Fitting procedure—actual and fitted result (o---o) is predicted;
———— is actual)

Figure 3.7.1 shows the actual and predicted values for the share indexes plotted versus the order of entry variable. Recall that predictions are obtained from our multivariate model so any deviation from the negative effect of order of entry (α_1 and α_4) reflects a covariance with positioning and/or advertising effects. For example, the third entry (Era) in the liquid detergent market achieved a predicted share higher than the second entrant due to a higher advertising value (1.1 versus 0.6). This more than compensated for the order of entry decline and raised the predicted share above that of Dynamo.

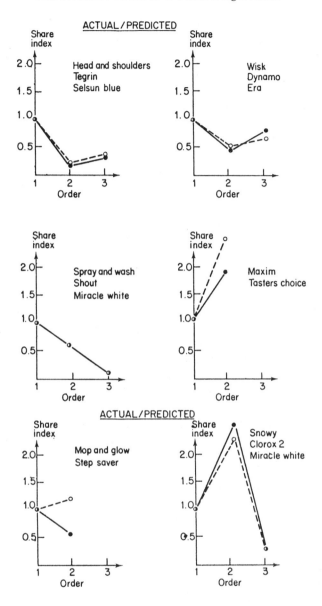

In assessing these fits, we calculate R^2 at 92 percent. Another measure of goodness of fit is to determine the portion of the cases where the model prediction corresponds to the turns in the actual data shown in Figure 3.7.1. There are 23 turns and the direction of actual and predicted agree for 22 turns or 96 percent of them.

Multicollinearity among the independent variables is low. Five out of six of the pairwise correlations are less than 0.1 and the sixth is only 0.31 (see Table 3.7.2). The parameter estimates are stable as variables are added to the regression. The order effect parameter is -1.57 ($t = 1.15$) when it is the only independent variable, -1.13 ($t = -1.44$) when the positioning variable (P) is added, -1.21 ($t = -2.45$) when the advertising variable (A) also is appended, and -1.30 ($t = -3.04$) with all the variables.

Table 3.7.2   Correlations among variables

	E	P	A	L
E				
P	−0.08			
A	0.02	0.31		
L	−0.01	−0.10	−0.04	

The estimates have been reviewed for adverse effects from leverage (Belsley *et al.*, 1980). Two variables are identified as having high leverage (Tegrin and Datril), but when they are removed the parameters (αs) change less than 5 percent from their original values and all *t*s remain significant.

In reviewing the regression results we find all variables are significant. The positioning variable is most significant followed by advertising and the order of entry parameters. In a stepwise regression the positioning variable was the first to be included and explained 76 percent of the variation. Adding advertising increased the R^2 to 82 percent and the order variables raised it to 88 percent. In each case the incremental variance explained was significant at the 10 percent level and all variables are significant when the full model is considered (Table 3.7.1).

Some care must be exercised in interpretation of the advertising and positioning coefficients. Although the advertising index (A) correlates highly with the share index, this may not be due to advertising causing share changes. In fact if advertising budgets were set by a rule such as 'advertising equals X percent of sales', the causative relationship is one of advertising being dependent on sales. Although the interpretation of the advertising coefficient must be cautious, this does not affect the interpretation of the order of entry coefficient (α_2). The variables are uncorrelated (see Table 3.7.2) and one can consider α_2 as a significant explanatory variable of the residual variance.

The positioning variable reflects the relative preference of brands given they were evoked. Such relative preferences, when scaled by β through logit procedures, provide good estimates of the probability of purchase given evoking—eqn (2). Since past choices among evoked brands are used to estimate β and the market shares are estimated based on the unconditional fractions of past purchases, there is a danger that the correlation would be inflated. However, this would be less than if the scaling parameter β were fitted along with the αs in eqn (2) by non-linear estimation procedures. The conservative view is to consider the positioning variable as removing a component of the variance due to correlation of unconditioned market share and probability of purchase conditioned by evoking. The positioning variable (P) is virtually independent of the order variable (see Table 3.7.2), so the threat to the construct validity of the order effect (α_2 and α_4) is low. The overall interpretation we draw from the fitting is that the order of entry effect is significant after considering the mediating effects of advertising and product positioning.

MANAGERIAL IMPLICATIONS

There are strategic implications from this study both for later entrants and pioneers. Later entrants should plan on achieving less share than the pioneering brand if they enter with a parity product. A preferred strategy may be to develop a superior product with either unique benefit features or a lower price. When this is backed by aggressive advertising spending a high share can be achieved. Although the best level of spending is not specified by our model, the advertising and entry parameters are important inputs to a profit-maximizing model (e.g. Urban, 1970, or Little, 1975).

Firms aiming at developing pioneering brands should be encouraged by the availability of a long-run market share reward for their innovation. Although the pioneer's share does decrease as each new firm enters, the pioneer retains a share differential. The size of this reward depends upon the presence and strategies of later entrants. The estimated values in Table 3.7.1 imply the innovators share will drop from 100 percent after the third entrant. This share decline will be greater if the other brands can achieve a superior positioning. The pioneer can minimize this risk by taking care to occupy the preferred positioning with its pioneering brand. This strategy pre-empts the competitor's ability to develop a superior positioning. If the pioneer does not carefully design its product, and an improved product is subsequently introduced and aggressively promoted by a competitor, the market share reward for innovation may be lost. The pioneer should also consider aggressively defending its brand with advertising, and thereby preventing competition from gaining an advertising dominance. In this empirical study, high advertising relative to the pioneer was correlated to competitive share gains. The pioneer could also consider entering a second brand in the category or developing a product line as a defense against competitive entries.

FUTURE RESEARCH

This exploratory empirical cross-category study of order of entry effects indicates the presence of market share rewards to pioneering brands. Our results are consistent with those found empirically by Bond and Lean (1977) and Whitten (1979) in industry studies of pharmaceuticals and cigarettes, and the theoretical work of Schmalensee (1982) and Lane and Wiggins (1981). We believe that this topic deserves additional attention from researchers.

One direction of further research is to conduct a predictive test of the model by applying it to a new sample of data. Another direction is to include additional variables. We hope to include price as a component of preference in our future studies. It would be useful to separate price as a variable and test its effects. Schmalensee (1982) hypothesizes that the order of entry penalty will be greater for higher-priced brands. Another variable that could be added is promotional spending. We have included advertising, but expenditures on promotion might explain more of the residual variance. Finally, introductory spending may explain some of the variation in the mature market shares analyzed here. We have only included the most current 3 years of advertising in our statistical analysis. An ideal data base would be a time-series for each brand with price, advertising, promotion (e.g. UPC or Nielson) along with survey measure of perception and preference. We are pursuing such a data base to enable a time-series cross-sectional analysis of the effects of order of entry.

A second line of research could be aimed at determining the behavioral and microeconomic bases for the order effects we have statistically identified. Schmalensee hypothesizes the reluctance of an individual to try a second entry if the pioneering product works as the core phenomena. It may be that the pioneer has occupied the best position—combination of benefits and price—so that later entrants who differentiate their products will not appeal to as many consumers. The pioneering product may be placed in premier place in an individual's memory so that later entrants will suffer a memory recall and evaluation disadvantage. Superior distribution and more shelf facings are often obtained by the pioneer; these effects of in-store awareness may explain some of the entry effects. The defensive strategies utilized by the innovator may create barriers to entry that penalize the share of new entrants. Research is needed to formulate and test alternative hypotheses. Historical and survey data will be useful but behavioral experiments based on information processing (Bettman, 1979) may be required to obtain a definitive understanding of the microphenomena.

Finally, we did not consider optimizing strategies in this paper. Explicit management science models could be built to maximize long-run profit. Works by Hauser and Shugan (1983) and Lane (1981) are relevant to setting the best defensive strategy for the pioneering brand. Extending these models for order of entry, equilibrium competitive conditions, and product lines are important research needs.

The phenomena surrounding order of entry are interesting research topics and important to firms in formulating new product strategies. Our study of frequently purchased consumer brands is a first step toward understanding the effects of order of entry on market response.

ACKNOWLEDGEMENTS

We would like to thank Management Decision Systems, Inc. for supplying the data for this study. Phil Johnson was especially valuable in generation and initial exploration of the data. Our thanks to Bill Robinson and our MIT colleagues for their comments and insights on our work.

REFERENCES

Bain, J. S., *Barriers to Competition*. Harvard University Press, Cambridge, MA, 1956.
Belsley, D. A., E. Kuh, and R. E. Welsch, *Regressive Diagnostics*. John Wiley, New York, 1980.
Bettman, J. R., *An Information Processing Theory of Consumer Choice* Addison-Wesley, Reading, MA, 1979.
Biggadike, R. E., *Entry Strategy and Performance* Harvard University Press, Cambridge, MA, 1976.
Bond, R. S., and D. F. Lean, 'Sales promotion and product differentiation in two prescription drug markets', *Economic Report* (Federal Trade Commission, Feb. 1977).
Hauser, J. R., and S. M. Shugan, 'Defensive marketing strategies', *Marketing Science*, 1983.
Lane, W. J., 'Product differentiation in a market with endogenous sequential entry', *Bell Journal of Economics*, 1981, 237–259.
Lane, W. J., and S. N. Wiggins, 'Quality uncertainty, repeat purchases and first entrant advantages'. Working Paper, Texas A&M University, Aug. 1981.
Little, J. D. C. 'Brand aid: a marketing mix model, structure, implementation, calibration and case study', *Operations Research*, **23**(4) (July–Aug. 1975), 628–673.
Little, J. D. C., 'Aggregate advertising models: the state of the art', *Operations Research*, **27**(4) (July–Aug. 1979), 629–667.
Mansfield, E., M. Schwartz, and S. Wagner, 'Imitation costs and patents: an empirical study', *Economic Journal*, **91** (1981), 907–918.
Schmalensee, R., 'Product differentiation advantages of pioneering brands', *American Economic Review*, **72** (June, 1982), 159–180.
Shocker, A. D., and V. Srinivasan, 'Multiattribute approaches for product concept evaluation and generation: a critical review', *Journal of Marketing Research*, **1**(2) (May 1979), 159–180.
Silk, A. J., and G. L. Urban, 'Pre-test market evaluation of new packaged goods: a model and measurement methodology', *Journal of Marketing Research*, **15**(2) (May 1978), 171–191.
Urban, G. L., 'Sprinter Mod. III: a model for the analysis of new frequently purchased consumer products', *Operations Research*, **18**(5) (Sept.–Oct. 1970), 805–853.
Urban, G. L., and J. R. Hauser, *Design and Marketing New Products* Prentice-Hall, Englewood Cliffs, N.J., 1980.

Von Hippel, E., 'Appropriability of innovation benefit as a predictor of the functional locus of innovation', *Research Policy*, **11** (Apr. 1982), 95–115.
Whitten, I. T., 'Brand performance in the cigarette industry and the advantage to early entry, 1913–1974'. Federal Trade Commission, Bureau of Economics, June 1979.

Strategic Marketing and Management
Edited by H. Thomas and D. Gardner
© 1985 John Wiley & Sons Ltd

3.8
An Extension of Market Segmentation: Strategic Segmentation

FREDERICK W. WINTER and HOWARD THOMAS
University of Illinois at Urbana-Champaign

INTRODUCTION

Marketing as a discipline is more developed than the fields of strategy, policy, and strategic planning. A strong research tradition in the behavioral and quantitative sciences, together with theories regarding exchange transactions, have contributed to this strong sense of identity currently lacking in the strategy area. Nevertheless, marketing has not cross-fertilized very effectively with other management disciplines such as organizational behavior, operations, finance, and control. This has not been true, however, in marketing's relationship with strategy in which there seems to be strong, genuine mutual interest.

This paper takes one of the more intuitively appealing aspects of marketing, the concept of market segmentation, and attempts to position its role within the strategic framework of the firm. Market segmentation has been much misunderstood since its formulation, but a new emerging view has major implications for strategic management.

THE CONCEPT OF SEGMENTATION

The concept of market segmentation was based on the theoretical foundations of Robinson (1948) and first introduced to the marketing community by Wendell Smith (1956):

> Segmentation is based upon developments of the demand side of the market and represents a rational and more precise adjustment of product and marketing effort to consumer or user requirements. In the language of the economist, segmentation is *disaggregative* in its effects and tends to bring about recognition of several demand schedules where only one was recognized before . . .

Market segmentation, on the other hand, consists of viewing a heterogeneous market (one characterized by divergent demand) as a number of smaller homogeneous markets in response to differing product preferences among important market segments. It is attributable to the desires of consumers or users for more precise satisfaction of their varying wants.

Overconcern for the past

Segmentation is an extremely appealing view of the marketplace in the sense that it recognizes heterogeneity on the part of consumers—heterogeneity in terms of awareness, attitudes, needs, wants, etc. Thus, it appeals to consumer behaviorists who study these differences and also to managers, who look for ways to simplify the complexities of the marketplace so that workable and profitable solutions can be derived.

Based on Smith's original work, market segmentation was concerned primarily with demand. Unfortunately early applications were concerned with demand of the past.

Smith's work was followed by a period labeled by one of the authors as '15 years of regression' (Winter, 1982). This is an appropriate label for two reasons. First, the standard segmentation method was to measure how much product was consumed and then relate this variable to demographic variables via multiple regression analysis. Secondly, it was 'regression' in the literal sense because it was a giant step backward from Smith's original contribution. The process of trying to identify the heavy user related poorly to the demand *schedules* to which Smith referred. Past consumption generated in one particular environment had very little to say about potential actions necessary to capture future demand.

Many examples exist today of marketers segmenting consumers based on behavior of the past. One example is 'product-form segmentation': "A marketer of dog food once described three segments in the industry: dry, moist, and semi-moist dog food." How does this representation help us market our products? Obviously, many different consumer segments converge on dry dog food for a variety of reasons. The dry dog food market may be composed of the price-sensitive segment, the convenience-oriented segment, or the nutrition-oriented segment. The marketing strategies adopted to capture each of these segments are likely to vary considerably. (For another view of how divergent segments might converge on one mix refer to Appendix 1.)

Lack of actionability

The formulation of segments on the basis of product form is not only an example of its focus on the past, it also illustrates early segmentation's lack of concern with actionability. Wind (1978) discusses this in terms of its importance for application.

The use of demographic variables in the formation of segments is another example of the lack of concern for actionability. If segments are defined in terms of old versus young, high income versus low income, there is very little that is obvious in terms of action. Sometimes demographics are correlated with other variables of actionability (e.g. price sensitivity) but why not use the actionable variable directly? Even industrial marketers who define segments on the basis of broad markets such as 'the automotive market', 'the mechanical goods market', and 'the chemical processors market' gain little in terms of actionability.

The stability of demographic segments is also troublesome. In different environments where segments can be expected to change, the static nature of demographic segments seems inappropriate. Haley (1968) states that demographic segmentation relies 'on descriptive factors rather than causal factors. For this reason they are not efficient predictors of a future buying behavior, and it is future buying behavior that is of central interest to marketers.' While Haley's view is even now basically correct, one new application of the use of demographics, pertaining to strategy, will be discussed in a later section.

Ignorance of cost realities

For a number of years, normative segmentation theory was founded on the principle of 'grouping consumers on the basis of similar demand elasticities'· An important paper by Tollefson and Lessig (1978) showed, via microeconomic analysis and simulation, that rules suggesting aggregation based on elasticities or response coefficients are not efficient. Instead a rule based on similar ideal marketing mixes yielded the optimum heuristic for aggregation. One reason for this is that demand-based procedures ignore the cost side of the equation; thus an aggregation by demand looks at only one component of the profit equation. However, the Tollefson and Lessig formulation viewed aggregation as a profit reducing strategy:

> Let D_{ij} be the profit reduction if segments i and j are aggregated, ignoring diseconomies related to the number of segments. The central core of the aggregation problem is the identification of the pair (i,j) for which D_{ij} is a minimum.

If the Tollefson and Lessig formulation is reasonable why would a firm not always segment at the individual level? Indeed the answer is that there may be substantial diseconomies associated with larger numbers of segments. Winter (1979) formulated this relation in terms of a fixed cost associated with the offering of a marketing mix (the fixed cost will vary depending on the marketing mix combination). Thus homogeneous subsegments may be aggregated in order to reduce costs. This may take the form of limiting the number of products produced, media used, or distribution outlets employed.

Other important considerations are constraints that have been modeled by Mahajan and Jain (1978):

> Finally in all the present approaches to normative segmentation the development of market segments and allocation of resources to these segments are considered as two independent questions. In fact, the two issues are closely intertwined and cannot easily be separated. It is meaningless to develop market segments which cannot be serviced with the available corporate resources or available marketing tools. The decision about the type and number of market segments should be imbedded in the overall resource allocation decision.

Although this is good in theory, practice which might follow from the Mahajan and Jain approach is difficult at best. It seems a little easier first to form segments (or they could be called subsegments) and then to aggregate these based on constraints. Thus 'homogenizing' is done first and followed by resource allocation later.

Summary

The significance of market segmentation has been reduced by applications which have focused on past (not future) behavior, ignored actionable alternatives, and have failed to consider resource constraints and the influence of production and technology on realistic cost functions. Accordingly it seems appropriate to offer a new definition of the concept of segmentation:

> Market segmentation is the recognition that groups or subsegments differ with respect to actionable properties which suggest that different marketing mixes might be used to appeal to the different groups. We then may aggregate these subsegments to reduce costs more than benefits (revenues) and this 'aggregation' is based on the fact that they both respond most to the same marketing mix. Subsegments may also be aggregated to satisfy constraints dictated by scarce resources or by management.

This concept states that unless the marketing mix were different (ideally) to different segments, the potential gain from segmentation is low.

THE INEVITABILITY OF THE SEGMENTED MARKET

There are few if any mature markets that do not recognize the existence of market segments by offering at least some marketing variations. The two essential elements that lead to segmentation strategies are heterogeneity of needs and wants, and competition. Even the telephone industry, with its near-monopolistic power, provides different services and demand-oriented pricing structures to meet different user needs. The form of competition can be brand, product form, or generic. Thus long-distance telephone calls must compete effectively with travel, florists, and even the mail service for the customer's dollars.

The period from when a new product is introduced until it is removed from the marketplace is called the product life cycle. Four stages are postulated: introduction, growth, maturity, and decline. Kotler (1980) refers to several options available to the marketing manager when his product reaches the maturity phase:

> the manager looks for new markets and market segments that have not yet tried the product . . . initiating calculated changes in the product's characteristics that will attract new users . . . stimulating sales through altering one or more elements of the marketing mix.

These segmentation practices occur because competition begins to segment the market and buyers' needs and wants grow more discriminating in response to the competition.

Kuehn and Day (1962) were first credited with introducing the concept of the majority fallacy. The majority fallacy recognizes that the majority of preferences among consumers will tend to draw the most competitors; thus a firm that enters the market at a later stage might be well advised to deal with a smaller niche of the market. Cox (1974) discusses the advantage of segmentation in terms of overcoming the low market share disadvantage implied by the Boston Consulting Group Growth-Market Share Matrix:

> Market segmentation—this is the key to the successful application of product portfolio strategy, for it provides the means of changing the category of any entry in the Growth-Share Matrix. Selection of the most appropriate market segments is directed by the matrix parameters of dominant share opportunity and high growth rates.

Competitive entry into market segments is both a reaction to, and a cause of, consumer heterogeneity. If consumers were not different in basic needs, then different wants could not result, and segmentation would be infeasible. Similarly, competitive offerings of differentiated products help redefine the wants exhibited by the consumer. For example, when automobiles were first introduced the automobile was compared to a horse. Obviously the wants which governed the choice of a 1909 black Ford were vastly different from the wants of a 'Sierra-Sunlight'-colored 1982 Ford Escort GL. The point is that competition has rendered discrimination on some attributes as meaningless—i.e. all cars have enclosed cabs with heaters.

Therefore, in a successful market, segmentation is inevitable. This paper will consider how the inevitability of segmentation can be considered during the early phases of a product's introduction as compared to the usual later phase. We will consider how segmentation can be appropriate for the dominant firm

as well as the dominated firm. Finally segmentation will be viewed as a way to
fine-tune the overall product portfolio.

Deterrents to segmentation

As mentioned earlier and as discussed in Appendix 1, cost is a primary
deterrent to multiple market mix strategies. This cost increase can be both a
unit cost increase and an increase in fixed costs.

Some of the Boston Consulting Group's (1968) work suggests that high
production runs and the benefits of accumulated experience yield lower unit
costs because of 'experience curve' benefits. Other benefits such as market
power (Buzzell *et al.*, 1975) could be lost when segmentation strategies are
invoked. Compounding this is the inventory–production run trade-off in
which high fixed costs with low demand result in higher unit costs (the fixed
cost of manufacturing is spread over fewer units) as well as a higher inventory
cost.

Fixed costs also multiply as a firm pursues a multi-marketing mix strategy.
Two products require two product managers instead of one. Two advertising
strategies utilizing different media may be required—this also precludes
media discounts. If different distribution strategies are to be employed, a
sales force will be used to establish the channels. Cost–benefit segmentation
concerns itself with the weighting of increased revenues against all production
and marketing-related sources of cost.

There are two approaches to this effect of costs on segmentation. The
passive solution is to accept the cost relationship and find the local optimum
level of segmentation given that constraint. The enterprising approach is to
search for the global optimum by considering ways in which the cost
constraints can be changed to permit more extensive segmentation.

Reducing the deterrents to segmentation

Several ways exist for a dominant first-in firm to defend itself against firms
that engage in niching strategies. These methods are based mainly on
anticipation of inevitable segmentation and the recognition of the strengths of
the dominant firm. In other words, 'compete where you have a differential
advantage'.

In anticipation of the inevitable, one can generally expect at least seven
different 'generic' segments that are potentially applicable to most products.
These are shown in Table 3.8.1. The task of the dominant firm, therefore, is
to make decisions in advance that allow it to hold a differential advantage in
as many of the segments as possible. For example, one potential advantage is
the cost advantage due to the experience curve. Therefore, in situations
where the experience curve applies, the dominant firm should seek to design

Table 3.8.1   Generic segments

Price-sensitive	Durability-oriented
Performance-sensitive	Distributor/retailer-sensitive
Status-conscious	Security-conscious
Convenience-oriented	

the product and manufacturing around the concept of keeping the experience curve advantage for as many segments as possible. This may involve some of the following:

(1) using standardized components as extensively as possible, particularly on components with potential experience curve gains;
(2) assembling standardized components as early as possible in the assembly process—this allows maintaining inventory of partially completed assemblies;
(3) favoring low fixed-cost production processes unless component standardization can be achieved (see Figure 3.8.1).

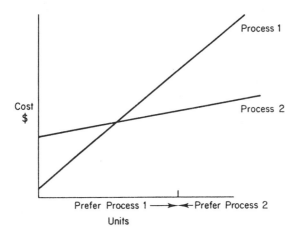

Figure 3.8.1   Indifference point shift between two manufacturing processes

In order to reduce the fixed cost associated with different promotional strategies some of the following tactics may need to be used and therefore anticipated.

(1) using instantaneous low fixed-cost methods of distribution such as manufacturing representatives;
(2) development of umbrella advertising approaches that are compatible with add-on strategies for the different segments;

(3) development of brochures and promotional materials that are expand-
able via use of inserts, etc.

In turn, a new firm to the market can consider these dominant firm normative
strategies in reverse. The new firm should look for segments where there exist
unsatisfied consumer needs *and* the low potential for a dominant firm to
enjoy a differential advantage. For example the costs of complexity or various
critical constraints may restrict the entry of the dominant firm. In terms of the
experience curve, this may mean evaluating which product components will
not serve additional segments. It may mean a thorough evaluation of the
dominant firm's manufacturing process which is heavily capital-dependent
and thus locked in to fixed-cost components. An example of looking for a
competitor's vulnerabilities is provided by Glueck *et al.* (1982):

> A strategy team for a heavy equipment manufacturer spent nine man-months
> reverse engineering the competitor's product, reconstructing his manufacturing
> facilities on paper, and estimating his manufacturing cost. This effort revealed
> that design improvement had produced a substantially lower-cost product for the
> competition and that no achievable amount of cost reduction could manufacture
> the company's product as cheaply. Strategic advantage, therefore, was not likely
> to be won in a price oriented bid for market share.

Of all the seven segments shown in Figure 3.8.1, the performance segment is
probably the most difficult for the dominant firm to adapt to, if it still wishes
to enjoy a differential advantage. For the dominant firm it is probably easier
to keep the standard component and reduce the price (and still preserve the
experience curve advantage) than it is to redesign and offer more performance. Similarly the status-conscious segment represents a probably gain to the
new firm, since previous sales levels decrease the status-satisfying potential of
the dominant firm.

SEGMENTATION AND ENVIRONMENTAL IMPACT

A market segment is really a group of homogeneous consumers who respond
in a similar fashion to a marketing mix. However, they respond in a particular
fashion *given* the current environment. Since the environment can change,
the response of segments can be expected to change as a function of the
environment.

It seems likely that consumers who are homogeneous in their response to
marketing stimuli are also homogeneous in their responses to the environment. For example, price-sensitive individuals may be similar in their
response to economic changes. Performance-sensitive consumers may not be
responsive to economic changes but may respond in a similar fashion to
technological changes. These are testable hypotheses that have yet to be

considered but should be the subject of further research on the dynamics of segment shift.

In industrial marketing there may be a use for reintroducing the concept of demographic segments, particularly with regard to industry specifications such as SIC codes. Because an industrial marketer's demand is a derived demand, response to environmental conditions may be similar within industry segments. It may still be worthwhile to segment further (on actionable bases) within these industry groups (e.g. 'automotive market—convenience oriented').

The implication of segments' differential responses to environmental conditions means that risks associated with marketing in each of these segments must differ. Because firms typically deal with multiple segments for a number of products, the overall product portfolio risk will be a function of the covariance between the sales to the different segments for the different products (see Howell and Winter, 1982). The magnitude of this covariance will be a function of the common environmental forces affecting the segments in which the firm competes. Table 3.8.1 shows that the firm can diversify by choosing to deal with different products, in different segments, and in different usage situations. The utilization of multiple marketing mixes for different segments can represent a form of diversification.

Thus, if one of the sources of a firm's 'differential advantage' is market power, concentration on the same product, the same segments, or the same usage situations may greatly magnify risk. If a firm's differential advantage is technology, manufacturing, financial power, or some combination, and this can be used for different products/segments/situations, then risk is not increased.

One obvious move is to diversify by investment in growth through new products. This diversifies a firm's portfolio by leaving the new enterprise not subject to the same technological forces, or the legal and economic factors which affect the product. A less than obvious diversification strategy is to target new buyers who use the product in different situations. Thus the two products or brands will not share common environmental forces which affect certain segments or situations in which the product is consumed.

CONCLUSIONS

In most competitive markets, segmentation is inevitable and an important weapon in seeking and maintaining competitive advantage. As Henderson (1979) says: 'most dramatically successful business strategies are based upon market segmentation and concentration of resources in that segment'.

The position taken in this paper is that segmentation can be an extremely important tool. First, however, *actionable* bases must be used. Second, we would argue for a broadening of the concept to one of 'strategic segmentation'. Strategic segmentation requires a focus upon the customer demand response, the cost and production systems which underlie the process of supplying customer demand, and the environments affecting both. Segmentation can thus be an important competitive strategy if it is recognized that, in many markets, the benefits of scale for the dominant producer may be reduced by the costs of complexity involved in a firm attempting to serve multiple market segments. However, a dominant producer who anticipates segmented markets may be able to tailor products and production systems so that, with minor modifications, certain common elements of the production process can generate the product output economically for multiple segments.

Strategic segmentation also implies a focus on competitive technologies. The conditions necessary for its application include not only an ability to differentiate customers, but also a 'production technology' which puts potential competitors in like segments at a relative disadvantage.

Henderson (1979) develops a philosophy for strategic segmentation based on the concept of strategic sectors:

> A strategic sector is one in which you can obtain a competitive advantage and exploit it. . . . Strategic sectors are the key to strategy because each sector's frame of reference is competition. The largest competitor in an industry can be unprofitable if the individual strategic sectors are dominated by smaller competitors.

Strategic segmentation offers a method for a firm to diversify its product-market portfolio by focusing on common environmental forces affecting product, segments, or situations for which the product is purchased. Thus a strategic view to segmentation can affect both return as well as risk.

It must be recognized, however, that the implementation of segmentation strategies in the corporate environment may not always be straightforward. Some organizations have structures which are flexible and can quickly adopt segmentation strategies to reinforce competitive strengths and cost advantages. Others, however, may have strongly entrenched organizational belief systems and premises which lead to implicit segmentation structures. Sometimes these implicit structures are counterproductive since the focused effort and investment ignores the realities of the marketplace and competition.

APPENDIX 1

Segmentation can be thought of as the disaggregation of the market into small subsegments followed by the assignment of a marketing mix appropriate for each segment. Thus, an indirect aggregation takes place if two subsegments are offered the same marketing mix. The motivation to offer two or more segments the same marketing mix is to spread the fixed cost associated with each marketing mix over more consumer units without much reduction in revenue. In formal terms this can be modeled in the following way.

We can consider overall profit Z as:

$$Z = \sum_{j=1}^{nm} \sum_{i=1}^{ns} X_{ij}GP_{ij} - \sum_{j=1}^{nm} w_j fc_j$$

or:

$$Z = \sum_{j=1}^{nm} \sum_{i=1}^{ns} X_{ij}(N_i C_j D_i P_{ij}) - \sum_{j=1}^{nm} w_j FC_j$$

subject to:

$$X_{ij} - w_j < 0 \qquad \text{for all } i, j$$

$$X_{ij} = 0,1$$

$$\sum_{j=1}^{nm} X_{ij} = 1 \text{ for all } i$$

where: X_{ij} = 0,1 assignment variable. If 1 it indicates marketing mix j is assigned to segment i

w_j = 0,1. If 1 marketing mix j has been assigned to at least one segment

GP_{ij} = gross profit before fixed costs associated with offering marketing mix j to subsegment i

N_i = number of consumers in segment i

C_j = contribution margin which is the price associated with marketing mix j minus the cost associated with mix j

D_i = per consumer (in segment i) demand of product class

P_{ij} = probability of brand (defined by mix j) purchase by member of segment i.

As shown in Figure 3.8.A1, the number of marketing mixes offered will affect both costs and revenues. If few subsegments are aggregated (many marketing mixes), revenue will have reached asymptotic levels, but costs will be very high. This shows the need for cost–benefit considerations. Table 3.8.A1, adapted from Winter (1979), shows that aggregation on the basis of appeal of similar marketing mixes can lead to aggregation of rather dissimilar subsegments: marketing mix 8 is offered to both subsegments 3 and 4 (in addition to mix 1 for subsegment 1 and mix 4 for subsegment 2). The implications of cost–benefit segmentation are the following:

(1) A marketing mix may be selected even though it is not optimal for any subsegment. (In the example, if the gross profit of mix 5 for subsegment III had been 107 instead of 38.4 neither subsegments III nor IV would be receiving the optimal marketing mix.)

(2) Subsegments are 'aggregated' because they respond most to the same

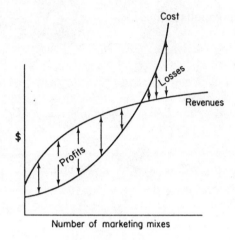

Figure 3.8A1

Table 3.8.A1   Segment–marketing mix profit matrix for gasohol market

Mix no.	D^1	Mix definition P^2	L^3	A^4	O^5	Market subsegments I	II	III	IV	Fixed cost FC (000)
1	S	70	L	5	89	592.4[6]	0	57.2	0	30
2	S	70	U	10	93	197.5	36.8	19.0	0	30
3	S	76	U	5	93	0.3	147.0	76.2	0	30
4	S	76	U	10	93	30.1	165.4	85.8	0	30
5	UC	70	L	5	93	209.6	0	38.4	72.0	50
6	UC	70	L	10	93	262.1	0	48.0	90.0	50
7	UC	76	L	5	89	0	0	0	234.0	50
8	UC	76	L	10	93	42.5	0	105.2	216.0	50
9	UN	70	L	10	89	713.9	0	0	0	160

Aggregate market (with arrows to Market subsegments)

[1] Distribution: S = Standard, UC = unbranded stations accepting credit cards, UN = unbranded stations not accepting credit cards.
[2] Price: 70 = 70c/gallon, 76 = 76c/gallon.
[3] Leaded/unleaded: L = leaded, U = unleaded.
[4] Alcohol content: 5 = % alcohol content, 10 = 10% alcohol content.
[5] Octane rating.
[6] Figures in matrix represent gross profit before fixed costs, π (000 omitted).
Source: Winter (1979).

marketing mix of those mixes to be offered. They may, in fact, have different response patterns. (Note that subsegments III and IV are drastically different, but marketing mix 8 is justified for both subsegments. This is totally compatible with the work of Tollefson and Lessig (1978) who argue that subsegments should *not* be aggregated on the basis of response elasticities.)

(3) Subsegments are not required to support individually the cost of a marketing mix.

(4) Factors such as selective accessibility are automatically considered and quantified. For example, if the market for one product variation is exposed to a wide variety of media, this in turn will be reflected in large numbers of homogeneous subsegments. Thus the marketer will weigh the revenue potential against the large fixed cost associated with a mass marketing strategy or the accumulation of multiple fixed costs associated with many marketing mixes differing in media schedules.

(5) There is no longer any need (or relevance) to specify target markets versus non-targets. Traditional non-target groups essentially reflect a low profit potential and thus receive little weight in the determination of the appropriate marketing mixes.

REFERENCES

Boston Consulting Group (1968). *Perspectives on Experience*. The Boston Consulting Group, Boston.

Buzzell, Robert D., Bradley T. Gale, and Ralph G. M. Sultan (1975). 'Market share—a key to profitability', *Harvard Business Review*, **53**(1) (Jan.–Feb.), 97–106.

Cox, William E. Jr (1974). 'Product portfolio strategy: a review of the Boston Consulting Group approach to marketing strategy', in Ronald C. Curhan (ed.), *1974 Combined Proceedings*, **36**, 465–470.

Glueck, Frederick, Stephen Kaufman, and A. Steven Walleck (1982). 'The four phases of strategic management', *Journal of Business Strategy*, **2**(3) (Winter), 9–21.

Haley, Russell I. (1968). 'Benefit segmentation', *Journal of Marketing*, **32** (July), 30–35.

Howell, Roy, and Frederick W. Winter (1982). 'A segmentation perspective of alternative growth strategies'. Working paper.

Henderson, Bruce (1979). *Henderson on Corporate Strategy* Abt Books, Cambridge, Mass.

Kotler, Philip D. (1980). *Marketing Management: Analysis Planning and Control*. Prentice Hall, Englewood Cliffs, N.J., pp. 205–206.

Kuehn, Alfred A., and Ralph L. Day (1962). 'Strategy of product quality', *Harvard Business Review*. (Nov.–Dec.), 101–102.

Mahajan, Vijay, and Arun K. Jain (1978). 'An approach to normative segmentation', *Journal of Marketing Research*, **15** (Aug.), 338–345.

Robinson, Joan (1948). *The Economics of Imperfect Competition*. Macmillan, London.

Smith, Wendell R. (1956). 'Product differentiation and market segmentation as alternative marketing strategies', *Journal of Marketing*, **21** (July), 3–8.

Tollefson, John O., and Parker Lessig (1978). 'Aggregation criteria in normative market segmentation theory', *Journal of Marketing Research*, **15** (Aug.), 346–355.

Wind, Yoram (1978). 'Issues and advances in segmentation research', *Journal of Marketing Research*, **15** (Aug.), 317–337.

Winter, Frederick (1979). 'A cost–benefit approach to market segmentation', *Journal of Marketing* (Fall), 103–111.

Winter, Frederick (1982). 'Market segmentation: a review of its problems and promise', from David Gardner and Frederick W. Winter (eds), *Proceeding of the 1981 Converse Symposium*, American Marketing Association, Chicago.

CHAPTER 4
Competitive Strategy and Strategic Competition

INTRODUCTION

Porter (1980) and Caves (1980) have been largely responsible for combining the diverse literatures of policy (Schendel and Hofer, 1979) and the economics of industrial organization (Scherer, 1980).

This literature is of particular relevance to those studying strategic marketing. It is relevant because it is consistent with the functional approach of Alderson (1965), the environmental approach (Holloway and Harcourt, 1974) and the systems approach to marketing (Fisk, 1967). The literature of competitive strategy and strategic competition can serve a useful integration function for these well-known approaches to marketing.

In particular, Porter stresses the importance of understanding the effects of industry structure upon the firm's competitive positioning and competitive strategy. Porter models an industry composed of firms engaged in competitive rivalry who are subject to a number of common competitive forces. Such forces include the threat of new entrants into the industry, the potential influence of new substitute products, and the pressures arising from the potential bargaining power of buyers and suppliers. Porter has clearly influenced many thinkers. For example, from a theoretical perspective motivated by the need to link policy and economics, Rumelt (1981) points out that the interesting phenomena of business policy, such as firm heterogeneity or entrepreneurship and risk-taking, were ignored in the traditional neoclassical theory of the firm. He argues for the development of a more encompassing strategic theory of the firm which focuses upon the firm as the organizing concept. In a more practical vein Porter has clearly influenced the thinking of leading strategic consultants, such as McKinsey, (Gluck *et al.*, 1982) and the Boston Consulting Group with its perspective on 'strategy in the 1980s'.

This chapter contains a brief review of the main concepts of competitive strategy, such as the analysis of industry structure and the concept of strategic groups. Their application to the analysis of strategic competition and the formulation of competitive strategy is also examined.

PORTER'S KEY CONTRIBUTIONS: STRUCTURAL ANALYSIS, STRATEGIC GROUPS, AND COMPETITIVE STRATEGY

It is useful to begin this review with a quote from Porter (1980) concerning the purposes underlying structural analysis and competitive analysis: 'The task of structural analysis in the long run is to examine each competitive force, forecast the magnitude of each underlying cause and construct a composite picture of the likely profit potential of the industry.' In a speech given to the North American Society of Corporate Planners (1981) he also suggests that effective competitor analysis has allowed less dominant companies to make inroads against stronger competitors in particular markets. Cases cited include the rejuvenated Miller Beer (following acquisition by Philip Morris) moving to the number two market share position against Anheuser Busch, and Polaroid's successful defense of its market position against Kodak's renewed onslaught with the instant camera.

Perhaps the most important initial step in any competitive strategy analysis is the need to understand the industry structure and the manner in which it may change over time. Five main characteristics are identified as being important in structural analysis; namely, entry and exit barriers; competitive rivalry; threats from substitute products, and the bargaining power of buyers and suppliers. Each of these will be examined below.

Entry of new participants into an industry (or the purchase of an existing competitor by a company with large resources) may change the competitive balance. This may occur because of the introduction of new products, pricing policies, and a whole range of other competitive strategies. However, entry by new firms is dependent upon their ability to afford the price of entry. For example, they may have to overcome a series of barriers to entry; that is, the set of industry characteristics and competitive factors possessed by existing competitors which must be matched by the new entrants. The costs of matching existing competitors may prove to be too high to some potential entrants. Others may be able to draw upon the capital resources of the parent company in order to ensure that an effective base and bridgehead is developed in that industry.

Clearly, the sources of entry barriers are related to such industry characteristics as the financial resources required for capital investment in the industry, the existence of significant economies of scale or cost experience effects, the need to establish and obtain appropriate channels for product distribution, the presence of differentiated products maintained by strong advertising and marketing programs, the possession of strong patents and product technology by existing competitors, and in some circumstances the impact of government regulations requiring registration or licensing of new entrants to enable them to manufacture the industry's product.

Note that entry barriers can change through time, e.g. R&D patents may expire and, in any case, barriers will not affect all potential entrants in the same way. Further, existing competitors may continually update their competitive positioning in order to make it more difficult for potential new entrants to consummate entry.

Competitive rivalry impacts existing competitors just as much as it does new entrants. One feature is that a range of strategies will be in evidence arising from the different strengths possessed by members of the industry, i.e. the firms in an industry are heterogeneous with respect to goals and strategies but it is also possible that they may cluster together into a number of strategic groups, defined by the adoption of similar or common strategies with respect to the competitive environment.

Competitive rivals will typically use their strategic strengths to consolidate their position within the industry. Their strategies will also depend upon the perceived degree of stability of the industry, i.e. the extent of entry and exit barriers. For example, if entry barriers are high and exit barriers are low (i.e. when there is a ready market for the assets and goodwill of existing businesses) then the profit potential of the industry is high, which in turn encourages firms to strengthen their positions and niches within the industry.

On the other hand, the ready existence of substitutes for the industry's product will severely limit the profit potential for the industry. Porter and Spence's (1982) article addresses the impact on the sugar market of the expansion of capacity for the sugar substitute, high-fructose corn syrup (a derivative and byproduct of the operations of such agribusiness firms as A. E. Staley, and Archer, Daniels Midland (ADM)).

Strong buyer groups can also affect industry profit potential. If they have significant power then they can attempt to bargain lower prices and/or argue for better quality and service at a given price. Certain companies may, therefore, attempt to sell to those buyers who cannot, through significant oligopoly power, bargain the price down to a relatively unattractive level.

Suppliers with power, either because they are few in number or because they can sell the commodity to a wide range of industries, will have the ability to raise raw material and commodity prices and somewhat limit an industry's profit potential. Firms may react to this by backward integration or by searching for a number of alternative supply sources or substitute raw materials.

Once the forces influencing the industry's competitive structure are understood, the company can compare its strengths and weaknesses with its perceptions about current and future competitive forces. By matching corporate strengths with environmental opportunities it can decide whether it would be wiser for it to compete through cost leadership, or through focusing its competitive position around a key set of resources or skills, or through adapting its skills to crucial customer needs which it perceives to be emerging over some future horizon. Its perspective should, therefore, be to monitor not only the existing competitive structure but also its predictions about industry changes and evolution through time.

Porter's concept of strategic groups is also extremely important for competitive positioning. A firm may try to match its strengths and weaknesses to the set of industry competitive forces but it may also try to match its competitive skills and resources against its perception of 'similar competitors', i.e. those against whom it monitors its sales, financial, and other target performance goals.

Porter (1980: 129) defines a strategic group within an industry as 'the group of firms in an industry following the same or a similar strategy along the strategic dimensions'. 'Heterogeneous' firms belonging to an industry can be divided into smaller groups called strategic groups, and the firms within each group can be considered relatively 'homogeneous'. If this concept is accepted, the performance of a firm will depend on the structural position of its strategic group relative to the other groups in the industry, and also on its position within the strategic group.

It should be noted that entry barriers protect firms in a strategic group not only from entry of those firms outside the industry, but also from entry of firms from other strategic groups attempting to move to a strategic group which offers more opportunities or less threats.

When a firm is attacked by a firm from another strategic group (in contrast to a new firm that tries to enter), Porter (1980: 134) says 'Mobility barriers provide the first major reason why some firms in an industry will be persistently more profitable than others. Different strategic groups carry with them different levels of mobility barriers, which provide firms with persistent advantages over others.'

In Porter's terms competitive strategy is the strategic action taken by a company to position itself optimally against the array of competitive forces and competitors, and in so doing developing a set of strategic moves to improve current competitive position and anticipate future changes in the competitive balance. (Additional features of competitive strategy formulation can be determined from Porter (1980), Hofer (1977) and Hofer and Schendel (1978). In particular, Hofer and Porter provide useful checklists of important strategic factors in market analysis, industry analysis, competitive analysis, supplier analysis, environmental analysis, and firm resource and capability analysis.)

RECENT CONSULTING CONTRIBUTIONS IN STRATEGIC COMPETITION AND COMPETITIVE STRATEGY

Porter's (1980) and Caves' (1980) work may have been the 'trigger' for the development of the new strategic competition focus of many consultants. On the other hand, the pioneering work of Bruce Henderson of BCG (1979) has undoubtedly been one of the major influences upon the emergence of the competitive strategy framework and the use of models, such as the experience curve, drawn from the industrial organization literature.

In this vein, it is useful to quote some paragraphs from a recent Boston Consulting Group note entitled 'Strategy in the 1980s'

> In the 1970s . . . The most successful companies achieved their success by anticipating market evolution and creating unique and defensible advantage over their competitors in the new environment.

They then argue that it is impossible, using simple rules or strategy positions, to determine the correct course for a business automatically:

> No planning system guarantees the development of successful strategies. Nor does any technique. The Business Portfolio (Growth/Share Matrix) made a major contribution to strategic thought. Today it is misused and overexposed. It can be a helpful tool, but it can also be misleading or, worse, a straight-jacket.

Their present work now focuses on strategic competition and competitive economics, and they express it in the following terms:

> The strategy requirements of any business are ruled by the competitive environment and the potential for change in that environment. Two factors in particular give one a sense of the nature of that environment. The first is the size of the advantage that can be created over other competitors. The second is the number of unique ways in which that advantage can be created. The combination of these two factors both gives a sense of the long term value of a business and dictates the strategy requirements.

The Boston Consulting Group then use a strategic box, based on these two dimensions, to categorize the industry type—fragmented, specialization, stalemate, and volume—in which particular businesses in the corporate portfolio compete. The focus is to develop the ability to create sustainable competitive advantages with a business portfolio, and also to change the basis of competition in anticipation of industry evolution or changing competitive trends. This point is reinforced in another BCG note entitled 'How to recognize the need for change'. Carl Stern notes that companies should be alert to signals of destabilizing influences in competitive environments. These signals can be detected from monitoring of such factors as the marketplace, channels of distribution, competitors, organizational changes, company financial performance, and, most important of all, the creativity and imagination emerging from managerial intuition.

CONCLUSIONS

The aim of strategic competitive analysis and models of strategic competition is to force the firm to establish its own strengths and weaknesses, to rate its position *vis-à-vis* competitors, to monitor all the industry and global environmental changes, to rate businesses in the corporate portfolio in relation to their competitive and market economics, and ultimately to select corporate strategies to meet corporate objectives concerning performance, growth, risk, and cost. It should be clear that this is appropriate for both the corporate level of planning as well as the business level where strategic marketing is focused.

This process is not easy. Creating viable strategic options to achieve sustainable long-term advantage requires creative managers and a good corporate culture. Writers such as Deal and Kennedy (1982) and Peters and Waterman (1982) have begun to identify organizational barriers to successful strategy implementation and have listed 'core value, focussedness and attention to detail' factors as amongst the attributes which may lead to corporate success and performance.

REFERENCES

Alderson, W. (1965). *Dynamic Marketing Behavior*. Richard D. Irwin, Homewood, IL.
Boston Consulting Group Newsletters (undated) 'Strategy in the 1980's', 'How to recognize the need for change'. Boston Consulting Group, Boston, Mass.
Caves, R. E. (1980). 'Industrial organization, corporate strategy and structure', *Journal of Economic Literature*, March, pp. 64–92.
Deal, T. E., and A. A. Kennedy (1982). *Corporate Cultures*. Addison-Wesley, Reading, Mass.
Fisk, G. (1967). *Marketing Systems: An Introductory Analysis*. Harper & Row, New York.
Gluck, F. W., S. Kaufman, and A. S. Walleck (1982). 'The four phases of strategic management', *Journal of Business Strategy*, 2(3), 9–21.
Henderson, B. (1979). *Henderson on Corporate Strategy*. Abt Books, Cambridge, Mass.
Hofer, C. W. (1977). 'Conceptual constructs for formulating corporate and business strategies'. Intercollegiate Case Clearing Hose (ICCH), Boston, #9-378-754.
Hofer, C. W., and D. E. Schendel (1978). *Strategy Formulation: Analytical Concepts*, West Publishing, St Paul, MN.
Holloway, R. J., and R. S. Hancock (1974). *The Environment of Marketing Management*. John Wiley & Sons, New York.
Peters, T. J., and R. H. Waterman Jr (1982). *In Search of Excellence*. Harper & Row, New York.
Porter, M.E. (1980) *Competitive Strategy*. Free Press, New York.
Porter, M.E. (1983). 'Analyzing competitors: predicting competitor behavior and formulating offensive and defensive strategy', in M. Leontiades (ed.), *Policy Strategy and Implementation*, pp. 192–209. Random House, New York.
Porter, M. E., and A. M. Spence (1982). 'The capacity expansion process in a growing oligopoly: the case of corn wet milling', in J. J. McCall (ed.), *The Economics of Information and Uncertainty*. University of Chicago Press, Chicago, IL.
Rumelt, R. P. (1981). 'Towards a strategic theory of the firm'. Working paper, Graduate School of Management, UCLA.
Schendel, D. E., and C. W. Hofer (1979). *Strategic Management: A New View of Business Policy and Planning*. Little, Brown, Boston, Mass.
Scherer, F. M. (1980). *Industrial Market Structure and Economic Performance*. Houghton, Mifflin, New York.

Strategic Marketing and Management
Edited by H. Thomas and D. Gardner
© 1985 John Wiley & Sons Ltd

Introduction to Conference Papers on Competitive Strategy

The literature on competitive strategy has already been reviewed in Chapter 4. The papers in this section are concerned with specific aspects of the field of competitive strategy and particularly the concept of strategic groups which has become one of the important research topics in the strategy field.

Hatten and Hatten examine the relationship of market share, profit, and market structure in the brewing industry. They probe the following issues using both strategic group and industry modes of analysis:

(1) the robustness of the market share–profit relationship;
(2) the information content of some alternate market definitions;
(3) the nature and stability of industry structure.

Their paper concludes with some guidelines for industry analysis. Note that Hatten and Hatten's study is a continuing element in a stream of research about strategic patterns, groupings, and market structure in the beer industry. These studies have been carried out by a series of researchers associated with Purdue University; namely: Arnie Cooper, Ken Hatten, Rich Patton, and Dan Schendel.

McGee, on the other hand, reviews both the concept of strategic groups and recent research evidence about its application. He argues that, for the business policy researcher and for the business strategist, strategic groups offer a distinctive slant on the identification of relative competitive position and suggest a systematic and comprehensive way of conducting a strengths and weaknesses analysis. He further suggests that the effect of strategic groups is to restore strategic decision to the center of the structure and performance arena and to re-emphasize the firm as an important unit of analysis.

One of the main purposes of Primeaux's study is to develop a method to identify the stage of the life cycle in which an industry is operating, and to determine whether all firms in the industry are in the same stage of the life cycle. The method involves using an investment behavior equation developed by Kmenta and Williamson to establish the investment behavior characteristics (and hence life cycle) of an industry as a whole. This same equation is then applied separately to strategic groups within the industry to determine the life cycle stage of each group. These groups are formed by using the well-known measure of the relative size of a firm in an industry as a proxy for its strategic group membership. As McGee and others point out, strategic groups can be formed in other ways—including the use of investment behavior variables as basic proxies for strategic group membership.

Ryans and Wittink develop another approach for identification of strategic groups based upon financial theory in general and the CAPM (capital asset pricing model) in particular. They explore the possibility that security price movements may be able to provide insight into the strategic group structure of some industries. The basic premise underlying their research is that firms in different strategic groups are likely to respond somewhat differently to disturbances from within and without the particular industry. Their results, based upon the airline industry, suggest that the approach is promising and should be researched in other industry contexts.

Williams is interested in the inferface between firms' marketing activities and their strategic management processes. In particular he focuses upon some strategic impacts on organizations which may result from choices in product market scope. Four areas are of interest: (1) the differential impact on organizations of product market strategies which lie at opposite ends of all firms' investment opportunity set, (2) the difference between using the product market matrix methodology to perform a structural analysis of an industry as opposed to using the methodology to manage the firm, (3) the kinds of managerial incentive problems that may follow an emphasis on certain kinds of investments, and (4) the intersection between the special marketing choices that a multi-product firm can make that are both strategic in nature and which also complicate the antitrust enforcement problem. These four areas are related in that they represent examples where the marketing function and the strategic management function can overlap in ways which blur the management boundaries of each.

Strategic Marketing and Management
Edited by H. Thomas and D. Gardner
© 1985 John Wiley & Sons Ltd

4.1
Some Empirical Insights for Strategic Marketers: The Case of Beer*

KENNETH J. HATTEN
Associate Professor, Boston University, School of Management

AND

MARY LOUISE HATTEN
Associate Professor, Boston College, School of Management

OVERVIEW

In this paper we show that market share and profit are not universally correlated and that various market share and profitability measures carry different, potentially important, information. We also show the profit impact of strategic marketing variables in the brewing industry, now a mature, high fixed-cost, concentrated industry, and suggest that the appropriate measure of managerial success in this industry is not profitability measured as return on assets but a company's share of industry profits. Profits earned count more than return on assets.

The Brewing Industry

As a site for industry analysis the brewing industry is a ready, interesting (and sometimes surprising) laboratory. Brewing is primarily a single-product industry, so its financial reports are the tracks of mostly single-business strategies. Developments in the industry have been remarkable since 1971. Major industry changes popularly attributed to marketing during the 1970s include:

(1) the $1 billion-plus Miller revitalization by Phillip Morris, famous for its marketing expertise in cigarettes;

---

* The authors gratefully acknowledge the significant contributions made by Mr Edward Black, Research Assistant in the Graduate School of Management, Boston College, in preparing and analyzing the data.

(2)   the decline of Schlitz accelerated by an advertising campaign ("You
       want to take away my Gusto?") which some felt was threatening to
       Schlitz's customers, and a beer of inconsistent quality;
(3)   the decline of Pabst;
(4)   the rise of Heileman, currently selling over 40 brands, and its bid to
       purchase Schlitz, the only major merger blocked by the FTC in the
       Reagan administration (to July 1982); and
(5)   reduced vitality at Coors and Olympia, the former once a marketing
       legend.

The industry has been concentrating since Prohibition, although the pace
seems to have accelerated during the 1970s. The number of brewers operating
in the US fell from 400 in 1950 to 90 in 1980 and the market share of the top four
brewers rose from 22 percent in 1950 to 75 percent in 1981.

   Such concentration seems to point to market share, and to marketing
strategy, as key factors for profitability and growth in the brewing industry.
Indeed, in recent years, a number of powerful regional brewers, such as Strohs,
have sought national distribution, suggesting that management may believe
market share or size brings profitability (Stroh's successful bid for Schlitz in
1982 and Schmidt's and Heileman's for Pabst, and Pabst's for Pittsburgh and
Olympia this same year support this hypothesis). Even Coors has widened its
distribution outside its original Western market. The industry is therefore an
interesting site to test the relevancy of some major concepts of strategic
marketing, particularly the market share—profitability relationship.

METHODOLOGY

As noted, this research is not an attempt to explain profitability in the brewing
industry; rather, it is an exploitation of the industry as a laboratory for industry
analysis. Our work was facilitated by our experience, a dissertation (Hatten,
1974), and subsequently a series of cases on Schlitz/Miller, Anheuser-Busch,
Olympia, and Heileman.

   The data base was assembled from public sources, the annual reports and
detailed 10K's of the brewers themselves, *Moody's, Advertising Age, The
Brewers' Almanac*, and the FTC report on the brewing industry (Keithahn,
1978).

   The data included in this research are substantially richer in the marketing
arena than the data used by Hatten (1974) and Patton (1976). Not only are
there advertising and state-level market share data to enhance our ability to
explore marketing strategy and market definition, but data on Coors, Miller,
and Schaefer as well—companies not represented in the earlier studies of this
industry. The firms in the data base included Anheuser-Busch, Associated,

Coors, Falstaff, Genessee, Grain Belt, Heileman, Lone Star, Lucky Lager, Miller, Olympia, Pabst, Pittsburgh, Rainier, Schaefer, and Schlitz.

Methodologically, we followed standard practice: we calculated a correlation matrix, examined scattergrams, and allowed theory to guide our selection of the parameters of the regression models we estimated to probe the market share–profitability relationship and market structure within the brewing industry.

Multicollinearity was a major characteristic of the data, although we attempted to limit its impact on the results by judiciously selecting non-collinear variables. As Farrar and Glauber (1967) point out, however, multicollinearity sometimes is a matter of 'how much'.

The heterogeneity–homogeneity trade-off is one we probed deeply, both across companies and over time using the Chow test (Chow, 1960), and the F/F_C ratio to guide pooling of firms (Hatten and Schendel, 1978). On this issue we depart from the usual practice in industrial economics and, in large measure, from practice in most industry analysis by using a statistical test to guide our pooling of firms into strategic groups, and not judgement alone.

RESULTS

Correlation analysis: market share, and profitability

One of our primary concerns in this research was to determine whether the conventional view that profitability and market share are highly correlated is particular to some circumstances. To this end, we calculated the correlation coefficients between five profitability measures and seven market share definitions (see Table 4.1.1 for variable definitions) and correlation coefficients; they apply to the full data base, that is, the industry, between 1952 and 1980.

Let us begin by examining the market share–profitability issue in the upper right of Table 4.1.1. The relationship between profitability and market share is weak in the brewing industry over this time period. Not only are the correlation coefficients between the usual market share and profitability measures low, but they differ measure to measure, implying that different measures carry different information.

Look at the left-hand side of Table 4.1.1. It is apparent that net profit on equity (ROE) and net profit on assets (ROA) are highly correlated, while operating income (OROA) is not highly correlated with either of them (Kuh and Meyer, 1955). Apparently a high OROA is not always associated with a high ROE or ROA. Leverage should, of course, lift ROE versus OROA, but which companies use debt? The larger companies seem more likely to use debt, since they have had the desire and opportunity to grow, and are probably perceived as lower risks by bankers.

Table 4.1.1 Brewing industry, 1952–80: profitability, profit, market share, correlation coefficients

	Net income on equity (ROE)	Net income on assets (ROA)	Operating income on assets (ROA)	Industry profit share (PROSHA)	Relative profit share (RELPRO)	US market share (bbl) (MSB)	US market share ($) (MSR)	Relative market share (bbl) (NRMCB)	Relative market share ($) (NRMCR)	Average state market share (bbl) (AVST)	Average state relative share (to leader) (AVSTR)	Average state relative share (to largest competitor) (AVSTRC)
ROE	.	0.92	0.76	0.41	0.40	0.17	0.19	0.19	0.19	0.07	−0.00	0.08
ROA		.	0.91	0.38	0.39	0.13	0.14	0.15	0.15	0.09	−0.01	0.11
OROA			.	0.38	0.39	0.16	0.18	0.17	0.17	0.16	0.06	0.18
PROSHA				.	0.90	0.88	0.89	0.81	0.79	0.60	0.47	0.53
RELPRO					.	0.87	0.90	0.93	0.90	0.51	0.44	0.45
MSB						.	0.99	0.92	0.86	0.48	0.40	0.37
MSR							.	0.95	0.92	0.50	0.43	0.39
NRMCB								.	0.98	0.40	0.39	0.31
NRMCR									.	0.40	0.39	0.30
AVST										.	0.92	0.97
AVSTR											.	0.87
AVSTRC												.

More significantly, however, profitability (all measures) is not highly correlated with profit share in the industry. This finding is important. Top management should be concerned with profits, earnings per share, and profit growth. That is, one of their objectives might be to get a disproportionate share of industry profits. Return on assets or return on equity can be manipulated for a time by changing the denominators (which actually means not growing or not reinvesting), but it is the numerator which does not lie and it is profit that funds growth.

Now move to the bottom right of Table 4.1.1, where the correlations between alternate market share definitions are displayed. Note that although national market shares measured in barrels and dollars are highly correlated, when relative national market shares are calculated, the revenue-based relative share, NRMCR, is less tightly linked to the barrel share measure, MSB. This implies that some companies pursue different revenue and barrel objectives than the others; they appear more interested in relative revenue standing than in selling barrels of beer—and the data shows Busch is one of these.

Now consider the relationships between national shares and state-by-state market shares. Correlation coefficients plunge from above 0.90 to as low as 0.30 for national relative revenue share, NRMCR, and the average state market share, AVSTRC. Obviously these two variables measure different competitive phenomena. First, the low correlations suggest that the brewers which dominate the national market do not dominate state or regional markets and that *some* small brewers, in fact, have relatively high regional power. Second, if we examine the correlations between profitability and national and state market shares, we find the state market share–profitability relationships are extremely low (and negative in one case), suggesting that regional market dominance is not sufficient for sustained profitability. This inference has serious consequences for companies whose marketing strategy has been regionally restricted. In 1982 these regionals may be trapped unprofitably in their once-safe niches, being devitalized by the slow competitive advances of the national brewers and the evolution of a national market.

To summarize, the results of the correlation analysis between profitability and market share in the brewing industry, are:

(1)   Market share is not strongly correlated with profitability in this industry, although marketing strategy has been perceived as being a significant contributor to business success in brewing.

(2)   There are alternate ways of measuring business success which have different implications: short-term profitability may not be closely linked with long-term industry profit positions.

(3) Multiple market share definitions carry information on marketing strategies: (past) state-level success is not closely linked with national dominance.

Scattergrams: market shares and information

Let us now focus on the information content of the different market share and profit measures. The profit share and relative state market share correlations suggest that geographic scope may affect profitability. Figures 4.1.1 and 4.1.2 show scattergrams of these relationships across the industry with different companies' data points labeled to help us interpret the data.

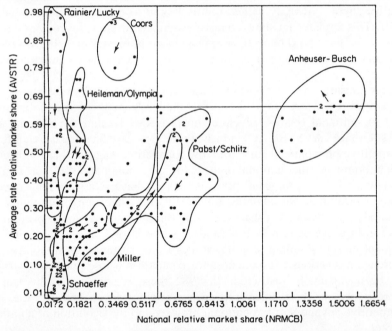

Figure 4.1.1   Average state relative share vs. national relative share, 1962–77

One of the most striking inferences we can make from these scattergrams is that Anheuser-Busch is pulling away from the industry. Figure 4.1.1 shows average state market share versus relative market share in barrels. Busch is penetrating the state markets, spreading geographically and intensifying its market penetration regionally. Figure 4.1.2 reveals more of Busch's strategy: it is steadily increasing its share of its markets to ultimately gain a dominant position state by state. If we examine Figure 4.1.2 again we can see the records of once-powerful regional brewers. Notice, for example, Rainier and Lucky

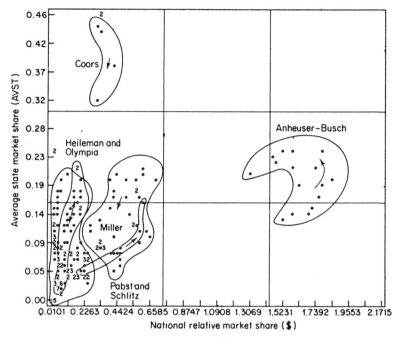

Figure 4.1.2   Average state market share vs. national relative share,
1962–77

which disappeared as independent companies after their market shares were
eroded by competition from the major national brewers (note Schaeffer's track
is inaccurate, because we have no data on the New York market).

Compare the X axes of Figures 4.1.1 and 4.1.2: it seems that Busch's share
of industry revenue is bigger than its share of industry barrel sales—the
implications for long-term wealth and power in the industry are obvious. The
remaining profits earned in the industry had to be split by the other brewers and
appear to have been insufficient to finance effective competition and long-term
growth for many. To document Busch's relative success consider the
competitive significance of its purchase of the new Schlitz plant in Syracuse,
New York, in February 1980, a plant which represented overcapacity to Schlitz
in spite of apparent likely future demand for Busch. Note too that in 1972
Busch earned an amount equal to 60 percent of total industry profits.

If the results for Anheuser-Busch are dramatic, the regionals' stories are also
telling. Coors in the past has been disproportionately profitable but recently
has been unable to sustain its profitability. It may follow the declining path that
afflicted companies like Lucky Lager and Rainier as the largest brewers
intensify their penetration of its once niche-like markets, and advertising
becomes a necessary but expensive marketing tool.

The patterns of these charts also suggest that Olympia's currently low profits and profitability may, in fact, be due to the same problem—the national brewers are now seriously eroding the market of the historically strong regionals of the West. As a consequence, Olympia may follow the fate of the other small brewers as the industry concentrates unless it can compete differently. For Olympia, 'competing differently' probably means moving out of its threatened niche and operating national-scale plants. Of course, such a change of strategy would require substantial capital and, since Olympia is marginally profitable, it is probably trapped long-term in an unviable position.

Heileman, too, may ultimately share the fate of Coors and Olympia unless it can establish and defend a position of back-up source or number two supplier to the beer distributors. Like Coors, Heileman's profitability has been high (ROE greater than 20 percent) but, unlike Coors, its share of industry profit has been low. How long it can operate as a conglomerate of regional breweries operating out of relatively small plants bought at a discount is a difficult question, but the company's thwarted efforts to acquire Schlitz and then Pabst suggest that top management wants to break out of its current regional strategic posture and grow at a faster rate—and that the company does not have sufficient wealth to expand except by the acquisition of weaker brewers.

Now, although our examination of these scattergrams was exploratory, it has led to some sensible questions for the management of different companies. Moreover, note how we reached this point—by probing, speculating on differences between one market share definition and another. The key to unlocking the information content of market share is to contrast and compare differently measured market shares and to find explanations for the differences or attribute meaning to them (Majaro, 1977).

There is, at least, one additional implication of these industry-wide scattergrams. Collectively, the scattergrams suggest that geographic scope differentiates companies. Since profitability appears to vary with scope it is reasonable to hypothesize different profit impacts of marketing strategies for companies with different geographic scopes.

Regression analysis: profitability, market share, and the 4 Ps

In this next section of the paper we examine the impact of market share on profitability when the effects of the major marketing variables, the 'four Ps', are controlled. We restricted the analysis to the 1962–77 period to take full advantage of the data collected for the FTC study, and to leave some unreliable advertising data and ancient history behind; 1952–62 in this case. Industry statistics have not been published by the IRS for years after 1976.

Theory in this case is straightforward. We attempt to explain profitability at the operating level, OROA, in terms of product, price, promotion, and place (marketing's four Ps) and market share.

The proxy for product here is number of brands, price is revenue/barrels sold (revenue is adjusted for diversification where necessary using 10K information), and promotion is restricted to six media advertising reported by *Advertising Age* measured as a rate, advertising dollars per barrel, and as an amount, relative share of industry advertising. Place is difficult. It would be valuable to have number of wholesalers per state, but out data base does not include this statistic. We have number of states per plant as an alternative spread measure. Finally, we use average relative state market share to measure market power in states served (at least those states encompassed by the FTC study*) and relative market share in barrels (NRMCB), to act as proxy for size. Following economic theory, a major hypothesis is that profitability will be negatively affected by the advertising variables. *A priori*, however, we did not hypothesize the signs of any other relationships, for example, plants or brands, since increases in these variables may represent both increased total costs and potential efficiencies lowering unit production costs, depending on management's skill.

Multicollinearity is a problem. Although the correlation matrices generated for these variables show it is generally not severe, some variables are severely correlated. For example, at the industry level, ADS/bbl and Relative Share of Industry Advertizing, RADSHC are correlated at the 0.54 level; these variables are conceptually and definitionally related; RADSHC and NRMCB are correlated at 0.85, since both measure market power and size. NRMCB and ADS/bbl are not highly correlated, however, having a 0.24 correlation coefficient.

The regression results for the industry, national, regional, and small brewer groups are shown in Table 4.1.2. These strategic groupings were based on industry tradition and the research of Hatten (1974) and Patton (1976).

The six equations in each set are intended as variations on the 'four Ps' theme, designed to collectively get around the multicollinearity problem. Generally, eqns (4), (5), and (6) are less affected since it is national market share which is highly correlated across the industry and within the strategic groups with advertising share RADSHC, States/Plants, Price, and with AVSTRC. This last variable is itself correlated negatively with advertising and brands, possibly due to the strategy of Coors, i.e. extreme regional dominance, a single brand and almost no advertising for many years.

National market share is significant and negative for the national group in equations inclusive of state share, AVSTRC, although it is positive for all the other regressions. Market share appears so closely correlated with other attributes of size that it is difficult not to agree with Rumelt and Wensley (1981) and Gale (1972), that market share is a proxy for many other managerially controllable assets. Although statistical theory in the face of multicollinearity

* Covering the period 1962–77 for 36 states. Notable exclusions are New York and Pennsylvania.

Part I

Table 4.1.2 OROA, 1962–77 (standardized βs, F stat)

Eqn.		Price	ADS/bbl	Brands	NRMCB	Plants	RADSHC	AVSTRC	State/plant	R^2	df
Industry											
1.	β	0.06	−0.08	−0.01	0.06			0.20	0.13	0.10	5,144
	F	0.53	0.77	0.02	0.46			3.98	2.12	3.15	
2.	β	0.05		ne	0.14		−0.12	0.21	0.12	0.10	5,144
	F	0.38			0.75		0.56	5.30	1.94	3.11	
3.	β	0.06	−0.06	−0.01	0.10		−0.05	0.19	0.13	0.10	7,142
	F	0.49	0.27	0.01	0.30		0.06	3.93	2.09	2.23	
4.	β	0.05	−0.02	0.05	0.43	−0.45				0.14	5,146
	F	0.30	0.06	0.36	14.74	14.49				4.87	
5.	β	0.03		0.07	0.32	−0.52	0.18			0.15	5,146
	F	0.11		0.69	4.83	16.00	1.13			5.12	
6.	β	0.04	−0.13	0.07	0.22	−0.54	0.34			0.16	6,145
	F	0.23	1.44	0.70	1.72	17.01	2.51			4.52	
Anheuser-Busch, Miller, Pabst, Schlitz											
1.	β	−0.58	−0.29	−0.56	−0.38			0.80	−0.14	0.56	6,53
	F	16.76	5.10	20.78	4.42			8.55	0.63	11.35	
2.	β	−0.70		−0.49	−0.31		−0.24	1.11	−0.09	0.54	6,53
	F	16.71		20.28	3.82		8.37	0.21	0.76	9.61	
3.	β	−0.59	−0.25	−0.56	−0.36		0.84	−0.08	−0.16	0.56	7,52
	F	15.71	2.60	20.68	3.82		8.37	0.21	0.76	10.46	
4.	β	−0.40	−0.45	−0.52	0.05	0.38				0.46	5,54
	F	10.56	12.90	17.72	0.01	8.83				9.25	
5.	β	−0.50		−0.36	0.35	0.44	−0.23			0.35	5,54
	F	15.11		8.20	5.33	6.46	1.54			5.85	
6.	β	0.40	−0.29	−0.51		0.33	0.10			0.46	5,54
	F	12.30	17.84	18.86		4.36	0.41			9.36	

Eqn.	Price	ADS/bbl	Brands	NRMCB	Plants	RADSHC	AVSTRC	State/Plant	R^2	df
Coors, Heileman, Olympia										
1. β	−0.47	−0.11	−0.13	0.96			−0.63	−0.20	0.29	6,26
F	5.27	0.24	0.37	4.85			1.62	1.06	1.78	
2. β	−0.40		−0.16	0.99		−0.26	−0.72	−0.15	0.33	6,26
F	4.16		0.63	5.52		1.87	2.41	0.62	2.15	
3. β	−0.42	0.24	−0.18	0.98		−0.41	−0.63	−0.16	0.35	7,25
F	4.42	0.55	0.77	5.33		2.13	1.73	0.66	1.89	
4. β	−0.25	−0.12	0.95	0.27	−0.99				0.40	5,27
F	1.92	0.46	7.78	2.06	9.14				3.63	
5. β	0.21		0.90	0.26	−0.97	−0.22			0.43	5,27
F	1.50		7.64	2.46	9.27	1.97			4.13	
6. β	−0.23	0.17	0.83	0.31	−0.93	−0.35			0.44	6,26
F	1.71	0.39	5.83	2.79	8.00	1.84			3.43	
Small brewers										
1. β	0.26	0.17	−0.39	−0.53			0.08	−0.04	0.39	6,19
F	1.07	0.44	2.57	1.83			0.08	0.02	1.99	
2. β	0.33		−0.32	−0.47		0.05		−0.03	0.37	5,20
F	1.96		2.50	2.47		0.05		0.01	2.38	
3. β	0.22	0.48	−0.41	−0.34		−0.35	0.08		0.40	6,19
F	0.89	0.92	3.14	0.96		0.41	0.08		2.13	
4. β	0.36	−0.33	−0.54	0.71	−1.37				0.67	5,22
F	6.57	4.22	12.19	8.98	24.36				9.12	
5. β	0.29	−0.38	−0.57	0.90	−1.39				0.69	5,22
F	4.91	5.26	14.31	10.79	26.20				9.65	
6. β	0.31	−0.09	−0.56	0.87	−1.41	−0.30			0.69	6,21
F	4.18	0.10	12.88	9.00	25.15	0.94			7.73	

cautions us not to make too much of the coefficients in spite of their significance levels, the reason we present them is to demonstrate that differences across groups are substantial.

Continuing with this theme, plants, which we used here as a proxy for wideness of distribution, appears to be positive for the nationals but for no others; and brands is positive for the regionals when the state data are not included in the equation, but for no others. Heileman is, of course, the major user of the multiple brand strategy in the industry and has enjoyed very high profitability for some years, indeed 26–27 percent ROE compared to Anheuser Busch's 17 percent.

Because of the multicollinearity present in the data, we need to be wary in extending this review of the coefficients and their signs, but it seems reasonable to note that:

(1) there appear to be substantial differences in the impacts of marketing variables on profitability between groups;
(2) the market share–profitability effect appears to be difficult to establish and probably varies across the brewing industry;
(3) national market share is very likely both a proxy for many corporate resources and the outcome of many decisions;
(4) in the brewing industry, the structure of competition may be primarily regional—if so, it is a competition of national brewers against regionals now isolated in once, but no longer, safe niches.

The structure of the industry is changing fundamentally. The small brewers are almost eliminated as viable competitors, while the regionals are being weakened by the competition of the nationals. The regional equations suggest that none of the regionals' generally used marketing strategies will enhance their profitability substantially. Heileman is the exceptional regional.

Heterogeneity in the brewing industry

Probing further, we decided to test the homogeneity of the groups which are still viable, the nationals and the regionals, using a simple four variable regression model, but in this case for the years 1962–80. The model and our findings are shown in Table 4.1.3a and can be compared with data from Hatten and Schendel (1977) which are also shown in Table 4.1.3b. What is notable is the differences between the two sets of results, even allowing for the different models in use. We see that:

(1) Anheuser Busch marketing is not homogeneous with any other national company, except Schlitz, in Table 4.1.3, 1962–80. Schlitz's overall strategy had been less homogeneous with Busch, 1952–71, than its

(a) 1962-80

Table 4.1.3 Homogeneity of US Brewers F/F_C

ROAO = f(Price, ADS/bbl, No. of brands, national relative market share in barrels)

	Anheuser-Busch	Coors	Heileman	Miller	Olympia	Pabst	Schlitz
Anheuser-Busch	·						
Coors	0.42	·					
Heileman	0.56	0.42	·				
Miller	2.67	0.45	4.81	·			
Olympia	4.41	1.34	1.37	3.50	·		
Pabst	1.23	0.24	2.43	1.57	3.31	·	
Schlitz	0.61	0.41	1.21	2.50	3.07	0.69	·

(b) 1952-71

ROE = f(No. plants, newness, capital intensity, no. of brands, price, receivables/sales, eight-firm concentration, size)

	Anheuser-Busch	Coors	Heileman	Miller	Olympia	Pabst	Schlitz
Anheuser-Busch	·	na		na			
Heileman	2.13		·	na			
Olympia	3.25	0.42			·		
Pabst	1.98	2.12	1.32			·	
Schlitz	0.72	1.40	2.13	1.78			·

marketing strategy has been 1962–80, suggesting that Schlitz may have been following the market leader more closely in recent years.

(2) Olympia was not homogeneous with Heileman in the 1962–80 period, although it had been for the earlier period. Heileman has employed a multiple-brand strategy successfully and more intensively over the later 1970s, particularly since 1977—up from 19 brands to 46 in 1980.

(3) Miller, Coors, Heileman, Pabst, and Schlitz appear to be a more homogeneous group in the later 1970s and 1980s than is implied by the traditional industry view or conventional wisdom which points to Anheuser-Busch, Miller, Pabst, and Schlitz as the nationals. 'Nationals' may no longer be the right label for these companies or Busch.

It is our view, therefore, that the industry may be restructuring more dramatically than many observers believe. It appears to be evolving into a three-tiered structure:

Anheuser-Busch
Miller, Strohs-Schlitz, Pabst/Olympia, Coors, Heileman
the rest

Given that Strohs-Schlitz and Pabst and Olympia are currently experiencing difficulties, it seems reasonable to expect some reduction in the second group's membership soon.

Why has this happened? Figure 4.1.3, we think, points to an explanation. Since shareholders require market returns, self-funded growth must be financed by extraordinary returns. As a clear winner, Anheuser-Busch's extraordinary returns have outdistanced its competitors and left them in the industry's dust. Market concentration may continue because few companies generate earnings sufficient to service the demand made available as smaller companies drop out of the industry. Anheuser-Busch has been earning a disproportionate share of industry profits for many years. Profit share and market share are correlated. When a large company like Anheuser-Busch is profitable, each sales dollar fattens its war chest faster than other companies and, we believe, thereby enhances its ability to grow still further.

Strategic marketing and brewing industry concentration

What is marketing's role in this saga of progressive industry concentration? Figure 4.1.4 points to one strategy Miller used to begin its climb to the number two contender position: it advertised. Its advertising seems to have led the other majors to match dollar for dollar, as the stretched shapes of the company clusters along the X and Y axes in Figure 4.1.4 indicate.

Busch's profitability, however, was less impaired by Miller's strategy than Pabst's or Schlitz's (or even Miller's). Figure 4.1.4 suggests why. On a per-unit

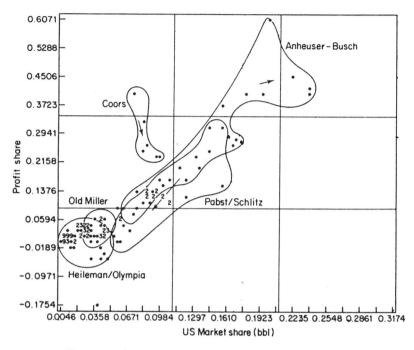

Figure 4.1.3   Profit share vs. barrel share, 1952–75

basis, Busch has been a more effective and a more efficient advertiser than its competitors. Given Busch's volume in 1980, 50 million barrels, it is easy to calculate what a $1 per barrel advertising saving means to Busch over its competitors—it goes a long way toward financing plant expansion and improvement. It may not be stretching our interpretation of the data too far to say that marketing efficiency has made Busch what it is, and marketing inefficiency, namely over- and under-advertising, has made some of its competitors what they are—marginal companies now prey to takeover. The lessons for strategic marketing are:

(1) all companies do not, cannot, and should not compete alike;
(2) all companies cannot make profits in the same way;
(3) managers must realize that a profitable strategy for the industry leader may not be profitable for them—following the leader is a dangerous game and strategy.

SOME GUIDELINES FOR STRATEGIC MARKETING

Marketing, the discipline, appears to have spent much energy pursuing a

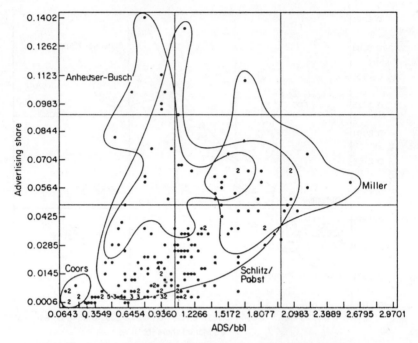

Figure 4.1.4   Advertising share vs. ADS/bbl, 1962–80

scientific rather than corporate point of view over recent years. Marketing research, for example, is more about market phenomena than day-to-day practice. Strategic marketing, therefore, may be untraditional in marketing because strategy is particular to products, businesses, corporations, and countries and the situations they are in. Strategy focuses on advantage, not phenomena.

Strategy is about developing, exploiting, and preserving competitive advantage. Because competition is, first, one-on-one, strategy requires many one-on-one analyses which management must integrate to understand the competitive environment; and theory can be helpful. For example the fundamental rules of competition are well known (if rarely practiced).

(1)   do what you do well;
(2)   pick competitors you can beat;
(3)   be sure the fight will pay off before you start it.

In other words, pick the game, know the rules, make the right moves, and keep score . . . and if you can, make the rules, too. In business, the score is dollars earned, but it is difficult to make the rules, decide on the appropriate competitive moves, and even the field of play simultaneously.

A major role for strategic marketing is to give management the information needed to better choose markets; that is, where and how to compete successfully. The type of information required goes beyond the analysis of markets to the analysis of industries. Management needs to know where profits are being made and how. It needs to know how competitors conceptualize their markets, and it needs to know where gaps in the market are.

During this research we have developed some guidelines for industry analysis which strategic marketers might find helpful:

Beware of oversimplifications

Beware of Type II errors: the costs of unknowingly betting your company on an inappropriate model are often high. Implicitly global phenomena like the market share/profitability relationship should be tested to determine whether they really apply in a particular competitive situation and to other companies like yours (those in your strategic group).

Not market share, but market shares

When you evaluate a company's competitive capabilities the concept of market share should be used creatively as an information source and an aid for diagnosis, not as a straightjacket. 'Market' is a working hypothesis and good strategic marketing necessitates a wide choice of market options. These options should be developed through consideration of not only customers, but competitors' strategies and the firm's internal capabilities. A single market definition can become a trap. A single view of market destroyed the *Saturday Evening Post* and Scripto, and may have been consuming Polaroid's competitive vitality through the latter 1970s and early 1980s. An alternative view can be productive and lead to new competitive insights.

Know who you compete with and who you compete like

Strategic groups fit between industry and market, and allow the analyst to distinguish between competitors and comparables. Companies in a strategic group serve similar markets, not necessarily the same markets, with similar resources but often using subtly different strategies to achieve different results. In analyzing competitors, therefore, be exhaustive about those you compete with, and especially those you compete *like*, since these companies' experiences may be relevant when your own strategy is being formulated—and be sure you probe differences as carefully as similarities. Group analysis can be used to preserve information; industry analyses too often compress it to the point where the real explanation of performance differences is lost.

292 *Strategic Marketing and Management*

Profit is what counts

It is dollars earned that matter, more than returns on assets or equity, for example. Be careful to monitor change in your industry's structure and try to determine the true direction of that change and its cause. Profitable niches can become no-growth traps when an industry restructures, and some large companies give growth priority. It is therefore important to monitor competitors' profits and growth rates as well as their, and your own, market shares and profitability.

To conclude, industry analysis is critical to strategic marketing because it examines the impact of market share, or power, on profits earned. It concentrates the firm's energies on locating opportunities to better exploit its strengths; that is, to use its resource capabilities and relationships to create value, the ultimate management task.

REFERENCES

Chow, Gregory C. (1960). 'Test of equality between sets of coefficients in two linear regressions', *Econometrica*, **28**(3) (July), 519–605.
Farrar, Donald E., and Robert E. Glauber (1967). 'Multicollinearity in regression analysis: the problem revisited', *Review of Economics and Statistics*, **49**, 92–107.
Gale, Bradley T. (1972). 'Market share and rate of return', *Review of Economics and Statistics*, **LIV** (Nov.), 4.
Hatten, Kenneth J. (1974). 'Strategic models in the brewing industry'. Doctoral dissertation, Purdue University.
Hatten, Kenneth J., and Dan E. Schendel (1975). 'Strategy's role in policy research', *Journal of Economics and Business*, **28**, 195.
Hatten, Kenneth J., and Dan E. Schendel (1977). 'Heterogeneity within an industry: firm conduct in the US brewing industry, 1952–71', *Journal of Industrial Economics*, **XXVI**(2) (Dec.).
Keithahn, Charles F. (1978). 'The brewing industry'. Staff Report of the Bureau of Economics, Federal Trade Commission, US Govt. Printing Office, Washington, DC, 1978.
Kuh, Edwin, and John R. Meyer (1955). 'Correlation and regression estimates when the data are ratios', *Econometrica*, **23**, 400–416.
Majaro, Simon (1977). 'Market share: deception or diagnosis', *Marketing*, Mar. 1977.
Patton, G. Richard (1976). 'A simultaneous equation model of corporate strategy: the case of the US brewing industry'. Doctoral dissertation, Purdue University.
Rumelt, Richard P., and Robin Wensley (1981). 'In search of the market share effect', *Proceedings of the Academy of Management*, p. 2.

Strategic Marketing and Management
Edited by H. Thomas and D. Gardner
© 1985 John Wiley & Sons Ltd

4.2

Strategic Groups: A Bridge Between Industry Structure and Strategic Management?

John McGee
Centre for Business Strategy, London Business School

FIRMS, INDUSTRIES, AND MARKETS

For many years there has been considerable discussion as to the most appropriate unit for analysis in industrial organization: the controversy still rumbles on. The economist is interested not only in the firm but often, indeed usually, in the analysis of movements in total output, of prices, of technical progress, and of industry performance measured in its sense of social performance. These matters require a unit of analysis and an analytical framework which extends beyond the confines of the firm. The perfect competition model permitted aggregation to the industry level, but in the process reduced the role of the firm to that of 'an automaton' (Lee, 1976). The identification of firm with industry and market was a simple affair. Firms belonging to an industry produced a single identical product which was sold in the same market. Presumably they used similar technical processes and bought from the same factor markets. therefore the firm belonged to a single identifiable industry which was in turn synonymous with its market since the producers were also the sellers. The new 'realism' of the monopolistic competition model restored the discretion and initiatory role to the firm but at the cost of the model's ability to analyse the main dimensions of business behaviour at the industry level.

Developments in oligopoly theory have done much to resurrect interest in the analysis of the firm and have filled the 'gaping hole' left by economists' traditional focus on the two polar cases of pure competition and pure monopoly by concentrating on interactions in markets where one firm's actions affect its rivals. However, the indeterminacy of the oligopolistic game within the traditional constrained optimization static equilibrium framework has made it difficult to focus the analysis on the industry or the market.

Typically the firm is multi-product, sells in more than one market, and has grown by diversification. The industry as conventionally understood produces a range of different products all of which are not close substitutes, and with a variety of technical production processes. Accordingly, it is unclear where the boundaries of the industry should be drawn. Two criteria are commonly used. The *market* criterion includes in an industry those products which are sufficiently similar as to be close substitutes in the eye of the buyer, the similarity being the familiar cross-elasticity of demand. The conceptual and, in particular, the empirical difficulties implicit in this definition led Triffin (1939) to preach abandonment of the concept of the industry as being inconsistent with the idea of product differentiation: 'The monopolistic competition writers resorted to the limping device of keeping intact, for the purposes of analysis, that concept of an industry which their study of differentiation showed to be untenable.' Triffin argued for a general equilibrium approach, a view which was later shared by Chamberlin himself (1951).

Andrews (1951), among others, argued strongly for the retention of the industry concept, advocating the classification of industries according to their similarity of processes—a *technological* criterion. In this view we look for breaks in the chain of cross-elasticities of supply (rather than demand) to identify the boundaries of the industry. However, the same problem remains—at what point in the spectrum of cross-elasticities, whether of demand or supply, does one draw the industry boundary line. Chamberlin advances the idea that an industry was not a definite economic entity but an analytical tool which could be used with varying degrees of generality.

The general conclusion to which economists have been driven is that the concepts of market and industry should be viewed as complementary and the emphasis employed should reflect the problems under consideration. According to Joan Robinson (1956): 'Questions relating to competition, monopoly and oligopoly must be considered in terms of markets, whilst questions concerning labour, profits, technical progress, localisation and so forth have to be considered in terms of industries'.

In an economic environment characterized by widespread product differentiation and technological change, it is not at all clear where one industry ends and another begins. Many large firms have the capability to make an extremely wide range of products, and can potentially enter and compete in a number of different industries. On purely technological grounds, products can be made which compete for the same customers, but which embody different technologies and which are produced by different processes. Again, it is difficult to tell to which industries some firms should be assigned in empirical investigations. In practice these insoluble problems are resolved case by case, the definitions employed being sufficient unto the day.

This paper continues to probe these old wounds. A concept of a finer grouping within that of the industry has recently found much currency. This appears to be a supply side concept in that it seeks to identify groupings or structures *within* industries, but it is in fact based on the observed similarity of behaviour of firms. These groups, *strategic* groups because the criteria by which we observe them are essentially long-term in nature and costly to reverse, are relatively tightly drawn structures within the more loosely drawn industry structure of conventional theory. If such groups exist they will clearly have implications for the patterns of competition within industries, will contribute to our understanding of oligopolistic interdependence, and may enrich the structure–conduct–performance paradigm of industrial organization theory. For the business policy researcher, and for the business strategist, strategic groups offer a distinctive slant on the identification of relative competitive position and suggest a systematic and comprehensive way of conducting a strengths and weaknesses analysis.

STRATEGIC GROUPS—THE EARLY DEFINITIONS

The term 'strategic groups' was coined by Michael S. Hunt in his doctoral dissertation (1972) to contribute to his explanation of the performance of the 'white goods' industry in the 1960s. Hunt observed that there were three sources of asymmetry between firms within the 'white goods' industry: the extent of vertical integration, degree of product diversification, and differences in product differentiation. This asymmetry resulted in four *strategic groups*: (i) full-line national manufacturers' brand producers, (ii) part-line national manufacturers' brand producers, (iii) private brand producers, and (iv) national retailers. His rationale for this grouping was that it 'minimized economic asymmetry within each group' (Hunt, 1972: 57). His contention was that the problems facing the potential entrant differed depending on which group he intended to enter, and Hunt therefore attempted to isolate 'barriers to entry to each strategic group' in a descriptive vein.

Howard H. Newman, in his doctoral dissertation (1973), applied the same principles in a statistical examination of 34 four-digit 'producer-goods' industries, all of which were related to 'chemical processes'. Michael E. Porter also analysed statistically a sample of 38 three-digit 'consumer-goods' industries in his doctoral dissertation (1973).

While Hunt had focused on strategic differences among competitors in their principal markets and delineated groups according to symmetry (homogeneity) of operations within the same basic businesses, Newman asserted that strategic groups can also be 'defined and identified by the relationship between the industry at hand and the activities carried out by its member firms outside that industry' (Newman, 1978: 418). It follows at once, he said, that those firms sharing the same basic business can be placed in the same strategic group while firms operating in the industry but having their principal business in a different industry form a different group. To a substantial degree, therefore, strategic groups 'turn out to be defined by their differing degrees of vertical integration with the market in question' (1978: 419). His analysis analysis showed 'that differing base industries and patterns of vertical integration sufficed to stratify rival sellers into subgroups', but, as he himself pointed out, it left 'open the question of what other operational factors may prove sufficient both theoretically and empirically for distinguishing them' (1978: 425).

Porter (1973) proceeded by 'using the relative size of a firm in its industry as a proxy for its strategic group membership', dividing firms in each industry into two categories that he called industry *leaders* and *followers*. He argued that:

> the leader/follower dichotomy may be particularly apt for dichotomising strategic groups in a sample restricted to consumer goods industries [because] while the configuration of strategic groups will vary from industry to industry, the leader group should encompass those strategic groups in the industry which are characterised by strategies potentially achieving economies of scale in production technology, vertical integration, captive distribution, in-house repair and service facilities, national advertising, and so on if these economies exist in the industry. The leader group should also encompass strategic groups with broad product lines and large sales forces. The follower group, on the other hand, is likely to encompass strategic groups composed of firms following specialist or narrow-line strategies, regional strategies, non-integrated strategies and so on. Thus the leader/follower distinction captures some of the variance among strategic groups (Porter, 1979: 220–221).

Kenneth J. Hatten, in his doctoral dissertation (1974) on the US brewing industry, 1952–71, paid greater attention to the methodology for establishing intra-group homogeneity and variance between groups. His contention was that the earlier researchers (Hunt, Newman, Porter) had focused on groups, not on firms, and in spite of considerable attention to the assumption of homogeneity within an industry across firms, they had not tested for homogeneity on a firm-by-firm basis. Hatten therefore began with case studies of firms in the brewing industry from which he concluded that brewers competed by allocating resources to two principal functional areas: manufacturing and marketing. He therefore specified an eight-variable model, relating return on equity (performance) to three manufacturing variables (number, age, and capital intensity of plants), three marketing variables (number of brands, price, and receivables/sales) and two structural variables (eight-firm concentration ratio, and firm size).

His first step in the statistical analysis was to develop disparate internally homogeneous groups.

> The process [he said] must begin with an untested assumption: since the current state of art in statistical theory cannot cope with simultaneous non-homogeneity across firms (sections) and across time, a decision must be made to assume

homogeneity over time or across sections. Since our interest was the firm and because it seemed more likely that the brewing industry would be homogeneous across time, the research began with that assumption (Hatten and Schendel, 1977: 101).

He argued that it was difficult to decide which firms to group with which others (because one firm may be homogeneous with one or more other firms), although it could be done in accord with *a priori* theory using criteria such as size (as Porter did) or types of market served. He overcame the difficulty by using a cluster programme to determine the distance between firms. Next he conducted a regression analysis that showed that there were important differences between the pooled estimates (the industry model) and the estimates made on the clusters (the disparate but internally homogeneous groups). The next step was to relax the assumption about industry homogeneity across time. The problem here was the selection of the right breakpoint (year); for this an institutional knowledge of the industry served as a guide.

Hatten and Schendel's (1977) conclusion was that 'attention to homogeneity' revealed information that would otherwise be obfuscated: they provided a methodology for isolating strategic groups. At the same time they argued that identification of strategic groups can help management evaluate proposed strategies and check the usefulness of conventional wisdom in specific competitive situations (Hatten *et al.*, 1978: 592). They stressed (p. 608) that:

> The notion of strategy leads to the expectation that, within a given industry or set of markets, different competitors with different resources should choose different means to attain their ends. Among other indications, this suggests that industry level models and indiscriminate pooling of data can produce results that are easily misled if used at the firm level. It also suggests that in the real world there really are different ways of 'skinning a cat', the firm too quick to copy a successful competitor, one which tries to emulate its competitors without careful thought, may overlook its own capabilities and work against its strengths.

One of the limitations of the Hatten study was that it was confined to firms competing in the same environment, the brewing industry being selected to control the product-market variable (diversification) at a low and non-significant level. With all chosen firms being undiversified, single-business units, the study was perforce reduced to one of 'business strategy' (strategy variables concerned with operations) and not 'corporate strategy' encompassing product-market and geographical diversification and horizontal and vertical integration.

The merit of these early contributions is their recognition that differences between firms do exist, and that they are the deliberate outcome of decisions made by firms. Groupings are therefore the result of strategic choices. Each of these contributions deployed the group concept in pursuit of the explanation of the level and variation of profits within an industry. The difficulty apparent is the *ad hoc* nature of the definition of strategic groups, product lines from Hunt, vertical integration from Newman, and relative size from Porter. Hatten paid attention to the methodological issues outlining a *process* by which homogeneity between firms could be tested. The issue of what dimensions to employ he resolved by case-study analysis of the firms involved. If strategic groups are to be something more than an *ad hoc* construction which can conveniently soak up some of the variability in the dependent variables in our analyses of industries then we need a more careful specification of the sources of dissimilarity between firms—a taxonomy.

A TAXONOMY OF MOBILITY BARRIERS

The natural way to assign firms to strategic groups is by reference to the characteristics of their competitive strategies with group members displaying similar strategies and differences between groups being relatively sharp. In Caves and Porter's words (1977) 'firms within a group resemble one another closely and recognise their mutual dependence most sensitively'. This begs the important question of how to identify the range of strategies available to a firm.

In industrial organization theory, the key characteristics of the structure of an industry are encapsulated in the idea of entry barriers, and market power is said to stem from the presence of structural or behavioural barriers to the entry of new competition. This argument applies also for strategic groups. A firm within a group makes strategic decisions which cannot readily be imitated by firms outside the group without substantial costs, significant elapsed time, or uncertainty about the outcome of those decisions. These barriers to casual imitation by firms outside the group, and the definition of group, requires the existence of such barriers.* Mobility barriers and the associated costs of mobility have become the accepted phraseology. Recognizing that these mobility barriers (or group-specific entry barriers) afford protection to group members, it is natural to envisage the key strategic variables as those which affect the height of mobility barriers.†

Classification of groups by their mobility barriers is an appealing idea which stresses the cost advantages enjoyed by group members and emphasizes the elapsed time as well as the investment expenditures required of would-be 'entrants' to overcome the barriers. In just the same way as in the traditional exposition of entry barrier theory, mobility barriers represent for the group members an investment in a collective, sometimes intangible, capital asset whose benefits are shared out between group members. *Ex ante*, the investment decision is risky in so far as the costs are irrecoverable. Resale

---

* See also the notion of 'uncertain inimitability' advanced by Lippmann and Rumelt (1981).
 † Rumelt (1981) goes further in explaining the uniqueness of firms by generalizing from mobility barriers to 'isolating mechanisms and the notion of 'idiosyncratic capital'.

markets may exist for plant and equipment, and for upstream supply companies, for example, but differentiation costs are not so easily recovered, nor are investments in R&D.

Mobility barriers can be expressed in the same form as conventional entry barriers; 'barriers to mobility between groups rest on the same structural features as barriers to entry into any group from the outside' (Caves and Porter, 1977). Thus the group counterpart expresses barriers either as absolute costs of movement from one group to another (becoming vertically integrated, for example), or as the operating cost penalty relative to the incumbents that the entrant must face. In either case the present value of the incremental costs associated with changing group membership detracts significantly from the profit margin available *before* taking into account any competitive reaction.

Sources of mobility barriers

Mobility barriers fall into three broad categories: market-related strategies, the characteristics of supply in the industry, and features specific to the ownership and management of the individual firm. *Market*-related strategies include the product line, its width and scope; the geographical coverage of the market and the nature of market segments served; the channels of distribution employed and the relationships with buyers; the technologies embodied in the product; and the nature and type of branding and product differentiation in general. These are clearly decision variables for the firm; but more than this, they represent strategic choices in so far as a competitive riposte requires an initial investment cost and some elapsed time before competition on equal terms becomes possible. Moreover, the 'investment' decision is risky in that it is not certain that equivalent or better market positioning can be acquired by the follower, or whether the market will respond to imitative strategies in the same way.

The characteristics of *supply* include the scale economies arising from size, whether in production, in marketing, or in administration; and the range of assets that could be invested in 'supply'—manufacturing capability, technological capability, marketing and distribution systems, and R&D expenditure. Scale effects are both conventional and familiar. More interesting, however, are the alternative investments in supply-side assets for the firm. These can be difficult to define with precision (what is an R&D capability?) and thus can be *difficult* to copy, certainly in the short run. The idea of supply capabilities relates directly to the idea of cross-entry and cross-elasticity of supply. Competition is often observed to spring from firms outside industry boundaries (e.g. Exxon entering the office automation industry) because these entrants possess the inherent capabilities to enter—for them the entry barriers are low—and moreover, they may have considerable latitude in their choice of entry point. The barriers to entry to the industry in general may be lower for some completely new entrants than the mobility barriers which impede the repositioning of incumbent firms.

Whereas supply capabilities may be generally available at a price, mobility barriers arising from the nature of the firm itself rest on characteristics internal to the firm.

The firm's organizational production function can be thought of as its organization structure and the skill of its management in employing it efficiently. Chandler (1962) has alerted us to the systematic relationship between strategic choices and organization structures, and Caves (1980) has recently surveyed the reverse set of relationships which run from the firm's organizational structure to its market behaviour. Management skills are intimately related to organization structure. It was Bower (1970) who highlighted the limitations on top management in formulating and implementing strategic choices. 'Definition and impetus in turn depend on the "situational context" of . . . lower level decision makers. Context consists of organisation structure, meaning not only the organisation chart assignment of responsibilities and powers but also the organisation's system of measuring and rewarding performance . . .' (Caves, 1980). These characteristics of structure, context, and skill are not easy to measure, particularly on only superficial acquaintance with the units of analysis. Williamson's (1970) formulation of Chandler's analysis of the two prototype structures—the functional and divisional—supplemented by Wrigley (1970) and Rumelt (1974)—provides some guidelines for assessment. As Caves indicates, these contributions highlight the subjective and firm-specific nature of the basic business, the bonds that link it to other parts of the corporate structure, and the organizational mechanisms for maintaining control and direction.

The *boundaries of firms* can be a rich source of diversity within an industry. The basic characteristics are the nature (related versus unrelated) and extent of diversification, the extent of vertical integration, and the nature of contracts with supplying firms or with customers. Contracts, whether for technology or for materials and components requirements, can yield significant operating advantages although the time horizon over which these can be enjoyed may not always be very long. Licensee arrangements may apparently confer temporary advantage but regarded as a form of accelerated learning they can result in a more durable form of technology advantage. Where significant cost savings are available from vertically integrated systems then it is common to observe that the large firms in an industry are all vertically integrated, although the extent varies according to local circumstances (*viz.* the pulp and paper industry). However, not all firms are big and these search for ways of offsetting the cost advantages of size, for example by providing high-quality, high-technology products to small insensitive segments of the market. One strategy offsets another by, for example, the raising of one mobility barrier against another strategic group. Diversification may create cost savings, for example the management of brands and families of brands across related markets or the sharing of technologies across similar industrial processes. Of much debate has been the proposition that there are economies of management arising from divisionalized structures and from synergies due to pooling of talents on related problems. Similarly diversification may reduce pockets of excess capacity in management and administration where management is purchased in indivisible lumps. Clearly, the extension or contraction of the firm's boundaries or any change in the nature of its contractual commitments requires time, is uncertain in its outcome, and is difficult to reverse. However, the boundary question is not merely one of unit costs, it is also one of risk. Conventional portfolio theory tells us that the pooling of uncorrelated risks reduces overall risk. In spite of the dissimilar nature of securities markets and the opportunity sets for corporate or business units, we may nevertheless see some significant risk reduction (e.g. lower risk of total default) from a diversified portfolio. This can be important in a number of ways. The perceived stakes may be quite different for diversified versus non-diversified companies and the nature of their competitive reactions may reflect this. The time horizon over which firms plan may differ and the initiatives they may consider may also vary. In general, the objectives of firms with different boundaries may differ systematically, may be reflected in their competitive behaviour, and could result in different levels of unit cost.

Ownership enables us to distinguish clearly between firms. The obvious characteristics are extent of shareholding both privately held and publicly quoted; nature of shareholders—family influence, country of origin, multinational, institutional holdings, and corporate interconnection; the nature of relationships with government—shareholding, long-term finance, subsidy, or other favoured treatment. Ownership matters because it affects the desired rate of return and the time horizon over which this is to be earned. Ownership may intrude on the celebrated divide between owners and managers in many more ways than conventional Anglo-American thought suggests. It can affect the definition of the business, in Abell's terminology—publicly owned industries in Europe are severely restricted in the diversification moves that they might consider. Cultural differences supported by different financial systems may result in much more broadly based, loosely held industrial groupings in Japan and West Germany, for example, than in the USA.

Firm-specific sources of mobility barriers are: organization structure and control systems, management skills and capabilities, the nature and extent of diversification versus vertical integration, and the nature of the firm's ownership and its connections with other power groups such as unions, consumer groups and regulators.

Mobility barriers—summarized in Table 4.2.1—are a corollary to the existence of strategic groups. A group structuring carries no meaning without costs attached to the imitation of strategy by other firms. Mobility barriers are thus decision variables of firms, and are a way of defining the set of key

Table 4.2.1   Sources of mobility barriers

Market-related strategies	Industry supply characteristics	Characteristics of firms
Product line	Economies of scale:	Ownership
User technologies	production	Organization structure
Market segmentation	marketing	Control systems
Distribution channels	administration	Management skills
Brand names	Manufacturing processes	Boundaries of:
Geographic average	R&D capability	firms
Selling systems	Marketing and	diversification
	distribution systems	vertical integration
		Firm size
		Relationships with
		influence groups

strategies available to a firm. The essential characteristic is cost disadvantage for non-member firms; the remedy probably involves investment expenditures on tangible or intangible assets with significant elapsed time before the investment comes to fruition. Moreover, the investment expenditures will be irreversible to the extent that intangible assets are being acquired, and there will typically be considerable uncertainty attached to the outcome of the investment expenditures.

IMPLICATIONS FOR RESEARCH

The existence of strategic groups has a number of implications for industrial organization, in particular the traditional theory of entry and for oligopoly theory. The generalization of entry barriers into mobility barriers allows a richer and more realistic portrayal of the process of entry and the motives for diversification (cross-entry). It also offers an explanation for persistent intra-industry differences in profit rates. The nature of oligopolistic interdependence is illuminated by the pattern of group memberships and the change of membership over time. In addition, strategic groups have some interesting parallels with theories of the growth of the firm, notably those advanced by Penrose (1959) and Downie (1958).

The structure–performance link

The most obvious, although probably the least productive, field of application for the strategic group concept is the traditional market structure–performance link. The general theory runs thus. The proposition that entry barriers generalize to mobility barriers explains why some firms in an industry persistently earn higher profits than others, and why firms adopt different strategies even though not all strategies are equally successful. Without mobility barriers firms with successful strategies could be quickly imitated by others, and firms' profit rates would tend towards equality at the margin except for relatively transient differences in firms' abilities to execute the 'best' strategy in an operational sense. The existence of mobility barriers means that some firms can enjoy systematic advantages over others, which can be overcome only by strategic breakthroughs that can lead to structural change in the industry.

The distribution of profit rates between an industry's member firms reflects two sets of structural influences. The first influence is that of general industry-wide traits while the second is that of the configuration of strategic groups within the industry—what Porter calls the structure within the industry. Strategic groups 'allow us to systematically integrate differences in the skills and resources of an industry's member firms and their consequent strategic choices into a theory of profit determination' (Porter, 1979: 216). The corollary of this is Newman's (1973) hypothesis that 'the basic structure–performance model should supply a better explanation of inter-industry variations in market performance for a group of homogeneous industries than for a group of heterogeneous industries'.

Indeed the bulk of the published work on strategic groups attempts to calibrate more accurately the relationship between market structure and performance by using groups as an intervening variable to sweep up some of the heterogeneity in observed rates of profit. Newman, for example, postulates that 'the complexity of the structure of strategic groups populating an industry exerts significant influence on its performance'. He went on to derive hypothesis about their influence on an industry's profitability and tested these on a sample of producer goods industries. He concludes that the complexity of group structures cannot be ignored in testing hypotheses about market structures, although other explanatory variables may also be required. Indeed the original work of Hunt, Newman, Porter, and Hatten was directed towards the explanation of the performance of firms and of industries. Hatten (1978) summarized his model as:

Performance $= f$ (controlled or strategic variables, non-controllable or environmental variables).

Caves and Porter (1977) conclude that the evidence to hand provides support for the hypothesis that group structures exist and systematically affect the distribution of profits within industries. There is room to be agnostic about the strength of the evidence here, particularly because of the unsystematic and *ad hoc* definition of group structures and the consequent difficulty in generalizing to other situations.

However, the main hypothesis is clearly of significance, namely that profits, and performance generally, differ systematically between groups. With the parallel claim that without intergroup immobility it is hard to explain persistent differences in performance between firms, there are important implications for antitrust policy.

This research is cast in the traditional mould of industrial organization (IO) where characteristics of market structure are hunted down, sorted, classified, and used to explain the performance of firms in an industry. The structure–performance link is the focus of attention with conduct being solved out as a mere intervening variable, reflecting the environment in which the industry operates. However, another important branch of the IO literature is oligopoly theory—the study of the outcome of competitive interactions in markets where one firm's actions directly affect its rivals. Oligopoly theory seeks to clarify and explain the link between structure and conduct (firm-to-firm rivalry). In general, IO theory suggests that some key structural characteristics condition the firm's range of choices of competitive strategy in the market (i.e. the firm's conduct). The small number of firms in an oligopoly emphasizes the zero–sum characteristics of competition and makes it difficult for any one firm to ignore the conduct of any other. Thus, strategic groups represent a finer analysis of industry structure with, it should be expected, implications for the patterns of rivalry between firms, and the types of rivalry that will take place. Similarly, the nature of the relationship between conduct and performance has received little attention relative to that lavished on the structure–performance connection. Caves (1980) has argued:

> Industrial organisation economists have only begun to incorporate strategic choice into their analyses of market structure, conduct and performance. The central hypothesis considered to date is that the more heterogeneous are the strategies chosen by an industry's oligopolistic members, the less effectively monopolistic will be the bargain they reach. The quality of performance associated with particular strategies could be investigated more effectively, and the performance dimensions should reach beyond allocative efficiency.

We might conclude from all this that closer attention to the nature of strategies pursued by firms captured in the term strategic groups will throw light on the much-worn structure–conduct–performance model and may even rescue it from generally agnostic conclusions that there are serious doubts whether profitability is simply related to market power.

It is now commonly observed that the structure–performance model is seriously deficient on its own (Hay and Morris, 1979: 226) and that more complex causal links need to be taken into account. Strategic groups may well be one of these links, but not likely to be the only one, let alone the major one.

The existence of group structures

The existing literature appears to justify the existence of group structures along its way to explaining differences in profit rates. However, it is appropriate to outline the main hypotheses and questions about the existence of group structures. First, sellers within an industry are likely to differ systematically in traits other than size, so that the industry contains groups of firms with different market behaviour characteristics. Second, mobility barriers are a counterpart of group structures and are an extension of conventional ideas about entry barriers. Mobility barriers arise from strategic decisions and stem from three main sources; decisions about strategies in markets, decisions about methods of supply, and decisions about the boundaries and organization of the firm. Third, how do strategic groups form?

Caves and Porter have pointed out the need to enlarge the theory of entry to a more general theory of the mobility or immobility of firms. The older theories of growth of the firm (Penrose, 1959 and Downie, 1958), were also concerned with dynamics of change and postulated limitations to the rate of growth of firms which stemmed from 'dynamic restraints'. Three broad categories of restraint were isolated: financial, arising from the need to build productive potential; demand, arising from the unit costs attached to the acquisition of new customers; and managerial, where management's ability to strategically plan and implement is subject to slow and costly development. The issue is one of the firm's inability to change and to grow. There are constraints on the ability of firms to change their market shares, to diversify, to innovate and so on. Dynamic restraints are an antecedent of mobility barriers even though they were conceived as firm-specific restraints. Like entry barriers before them (Bain, 1956), there is a need for formal definition and exposition of mobility barrier theory together with empirical estimation of the nature of these barriers and their implications for group structures.

The observation of strategic diversity within an industry, and the corresponding claim that this has a significant bearing on market behaviour, is central to the theory of strategic groups. Without this diversity, and without some clustering of strategic choices, there is no group phenomenon to investigate. Mobility barrier theory as outlined in this paper is some contribution to a taxonomy of strategic choices. Caves (1980) called for a taxonomy that transcends the corporate issues of diversification and integration and considered instead the strategies available within given markets. Mobility barriers require strategic choice, and the identification of mobility barriers (like the identification of entry barriers before them) can lead to a classification and taxonomy of strategic groups.

Porter (1979) provides three explanations of the formation of strategic groups: (1) investments in building mobility barriers are risky and firms have different risk-aversion postures; this leads to different groups defined in terms of R&D and advertising outlays as defensive mobility barriers; (2) business units which differ in their relation to a parent company may differ in goals in ways that lead to strategy differences; (3) historical development of an industry (nature of demand, production technology, product characteristics, etc.)

bestows differential advantages/disadvantages on firms. A fourth possible explanation, relegated by Porter (1979: 217) to a footnote, is exogenous causes such as technological change:

> Changes in the structure of the industry can either facilitate group formation, or work to homogenise groups. For example, technological changes or changes in buyer behaviour can shift industry boundaries bringing entirely new strategic groups into play in the industry by increasing or decreasing product substitutability and hence shifting relevant industry boundaries.

Porter merely hints at the effect of technical change on group formation. An equally important empirical question is whether technological change impacts differently on different strategic groups; *viz.* does technological change affect the mobility barriers surrounding one group to a lesser or greater extent than the barriers (same or different barriers) surrounding another group? If so, does this differential impact explain performances? This question has not so far been addressed empirically.

Entry theory and mobility of firms

In traditional entry theory the potential new entrant's investment decision is based on three elements covered by the standard limit-price models:

(1) the rents presently earned by the market's occupants;
(2) the structural or static entry barriers identified by Bain;
(3) the incumbent's expected reactions to entry;

and also three other elements that vary from industry to industry and from time to time:

(4) other members of the queue of potential entrants, and their likely behaviour;
(5) any relevant resources already in the hands of the entrant; and
(6) the irreversible costs of gathering information and making the decision.

Moreover, the new entrant is a new firm which makes its investment choices in accord with the above elements. Because the industry is assumed to be a monolithic, homogeneous unit, no other movement or positioning of firms within the industry is considered; the relevant entry barriers taken into account are only those that surround the industry as a whole. However, in reality entrants into an industry (and these may be entirely new firms or firms already established elsewhere) may enter one or another *segment* of a given industry, and firms already operating in one segment may shift to another. Movement in and out of segments is determined not by the industry-wide *entry barriers* but by *mobility barriers* surrounding particular segments where these particular segments within the industry are *strategic groups*.*

The presence of strategic groups also raises the possibility of entry *paths*.†
Quoting Caves and Porter (1977: 255) again:

> Conventional entry theory has the unsatisfying property of positing that the firm chooses to enter at some scale x in the industry, and that this choice is independent of its future plans. If the firm will in general alter position within its industry after entry, and if it is not completely ignorant of this possibility when it makes its entry choice then the initial entry plan will rationally include some provision for expected future moves, as may a going firm's intergroup shift.

Formulating the entry process as an investment decision made under uncertainty, particularly about the potential competitive riposte, and by recognizing that subgroup structures within an industry impede intra-industry mobility, traditional entry theory can be generalized into a theory of mobility barriers that takes a consistent and comprehensive view of the decision-making behaviour of both nascent and going firms. 'This "new view" is designed primarily as a framework for empirical analysis and research in the field of industrial organisation' (Caves and Porter, 1977: 261).

To summarize, there are some hypotheses about the process of entry which merit attention. First, the group-specific character of mobility barriers has strong implications for the entry of firms from outside the industry. In particular, the presence of groups raises the possibility of entry paths involving a sequence of moves before a settled position within the industry is achieved. Where capital requirements are large, firms will seek to minimize risk by indirect or circuitous moves which place only limited amounts of capital at risk at each stage. In general, entry will be targeted at a particular group or at the creation of a new group. Second, the queue of potential entrants to a group

---

* Entry into one strategic group (segment) within an industry may be easy (because of low mobility barriers) even though entry barriers surrounding the whole industry might be high. An example of this is furnished by Brock (1966: Chapters 1–5), who found dramatic differences in the height of barriers by way of capital requirements, economies of scale, and the product differentiation between integrated system producers of mainframe computers and peripheral suppliers to the computer industry. Despite the rapid growth of the integrated system segment from 1960 to 1973, no entry occurred (high mobility barriers), while numerous entrants came into the peripheral supply segment. See also Shaw and Sutton (1976).

† 'Entry is likely to occur along a circuitous path into groups whose capital requirements for entry are large: if large lumps of capital pose a major entry deterrent, it makes sense to go for bite-sized pieces. Investments in vaulting entry barriers are irreversible in differing degrees, a condition that favours a strategy of circuitous entry. Outlays for production facilities and other tangible assets are largely reversible entry costs, while outlays for product differentiation and other intangibles are fully irreversible (most risky). Thus, it may be optimal to enter groups characterised by tangible asset outlays (e.g. producing for private label with no advertising outlay) first and groups requiring more risky intangible asset outlays only after a viable base in the industry is attained: the lower-risk barriers are vaulted earlier' (Caves and Porter, 1977: 256). In the office reprographics industry, the Japanese firms appear to have followed this circuitous entry path (Ghazanfar, unpublished PhD thesis, 1982).

will, in general, consist of established firms in other industries, going firms in other groups, and entirely new firms. The position in the queue will depend on the structural mobility barriers as modified and extended by the incumbent firms' choice of barrier-raising investments. Third, going firms outside the industry will be the major potential competitors for the oligopolistic core of dominant firms protected by product differentiation and absolute cost barriers. Correspondingly, new firms—the traditional entrant of Bainsian theory—will sprout in the competitive fringe of oligopolistic markets. Fourth, incumbent firms deter entry by investing in the creation of new mobility barriers.

The traditional theory of entry has a number of well-known serious limitations. These difficulties arise from an over-narrow definition of 'entry'. Thus, Bain concentrates on entry by new firms. He neglects take-overs, cross-entry, vertical integration, and additions to capacity by existing firms. The group concept allows a richer portrayal of the entry process from which we can observe types of entrant, patterns and paths of entry, the effect of entry on the evolution of the industry, and the manner in which cross-entry spurs the parallel development of separate industries.

Patterns of rivalry

In traditional oligopoly theory goal congruence among firms is assumed even when the problems and costs of communication and the detection of cheating are discussed (Stigler, 1964). By contrast, the strategic groups thesis argues that not only may there be very little goal congruence to start with, but that other differences (e.g. customers, suppliers, distribution channels) which contribute to strategic grouping within the same industry make the formation of oligopolistic consensus even more difficult. As asymmetry increases, in other words as the number of observable strategic groups increases, collusion becomes all the more improbable. The industry becomes segmented but does not disappear because cross-elasticities of substitution between products remain unchanged. Oligopolistic interdependence and homogeneity of firms become recognizable not at the industry level but at the strategic group level.

Following Caves (1980: 89), the more heterogeneous are the firms' strategies, and the larger and more differentiated are the strategic groups, then the less likely and less effective will be any oligopolistic collusion. Just as industrial organization coupled with oligopoly theory offers a systematic model for assessing the nature of competition and the patterns of competitive interaction (Porter, 1980: 611), then strategic groups provide a supplementary framework in which the ability to compete can be put alongside actual market behaviour. Research into conduct* generally concentrates on the pervasiveness of co-ordination and cross-adaptation of price, product and sales promotion policies, and the presence or absence of, and extent of, predatory or

---

* Bain defines conduct as 'patterns of behaviour which enterprises follow in adapting or adjusting to the markets in which they sell' (Bain, 1968: 9).

exclusiary tactics against established rivals or potential entrants. Cross-sectional studies, as well as industry-specific case-studies, will no doubt be capable of detecting the extent to which alternative configurations of groups weaken the potential for collusion.

Patterns of rivalry between groups are only tentatively approached by the weak assertion that it all depends on market interdependence. Where groups are defined by market-related characteristics such as product line or distribution channels, then market interdependence is likely to be lower rather than higher. Where group configurations arise from non-market sources then the potential for market overlap will be that much greater.

Rivalry is usually, though not exclusively, used to refer to a single period cross-sectional portrayal of competitive interaction. The pattern of rivalry played out over long periods of time is captured under headings such as life cycle theories of the firm, and is usually offered in a supporting role to the principal actors such as technology, development of markets, and growth of firms. Schumpeter (1934) and Downie (1958) gave starring roles to the competitive process. Downie set up a crude model of the competitive process. The first part of his model specified a 'transfer mechanism' whereby the more efficient firms steadily encroach on the market share of the less efficient, the extent of the transfer being dependent on the extent of dynamic restraints which make more costly the development of capacity and the capturing of new customers. The second part was an 'innovation mechanism', a counterforce to the transfer mechanism. This is the process whereby the efficient firms responding to their diminishing market shares actively seek to reverse the process by (perhaps) innovating with more flexibility and enthusiasm than their competitors. The transfer mechanism then starts up again in the opposite direction. The driving force behind this is that 'the most fundamental characteristic of a capitalist economy is growth and change . . . [it] is characterised by a restless urge to do better, to change the conditions lest, through inactivity, they are changed against you' (Downie, 1958).

In this sense Downie's model is Schumpeterian in style and insists that the analysis of the individual firm be set in the context of the competitive process. His object of study is in fact the competitive process in which he sees oligopolistic interdependence and continuous change to be playing key roles. The theory which emerges argues that the maximum sustainable rate of growth is set by the interaction of two dynamic restraints: the financial (funds to acquire capacity) and demand (costs of acquiring new customers). Downie's process shows gains being made by the more efficient with the less efficient submitting or riposting with innovation and change to alter the nature of the game and the relative positions of the combatants.

In general, however, oligopoly theory has lacked a 'realistic' testable framework within which patterns of rivalry can be observed over time. The various theories have been unique constructs and the multitude of case-studies have lacked generality. Strategic group analysis conducted longitudinally may provide us with a framework to allow the categorization of strategic changes, an objective analysis of the position of a firm within an industry, and a way of assessing industry evolution. The prospect, however, merely tantalizes. Group analysis requires further taxonomy development before group structures can be compared intertemporally. Strategic groups, like game theory, may remain an elegant and inspired form of language, but we should beware the empty boxes within the matrices.

The principal hypotheses that merit attention are: group members are likely to respond in similar ways to disturbances from outside the group; the effect of groups on rivalry depends on the number and size distribution of groups and on the market interdependence between groups; and firms within a given group can recognize mutual dependence and co-ordinate their behaviour more effectively than can firms in different groups.

The theory of growth of the firm

Strategic groups has interesting parallels with the theory of growth of the firm as first articulated by Downie, Penrose, and Marris more than 20 years ago. Downie sought to explain the sources of efficiency dispersion within an industry, the consequences for competition, and the role of innovation in the competitive process. His contribution was to link growth of the firm and profitability, and to put growth firmly in the context of the competitive process in which he had a clear place for oligopolistic interdependence. Downie's view of the innovation mechanisms has been criticized for its apparent unreality in ascribing innovation to the less efficient firms, but it requires only to add mobility barriers and patterns off cross-entry to recover his basic results.

Penrose bypassed the industry entirely and concentrated on the firm.* She regarded the principal dynamic restraint to be internal to the firm, managerial in nature. Her contribution has often been deemed to be more behavioural than economic but she emphasizes above all the long-run, strategic aspects of managerial activity—diversification, innovation, and merger. Her concern is with the limited ability of the management team to plan and implement strategic change without incurring higher costs. Both in Penrose and elsewhere in the literature is an unfamiliar but fundamentally economic notion of an organizational production function. 'The output is the ability to reallocate the firm's complement of fixed factors . . . in response to unexpected disturbances' (Caves, 1980). Penrose regards the growth of the firm as limited only in the long run by its internal management resources. Moreover she regards the general direction of expansion as determined by inducements and obstacles to expansion where these look remarkably like mobility barriers and demand changes. It is implicit (according to Lee, 1976) in the whole of Penrose's presentation of her theory that diversification is the normal way in which firms

---

* Likewise, Rumelt also bypasses the industry in his 'Strategic theory of the firm' (1981).

grow and not merely a reaction to the saturation of existing markets. If indeed the firm is to be conceived as a pool of productive resources organized within an administrative framework, then indeed the set of productive services which these resources can render are as significant a driving force behind the direction of expansion of the firm as are demand shifts external to the firm.

'Distinctive competence' is a phrase much used by policy analysts. It is usually taken to refer to those unique and distinctive features of an organization which can be translated into a competitive advantage in the market. The thrust of the Penrose argument is that certain organizational and managerial characteristics facilitate successful corporate strategy initiatives and the subsequent development of corporate structures.

From this background we can pose some particular hypotheses: strategic groups allow us to examine the interrelation between business units and their corporate parents and their corporate siblings in analysing the evolution of industries; strategic groups provide a means for analysing changes in industry structure over time, and can provide predictions of the mechanisms by which structural change will be affected; changes in strategic groups and in mobility barriers can eventually be brought about by rates of profit which differ systematically between groups.

CONCLUSIONS

The theory of strategic groups and associated mobility barriers is related to the structure of industries and the strategic market behaviour of firms within their industries. The group concept appears to be a supply-side concept in its role defining structures within industries, but is in all its essentials a market behaviour or conduct concept, fitting neatly between the supply idea of an industry and the demand idea of a market. The defining characteristics of strategic groups arise from the mobility barriers which protect the groups. The three sources of mobility barriers are market-related strategies, general supply characteristics of the industry, and the organizational and boundary choices of the firm—each of them being decision variables for the firm.

Strategic groups pose a number of interesting research challenges. The first to be explored, and most obvious one, is the contribution it makes to the market structure–performance link. Of more promise are other areas: the existence and evolution of group structures and their relationship to the evolution of industries, their contribution to the theory of entry, the queue of potential entrants and the alternative entry paths, the patterns of rivalry in oligopolistic markets, and our understanding of the growth and evolutionary patterns of firms.

The emergence of the strategic group concept and the increasing research attention being paid to the boundary areas between industrial organization, strategic marketing, administrative behaviour, and strategic management suggests closer attention to the firm as the unit of analysis. The difficulty of applying rigorous research techniques in the area of strategic decision-making is extreme. The problems of controlling for exogenous variables, the lack of comparability among the units of analysis, and the disparate nature of these units, and the changing nature of opportunity sets and the environment generally restricts the ability of researchers to make causal connections between sets of variables. All these problems are compounded by the lack of suitable data bases for research.* We may very well see a continuing trend towards in-depth studies of firms and their industries in an attempt to apply control procedures to fewer variables and to explore the character and texture of strategic choices in ways impossible for statistical analysis to achieve. The effect of strategic groups is to restore strategic decisions to the centre of the structure and performance arena and to re-emphasize the firm as an important unit of analysis.

REFERENCES

Andrews, P. W. S., 'Industrial analysis in economics', in P. W. S. Andrews, and T. Wilson (eds), *Oxford Studies in the Price Mechanism*, Oxford University Press, Oxford, 1951.

Bain, J. S., *Barriers to New Competition*, Harvard University Press, Cambridge, Mass., 1956.

Bain, J. S., *Industrial Organisation*, 2nd edn. Wiley, New York, 1968.

Brock, C., *The Control of Restrictive Practices from 1956*. McGraw-Hill, London, 1966.

Caves, R. E., 'Industrial organisation, corporate strategy, and structure: a survey', *Journal of Economic Literature*, **18**(1) (1980), 64–92.

Caves, R. E., and M. E. Porter, 'From entry barriers to mobility barriers: conjectural decisions and contrived deterrence to new competition', *Quarterly Journal of Economics*, **91** (1977), 241–262.

Caves, R. E. and M. E. Porter, 'Market structure, oligopoly and stability of market shares', *Journal of Industrial Economics*, **XXVI**(4) (June 1978).

Chamberlin, E., 'Monopolistic competition revisited', *Economica*, 1951.

Chandler, A. D. Jr, *Strategy and Structure: Chapters in the history of the Industrial Enterprise*. MIT Press, Cambridge, Mass., 1962.

Downie, J., *The Competitive Process*. Duckworth, London, 1958.

Ghazanfar, A., 'Analysis of competition in the office reprographics industry in the U.K.'. Forthcoming PhD. thesis, London Business School.

Hatten, K. J., 'Strategic models in the brewing industry'. Unpublished doctoral dissertation, Harvard University, 1974.

Hatten, K. J., and D. E. Schendel, 'Heterogeneity within an industry', *Journal of Industrial Economics*, **XXVI**(2) (1977), 97–113.

Hatten, K. J., D. E. Schendel, and A. C. Cooper, 'A strategic model of the U.S. brewing industry: 1952–1971', *Academy of Management Journal*, **21**(4) (1978), 592–610.

Hay, D. A., and D. J. Morris, *Industrial Economics: Theory and Evidence*. Oxford University Press, Oxford, 1979.

* Honourable exceptions to this are the PIMS Program of the Strategic Planning Institute, and the Program for Industry and Company Analysis (PICA) at Harvard.

Hunt, M. S., 'Competition in the major home appliance industry, 1960–1970'. Unpublished doctoral dissertation, Harvard University, 1972.

Lee, T., 'Industrial and market structure', in Devine, Jones, Lee, and Tyson (eds), *Introduction to Industrial Economics*. Allen & Unwin, London, 1976.

Lippmann, S. A., and R. P. Rumelt, *Efficiency Differentials under Competition: A Stochastic Approach to Industrial Organisation*. UCLA, 1981.

Marris, R., *The Economic Theory of Managerial Capitalism*, Macmillan, London, 1964.

Newman, H. H., 'Strategic groups and the structure/performance relationship: a study with respect to the chemical process industries'. Unpublished doctoral dissertation, Harvard University, 1973.

Newman, H. H., 'Strategic groups and the structure/performance relationship', *Review of Economics and Statistics*, **60** (1978), 417–427.

Penrose, E. T., *The Theory of the Growth of the Firm*. Basil Blackwell, Oxford, 1959.

Porter, M. E., 'Consumer behaviour, retailer power, and manufacturer strategy in consumer goods industries'. Unpublished doctoral dissertation, Harvard University, 1973.

Porter, M. E., 'The structure within industries and companies' performance', *Review of Economics and Statistics*, **61** (1979), 214–227(b).

Porter, M. E., 'The contributions of industrial organisation to strategic management', *Academy of Management Review*, 1981.

Robinson, J., 'The industry and the market', *Economic Journal*, 1956.

Rumelt, R. P., *Strategy, Structure and Economic Performance*. Division of Research, Harvard University Graduate School of Business Administration, 1974.

Rumelt, R. P., 'Towards a strategic theory of the firm'. Paper prepared for a conference on Non-Traditional Approaches to Policy Research, Graduate School of Business, University of Southern California, 1981.

Schumpeter, J. A., *The Theory of Economic Development*. Harvard University Press, Cambridge, Mass., 1934.

Shaw, R. W., and C. J. Sutton, *Industry and Competition*. Macmillan, London, 1976.

Stigler, G. J., 'A theory of oligopoly', *Journal of Political Economy*, 1964, p. 72.

Triffin, R., *Monopolistic Competition and General Equilibrium Theory*. Harvard University Press, Cambridge, Mass., 1939.

Williamson, O. E., *Corporate Control and Business Behaviour*. Prentice-Hall, Englewood Cliffs, N.J., 1970.

Wrigley, L., 'Divisional autonomy and diversification'. Unpublished DBA thesis, Harvard Business School, 1970.

Strategic Marketing and Management
Edited by H. Thomas and D. Gardner
© 1985 John Wiley & Sons Ltd

4.3
A Method for Determining Strategic Groups and Life Cycle Stages of an Industry

WALTER J. PRIMEAUX, JR
University of Illinois at Urbana-Champaign

INTRODUCTION

For some time it has been accepted that products go through stages in a life cycle. In a similar way firms and industries are also thought to move through life cycles. Yet the concept is somewhat ambiguous and not much is known about the nature of the life cycle or how it affects firms in a particular industry. The purposes of this study are to present an approach for gaining a better understanding of the industry life cycle and to suggest a method for developing hard data for gaining a better understanding of the concept.

PREVIOUS STUDIES

The life cycle

The importance of both the industry life cycle and strategic group concepts is well documented in the strategic management and policy literature. Porter (1980: 157) explains that there is some controversy about whether the life cycle applies only to individual products or to whole industries.* In this reference Porter takes the position that the life cycle applies to industries. The notion is that industry growth follows an S-shaped curve because of the process of innovation and diffusion of new products. He also explains that the life cycle concept has attracted some criticisms. First, the length of the stages varies widely from industry to industry; it is often not clear what stage of the life cycle an industry is actually in (Porter, 1980: 158). The usefulness of the concept as a planning tool, according to Porter, is diminished because of this problem. A

---

* The industry life cycle and the market or industry evolution cycle are essentially the same thing. See also: Biggadike (1981: 631) and Porter (1981: 609–620).

second criticism is that industry growth does not always go through the S-shaped curve. Sometimes stages are skipped and sometimes industry growth revitalizes after a period of decline (Porter, 1980: 158). The third criticism of the industry life cycle is that companies can affect the shape of their growth curve through product innovation and repositioning (Porter, 1980: 162). Porter explains that if a company takes the life cycle as given, it becomes an undesirable self-fulfilling prophesy. Patz (1981: 127–130); Rumelt (1979: 204–206, 208–209, 211–212, 215); and Cooper (1979: 318–325) also discuss the industry life cycle as it relates to strategic management.

Porter (1980: 162) also explains that the nature of competition associated with each stage of the life cycle is different for different industries. Some industries start off highly concentrated and remain so; others are concentrated for a significant period and then change to a lower level of concentration. Others begin highly fragmented; later some consolidate and some do not. Although Porter does not make any reference to the fact, these changing patterns may have significant implications for strategic groups within an industry. This possibility will be discussed later. Porter also mentions that the same changing patterns apply to advertising, R&D expenditures, degree of price competition, and most other industry characteristics. Moreover, he argues that 'divergent patterns such as these call into serious question the strategic implications ascribed to the life cycle' (Porter, 1980: 162).

The strategic group concept

Newman (1978: 417–427) and Porter (1979: 215–227) both discuss the strategic group concept. Although these studies investigated different questions, they are both concerned with the importance of examining strategic groups within a given industry instead of the group as a whole, to obtain more meaningful information concerning firm strategy.

> If corporate strategies can differ persistently among direct market rivals, we can speak of strategic groups—each group consisting of firms highly symmetrical in their corporate strategies—as a *stable* element of market structure (Newman, 1978: 417–427).

Porter (1979: 215) explains that an industry is composed of a cluster of firms, each group following similar strategies in terms of key decision variables. The group may consist of a single firm or all firms in the industry.

The dynamics described by Porter (1980: 162 and 136) could lead one to the conclusion that strategic groups could be different for each phase of an industry's life cycle; this conclusion follows from his discussion. He further explains that an industry may contain several strategic groups. Entry barriers protect members of a strategic group from entry by an outside firm and also provide barriers to members of an industry shifting strategic positions from one strategic group to another (Porter, 1980: 133).

Rumelt (1979: 204–206, 208–209) mentions both the life cycle models and the strategic group models as fruitful areas for further research. He acknowledges that the strategic group concept represents a beginning of the move away from equating structure with concentration, but he explains that further work is required. Regarding the life cycle concept, he says that the application of a Hatten–Patton type of method to a competitive group in the growth phase and then again in the maturity phase of the life cycle would be a worthy study (Rumelt, 1979: 212). The objective of this particular study is different from Hatten and Patton's studies; however, this work does represent an attempt to integrate strategic group theory into industry life cycle theory. Moreover, it provides an attempt to establish a technique which will be useful for determining the phase of the life cycle an industry is in, at a point in time, without requiring previous or future information.

THE THEORY

The industry life cycle

Firms and industries go through a life cycle similar to that attributed to products which is described in Rink and Swan (1979: 219–242). Grabowski and Mueller (1975: 401) argue that investment behavior by a firm follows a life cycle. Kmenta and Williamson (1966: 172–181), in their study of the railroad industry, established that investment in that industry did follow a life cycle pattern which consisted of a three-stage pattern; an early period of adolescence (1872–95), a middle period of maturity (1896–1914) and '...discarding the unusual war years of governmental control a final period of senility, 1922–41' (Kmenta and Williamson, 1966: 173).

These studies seem to provide adequate bases for a life cycle which causes firms within an industry to adjust their investment strategy.

The life cycle behavior of investment is inherent in the table in Porter (1980: 160). The author attributes to Patton (1959) the idea that in the growth stage undercapacity would occur, and to Staudt *et al.* (1976) along with Wells (1972) the notion that a shift towards mass production would be expected in that stage.

Porter (1980: 160) also attributes to the maturity stage some overcapacity, according to Levitt (1965); and a movement toward optimum capacity, according to Smallwood (1973). Porter's table also shows stability of the manufacturing process, according to Catry and Chevalier (1974); and movement toward long production runs with stable techniques, according to Wells (1972), in the mature stage of the life cycle.

Porter (1980: 160) states that for the decline stage of the life cycle substantial overcapacity would exist, from Levitt (1965) and Patton (1959).

The significant thing for our purpose is to note that these characteristics and conditions cited by previous authors would all affect investment strategy within a firm and within an industry, as an industry moves from one stage of the life cycle to another.

The strategic group concept and the industry life cycle

Fizaine (1968: 606–620) examined 1183 establishments in the French economy and found that age is a better explanatory variable than size in determining growth. Mueller (1972: 210) concludes from these results that '...young firms grow faster than old ones regardless of their size, and that large and small firms of the same age have the same growth rate'. These results seem to have significant implications for the strategic group concept, as it relates to the industry life cycle. That is, newer firms (young firms) would tend to grow faster than older-established firms. Consequently, newer entrants into an industry are not necessarily in the same stage of the industry life cycle as the older-established firms. Moreover, it is very clear from Newman (1978: 417–427) and Porter (1979: 214–227) that all firms within an industry are not within the same strategic group. It follows, therefore, that all firms within an industry need not be in the same stage of the industry life cycle! This likelihood is consistent with the earlier comment attributed to Porter (1980: 162), that concentration changes as industries develop, as does the level of fragmentation. These changes, too, indicate pressure moving firms toward different stages of the life cycle as well as toward membership in different strategic groups within the same industry.

As mentioned by Porter (1980: 158), Shepherd (1979: 193) 'The "normal" life cycle is occasionally broken, as new conditions change a mature industry back into a young one. Still age often explains much of an industry's structure, behavior, and degree of flexibility'. Shepherd's comment is not inconsistent with the position taken here; that is, the industry life cycle may change. However, neither Shepherd nor any previous author, to my knowledge, has mentioned the possibility that all firms within an industry may not be in the same stage of the life cycle, or that different strategic groups may be in different stages of the industry life cycle.

METHOD

As mentioned earlier, one of the main purposes of this study is to develop a method to identify the stage of the life cycle in which an industry is operating, and to determine whether all firms in that industry are in the same stage of the life cycle.

One might suggest several different approaches to answering the above questions. However, it is highly likely that the suggested approach to providing an answer would involve considerable judgement on the part of the investigator.

One essential characteristic of the method suggested here is that it is, to the greatest extent possible, free of judgement on the part of the investigator; neither does it rely on responses to questionnaires where firms 'tell' you the stage of the life cycle they are in, nor does it depend upon judgement of the investigator in observing the behavior of the firm. Instead, hard data, accompanied by the use of rigorous statistical methods, reveal the answers to the questions.

Firm data are readily available to researchers through Compustat tapes and similar sources. Individual firm data, of course, can be summed to obtain industry data. So the researcher has access to both industry and firm data. Even if all data are not actually available for all firms in a given industry, an aggregation of the available data will provide information which is truly representative of the industry. In the final analysis, that is what really matters.

The next step in the process is to search the literature for some good statistical models which have been developed to examine certain firm or industry behavior. In this phase, I am suggesting that one could benefit substantially by reviewing the economics, management, marketing, management science, and finance literature. These disciplines all have much common ground; if there is a useful method or model in another discipline, we should be willing and eager to accept and adopt it for our purposes, assuming it is a valid approach and adaptable for our purposes.

To illustrate the main point in the previous paragraph, the following discussion focuses attention on the specific problems posed in this paper; and it illustrates a sound approach to answering the questions posed earlier.

Investment behavior is one important indicator of the industry life cycle. Porter (1980: 163) mentions that:

> ...instrumental in much industry evolution are the investment decisions by both existing firms in the industry and the new entrants. In response to pressures or incentives created by the evolutionary process, firms invest to take advantage of possibilities for new marketing approaches, new manufacturing facilities, and the like, which shift entry barriers, alter relative power against suppliers and buyers and so on.

The main points for our purpose is that investment decisions are a key variable and that firms adjust this variable as industry evolution takes place, according to Porter.

Lawrence Klein (1951), a Nobel Prize-winning economist and excellent econometrician, developed a model of investment behavior in the railroad industry. Klein's objective was to model the investment behavior which actually took place in the industry from 1922 to 1941. He developed two alternative specifications which were able to explain between 0.903 and 0.941 percent of variations in investment in the industry.

Kmenta and Williamson (1966: 172–181) in a subsequent study explained that, although Klein's model had important merit, his estimates could have been improved if he had focused attention on the stages of the life cycle of the railroad industry. They used some new data which had recently become available and tested Klein's model. Then they used the same data in their new life cycle model. The results were that they did, indeed, improve upon the estimates which came from Klein's model. The significant fact is that they essentially established that there had been life cycle stages in the railroad industry. They used a three-stage cycle: growth, maturity, and senility. Kmenta and Williamson (1966: 180) explain that their analysis could probably be readily adapted to study other industries for which we now have time series data.

The equations used in the Kmenta and Williamson paper are as follows:

Stage of adolescence

$$I_t^N = A + B_1 X_{t-2} - B_2 K_{t-2} + B_3 \left(\frac{\pi^*}{K}\right)_{t-2} + B_4(\pi^*_{t-1} - \pi^*_{t-2}) + \hat{U}_t \quad (1)$$

Stage of maturity:

$$I_t^N = A + B_1 X_{t-2} - B_2 K_{t-2} + \hat{U}_t \quad\quad\quad (2)$$

Stage of senility:

$$I_t^N = A - B_1 K_{t-1} + B_2 \pi^{**}_{t-1} + \hat{U}_t \quad\quad\quad (3)$$

Where: I^N = net investment deflated by q (millions of dollars)
$\quad\quad X$ = operating revenue deflated by q (millions of dollars)
$\quad\quad K$ = capital stock deflated by q (millions of dollars)
$\quad\quad \pi^*$ = net operating income excluding depreciation deflated by q (millions of dollars)
$\quad\quad \pi^{**}$ = net income deflated by q (millions of dollars) and π^*/K in (1) is given in percentage rates
$\quad\quad q$ = railroad construction index; 1929 = 100.

The kind of research undertaken by Kmenta and Williamson is very valuable and useful to those who are concerned and interested in questions of policy and strategy. Moreover, in this particular work, researchers have a vehicle for answering some very important questions concerning the industry life cycle.

At the beginning of this discussion I wish to acknowledge that many readers have the ability to 'build their own' econometric models. That point is not at issue. The fact is that it is possible to adapt previously published research, which has already been given the 'stamp of approval', to further develop some insight into previously unanswered questions.

With the Kmenta and Williamson work we have a model of industry life cycle investment behavior. The authors are excellent econometricians so it is fairly safe to assume that the work is sound. This being the case, if one used their model to develop multiple regression equations for any given industry, one of the three life cycle equations would best fit the data of the industry being examined. That equation would indicate the investment behavior within the industry and would identify the stage of the life cycle of that industry.

APPLICATION OF THE TECHNIQUE

This section presents an application of the method discussed above by using actual data for firms in the petroleum industry.*

This practical application involves the following steps. The research begins with available data since World War II; 1961–80, representing 20 years of operation. The raw firm data for the petroleum industry were taken from Compustat tapes. These firm data were summed to obtain industry data. Then the three investment life cycle equations from Kmenta and Williamson were individually estimated with the same industry data. The model of the stage which best reflects industry investment behavior would identify the stage of the life cycle the *industry* is actually in. This approach would permit a researcher to gain a better understanding of the investment strategy and behavior of the industry as a whole; in a real sense, the industry life cycle stage would be identified.

Table 4.3.1 presents multiple regression equations for the petroleum industry for the three different stages of the industry life cycle presented by Kmenta and Williamson; their model was modified to add an interest rate variable (r_{t-1}) and a research and development variable (t). Neither variable was included in their railroad industry study because it was thought that the effects would be unimportant, given the industry being examined. Obviously, an adaptation of the models to most other industries would require R&D and interest rate variables.†

The *industry* equations are (1), (4), and (7). The results show that equation (1), representing the adolescence stage of the industry life cycle, seems to best fit the industry data. That is, according to $\bar{R}^2$, the adolescence equation explains a greater percentage of change in net investment for the whole petroleum industry (0.79) than either the maturity stage (0.25) or the senility

---

* The method is most useful for firms with a minimum degree of diversification. Of course it is possible to control for diversification differences, to some extent.

† The interest rate proxy variable (r_{t-1}) is the real corporate bond rate, lagged 1 year. Specifically, the industrial average was used for the industry equations; the triple A (AAA) rate was used for the leading firms; and the double A (AA) rate was used for the following firms. The R&D variable is a time trend variable (1 in the first time period, n in the final time period). An additional modification of the Kmenta and Williamson model involved the price deflator, q. For this study, q is the implicit price deflator for producers' durable equipment.

Table 4.3.1 Multiple regression equation of life cycle stages, petroleum industry

$$I_t^N = A + B_1 X_{t-2} - B_2 K_{t-2} + B_3\left(\frac{\pi^*}{K}\right)_{t-2} + B_4(\pi^*_{t-1} - \pi^*_{t-2}) + B_5 r_{t-1} + B_6 t + U_t$$

Adolescence stage

	A	B_1	B_2	B_3	B_4	B_5	B_6	$\bar{R}^2$	DW
(1) Industry	5875.2 (5332.4)	0.126 (0.041)***	-0.163 (0.167)	-22454 (16050.0)	0.056 (0.129)	57.497 (284.36)	121.71 (662.34)	0.795	1.964
(2) Leading firms	1053.2 (4566.9)	0.041 (0.084)	0.004 (0.334)	-4833.6 (4840.9)	-0.128 (0.149)	-38.947 (135.51)	49.786 (411.95)	0.316	2.117
(3) Following firms	6828.7 (3085.7)**	0.176 (0.047)***	-0.398 (0.151)*	-28422.0 (17082.0)*	0.145 (0.170)	6.912 (221.03)	423.16 (402.84)	0.810	2.018

$$I_t^N = A + B_1 X_{t-2} - B_2 K_{t-2} + B_3 r_{t-1} + B_4 t + U_t$$

Maturity stage

	A	B_1	B_2	B_3	B_4	$\bar{R}^2$	DW
(4) Industry	-290.67 (1545.9)	0.047 (0.037)	-0.014 (0.179)	307.37 (159.80)**	355.14 (714.94)	0.251	2.002
(5) Leading firms	-254.25 (3886.3)	0.040 (0.061)	0.041 (0.285)	57.734 (100.85)	-24.734 (327.75)	0.356	2.088
(6) Following firms	-991.36 (1257.0)	-0.034 (0.044)	-0.222 (0.174)	159.09 (120.76)	1671.0 (811.13)**	0.230	2.017

$$I_t^N = A - B_1 K_{t-1} + B_2 \pi^{**}_{t-1} + B_3 r_{t-1} + B_4 t + U_t$$

Senility stage

	A	B_1	B_2	B_3	B_4	$\bar{R}^2$	DW
(7) Industry	-5.742	-0.112	0.120	275.28	936.01	0.314	1.954
	(1711.8)	(0.200)	(0.250)	(161.01)*	(475.21)**		
(8) Leading firms	2719.0	-0.199	0.154	64.288	215.19	0.436	2.031
	(1638.5)*	(0.165)	(0.382)	(75.792)	(87.747)**		
(9) Following firms	-4544.0	-0.180	0.303	263.41	45732.0	0.189	1.790
	(5699.0)	(0.174)	(0.231)	(104.47)**	(56536.0)		

*** Significant at 1 percent level.
** Significant at 5 percent level.
* Significant at 10 percent level.
Standard errors are in parentheses.

stage (0.31). From these results, then, a researcher would identify the petroleum industry (that is the aggregate of all firms) as being in the adolescence stage of the industry life cycle. This approach clearly constitutes an important aide for a better understanding of the industry life cycle.

The above discussion does explain how an industry life cycle can be identified; however, it does not explain whether or not all firms within an industry are in the same stage of the life cycle. An adaptation of the strategic group concept, along with the procedure discussed above, was used to generate further useful information and answer this question.

The procedure followed by Porter (1979: 214–227) was employed to identify the strategic groups in the petroleum industry. Porter divided each industry sample into two parts. He used the relative size of a firm in its industry as a proxy for its strategic group membership (Porter, 1979: 220). The firms in each industry were divided into two categories: leaders and followers. Leaders were defined as the largest firms in the industry (accounting for approximately 30 percent of industry revenue). Remaining firms constituted the follower group. After the segmentation was made to determine the strategic groups within the industry being examined, the three life cycle investment equations were run for each strategic group. If the two strategic groups were in the same stage of the life cycle, the same investment life cycle stage equation would explain best the investment behavior of both groups; if, however, one life cycle equation explains best one strategic group's investment behavior, and another explains the investment of the other strategic group, the conclusion would be that they are in two different stages of the industry life cycle.

Equations (2), (3), (5), (6), (8) and (9) in Table 4.3.1 present the results of the strategic groups' multiple regressions for the petroleum industry. From these equations it is possible to determine the stage of the industry life cycle of each strategic group. Equation (8) is clearly the best equation for the leading firm, with $\hat{R}^2$ of 0.43. This indicates that the leading firms in the petroleum industry reflect investment behavior characteristic of the senility stage of the industry life cycle. The following firms, in contrast reflect investment behavior characteristic of the adolescence stage. This is determined from the highest R^2 for following firms, generated by equation (3), which is 0.81.

In summary, for the petroleum industry used in this illustration, the industry as a whole reflected investment behavior characteristic of the adolescence stage of the industry life cycle; the leading firms reflected investment behavior characteristic of the senility stage, and the following firms reflected investment behavior characteristic of the adolescence stage. The reasons for the difference in investment behavior between members of the two strategic groups is that the following firms are the younger firms. As Mueller (1972: 210) explained, young firms grow faster than old ones regardless of size. The leading firms clearly reflect different investment behavior from the following firms; consequently, they are in a different stage of the life cycle.

The essential point for our purpose is that multiple regression equations and data have been used to make these identifications instead of less objective methods. Overall, the results show: (1) the method proposed here is useful for identifying the stage of the life cycle an industry is in, (2) the method is useful for determining the life cycle stage strategic group members are in. The results also show: (1) all members of strategic groups need not be in the same life cycle stage, (2) the industry life cycle and the life cycle of each strategic group could differ, although one strategic group did match the industry in the illustration presented here.

A question may be raised about the validity of Porter's designation of 30 percent representing the leading group. In fact, he refers to the 30 percent designation as arbitrary (Porter, 1979: 220). Indeed, it may be that instead of two strategic groups, three may exist; and the appropriate breakdown should be, say, one strategic group accounting for 20 percent of sales, another accounting for 30 percent of sales, and another accounting for 50 percent.

The results from this alternative strategic group designation could surpass the results of the Porter (1979) analysis. More than likely, some industries will be represented best by three strategic groups, while others will be best identified with two, as Porter (1979: 221) suggests. As McGee (1984) indicates, there are also other methods for determining strategic groups. Porter's (1979) basic designation was arbitrarily selected for this example. The technique explained here readily permits statistical tests to assess the efficacy of one method of strategic group determination versus available alternatives.

One might still remain unconvinced, even after the industry life cycle stage has been identified and a determination made concerning the applicability of the life cycle to the strategic groups in the industry. One might assert that, even though the equations make the identifications from hard data, the *real* life cycle may be different from the one indicated. This type of skepticism cannot be easily overcome. One can certainly conclude that the results do mean that the firms, as a strategic group within an industry, are behaving as if they are in a certain stage of the industry life cycle, with respect to their investment decisions. These conclusions would follow from the hard data and the rigorous statistical analyses which are used. Admittedly, the analyses may not generate conclusive proof; however, the results should certainly be more credible than judgements made from instinct, hunch, speculation, or even firm surveys.

Given several studies of the type suggested here, we should be able to make much stronger industry analyses and understand better industry life cycles and strategic groups. This conclusion follows because the composition of strategic groups is probably not independent of the industry life cycle, yet previous analyses have tended to assume that is the case.

CONCLUSIONS

In contrast to methods which rely on hunch and speculation to identify the industry life cycle or the strategic groups of an industry, the method advocated in this study is dependent upon rigorous statistical analysis. Although researchers could develop their own econometric models to make desired identifications, models which have been developed by previous research may be readily adaptable to answer relevant questions.

Although the primary focus here has been upon the industry life cycle and strategic groups, it is almost certain that other important questions, of interest to the study of strategic management, could also be answered in a similar fashion. This basic approach could substitute rigor for subjective judgement wherever it is used.

An additional point can be made concerning the value of industry life cycle analyses. Kmenta and Williamson (1966) show the importance of examining industry data with life cycle models. Their analysis provides rather strong evidence that those concerned with industry analysis and strategy must take the industry life cycle concept seriously. This conclusion follows from their whole analysis and is adequately summed up in one of their final comments: 'All of this suggests considerable potential for the life-cycle approach as contrasted to models which disregard the stage of industry development' (Kmenta and Williamson, 1966, p. 180).

REFERENCES

Biggadike, E. Ralph, 'The contributions of marketing to strategic management', *Academy of Management Review*, Oct. 1981, pp. 621–632.

Catry, B., and M. Chevalier, 'Market share strategy and the product life cycle', *Journal of Marketing*, Oct. 1974. (Cited by Porter, 1980: 160–161.)

Cooper, Arnold C., 'Strategic management: new ventures and small business', in Dan E. Schendel and Charles W. Hoffer (eds), *Strategic Management: A New View of Business Policy and Planning*. Little, Brown & Co., Boston, 1979.

Fizaine, Francoise, 'Analyse Statistique de la Croissance des Entreprises Selon l'age et la Taille', *Revue d'Economie Politique*, July–Aug. 1968, pp. 606–620.

Grabowski, Henry G., and Dennis C. Mueller, 'Life cycle effects on corporate returns and retentions', *Review of Economics and Statistics*, Nov. 1975, pp. 400–409.

Klein, L. R. 'Studies in investment behavior'. Universities-National Bureau Committee for Economic Research. *Conference on Business Cycles*. National Bureau of Economic Research, 1951 (New York, 1966).

Kmenta, Jan and Jeffrey G. Williamson, 'Determinants of investment behavior: United States Railroads, 1872–1941', *Review of Economics and Statistics*, May 1966, pp. 172–181.

Levitt, T., 'Exploit the product life cycle', *Harvard Business Review*, Nov./Dec. 1965. (Cited in Porter, 1980.)

McGee, John, 'Strategic groups: a bridge between industry structure and strategic management'. This volume, Chapter 4.2, 1984.

Mueller, Dennis, C., 'A life cycle theory of the firm, *Journal of Industrial Economics*, July 1972, pp. 199–218.

Newman, Howard H., 'Strategic groups and the structure–performance relationship', *Review of Economics and Statistics*, Aug. 1978, pp. 417–427.

Patton, Arch, 'Stretch your product's earning years', *Management Review*, June 1959. (Cited in Porter, 1980.)

Patz, Alan L., *Strategic Decision Analysis*. Little, Brown & Co., Boston, 1981.

Porter, Michael, E. 'The structure within industries and companies' performance', *Review of Economics and Statistics*, May 1979, pp. 214–227.

Porter, Michael E., *Competitive Strategy*. The Free Press, New York, 1980.

Porter, Michael E. 'The contributions of industrial organization to strategic management', *Academy of Management Review*, Oct. 1981, pp. 609–620.

Rink, David R., and John E. Swan, 'Product life cycle research: a literature review', *Journal of Business Research*, Sept. 1979, pp. 219–242.

Rumelt, Richard P., 'Evaluation of strategy: theory and models', in Dan E. Schendel and Charles W. Hoffer (eds) *Strategic Management: A New View of Business Policy and Planning*. Little, Brown, & Co., Boston, 1979.

Schendel, Dan E., and Charles W. Hoffer (eds), *Strategic Management: A New View of Business Policy and Planning*. Little, Brown, & Co., Boston, 1979.

Shepherd, William G., *The Economics of Industrial Organization*. Prentice-Hall, Englewood Cliffs, N.J., 1979.

Smallwood, J. E., 'The product life cycle: a key to strategic market planning', *MSU Business Topics*, Winter 1973. (Cited in Porter, 1980.)

Staudt, T. A., D. Taylor, and D. Bowersox, *A Managerial Introduction to Marketing*, 3rd edn. Prentice-Hall, Englewood Cliffs, N.J., 1976. (Cited in Porter, 1980.)

Wells, L. T., Jr. 'International trade: the product life cycle approach', in L. T. Wells, Jr. (ed.), *The Product Life Cycle in International Trade*. Harvard Graduate School of Business Administration, Cambridge, Mass., 1972. (Cited in Porter, 1980.)

Strategic Marketing and Management
Edited by H. Thomas and D. Gardner
© 1985 John Wiley & Sons Ltd

4.4
Security Returns as a Basis for Estimating the Competitive Structure in an Industry

ADRIAN B. RYANS
School of Business Administration, University of Western Ontario, London, Canada

AND

DICK R. WITTINK
Graduate School of Management, Cornell University, Ithaca, N.Y.

INTRODUCTION

In recent years there has been an increasing emphasis on the role of the structure within industries on the performance of the firms in the industry. Porter (1979) has argued that a firm's performance depends on general industry factors, such as market growth rate and the power of buyers and suppliers, the strategic group to which the firm belongs, and the firm's position within its strategic group. A strategic group is defined as a group of firms within an industry that follows similar strategies with respect to key business decision variables (Porter, 1979: 215). As the subsequent literature review will suggest, one of the difficulties in using the strategic group concept in research has been the difficulty in identifying the strategic groups in an industry. The purpose of this paper is to explore the possibility that security price movements may be able to provide insight into the strategic group structure of some industries.

The growing emphasis in the industrial organization literature on the importance of strategic groups in strategic decision-making appears to be borne out by some fragmentary empirical evidence. Newman (1978) argued that if an industry is composed of a more complex and heterogeneous set of strategic groups, it will be a more competitive industry. A heterogeneous set of strategic groups implies different effects of, and responses to, common environmental disturbances, thus making it difficult to establish and maintain any tacit agreements between the firms in the industry. Thus, he concluded that the basic structure–performance model would do a much better job of explaining inter-industry variations in market performance for a group of industries with few important strategic groups (homogeneous industries) than for a group of industries with many strategic groups (heterogeneous industries). In his empirical test of this proposition, using 34 four-digit Standard Industrial Classification (SIC) industries from the chemical and process industries, Newman was able to demonstrate that a model relating company performance to industry concentration, market growth, capital–output ratio, degree of vertical integration, and industry strategic group heterogeneity had high explanatory power for industries relatively low in strategic group heterogeneity, and low explanatory power when strategic group heterogeneity was high. Newman identified the strategic groups in the 34 industries from a qualitative examination of company and industry data.

Porter has carried the reasoning further and has argued that a firm will have higher profits, if it is located in a strategic group that has few members, high mobility barriers and is well insulated from inter-group rivalry, is in a strong bargaining position with respect to both suppliers and customers, and faces little direct competition from substitute products (Porter, 1979: 219). Porter then attempted to subject his theory to an empirical test. Unfortunately, he was not able to obtain direct measures of all the hypothesized influencing variables. His proxy for strategic group membership was whether the firm was an industry leader (operationally defined as one of the largest firms in the industry which in aggregate accounted for 30 percent or more of industry sales), or an industry follower (other firms in the industry excluding 'fringe' firms). His final sample consisted of 38 consumer goods industries. He argued that in these types of industries his leader/follower dichotomy may well capture some of the variance among strategic groups, since large firms are likely to be vertically integrated, with broad product lines, large sales forces, and make use of national advertising, whereas followers will probably not have this type of strategy. Based on these hypothesized differences between the leader and follower groups, he argued that different aspects of industry structure will provide mobility barriers or affect the pattern of rivalry for different strategic groups. Hence, different structural models should be appropriate for explaining average firm profitability in the leader and follower groups. In the separate regression analyses of leader and follower rates of return, Porter (1979) found, as hypothesized, that different sets of variables seemed to be related to firm profitability in the two groups. For example, consider one of the major models estimated by Porter. For the leader group of firms he found that the advertising to sales ratio, and a variable reflecting the cost disadvantage of small-scale plants, had a significant positive impact on average firm profitability. For the follower group, industry growth, eight-firm concentration ratio, and capital requirements had a significant positive impact on average firm profitability. Thus, Porter concluded that the structure within industries does have an important effect on the factors affecting firm profitability.

Both the works of Newman (1978) and Porter (1979) provide fragmentary empirical support for their contentions that understanding the strategic group structure within an industry can be important for understanding the profitability of the firms within an industry. Clearly, one of the major deficiencies in this research to date has been the difficulty of identifying the strategic group structure within an industry. Newman (1978) had to rely on a large-scale qualitative and quantitative analysis of a variety of data sources, including corporate filings with the Securities and Exchange Commission, trade publications, and a variety of industry sources, to identify the strategic groups in the 34 industries in his sample. As discussed above, Porter (1979) used a cruder procedure, assuming that 'leader' firms and 'follower' firms in his industries were likely to be in different strategic groups.

If an industry is composed of a number of subgroups of firms ('strategic groups') which have similar business strategies and which are likely to be affected by, and to respond somewhat differently to, disturbances from inside or outside the industry, this may provide a possible basis for the identification of the strategic groups within an industry. One way the effects of disturbances and the responses of firms to disturbances is likely to manifest itself is through the prices of a firm's stock. If markets are efficient the anticipated effects of disturbances and firms' likely responses should be reflected in the movement of their stock prices. If two firms are in the same strategic group, then their stock prices should tend to move together. Some of this similarity may be captured in the betas of their securities. There is evidence, for example, that a firm's capital structure and operating leverage are related to the beta of its securities (Foster, 1978).

The use of security price movements as a means of identifying strategic groups within industries has a number of important advantages:

(1) Security price data are 'hard' data and, hence, the determination of industry structure is less dependent on qualitative judgements such as those used by Newman. In a way, the stock price data reflect the collective wisdom of numerous analysts making investments on the basis of their judgements. The 'face validity' of the structure uncovered by the quantitative analysis of the security price data can be assessed by persons familiar with the qualitative data on the industry structure.

(2) Security price data are readily available for most, if not all, firms in a given industry. If daily stock return data are used, about 250 observations per firm are available in a 1-year period. This is advantageous if we are attempting to test if the structure of the industry is stable or is changing over relatively short periods of time.

The major potential disadvantages of the use of security price data are the following:

(1) The approach makes most sense in industries where most of the participants are basically one-industry firms. If this is not the case, then the security price movements will reflect a complex aggregation of the effects of events in all the industries in which the firm participates. However, many important industries are composed of basically single-industry firms. For example, steel, oil, aluminum, public utilities, airlines, office equipment, and banking industries are largely (but certainly not exclusively) composed of firms heavily committed to one industry.

(2) In order for the latent structure in the industry to manifest itself, some internal or external disturbances that affect the strategic groups differentially need to occur. Ideally, we need a range of different types of disturbances so small differences in strategic posture will be evidenced. Generally, if the study period encompasses a reasonable length of time, this should not be a problem for most industries, which in recent years have been afflicted by raw material shortages, rapid escalations in energy costs, varied macroeconomic environments, changing customer needs, increased foreign competition, and the usual array of moves by various competitors. The length of the study period that will be necessary to assess the strategic group structure of an industry will vary depending on how exposed the industry has been to these external and internal forces.

AIRLINE INDUSTRY

The airline industry was selected for study here. While some of the companies in the US air transportation industry have significant non-air transportation businesses (e.g. at the time of the study, Pan-American owned Intercontinental Hotels, which accounted for 9 percent of its revenue in 1979), most are essentially one-industry companies.

The industry has a history of unusually wide variability (across firms) in the profitability of the individual firms (Fruhan, 1972), and this wide variability continues to this date. This suggests great heterogeneity in terms of market environments and business strategies, and perhaps the presence of several quite different strategic groups within the industry. With the gradual deregulation of the domestic US air transportation beginning in 1978, and the lessened involvement of the Civil Aeronautics Board in the industry, several airlines adopted quite different growth strategies. Thus, we should expect to observe changes in the industry structure in the years following the deregulation decision. In many ways the strategic group structure of the airline industry is difficult to discern. There are no obvious clear strategic groups other than the dichotomy between the large trunk airlines and the smaller regional airlines, to which analysts sometimes refer (Forbes, 1981). Different geographic markets are growing at quite different rates and all companies tend to have strength in only a limited number of geographic markets, and no two airlines have strength in identical geographical segments. Thus, uncovering the strategic groups in the air transportation industry is likely to be a challenging task.

The study included all certified air transportation companies listed on the New York or American Stock Exchanges for the calendar years 1977 to 1979. Twenty-two airlines met these criteria. The Center for Research in Security Prices (CRSP) stock returns files were used in the analysis. The period included in the study included a 21-month period prior to the signing of the Airline Deregulation Act in October 1978, and the first year or so of experience operating in an increasingly less regulated environment. Many airlines began implementing their deregulation strategies in 1979. For example, United Airlines had made significant changes in its route structure by mid-1979 (*Business Week*, 1980). Thus, the new strategies were becoming apparent to analysts and investors during the time period included in the study and the change in strategy should thus be starting to be reflected in stock market prices by the end of the period studied here, if analysts and investors react to the changes in strategies rather than wait for the ultimate effects on performance to be available.

In this exploratory study it was decided to analyse the data separately for each calendar quarter. Given daily stock price data, each quarterly observation was based on approximately 62 daily observations. Three months was chosen because it provided a reasonable number of observations for estimation of the market model, and yet it represented a period short enough that major structural changes in the industry were unlikely to have occurred within the period.

THE MARKET MODEL

In order to study the competitive structure of an industry using correlations in security return movements between pairs of companies, a preliminary step was taken by removing the movement that is common to all securities traded on an exchange. Thus, the analysis reported here is 'free' of movement in the market as a whole. Instead of using a popular market measure such as the Dow Jones Industrial Average or Standard and Poor's 500 Composite Index, we used the simple average return across all securities traded on the New York Stock

Exchange. The market model is*:

$$r_{i,t} = \alpha_i + \beta_i r_{m,t} + u_{i,t} \tag{1}$$

where: $r_{i,t} \quad = \dfrac{p^*_{i,t} - p^*_{i,t-1} + d_{i,t}}{p^*_{i,t-1}}$

$p^*_{i,t} \quad = p_{i,t} \times s_{i,t}$

$s_{i,t}$ $\begin{cases} = z/y \text{ if a } z \text{ for } y \text{ stock split takes place on day } t \text{ for security } i \\[1em] = \dfrac{100 + x}{100} \text{ if a } x \text{ percent stock dividend is paid on day } t \text{ for security } i \end{cases}$

$r_{m,t} \quad = \dfrac{\sum\limits_{i=1}^{n} r_{i,t}}{n}$

$p_{i,t}$ is the price of security i on day t

$d_{i,t}$ is the dividend, if any, paid on day t for security i

$u_{i,t}$ is a random disturbance for security i at time t

$r_{m,t}$ is the return on the market portfolio on day t

n is the number of securities used to obtain the return on a market portfolio.

However, it is not inconceivable that the parameters, unique to each security, also vary systematically over time. Given our interest in studying the competitive structure for each of twelve quarters separately, it seems appropriate to adjust for market variation separately for each quarter if the parameter estimates are statistically significantly different across the twelve quarters. We note also that the market model, under certain conditions, is equivalent to the capital-asset pricing model (Sharpe, 1964; Lintner, 1965). In the context of this model it is easy to argue for systematic changes in at least the slope parameter of the model.

* The estimation of the market model using daily data does lead to problems due to the non-synchronous trading problem (Scholes and Williams, 1977). In this exploratory paper no attempt was made to deal with this problem. Research by Alexander and Chervany (1980) suggests that 48–72 months of data are optimal for the estimation of beta for portfolios. Here, we have approximately 62 daily observations to estimate the beta for each airline. It is possible that Alexander and Chervany's results may be partly dependent on the time interval of the data. Furthermore, research by Sharpe and Cooper (1972) suggests that betas are not very stable over 5-year and even 1-year periods (again, monthly data were used). We would certainly expect betas to be unstable in the airline industry over time periods similar to those discussed by Alexander and Chervany.

Homogeneity tests*

To test the homogeneity (stability) of the parameters over time, we compared the following three models with the model in equation (1).

$$r_{i,t} = \alpha_{iq}^{I} + \beta_{iq}^{I} r_{m,t} + u_{i,t}^{I} \tag{2}$$

$$r_{i,t} = \alpha_{iq}^{II} + \beta_{i}^{II} r_{m,t} + u_{i,t}^{II} \tag{3}$$

$$r_{i,t} = \alpha_{i}^{III} + \beta_{iq}^{III} r_{m,t} + u_{i,t}^{III} \tag{4}$$

where a q subscript refers to a parameter that is allowed to vary from quarter to quarter.

Using model comparison tests, we obtained the following F-values:

$$\begin{array}{lll} (2) \text{ vs. } (1) & F_{504,16848} = 1.11 \\ (3) \text{ vs. } (1) & F_{252,17100} = 0.65 \\ (4) \text{ vs. } (1) & F_{252,17100} = 1.50 \; (p < 0.01) \end{array}$$

Based on the statistical evidence it appears that model (4) should be adopted. Thus the slope coefficients, but not the intercepts, are allowed to vary from quarter to quarter.

To see if a more parsimonious model might capture the variation in the slope coefficients over time, we estimated the following model:

$$r_{i,t} = \alpha_{i}^{IV} + (\beta_{i}^{IV} + \beta_{q}^{IV}) \, r_{m,t} + u_{i,t}^{IV} \tag{5}$$

In equation (5) the slope coefficients are allowed to vary over time but in identical (additive) ways for each security. Thus, while each security has its unique slope coefficient, a quarter-specific constant is added, the constant being the same for all securities. Although model (5) compared favourably to model (1), with $F_{11,16598} = 6.92$, model (4) is still superior to model (5) based on $F_{231,16367} = 1.28$. Thus, we use the residuals from model (4) as a basis for estimating the structure in the airline industry.

To provide some insight into the relation between the return on an airline security and the market return, for the period 1977–79, we have summarized the parameter estimates for model (1) in Table 4.4.1. The goodness-of-fit (R^2) values for model (1) vary from 3.6 percent for Hawaiian Airlines to 28.4 percent for Braniff. Only for two airlines, Hawaiian and KLM, is the slope coefficient less than one. This coefficient is a measure of the systematic risk associated with investments in the firm's common stock. The small slope coefficient for these two airlines seems quite reasonable, since the former is a member of a duopoly and faces little competition from other modes of transportation, and the latter is the national flag carrier for the Netherlands

---

* The homogeneity tests were carried out using two additional airlines: Piedmont and Texas International Airlines. However, since only a limited number of observations were available for each of these firms, they were excluded from the analysis of industry structure.

Table 4.4.1   Parameter estimates by airline for model (1) and R^2 values for models (1) and (4)

	Model (1)			Model (4)
	$\hat{\alpha}_i$	$\hat{\beta}_i$	R_i^2	R_i^2
Alaska	−0.000(−0.23)[a]	1.19 (6.44)	0.052	0.056
American	−0.002(−2.16)	1.80(15.17)	0.234	0.261
Braniff	−0.002(−2.36)	1.93(17.29)	0.284	0.291
Continental	−0.001(−0.94)	2.05(13.90)	0.204	0.212
Delta	−0.001(−1.96)	1.11(16.90)	0.274	0.343
Frontier	−0.000(−0.05)	1.31(10.62)	0.130	0.154
Northwest	−0.001(−2.15)	1.59(17.19)	0.281	0.321
Ozark	−0.000(−0.41)	1.36 (8.25)	0.083	0.097
PSA	0.000 (0.42)	1.43 (9.92)	0.115	0.129
Seaboard World	0.001 (0.81)	1.28 (6.38)	0.051	0.070
Southwest	0.001 (0.67)	1.16(10.62)	0.130	0.146
Tiger	−0.001(−1.02)	1.78(16.00)	0.253	0.276
TWA	−0.001(−1.42)	2.18(16.59)	0.267	0.272
United	−0.001(−2.10)	1.58(15.85)	0.250	0.265
US Air	−0.001(−0.92)	2.05(12.35)	0.168	0.196
Western	−0.001(−1.24)	1.74(13.16)	0.187	0.212
Eastern	−0.002(−1.91)	2.05(15.50)	0.242	0.254
Pan-American	−0.001(−1.07)	1.68(11.97)	0.160	0.176
Hawaiian	−0.000(−0.07)	0.74 (5.32)	0.036	0.053
KLM	−0.000(−0.64)	0.73 (7.77)	0.074	0.095
National	0.001 (1.21)	1.11 (8.48)	0.088	0.146
Republic	−0.001(−0.79)	2.01(13.46)	0.194	0.209

[a] The number in parentheses is the computed t-ratio.

and thus enjoys a somewhat protected position. The highest slope coefficient was obtained for TWA, suggesting that this airline company has a particularly high systematic risk. In the last column of this table we show the R^2 values obtained for model (4). Compared to model (1), the goodness of fit was increased moderately with the values for model (4) ranging from 5.3 percent for Hawaiian to 34.3 percent for Delta. The increases in fit appear to be most dramatic for Delta and National.

It would not be very useful to present the changes in slope coefficients over time for each company separately. However, some indication of the nature of these changes, on the average, is provided by the estimates of β_q in model (5) for the quarters 2,3,...,12,* as shown in Table 4.4.2. The most dramatic change in the slope coefficients is observed for quarters six and seven. For those quarters (April–September 1978), the *systematic risk* for the average

* To avoid linear dependence, eleven dummy variables were used with the first quarter functioning as the base to which other quarters were compared.

Table 4.4.2 Parameter estimates for common time variation in model (5)

Quarter (q)	Time period	$\hat{\beta}_q$
2	Apr.–June 1977	0.20 (0.86)[a]
3	July–Sept. 1977	−0.32(−1.26)
4	Oct.–Dec. 1977	0.09 (0.43)
5	Jan.–Mar. 1978	−0.19(−0.87)
6	Apr.–June 1978	0.46 (2.21)
7	July–Sept. 1978	0.55 (2.63)
8	Oct.–Dec. 1978	0.08 (0.46)
9	Jan.–Mar. 1979	0.01 (0.06)
10	Apr.–June 1979	0.13 (0.61)
11	July–Sept. 1979	0.24 (1.13)
12	Oct.–Dec. 1979	−0.34(−1.88)

[a] The number in parentheses is the computed t-ratio.

airline security is substantially higher than it is for the first quarter. Interestingly, these are the quarters just prior to the final congressional decision to end all airline route regulation by 1981, when there was a great deal of uncertainty about the exact extent of deregulation and the effects of deregulation on the various airlines. Although not quite as dramatically, quarters three and twelve show less variation in return for the average airline compared with the first quarter.

ANALYSIS OF THE RESIDUALS

Having eliminated the part of the variation in the security returns that is systematically related to the variation in return on a market portfolio, the residuals from the regression analysis were next examined. Here the objective was to determine if there are subgroups of airline companies which share a common pattern in the security price movement (after eliminating the market return variation). Before conducting any sort of analysis of the correlation matrices obtained by correlating the residuals between airlines for all the observations in a quarter, the correlation matrices were first tested to determine if there appeared to be significant correlations between the variables. The sphericity test developed by Bartlett was used for this purpose (Green, 1978: 361). In this test the null hypothesis is based on the fact that if the universe from which the sample is drawn is made up of mutually uncorrelated variables, then the determinant of the population correlation matrix should be one.*

Using the correlation matrix for the residuals across all twelve quarters, we obtained $\chi^2_{231} = 1710$, which, using the normal approximation ($z = 37$), is

* Note that we expect that a similar null hypothesis expressed for security returns before elimination of the market return variation would be rejected quite easily.

highly significant. When χ^2 was computed separately for each quarter, each was also found to be highly significant. Thus, it seems appropriate to examine the residuals further.

Factor analysis

The nature of the data matrices on which the correlation matrices were based suggested that an S-type factor analysis might be a useful first step in the data reduction process. Principal components analysis was used for the data pooled over the twelve quarters, as well as for each quarter separately. Horn's criterion (Horn, 1965) was applied to determine the number of factors that should be retained. Application of this criterion involves a comparison of the set of eigenvalues obtained from the factor analysis of the sample data with a set of eigenvalues obtained from the factor analysis of random data (i.e. a correlation matrix that differs from an identity matrix due to sampling error). Although there is some evidence to suggest that it may be sufficient to use one single set of 'random' eigenvalues for a given problem (Crawford and Koopman, 1973), we used average 'random' eigenvalues for 100 independently generated correlation matrices.

In order to determine how many factors should be retained, Horn proposed to compare the magnitudes of the eigenvalues for the sample data with the eigenvalues for the random data. In order to retain a factor the eigenvalue for the real data would have to exceed the corresponding eigenvalue for the random data. The results for the data pooled across all twelve quarters, and the average values for analyses done separately on each quarter, are shown in Table 4.4.3.*

---

* It should be noted that an alternative criterion, commonly used in applications of factor analysis, is to retain all factors with eigenvalues in excess of one (Green, 1978: 368). If this rule had been applied here seven or eight factors would have been identified (for the random data, nine or ten factors would be identified). Clearly, the specific rule employed can have a dramatic impact on the number of factors retained. Although Horn's criterion seems preferable over the simplistic 'eigenvalue greater than one' rule, it should be noted that Horn's criterion is somewhat conservative. Specifically, by definition, the sum of the eigenvalues $\left(\sum_{i=1}^{I} \lambda_i = I \right)$ equals the number of variables. Then, if (at least) one factor exists (i.e. $\lambda_{1s} > \lambda_{1r}$, where s refers to sample data and r refers to random data), the average magnitude of the remaining eigenvalues for the sample has to be smaller than the average magnitude of the remaining eigenvalues for the random data. For example, for the pooled data, $\lambda_{1s} = 3.75$ and $\lambda_{1r} = 1.32$. Then, $\bar{\lambda}_s = \dfrac{I - \lambda_{1s}}{I - 1} = 0.87$ and $\bar{\lambda}_r = \dfrac{I - \lambda_{1r}}{I - 1} = 0.98$, for $I = 22$. One could argue that a new set of random eigenvalues should be generated, given that one factor has been extracted. Indeed, Crawford and Koopman found that Horn's criterion tended '... to underestimate the population number of factors following principal components analysis ...' (1973: 123). However, in their study the underestimation amounted to approximately one factor. Here, the effect could be more pronounced.

Table 4.4.3   Eigenvalues for real data pooled and average eigenvalues for separate quarters compared with eigenvalues for random data

Factor	Pooled data across all twelve quarters[a]		Separate analysis of each quarter[b]	
	Real data	Random data	Real data	Random data
1	3.75	1.32	4.04	2.27
2	1.35	1.27	2.07	2.00
3	1.20	1.23	1.77	1.83
4	1.15	1.19	1.60	1.69
5	1.09	1.16	1.45	1.53
6	1.07	1.13	1.33	1.41
7	1.02	1.10	1.19	1.29
8	0.99	1.08	1.10	1.20
9	0.95	1.03	0.98	1.10
10	0.94	1.00	0.89	1.02
11	0.88	0.98	0.81	0.93
12	0.88	0.96	0.74	0.86
.	.	.	.	.
.	.	.	.	.
.	.	.	.	.
22	0.53	0.72	0.15	0.21

[a] The sample size is 747.
[b] The sample size varies slightly from quarter to quarter; for the random data, 63 was used as the sample size.

The results presented in Table 4.4.3 for the pooled data and the average results for the twelve individual quarters both suggest that two factors should be retained. The individual analyses of the results for each quarter, again using Horn's criterion, are shown in Table 4.4.4. These results suggest that one, two, or three factors are appropriate depending on the particular quarter. Only in one quarter, the first quarter in 1979, are three factors apparently present.

The factor loadings for all 22 airlines based on the factor analysis of all twelve quarters of data are shown in Figure 4.4.1. Most of the 'trunk' airlines, those with major transcontinental routes, do tend to have similar loadings on the factors and are grouped together. Eastern Airlines, another trunk carrier but one with its route structure having a predominant north–south orientation, is located at some distance from the main group of trunk carriers. KLM has a quite different pattern of loadings to the other airlines and occupies an isolated position. Hawaiian Air and Seaboard World Airways are also quite isolated from other airlines. Again, this makes sense since Hawaiian Air is the dominant carrier in an isolated market, and Seaboard World Airways is primarily an air

Table 4.4.4   Apparent number of factors present in data

Quarter	Number of factors present in data[a]	Quarter	Number of factors present in data[a]
1	2	7	2
2	1	8	1
3	2	9	3
4	1	10	2
5	2	11	2
6	2	12	1

[a] Using Horn's criterion.

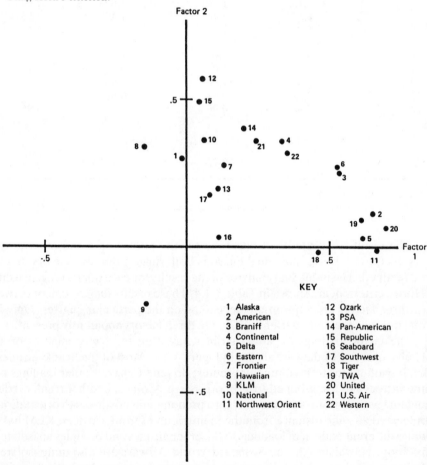

Figure 4.4.1   Plot of factor loadings of each airline based on all twelve quarters of data

freight carrier. Tiger International, while also primarily an air freight carrier, is located much closer to the trunk carriers. The two primarily intrastate commuter airlines, PSA and Southwest Airlines, also have very similar loadings on the two factors. It is also interesting to note that Pan-American World Airways and National Airlines, which merged in January 1980, had very similar loadings on the two factors.

When the factor analysis results of the quarterly data were examined, a good deal of instability was in evidence. Nevertheless, there appeared to be a considerable amount of continuing structure in the data. The trunk airlines were generally positioned quite close to each other in terms of factor loadings—Delta and Northwest Orient, in particular, were almost always in quite close proximity. As one measure of the over-time stability of loadings, the correlation between the loadings on the first principal components, prior to rotation, for all quarters were computed. The results shown in Table 4.4.5 suggest considerable stability from quarter to quarter.

Table 4.4.5 Correlation of airline loadings on first principal component across quarters

Quarter	1	2	3	4	5	6	7	8	9	10	11	12
1	1.00											
2	0.80	1.00										
3	0.72	0.79	1.00									
4	0.43	0.53	0.52	1.00								
5	0.76	0.85	0.73	0.39	1.00							
6	0.68	0.77	0.53	0.40	0.71	1.00						
7	0.44	0.35	0.19	0.48	0.35	0.53	1.00					
8	0.49	0.64	0.44	0.18	0.71	0.82	0.58	1.00				
9	0.58	0.80	0.70	0.68	0.68	0.66	0.46	0.60	1.00			
10	0.80	0.79	0.73	0.60	0.82	0.64	0.40	0.52	0.68	1.00		
11	0.60	0.59	0.46	0.41	0.71	0.59	0.54	0.61	0.71	0.67	1.00	
12	0.70	0.74	0.68	0.29	0.78	0.61	0.42	0.72	0.58	0.74	0.67	1.00

Cluster analysis

In order to see if other data reduction techniques might provide additional insights into the structure of the airline industry, the overall correlation matrix of residuals and the quarterly correlation matrices of residuals were submitted to the HICLUS cluster analysis program (Johnson, 1967). The diameter method was used in the development of clusters, so at any point when a new cluster was formed, the 'distance' between that cluster and any other object or cluster was defined as the maximum distance between any object in the newly formed cluster, and the other object or the most dissimilar object in the other cluster.

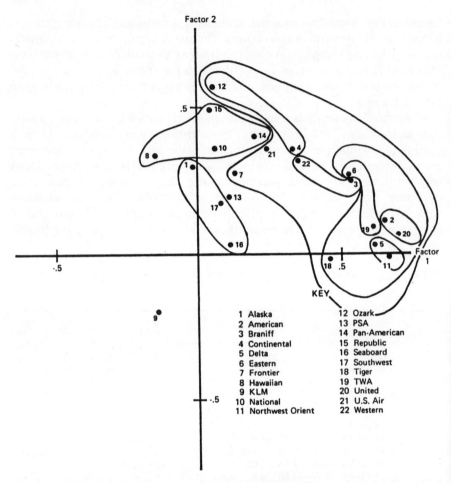

Figure 4.4.2   Results of cluster analysis of all twelve quarters of data superimposed
on plot of factor analysis loadings

The results of the cluster analysis of the correlation matrix based on the overall 3-year correlation matrix are shown superimposed on the factor loadings data in Figure 4.4.2. As this figure suggests, the initial clusters formed were sub-clusters of the major trunk airlines. It was only later that the Braniff and Western, National and Pan-American, and Ozark and Continental clusters were formed. Several of the airlines were isolates until fairly late in the clustering process; i.e. KLM, PSA, Seaboard, and Hawaiian. Generally, as would be expected, the cluster analysis results tended to reinforce the factor analysis results.

In order to try to provide a summary of the cluster analysis results for the twelve individual quarters, a consistent, but arbitrary, clustering criterion was selected and the composition of the clusters at this level summarized. One simple

Table 4.4.6 Number of times airlines appear in the same cluster—all twelve quarters

		1 Alaska	2 American	3 Braniff	4 Continental	5 Delta	6 Eastern	7 Frontier	8 Hawaiian	9 KLM	10 National	11 Northwest	12 Ozark	13 PSA	14 Pan-American	15 Republic	16 Seaboard	17 Southwest	18 Tiger	19 TWA	20 United	21 US Air
Alaska	1																					
American	2	0																				
Braniff	3	1	2																			
Continental	4	3	2	3																		
Delta	5	0	7	3	2																	
Eastern	6	1	4	6	2	5																
Frontier	7	1	1	2	2	1	3															
Hawaiian	8	0	0	3	0	1	2	4														
KLM	9	1	0	2	1	1	0	1	3													
National	10	1	2	5	2	3	4	2	2	0												
Northwest	11	0	9	2	2	8	5	2	1	1	3											
Ozark	12	2	2	4	4	2	2	3	0	2	1	2										
PSA	13	1	3	3	2	1	2	0	1	3	2	3	1									
Pan-American	14	0	3	4	1	3	5	1	4	1	3	4	0	2								
Republic	15	4	1	2	3	2	3	0	4	0	2	1	4	3	2							
Seaboard	16	3	2	1	2	1	0	1	1	0	1	0	2	1	1	2						
Southwest	17	5	1	1	1	0	1	0	1	0	2	0	1	1	2	2	3					
Tiger	18	1	5	2	2	3	2	2	1	1	0	3	1	2	4	2	3	4				
TWA	19	0	8	4	2	8	6	1	1	0	4	7	1	2	4	3	2	2	6			
United	20	0	8	4	2	8	7	1	1	0	5	9	1	3	3	3	1	1	4	9		
US Air	21	2	2	3	2	3	4	1	2	0	2	3	3	1	2	3	0	3	2	2	2	
Western	22	2	3	5	5	5	6	2	2	0	3	3	2	2	6	2	1	2	3	3	2	2

way to summarize the clustering results was to count the number of quarters each possible pair of airlines appeared in the same cluster. The results for a clustering criterion of 0.00 are shown in Table 4.4.6. A clustering criterion of 0.00 indicates that the minimum correlation between the residuals of any two airlines in a cluster was 0.00

The overall results are similar to those found heretofore—the trunk airlines frequently are located in the same cluster. When American, Delta, Northwest Orient, TWA, and United are considered, the minimum number of times any pair of these appears in the same cluster is seven out of the possible twelve times. Frequently, pairs of these airlines are in the same cluster 75 percent of the time. On the other hand, KLM seems to be a clear isolate—it is never in the same cluster with any airline more than 25 percent of the time. Some of the regional airlines, and the intrastate airlines, have no consistent pattern of clustering, although their most frequent cluster partner is often another similar airline; e.g. Southwest Airlines and Alaska, and Frontier and Hawaiian.

Some of the more interesting findings in the analysis that led to Table 4.4.6 were some of the apparent trends in the clusters which particular airlines joined. For example, both Eastern and National were initially quite likely to be in clusters with the major trunk airlines, but over time the probability of this seemed to drop. In the first four quarters National Airlines was always in the same cluster as United and TWA, and was in the same cluster as Delta and Northwest Orient in three out of these four quarters. In the final seven quarters it *never* appeared in the same cluster as any of these four airlines.

DISCUSSION AND CONCLUSIONS

The primary purpose of this research was to determine if the movements of security prices could provide any insights into the strategic group structure of an industry. The basic premise underlying this research is that firms in different strategic groups are likely to respond somewhat differently to disturbances from within and without the particular industry. If this is correct, then the stock prices of firms within the same strategic group are likely to move together and in a different pattern than those firms in a different strategic group. The exploratory research reported here was conducted on the airline industry, an industry with an apparently ill-defined strategic group structure. A basic conclusion that can be drawn, based on the empirical results reported in the last section, is that there does appear to be information contained in the residuals from the application of the market model to each individual airline's stock prices. The analysis of the correlations of these residuals using both factor analysis and cluster analysis does suggest a structure for the industry that has good face validity in that the major trunk airlines do appear to be grouped together and airlines that one might suspect would not belong to a strategic group are isolates in the analysis. An analysis of the quarterly data also suggests some systematic movement of individual airlines with respect to particular strategic groups. The results of this exploratory study do suggest that the approach does hold promise and is worth pursuing further.

In further research in this area there are some obvious methodological and substantive issues to pursue. From a methodological viewpoint one of the major problems is that minor changes in the correlations can have significant effects on the results. This is particularly true in the case of cluster analysis, where minor changes in a couple of correlation coefficients can lead to substantially different clusters. This problem becomes particularly serious when we are trying to look at changes in industry structure from one time period to another—we need to be able to distinguish trends from noise. While this seemed to be a major problem, given the airline data, this may not be as serious an issue in some other, less dynamic, industries.

From a substantive viewpoint a host of interesting issues remain to be addressed. It would seem useful in the long run to try to identify the kinds of strategic moves that are viewed by the market as affecting the strategic posture of the firm and causing a firm to move toward or away from a strategic group. Investigation of environmental and competitive moves, and the effects they have on industry structure, would also be interesting. In the airline industry there has been a number of events of this type: Eastern's entry into the transcontinental market in a major way in 1980, large increases in fuel costs in 1979, and major mergers (e.g. Pan-American and National in January 1980). Various measures of structure are available including the number of significant factors present and the number of strategic groups present in the industry.

We are presently beginning some research of this type by content analysing references to articles on the airline industry in the *Wall Street Journal Index*. We will then attempt to relate indicators of changes in industry structure to the number and type of events reported.

In summary, this exploratory research has suggested that stock market prices may provide fruitful information about industry structure. Much methodological and substantive work needs to be undertaken before this promise will be fulfilled.

ACKNOWLEDGEMENTS

The authors gratefully acknowledge the invaluable assistance of Bruce Zweig and Julia Nutter, both doctoral students in Marketing at the Graduate School of Business, Stanford University.

REFERENCES

Alexander, Gordon J., and Norman L. Chervany, 'On the estimation and stability of beta', *Journal of Financial and Quantitative Analysis*, **15** (Mar. 1980), 123–137.

Business Week, 'Flying a risky new route for United', 18 August, 1980, pp. 78–82.

Caves, R. E., and M. E. Porter, 'From entry barriers to mobility barriers: conjectural decisions and contrived deterrence to new competition', *Quarterly Journal of Economics*, **91** (May 1977), 241–261.

Crawford and Koopman, 'A note on Horn's Test for the number of factors in factor analysis', *Multivariate Behavioral Research*, 8 (Jan. 1973), 117–125.

Forbes. 'Airlines', 5 January, 1981, pp. 144–146.

Foster, George, *Financial Statement Analysis*. Prentice Hall, Englewood Cliffs, N.J., 1978.

Fruhan, William E., Jr, *The Fight for Competitive Advantage: A Study of the United States Domestic Trunk Air Carriers*. Harvard University Press, Boston, Massachusetts, 1972.

Green, Paul E. *Analyzing Multivariate Data*. The Dryden Press, Hinsdale, Ill., 1978.

Horn, J. L. 'A rationale and test for the number of factors in factor analysis', *Psychometrika*, **30** (1965), 179–186.

Johnson, S. C., 'Hierarchical clustering schemes', *Psychometrika*, **32** (1967), 241–254.

Lintner, J. 'The valuation of risk assets and the selection of risky investments in stock portfolios and capital budgets', *Review of Economics and Statistics*, **47** (Feb. 1965), 13–37.

Newman, Howard H. 'Strategic groups and the structure–performance relationship', *Review of Economics and Statistics*, **60** (Aug. 1978), 417–427.

Porter, Michael E., 'The structure within industries and companies' performance', *Review of Economics and Statistics*, **61** (May 1979), 214–227.

Porter, Michael E., *Competitive Strategy*. Free Press, New York, 1980.

Scholes, Myron, and Joseph Williams, 'Estimating betas from non-synchronous data', *Journal of Financial Economics*, **5** (Dec. 1977), 309–328.

Sharpe, William F. 'Capital asset prices: a theory of market equilibrium under conditions of risk', *Journal of Finance*, **19** (Sept. 1964), 425–442.

Sharpe, William F., and Guy M. Cooper, 'Risk-return classes of New York Stock Exchange common stocks, 1931–67', *Financial Analysts Journal*, **28**, (Mar.–Apr. 1972), 46–54.

Stewart, David W., 'The application and misapplication of factor analysis in marketing research', *Journal of Marketing Research*, **18** (Feb. 1981), 51–62.

4.5

Organizational Impact of Product Market Choice*

JEFFREY R. WILLIAMS

Carnegie–Mellon University, Graduate School of Industrial Administration, Pittsburgh, Pennsylvania 15213

INTRODUCTION

The purpose of this paper is to explore some aspects of the interface between the marketing activity of firms and firms' strategic management. Businesses are increasingly willing to define their product market scope in response to their understanding of the economics that drive competition in the markets in which they compete (see Abell, 1980). This has had at least three beneficial effects. First, it has moved marketing a bit closer to industrial organization and conversely. Second, it has provided a normative economic structure in which to do research and practice what is coming to be called strategic management. Finally, it may have made firms more profitable and affected the way they compete (this last point is no doubt subject to debate).

This product-market orientation follows from the nature of the environmental and competitive forces that characterize the modern firm's business climate. For some, shorter life cycles and more complex technology make the institutionalization of adaptive behavior more important if the firm is to formalize the profitable introduction and disposal of technology. For others, risk measurement and risk management techniques are felt to be increasingly important because future anticipated cash flows are characterized by increased uncertainty. For still others, more consideration is given to the need to purchase long-run competitive strength at some expense of short-run profits. The proliferation of the multi-product firm has added to the complexity of the management task.

A few management tasks can be specified that fit more the domain of strategic management than any other management function. The strategic

---

* This paper is a revision of an earlier version which was presented at a conference at the University of Illinois, 10–11 May 1982. This version has benefited from helpful comments by Howard Thomas, Robert Kaplan, and Allan Shocker.

management responsibility includes decisions that have an expected impact across more than one business unit and, as a result, the effects on the organization are intertangled. Examples include situations where the firm considers itself to be capital-constrained, so the decision to do more in one area by necessity means doing less in another area. Another example is where shared costs, experience, and technology between formally distinct business units actually make them dependent upon each other in an economic sense. The strategic management function is responsible for decisions which are likely to displace the firm along the risk–return spectrum and change investors' perceptions of the firm's non-diversifiable risk. Other strategic decisions may change investors' perceptions of bankruptcy risk. Examples include the choice of a technology with different cash flow characteristics and decisions which result in a change in the firm's financial capital structure (a change in the debt level, for example).

The strategic management function is also responsible for the extent of vertical integration and horizontal diversification because these decisions are at the center of the firm's corporate structure. Examples include decisions as to whether the production process is fully integrated or whether to rely on purchased subassemblies; also the extent to which the firm diversifies into related and non-related products and markets. A fourth strategic management area includes the structuring of incentive plans which govern patterns of managerial behavior. This is because the firm's top management is responsible for the extent of incentive incompatibility which may exist between the firm and its external capital markets; that is, the extent to which individuals in the firm are motivated toward goals which are not in the interests of stockholders. These areas of responsibility are not an inclusive list of the responsibilities of strategic management, but they can provide guidelines to some of the interesting marketing and strategic management interfaces.

STRATEGIC IMPACT OF PRODUCT-MARKET CHOICE

During the last decade there was a rapid adoption of product market matrix resource allocation models. Two popular forms are the Boston Consulting Group 'growth-share' model, and the McKinsey and Company 'attractiveness–strengths' model (the following discussion is not intended to imply that these two frameworks represent the only planning aids available from these two firms). These models offered a method of allocating firm resources which gave explicit recognition to the importance of industry and market structure. They implicitly offered a way of judging the structural fit of the firm's organization to the structure of its markets. They also included a method for balancing the term structure of the firm's real assets and, in so doing, minimizing bankruptcy risk. In some cases, no doubt, the rapid acceptance of these models resulted in their misapplication despite an incomplete understanding of their underlying economics.

Either product portfolio management (PPM) methodology can be used to illustrate competitive advantage. In the context of the PPM methodology, as investments appear further to the left along the horizontal axis, real asset (as opposed to financial asset) investments reflect one or both of the following characteristics: (1) increased productivity, as firms maximize efficiency around a production function which shows experience curve effects, or (2) increased profit margins per unit, from the effects of increasing brand and market power relative to competitors. The result in either case is increasing ROI due to the effects of increased production efficiency or increased market power. These are measures of relative competitive advantage which follow from the competitive supply situation existing in the market.

Placement of investments along the vertical axis in either matrix methodology reflects the market's demand structure. Placement of projects higher up the axis may reflect increasing rates of change of customer preferences if the axis measures growth rates (the growth–share PPM methodology). In these cases an increased payout horizon results from newer investments. Organizational uncertainty also may be greater due to assets being in earlier phases of their technological life where total risk per dollar may be higher, (however, in early phases of technological development much of this risk may be diversifiable, so investors' required rates of return may be at their lowest*). What may result in early stages are incentive problems between the firm and the capital markets.

Although both product portfolio models have a macro orientation toward the firm's internal markets for physical and human capital, the models are otherwise quite different. Each is based on a distinct underlying logic and each has a different investment scope, set of limitations, and potential range of benefits. The two models also have a different emphasis toward the relationship between investment content and the process of decision-making, and this leads to a different strategic management orientation. Finally, although not usually stated by their builders and users, the use of one technique over the other may place firms on different positions on the risk–return trade-offs of concern to investors. Each of these possibilities will be discussed in order.

In general, both models prescribe roughly the same patterns of resource allocation as a function of technological evolution and company competitive advantage. Resources should be concentrated on products and markets where the firm can build or maintain profitable barriers to entry, so that, over time as the market matures, a sustainable competitive advantage can be maintained through market maturity. As the equilibrium market price falls below

---

* Williams (1983) argues that during the evolution of commodity-type process technologies (steel, chemicals, auto, fire) the total risk of projects decrease while the systematic risk that matters to investors increase.

production costs, the supporting assets should be divested gradually. Both techniques allow simultaneous comparison of many products, markets, and relative competitor positions, so both are designed for competitor analysis, in a way that encourages managers to look outside their businesses. Both emphasize an interdependence and implicit balance between growth, stability, profits, and cash flow, and both have a bias toward internal funding (although neither approach excludes the addition of new debt). Either approach may be employed at the corporate, business, or functional levels. In these ways both models help the manager with difficult strategic problems, and this helps to explain why these models first proved popular with strategy advisors.

GROWTH–SHARE COMPETITION

In the growth–share framework the emphasis on growth rate and market share implies a production-skill focus toward investments and toward competition. The products should be of a commodity nature so that as competition moves toward a less dynamic and more steady-state equilibrium, there will be a relatively high probability that the production process can be rationalized around a central product technology. This will permit little chance of differentiation or segmentation by rivals of significant amounts of the market. This is important because in the absence of a uniform product technology the benefits of experience curve effects are diminished. Similarly, in the absence of experience-based dominance, the justification for the growth–share heuristic is less evident. So the growth–share framework makes more sense when the product is standardized and the supporting process technology is expected to yield an experience curve with a relatively steep slope. Conversely, when the product technology is uncertain, the process technology leads to an experience curve of narrow slope, or there exist many ways to segment the market, then other means besides the race for market share are acceptable ways to compete.

The growth–share heuristic puts a good deal of emphasis on the benefits of first-mover advantages and implicitly assumes that process technology is not readily diffusible throughout the industry. Under these assumptions the firm must decide to commit to a product and its supporting production process and do so faster than competitors, or risk being an experience curve follower (higher-cost producer) for the life of the product–process technology combination. The emphasis on first-mover advantages is also consistent with an assumption of growth markets with sufficient market absorption potential to accept the rapid output of volume required by the growth–share-based production strategy.

The growth–share view of competition also implies an organizational emphasis on the R&D and the production segments of the firm's value-added chain. Commitment to this kind of strategy suggests a good deal of managerial attention to the rationalization of the production line, value engineering (internal component redesign to reduce costs), and the quality circle concepts that the Japanese use so well and with which American firms are experimenting.

Large amounts of capital may also be required to play in this game. Access to capital may be made more difficult when accounting losses are required to build competitive advantage long before the results of market dominance appear on the firm's income statement. In those cases where first-mover advantages are possible, and in the presence of imperfect capital markets, the large or multi-product firm may have the advantage in access to resources. Most likely, the firm will have to concentrate on fewer segments of the business, broadly defined, in order to prevail in the long run. Because this reduces cash flow diversification, the chances of bankruptcy may increase.

Two elements that must be successfully managed in the growth–share strategy are an unexpected change in product or process technology, and transfer of dominant technology to a competitor. The presumed reward is that if the firm is successful it will have established a defensible cost advantage and a formidable barrier to entry which can lead to high profits. Nevertheless, the risk is considerable because, if technology does not evolve as expected, the firm may be saddled with undepreciated assets which are obsolete in economic terms.

To the extent that, the use of the growth–share matrix as a resource allocation heuristic may place these firms in higher-risk product-market segments, the choice of the decision model and the model's product-market orientation has strategic significance. At the very least, when used as a marketing tool the larger organizational impacts need to be emphasized The growth–share framework requires constant attention toward cost-based competition and the risks and benefits of barriers to entry that can accrue from first-mover advantages.* The point of all this is that the growth–share model is less the natural domain of the marketing manager than is generally suggested in the marketing literature.

ATTRACTIVENESS–STRENGTHS COMPETITION

The 'attractiveness–strengths' allocation model, in contrast, has more of a natural marketing orientation. This is so for several reasons, which relate to both decision process and decision content. Choice of this model to analyze a market is based on the assumption that a multitude of attributes in product-market space can be employed by rivals to provide a sustainable competitive advantage. This technique is more sympathetic to the possibilities that in the

---

* Spence (1981) models the effects on industry structure that may accrue with the learning curve and competition.

firm's value-added chain of products and services a multitude of opportunities create competitive advantage and yield defensible market niches. The focus of competition is on almost anything except growth–share volume-based cost advantage and commodity–form process technology.

Some of the generalizable economic characterisitics of products and markets which justify this model include cases where the basic technology is expected to exhibit a more narrowly sloped (experience curve) process productivity. Then, by default, 'non-cost' elements of competition take on relatively more importance. Of course, the economist (or good businessman for that matter) will point out that there is no such thing as 'non-cost competition'; that is, all elements of competition can be reduced to quality–cost relationships. In this context the term 'non-cost' refers to costs that are difficult to assign on a per-unit basis, such as quality differences, or staff or product loyalty, or costs that change relatively little with increases in volume. This non-cost orientation is compatible with slower growth segments, in that little differential competitive advantage is gained from further cost reduction through experience curve effects.

This procedure should also be more appropriate when the product-market space permits many variations of the basic product technology. The designs of product features that appeal to different customer segments are employed to gain for each firm a sustainable competitive advantage, with each variation based on successfully differentiated variations of the commodity form.* Smaller firms may engage in profitable niche maintenance strategies for extended periods, even though in a broader sense, they are operating further behind the market leader on the industry-wide technology experience curve. Niche maintenance strategies are generally defensible only so long as volumes are low enough as to discourage competitive entry by larger firms and the differentiated value-added cannot easily be copied by the larger-volume producers.

For the competing organization, the investment orientation and risk–return trade-offs may also be less uncertain and less dynamic. The adoption of a 'wait-and-see' position may be less likely to result in a non-competitive position in the long run. There is less need to take the risk of investing quickly under uncertainty in return for anticipated first-mover advantages. Instead, follower strategies segment the market in a variety of ways. These include brand loyalty, product quality or product features, people or service, geography, or job-shop skills. As a result of all these factors acting together or separately, the use of the attractiveness–strengths resource allocation model and the choice to compete in these ways should, on average, have less impact on the risk–return structure of the firm.

---

* Hall (1980) offers a model of industry structure which traces high profitability in mature businesses either to the most efficient producers or to highly differentiated producers.

Additionally, because the attractiveness–strengths framework puts relatively more emphasis on identifying customer preferences, the importance of advertising in differentiating products, and the importance of distribution and service in satisfying customer needs (in contrast to the production and finance orientation which characterizes the growth–share framework), this model should impart relatively more responsibility to the marketing manager to add value to the product.

PRODUCT-MARKET CHOICE AND INCENTIVE INCOMPATIBILITY

Certain kinds of investments require special attention to managerial behavior where the potential for incentive incompatibility is increased. The use of short-run profit incentive structures, such as ROI control or earnings per share bonus plans, are incompatible with certain elements of the growth–share framework, particularly in the high-growth categories. Pricing below production costs in the short run produces accounting losses in the current period. If experience effects are expected to be strong, it can be argued that these negative cash flows are an investment in the 'organizational capital' of the firm and justifiable by the value-maximizing firm. This is so where experience curve-based competition puts particular emphasis on organizational learning and building organizational capital even in the face of what may be severe price competition on the part of rivals who view the situation in much the same way. Under short-run profit incentive plans there can be a tendency in these competitive situations to overprice and underinvest in order to improve reported profits. The result can be that the firm liquidates its strategic position too quickly in a competitive sense and, under the right conditions, too soon to maximize firm value.

ROI-based incentive plans are less inconsistent with attractiveness–strengths product-market choices in the sense that this approach puts less emphasis on rapid capital expansion under uncertainty, rapid learning, and pricing below short-run cost. The possibilities are fewer that short-run 'losses' in accounting terms can be justified as an investment in the firm's organizational capital. Where incentive incompatibility is less as with the use of the attractiveness–strengths model, this problem should cause less of a need to occupy the attention of the firm's strategic management.

MARKET ANALYSIS vs. PORTFOLIO MANAGEMENT

Another area where the use of the portfolio models can blur the responsibilities between marketing and strategic management is in cases where the models are used to understand external market structure (lets call this market structure analysis, MSA) or instead used to manage the firm's internal structure (what we have been calling product portfolio management, PPM). When employed to judge each business unit's competitive position (MSA) some of the essential features of the decisions being made are, in the context of industrial organization economics*:

(1) definition of the industry (group of competing products);
(2) extent of industry concentration (monopolistic vs. oligopolistic vs. perfect competition);
(3) extent of presumed barriers to entry and exit (extent of competitive advantage);
(4) analysis of basic value-added (core skill analysis);
(5) extent to which the product-market space is capable of being segmented (number of genuinely differentiable end-user preferences that comprise the broad product-market space).

In all these cases the emphasis is on understanding the basis upon which a single product competes with another, the relative competitive advantage which each producer brings to the market, and the overall attractiveness of each individual market segment. The proper resolution of these questions is essential to the formulation of a sound business unit strategy. The marketing function can help answer all of these questions.

There is another set of duties for which the responsibility is more clearly that of strategic management. In contrast to MSA, the portfolio methodology can be used to manage a portfolio of assets (PPM). Here it is better suited to address the following issues:

(1) optimal corporate growth rates (funding vs. payout patterns);
(2) shared experience between formally independent business units (organization structure audit);
(3) optimal balance with respect to the term structure (age) of real assets (extent of bankruptcy risk);
(4) mix of total firm risk from mature (known) technologies as opposed to emerging technologies (this may affect the placement of the firm on the securities market line).

Under the criteria set up earlier, these decisions have a strategic impact on the organization. No single functional area (marketing, finance, systems, production, or human resources) is equipped by virtue of its local knowledge or responsibilities to answer these sorts of questions. In all of these cases, interface between the functional and strategic areas is necessary to success, but

---

* For a synopsis of the industrial organization literature as it can be applied by practicing managers, see Porter (1980).

ultimate responsibility lies with general management, and in some cases the board of directors. In the literature, whenever these sorts of decisions are treated as something other than strategic, what results is an inaccurate and dangerous inference to the reader at both the normative and descriptive level.

PUBLIC POLICY IMPLICATIONS

The widespread use of the MSA and PPM methodologies by rivals may more easily facilitate between them the signalling of product choice strategies (Williams, 1981). If so, this can have public policy implications for the performance of markets. When the players in any rivalrous contest know the rules of the game better, they tend to play against each other in more intelligent ways. As our models of industrial organization and market behavior get better, the more important rules of economic contests will become clearer. Whether or not the resulting behavior of firms will result in 'more or less competition', traditionally defined, depends on a complex set of conditions. The ability of all rivals to understand more clearly how each competes in an industry and to convey this understanding to each other makes it easier for the players to divide up a market according to whatever competitive advantage each player brings to the game. Whether society is better off with more or less product variety is far from clear.* Uncontested competitive advantage may yield increased efficiency, but also conveys the opportunity to exercise monopoly power. Under what conditions firm surplus or consumer surplus is maximized is a complex question, but may become increasingly necessary to answer as managers and academics better understand what can be thought of as 'the rules of economic combat'.

SUMMARY

These comments have been intended to specify how the choice of decision models can have a strategic impact on firms. There may be generic types of strategies that place the firm in different risk classes, affect the firm's organization in a structural way, and raise incentive problems which can serve as obstacles to good performance. Other aspects of the marketing decision may have subtle antitrust implications. It has been argued that in most cases these kinds of decisions, by necessity, are the responsibility of the firm's strategic management. In no cases should these distinctions imply the exclusion of marketing management or any other discipline. In all cases firms will be more effective competitors to the extent that they effectively manage the interfaces.

---

* A survey of the social benefits of product differentiation, market structure, and competition is provided in Scherer (1980) Chapter 14.

356   *Strategic Marketing and Management*

REFERENCES

Abell, Derek F. (1980). *Defining the Business*, Prentice Hall, Inc., Englewood Cliffs, N.J.
Hall, William K. (1980). 'Survival strategies in a hostile environment', *Harvard Business Review*, Sept.–Oct., pp. 75–85.
Porter, Michael E. (1980). *Competitive Strategy*, The Free Press, division of Macmillan, New York, N.Y.
Salop, Steven C., (ed.), (1981). *Strategy, Predation, and Antitrust Analysis*, Bureau of Economics, Bureau of Competition, Federal Trade Commission, Washington, DC.
Scherer, F. M. (1980). *Industrial Market Structure and Economic Performance*, 2nd edn. Rand McNally College Publishing Co., Chicago, Il.
Spence, A. Michael (1981). 'The learning curve and competition', *Bell Journal of Economics*, Spring, pp. 49–70.
Williams, Jeffrey R. (1981). 'Product portfolio management, competition, and public policy', Office of Policy Planning, Federal Trade Commission, *Policy Planning Issues Papers Series*, Washington, DC.
Williams, Jeffrey R. (1983). 'Technological evolution and competitive response', *Strategic Management Journal*, January–March, pp. 55–66.

Strategic Marketing and Management
Edited by H. Thomas and D. Gardner
© 1985 John Wiley & Sons Ltd

CHAPTER 5
Analytical Models in Strategy

INTRODUCTION TO CONCEPTUAL FRAMEWORK

Many of the planning techniques and approaches advanced in the strategy literature have been discussed in Chapters 2 through 4. Approaches such as PIMS, BCG (growth/share matrix and experience curve) and competitive analysis which have found ready application in the marketing strategy literature have also been reviewed. The PIMS and BCG approaches have a rational–empirical (i.e. data-analytic) perspective, whereas Porter's industrial organization-based approach has a more rational–interpretive (i.e. deductive) perspective and is close to the tradition of analytic modeling well represented in the management science, decision science, and econometric literature.

The analytic modeling tradition has also been an important influence upon the development of marketing thought and theory. Writers such as Chakravati *et al.* (1979), Larreche and Srinavasan (1982), Lilien (1979), and Little (1970) have made rich contributions, using analytic modeling approaches such as decision calculus, to the resolution of marketing strategy problems. Fitzroy (1976) and others have provided extensive reviews of analytic models for marketing management.

Specific analytic modeling techniques will not be examined in this chapter. Instead the focus will be upon indentifying the strengths and weaknesses of the analytic modeling approach to strategy and examining its usefulness in the context of strategy formulation (whether it be at the corporate level or at the business level where marketing concerns may be more important).

Analytic modeling

The analytic modeller grounded in the management science/operations research tradition typically develops a single planning problem formulation generally based upon mathematical representations of underlying theories and problem structures. These models are typically subjected to deductive solution to discover 'optimal solutions' (see Hillier and Lieberman, 1980; Wagner, 1969). In some circumstances, such as for example many risk analysis models (Hertz and Thomas, 1983), the model is seen as an experimental tool and 'simulations' of the 'modeled world' are carried out in order to develop better insight about and understanding of the policy problem. In recent years the literature on strategy has seen an increasing number of attempts to apply analytic models to strategy problems (for example, Thomas, 1982; Karnani, 1982; Porter and Spence, 1983; Hofer and Schendel, 1978; Rao and Rutenberg, 1981).

Mason and Mitroff (1981: 288–289) make some important comments about the role played by analytic models in the context of business policy-making. They identify three phases in the use of analytic models in strategy. The first they characterize as outright rejection by strategists on the grounds of irrelevance or inapplicability. Analytic models, in this vein, are seen as valid for addressing well-structured problems but not the ill-structured problems (or 'wicked problems of organized complexity' in Mason and Mitroff's terms) that are strategy's fare. The second phase involved a rather grudging, superficial acceptance in which models were accepted as reasonable representations of the 'real world'. In the third phase, which is still under way, models are increasingly viewed as aids for strategic thinking processes. There is now clear evidence that modellers recognize the role of judgement in framing problems (Tversky and Kahneman, 1981) and accept that several alternative models, based upon different assumption sets and 'views of the world' can be constructed to help the strategist view the problem from a number of different perspectives. Clearly in this third phase the strategic inquiry system has become more complex and multi-dimensional and closer to the inquiry systems proposed by Churchman (1971). That is, systems in which several views about the problem are held, and from which it is believed that synthesis and consensus about problem formulation is achieved through discussion and debate about alternative viewpoints.

This changing view of the role of analytic modeling can be seen as a trend in the literature related to analytic modeling in strategic management. For example, Hofer and Schendel (1978) point out that continuing evolution of modeling approaches and the development of ever more sophisticated models (e.g. allocation models such as mathematical programming and portfolio models) is a reflection of managerial drive to improve performance in ever-changing and more complex micro- and macro-environments. Analytic strategy models were developed in a rather independent fashion and were changed in reaction to the perceived weakness of the then existing variants. Consequently, while many models are now available, several seem impractical and narrowly based when applied to strategic management processes. Hofer and Schendel (1978) stress the need to evaluate approaches and examine how they may be applied to clarify the unified, broadly based strategic management process. In this vein, the subsequent sections examine the role of analytic models in the strategic management process and comment briefly upon their usefulness.

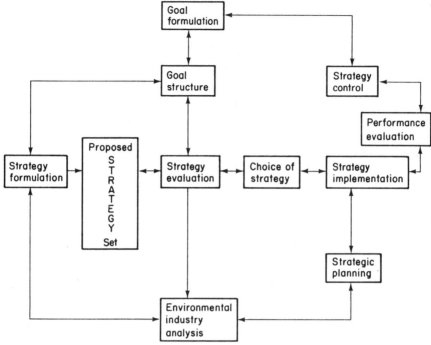

Figure 5.1 Strategic management paradigm (Adapted from Schendel and Hofer, 1979)

Strategic management processes

Our discussion of analytic models is focused around the best-known organizing paradigm for the strategic management field (Schendel and Hofer, 1979) and which is shown in Figure 5.1. Given this paradigm and its related concepts of normative strategy formulation, the processes involved in that formulation can now be examined.

Articulation of goals and goal structures

Assuming that a firm or organization, whether profit-making or non-profit-making (e.g. charities, etc.) is purposive (Thompson, 1976: 83) its overall goal definition will originate from the firm's purpose. Yet it is empirically obvious that 'purposive' does not necessarily connote only one purpose—there may be a few or many. Hence the definition of broad goals within the context of a multi-dimensional framework raises the issue of how goals are structured and articulated.

Ansoff (1965: 3) defines the firm (in the profit or business sense) as 'an economically or "money" motivated purposive social organization', and thus deduces that 'a set of objectives or purposes can be identified in most firms, either in explicit form as a part of the firm's business plan, or implicitly through past history and individual motivations of the key personnel'. It seems irrelevant to the substance of his argument whether he applies his definition to a profit- or non-profit-making enterprise, since his substantive point is the existence of a social organization for a given purpose or set of complex purposes.

Ansoff and Thompson thus define two possible starting points for the articulation of goals and goal structures. Ansoff implicitly looks to the origin of the organization and the purpose of its formation, whilst Thompson accepts either the Ansoff view or the fact that at any given point in time the goal(s) and goal structure of a firm can be inferred from its antecedent actions. Thompson's main purpose, though, is the analysis of the strategy and structure of complex organizations; Ansoff merely postulates a more generalized position.

Following Thompson's definition of goals as the organizational objective of moving from a given domain(s) to some intended future domain(s), the articulation of goals becomes the process of defining those intended future domain(s). From this generalization stem two possible processes of goal articulation—either the organization itself defines its present domain(s) and intended future domain(s), which is by no means a trivial problem, or the outsider makes extra-firm inferences from the firm's past actions and any announced intention.

Clearly, direct goal articulation by the organization itself is the logical normative process. It may take a simple or naive form of defining intended future domain(s), or it may take the detailed analytical form of multi-attributed utility preference (Keeney and Raiffa 1976) to arrive at an articulated and compatible goal-set looking to a number of future time horizons and related intended future domains both longitudinally and cross-sectionally (i.e. at each given time horizon point). Alternatively, in the absence of explicit goal articulation, inferences can be made (both within the organization and from the outside) as to the general definition of the organization's existing domain(s) and the implications stemming from that as to its likely or probable future domain(s). Clearly the latter articulation is significantly less definitive than the former, yet both aspects, it would seem reasonable to assume, can be constructively pursued. Such indirect assessment may be inferred from the basis of the organization's pattern of past and present behavior and probable outcomes of the organization's behavior and inferred attitudes and values, etc.

However, contained within the concept of the organization being purposive, is the subsumed idea that such purposiveness is not a total intra-organizational concept, but rather that the purposive concept relates to the relationship between the organization and the society and societal environment in which it exists (Galbraith, 1969).

Thus, the issues of goals and goal structure articulation fall into two main categories viz:

(1) societal aspirations and environmental constraints—in addition inter-organizational relationships, where, for example, joint ventures are common, may be significant;
(2) intra-organizational aspirations with possible constraints imposed by societal aspirations and other firm characteristics.

It therefore follows that the articulation of organizational goals and goal structures depends not only on the aspirations of the organization itself but also upon its environmental, societal and inter-organizational interfaces. To seek to articulate organizational goals without regard to surrounding interfaces is to ignore reality and related risks of unforeseen conflicts or to gamble on undetermined probabilities that societal, environmental, and organizational goals will fortuitously coincide. This is an uncertain proposition even in a state-controlled economy, let alone a free-enterprise system, particularly with all the economic and social uncertainties of the 1980s.

Thus, an organization cannot seek to articulate a goal structure without having careful and detailed regard to its various societal and inter-organizational interfaces. A mining company cannot plan to construct mines without having regard to both law and lobbies on issues such as environmental protection or with planning and government regulation; nor can it plan goals without considering possible changes in technology, product markets, pricing predictions, export (or import) restrictions, etc. Hence, any articulated goal structure must allow for, and take account of, environmental and societal constraints both actual and potential.

Environmental analysis

Thompson referred to the present domains in which an organization operates, and its intended future domains. Andrews (1971: 59) follows a similar line but expands the concepts of future domains into 'the identification of a range of strategic alternatives . . . [and] the complexity and variety of the environmental forces which must be considered, and the problems of accuracy in assessing company strengths and weaknesses'. He states that

> the environment of a company in business, like that of any other organic entity, is the pattern of all the external conditions and influences that affect its life and development. The environmental influences relevant to strategic decisions operate in a company's industry, the total business community, its city, its country, and the world. They are technological, economic, social and political in kind (Andrews, 1971: 60) (see also Christensen *et al.*, 1965: 229).

A similar view is expressed by Schendel and Patton (1978: 1611) who suggest that 'strategy can be viewed as a pattern or a positioning of resources of the firm relative to its environment, all to achieve desired performance outcomes'.

Many other writers express similar views and stress the importance of analyzing the interface between the firm and its environment. The magnitude of the environmental analytic problem and the related issues of the firm's interface with that environment is emphasized by Ansoff (1979). He draws attention to the nature of turbulent environments and the implications of such turbulence on the strategic management processes of the firm. Turbulence produces both surprises and discontinuities in the strategic management processes, particularly in more recent times, and thus adds a major complex dimension to the issue of the interface between the firm and its environment. This environment interface is further emphasized in its political aspects (*inter alia*) by Newbould and Luffman (1978) who point out the increasing involvement of government in business and the consequential increasing need for business to take account both of the broad aspects of government policy and the narrower aspects of government regulation as it affects the government--business interface and the related environmental aspects of strategy formulation. They further seek to chart the main factors which might constitute successful business policies.

Fahey and King expand the concept of environmental scanning (1977: 62) in terms of three scanning approaches 'irregular, regular, and continuous'. More 'continuous' environmental scanning implies a more pro-active adaptive organizational stance. The other extreme of 'irregular' scanning suggests a more reactive, crisis-oriented organizational type. Either way, scanning provides the organization with a descriptive analysis of its existing environment and may also predict and analyze the organization's options in relation to the changing environment.

Andrews (1971: 72) provides a summary of an environmental scanning model where he quotes Aguilar (1967) who developed a four-mode model:

(1) Undirected viewing—the exposure to information without purpose, or knowledge of what issues might be raised.
(2) Conditioned viewing—directed exposure, not involving active search, to an identified area or type of information by implying sensitivity to kinds of data and the readiness to assess their importance.
(3) Informal search—limited and unstructured effort to get specific information for a specific purpose.
(4) Formal search—deliberate effort following pre-established methodology to secure specific information relating to a specific issue.

'Environment' is used in this section not only in the sense of the world and national surrounding economy of the firm, but also to include international, national, and local societal issues, regulatory authorities and technological developments (Drucker, 1958: Chapter 4). Thus, it includes all of those factors which surround the firm and create the totality of the 'world', 'state', or 'situation' in which the firm finds itself operating and in which it has to plan its future operations given that some at least, if not all, of the surrounding environmental factors are changing or are subject to change during the period of the firm's planning horizon. This, in turn, implies probabilistic assessments of changes in environmental factors and of the likely extent or magnitude of such changes. The assessment of such changes can be undertaken via a whole range of forecasting methods (Chambers, 1974), as well as subjective probability forecasting. Such an environmental scanning process is a valuable initial phase step in what Ackoff sees as 'evaluative' and 'innovative' aspects of strategy formulation.

Industry analysis

Another integral part of the strategy formulation process is that of industry analysis and, in particular, the structural analysis of industries (Porter, 1980: Chapter 1). Ackoff sees the development of a 'model of the firm' contained within which are models of 'supply'. 'distribution and sales links', 'the consumer', and 'competition'. The firm's strategy formulation process must also take account of the industry in which it operates and expectations of change within that industry.

This, of course, provokes the whole issue of the structure of that industry and the position held by the firm in that industry; i.e. the nature of its competitive position and edge within a differentiated oligopoly. These issues are not pursued here but are well-detailed in Scherer (1980) and Stigler (1970) (see also Caves, 1980: 64–92). The importance of market share as a source of profit growth is emphasized in the Boston Consulting Group literature on the product portfolio and in the same group's emphasis on the experience curve as a corporate growth strategy. Scott (1973: 133) and Rumelt (1974) add further dimensions to corporate strategy formulation processes in the industry analysis area, both in terms of market share and diversification strategies (into both related and unrelated businesses following the developmental stages of single and dominant product businesses). These sources illustrate the increasing influence of expanding research in the industrial organization field (Porter, 1980) which focuses on strategic industry issues reinforcing industry analysis as an important element in normative strategy formulation processes.

Together with this analytical framework is the further aspect of the profit impact of market strategies (Buzzell *et al.*, 1975; Schoeffler *et al.*, 1974) and the related cautionary note on the risk of over-extension of the firm in its market share strategies (Fruham, 1972).

It should be emphasized that the definition of an 'industry' is by no means clear (e.g. King, 1966: 39). The term is usually used either loosely or on a conceptual basis in both economics and corporate strategy literature. What are the factors and components which precisely define the term 'industry'. For example, an examination of public companies on the major stock exchanges shows that most companies are conglomerate or agglomerate in character (i.e. being dominant product, related product or unrelated product types of firms, within the context of Rumelt's taxonomy of firms (Rumelt, 1974: 11) rather than single-product firms. Here, conglomerate is used in Rumelt's sense of related product firms and agglomerate in the sense of unrelated firms. The differentiation, though, is semantic rather than substantial and generally 'conglomerate' is used here to cover both types of firms, and more generally the multi-product, multi-activity kind of firm. The existence of the single-product firm is acknowledged, although it is only generally toward the tail end (by size, measured in terms of market capitalization) one finds companies engaged in a single activity.

Thus, the strategy formulation process is commonly a problem faced by complex (including conglomerates and agglomerates) and/or diversified companies (cf. Vancil and Lorange, 1975: 81f.) but, in principle the problem similarly exists for the single-product firm. For complex firms an analytical process of breaking down the firm into its business segments (sometimes described as strategic business units) is a prerequisite for the industry analysis process; i.e. each business segment of the firm needs to be analyzed in relation to the business, industry, or market in which it is involved and in which it competes. The 'industry' to which each business segment is related may in turn be local, regional, national, or international, depending on the nature of the business, its product(s), and the relevant market place (Figure 5.2). The 'industry' may be further decomposed in the sense that, for example, a small producer may be concerned with only the local marketplace whilst a large producer may be concerned with some or all of the tiers of the market and the related variety of factors which may determine or affect each of those tiers.

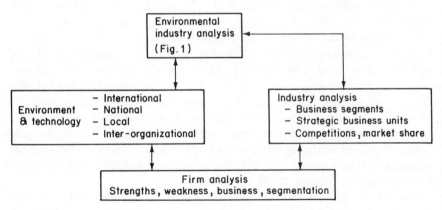

Figure 5.2   Segmentation analysis

However, to talk of this aspect of industry analysis is to examine only the output or product end of the industry. Any substantive and rational analysis of an industry must consider not only its structure and output (referred to above), but also its inputs and any related peculiarities on inputs into a given industry, together with the possibilities of industry factors restricting the firm's flexibility in strategy formulation.

The inputs to any industry constitute a substantial part of the industry analysis process of normative strategy formulation. It is in this area that many factors emerge, such as comparative advantages in the supply of materials, the degree (and cost or benefit) of vertical integration (Williamson, 1975: Chapter 5), and the related issues of cost structures of vertically integrated firms (in the supply of materials context) compared with competing suppliers of final product which are not vertically integrated or, at least, not to the same extent.

The next aspect is naturally the state of (i.e. supply of and demand for) labor, and its related skill level in a given industry (Williamson, 1975: Chapter 4). Considerable work has been undertaken in this area recently, both at the theoretical and empirical level (cf. Fisher, 1971: Chapters 2, 3, and 7; Phelps-Brown, 1969: 93f.). The significance of wage differentials in relation not only to job differentials, but also to 'regional differentials, and industry differentials' (Phelps, 1967: 470) form a significant aspect of the labor content of industry analysis. (Further empirical studies include Ostry and Zaidi, 1979, and others.) Similarly rigidities in the wage/labor system may also constrain the firm's flexibility to formulate strategies.

A further major aspect of the industry analysis process of normative strategy formulation is the aspect of capital—what is the positioning (in risk and return terms) and the related freedom of access to capital markets of a given firm (having some business segment involved) in a given industry—does it have a comparative advantage or disadvantage in those capital markets in relation to its competitors—can it raise such capital as it needs for its strategic goals, etc.? (Foster, 1978: Chapter 5; Copeland and Weston, 1979: Chapter 12).

From the foregoing brief outline it can be seen that the process of industry analysis is itself complex and possibly many-faceted, and must necessarily constitute an integral part of the normative strategy formulation process.

Analysis of the firm

In relation to Thompson's observation of goals as moving a firm from a given domain to an intended future domain, a number of firm-specific problems arise requiring their own particular analysis. The 'intended future domain' cannot be a dream, an ideal, or a total impossibility. It must be realistic or within the realms of realism (i.e. some degree of idealism may be involved) and, further, it must be within the reasonable (even if optimistic) capabilities of the firm itself. The firm must know its abilities, its distinctive competencies, its analytic skills, and its strengths and weaknesses (Christensen *et al.*, 1965: 8). These skills strengths, weaknesses, etc. include not only the ability of a firm to produce a product, but also the further and wider aspects of its production, marketing, financial, and managerial abilities; its R&D programs and prospects; its attitude and abilities to cope with growth, contraction, changing environments and all of those related problems and their ramifications. The more complex (both product-wise and organizationally), the more segmented or diversified the firm, the more it is forced into a detailed self-appraisal if it is effectively to formulate strategies for its movement from a given domain toward some intended future domain. In this area the firm must analyze the actual and future or potential profitability of each of its business segments, product lines, geographic areas of operations, etc.

It therefore becomes apparent that a detailed analysis of the firm itself forms an integral part of the normative strategy formulation process. This follows logically from Thompson's goal determination analysis, in which is contained the implicit assumption that it is the firm itself (at least in the going-concern context) which is the key decision-making entity. Even though constrained by externalities, the firm (within the context of the Rumelt taxonomy, referred to earlier) can operate as a decision-making unit(s) within the general area of comprehensive rationality, 'bounded rationality' and 'uncertainty–complexity' (Williamson, 1975: Chapter 2, p. 40). Reinforcing the concept of the firm as the key decision-making unit are the constraints within which it must operate. These may involve environmental constraints and governmental (and other e.g. stock exchange) regulations or issues concerned with the complexity of a given firm. Thus, it is necessary to examine both external and internal constraints which affect the firm's strategic flexibility.

In relation to internal constraints, major issues arise in relation to the structure of the firm and its ability to be dynamic and progressive, or its flexibility to do so (Chandler, 1962; Donaldson, 1980). In other words, the more bureaucratic an organization's structure is, the more that structure is likely to limit the firm's ability to be flexible in its strategy formulation processes (see March and Simon, 1958: 81–82). Similarly, industry factors such as cartels, industry–union agreements, industry regulation (voluntary by agreement or imposed by external regulation) will constrain the firm's flexibility to make decisions in relation to its strategy formulation processes. However, though constraints may exist, the fact remains that the firm itself has to formulate its own strategies to use and expand (or contract) the resources over which it has command or control. Since the focal decision-making unit is the firm itself (and segmented units within the firm), with varying degrees of autonomy but finally adding up to the totality of the firm(s), it is therefore at the firm level that normative strategy formulation processes must be developed, appraised, and put into effect.

INTRODUCTION TO ANALYTIC APPROACHES FOR STRATEGY FORMULATION AND EVALUATION

It is apparent that strategy formulation, normatively, is a highly complex process. Given the constraints of the firm's risk and return, its attitude toward maximizing or optimizing versus satisficing, etc. (Ackoff, 1970: Chapter 1), the varying elements of uncertainty contained within each of the 'independent variables', the firm is ultimately confronted with a feasible range of options for strategic choice. These strategic options assume the choice of an appropriate time horizon. The time horizon contemplated by the strategy formulation process may be arbitrary (i.e. some period which management sees as desirable, reasonable, or in some way feasible—a purely judgemental situation); or it may be determined by some focal lead-time such as new plant construction, new product development; or, again, it may be controlled by some finance factors such as due dates for maturity of debt.

In those cases, time horizons for strategy formulation tend to be pragmatic rather than normative. If such horizons are to be normative and thus related to a normative strategy formulation process, then they must, by definition, relate to the goal determination process and envisage the time a firm will take, or may expect to take, to move from its given domain to its intended future domain. This too, by definition, envisages a longer-term strategic formulation and implementation process.

Evaluation and development of normative strategy formulation processes are seen here as conjunctive functions. This means that, given a set of goals or possible goals, no strategy for their achievement can be developed without concurrently being evaluated, tested, and subjected to sensitivity analysis. Such evaluation attempts to ensure that a given strategy is feasible and goal-congruent or can reasonably be expected to be so, prior to its adoption and implementation.

Finally, two views of normative strategy formulation and evaluation are examined. First, there is the 'intra-firm' aspect, i.e. the techniques which can be adopted within the firm using internal data, as well as all other necessary and obtainable data. The emphasis in this situation is thus on the normative strategy formulation process itself (and its related evaluation). The second is the 'extra-firm' aspect, i.e. the techniques and processes which can be normatively applied from an external position to examine the firm's strategies. Normally, published financial data for the firm and other relevant publicly available data are used to analyze and infer a firm's strategies and predict future strategic developments.

'Extra-firm' strategy evaluation is, by definition, not a part of a firm's normative strategy formulation process. However, the consequent deductive–predictive implications for strategy outcomes and the inferred strategy formulation process are essential to many parties external to the firm. For example, investors (present or potential), including those interested in a possible takeover seek appraisals of the long-term potential of the firm as an investment. Competitors and lenders likewise seek longer-term predictive evaluation of a firm's strategies, their origins, possible outcomes, and likely future trends.

Similarly, in relation to extra-firm analysis, Grabowski and Mueller postulate two different models; *viz.* 'a firm maximizing stockholder objectives will exhibit different behavior in its expenditure decisions from one pursuing managerial goals', i.e. motivational differences (Grabowski and Mueller, 1972: 9). The Grabowski–Mueller hypothesis is not pursued at this point; nor is their testing replicated herein, but their work is quoted in support of the purpose and concept of extra-firm as well as intra-firm strategy evaluation.

STRATEGY FORMULATION AND EVALUATION PROCESSES

Judgemental processes

It is often the situation 'that people rely on a limited number of heuristic principles which reduce the complex tasks of assessing probabilities and predicting values to simpler judgemental operations. In general, these heuristics are quite useful, but sometimes they lead to severe and systematic errors' (Tversky and Kahneman, 1974: 39). Such processes of making judgements under uncertainty are examples of heuristic problem-solving. Heuristic principles have commonly been identified in the choice and decision phases of strategy formulation. For example, Simon (1964) suggests a heuristic based upon a satisficing concept, whilst Lindblom (1959) suggests a 'muddling through' type of concept. Either way these choice criteria represent attempts by managers to simplify, in cognitive terms, the complexity of the decision process. Frequently in the small business environment, and sometimes in the larger business environment, the one-man entrepreneur exists. In these situations the entrepreneur, perhaps aided by some surrounding executives, formulates strategy on an intuitive basis or on the basis of some form or set of heuristics. Sometimes such strategy formulation is quite long-term, sometimes its long-term appearance is only form rather than substance. However, it cannot be denied that some such judgemental strategy formulation (e.g. Henry Ford and the T-model Ford) has been successful.

However, judgemental processes or heuristics fall short in many directions. There are built-in problems of bias (Armstrong, 1978: 74, 81), as well as problems of reliance on the intuitive ability of the entrepreneur coupled with the generally subjective character of such heuristics for strategy formulation. Further, strategy formulated on such a basis is difficult if not impossible to evaluate, because of the lack of data which would be necessary for a full and adequate appraisal. This is not to deny that situations arise in the process of strategy formulation where judgement has to be exercised, particularly in areas which are qualitative rather than quantitative. However, in such cases, some form of probabilistic assessment, perhaps of the risk analysis type (Hertz and Thomas, 1983), of possible strategic alternatives or outcomes can often be made and, coupled with some form of sensitivity analysis and managerial dialogue, a reasonable solution may be determined.

In summary, then, judgemental processes tend to be qualitative and subjective and frequently are not capable of evaluation. However, the role of judgement is inextricably intertwined with the quality and nature of the 'expert' who provides the judgement. What constitutes an 'expert', and how such a character can be identified and evaluated, is the subject of much research in behavioral decision theory (Hogarth, 1980).

Analytical processes

The term 'analytical processes' is used here to describe processes which are more formalized and systematic than pure judgemental heuristics. These processes envisage a decomposition of the component problems of strategy formulation and the application of some systematized methodology such as the decision or economic analysis approach to the aspects of problem decomposition, assessment (both qualitative and quantitative) of probable outcomes of possible options, and recomposing these sub-routines into an overall firm strategy formulation. Such analytical processes may be applied internally within the firm or externally from, say, the point of view of an investment analyst concerned with evaluation of an investment.

Analytical processes envisage situations where strategy formulation components can be segregated and analyzed by a variety of means, both subjective (or qualitative) and objective (quantitative). In a broad sense the analytical approach is considered as a method better developed than pure judgemental forecasting, but, in varying degrees, less formalized than the mathematical approach discussed below.

Formal modeling processes

Models may be defined as

> a system of postulates, hypotheses, information, data, and inferences delineated as a descriptive, predictive, and/or normative representation of reality or the state of affairs. Models are designed and constructed for purposes of solving both simple and complicated problems of real life, as a system of imitation, simulation, and abstraction of reality. Therefore models can be classified differently, depending upon different taxonomical schemes. Based upon structures, for example, we have iconic, analog, and symbolic models, whereas on uncertainty references,

deterministic, probabilistic, and game theory models. (Ishikawa, 1975: 3).

In this section the models of prime concern are formal models referred to here as mathematical models—the term being used in a generic sense to include models based on some mathematical or quantitative form whether it be simplistic, econometric, or probabilistic/uncertainty-oriented.

Mathematical models can be developed for corporate planning on both an intra-firm and extra-firm basis (Grabowski and Mueller, 1972: 9). These models can range from the simple or naive to the complex corporate planning models expounded by Naylor (1979: Chapter 1). Whilst Naylor refers to a 'planning model', models here are discussed only in so far as they relate to strategy formulation and evaluation processes. The object of such models is to quantify and relate all of the significant independent variables, both quantitative and qualitative, to the attainment of the firm's goals which may be to maximize shareholder net worth. The value of such models is that they can incorporate both quantitative and qualitative data, measure their outcomes, and provide a basis for evaluation in the form of sensitivity analysis both in terms of probabilities of given variables falling within a given range or distribution, and in terms of significance testing of each of the variables.

Such models can range from the naive random walk plus residual analysis (Foster, 1978: 83–85) to the complex corporate planning models examined by Naylor. The sophistication of the model is dependent upon the purpose for which it is used, the level and quality of data available (e.g. intra-firm versus extra-firm), the cost/benefit of the model, and the availability of appropriate computer facilities.

Mathematical modeling techniques follow the sequence of the normative strategy formulation process, i.e. environmental scanning assessment, industry assessment and firm-level analysis, and predictions of possible (probabilistic) strategy outcomes. Different kinds of models and modeling techniques may be appropriate for different purposes. For example, models constructed on an extra-firm basis with a relatively limited data base are likely to be less complex than intra-firm modeling processes where the data base is substantially greater (Naylor, 1979).

At the environmental level, models may take a form as complex as that of the class of econometric 'national' models, examples of which are the Brookings model (Intriligator, 1978: 444) or the Wharton model (Intriligator, 1978: 441) in macroeconomic forecasting of the US economy. Some other countries, including Australia (Federal Treasury) have attempted to build certain macroeconomic models to provide some analyses of trends in the economy. However the focus of those models tends to be short-term and less useful for firms in formulating strategy (see Intriligator, 1978: 444–447). Therefore firms—may increasingly require the development of environmental and econometric models which are more firm-specific in their purpose.

Technological forecasting both generally and with specific reference to corporate planning, is discussed in Wills *et al.*, 1969: Chapters 1–6. It is concluded that the firm has to isolate and plan for the changing technological factors which are, may be, or could become, relevant to the strategy formulation and evaluation processes of a given firm (and/or business segments of that firm).

Delphi-type approaches may also be used at the environmental–technological level. They are frequently combined with indicators which are available such as a variety of OECD publications on the international level (generally shorter-term) together with longer-term trend predictions such as the Club of Rome (Tinbergen *et al.*, 1976). In such areas of uncertainty and probability estimation, decision theory provides a framework within which the firm can postulate probabilities of outcomes of such options as it foresees (Moore and Thomas, 1976: 39–41).

Industry-level analysis can be handled using mathematical modeling approaches. Industry trends in terms of variables such as volume, product, price, etc. can be formed into mathematical models as part of the strategy formulation process. Recent industry models include a petrochemical price forecasting analysis (Stobaugh and Townsend, 1975) and a strategic analysis of the US brewing industry modeling industry trends, market shares, etc. This revealed 'significant relationships between purpose, strategy and the environment in which a firm operates,' and characteristics of the industry in which it competes' (Hatten *et al.*, 1978: p. 608).

Mathematical modeling processes lead similarly back to the firm level of analysis, since in both environmental–technological and industry areas, the relevant factors are those which relate to the firm, its options, strategies, and feasible range of intended future domains. Hence, the logical conclusion is that the modeling process has to be designed and developed in relation to the relevant decision-making unit which is the firm itself.

Given the output of the mathematical models of the broad economic, technological and industry environments, the firm can incorporate their findings into its own strategic models. Such models indicate trade-offs to be made between incompatible goals, and provide a basis for strategic formulation and subsequent performance (Schendel and Patton, 1978: 1620).

At the firm level, a number of modeling processes have been developed. Most of these relate to the intra-firm type of models and require intra-firm data. Heenan and Addleman (1976: 32–62) discuss the application of multivariate analysis techniques to a number of intra-firm decision areas including marketing strategies, credit risk determination, employee reward systems, etc. These writers consider the application of aspects of mathematical modeling to particular decision areas and the related predictive ability of such modeling processes. In the present context of strategy formulation and evaluation processes, Heenan and Addleman indicate means of decomposing strategic decision problems into sub-units which can be separately analyzed, simulated, and predicted. (Interestingly, this decomposition process is one of the central elements of the decision structuring phase of decision analysis.) Their work could be carried further in the sense of reintegrating their decomposed analytical–predictive modeling methodology into the firm's total strategy formulation and evaluation processes to consider the totality of the firm and its strategies.

Some integrative modeling work has been carried out by Mueller, among others. Mueller notes that

> in formulating policy recommendations one must be aware of these interactions [which are numerous and result from the simultaneity of decisions] not only in order to avoid undesirable side effects which might stem from a given policy, but also to be certain that these interactions do not actually result in a negation of a policy's primary goal (Mueller, 1967: 58).

Mueller propounds the concept of a detailed intra-firm econometric modeling and simulation process as a means of policy formulation and evaluation. Eliasson (1976), also emphasizes that the corporate modeling process is an integral part of the whole corporate strategic planning process which links businesses and divisions into a total firm perspective.

Another study developed a model which linked an 'extra firm' model of the Canadian economy with a firm-level model. This study involved the use of a significant amount of extra-firm data. The model was developed for strategic planning purposes (MacIntosh *et al.*, 1973: 48–60). This modeling process demonstrates the effectiveness of predictions from strategic plans using both general economic data and firm-specific data.

Mathematical modeling processes may be used therefore to provide a substantive basis for strategy formulation and evaluation processes. In comparison with other methods, on both an intra- and extra-firm basis, their ability to describe, analyze, and predict is often greater than other processes. It is not suggested that such models remove the need for further judgement, appraisal, and analysis. However, it is argued that they can provide a basis for better measuring and understanding of possible outcomes of strategy options.

Thus it is contended that mathematical modeling processes might form an integral part of normative strategy formulation and evaluation processes of the firm, its industry(ies), and environment. It is also postulated that since the strategy decision-making process is an ongoing process, so too is the modeling process, and that given such modeling processes, the firm may well be able to develop better decision rules not only for strategy formulation and evaluation, but also for subsequent strategy performance evaluation and strategy changes.

It seems reasonable to conclude that the use of mathematical modeling processes on an extra-firm basis might provide improved insights into the strategies of a given firm and the possible range of outcomes of those strategies.

As a result, even with a limited data base, more effective analysis and predictions of present and likely future domains of a given firm might be developed from mathematical modeling processes than can be obtained from judgemental, analytical, or other less sophisticated forms of strategy analysis.

SUMMARY AND CONCLUSIONS

The purpose of this discussion has been to review strategic management techniques and processes and to draw attention to some of the literature relating to strategic management issues. The literature covers a broad range of topics, all of which are not discussed here. However the major topics have been examined in order to outline the processes and the many ramifications of normative strategic planning, formulation, and management.

Specifically, the argument put forward is that formal or mathematical modeling processes should be developed both on an intra-firm and extra-firm basis. This is because they provide useful techniques and methodology not only for the normative strategy formulation and evaluation processes of the firm, but also for subsequent performance measurement and control and, where and when necessary, revision of the strategic plan itself.

Finally, it is concluded that from an extra-firm aspect, formal or mathematical models of a firm's strategy and performance can be constructed so as to provide a more sound basis for interested parties external to the firm to analyze the direction in which the firm is headed and the probable range of future (longer-term) outcomes of its present strategies. Thus, improved insights into the longer-term effects of the firm's adopted strategies and policies may be provided.

REFERENCES

Ackoff, R. L. (1970). *A Concept of Corporate Planning*. Wiley-Interscience, New York.

Aguilar, F. J. (1967). *Scanning the Business Environment*, Macmillan, New York.

Andrews, K. R. (1971). *The Concept of Corporate Strategy*. Dow Jones-Irwin, New York.

Ansoff, H. I. (1965). *Corporate Strategy*. McGraw-Hill, New York.

Ansoff, H. I. (1979). *Strategic Management*. John Wiley, New York.

Armstrong, J. S. (1978). *Long Range Forecasting from Crystal Ball to Computer*. John Wiley, New York.

Boston Consulting Group, *The Product Portfolio and The Experience Curve Revisited*. Boston Consulting Group, Massachusetts.

Buzzell, R. D., B. T. Gale, and R. G. M. Sultan (1975). 'Market share—a key to profitability', *Harvard Business Review*, January–February 1975, 97–106.

Caves, R. E. (1980) 'Industrial Organization, corporate strategy and structure'. *Journal of Economic Literature*, **XVIII**.

Chakravarti, D., A. Mitchell, and R. Staelin (1979). 'Judgement based marketing decision models: an experimental investigation of the decision calculus approach', *Management Science*, **25**(3) (Mar.) 251–263.

Chambers, J. C. (1974). *Executive's Guide to Forecasting*. John Wiley, New York.

Chandler, A. D. (1962). *Strategy and Structure*. MIT Press, Massachusetts.

Christensen, C. R., K. R. Andrews, and J. L. Bower (1965). *Business Policy*. Irwin, Homewood, Ill.

Churchman, C. W. (1971). *The Design of Inquiring Systems*. Basic Books, New York.

Copeland, T. E., and J. F. Weston (1979). *Financial Theory and Corporate Policy*. Addison-Wesley, Reading, Massachusetts.

Donaldson, L. (1980). 'Strategy and Structure: a Critical Analysis'. Unpublished working paper, Australian Graduate School of Management, University of South Wales.

Drucker, P. F. (1958). *Technology, Management and Society*. Harper & Row, New York. (Rev. edn, 1970.)

Eliasson, G. (1976). *Business Economic Planning*. John Wiley, New York.

Fahey, L., and W. R. King, (1977). 'Environmental scanning for corporate planning', *Business Horizons*, **20**(4).

Fisher, M. R. (1971). *The Economic Analysis of Labour*. St. Martin's Press, London.

Fitzroy, P. T. (1976). *Analytical Methods for Marketing Management*. McGraw-Hill, New York.

Foster, G. (1978). *Financial Statement Analysis*. Prentice-Hall, Englewood Cliff, N.J.

Fruham, W. E. (1972). Pyrrhic Victories in Fights for Market Share. *Harvard Business Review*, September–October 1972, 100–107.

Galbraith, J. K. (1969). 'The goals of an industrial system', in H. I. Ansoff (ed.), (1978). *Business Strategy*, Penguin, Harmondsworth, UK.

Grabowski, H. G., and D. C. Mueller (1972). 'Managerial and stockholder welfare models of firm expenditures', *Review of Economics and Statistics*, **54**.

Hatten, K. J., D. E. Schendel, and A. C. Cooper (1978). 'A strategic model of the US brewing industry: 1952–1971', *Academy of Management Journal*, **21**(4).

Heenan, D. A., and R. B. Addleman, (1976). 'Quantitative techniques for today's decision makers', *Harvard Business Review*.

Hertz, D. B., and H. Thomas (1983). *Risk Analysis and its Applications*, John Wiley, Chichester, England.

Hillier, F. S., and G. J. Lieberman (1980). *Introduction to Operations Research* (3rd edn). Holden-Day, San Francisco, CA.

Hofer, C. W., and D. E. Schendel (1978). *Strategy Formulation: Analytical Concepts*, West Publishing, St. Paul, MN.

Hogarth, R. M. (1980). *Judgement and Choice*. John Wiley, Chichester, England.

Intriligator, M. D. (1978). *Econometric Models, Techniques and Applications*. Prentice-Hall, Englewood Cliffs, N.J.

Ishikawa, A. (1975). *Corporate Planning and Control Model Systems*. New York University Press, New York.

Karnani, A. (1982). 'Equilibrium market share: a measure of competitive strength', *Strategic Management Research*, **3** (Jan.–Mar.) 43–51.

Keeney, R. L., and H. Raiffa (1976). *Preference Amongst Multiple Conflicting Objectives*. John Wiley, New York.

King, B. J. (1966). Market and Industry Factors in Stock Price Behavior, *Journal of Business*.

Larreche, J. C., and V. Srinavasan (1982). 'Stratport: a model for the evaluation and formulation of business portfolio strategies', *Management Science*, **28**(9) (Sept.) 979–1000.

Lilien, G. L. (1979). 'ADVISOR 2: modeling the marketing mix decision for industrial products', *Management Science*, 25(2) (Feb.), 191–204.

Lindblom, C. E. (1959). 'The Science of "Muddling Through" ', in H. I. Ansoff (ed.) *Business Strategy*. Penguin, Harmondsworth, UK.

Little, J, D, C, (1970). 'Models and managers: the concept of a decision calculus', *Management Science*, 16(8) (Apr.), B466–B485.

MacIntosh, N. B., H. Tsurumi, and Y. Tsurumi (1973). 'Econometrics for Strategic Planning', *Journal of Business Policy*.

March, J. G. and H. A. Simon (1958). *Organizations*. John Wiley, New York.

Mason, R. O., and I. I. Mitroff (1981). *Challenging Strategic Planning Assumptions*, John Wiley, New York.

Moore, P. G. and H. Thomas (1976). *The Anatomy of Decisions*. Penguin, Harmondsworth.

Mueller, D. C. (1967). 'The firm decision process: an econometric investigation', *Quarterly Journal of Economics*.

Naylor, T. H. (1979). *Corporate Planning Models*. Addison-Wesley, Massachusetts.

Newbould, G. D. and G. A. Luffman (1978). *Successful Business Policies*, Gower Press, Farnborough, England.

Ostry, S. and M. A. Zaidi (1979). *Labour Economics in Canada*. Macmillan, Canada.

Phelps Brown, E. H. (1969). *The Economics of Labour*, 5th edn. Yale University Press, New Haven, CT.

Phelphs, O. W. (1967). *Introduction to Labour Economics*, 4th edn. McGraw-Hill, New York.

Porter, M. E. (1980). *Competitive Strategy*. Free Press, New York.

Porter, M. E., and A. M. Spence (1983). 'The capacity expansion process in a growing oligopoly: the case of corn wet milling', in J. J. McCall (ed.), *The Economics of Information and Uncertainty*. University of Chicago Press, Chicago.

Rao, R. M., and D. P. Rutenberg, (1981). 'Preempting an alert rival: strategic timing of the first plant by analysis of sophisticated rivalry', *Bell Journal of Economics*, 12 (Spring), 412–428.

Rumelt, R. P. (1974). *Strategy, Structure and Economic Performance*. Harvard University Press, Cambridge, Mass.

Schoeffler, S., R. D. Buzzell, and D. F. Heany (1974). 'Impact of strategic planning on profit performance', *Harvard Business Review*, March/April 1974, 137–145.

Schendel, D., and G. R. Patton (1978). 'A simultaneous equation model of corporate strategy', 25(15).

Schendel, D. E., and C. W. Hofer (1979). *Strategic Management: A New View of Business Policy and Planning*. Little, Brown, Boston, Mass.

Scherer, F. M. (1980). *Industrial Market Structure and Economic Performance*. Houghton-Mifflin, New York.

Scott, B. R. (1973). 'The industrial state: old myths and new realities', *Harvard Business Review*.

Simon, H. A. (1964). On the Concept of an Organizational Goal, Reprinted in [8].

Stigler, G. J. (1970). *The Organization of Industry*. Irwin, Homewood, Ill.

Stobaugh, R. B., and P. L. Townsend (1975). 'Price forecasting and strategic planning: the case of petrochemical', *Journal of Marketing Research*, XII.

Thomas, H. (1982). 'Screening policy options: an approach and a case study example', *Strategic Management Journal*, 3(3), 227–244.

Thompson, J. D. (1976). *Organizations in Action*. McGraw-Hill, New York.

Tinbergen, J. (Co-ordinator), A. J. Dolman (ed.) and J. Van Ettinger (Director) (1976). *Reshaping the International Order*. Hutchinson, London.

Tversky, A., and D. Kahneman, (1974). 'Judgement under uncertainty: heuristics and biases'. Reprinted in Kaufman, G. M. and H. Thomas (eds.), (1977). *Modern Decision Analysis, Selected Readings*, Penguin, Harmondsworth.

Tversky, A., and D. Kahneman (1981). 'The framing of decisions and the psychology of choice', *Science*, **211**, 453–458.

Vancil, R. F., and P. Lorange (1975). 'Strategic planning in diversified companies'. *Harvard Business Review* and reprinted in P. Lorange and R. Vancil *Strategic Planning Systems*, Prentice-Hall, Englewood Cliffs, N. J., 1977.

Wagner, H. M. (1969). *Principles of Operations Research*. Prentice-Hall, Englewood Cliffs, N.J.

Williamson, O. E. (1975). *Markets and Hierarchies: Analysis and Antitrust Implications*. Free Press, New York.

Willis, G., D. Ashton, and B. Taylor (1969). *Technological Forecasting and Corporate Strategy*. Elsevier, New York.

Strategic Marketing and Management
Edited by H. Thomas and D. Gardner
© 1985 John Wiley & Sons Ltd

Introduction to Conference Papers on Analytic Modeling

Chapter 5 reviews the role of analytical modeling in strategy and gives a thorough insight into applications of analytic models to strategy problems. In this section three papers which demonstrate very specific analytic models are presented. Two, by Hertz and Thomas and Lock and Thomas, reflect the decision analysis as policy dialogue approach for strategy formulation. The third, by Wensley, insightfully addresses implementation issues and discusses the effective organizational use of analysis in strategic marketing.

Hertz and Thomas examine how decision and risk analysis may be applied to a new product and facilities planning problem. The discussion describes the risk analysis process, and presents the step-by-step approach used by the project team. The initial results of the analysis are presented and discussed by the team in a process of policy dialogue. It is shown that the project team questioned a number of project assumptions (particularly in the marketing area) and expressed concern about the perceived vagueness of the firm's objectives. Further analyses and examination of the relationship of the Egg'N Foam project to the firm's growth path led to a strategy recommendation. The linkage between risk analysis and strategy is also stressed at various points in the paper.

Lock and Thomas present an example of the application of decision-theoretic multi-attributed utility approaches in a rather different context for marketers, namely, strategy determination at the business unit level. Marketers are more aware of the application of these approaches to product concept evaluation and generation. The example given in the paper is of an ill-structured strategy problem involving choices between strategic options facing a British subsidiary of a multi-national company operating in the shoe industry. The dialogue process leading to the structuring of the problem, and the simulation programmes representing the options, are described. Conjoint analysis is used to elicit preferences across the multiple criteria, and the actual choice made is compared with the choice predicted by the models

Wensley, in an extremely interesting and thoughtful paper which ranges over the entire field of marketing strategy, offers some organizational and other criteria for justifying the role of analysis in marketing decision-making. He argues that various forms of analysis are required. At the local unit level a range of different analytical approaches, which provide different and sometimes conflicting answers, are required rather than one comprehensive approach. In the interaction between local and corporate management forms of analysis are required which aid both parties in exploring crucial market-based assumptions. To aid this process, echoing a theme in the two previous papers, he states that forms of marketing analysis need to be created which can assist in creating an effective management policy dialogue.

Strategic Marketing and Management
Edited by H. Thomas and D. Gardner
© 1985 John Wiley & Sons Ltd

5.1

Decision and Risk Analysis as Policy Dialogue Processes: A New Product and Facilities Planning Problem, CCA Company's Egg'N Foam Project*

DAVID B. HERTZ

Institute of Artificial Intelligence, School of Business, University of Miami at Coral Gables

AND

HOWARD THOMAS

Department of Business Administration, University of Illinois at Urbana-Champaign

INTRODUCTION

The paper discusses the role of risk analysis in relation to the Egg'N Foam project—a potential investment opportunity in the plastic egg carton market. The step-by-step nature of the application of risk analysis is illustrated (see Hertz and Thomas, 1983), and the procedures adopted at each stage are described.

Risk analysis (Hertz, 1979) was originally presented as an useful addition to the range of techniques used in financial evaluations. It was seen as a logical extension to sensitivity analysis (Rappaport, 1967), and a means of explicitly taking account of uncertainty in financial forecasts. The proposition that risk and uncertainty could be more accurately defined by a simulation of input variables became widely accepted. It was emphasized, however, that risk analysis was a strategic decision aid and that eventually managerial judgement would be required in both input estimation and decision.

Although it was interpreted by some readers as an argument about methodology in investment appraisal, that was not the main purpose. Rather, it was intended to provide a cautionary note to businessmen to examine the

---

* This problem is somewhat disguised in regard to project chronology and magnitudes of input data, but the problem structure and new product area is unaltered. A more detailed description of the problem, including all data inputs, is available from the authors.

data and assumptions surrounding investment proposals and other decision problems, given the pervasive uncertainties in both business and other environments. For example, risk analysis is increasingly seen as a necessary and useful adjunct to a strategic planning and thinking process (Gluck *et al.*, 1980; Hogarth and Makradakis, 1981). It is viewed as an approach for forecast/uncertainty-based planning (Stage II/III of Gluck's four stages of strategic planning) in which an understanding of project risk, cash flow projections and future scenarios is developed.

Subsequent sections of this paper will examine various aspects of the problem relating to the Egg'N Foam project. The problem structure will be outlined in flow diagram form with the problem assumptions stated and an initial sensitivity analysis performed. Investment alternatives will then be developed, subjective probabilities assigned and the results of the risk analysis presented, Finally, the process of policy dialogue about the strategy to be chosen will be demonstrated and the conclusions summarized.

Various decision alternatives were considered. These ranged from abandonment to expansion strategies. Abandonment would involve the loss of the pilot plant; expansion strategies involved both the larger plants (known as superplants) and a series of smaller plants.

The risk analysis approach involved three sets of people. The management group at CCA, the CCA project team (charged with the responsibility for project evaluation), and the consultants (providing technical expertise and guidance). An extremely interesting part of the process was the dialogue about choice and implementation which developed between the project team and CCAs management group.

Strategic risk analysis and policy dialogue

An underlying theme in this paper is that risk analysis can help *strategic thinking* by encouraging constructive dialogue and debate about the policy options. In such a dialogue process risk analysis is seen as an input for the strategy development process, aiding strategy formulation, evaluation, choice, and implementation. Therefore, no distinction is drawn between strategic risk analysis and strategy formulation. Instead, analysis and formulation are parts of a policy dialogue process which is iterative, adaptive, and flexible. This dialogue involves managerial consideration of problem and policy formulation through a continual re-examination of potential alternative strategies and problem assumptions.

The role of strategic risk analysis in policy formulation and choice should therefore be to force hard thinking about the problem under consideration. It should highlight the alternatives to be considered, examine the changing secondary effects, and anticipate the nature and extent of the impact of uncertainty for contingency planning. It is recognized that an initial risk analysis is no more than a first attempt at problem understanding. It should encourage controversy, and allow members of the decision-making group to discover where basic differences exist about problem assumptions, values, and uncertainties. This controversy should encourage critical comment and review and force the re-analysis. Hopefully, after considerable dialogue the quality and level of debate should facilitate compromise and consensus around a reasonable problem solution.

The role of strategic risk and decision analysis is examined in the following sections by means of the discussion of a strategic investment decision faced by the CCA company. Questioning and challenging of analytic assumptions is evident in the process of managerial dialogue about strategic choice.

THE CCA COMPANY'S EGG'N FOAM PROJECT

The Egg'N Foam project at CCA involved various issues. It represented a large investment by the company, a totally new market area, and a completely new product for CCA. CCA had been developing Egg'N Foam, which was a plastic package produced as a competitive substitute for paper egg cartons, for several years. The product design had been refined and a pilot plant in Pennsylvania had been operational for some time. The project involved substantial amounts of uncertainty.

The project team selected to work on the Egg'N Foam decision consisted of representatives from the Research and Development Division, Plastics Division, and Corporate Controller's Office. Those involved had been associated with the Egg'N Foam project for many years, and were very familiar with the development, production, and marketing aspects of the project.

The step-by-step approach used by the project team to study the attractiveness of investing more funds in Egg'N Foam is discussed in the following section.

THE RISK ANALYSIS PROCESS

Developing the flow chart and problem structure

The first step in applying risk analysis to Egg'N Foam was to construct a flow chart of the investment analysis. The basic economics of the investment project were assessed and then each element was entered in a simple chart. The initial Egg'N Foam flow chart shown in Figure 5.1.1 consisted of six elements representing: (1) the total market size for egg cartons, (2) CCA's foam market share, (3) selling price, (4) manufacturing cost, (5) total overheads, and (6) investment base.

The initial flow chart was then expanded backward to encompass a large set of input factors. A value was established for each factor, analyzing the determinants of that value, questioning the validity of the determining factors and, where possible, exploding the elements into further detail. This produced

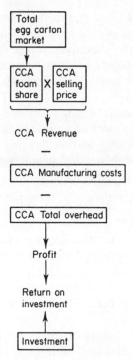

Figure 5.1.1   Initial flow chart, Egg'N Foam

a flow diagram of all the factors relevant to determining the profitability of Egg'N Foam.

The final flow chart for Egg'N Foam is considerably more detailed than the initial chart. The manufacturing costs, overhead costs, and investment base, were all expanded into a substantial number of inputs. However, the unavailability of sufficient market data limited the amount of analysis which could be undertaken on the marketing elements (i.e. market size,* market share, and price).

Stating the assumptions

Upon completion of the flow chart the assumptions underlying each of the factors were stated explicitly and recorded. This step was particularly

---

* For the purpose of this study, the total market for egg cartons has been divided into five regions. Each represents a market that could be covered by the output from *one* Egg'N Foam plant. The West Coast was excluded from the analysis because entering this market was considered to be a separate decision not related to building plants in the other four regions. Egg'N Foam cartons cannot be shipped to the West Coast as the freight costs are too high.

important because it placed a limit on the amount of detail required to substantiate the data inputs. For example, if the project team assumed CCA would capture a 10 percent share of the carton market, little data would be needed to estimate CCA's sales volume. However, it is important to verify the reliability of such assumptions. Invalid assumptions can result in misleading and inaccurate conclusions from analytic models. Thus, verification of assumptions is an integral and important part of the phase of stating the assumptions.

The Egg'N Foam project team was able to verify the validity of most of the data. This included information about equipment rates as supplied by Research and Development Division personnel, as well as forecasts of total egg production as supplied by the US Department of Agriculture. Nevertheless, further study was considered necessary to determine the accuracy of some of the data and assumptions. In particular, more specific information was required about the percentage of eggs cartoned, as well as future Egg'N Foam sales volume and price.

Analyzing sensitivity

The next step in the analysis was to construct a non-probabilistic computer model based on the flow chart. The model was built for a single plant, as each region represented a similar-size market that would support a single plant operation. The model performed all the calculations indicated by the flow chart and provided answers in terms of the return on investment and cash flows.

The model was also used to determine the sensitivity of investment returns and cash flows to changes in input variables. Questions put to the team included: 'What would happen to the discounted rate of return if the price dropped by $0.50 per thousand cartons?', or 'What would happen, say, if the thermoformer cycle time (in the production process) were improved to $4\frac{1}{2}$ seconds?'. The results of the sensitivity analyses on Egg'N Foam are shown in Figure 5.1.2. Changes in two factors—caliper (or thickness) and demand—had a dramatic effect on the rate of return, whereas changes in the value of other factors had only minor impact on profitability. The high sensitivity of the investment return to changes in caliper* and demand indicated the extreme importance of the accuracy of the assumed sales volume of Egg'N Foam.

The sensitivity analysis also helped to identify the optimal plant operation because it permitted the team to use the computer to experiment with different equipment combinations and plant sizes. The sensitivity analysis suggested that in the case of Egg'N Foam one extruder could support two

---

* This is because caliper increase reduces the physical capacity of the plant.

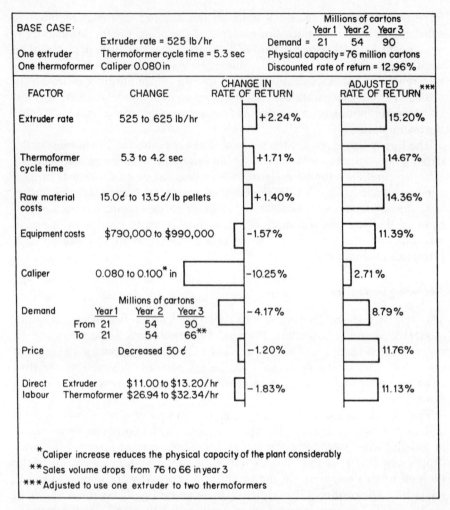

Figure 5.1.2   Sensitivity of investment return to changes in major input factors

thermoformers instead of one thermoformer. It also demonstrated the feasibility of building larger plants containing two extruders and four thermoformers.

Developing investment alternatives

Following the sensitivity analysis, the single plant model was used as a building block in constructing investment strategies for Egg'N Foam.* The team

* The input data that were used for each strategy can be obtained from the authors.

developed four alternative strategies for CCA in the egg carton market. Two strategies involved building superplants, each containing two extruders and four thermoformers; the other two strategies called for small plants, each containing one extruder and two thermoformers.

The two superplant strategies† and the two small plant strategies differed in speed of market entry. On the one hand, a slow, conservative investment pace was suggested by strategies drawn up for both the small and superplants, requiring the addition of thermoformers only after the demand for the output of existing equipment was firmly established. However, the other strategies assumed that CCA should act as quickly as possible to acquire equipment, hire, and train the necessary manpower, and open the plants. The four strategies are shown in Figure 5.1.3 and are expressed in terms of the timing and sequence of equipment installation by plant location.

Assigning the probabilities

Probability information on input factors was obtained next. Subjective probabilities were developed for the five inputs of the model that had either a significant impact on profitability, or a considerable degree of uncertainty. Three inputs related to the production process—namely extruder rate, thermoformer cycle time, and caliper—whereas the other two—price and demand—were marketing variables.

The probability distributions obtained using the fractile assessment method suggested by Raiffa (1968) represented the best judgement of those CCA personnel who were most knowledgeable about the Egg'N Foam situation.

It should be stressed that the probability assessors felt quite confident about their short-term forecasting abilities (for, say, the next 3 years), but found it more difficult to think about future events (over a 3–10-year horizon) which would impact upon their longer-term assessments. In order to structure their thought processes, certain assumptions were made which were the basis for their probability assessments over the future 10-year period.

With the three production variables it was assumed that technological and design advances would improve the performance of extension and thermoformer equipment, and enable caliper thickness to be better and more uniformly controlled. It was anticipated that such new equipment would be introduced approximately 2–3 years after product adoption.

In the case of the assessment of marketing variables, much stronger assumptions were made. Based on current evidence it was felt that the price of a carton would decline linearly in real terms over the time horizon. Estimates of demand were based on the assumption that CCA would be able to capture a 10

† Superplant strategy assumes construction of two plants to serve the four regions, while the small plant strategy assumes construction of four plants.

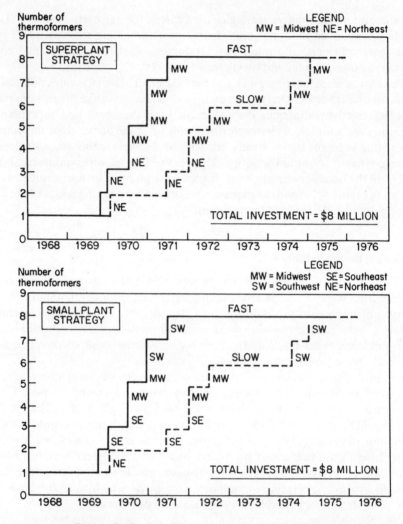

Figure 5.1.3   Investment strategies for Egg'N Foam

percent market share in 6 years with the 'fast' strategy, or in 10 years with the slower strategy.

Results of the 'first pass' risk analysis

The results of the probabilistic risk analysis are shown in summary form in Table 5.1.1. Figure 5.1.4 shows the cumulative density functions (CDFs) for net present value for each of the strategies. The performance measures shown in Table 5.1.1 are net present values. Columns 4 and 5 present two possible

Table 5.1.1 Results in terms of NPV

| Strategy | Point estimate ($m.) | Risk-analysis Simulation ($m.) | | Probability (NPV > 0) | NPV such that 95% probability of exceeding that value ($m.) |
		Mean	Standard deviation		
1	4.12	3.53	0.84	0.99	2.0
2	0.85	0.74	0.45	0.94	0
3	2.90	0.94	1.37	0.88	−2.0
4	−1.38	−1.70	0.68	0	−3.0

Notes:
(a) Discount rate in simulation calculation is assumed at 5% net-of-tax; i.e. the riskless rate.
(b) Point estimate calculation made using most likely values for each input variable and CCA's appropriate net-of-tax risk-adjusted rate of return.
(c) Strategy 1 = super-fast; strategy 2 = super-slow; strategy 3 = small-fast; strategy 4 = small-slow.

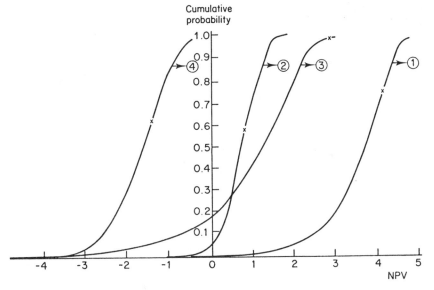

Figure 5.1.4 Graph of CDF for NPV for each strategy

choice criteria for each strategy. These are the probability that the net present value is positive, and also the value of NPV such that there is a 95 percent probability of exceeding that value. Using these criteria it would appear that strategy 4 could be eliminated immediately.

Using principles of stochastic dominance, it would also appear that strategy 1 dominates all other strategies. Therefore, strategy 1 is recommended.

However, as a contingency plan, strategy 2 appears to be the next best alternative if, in the first 4 years, the market growth projections are revised downwards considerably.

Policy dialogue

Following the initial risk analysis the dialogue about strategy choice between the project and management teams at CCA focused around two main concerns. Although it was agreed that the sensitivity and risk analyses had aided the process of strategy evaluation, it was felt that further discussion and review was necessary prior to strategy choice. Much controversy centered around the inadequacy of the processes of problem identification (including key assumptions), and the lack of specificity and clarity about CCA's objectives. The strategic issues raised are outlined in subsequent paragraphs.

Problem identification

Typical critical comments from management included:

> The team seems to have considered heavily technologically oriented strategies, i.e., concentration on plant size and speed of introduction for the product. Little emphasis was placed on interpreting the demand picture, which seems to suggest that marketing related strategies have either not been considered or assumed away.

or:

> Why should the first step . . . be to construct a flow chart?

or:

> The team's effectiveness might improve if its composition were better balanced, with the addition of some marketing personnel.

In general it was felt that some problem assumptions and inputs should be examined and questioned more closely prior to a more effective 'structuring' of the risk analysis model. It was agreed that both the initial listing of assumptions and the sensitivity analysis in Figure 5.1.2 provided a valuable starting point for examining problem structure and the influence of problem assumptions.

Some further observations were made about the assumptions. First, why did the CCA project team assume that CCA would produce their own sheets of foam when the option of purchasing from an outside source might be a worthwhile and cost-effective alternative? Second, what additional correlation effects (with their attendant measurement complications) should be included in the model in relation to price elasticity, demand, production rates, etc.? Third, why were market assumptions taken more or less as given, thus reducing

CCA's decision to an apparent choice between one of four production strategies and ignoring market-related strategies?

After much discussion it was agreed that the greatest weakness concerned the marketing assumptions adopted in the model and the level of empirical or research effort available to support these assumptions. Some of the questions raised about the treatment of marketing were:

(1)   That market share will be 10 percent by 1978. (Should there be a spread of possible values?)
(2)   That no manufacturer other than Diamond National would enter the market before 1978.
(3)   That paper carton manufacturers would not react violently to their share being cut in 10 years from 50 percent to 5 percent. (Why would they not start a price war? Could they afford to do so?)
(4)   That pricing must be at a predetermined level for paper cartons. Why not, for example, consider the adoption of penetration pricing policies to gain share in an aggressive manner?
(5)   That market forecasts are assumed correct. Has any attempt been made to check their methodology and forecast accuracy?
(6)   That selling would be undertaken by the plastics marketing department. It seemed that the transfer price would become an increasingly important motivating factor; this might indicate the need to establish a separate department for marketing Egg'N Foam in the carton market.

Two other financial management assumptions were seen to require further justification. First, that working capital could not be regarded as a single predetermined value. The amount required would depend upon the level of plant capacity, the accuracy of demand predictions (e.g. a stock pile-up might occur), the speed of payments by debtors and many other, as yet unknown, factors. Second, the influence of inflation could not be ignored. It may affect foam more than pulp, or vice-versa, seriously changing the competitive balance within CCA. This might lead to shortfalls in short-term cash flow, leading to an increase in short-term loans or in the time to settle suppliers' accounts.

Specificity and clarity of objectives

The management felt that the project team was also uncertain about the criteria by which choice should be made in relation to the available strategies. It was suggested that attention should be directed toward the criterion for strategy choice in relation to CCA's overall portfolio of investments, both current and projected. The main concern was to relate single project risk to the firm's overall risk, and to handle strategic issues. For example, the issue of whether the CCA Egg'N Foam project would be too risky, not only in the sense of variability of returns, but also in terms of its effect on the firm's portfolio of projects, i.e. its long-term capital assets. Senior managers commented that the carton project might focus too great a proportion of the company's resources (financial, managerial, production, and marketing) on a single project, to the detriment of other possible alternatives. This might weaken the firm's competitive edge in other strategic areas.

Conclusions of the initial policy dialogue

It was agreed that certain tasks could be better performed by management than by the project team. It was suggested that the project team, (perhaps better balanced with additional marketing and financial expertise), should generate appropriate alternative strategies in line with management policy. Some form of strategic evaluation could be carried out later, using risk measures agreed jointly with management. Management's task should be to define guidelines for the range of strategies to be considered, and to direct the project group in the decision-making task. A managerial dialogue process involving the consideration of other factors and attributes should ultimately determine the final strategy choice.

It should be emphasized that both groups stressed the importance of management's role in the problem-finding and formulation process. It was felt that the current strategy set had an overly production/R&D character. It was also agreed that the range of strategies for consideration should focus on a close scan of the internal and external environment, as well as a screen of potential competitive market and technological uncertainties.

As a result, the following recommendations were made concerning further strategy formulation and evaluation through the analytic process. First, that greater attention should be paid to the influence of competition, competitive reaction, and marketing forces on the Egg'N Foam decision. In other words, marketing/production mix combination strategies should be developed. Management felt that the most sensible approach would be to develop a number of marketing scenarios (using a Delphi-type approach) and, if appropriate, carry out a simulation of each scenario. For example, scenarios of the following type should be developed in association with each of the set of production alternatives:

(1) steady price;
(2) failure of the market to grow meaningfully;
(3) tough competitive reaction, e.g., price war initiated by Diamond National and others;
(4) a price war started by CCA to discourage other potential market entrants—i.e. an attempt to build up share quickly;
(5) consumers preferring paper-based to plastic cartons.

Second, that attention should be given in model development to working capital and cash flow management. For example, inflation effects and their impact on potential cash flow generation needed to be examined thoroughly. Third, that the output of the analytic process should be presented in terms of a series of performance measures (essentially indicator variables) over the project time-horizon (15 years). This recommendation developed from the belief that the influence of contingencies on a series of measures such as cash flow and sales projections and NPV measures, would give valuable input to the process of strategy choice. The performance measures suggested were:

(1) total $ sales;
(2) cash flow profile;
(3) gross profit as a percentage of sales;
(4) net profit after taxes;
(5) net profit as a return on investment;
(6) net present value;
(7) further sensitivity analysis of results to key changes in input factors.

Subsequent policy dialogue

Management reviewed the subsequent output of the risk analysis, which showed that strategy 1 (super-fast) was still dominant, except under adverse marketing and financial scenarios, when strategy 2 would be preferred. The marketing scenarios also demonstrated that CCA had a competitive strength with the plastic carton. As a result, if it adopted an even more aggressive capacity-building strategy, it might be able to obtain both the dominant market share position, and the lowest relative cost position. This information provided an additional interesting discussion topic.

The management group commented upon the usefulness of the marketing and financial (e.g. cash flow) probabilistic forecasts provided by the 'second-pass' risk simulation. Quite apart from providing a better understanding of the influence of uncertain events on their business activities, it was also felt that it gave an insight into the relationship between this project and the firm's portfolio of activities.

As the project's NPV (for strategies 1 and 2) was positive when discounted at the required risk-adjusted rate (determined from modern capital-asset pricing theories), then the project should certainly merit acceptance in portfolio terms. This was reinforced by the strategic aspects of the risk simulation, which enabled management to judge the project's viability under a range of alternative future scenarios. Indeed, managers commented that the confirmatory positive indications of the set of performance measures under the range of scenarios enabled them to better understand the project and assess its competitive potential.

Whilst generally in favor of project acceptance, a closer examination of CCA's goals was desired. First, it was felt important to ensure that this project was compatible with the firm's long-term growth plans and objectives. Second, in order to develop this strategic thinking process, it was decided to simulate the firm's portfolio (with the inclusion of either strategy 1 or strategy 2) over a 5–10-year horizon in terms of profitability and cash flow objectives. It was hoped that this would highlight other business areas with future potential for decline/growth, and assess cash flow and financial implications for the Egg'N Foam project.

This subsequent portfolio analysis showed sound long-term viability, and gave strength to the management's view that some diversification into foam cartons was a related-business diversification which gave the firm a useful competitive edge. It was also felt that it would be complementary in skills and growth potential to the firm's recent diversifications into the poultry processing and broiler chicken manufacturing areas.

Risk analysis as a strategic inquiry system

It is important to emphasize the link between risk analysis and strategic management. This can be conceptualized in terms of Churchman's (1971) development of inquiry systems. The initially envisaged risk analysis process (see Figures 5.1.1 and 5.1.2) is a simple, somewhat naive form of a Leibnitzian inquiry system. In other words, a single 'optimal' problem formulation is developed and data are collected to support this single 'view of the world'. After the first-pass risk analysis the ensuing policy dialogue indicated, *inter alia*, that increased effort should be directed toward focused questioning of assumptions, scenarios, and product market concepts. Indeed managers took 'devil's advocate' positions in their advocacy of extreme scenarios and alternative project assumptions. Note that the use of risk analysis in the questioning and debate process indicates a significant change in the character of inquiry system. The problem formulation system is now more complex and multi-dimensional, and is much closer to Churchman's (1971), Kantian, and Hegelian forms of inquiry system. This arises because the problem is viewed from several perspectives and because it is anticipated that synthesis and consensus about problem formulation should be achieved through a process of group debate and dialogue. Further 'passes' of risk analyses aid strategic dialogue by generating additional information for debate about the possible consequences of alternative assumptions, problem formulations, and future scenarios. This should lead to a continual review and updating of strategy options and, following debate, lead to a resolution of conflicting viewpoints.

SUMMARY, CONCLUSIONS, AND STRATEGIC IMPLICATIONS

The value of risk analysis in a facilities planning decision is examined here in relation to a disguised recent planning situation called Egg'N Foam. In essence, following Gluck *et al.* (1980), risk analysis is presented as Stage II/III of a sensible strategic thinking process. It is seen as a vehicle for forecast/uncertainty-based planning, in which an understanding of future scenarios, cash flow projections, and synergies between marketing and production activities is developed. This also enables managers to search more creatively in order to identify the menu of strategic options.

The strategic risk analysis presented here differs from that presented by some other authors in the same area (e.g. Spetzler and Zamora (1974); Buffa (1980)) in terms of its treatment of risk preference and criteria for strategy choice. Risk preference involves the decision-maker's attitude toward risk, and is commonly handled via utility function assessment and certainty equivalence concepts. In this instance the management group felt uncomfortable with the utility concept, even though they regarded risk preference as a policy question. They preferred to treat risk preference through a number of 'lenses', i.e. by examining the risk simulation output in mean/variance terms, in terms of 'risk of ruin' criteria (i.e. prob. NPV > 0), and by looking at future cash flow profiles. In addition, they accepted that a project with a positive NPV, when discounted at an appropriate 'risk-adjusted' rate, would increase the value of the firm in portfolio terms.

Management also felt that for strategy choice, both the project and the firm's portfolio should be examined in terms of a number of performance measures (cash flow, NPV, sales) specified over the 15-year project time horizon. This criterion of policy choice, specified in terms of a time stream of indicator measures (cash flow, etc.) rather than in terms of a single criterion (such as expected utility), is consistent with the work on preferences over time (see Bell, 1977 and Meyer, 1976).

In terms of strategic implementation this risk analysis approach was successful. The value of risk analysis lies in encouraging policy dialogue amongst the management group about future uncertainty impacts. The continued questioning of assumptions and problem formulation is seen as essential for the effective formulation and evaluation of alternative strategy positions. By such continued questioning and dialogue, a meaningful consensus about strategy choice emerged. This consensus process, which involved 'three passes' of a risk analysis process, could not have been achieved without adaptive mechanisms and flexibility being built into the process during the course of dialogue and successive risk analysis passes. The outcome interestingly was to follow strategy 2, the super-slow strategy, with the proviso that should the market take off rapidly, a contingency plan for quickly adding further capacity should be immediately activated.

REFERENCES

Bell, D. E. (1977). 'A decision analysis of objectives for a forest pest problem', in Bell, D. E., Keeney, R. L., and Raiffa, H. (eds), *Conflicting Objectives in Decisions*. John Wiley, New York.

Buffa, E. S. (1980). *Modern Production/Operations Management*, 6th edn, p. 108. John Wiley, New York.

Churchman, C. W. (1971). *The Design of Inquiring Systems*. Basic Book, New York.

Gluck, F. W., S. P. Kaufman, and A. S. Walleck (1980). 'Strategic management for competitive advantage', *Harvard Business Review*, July/Aug., pp. 154–161.

Hertz, D. B. (1979). 'Risk analysis in capital investment', *Harvard Business Review*, **57**, September/October 1979, pp. 169–181 (originally printed in Harvard Business Review, 1964).

Hertz, D. B.. and H. Thomas (1983). *Risk Analysis and its Applications*. John Wiley, Chichester.

Hogarth, R. M., and S. Makradakis (1981). 'Forecasting and planning: an evaluation', *Management Science*, **27**(2) (Feb.) 115–139.

Meyer, R. F. (1976). 'Preferences over time', Chapter 9 in R. L. Keeney and H. Raiffa (eds), *Decisions with Multiple Objectives*. John Wiley, New York.

Raiffa, H. (1968). *Decision Analysis*. Addison-Wesley, Reading, Mass.

Rappaport, A. (1967). 'Sensitivity analysis in decision-making', *Accounting Review*, July, pp. 441–456.

Spetzler, C. S., and R. M. Zamora (1974). 'Decision analysis of a facilities investment and expansion problem', in *Readings in Decision Analysis*. Stanford Research Institute, Palo Alto.

5.2
Applying Multi-Attributed Decision Analysis Models to Policy Formulation

ANDREW R. LOCK
School of Business, Kingston Polytechnic, Kingston-upon-Thames, England

AND

HOWARD THOMAS
Department of Business Administration, University of Illinois at Urbana-Champaign

In the marketing field decision analysis has generally been applied to problems of a tactical rather than strategic nature. Day (1964) gives a number of early applications including Green's seminal (1963) paper on the solution of a pricing problem. Further examples may be found in Newman (1971), Brown *et al.* (1974) and Moore *et al.* (1976).

In all of these situations, however, solutions were defined in terms of the single criterion, expected monetary value (EMV), with an *ad hoc* discussion of risk in terms of variance of outcomes. EMV has been recognized as an unsatisfactory criterion in complex risky situations (such as strategic decision problems) and in principle has been supplanted by expected utility. Recent developments have expanded the structure to cover multiple criteria and in the decision analysis field this has come to be known as the multi-attribute utility (MAU) approach (Raiffa, 1968b; Keeney and Raiffa, 1976).

There has been a parallel, primarily psychometric, development in the analysis of riskless choice across multi-attributed alternatives. In marketing this has been applied to problems of consumer preferences and choice using, in particular, conjoint analysis (see for example Green *et al.*, 1972; Green and Wind, 1973; Shocker and Srinivasan, 1979). However, neither these techniques nor the MAU/decision analysis approach have made much impact on the treatment of strategic problems in marketing and business in general (Lock and Thomas, 1978; Behn and Vaupel, 1976). Some of the difficulties involved in applying analytic techniques to complex problems are discussed in Kaufman and Thomas (1977) and Kunreuther and Schoemaker (1980).

The goal of the case-study analysis reported in this paper was to test the feasibility and practicality of a multiple-criterion approach to a strategic problem using decision simulation to model the strategy options, and conjoint analysis to elicit preference functions. These are embedded in a policy dialogue process using the analytic techniques as aids for structuring complex problems and improving decision-makers' understanding of underlying interrelationships (Humphreys and McFadden, 1980; Jungermann and von Ulardt, 1982). In situations with multiple decision-makers it provides a basis for dialogue, discussion, and eventual consensus. Learning also occurs, which improves the effectiveness of decision-making in subsequent situations. The use of models to represent decision problems is similar to Little's decision calculus (Little, 1970). However the current approach emphasizes preference analysis involving the explicit use of MAU models to assist the decision-maker to use and develop an acceptable overall criterion function.

A MARKETING STRATEGY PROBLEM AT THE STRATEGIC BUSINESS UNIT (SBU) LEVEL

In mid-1976, Bally (UK) Ltd. were considering the future of their men's shoe business. This was precipitated by the decline in the sales of shoes manufactured by the Swiss parent company over a 15-year period, due largely to the relative fall in the value of the pound. Bally shoes were sold both through the company's own stores and other mainly independent shops. The company specialized mainly in ladies' shoes, which were manufactured at Norwich in the UK as well as being imported from Switzerland.

The problem was discussed at length in a dialogue between one of the authors and the decision-makers within Bally. Notes were taken at each meeting and these were used as a basis for subsequent discussion.

STAGES OF THE ANALYSIS

The study was performed in the following chronological order:

(1) The range of options and criteria were elicited in discussions with managers.
(2) The structure of the options and their associated stochastic models were derived on the basis of further conversations.
(3) The input data were collected by means of questionnaire and interview.
(4) A two-stage rating exercise was completed by one decision-maker.
(5) Simulation programmes were constructed for the policy options.
(6) The output of the programmes was checked for consistency.
(7) The outcomes from the revised programmes were computed and summarized. These were presented to the two decision-makers.
(8) Experiments were designed to elicit preference judgements on the basis of the range of outcome values for the undominated options.

(9)   The second decision-maker completed the experiments and filled in a rating questionnaire on the qualitative attributes.
(10) The rankings for the experiments were processed using a conjoint analysis algorithm.
(11) The selected preference model was applied to the simulation outcomes. Value scores for the options were computed on a number of comparative bases.
(12) The derived solution was examined to determine its relative stability.
(13) The overall effectiveness of the study was considered in the light of the actual decision taken.

THE RANGE OF OPTIONS

A number of possible basic strategies were identified:

(1)   Do nothing—continuing with sales of Swiss shoes and limited imports from Italy.
(2)   Expand buying-in of Italian shoes.
(3)   Persuade the parent company to reduce the transfer price.
(4)   Import parts from Switzerland for assembly in England
(5)   Manufacture men's shoes in their existing Norwich factory.
(6)   Start a new manufacturing operation elsewhere.
(7)   Subcontract to a small manufacturer. This would involve the transfer of some skills and technology.
(8)   Purchase a small shoe manufacturer.

These options were made more complex by other decision variables such as choice of price or manufacturing capacity. These were not necessarily mutually exclusive and were thus referred to as policy components or options rather than alternatives.

It was felt that the construction of a total company model was not feasible at this stage, and it would be more profitable to develop sub-models for each of the policy components.

DECISION CRITERIA

It became clear from the dialogue process that there was a wide range of aspects to the determination of preferences amongst the options. In part this is characteristic of strategic decision problems. In this case it is particularly marked because as a wholly-owned subsidiary, Bally had to consider factors which were highly valued by the Swiss parent. These included the desire to maintain volume at the Swiss plants and the international brand image. The following list of criteria emerged:

(1)   Contribution and its configuration through time.
(2)   Investment requirements (including working capital).
(3)   Market share/pairage.
(4)   Speed of erosion of volume and rate of recovery.
(5)   Bally image—the brand and its survival.
(6)   Feasibility of manufacture of Bally shoes in the proposed way.
(7)   Impact on the retail business and its possible expansion.
(8)   Impact on the wholesale business (60 percent of current volume).
(9)   Effect on the Swiss parent.
(10) Ability to present a full range.
(11) Bally (UK) corporate objectives.
(12) Demands on managerial resources and skills.

In addition a financial constraint was imposed such that any option under consideration should have an expected rate of return greater than 22 percent after interest and tax.

The above list contains some overlap and the criteria (1) through (4) require some form of measurement to be defined. As the decision-makers wished to consider the retail and wholesale/manufacturing businesses separately, net cash flow measures through time were produced for both. The third and fourth criteria were represented by the evolution of forecast sales volume through time. These three derived criteria, namely, *cash flows for wholesaling, cash flows for retailing* and *total sales volume* through time represent the quantitative measures used for the conjoint analysis exercises. It had originally been intended to use the approach for all the attributes, but difficulties were encountered in persuading the decision-makers to perform the exercises. As they were particularly interested in the configuration of outcomes through time, simple summary measures (e.g. NPV) were unsuitable, and it was decided to consider the first 5 years' results separately.

DESIGN OF THE RANKING EXPERIMENTS

Ranges were obtained from the simulation output for the undiscounted cash flows for wholesaling activities (including manufacturing where appropriate), for retail activities, and for total sales volume for each of the 5 years 1977–81. Even this reduced set contained 15 attributes. It is evident from the literature (Slovic and Lichtenstein, 1971; Shepard, 1964) that subjects are unable to deal with such a large number simultaneously. Thus it was necessary to divide them up into subsets to be considered separately. To be able to re-aggregate the subsets they need to overlap.

Each subset was limited to three attributes which subjects tend to find a relatively easy number to deal with. Larger numbers were avoided because they would prevent the introduction of interaction variables into the analysis. Significant interaction variable coefficients would indicate the presence of utility dependence between attributes. It was, however, a central hypothesis that a simple linear model would prove an adequate representation.

It was also decided to use three levels on each attribute to generate the hypothetical alternatives for the ranking experiments. All possible combinations of three levels on three attributes yields 27 alternatives. Lock (1979) had previously considered a Latin square design with four levels, but had found it less satisfactory. The mean outcomes on each attribute were taken for each policy component, omitting dominated options. The highest and lowest were identified and rounded. The third value was derived by approximately bisecting the interval between highest and lowest. The resultant combinations were examined to check that real trade-offs had to be made to order them.

Table 5.2.1   Attribute levels for the composite experiment

	Level 1	Level 2	Level 3
Wholesale/manufacturing, year 1	−£500,000	−£200,000	£50,000
Retail cash flows, year 1	£270,000	£400,000	£530,000
Sales volume, year 1	85,000	135,000	180,000

As an example of the attribute values used for the hypothetical alternatives, the values for the composite model are shown in Table 5.2.1. The composite experiment combines the first-year values in order to estimate the trade-offs over the whole set of quantitative attributes. The instructions given to the subject emphasized the assumptions underlying the figures presented. The alternatives were printed on cards (4 × 3 inches) and shuffled before being given to the subject.

A CAVEAT

Some of the subjects were reluctant to participate in the exercises. It became evident that the exercises were perceived as tedious, potentially time-consuming, and possibly rather demeaning. They were also not seen as part of the analysis process, which was considered completed when the simulation output was presented to the decision-makers. This must, in part, be attributed to a failure to clarify adequately the nature of the process at the outset and to combine it into the 'informal contract'.

On a more general level, there were significant implications in the derivation of a formal multiple criterion model of preference. In this process the decision-maker is placed in the hands of the analyst; the analyst's structuring of the problem and the approach will not necessarily be an exact reflection of his or her views. The power and role of the analyst are likely to prove major issues in practical applications. these are only likely to be resolved by decision-makers acquiring greater formal technical competence. It also requires the adoption of a paradigm for decision analysis as an aid for formulation and as an information-gathering basis for a strategic inquiry system about options involving a mixture of policy dialogue, debate, and creative analytic inputs.

THE RANGE OF MODELS TESTED

Various models for the observed preference orderings were investigated, all of which could be fitted with the non-metric regression package that was available. Pilot studies (reported in Lock, 1979) had indicated that a linear additive model would perform well, but it was desirable to compare its performance with alternative functional forms. In all the models listed below, x_i denotes the value for the ith attribute, w_k the weight attached to the kth term and x_{ij} is a binary variable, equal to 1 for the jth level on the ith attribute and zero otherwise. $U(X)$ denotes the utility attached to a vector of attributes X. The following models were considered:

(1)   Linear additive

$$U(X) = \sum_{i=1}^{m} w_i x_i \tag{I}$$

The linear additive model implies risk neutrality and additive utility independence of the attributes. A wide variety of studies attest to its power in representing human judgements. It also enables us to test a discounting model for the configurations over 5 years. For this to hold the ratios w_i/w_{i-1} should be all equal and less than 1.

(2)   Simple analysis of variance

$$U(X) = \sum_{i=1}^{m} \sum_{j=1}^{n} w_{ij} x_{ij} \tag{II}$$

This perhaps the most common conjoint analysis model, typified by Kruskal's MONANOVA algorithm (Kruskal, 1964a,b). The w_{ij} give the part-worths of the attribute levels. The model is additive but permits the possibility of non-linearity on the attributes.

(3) Square root

$$U(X) = \sum_{i=1}^{m} w_i(x_i)^{1/2} \tag{III}$$

Bernoulli (1738) proposed the square root model as a simple representation of risk aversion. The attributes have to be transformed to be positive.

(4) Logarithmic

$$U(X) = \sum_{i=1}^{m} w_i \cdot \ln(x_i) \tag{IV}$$

This also requires the transformation of attributes to be positive, and satisfies risk-aversion requirements by being concave downwards. It is also a transformation of a multiplicative (or approximation to the conjunctive) model.

(5) The ideal point model
If an ideal level or goal on each attribute is defined as x_i^*, and utility is seen as being inversely proportional to the weighted Euclidean distance from the ideal point, we obtain the function (V.1) which multiplies out to (V.2).

$$V(X) = -\sum_{i=1}^{m} k_i(x_i^* - x_i)^2 \tag{V.1}$$

$$V(X) = -\sum_{i=1}^{m} k_i(x_i^{*2} - 2x_i^*x_i + x_i^2) \tag{V.2}$$

By fitting the model (V.3), the equivalence of the two models can be seen immediately, with $w_i = +2k_ix_i^*$ and $w_{i+m} = -k_i$, which permits solving for x_i^*.

$$U(X) = \sum_{i=1}^{m} (w_ix_i + w_{i+m}x_i^2) \tag{V.3}$$

(6) Linear additive with interaction terms
It is frequently felt that human judgement is configural rather than simply additive (Hoffman, 1968), though there is substantial evidence that a linear model explains much of the variance even with an underlying configural model (Yntema and Torgerson, 1961). In the case of a three-attribute model we have equation (VI).

$$U(X) = \sum_{i=1}^{3} w_ix_i + \sum_{i=1}^{3}\sum_{j=i+1}^{3} w_{ij}x_i \cdot x_j + w_7x_1 \cdot x_2 \cdot x_3 \tag{VI}$$

(7) Linear additive with higher powers
This is a more general form of (V.3) with the possibility of including cubic or higher-powered terms.

(8) Linear plus logarithmic
This combines models (I) and (IV). Given the problem of transforming the attributes to be positive and the strange function resulting from taking the antilog, this is essentially an arbitrary model.

(9) Linear differences
This looks at the change from one period to the next, and would represent the situation where subjects looked favorably on alternatives showing improvements from one period to the next. The basic model in (IX.1) is fitted by the equation (IX.2) where $w_0 = 0$. It has one less parameter than equation (I) and is more constrained for a given attribute set.

$$U(X) = \sum_{i=1}^{m-1} w_i(x_{i+1} - x_i) \tag{IX.1}$$

$$U(X) = \sum_{i=1}^{m} (w_{i-1} - w_i)x_i \tag{IX.2}$$

(10) Logarithmic difference

$$U(X) = \sum_{i=1}^{m-1} w_i \cdot \ln(x_{i+1} - x_i) \tag{X}$$

Like the linear difference model, this reduces to the logarithmic model with one less parameter.

CRITERIA FOR DISTINGUISHING BETWEEN MODELS

Kruskal (1964a,b) presents a measure of goodness of fit, the stress value, lying in the interval (0,1), where 0 is perfect fit. A stress value in the region of 0.05 to 0.08 was identified as a stopping value. Given equal stress, the principle of parsimony would lead to the choice of a model with fewer independent variables. Some of the models have significant correlations between some of their independent variables. As this introduces biases in the fitted weights, one would prefer, *ceteris paribus*, an alternative model.

Whilst there do not exist formal tests of significance for reductions of stress resulting from the inclusion of extra variables, it is nonetheless possible to conclude that, say, a five-point reduction in stress is insufficient to justify the addition of three variables. It is also possible to examine the change in rank correlation between the observed and fitted orderings.

Further considerations relate to the apparent significance of the computed coefficients. Again some circumspection is required as the distribution of the weights is distorted by the subroutine adjusting the basic regression formulation into a best ordinal fit to the observed ordering. It is also desirable to look at the signs and relative magnitudes of the fitted weights and to compare them with *a priori* expectations. For example, one would be reluctant to incorporate in a prescriptive model partial utility functions exhibiting risk preference.

RESULTS OF THE CONJOINT ANALYSIS

The composite and sales experiments both yielded such very low stress values (≤ 0.03) for the linear additive model that there was no need to fit more complex models. The wholesale experiments exhibited moderate linear fits (stress 0.22 and 0.17), but the reduction in stress from the addition of up to 4 extra terms was in the 0.03–0.04 region. This was not considered sufficient to justify a more complex model. Also, the pattern of weights was supported by other analyses including the ANOVA. The weights peaked in the third year, with weights for years 4 and 5 greater than or equal to those in the first 2 years. These are inconsistent with conventional discounting of future cash flows, and may be related to the widespread managerial concern with seeing returns from policies in the medium term, when the success of a strategy might be evaluated. (This is true in the British managerial context, but may be less marked in the US where more immediate performance is valued.)

The retail experiments presented rather more difficulty. None of the fitted models were in any sense satisfactory, and there were consistently counter-intuitive signs. Some interactive experimentation was performed, varying the linear weights and examining the effect on the rank correlation coefficient. This showed distinct local maxima. However, further examination showed that a set of ordering rules seemed to have been used. Firstly, the alternatives were ordered by magnitude ordering on the attributes (P denotes 'is preferred to'):

$$(x_3 > x_2 > x_1) \, P \, (x_3 > x_1 > x_2) \, P \, (x_1 > x_3 > x_2) \, P$$
$$(x_2 > x_3 > x_1) \, P \, (x_2 > x_1 > x_3) \, P \, (x_1 > x_2 > x_3)$$

Within each of these categories, the alternatives were ranked, first on the basis of the third attribute magnitude, then on the second, and finally on the first. Thee resultant rank correlations were 0.985 and 0.98 respectively. Even these could have been improved, as it was observed that conditional preferences on the first attribute were inversely related to its magnitude. The problem with this set of rules is that it is not readily integrated with other preference models. Also, being partly lexicographic, it fails to satisfy reasonable criteria for a rational decision model (Fishburn, 1968).

Why should a protocol like this be adopted in this case, when adequate trade-offs could be deduced for the other experiments? It may relate to the distance of the phenomena from the decision-maker, as these were figures with which he was familiar as a board member rather than in a day-to-day managerial capacity. Subjects may fall back on formal rules in the absence of familiarity with the choices under consideration. A more pessimistic view would be to attribute it to boredom or disinterest. Evidence from other applications suggests that holistic ranking exercises fail intermittently in similar circumstances.

There remained the problem of selecting a metric model to incorporate in the overall preference function. A linear model with weights slightly adjusted from the interactive variation was chosen.

APPLICATION OF THE AGGREGATE MODEL TO THE SIMULATION OUTCOMES

Given the doubts attached to the results from the retail experiments, it was decided to test several alternative linear models. The first was the one actually derived from the analysis. The second combined the mean of the actual 5 years' results with the derived composite weights. This corresponds to equally weighting across the years. The third also used the composite weights but the annual results were discounted at a risk-free rate of 14 percent. The final model used equal weights for all 15 attributes.

All four yielded identical orderings for the first five policy components, which suggests that, given the estimates, the model is very stable. Rank correlations were computed for the first model versus the other three, and were found to be 0.927 with the weighted means, 0.824 with the weighted discounted model, and 0.983 with the equal weights one. The final one is particularly interesting as, although it may not seem appropriate to weight sales in units equally with contribution in pounds, the resultant correlation with the derived model is better than the other two. This must to a large extent be ascribed to the monotonic relationship that largely holds between sales and contribution for each policy alternative (cf. Newman, 1977).

The most preferred single component was found to be the assembly of Swiss parts in Norwich with a price of about £26 (for 1977). Such a policy was compatible with marketing Italian branded and unbranded shoes, but meant some cannibalization of existing Swiss sales. Some doubts were also expressed about the cost estimates, particularly the basic investment. The next favoured policy was the link with another company, which was compatible with both Swiss and Italian sales. If the derived score for Swiss imports is deducted from the difference in scores for the assembly in Norwich option and the link with another company, a residual difference remains which, if fully accounted for by increased manufacturing investment, amounts to about £1,190,000. This is rather larger than was thought likely. Also, the first option would not actually result in total cannibalization of Swiss sales.

The close agreement between the different models suggests that little would be gained by using more complex ones. Do such similar results justify the universal use of, say, an equal weighting model for strategic decisions with multiple criteria? In this case there was sufficient evidence that the weight for sales volume was significantly lower than those for the cash flows. There were also strong indications against the equal weighting of the results for individual years. In most business situations there is a distinct hierarchy of relative weights, and the indiscriminate use of equal weights could lead to markedly non-optimal decisions. Newman (1977) shows that differential weights may make a difference if some of the attributes are negatively correlated. It may also be necessary to justify recommendations with rather more ritual than the equal weight model supposes. The reluctance of decision-makers to accept the encapsulation of their decision-making by simple models is amplified by the contrast between their difficulties faced with complex multi-attributed decisions and a model eliminating judgemental input into the preference process. Finally, equal weighting is sufficiently distant from the concept of cardinal utility for differences in scores to have little meaning. The decision analysis process focuses as much on sensitivity testing of the parameters on the basis of utility differences as it does on the precise answer, or on the method used to derive the utility function.

OTHER FACTORS

To a large extent the orderings resulting from the rating models reflected the particular areas of interest of each decision-maker, suggesting biases due to halo effects. The second rating exercise used criteria that were not covered by the conjoint analysis exercises. It produced results that favoured manufacturing options and was broadly consistent with the results from the derived model. It would have been difficult to reconcile wholly inconsistent results from the two approaches, as the use of the rating method was partly a fallback after it had proved impossible to implement the full assessment process.

Rating methods are most effective in assessing the importance of attributes, rather than in generating actual attribute scores in the context of complex strategic decisions. Apart from response biases and halo effects, such methods seem to be a gross under-utilization of the potential information available, given the expected value of decision analysis in this type of situation (cf. Watson and Brown, 1978). They do have a role in pre-screening options for further analysis (Lock and Thomas, 1982).

WHAT ACTUALLY HAPPENED?

By the end of the process a preferred policy had emerged. After considerable discussion the option to assemble Swiss parts was felt to be infeasible for several reasons:

(1)   space previously available in the factory had been partially taken up by other activities;
(2)   the Swiss management was unlikely to accede;
(3)   if new capacity were needed, it would render the option less attractive than other manufacturing options;
(4)   it was still felt that the investment costs had been underestimated.

Accordingly discussions were opened with a UK company, initially with a view to Bally selling their products, with the later possibility of a licensing agreement to produce branded shoes.

In the event, while some products were marketed, the licensing option was effectively superseded by the events of 1977. The value of the pound versus the Swiss franc stabilized at a higher level than anticipated and it also appreciated against the Italian lira. This meant that there would be a much more gradual decline in sales of Swiss shoes than had been predicted. Further, for similar buying-in prices, British-made shoes would not match Italian quality, except for some strictly traditional lines. The link with a British company was useful in terms of breadth of sales lines, but the risks in transferring highly marketable skills were unjustified by the small expected volume in the new circumstances.

THE USEFULNESS OF DECISION ANALYSIS IN THIS CASE

The simulation models of the various policy options were effective in highlighting the characteristics of the various strategies. They were perceived as particularly useful for understanding the structure and characteristics of the decision problem and formed the basis for a useful debate about the relative merits of the options. They illustrated the high costs of the manufacturing options and also showed that the retail business would be the main cash generator from new projects, because of the low costs of taking up spare capacity in existing retail outlets.

These models, together with the main analysis of preference, showed that many of the strategies and sub-strategies could be eliminated using reasonable dominance rules, leaving the decision-makers with relatively few strategies to make a final choice, and more structured information on which to do so. For smaller problems, the cost and effort of developing such simulation models might be harder to justify, however.

The reluctance on the part of the decision-makers to participate in the preference measurement exercises leaves the analysis in an unsatisfactory state. It has been attributed to the possible perception of the tasks as tedious, simplistic, and possibly demeaning. An additional contributory factor may have been the status and role of the analyst. Given the complexity of the output of the simulation programmes, it represents a distinct reduction in information use and in the analysis of preference. With hindsight the self-administration of methods for preference analysis as proposed by Edwards (1976) would probably have improved the process of preference measurement.

CONJOINT ANALYSIS: ADVANTAGES AND DISADVANTAGES

Wind and Saaty (1980) observe that the determination of the relative importance of corporate objectives is an area in which it would be possible to use either Saaty's analytic hierarchy process (AHP) or conjoint analysis, but that there have been few, if any, such applications of the latter. There are significant differences between the AHP approach and the one in this study. Here simulation methods have been used to generate distributions of outcomes for each policy component on each objective. AHP uses pairwise comparison matrices with a nine-point scale to establish both relative objective weights and relative performance scores on objectives. It thus relies effectively on a rating-type input as opposed to actually modeling alternatives. This suggests a possible contrast with MAU approaches whereby the latter are appropriate for detailed analysis, with AHP used as a screening device. In the treatment of actual preference models, AHP is constrained to a set of linear weights, constrained also by the basic nine-point scale input. The evidence from this study and elsewhere suggests that this is not too severe, though it does take one sufficiently far from cardinal utility to make one a little uneasy with sensitivity analysis on score differences. Both methods presuppose a hierarchy of objectives whereby an overall goal—corporate mission and well-being—is broken down systematically to a level at which the components become measurable (see Keeney and Raiffa, 1976: 41 *et seq.*).

The main advantage of conjoint analysis relative to many other utility assessment methods is that it uses preference judgements and thus avoids many problems of intransitivity and poor identification associated with indifference judgements. Preference judgements yield a set of inequalities that can give accurate estimates of trade-off weights, which are ratio-scaled and satisfy the requirements of true relative scaling for linear additive utility functions. Similarly polynomial conjoint analysis models yield interval-scaled utility functions. Furthermore, alternative methods for eliciting utility functions are frequently based on lotteries or gambles (Hull *et al.*, 1973). These tend to compound the assessment problem for the respondent and introduce a further potential source of error. Riskless assessment methods enable the subject to focus on the relationship between the attributes under consideration.

There is, however, the problem of feasibility. The assessment requirements effectively constrain individual exercises to three or four attributes, which for most practical problems necessitates a partial disaggregation of the problem. The ordering requirement placed upon the subject is not excessively onerous given reasonable provision of instructions and cards for shuffling. It does require significant involvement on the part of subjects, and it breaks down when subjects cease to relate to the material. The result is an ordering protocol similar to that observed in the study.

A significant advantage of conjoint analysis is the separation of the assessment of preference from the establishment of attribute values. Hammond and Adelman (1976) show the effectiveness of this separation in the context of a controversial community decision problem. A similar separation seems crucial within the strategic business decision situation, where the participants are likely marked response biases and prejudices in favor of specific courses of action.

The algorithm used is capable of fitting a number of functional forms to the observed orderings. This permits the testing of a number of models that include interaction terms, providing useful measures of utility dependence between attributes. Strictly to justify partial or complete disaggregation, some testing for dependence is necessary. Conventional approaches (Keeney and Raiffa, 1976), mainly gamble-based, create difficulties in terms of the types of questions asked and the additional set of tasks for the decision-maker.

The problem of experimental design is a potential restriction on practical use. The selection of attribute levels to be permuted will to a large extent dictate the fixity of the solution. In extreme cases it may cause confused judgements yielding high stress values and unsatisfactory weights. It is important to use a range of attribute values which accurately reflect the outcomes of the set of efficient (i.e. undominated) alternatives.

IS THE CONCEPT OF A CORPORATE UTILITY FUNCTION MEANINGFUL?

In effect, we are postulating a corporate utility function for the purpose of selecting an optimal strategy. In order to derive such a function it is necessary to incorporate the judgements of one or more decision-makers, who typically act as agents rather than principals. They have preference structures which represent 'managerial' interests rather than the ill-defined corporate one. For example, an individual decision-maker might exhibit a greater degree of risk aversion than is desirable from a corporate point of view. As a consequence, one has to decide how far to pursue variance in the decision-maker's judgements and whether the derived models are an adequate proxy for the corporate interest.

In this study the final choice of policy was remarkably robust to changes in the parameters of the utility function. This helps to reduce the tensions between the positive and normative aspects of a decision analysis of this nature. The elements of judgement required of the analyst—the degree of complexity of model to fit to a subject's judgements, and the acceptance or rejection of a particular model—makes it easy for the analyst to impose his or her own structure and judgements, possibly at the expense of those of the decision-makers and of the corporate interest. The professional defense in this situation is quite specific; that the models are explicit and capable of external criticism and manipulation, in contrast to the processes that they replace.

CONCLUSIONS

There are clear difficulties in generalizing from a single case-study. Strategic decision problems are usually one-offs and conventional criteria for adequacy of evidence are frequently hard to apply. It is not impossible to draw conclusions, however (cf. Campbell, 1975). Numerous studies of personal judgement and decision-making attest to the power of MAU models, usually simple linear ones, in representing judgements and aiding problem formulation and structuring (a useful summary of some of this material is to be found in Hogarth, 1980). It is not intended to argue that the approach taken is necessarily an ideal one. However, with certain reservations it appeared to be both feasible and practicable as a method for analyzing policy options in detail. Many of the benefits of the approach are common to all methodologies that involve the structuring and analysis of problems. In the context of decisions with large potential opportunity losses, it appears desirable to use as much information as is available to model the alternatives facing decision-makers. Simulation is particularly useful in this respect and is quite easily adapted to provide output on multiple attributes.

The discrepancy between the policy selected by the analysis and the actual decision taken provides an insight into the decision process. It can be described as a policy dialogue in which analysis is used to structure the problem and provide an understanding of the impacts of uncertainty and problem assumptions upon the various policy options. In addition, decision-makers can explore their preferences on a broad range of criteria and familiarize themselves with dealing with multiple attributes. Sensitivity analyses can also be used to test the stability of any solution and identify alternative solutions if circumstances change. In the actual study, the change of strategy resulting from exchange rate outcomes outside the assessed distributions is a case in point.

The fact that decision-makers may not adopt the policy proposed by a particular analysis does not necessarily mean that the exercise is a failure. It seems that participants gain an enhanced understanding of the problems facing them and feel more confident in their actual choice of policy. By presenting alternative viewpoints and solutions, analytic approaches to strategic decision-making provide inputs and stimuli for processes of dialogue and dialectical debate which improve the process of policy and the quality of the final decision.

ACKNOWLEDGMENT

We would like to thank Bally (UK) Ltd. for their kind permission for the publication of the case-study.

REFERENCES

Behn, R. D., and J. W. Vaupel (1976). 'Why decision analysis is rarely used and how it can be'. Working Paper. Center for Policy Analysis, Institute of Policy Analysis and Public Affairs, Duke University.

Bernoulli, Daniel (1738). 'Specimen theoriae novae de mensura sortis'. *Commentarii Academiae Scientiarum Imperialis Petropolitanae*, pp. 175–192. Translated by L. Sommer (1954). *Econometrica*, **22**, 23–36.

Brown, Rex V., Andrew S. Kahr, and Cameron R. Peterson (1974). *Decision Analysis for the Manager*. Holt, Rinehart & Winston, New York.

Campbell, Donald T. (1975). ' "Degrees of freedom" and the case study', *Comparative Political Studies*. **8**, 178–193.

Day, R. L. (ed.) (1964). *Marketing Models—Quantitative and Behavioral*. International Textbook Company, Scranton PA.

Edwards, Ward (1976). 'How to use multi-attribute utility measurement for social decision-making'. SSRI Technical Report, 001597-1-T. Social Science Research Institute, University of Southern California, CA.

Fishburn, P. C. (1968). 'Utility theory', *Management Science*, May, pp. 335–378.

Green, Paul E. (1963). 'Bayesian decision theory in pricing strategy', *Journal of Marketing*, Jan., pp. 5–19.

Green, Paul E., Frank J. Carmone, and Yoram Wind (1972). 'Subjective evaluation models and conjoint measurement', *Behavioral Science*, pp. 288–299.

Green, Paul E. and Yoram Wind (1973). *Multi-Attribute Decisions in Marketing: A Measurement Approach*. Dryden Press, Hinsdale IL.

Hammond K. R., and L. Adelman (1976). 'Science, values and human judgment', *Science*, **194**, 389–396.

Hertz, David B. and Howard Thomas (1982). *Risk Analysis and its Applications*. Wiley, Chichester.

Hoffman, P. J. (1968). 'Cue-consistency and configurality in human judgment', in B. Kleinmuntz (ed.), *Formal Representations in Human Judgment*, pp. 53–90. Wiley, New York.

Hogarth, Robin M. (1980). *Judgement and Choice: The Psychology of Decision*. Wiley, Chichester.

Hull, John C., Peter G. Moore, and Howard Thomas (1973). 'Utility and its measurement', *Journal of the Royal Statistical Society, Series A*. **136**, 226–247.

Humphreys, Patrick C., and Wendy McFadden (1980). 'Experiences with MAUD: aiding decision structuring versus bootstrapping the decision maker', *Acta Psychologica*, pp. 51–69.

Jungermann, Helmut, and Ingrid von Ulardt (1982). 'The role of the goal in representing decision problems'. In Humphreys, P. C. and A. Vari (eds.). *Analysing and Aiding Decision Processes*. North-Holland, Amsterdam.

Kaufman, Gordon M., and Howard Thomas (eds.) (1977). *Modern Decision Analysis*. Penguin, Harmondsworth.

Keeney, Ralph L., and Howard Raiffa (1976). *Decisions with Multiple Objectives: Preferences and Value Tradeoffs*. Wiley, New York.

Kruskal, J. B. (1964a). 'Multi-dimensional scaling by optimizing goodness of fit to a non-metric hypothesis', *Psychometrika*, pp. 1–28.

Kruskal, J. B. (1964b). 'Non-metric multi-dimensional scaling: a numerical method', *Psychometrika*, pp. 115–129.

Kunreuther, Howard C., and Paul J. H. Schoemaker (1980). 'Decision analysis for complex systems: Integrating descriptive and prescriptive components'. Working Paper. Department of Decision Sciences, University of Pennsylvania.

Little, John D. C. (1970). 'Models and managers: the concept of a decision calculus', *Management Science*, Apr. pp. B466–B485.

Lock, Andrew R. (1979). Multiple criterion strategic marketing problems: an analytical approach. Unpublished doctoral dissertation, London Business School.

Lock, Andrew R. (1982). 'A strategic business decision with multiple objectives: the Bally men's shoe problem', *Journal of the Operational Research Society*, Apr., pp. 327–332.

Lock, Andrew R., and Howard Thomas (1978). 'An appraisal of multi-attribute utility models in marketing', *Management Bibliographies and Reviews*, **4**, 117–130.

Lock, Andrew R., and Howard Thomas (1982). 'Screening multi-attributed marketing strategy alternatives'. Working Paper. Department of Business Administration, University of Illinois at Urbana-Champaign.

Moore, Peter G., Howard Thomas, Derek W. Bunn, and Juliet M. Hampton (1976). *Case Studies in Decision Analysis*. Penguin, Harmondsworth.

Newman, J. G. (1977). 'Differential weighting in multi-attribute utility measurement: When it should not and when it does make a difference'. *Organizational Behavior and Human Performance*, **20**, 312–325.

Newman, J. W. (1971). *Management Applications of Decision Theory*. Harper & Row, New York.

Pratt, John W. (1964). 'Risk aversion in the small and in the large', *Econometrica*, **32**. 122–136.

Raiffa, Howard (1968a). *Decision Analysis*. Addison-Wesley, Reading, Mass.

Raiffa, Howard (1968b). *Preferences for Multi-Attributed Alternatives*. Rand Monograph RM-5868. Rand Corporation, Santa Monica, CA.

Shepard, R. N. (1964). 'On subjectively optimal selection among multi-attribute alternatives', in M. W. Shelly and G. L. Bryan (eds), *Human Judgments and Optimality*. Wiley, New York.

Shocker, Allan D., and V. Srinivasan (1979). 'Multiattribute approaches for product-concept evaluation and generation: a critical review', *Journal of Marketing Research*, **16** (May), 159–180.

Slovic, Paul, and Sarah Lichtenstein (1971). 'Comparison of Bayesian and regression approaches to the study of information processes in judgment', *Organizational Behavior and Human Performance*, **6**, 649–744.

Toda, Masanao (1976). 'The decision process: a perspective', *International Journal of General Systems*, pp. 79–88.

Watson, Stephen R., and Rex V. Brown (1978). 'The valuation of decision analysis', *Journal of the Royal Statistical Society, Series A*. **141**, 69–78.

Wind, Yoram, and Thomas L. Saaty (1980). 'Marketing applications of the analytic hierarchy process'. *Management Science*, July, pp. 641–658.

Yntema, D. B., and W. S. Torgerson (1961). 'Man-computer co-operation in decisions requiring common-sense'. *IEEE Transactions on Human Factors in Electronics*, **HFE-2**, 20–26.

5.3

Strategy as Maintaining a Viable Organizational Entity in a Competitive Market

ROBIN WENSLEY
London Business School

The overall strategic direction of the diversified firm must be concerned with both the economic viability of its constituent units with respect to their individual markets and also the maintenance of an overall corporate entity or identity. It is perhaps no accident that the former aspects have become developed in the context of marketing strategy whilst the latter have tended to be the purview of organizational behaviour. Even when issues of both decision process and organizational design are raised within the area of marketing strategy the concern often remains exclusively one of economic viability. Hence some of the prescriptions in these areas can be dangerously partial because they fail to recognize the equal importance of corporate identity. Equally a concern for such issues raises crucial questions about the relationship between various forms of analysis in marketing strategy and the overall model of strategic direction itself.

In this paper we will first consider the overall concept of strategy in a business context, and how such concepts influence the role of marketing strategy. We will then consider how the overall balance between unit viability and corporate identity is achieved through various organizational forms, and the implications of such solutions in the context of a complex competitive market. A better understanding of the responsibilities of both corporate and local management, and how such levels interact, provides a framework in which various key issues in marketing strategy can be addressed. In particular, first, the strategic relevance of the information system at both local and corporate levels, which is often based on accounting data and restricted by the existing organizational structure. Second, the problem of ambiguity in the appropriate unit of analysis where simple organizational reporting needs often conflict with a balanced view of the interaction between cost structure, customer segmenta-

Strategic Marketing and Management

tion, and competitor positions. Finally we will consider the implications of such an approach for the criteria to be applied to forms of analysis in strategic marketing.

THE CONCEPTS OF STRATEGY

Two dominant traditions have influenced thinking about the meaning of strategy in a business context: the military perspective and an ecological view. One of the earlier examples of such comparisons is to be found in Anthony (1965) and there have been a number of more recent works emphasizing the application of military strategy principles to a business context (Henderson, 1979; Widmer, 1980; Kotler and Singh, 1981).

The military generally start with, amongst others, two crucial assumptions: that certain resources are only available from captive suppliers, and that conflict can be seen in terms of direct readjustment of territorial boundaries at the expense of the enemy. Neither of these assumptions apply with the same force in a business context, although it must be admitted that even in military terms there is a distinction between the direct territorial approach of a Clausewitz and the more subtle oriented approach of a writer like Sun Tzu (Griffith, 1963). Of couse, there are critical resources in a business context analogous to the military resources of men, materials, and supplies but there is also generally a third party open to negotiation for the supply of such resources at a market price when they are required. Patton could not find an alternative supplier for gas for his tanks but most corporations can raise further cash from outsiders if they suddenly happen on a new, attractive investment opportunity. Life is not quite as simple as this: in particular short-term problems may mean that the cost of such cash turns out to be high and a financial policy of maintaining some level of cash reserve against such eventualities can prove prudent.

On the other hand, in the longer term this would suggest that we should be more concerned to conserve those business strategic resources for which the external supply market is likely to be either poor or expensive. Hence marketing capabilities and know-how should perhaps be the basis for some forms of strategic analysis rather than the almost exclusive focus on cash which underpins a number of recent forms of marketing strategic analysis (Wensley, 1981).

The military model of one-on-one competition over territory contrasts very directly with the ecological model which is concerned with the survival characteristics of various species types (Hannan and Freeman, 1977). One useful distinction in the ecological analogy relates to the means for species to coexist: in particular, the distinction between r-types (broadly, those that survive on the basis of their rapid rate of reproduction) and k-type species (broadly, those which depend on their abilities as specialists within an ecological niche). In a market context there is some equivalence to the growth patterns of new markets in which in the early stages we are concerned with broad volume expansion whilst in a maturing market specialization and segmentation become dominant issues. The difference lies in the fact that there would appear to be no fundamental constraint preventing an '*r* type' firm undergoing meta-morphosis to a '*k* type' one or vice-versa as market conditions change. It does, however, seem to be true that such changes are in practice both difficult and very costly (Abernathy and Wayne, 1974; Cooper and Schendel, 1976). Hence the issue of deciding the balance between specialization and adaptability: the problem being that it is much easier to recognize the criteria for a good specializer than a good adapter before the event. This may suggest that it is much more important to have a particular strategic focus at any one time but also, as an integral part, a means of assessing the continuing relevance of such a focus. We will return to this particular concern when we consider some of the choices in organizational form.

Both ecological and military strategies also raise basic questions about the nature of strategy itself. Indeed the ecological approach raises questions about any element of purposeful choice at all: successful survival of a particular species can hardly be ascribed to its strategy in any meaningful sense. Aldrich (1979) has therefore argued that strategic choices open to organizations are fairly restricted compared with the view of Child (1972) that strategic choice encompasses real choices about organizational form and process as well as product-market selection and measures to manipulate the firms environment. The ecological notion of a niche, although it has recently been adopted by strategists, (Henderson 1983) actually raises a number of further issues about the underlying failure of the relationship between the firm and its environment (Boxer and Wensley 1983). In the military context, too, there are obvious concerns: there is a wide recognition that what happens on the actual battlefield is almost always confused and dependent on the judgement of the local commanders. Napoleon is, for instance, reputed to have said 'No strategy ever survived a battle.' In response to some of these concerns, military strategists have often applied themselves to general overall issues, recognizing that the brilliance of an individual field commander may often mean success against the rather weak strategic rules.

Such rules themselves have focused on two separate aspects: external behaviour with respect to the enemy and the maintenance of internal strength. The external issues—those of massing, surprise, and logistics—have clear relevance in a competitive strategy context and have indeed been often considered. The internal dimension has, however, been less widely addres-sed. Yet military strategists have recognized that success is as much a function of the psychological strength of one's own troops as their actual level of hardware support. It is the maintenance of this balance between external and internal concerns that we wish to look at more closely in a business context. In such a context, however, the actual issue appears in a rather different guise. The problem becomes one of balancing the need for economic viability, in a range of distinct markets against diverse competition with the need for a corporate identity.

ECONOMIC VIABILITY AND ORGANIZATIONAL IDENTITY

A diversified firm operating in a range of product-markets faces strong pressures to decentralize management so that resources can be set at the most efficient level for each specific activity. In a competitive market such pressures on other competitors are self-reinforcing: as the competition becomes more efficiently targeted on a particular product-market so commercial survival depends on matching such improvements. This is not to suggest that in certain instances there may not be sound economic reasons for maintaining a significant degree of central control. In the context of multinational enterprises, for instance, Doz (1980) has coined the term 'economic imperative' to cover the requirements for integration and rationalization to achieve continued economic success. Such a situation is most common when product-markets are spanned by crucial technological requirements, in the form of either very large economic plants or research and development, with limited if any access to alternative sources of supply besides those developed within the firm. In many other instances, however, the 'economic imperative' for the diversified firm is towards greater decentralization rather than centralization. Such pressures therefore raise questions as to the rationale and mechanisms that hold these diverse product-market operations together.

Lawrence and Lorsch (1967) in their original study claimed to have shown that a high-performing organization was one in which the degree of differentiation was matched to the environmental demands but balanced by the complexity of the integrative devices. However, two concerns arise when this work is considered in the context of organizational design for the multi-product, multi-market firm. First, the linkage they established between organizational design variables and measures of economic performance was fairly tenuous given the small size of their sample. Second, the differentiated units that they studied were activities such as research and development units, and sales. Such units could not, except from an extreme economic viewpoint, be hived off in the same way as individual product-market units in a more diversified firm. Allen (1970) did extend their work to such relationship between divisions and headquarters in highly diversified firms. On the basis of a sample of two it is interesting that differentiation became defined in terms of required product-market diversity, and integration was seen much more in terms of achieving control over total profitability and funds flow.

Lawrence and Lorsch (1967: 11) originally defined both differentiation and integration:

Differentiation as we define it in this study—the difference in cognitive and emotional orientation among managers in different functional departments . . . we define integration—the quality of the state of collaboration that exists among departments that are required to achieve unity of effort by the demands of the environment.

From a marketing and economic point of view the important distinction is that they were not concerned with differentiated outputs for the organization *per se* but with the different ways of thinking and working in various units. Hence we are not dealing with the more simple problem of producing a range of products for different market segments which might be open to analysis and solution by technical means. We are dealing with situations in which different market areas demand different ways of thinking and hence managing.

However, from the strategy perspective we can also argue that if these different market areas require such different types of market management, we should question whether they should be put under one organization at all: they could be split off as separate entities. A good example of this has been in the grocery retail business in the UK. The major manufacturers have generally decided that the business of running retail outlets requires such a different managerial style that such activities are best hived off and relationships conducted through the external market system. Hence Ranks Hovis McDougall disposed of Wheatsheaf in the 1960s and Unilever of MacFisheries in the 1970s. It will be interesting to discover whether Texas Instruments, or indeed a number of other major electronics manufacturers, are not forced to come to the same conclusion in the US in the long run.

Hence, an obvious option to be considered alongside the Lawrence and Lorsch solution of more and more complex integrative devices is in fact to hive off the differentiated activities completely so that resource allocation choices between them are mediated solely by the external capital market. Alternatively we can consider the nearest internal solution to this option: that of an internal capital market between autonomous business units.

The choices of organizational form in response to an increased requirement for differentiated activities to sustain economic viability move in two directions: we can either develop complex matrix structures so as to retain the required complexity of integrative devices, or we can choose to simplify the integrative mechanisms substantially so that the only significant linkage becomes one related to cash flows in a strategic business unit (SBU) structure (Galbraith and Nathanson, 1978). To consider the long-term viability of the latter option we must look more closely at the choice between an internal and an external market.

EXTERNAL VERSUS INTERNAL MARKETS

It is crucial if we are to assess the long-term viability of the SBU organizational form that we recognize the extent to which, in its pure form, it represents the adoption of an internal rather than an external market mechanism to facilitate resource allocation decisions between the various units.

Williamson's work (1975), with its focus on transaction costs, addresses very directly the issue of the comparative advantages of external and internal markets. In one sense we can argue that internal markets are merely a more exaggerated response to the problems of building goodwill and trust which we commonly observe in stable industrial markets. The transaction cost approach emphasizes the problems inherent in the high degree of potential opportunism and the difficulties in developing enforceable contingent contracts which make the recourse to the external market more costly than the internal solution. We must always recognize that the external market option is available and that in choosing to organize certain commercial relationships within the firm assumptions are being made about the relative effectiveness of the external market.

This concern is particularly relevant in the case of the multi-divisional structure which Williamson characterizes as an internal capital market. Given a number of relatively independent divisions or indeed SBUs, we must consider why one should draw a boundary round them and treat them as one organizational entity at all. After all, if they are really totally independent the logic would be to place them on the external capital market and indeed there is some evidence from the current popularity of spin-offs that this course of action may well have value in certain instances.

Williamson, however, argues that under certain circumstances we can expect an internal capital market to perform more effectively than an external one. He considers such potential efficiencies in terms of the economics of both control and also of atmosphere. He also argues that economists are in general uncomfortable with the concept of atmosphere and, indeed, most of his own analysis of the potential benefits of an internal organization are expressed in control terms. In general he argues that corporate management can have comparative advantages in terms of access, audit, and adaptation in their management of subsidiaries. They have much better access to unit information than the external market, a facility to conduct an audit on a more cooperative rather than competitive basis, and finally the means to encourage adaptation in current activities rather merely to dispose of the relevant assets. Corporate realists might argue that he underestimates the tensions between corporate and divisional management (Prahalad and Doz, 1981; Doz and Prahalad, 1981) whilst market purists might argue that the extent to which such managers behave in a cooperative fashion is merely a reflection of their mutual collusion against the interests of their shareholders. If therefore we have doubts about even the value of the potential benefits defined by Williamson, we must, *a fortiori*, have bigger doubts about the long-run viability of the internal capital market and hence the maintenance of an organizational boundary around such independent SBUs.

It is, of course, possible to suggest other benefits that Williamson has not emphasized: for instance, the opportunities for regrouping units in response to changing circumstances and a means whereby investment options can be developed in a less hostile environment. Such potential benefits are, however, not totally consistent with the view that business strategy should be seen in terms of resource allocation decisions between independent business units. We will return later to some of the implications of such changes. We can also develop the transaction cost approach in a somewhat different manner and consider a viable organizational entity as one which encompasses those sets of transactions which can be conducted on a more efficient basis within a single organization rather than mediated through the market mechanism. To consider the implications of such a definition we must look more closely at the choice between institutional and market relationships.

INSTITUTIONAL VERSUS MARKET RELATIONSHIPS

In marketing experience it is common to observe that relationships between buyer and seller are long-established, mutually advantageous, and maintained by both parties. It is clear that the distinction between the totally depersonal- ized market relationship of the pure market and institutional transactions within the organization actually becomes much less marked in practice. This has led a number of writers to comment on the reworked nature of interorganizational relationships, particularly in the context of distribution channels (Hammarkist *et al.*, 1982).

From a marketing strategy perspective a viable organizational entity will be one which satisfies its diverse markets in an economically efficient way, as well as one which maintains sustainable boundaries around its activities. Two broad criteria should influence our judgement about the sustainability of such boundaries.

First, we must consider the extent to which there is a case for an institutional rather than a market-based transaction. If one of the parties is required to undertake an idiosyncratic investment and can only reap the benefit by a commercial arrangement with another party, then there is a significant risk of opportunism and the need to establish some norm of reciprocity to ensure an efficient transaction.

Second, we can consider the nature of sustainable organizational bound- aries; the concept of a boundary implies some sort of barrier which makes crossing difficult. Hence sustainable organizational boundaries appear to be strongly related to the concept of mobility barriers as developed by Caves and Porter (1977). A mobility barrier is a limitation that is placed on others who seek direct imitation of the successful. Such barriers can obviously arise in a number of ways of which the most obvious is legal restrictions.* Other forms of

---

* This definition of legal barriers to imitability might suggest that they are inevitably against the public interest. In fact we must recognize that an *ex post* mobility barrier is merely the *ex ante* guarantee of security from imitation that makes it economic for the entrepreneur to take the initial risk (Demsetz 1982).

mobility barrier can be interpreted as a result of 'uncertain imitability' (Lippmann and Rumelt, 1980). The problem from a strategy perspective is the extent to which such barriers are recognizable before, rather than after, the development of the market (Wensley, 1981).

In general, however, with specific exceptions in the cases of corporate branding and to a lesser extent specific distribution channels, an investigation of idiosyncratic investments and imitability will tend to focus at the individual business unit level rather than the overall corporate entity. The problem, therefore, of understanding the basis for sustainable boundaries around the overall organization rather than its constituent businesses remains.

CURRENT CHOICES IN ORGANIZATIONAL FORM

Strategic business unit structures have been enthusiastically adopted by various organizations (Hall, 1978). However, as Day (1981a) recently commented, a great deal has been written about the desirability of SBU structures but very little on how to decide appropriate groupings. The preceding analysis also suggests that if they are held together solely by financial control and investment appraisal then they will, in the long run, prove less effective than separate independent entities.

In many such situations, however, the matrix form of organization seems to offer no real solution. Experience suggests that although the matrix does provide a means whereby selected critical perspectives and conflicts rise to the surface it does not encourage resolution of such conflicts at lower levels in the organization. As a result senior management tend to become overloaded and often face a number of difficult choices (Prahalad, 1976; Peters 1979).

The failure to resolve such problems is not, however, a reflection of poor managerial performance at lower levels despite the entreaties from many academics for better 'understanding' amongst these very managers (Davis and Lawrence, 1978). The managers understand only too well: the problems that they face are of a different order. They represent clashes between the demands of individual products, market developments, and technology: the choices to be made will indeed determine the strategic direction of the company but they cannot be made purely by finding the mid-point in the argument. Matrix structures are therefore an effective means of surfacing such conflicts but not of resolving them. In a similar manner one can also consider particular forms of decision process designed to surface crucial strategic assumptions (Mason, 1969; Mitroff and Emshoff, 1979; Mitroff and Mason, 1980). In this sense the choice lies between building such a process into the overall organizational structure or reintroducing it for each particular decision. Both approaches assume that the actual process of argument and dialogue will resolve the particular conflicts that arise, whereas the SBU structure generally avoids the problem by imposing pre-emptive decisions before the alternative options are even surfaced.

Because any matrix needs to be designed to represent critical dimensions for future decisions there are further problems in determining the actual number and nature of the relevant dimensions. In one particular instance recently, involving computer equipment, we identified five obvious matrix dimensions: industry end-user, product, geography, application, and technology.* Any even workable matrix structure would mean that certain dimensions would have to be eliminated or at least given a very subordinate role.

What choices do we therefore have between the economic inefficiency of the matrix structure and the long-term threat to organizational identity of the SBU system? Although Weitz and Anderson (1981) recognize two critical elements in their contingency view of organizations—unpredictability and interconnectedness in the environment—they still end up with a choice between such options.

In one sense, however, the choice of organizational form brings us close to one element in the nature of organizational survival. The problem is about building an organization that can, over time, both exploit an effective strategy and at the same time continue to monitor the relevance of the strategy; a concept very akin to that developed by Schon (1975) in 'double-loop learning'. Hence Peters (1979) emphasizes how organizations have to adopt temporary focusing devices, often dependent on a visionary CEO, to assess the continued relevance of the existing organization without losing a long-term sense of direction. Such a solution can hardly be described, however, as ideal: visionaries, after all, have also been known to be wrong.

If we return to the argument that economic viability depends on units which can compete effectively in their own product-markets then the underlying problem is that we are looking at the wrong methods to achieve identity and coherence within such a diversified unit structure. The cash and resource allocation system common to the SBU approach is designed to differentiate units rather than hold them together. On the other hand the co-ordinators and committees of the matrix structure often hinder economic viability by increasing costs and delaying decisions. Other means of integration are also possible, however, based more directly on the concept of the economics of atmosphere which was discussed above in the context of Williamson's (1975) work. We have chosen to designate such activities means to secondary integration, to distinguish them from the more recognized methods for linking together diverse product market units via cash and resource control.

---

* Not surprisingly such a list is close to that suggested by Garda (1981), for strategic segmentation: customer use, production economics, geography, buying factors and customer size.

A CONCEPT OF SECONDARY INTEGRATION

Primary integration based on cash and resource control within a SBU structure is unlikely to assist corporate management in their attempt to achieve better economic performance from the business units than could be expected if such units operated independently. The evidence of both the realities of orgnizational decision processes (Bower, 1970; Hall, 1973) and also the nature of crucial information about specific commercial opportunities (Day, 1981b; Wensley, 1982) emphasizes the extent to which unit management has the commercial advantage. In making resource allocation choices corporate management would appear to face an invidious choice (Boxer and Wensley 1984): they either have to second-guess their local management on the basis of more limited information, or else go through a ritual in which they ask a few standard questions and then accept the underlying assumptions.

There are other areas of concern to be considered: that of monitoring the continued commercial relevance of the unit designations; a focus on the development of better options for resource allocation choices (rather than on the allocation problem between available options), and the development of more effective local management. A focus on such activities in the relationship between local and corporate management would suggest a rather different set of concerns than that implied by the more common concept of integration in terms of resolving various forms of direct resource conflict. It is perhaps no surprise that Ohmae (1981) argues that many experts have failed to recognize the real strength of Japanese industry which lies in such things as individual development, structured flexibility, group harmony, and a respect for the detailed knowledge at the operating level. Similarly Ouchi (1981) draws Japanese comparisons in his Theory *z* organization to argue that a sense of identity and corporate commitment can overcome complex and expensive control problems.

Such an approach does imply rather different behaviour by corporate management. Encouraging both the development of options and also diverse parts of the corporation to get together, when they appear to be working on similar problems, suggests a role for top management as 'fixers'. As good fixers they should be much less concerned with public displays of power through formal rejection of resource proposals and much more concerned with being aware of the embryonic and informal ideas being developed in their divisions: perhaps Marcus Seiff was not getting it all wrong when he first decided to spend a significant amount of his time with his store assistants on his vists to Marks and Spencer's stores as well as the local management.

We will now consider how this rather different view influences three key issues in marketing strategy: the role of the information system in helping maintain flexibility of organizational form; the appropriate unit of analysis for commercial performance, and the criteria to be applied to various forms of analysis.

MAINTAINING FLEXIBILITY IN ORGANIZATIONAL FORM

The appropriateness of any existing organizational structure can only be tested if forms of information are available which are not constrained by the existing structure itself. In practice we often return to the limitations of the accounting system, with its failure to reflect crucial market factors (Simmonds, 1982). More fundamentally, the accounting information system often represents the dominant influence in the symbolic domain for many managers whereby they both make sense of, and action choices in, the physical domain (Boland, 1979; Hopwood, 1978).

It is the potential distinction between the range of forms of information, from computerized systems to the archetypal back of the envelope, that make up any individual's symbolic domain and the physical domain (Boxer and Wensley, 1981), which enables us to revisit the Lawrence and Lorsch (1967) definition of differentiation in a rather different way. They saw differentiation as the problem of differences in cognitive orientation amongst different managers: the cognitive orientation for each manager was fixed. By uncoupling the symbolic domain from the physical one, in that it is no longer merely a reflection, we can provide the facility whereby individual managers can develop and explore different cognitive orientations themselves.

Hence the diagnostic process can only develop to challenge the appropriateness of the current physical domain if information can be built up in ways which cross the organizational structure. In many marketing organizations this involves a move away from the bias towards cost and profit data and a greater emphasis on market and competitive performance (Simmonds, 1981). It often also involves a total change in the dimensions used. In the recent case of a UK regional brewery, for instance, we discovered that organizational reporting was, effectively, along different elements of asset ownership: with distinctions between both managed and tenanted outlets for the tied trade and between clubs and retail outlets for the 'free' trade. Marketing information, however, was in terms of brands and products: bitter, lager, wines and spirits. Although the problem of merely relating performance between one set of data and another was severe, neither set of dimensions really addressed the crucial market benefits to either consumers or owners of independent outlets.

In one sense these concerns are similar to those expressed by Little (1970) in his original concern for 'decision calculus' models which has led to such approaches as STRATPORT (Larreche and Srinivasan, 1981) in strategic marketing. However, the problem with such approaches is they often fail to start with the market assumptions of the user: the language of market response functions is rarely the language of marketing executives. Equally, such approaches are in fact often a strong reflection of the existing organizational structure. Hence we need to develop information systems which are much more capable of responding to the conceptual models of individual managers, and which may well span a number of established organizational or indeed product-market boundaries.

THE UNIT OF ANALYSIS

The crucial issues in the design of the information system can also be intepreted in terms of common problems of deciding the appropriate unit for strategic analysis, addressed by Cravens and Lamb (1982). The problem is that specific choices have to be made for organizational and control purposes, often in fact on the basis of assets and hence cost structures, whilst longer-term strategic relevance depends on the interaction between such asset structures, the developing customer segments, and competitive behaviour. In our experience an analysis of the relationship between, for instance, cost elements and served market segments often provides useful information but fails to indicate a single answer to the unit of analysis question.

We should therefore address the unit of analysis issue from the three different perspectives, broadly characterized as cost structure, customer segmentation, and competitor portfolio. As we have discussed earlier, however, it should be possible to interpret the results of such an analysis in one perspective into another, since the competitive marketplace provides the mechanism whereby long-run profits can only be achieved through a sustainable competitive advantage. In particular such considerations mean that what appears as a desirable investment from a strategic marketing perspective should also prove to be one which shows a positive net present value in financial analysis (Brealey and Myers, 1980).

FORMS OF ANALYSIS IN STRATEGIC MARKETING

We can justify any form of analysis in decision-making on one of two criteria: it either reflects well-established empirical regularities which should be considered in the particular decision, or else it helps to test the implicit or explicit models being used by the relevant executives against the available data. On top of this, we have implied some further criteria in the case of strategic marketing analysis.

First, we have to consider the choice between the development of a number of independent, relatively simple forms of analysis compared with a single comprehensive approach. The problem with the latter approach is that the process required may both restrict the development of options and also fail to reflect crucial ambiguities in the information about the competitive market. For instance, the development of the analytical hierarchy process, proposed by

Wind and Saaty (1980) requires both a strong belief in the value of procedural rationality (Burton and Naylor, 1980), for which there is little evidence (Mintzberg *et al.*, 1976), and also a strong focus on the resource allocation role of top management, contradicting the concerns raised above.

Second, we need to consider the related issue as to the extent to which the forms of analysis impose a very specific structure on the problem or alternatively provide a means for exploring crucial assumptions. It is often the case that the process of decision-taking is the means whereby choices are made between contradictory forms of analysis (Lindblom, 1959, 1977). Complex portfolio approaches may introduce greater computational power and hence bigger models, but may also be of limited long-term value because they fail to reflect the actual political context within which strategic decisions are taken.

Third, there is a need for a more effective comparison between the results of, on the one hand, market-based analysis and, on the other, financial appraisal of individual investment projects (Wensley, 1981; Wensley, Barwise and Marsh, 1984). As discussed above, the competitive marketplace provides the means whereby both the value of productive assets and also particular product-market segments can be determined. The process may, of course, be untidy but as Woodward (1982) has observed the problem of a turbulent environment for some organizations is merely the reverse side of a commercial opportunity well taken by others. A more effective comparison of marketing and finance perspectives at the operating level should mean that marketing strategy considerations are influential at the point where it really matters: when money is being spent.

Fourth, there is the continuing concern of relating operating activities to strategic requirements. As suggested above this can partly be resolved by encouraging more effective project evaluation at the operating level. Beyond this there is perhaps a danger that we too readily assume that strategy, by definition, dominates operations. After all, despite Drucker's impressive rhetoric, there is actually very limited evidence that 'doing the right thing is more important that doing things right'. We could equally well argue that 'doing things right makes it the right thing to do'. Hence, as discussed, top management faces an uncomfortable dilemma: they inevitably have less information about product-market specifics than their own local management, but often find themselves in the apparent role of deciding between various options in product-market terms. In effect it has been argued above that the way out of this dilemma is to reinterpret the crucial priorities for corporate management.

Corporate management must be concerned with the degree to which the overall organization is designed to reflect the desired strategic direction. This is distinct from the question of individual resource allocation choices since these will arise within the structure at a later date. Marketing analysis in this context should provide guidelines as to those areas which need to be integrated internally and those where interrelationships can be conducted on an internal or external market basis. In the context of individual resource allocation choices it has been suggested that corporate management needs, in effect, to work with local management rather than wait and then choose between the proffered options. This would suggest that, in general, the consensus development process (Nielsen, 1981; Simmonds, 1982) is much more likely to be effective than the conflict-based approach (Doz and Prahalad, 1981). To aid this process, we need to develop forms of marketing analysis which can assist in creating an effective dialogue.

CONCLUSION

Strategy in a business context must reflect a concern for both economic viability and the maintenance of an overall organizational entity. Whilst such concerns are recognized in military strategy, there is also a clear recognition that it is more important to respond to the specifics of any situation rather than set unalterable rules before battle is joined.

A competitive market perspective throws a rather new light on a number of current organizational design issues. Careful justification has to be made, not only for the choice of strategic business unit designations, but also for the decision to retain them within the corporate entity. Within such an SBU structure we need to establish various systems designed to exploit the potential benefits of a corporate entity. These include a flexible information system, a means of encouraging the development of new options, and an effective process of local management development.

Various forms of analysis are required in the area of marketing strategy. At the local unit level a range of different and sometimes conflicting answers, are required rather than one comprehensive approach. In the interaction between local and corporate management we require forms of analysis which aid both parties in exploring crucial market-based assumptions.

REFERENCES

Abernathy, William J. and Kenneth Wayne (1974). 'Limits of the learning curve', *Harvard Business Review*, **52** (Sept.–Oct.), 109–119.
Aldrich, Howard E. (1979). *Organisations and Environments*. Prentice Hall, Englewood Cliffs, N.J.
Allen, Stephen A. III, (1970). 'Corporate–divisional relationships in highly diversified firms', in Jay W. Lorsch and Paul R. Lawrence (eds), *Studies in Organisational Design*. Richard D. Irwin, Homewood IL.
Anthony, Robert N. (1965). *Planning and Control Systems: A Framework for Analysis*. Division of Research, Graduate School of Business Administration, Harvard University, Boston, (in particular Appendix B: Caplan, Robert H., 'Relationship between principles of military strategy and principles of business planning').
Brealey, Richard, and Stewart Myers (1980). *Principles of Corporate Finance*. McGraw-Hill, New York, N.Y.

Boland, Richard J. (1979). 'Control, causality and information system requirements', *Accounting, Organisations and Society*, **4**(4), 259–272.

Bower, Joseph L. (1970). *Managing the Resource Allocation Process*. Division of Research, Graduate School of Business Administration, Harvard University, Boston.

Boxer, Philip and Robin Wensley (1983), 'Niches and Competition: The Ecology of Market Organization', Research in Marketing Series, 83/8, London Business School, December.

Boxer, Philip, and Robin Wensley (1984), 'The Need for Middle-Out Development of Marketing Strategy', *Journal of Management Studies*, (forthcoming).

Burton, R. M., and T. N. Naylor (1980). 'Economic theory in corporate planning', *Strategic Planning Journal*, **1**(3), 249–263.

Caves, R. E., and M. E. Porter (1977). 'From entry barriers to mobility barriers: conjectural decisions and contrived deterrence to new competition', *Quarterly Journal of Economics*, **XCI** (May), 241–261.

Child, John (1972). 'Organisation structure, environment and performance—the role of strategic choice', *Sociology*, **6** (Jan.), 1–22.

Cooper, A. C., and D. Schendel (1976). 'Strategic responses to technological threats', *Business Horizons*, **19** (Feb.), 61–69.

Cravens, D., and C. Lamb (1982). 'Defining and selecting strategic marketing planning and control units'. AMA Strategic Marketing Workshop, Illinois, May.

Davis, Stanley M., and Paul R. Lawrence (1978). 'Problems of matrix organisations', *Harvard Business Review*, **56**(3) (May–June), 131–142.

Day, George S. (1981a). 'Analytical approaches to strategic market planning', in Ben M. Enis and Kenneth J. Roering (eds), *Review of Marketing*. American Marketing Association, Chicago.

Day, George S. (1981b). 'Strategic market analysis and definition: an integrated approach', *Strategic Management Journal*, **2** (July–Sept.), 281–299.

Demsetz, Harold (1982), 'Barriers to Entry', *The American Economic Review*, **72**(1), March, 47–57.

Doz, Yves L. (1980). 'Strategic management in multinational companies', *Sloan Management Review*, Winter, 27–46.

Doz, Yves L., and C. K. Prahalad (1981). 'Headquarters influence and strategic control in MNCs', *Sloan Management Review*, Fall, pp. 15–29.

Galbraith, Jay R., and Daniel A. Nathanson (1978). *Strategy Implementation: The Role of Structure and Process*. West Publishing, St Paul, MN.

Garda, Robert A. (1981). 'A strategic approach to market segmentation', *McKinsey Quarterly*, Autumn, pp. 16–29.

Griffith, Samuel B. (1963). *Sun-Tzu—The Art of War*. Oxford University Press, London.

Hall, William K. (1973). 'Strategic planning models: are top managers really finding them useful', *Journal of Business Policy*, **3**(2), 33–42.

Hall, William K. (1978), 'SBUs: hot, new topic in the management of diversification', *Business Horizons*, Feb., pp. 17–25.

Hammarkist, K. O., H. Hakansson, and L. G. Mattsson (1982). 'Markets as Networks: an approach to the analysis of specific marketing situations'. Annual Meeting of the European Academy for Advanced Research in Marketing, Antwerp.

Hannan, Michael T., and John Freeman (1977). 'The population ecology of organisations', *American Journal of Sociology*, **82**(5), 929–965.

Henderson, Bruce D. (1979). *Henderson on Corporate Strategy*. Abt Books, Cambridge, MA.

Henderson, Bruce D. (1983), 'The Anatomy of Competition', *Journal of Marketing*, **47**(2), 7–11.

Hopwood, Anthony G. (1978). 'Towards an organisational perspective for the study of accounting and information systems', *Accounting, Organisations and Society*, **3**(1), 3–13.

Kotler, P., and R. Singh (1981). 'Marketing warfare in the 1980s', *McKinsey Quarterly*, Summer, pp. 62–81.

Larreche, J. C., and V. Srinivasan (1980). 'STRATPORT: A decision support system for strategic planning'. Research Paper No. 573, Graduate School of Business, Stanford University, CA.

Lawrence, Paul R., and Jay W. Lorsch (1967). *Organisation and Environment: Managing Differentiation and Integration*. Division of Research, Graduate School of Business Administration, Harvard University, Boston, MA.

Lindblom, Charles E. (1959). 'The science of "muddling through" ', *Public Administration Review*, **19** (Spring), pp. 79–88.

Lindblom, Charles E. (1977). *Politics and Markets*. Basic Books, New York, N.Y.

Lippmann, S. A., and R. P. Rumelt (1980). 'Uncertain imitability and market structure', UCLA Working Paper.

Mason, R. O. (1969). 'A dialectic approach to strategic planning', *Management Science*, **15**(8), (Apr.), B403–B413.

Mintzberg, H. D., D. Raisinghani, and A. Theoret (1976). 'The structure of unstructured decision processes', *Administrative Science Quarterly*, June 1976, pp. 246–275.

Mitroff, Ian I. and J. R. Emshoff (1974). 'On strategic assumption-making—a dialectic approach to policy and planning. *Academy of Management Review*, **4** 1–12.

Mitroff, Ian I., and Richard O. Mason (1980). 'Structuring ill-structured policy issues: further explorations in a methodology for messy problems', *Strategic Management Journal*, **1**, 331–342.

Nielsen, Richard P. (1981). 'Towards a method for building consensus during strategic planning', *Sloan Management Review*, Summer, pp. 29–40.

Ohmae, K. (1981). 'Myths and realities of Japanese corporations', *McKinsey Quarterly*, Summer, pp. 2–20.

Ouchi, William G. (1981). *Theory Z: How American Business Can Meet the Japanese Challenge*. Addison-Wesley, Menlo Park, CA.

Peters, Thomas J. (1979). 'Beyond the matrix organisation', *McKinsey Quarterly*, Autumn, pp. 10–25.

Phillips, Lynn W. (1981). 'Assessing measurement error in key informant reports: a methodological note on organisational analysis in marketing', *Journal of Marketing Research*, **XVIII** (Nov.), 395–415.

Prahalad, C. K. (1976). 'Strategic choices in diversified MNCs', *Harvard Business Review*, July–Aug., pp. 67–78.

Prahalad, C. K., and Yves L. Doz (1981). 'An approach to strategic control in MNCs', *Sloan Management Review*, Summer, pp. 5–13.

Schon, Donald A. (1975). 'Deutero-learning in organisations: learning for increased effectiveness', *Organisational Dynamics*, Summer, pp. 2–16.

Simmonds, Kenneth (1981). 'Strategic management accounting'. ICMA Working Paper, London Business School, London, England.

Simmonds, Kenneth (1982). 'Global strategy and the control of market subsidiaries', *Research in Marketing Series*, **82**(7), London Business School, London, England, July.

Weitz, Barton, and Erin Anderson (1981). 'Organising the marketing function', in Ben M. Enis and Kenneth J. Roering (eds), *Review of Marketing 1981*. American Marketing Association, Chicago, IL.

Wensley, Robin (1981). 'Marketing strategy: betas, boxes or basics', *Journal of Marketing*, **45** (Summer), 173–182.

Wensley, Robin (1982). 'PIMS and BCG: new horizon or false dawn?', *Strategic Management Journal*, **3**, 147–158.

Wensley, Robin, Patrick Barwise and Paul Marsh, 'Strategic Investment Decisions', *Research in Marketing*, JAI Press [forthcoming]

Widmer, H. (1980). 'Business lessons from military strategy', *McKinsey Quarterly*, Spring, pp. 59–67.

Williamson, O. E. (1975). *Markets and Heirarchies: Analysis and Anti-Trust Implications*. Free Press, New York, N.Y.

Wind, Y., and T. Saaty (1980). 'Marketing applications of the analytical hierarchy process', *Management Science*, July, pp. 641–658.

Woodward, S. N. (1982). 'The myth of turbulence', *Futures*, Aug., pp. 266–279.

Strategic Marketing and Management
Edited by H. Thomas and D. Gardner
© 1985 John Wiley & Sons Ltd

CHAPTER 6
Generic Strategic Marketing Prescriptions

INTRODUCTION

The most visible planning tools in current marketing literature are frameworks involving product and business portfolios. Such portfolio approaches are referred to in many of the papers in this volume. They have also appeared in many marketing textbooks and have been the subject of much debate and, unfortunately, much misunderstanding.

The growth/share matrix approach of the Boston Consulting Group was an innovative and forward-looking approach to the increasing complexity of the competitive environment. This well-known approach combined the implications of the experience curve with a well-articulated relationship between market share and profitability. Of similar vintage and familiarity is the business assessment array closely associated with General Electric. This approach focuses on the strategic dimensions of industry attractiveness and business strengths. At least seven other product and business portfolios exist (Wind and Mahajan, 1981). These include the business profile matrix, directional policy matrix, product performance matrix, conjoint analysis-based approach, analytic hierarchy process, risk/return model, and stochastic dominance.

Many articles have been written about the portfolio approach and several are of particular relevance to those interested in marketing strategy because they address and question the value of market share which is one of the major assumptions of the growth/share matrix approach. For example, if a rather superficial understanding of the relationship between market share and profitability is taken, it is likely that one of two competitive strategies for products and/or businesses will be adopted. Attempts could be made to increase market share so that the share obtained is either the largest or second-largest. Alternatively, that particular product or business could be dropped and a search undertaken for an alternative that would offer an opportunity to achieve a dominant position.

If these generic prescriptions were adopted, a firm with potentially dominant business share position would drive for market share (itself an *outcome* variable not a *strategic* variable) with the expectation that increased ROI would follow. Similarly if a product or business was not in a dominant position, or could not readily become dominant, it was often sold or otherwise liquidated. Yet the Boston Consulting Group, in its writings, had always maintained the viability of a third option; namely, to focus resources upon leadership in a market segment or segments. It appears that although BCG always stressed the strategic segmentation focus, many firms did not understand the strategy of segmentation. Fruhan (1972) confirms the weakness of the uncritical acceptance of market share dominance in his article about 'Pyrrhic victories in the fight for market share'. However, an important offshoot of this use of product and business portfolios was the attempt to better define markets (Porter, 1980). At one extreme it would be possible to define a market so narrowly that your own product or business was the dominant firm. However the search to better define markets has had a positive effect on the practice of marketing.

GENERIC STRATEGIES: SOME SUGGESTIONS

Out of this background have come four articles specifically questioning the assumption of the need to be dominant in a market to maximize profitability. These are refinements of the generic prescriptive strategies previously discussed. The first article suggests that while being dominant in a market is likely to generate high profits as well as leadership, power, and glory, it can present many problems (Bloom and Kotler, 1975). In this article, entitled 'Strategies for high market-share companies', Bloom and Kotler argue that 'the company that acquires a very high market share exposes itself to a number of risks that its smaller competitors do not encounter' (Bloom and Kotler, 1975: 63). The risks occur in the form of attacks by smaller competitors, consumers who tend to focus complaints on large companies if something goes wrong, and the government and its antitrust activities.

Bloom and Kotler's arguments are based on the belief that: 'Much has been written about how a company should go about attaining increases in market share, but little about what it should do once it has attained a large share' (Bloom and Kotler, 1975: 65). As a partial solution the following three-step procedure is suggested:

(1) estimate the relationship between market share and profitability;
(2) estimate the amount of risk associated with each share level;
(3) determine the point at which an increase in market share can no longer be expected to bring enough profit to compensate for the added risks to which the company would expose itself (Bloom and Kotler, 1975: 65).

If carried out carefully, this three-step procedure should yield its optimal market share.

Given the optimal market share size, several strategies for attaining or maintaining this optimal share are presented. Most companies will discover, according to Bloom and Kotler, that they should build share. Share-building strategies which are recommended are based on product innovation, market segmentation, distribution, distribution innovation, and promotional innovation. If share maintenance is the appropriate strategy because market share is optimal, then product innovation and market fortification is recommended to prevent competitors from eroding market share. An alternative strategy would be to reduce share by demarketing (Kotler and Levy, 1971). A risk reduction strategy is appropriate for firms that have a high share but believe it is dangerous because of threats from competitors and government. Risk reduction can be carried out by pacifying competition, forging a link with the government, public relations, diversification, and improving social responsiveness.

It is argued therefore that 'the optimal market share is a function of both profitability and risk, and that any success in reducing the risk surrounding a high share is tantamount to optimizing that share' (Bloom and Kotler, 1975: 70). The Bloom and Kotler article goes a long way toward pointing out that the growth/share matrix approach is more descriptive than prescriptive.

A second article also questions the universality of the relationship between market share and profitability advanced in the PIMS Newsletters. 'Strategies for low market share businesses' opens with two strong statements that are the central thrust of the article (Hamermesh *et al.*, 1978: 95). The authors suggest firstly that: 'many of the inferences that both managers and consultants have been drawing from this finding are erroneous and misleading'. They then argue that: 'In many industries, companies having a low market share consistently outperform their larger rivals and show very little inclination to either expand their share or withdraw from the fight' (Hamermesh *et al.*, 1978: 95). Using Burroughs Corporation, Crown Cork & Seal Co., Inc., and Union Camp Corporation as units of analysis, they emphasize that it is not necessarily market share dominance that determines profitability. The profits of these three firms are the result of four characteristics: 'they carefully segment their markets, they use research and development funds efficiently, they think small, and their chief executives' influence is pervasive' (Hamermesh *et al.*, 1978: 98). Although lack of dominance in a market is not necessarily seen as a handicap, the article does suggest that the less dominant a firm is, the more problems it faces. However the article does emphasize that small is not necessarily bad.

A third, and more recent, article points out where the real problem lies with generalizations such as those relating to market share and profitability. This article is highly critical of the 'implicit causal theory' approach used to justify prescriptions based on PIMS data (Camerer and Fahey, 1983). It is argued that regression analysis using the PIMS data base has often ignored the inherent limitations of regression analysis. Camerer and Fahey are particularly critical of the use of regression analysis because of the general absence of theory testing (Camerer and Fahey, 1983: 3–5). It is suggested that researchers act as if they are using an explicit theory when in fact they are using an implicit theory. Consequently, prescriptions are made, using results of the regression analysis that may or may not apply in a given situation. It could be argued then that those PIMS researchers who have followed this implicit causal theory route have created problems which might not have occurred if some attempt had been made to incorporate even the most elementary concepts of marketing theory.

The questions which should have been asked by these PIMS researchers are those asked of every Ph.D. candidate defending an analytical dissertation:

(1)   Do the results have universal or specific application?
(2)   What is the underlying theory supporting this phenomenon?
(3)   Are there alternative hypotheses?

As Camerer and Fahey say: 'Alternatively, we can ask what assumptions "predict" the share–profitability correlation without justifying the PIMS prescriptive advice' (Camerer and Fahey, 1983: 9). They suggest that two classes of theories would predict a share–profitability correlation. The first is a direct or behavioral effect and the second are stochastic effect theories. They also argue that 'the behavioral interpretation of the share–profitability correlation must be coupled with an assumption of disequilibrium in order to make the PIMS advice valuable' (Camerer and Fahey, 1983: 11). This argument is certainly counter to the widely held equilibrium theory in economics. Therefore it becomes both a hypothesis and a large question mark that must be applied to any implicit causal theory of share–profitability correlation.

Woo and Cooper (1983) report a study that attempts to overcome some of the criticisms leveled by Camerer and Fahey. In this study low market share businesses that are a part of a larger corporate portfolio are examined. Using the developing stream of research on corporate characteristics as determinants of business-level performance, several corporate characteristics were hypothesized to be explanatory variables. Although the findings from this type of research may not yet be considered explicit theory, they are consistent with other findings of the behavioral effect theories.

The specific corporate characteristics hypothesized to explain successful low share businesses are:

portfolio characteristics;
relatedness to other businesses in the corporation;
corporate financial strength.

Using discriminant analysis, successful low-share businesses were compared with ineffective low-share businesses and also with effective high-share businesses. The findings suggest that effective low-share businesses were relatively high-growth businesses within their corporations. Also, in comparison with ineffective low-share businesses, their parent corporations had stronger financial positions and the effective low-share business had a higher level of internal sales. Effective low-share businesses differed from effective high-share businesses as well: low degree of relatedness to other internal divisions, higher level of internal purchases, and greater diversity of their parent corporations (Woo and Cooper, 1983: 16–17).

Part of the confusion in marketing literature surrounding the use of product and business portfolios is that the level of analysis is paid scant attention. Confusion also is created by failing to distinguish carefully between the prescriptive and descriptive nature of the various approaches. A recent article assists in overcoming the potential confusion by outlining seven steps to follow in evaluating or designing a portfolio approach (Wind and Mahajan, 1981). This particular approach is of interest to the study and practice of marketing because it helps clarify the distinction between descriptive and prescriptive approaches and level and unit of analysis. Based on their analysis, Wind and Mahajan conclude that tailor-made approaches are superior for the same reasons mentioned in the four articles discussed above, but also because it is possible to include what is conceptually desirable in an industry and for a firm with its particular strengths and weaknesses. They also suggest that the tailor-made approach stimulates management's creativity, helps gain an advantage over competitors by making it difficult for them to analyse the firm's actions, and finally can be as prescriptive as desirable.

Without explicitly stating their views, it seems clear that each of these articles is arguing for a contingency approach. From both a theoretical and practical viewpoint, a contingency approach is necessary if we are to avoid simplistic solutions.

TOWARDS A CONTINGENCY APPROACH

A step toward the contingency approach is often referred to as competitive analysis. While the techniques of competitive analysis are certainly not new because of the significant contribution of industrial economics, awareness of the general approach of competitive analysis has been heightened by the popularity of the writings of Michael Porter. For Porter 'the essence of formulating competitive strategy is relating a company to its environment' (Porter, 1980: 3). Competition is more than the current competitors, more than your current products and markets. 'Rather, competition in an industry is rooted in its underlying economic structure' (Porter, 1980: 3).

The industry analysis approach of Porter seems to have two main contributions to marketing as it grapples with a contingency approach to marketing strategy. They are his concepts of generic competitive strategies and generic industry environments.

Porter says what Hamermesh *et al.* (1978) only hinted at:

> In coping with the five competitive forces, there are three potentially successful
> generic strategic approaches to outperforming other firms in an industry:
> 1. overall cost leadership
> 2. differentiation
> 3. focus (Porter, 1980: 35).

Note that Porter does not talk about market shares. Rather he talks about such terms as creating a defendable position and outperforming competitors.

Porter lays a good foundation for a contingency-based approach to marketing strategy. He suggests that:

> industry environments differ most strongly in their fundamental strategic
> implications along a number of key dimensions:
> 1. industry concentration
> 2. state of industry maturity
> 3. exposure to international competition (Porter, 1980: 191).

Three of the generic industry environments described by Porter are very familiar to students or practitioners of marketing because of their foundation in the organizational and product life cycle concepts. These generic industry environments are first, emerging industries, second, the transition to industry maturity; and, third, declining industries. It is in these environments that the portfolio approach to product and business planning is most likely to have application. However, due to the complexities of each environment a contingency approach seems very much in order. This certainly would be consistent with the thinking of Wind and Mahajan (1981).

The fourth generic environment is not as familiar. The generic environment of fragmented industries is that type of environment in which no firm has a significant market share and hence there is an absence of market leaders. Much marketing theory seems to assume market leadership. Therefore, this generic environment has seemingly received scant attention in the literature.

The fifth generic environment is global industries. Peter Drucker, in *Managing in Turbulent Times*, suggests that the trend toward global competition represents the most significant structural change facing businesses and governments today (Drucker, 1980). Porter, like Drucker, makes a distinction between international competition and global competition. 'A global industry is one in which the strategic positions of competitors in major geographic or national markets are fundamentally affected by their overall global positions' (Porter, 1980: 275).

It is in the generic environment of global industries (Hout *et al.*, 1982) that the most creative applications of the product and business portfolio concept must be sought and applied. Simplistic descriptions will not be adequate.

Rather, sophisticated approaches using a contingency-based analysis will be of absolute necessity.

Many other authors and articles could have been referenced in this section. However, rather than undertake an exhaustive discussion the intention was to underline the observation that simple, descriptive techniques are severely limited. They are especially limited at the marketing action level because of the lack of prescription. Thus it seems essential to devote greater time and energy to exploring contingency-based approaches to marketing strategy.

REFERENCES

Bloom, Paul N. and Philip Kotler (1975). 'Strategies for high market-share companies', *Harvard Business Review*, **53**(6) (Nov.–Dec.), 63–72.

Camerer, Colin, and Liam Fahey (1983). 'The regression paradigm: a critical appraisal and suggested directions'. Paper presented at Significant Developments in Strategic Management—Business Policy Conference, University of Texas, Arlington, Feb.

Drucker, Peter (1980). *Managing in Turbulent Times*. Harper & Row, New York.

Fruhan, W. E. Jr., (1972). 'Pyrrhic victories in the flight for market share', *Harvard Business Review*, **50**, (September/October) 100–107.

Hamermesh, R. G., M. J. Anderson, and J. E. Harris (1978). 'Strategies for low market share businesses' *Havard Business Review*, **56**, (May/June), 95–102.

Hout, T., M. E. Porter, and E. Rudden (1982). 'How gobal companies win out', *Havard Business Review*, **60** Sept./Oct.)

Kotler, Philip and Sidney J. Levy (1971) "Demarketing, Yes, Demarketing," *Havard Business Review*, **49** (b) (Nov-Dec.)

Porter, Michael E. (1980). *Competitive Strategy*, The Free Press, New York.

Wind, Yoram, and Vijay Mahajan (1981). "Designing product and business portfolios"' *Harvard Business Review*, **59** (Jan/Feb.), 155–165.

Woo, Carolyn Y. and Arnold C. Cooper (1983) 'Corporate settings of effective low share businesses', (this volume) Chapter 6.3).

Introduction to Conference Papers on Generic Strategies

Chapter 6 presents some of the literature on generic strategies and provides a background for the papers in this section. Issues treated range from growth strategies for small-share firms to marketing strategies used by the Japanese.

Kotler and Fahey attempt to provide an insight into Japanese marketing strategy. They conclude that the Japanese are now much better marketers than they were in the 1960s or early 1970s. Yet they point out that the Japanese have not invented any new marketing practices. Neither can their marketing process and success be simply attributed to their alleged penchant for predatory pricing and other questionable practices. They suggest that an understanding of Japanese marketing practices is a necessary prerequisite for US marketers in formulating their competitive battles and strategies with Japanese companies.

Stasch and Ward indicate that recent literature on successful marketing strategies for small-share firms in mature markets suggests two basic courses of action: focus on fast-growth segments and/or develop specialized niches with highly differentiated offerings. They point out that their study demonstrates that three 'refinements' to these two basic courses of action may be needed in order for the small-share firm to successfully achieve growth: (1) maximise competitive differences; (2) minimize competitive response; and (3) develop secure distribution advantage.

Woo and Cooper examine the corporate settings associated with successful low-share businesses. Through discriminant analysis, these businesses are contrasted with: (1) ineffective low-share businesses and (2) effective high-share businesses. Members of the target group appeared to be realatively high-growth businesses within their corporate portfolios. They differed from their ineffective counterparts in the stronger financial position of their parent corporations and in their higher level of internal sales. They differed from effective high-share businesses in their low degree of relatedness to other internal divisions, their higher level of internal purchases, and the greater diversity of their parent corporations.

6.1
Japanese Strategic Marketing: An Overview

PHILIP KOTLER AND LIAM FAHEY
J. L. Kellogg Graduate School of Management,
Northwestern University,
Evanston, Illinois 60201

The intent of this paper is to provide a brief overview of the role of marketing in the success of Japanese firms in the world marketplace. Despite an avalanche of literature on the Japanese way of doing business,* the role of marketing has received negligible attention. Indeed, it is our contention that most people in business, government, and academia have, perhaps unwittingly, downplayed on the importance of marketing in Japan's success.

Our thesis is that marketing is clearly one critical factor among several contributing to Japanese business success, and that marketing must be included in any attempt to provide a full and complete explanation of Japan's success. Japanese firms have demonstrated the capacity to improve their marketing know-how and skills over time, to the point that they are now at least as proficient in marketing as many of their US competitors. Although the Japanese do not follow a uniform marketing approach across markets, a number of patterns and themes in their marketing strategies are evident.

The discussion of Japanese marketing strategy which follows is based upon intensive study of the marketing approach adopted by Japanese firms in a wide variety of industries with particular emphasis upon their entry into the US marketplace and the consequent evolution of their competitive strategy. The focus of this effort has been to trace the scope and direction of the marketing strategy of individual Japanese firms and then to search for commonalities and differences across the strategies.

---

* See Ezra F. Vogel, *Japanese Number One: Lesson for America*, Harvard University Press, Cambridge, Mass.; Richard T. Pascale and Anthony G. Athos, *The Art of Japanese Management*, Simon and Schuster, New York, 1981, and William G. Ouchi, *Theory Z: How American Business Can Meet the Japanese Challenge*, Addison-Wesley, Boston, Mass., 1981.

442 *Strategic Marketing and Management*

JAPANESE MARKETING STRATEGIES

Japanese marketing strategy is characterized by flexibility, incrementalism, and integration. Contrary to popular impressions the Japanese do not follow a uniform marketing approach accross markets.Individual firms manifest a deep-seated capacity to modify their marketing approach. The incremental nature of much of their marketing efforts is perhaps an outgrowth of their flexibility: they adapt to the environmental circumstances confronting them by learning as they go. However, at any point in time the marketing strategy elements of Japanese firms are in 'synch' with each other; they vigorously implement an integrated package of marketing activities, frequently endeavouring to out-compete their competitors on a number of dimensions simultaneously.

Japanese marketing focuses upon the management of product-market evolution. While they compete intensely at the level of marketing tactics, a strategic thrust pervades their marketing efforts. They manage not only the product life cycle of individual products, but the evolution of a complex of product lines and items. What markets are entered, the sequence in which they are entered, and how they are entered are carefully orchestrated.

However, it must be emphasized that Japanese marketing strategy is not predicated upon new marketing principles or techniques. The fountainhead of Japanese marketing success is that they have devoted themselves to thoroughly understanding and applying the existing textbook principles. The ultimate irony for the US is that the Japanese came to the US to study marketing and went home understanding its principles better than most US companies did.

We will characterize Japanese marketing strategies in three stages of market competition: (1) entering a product-market; (2) developing and penetrating a product-market; and (3) maintaining an established position in a product-market.

Japanese market-entry strategies

The key to successful market entry is (1) entering the right markets and (2) entering them right. Japanese firms are skilled in both areas.

Japan as a nation carefully chooses which industries or markets to enter. The emphasis upon choice is captured in the notation of 'targeted' industries. Government and industry mutually recognize important or potentially important industries as high priority areas for national resource commitments. 'Targeted' industries represent the focus of Japanese industry development policies.

A number of factors are desired in the choice of targeted industries: high labor skills, high labor intensity, relatively small natural resource requirements, relatively low raw material import requirements, potential for technology development, high value-added content, and large export potential. It is thus not surprising to find that consumer electronics was one of the initial targeted industries, or that computers, microprocessors, and semiconductors are now receiving heavy emphasis.

The Japanese have long recognized that economies of scale and experience curve effects become more potent through developing new product concepts and existing product modifications that are matched to substantial pockets of unmet demand. They have also sought product-markets which exhibit weak or complacent competition. Such has been the Japanese experience in calculators, watches, radios, televisions, and autos. Product-market sectors are chosen which facilitate product-market development and not simply the capturing of existing markets. A major intent is to establish a beach-head from which related product-market sectors can be attacked.

Once they have identified the right market segment to enter, the Japanese employ a variety of marketing approaches to gain initial market penetration. One common strategy is to bring out smaller, frequently stripped-down versions of standard products. Thus, Honda and Yamaha entered the US market with their smaller and easier to operate motorcycles. Sony, Panasonic, and other Japanese television manufacturers entered the US marketplace with television sets that were much smaller than those sold by US firms. Canon, Sharp and Ricoh entered the copy machine market by offering smaller copying machines than Xerox. US market leaders prefer to sell large versions of their products (more profit). These small Japanese products were not initially seen as competitive threats by many US firms. Harley Davidson, the leading US motorcycle manufacturer, dismissed the small Hondas pouring into the US as toys.

In some industries the Japanese broke into the US market by offering innovative features to attract customers. Seiko pushed the development of the quartz digital watch as an alternative to the mechanical watch. In the hand calculator market, Casio, Sharp, and others offered various new features, such as calculators with melodies or with clocks, multifunctional calculators, and so on.

The Japanese have also cracked into many markets by offering not more but less at a substantial cost savings. They entered the medical electronics equipment market with a low-cost, stripped-down version of competitors' equipment; thus Toshiba introduced and X-ray computerized CT scanner that is 40 percent cheaper than GE's model that omits some costly features that customers will not miss.* American manufacturers prefer to build sophisticated features and charge customers more. The Japanese have used the low-priced, stripped-down strategy to enter other markets, such as large appliances, television, copying machines, and so on.

* Japan: Undercutting the West in Medical Electronics', *Business Week*, 27 April, 1981, pp. 52ff.

A very heavy emphasis upon product quality and after-sales service has marked the market entry strategy of many Japanese firms. This is in part a consequence of the competitive battles many Japanese firms have long had to wage in their domestic marketplace. It is also in part a consequence of their awareness of the poor image in terms of quality which Japanese products suffered from in the early post-World War II era. In short, across all industries, Japanese firms have tried to produce higher-quality products than their foreign competitors in terms of product performance, utility for the customer, conformance to standards and specifications, lower need for repairs and service, etc. For example, it has frequently been asserted that Japanese cars need substantially fewer repairs than US cars.*

Despite their emphasis upon quality (or perhaps because of it), the Japanese stress after-sales service. They establish an adequate number of service centers so that products can be quickly repaired; good customer relationships can be developed; customer complaints can be handled; and direction and advice can be given to distributors, dealers and retailers. Nissan Motors, for example, having carefully studied the US market, and especially the experience of European firms, developed an extensive parts and service network to assure customers of prompt and efficient service.

Aggressive pricing has characterized many Japanese market entry strategies. Of course, aggressive pricing has been used in conjuction with the other market entry strategy elements noted above. Pricing well below prevailing competition has marked the Japanese entry into many product-markets: radios, televisions, autos, copiers, motor cycles, construction equipment, etc. Transistor radios provide a dramatic illustration of aggressive pricing: Japanese firms introduced three transistor radios at $14 per unit when US producers were marketing six transistor radios at $60 per unit. The Japanese later lowered their price down to $3.75 per unit, one result of which was the withdrawal of many of their competitors from the market. Komatsu entered the US market with superior equipment and services but priced its products much lower than those of Caterpillar, the world's largest manufacturer of construction equipment.

It should also be noted that the Japanese have frequently been accused of engaging in 'predatory' or discriminatory pricing practices. Many of their products have initially been sold in the US at prices lower than those charged in their domestic market. It should also be noted, however, that price is only one of the ingredients which has contributed to their success, albeit a most significant one.

The Japanese quickly learned that having a quality product, competitively priced and high after-sales service was not sufficent: the product must be distributed and promoted. Indeed, it was in the areas of distribution and promotion that the Japanese really had to learn and understand 'the American

---

* Robert E. Cole, 'The Japanese lesson in quality', *Technology Review*, July 1981, pp. 29–40.

way'. Not surprisingly, it was in those two areas that the Japanese made most use of US organizations — distributors, advertising agencies, native US sales representatives — to achieve their own ends.

To obtain initial market penetration Japanese firms used a variety of distribution approaches. In consumer electronics (e.g. televisions, radios) a number of Japanese firms used a one-step distribution system as opposed to the two-step system employed by many US firms. In the early years of Japanese involvement in the US marketplace, some Japanese firms sold through US producers, sometimes using American brand names. Sony, for example, began exporting its transistor radio through American companies in the 1950s before it established its own distribution network. Some Japanese firms initially utilized private labels, i.e. selling their product under the name of the distribution channel; this approach was very successfully employed in the television industry. Some other Japanese firms relied on US independent distributers or dealers to handle distribution and selling functions during the early period of market entry.*

Japanese market development and penetration strategies

Entering a market is one thing; achieving market penetration and ultimately attaining market dominance is something else. Yet the latter is not only what many Japanese firms have striven for, but have realized. Their drive for product-market dominance takes two related foci: product development strategies in the form of product improvement; product upgrading and product proliferation; and market development strategies such as market segmentation, market sequencing, and market flexibility. While these foci are related sides of the same coin, each merits separate discussion. It is the effective integration of the two which makes the Japanese such formidable competitors.

Japanese companies have distinguished themselves by their commitment to continuous product improvement. They constantly seek competitive advantage through product improvement. Their extensive market and customer intelligence networks are oriented to identifying potential improvements in product functionality, performance, style, appearance, features, and quality. This is frequently matched by extensive product development and testing procedures. Of course it has frequently been asserted that Japanese companies take their competitors' products apart to identify potential product improvements.

Examples of product improvement abound. If one examined the successive annual models of the Mazda RX-7 sports car, one would observe continuous improvement of product features, not just annual style changes. A long series of product modifications predicated upon technology advances has characte-

* See *The US Consumer Electronics Industry and Foreign Competition*, US Department of Commerce/Economic Development Administration, May 1980.

rized the strategy of Seiko and Casio in the watch industry. A sequence of product improvements has also marked Canon's chequered attempts to penetrate the copier market. Even in some high-technology areas, such as semi conductors and computers and electronic medical equipment, Japanese commitment to product improvement has catapulted them beyond many of their US competitors in terms of product performance, reliability, and features.

Japanese firms, once they gain a toehold in the market, practice product upgrading. They stretch their line toward the upper end of the market, while not abandoning the lower end. Product uprgading has typified the market penetration strategy of most of the well-known Japanese success stories in the US marketplace: autos, televisions, motor cycles, watches, copiers, etc. For example, Datsun and Toyota have continuously upgraded their product, successively reaching and penetrating higher price points in the auto market. Indeed, Datsun and Toyota have been studying the luxury car market (Mercedes, BMW, etc.) with an eye toward eventually introducing their own luxury automobiles.

For many Japanese companies a strategy of product proliferation has gone hand in hand with product improvement and upgrading. They put out multiple versions of the product to appeal to different end-users, tastes, and income classes. Product proliferation may serve a variety of purposes: it helps tie up distribution; it provides a presence in many different market sectors, thus forcing competitors to fight on many fronts simultaneously; and it may serve as a barrier to entry, deterring prospective entrants. These are some of the problems which Swiss and US watch manufacturers have faced in confronting the Japanese; Seiko, for example, markets over 2300 different watches. Casio, Sharp, and others produce a great variety of hand calculators showing different styles, features, sizes and so on. Canon offers a wide variety of selections around its basic models. It is also interesting to note that at the time that other foreign auto manufacturers (e.g. Volkswagen) were reducing the diversity of their product lines, Japanese manufacturers were significantly extending theirs.

Implicit in these product strategies are market considerations. Product development and modification anticipates and responds to market changes. Market segmentation and sequencing are integrally related to product improvement, upgrading, and proliferation. Products and markets evolve together. Particularly noteworthy in the conduct of many Japanese firms is their market flexibility: the capacity to adapt their marketing approach to market conditions and market evolution. The Japanese have clearly distinguished themselves across many markets in their ability to marry product development and market development.

Market segmentation and sequencing are evidenced in the US market penetration strategy of almost every Japanese firm. Toyota and Honda initially attacked the California market and in a series of geographical expansion moves eventually covered the entire US market. A number of Japanese firms have built their presence in the US marketplace through carefully sequencing their penetration of distribution channels. Many consumer electronics firms initially developed relationships with very large retail chains (sometimes via private label, sometimes under their own brand name) and they worked their way down to the level of smaller independent outlets.

The Japanese approach to market segmentation and sequencing, at both the national and individual firm levels, is well illustrated by their patient work in the computer market. The Japanese government's effort to help develop the computer industry has been a long-term project that gained much of its impetus in 1970 in response to IBM's introduction of its large 370 series of mainframes. MITI (the Ministry of Trade and Industry) then organized Japanese computer manufacturers into three groups: Futjitsu and Hitachi were to focus on large IBM-compatible mainframes; Mitsubishi and Oki Electric Industry Co. would concentrate on small IBM-compatible computers, and NEC and Toshiba were told to design their own computer architecture. Although these companies are all much more diverse now in their current product lines, the initial concentration or market focus appears to have helped strengthen their catch-up efforts in computer technology.

Japanese firms committed themselves to the development of computers that were 100 percent plug-compatible with IBM, but considerably lower in price. They were sold initially to sophisticated companies in Japan who owned IBM equipment but wanted to get more value for their money. These firms gained valuable customer experience and continuously improved their product.

Market sequencing lies at the core of Fujitsu's onslaught on the world market. They chose Australia as its major initial foreign market. They are using Australia as a test market because it resembles Western markets and yet it is isolated from the West so that any mistakes will not necessarily be broadcast elsewhere. They hire and train Australians to do the selling and give them a lot of autonomy.

Fujitsu and many other Japanese computer manufacturers have begun to enter the US market with particular emphasis upon the smaller (personal computer) end. Their market development and penetration strategy seems to be following a path adopted by other Japanese industries such as copiers, televisions, autos, and motor cycles: develop brand name awareness, reliability, service, etc., in the small end of the product scale and then eventually move up into larger computers — ideally trading up customers into larger systems.

Central to the marketing sequencing strategy of many Japanese firms is the use of their domestic market for product development and testing before they hit the US marketplace. Their experience in the Japanese market provides insight into customer preferences, product deficiencies, and effective marketing strategies. Japanese copier manufacturers, for example, spent many years developing their product in Japan before they entered the US market.

Market flexibility refers to the capacity and willingness of Japanese firms to manage and change their marketing mix over the life cycle of product-markets. Japanese firms are adept at using a multiplicity of competitive weapons with varying degrees of emphasis — price, product quality, product features, service, distribution promotion — to penetrate and win markets. This flexibility is cultural. Buddhist thinking emphasizes that nothing is permanent, that life is ever-changing. Samurai warriors in Japan learned several martial arts — judo, karate, aikido — always choosing the best means to attack or defend. A Japanese company will sometimes attack with a karate blow aimed at a competitor's weaknesses and at times with an aikido side-step, taking advantage of the force created by a competitor. The game of GO, originated by the Chinese and perfected by the Japanese, provides a mental training in long-range strategic thinking, the principles of indirect attack and encirclement, and the need for opportunistic replanning. Thus Japanese culture provides deep models for flexible marketing warfare.

The emphasis within the mix of competitive weapons is typically adapted by the Japanese in accordance with their market penetration. In early efforts to achieve market penetration, price to the ultimate consumer and margins to the distribution chain are often dominant. Special product features are also frequently emphasized. These have been the characteristics of their early penetration efforts in calculators, watches, radios, televisions, stereo equipment, and farm equipment. As they penetrate these markets, brand identification, more varied forms of distribution, and service have often gained in importance.

Japanese marketing flexibility is also exhibited in their handling of individual marketing variables. Product change and development has already been noted. Toyota's product strategy reveals continuous product change as they have moved from the low end to much higher regions of the auto market. Relatedly, the Japanese raise their prices as their products gain acceptance. Sony's penetration of the television market is a good example: Sony initially priced their television sets below American prices, but continued to raise prices as they gained market penetration and have for sometime now higher prices than almost all their competitors. As has already been noted, Japanese firms modify and adapt their distribution system as they acquire market share.

Market maintenance

The Japanese now dominate many product-market sectors, and are rapidly moving toward dominating many others. Protecting their leadership position presents the Japanese with a quite different strategy challenge than attaining that position: they will increasingly find themselves in the role of prey rather than preditor. Maintaining their market dominance or a significant presence will require quite different strategies than those which achieved that dominance or presence.

This is so in large measure due to the concerted responses to the Japanese challenge now being mounted by such US firms as IBM, Xerox, Kodak, RCA, Motorola, and Texas Instruments, and major European firms such as Philips. These and other firms have begun to plan for and fight competitive battles against the Japanese; in some instances attempting to beat them at their own game. It is not uncommon now for US firms to send teams of managers to Japan to study Japanese business practices.

In many respects the Japanese market maintenance strategy seems to involve doing more of what won them the markets — product development and market development. The Japanese continue to pour money into product improvement, upgrading, and proliferation in such industries as watches, televisions, audio and stereo equipment, calculators, autos, and copiers; US and foreign firms find it difficult to compete. The Japanese pursue market segmentation, sequencing, and flexibility to ensure that no major windows of opportunity are left open to foreign competitors.

In other respects Japanese market maintenance strategy reveals some major new thrusts. It is less dependent upon product imitation and minor product improvements; it reflects much more involvement in genuine innovation. This is true in product-market sectors where the Japanese are now major actors — television, autos, cameras, and stereos — and, perhaps more significantly, in newly emerging market sectors such as video-tape recorders and discs and non-film-using cameras. In these emerging market sectors their leadership is in large measure a consequence of their own technology development and not mere imitation or adaptation of products initially developed and marketed by US manufacturers.

In many respects the real battle between US and Japanese firms is only now beginning. No longer are US firms willing to treat the Japanese lightly or question their strategic astuteness or willingness to pursue their goals. Indeed, major US firms such as IBM, Xerox, and Texas Instruments have initiated major reorganizations specifically to better combat the Japanese. These firms do not plan to give the Japanese a free hand in major market sectors as previously occurred in televisions, radios, motor cycles, and autos.

How can US companies compete with Japan?

American companies are scrambling to find ways to defend their markets against further penetration by Japanese competitors. General Motors, Xerox, Zenith, and other companies acknowledge their fatal error in letting the Japanese gain strong footholds in their markets. Now that Japanese companies have earned well-respected names in the world market, what can US companies to to contain them? Our comments here will address marketing specific issues.

In short, US firms competing against the Japanese — or anybody else — must adopt a systematic and integrated approach to their marketing activities and to how marketing relates to all other corporate activities. Marketing is a vital link in the chain but the many interdependencies between it and other functional areas and corporate tasks must be fully recognized. A number of points can be made.

Product-markets must be systematically and creatively identified, developed, and managed. For many US companies this will entail nothing short of embracing a new way of thinking about, and doing business. For some US firms it will mean rediscovering that which made them innovative, dynamic market leaders. Essentially, US firms must renew or acquire an entrepreneurial marketing culture.

Managing product-market evolution is the name of the game. Well-known market segmentation principles must be employed: otherwise major market 'windows' will be left open to the Japanese and worse, major market sectors will be conceded without a fight. Also 'milking' current product-market successes without devoting substantial reserves to the creation of tomorrow's product-markets is a recipe for failure. If US companies fail to develop new product-market sectors, they will find themselves always responding to the market initiatives of the Japanese.

US firms can no longer afford to concentrate on product development to the relative neglect of market development. One without the other is much more likely to leave open windows of opportunity for competitors. The fusion of the two is necessary to move successfully from marketing copiers to marketing office work systems, a challenge currently facing Xerox and many other firms. A similar challenge confronts RCA, Zenith, and others moving in from televisions to video recorders/discs to home entertainment centers.

Effective exploitation of product-market management implies that firms must learn new marketing skills and relearn old ones. Pricing, sales, distribution, promotion, and service approaches need to be adapted to changing market conditions as product-markets evolve. Selling complex office systems requires quite different skills than selling copiers. Identifying and developing markets requires quite different skills than selling in well-established markets.

Whether in choosing and developing new product-markets, exploiting mature product-markets or learning new marketing skills, US firms must carefully identify and exploit their competitive strengths and advantages. These strengths and advantages must be appraised in the context of what customers, retailers, and distributors need, want, and appreciate. Many US firms have allowed their traditional comparitive strength in research and development to wane and by not continuing to match their technical expertise to customer needs and values. Perhaps, much worse, many US firms have permitted the Japanese to outdo them in designing distribution systems, establishing service networks, providing retailer credit, and creating product and company image.

Marketing decisions are made in an organizational context. How these decisions get made is quite different in US and Japanese firms. Marketing and other corporate functions can no longer remain as isolated centers of decision activity; they must be integrated. The key question no longer can be: Can marketing and manufacturing co-exist? but rather how can they be made into congenial bedfellows? Automation, experience gains, reduction of components counts, and so on produce little gain if the firm is serving the wrong product-market sectors. Their current acclamation notwithstanding, quality circles are of little assistance in choosing product-market segments and designing appropriate marketing strategies.

Implicit in the adoption of a marketing culture is the emergence of a managerial ideology or frame of reference quite different from that which has traditionally prevailed in many US firms. Nothing can be treated as sacrosanct. Managers must start questioning well-known 'facts', principles, practices, and deeply held assumptions and start observing what is happening to customers, competitors, and distributors in the marketplace. A new mind-set is needed to lead US firms to invest, innovate, and seek leadership in the marketplace through the creation of customer value.

CONCLUSION

Marketing has contributed to Japanese success. The Japanese are significantly better marketers now than they were in the 1960s or early 1970s. Yet they have not invented any new marketing practices. Neither can their marketing process be simply attributed to their alleged penchant for predatory pricing and other questionable practices. Nor can US and other foreign firms simply resort to such behaviour if they hope to outcompete the Japanese.

Strategic Marketing and Management
Edited by H. Thomas and D. Gardner
© 1985 John Wiley & Sons Ltd

6.2

Growth Strategies for Small-Share Firms in Mature Industries: Some Refinements of the 'Fast Growth Segment–Highly Differentiated Niche' Theme

STANLEY F. STASCH AND JOHN L. WARD
Loyola University of Chicago, Chicago, Illinois 60611

The popular acceptance of The Boston Consulting Group's growth-share matrix and other 'portfolio grids' as an aid in the evaluation of the attractiveness of opportunities has brought forth numerous articles and debates on *if* and *how* small-share firms in mature markets can improve their situation. The frequently recommended general strategies for such firms include:[*]

(1) plan a total exit;
(2) reduce the product-market scope selectively for more profitable operations;
(3) change the 'economics' of industry production to obsolete dominant competitor's 'experiences';
(4) introduce a new product technology; and
(5) increase market penetration against stronger competitors via *superior marketing strategy*.

This paper discusses the literature and some findings from our research on the *marketing strategies* which can help small-share firms in mature markets *gain profitability*.

The issue is an important one for many firms. After all, the vast majority of all firms or product-lines face the difficult question of how to cope with no better than second position in a mature or soon-to-be mature market. Until recently,

---

[*] For example, see Hofer and Schendel (1977), Rothschild (1979), and Abell and Hammond (1979).

453

most of the 'clichés' and 'rules-of-thumb' have suggested that, except for a very few, their potential is unexciting. Our research identified a number of small-share firms who successfully improved their market shares through the use of aggressive marketing strategies. This paper reports the lessons we have learned from studying their efforts and their circumstances, and relates our findings to the recent literature.

THE THEME

Table 6.2.1 summarizes the theoretical and empirical literature regarding strategies which small-share firms can use to gain share. The literature suggests that there are two such strategies:

(1)   invest selectively in fast growth market segments; and/or
(2)   seek and develop specialized niches with a highly differentiated offering.

Note that each study offers some hope for small-share firms in mature markets through the marketing strategies of *segmentation* and/or *differentiation*. Consequently, there is some consensus that the most likely growth strategies for small-share firms in mature markets are those of focusing on growth and/or stressing differentiation.

DESCRIPTION OF RESEARCH

This paper is based on a research project whose objective is to identify which specific marketing strategies (e.g. cut price, change product form, use new channels) in what market and competitive enviroments have the best chance for success. To date, some 50 marketing strategy case histories have been obtained from sources generally believed to be reliable by most academicians and business practitioners — business publications, cases for classroom use, personal experiences, and other sources such as security analysts. A number of sources — often more than 10 — are used in the compilation of each case history. All of these case histories have been classified according to (1) the competitive and enviromental *situation* faced by the different firms, (2) the marketing *strategies* they used in those situations, and (3) the *results* of those strategies. Thus, the research can be presented schematically as follows:

$$\text{Situation} + \text{marketing action} \rightarrow \text{results}$$

The *competitive and enviromental situation* of each marketing strategy case history is classified according to 22 situational factors.* In order to assure

---

* For a more complete discussion of the 22 situational factors, see Ward and Stasch (1980a).

Table 6.2.1   Strategies for small-share competitors in mature industries

Reference	Marketing strategy recommendations	Other strategic recommendations
Hammermesh *et al.* (1978)	Seek creative segmentation	Maintain top-quality management Manage controlled growth Spend efficiently on R&D
Woo and Cooper (1979)	Avoid head-to-head competition Stress just one market differentiating variable Don't have equal product-line breadth as competitors Provide relatively high quality for moderate price (good value)	
Buzzell and Wiersema (1981)	Focus on smaller, narrowed segments less influenced by scale (i.e. service, capitive, regional, etc.) and where product redesign possible Keep marketing expenses low Emphasize quality Avoid aggressive competitors	
Hall (1980)	Provide highly differentiated product	Have lowest costs
Hammermesh and Silk (1979)	Select growth segments Provide high-quality products Provide innovative products	Maintain efficient production and distribution
Leavitt (1980)	Differentiate product-service offerings	
Hofer and Davoust (1977)	Specialize in offerings Seek market niches Invest in growth segments Prune product lines	Consider exit Don't rock the boat Minimize investment
Ward and Stasch (1980b)	Provide meaningful and significant competitive differences Attack lethargic competitors	
Strategic Planning Institute (1979)	Select defensible segments Have broader or narrower product line than competition Develop high-quality differentiation Introduce relatively more new products	Minimize R&D
Boston Consulting Group (1968)	Focus on differentiated, protected niches Invest aggresively in fast growth segments	Combine related businesses Change production or distribution 'economics' in industry

consistency from one case history to another during the data collection activity, a questionnaire type of data collection form which incorporates the 22 situational factors was devised. In addition, all but four of the situational factors have been categorized (e.g. there are 10 pre-established size categories for the situational factor of 'size of industry') — a procedure which we feel encourages both consistency and objectivity.

Each firm's *marketing strategy* is classified according to the action taken with respect to the market, product, price, distribution, advertising, promotion, and creative communication or positioning. In addition, each firm's marketing action is classified according to the advantage it is attempting to stress or the disadvantage it is attempting to overcome.

Finally, the *results* of each strategy are recorded in terms of the changes in market share, sales, or profits which are associated with the pre- and post-strategy time periods. These types of information are the raw data being used to study the effectiveness of various marketing strategies in different situations.

SOME REFINEMENTS

Compared with the studies listed in Table 6.2.1, our research explored in greater detail the competitive circumstances and marketing strategies of firms which have successfully implemented the 'growth segment – differentiated niche' theme. As a result, we have observed some interesting 'refinements' to this theme.

Among the small-share companies which we studied, success often seemed at least partially attributable to the following three factors.

(1) their strategies included some effort to maximize the competitive differentiation between themselves and their competitors;
(2) their strategies were ones which tended either to minimize or avoid competitive response;
(3) they developed a significant distribution 'advantage' to help secure their accomplishments.

In each of the case studies it was noted that at least two (and occasionally all three) of these factors were present.This suggests that, to be successful, small-share firms probably must do more than just pursue the two basic strategies of seeking growth segments and/or developing differentiated products. It may be that the above three factors are 'refinements' to the two basic strategies which are as important as the two basic strategies themselves. In fact, it seems that success is more likely to be assured as more of these 'refinements' are incorporated into the 'growth segment – differentiated niche'

Table 6.2.2 Exploiting the 'growth segment–differentiated niche' theme

Maximize difference between self and competition	Develop a strong brand identity Create a new product form Add a new competitive variable to industry's traditional competitive marketing mix or format
Minimize likelihood of competitive response	Start early in small segments Compete where competitive impact is against many products or competitors Compete where competitors fear their response hurts them more than you
Solidify position with distribution advantage	Gain channel support with broader product line Develop direct, self-controlled distribution

strategy. Table 6.2.2 outlines some suggestions on how a small-share firm can employ these three 'refinements'

MAXIMIZE DIFFERENCE BETWEEN SELF AND COMPETITION

It appears that little will be gained if a small-share firm only duplicates, or copies, the success formula used by the dominant competitor. The small-share firm is much more likely to attract the attention of consumers and distributors by creating a large difference between itself and its major competitors. It can do so in at least three ways.

Create a brand identity synonymous with newer product forms or highest quality

In virtually each case we studied the small competitor went to considerable expense and determined effort to select and develop a brand name which became identified with the product form and/or with the highest quality. Successful examples of building a brand name to be synonymous with newer product forms include Miller's Lite (for a type of beer known as 'light'), Mr Coffee (for a new type of coffee-brewing device), Perrier (for naturally carbonated mineral water), and BIC (for inexpensive, disposable ballpoint pens). Entermann's (in bakery goods) and Heublein's Smirnoff (in vodka) are examples of developing unique quality images for very established but quickly growing product forms.* (These and other examples are shown in the first column of Table 6.2.3.)

* Because of the large number of sources of information used to compile these cases, references are not listed. (For example, 32 sources of information were used in the six cases just mentioned in this paragraph.)

Table 6.2.3 Examples of 'refinements' in selected cases

Company and brand	Maximize difference			Minimize response			
	Establish strong brand identity (1)	Product form (2)	'Rules of game' (3)	First vigorous entrant (4)	Take from many competitors (5)	Make response 'hurt' competition more (6)	Establish distribution advantage (7)
Hanes' L'eggs	Yes	One size fits all	Direct, consignment delivery	Yes	Many brands and private labels	Competition strong in different form – less disposable	Direct delivery and personal shelf management
Quaker Oats Tender Chunks	Descriptive name	Soft-dry			Both dry and moist which are different forms	'Straddles' both dry and wet foods with new form	
Lorillard's Kent Golden Lights	Lo-Tar			First	Many, many brands	Competitive response lends attention to lo tar option	
Mr Coffee	Synonymous	New method			Many forms of making coffee		

Miller's Lite	Synonymous	Less filling	Full line and niche definitions		Many competitors and brands		Provided full line
Heublein's Smirnoff	Top quality	New mixed drinks	Advertising to support premium price	Yes	Many competitors and brands		Provided full line
Entermann's	Top quality	Fresh baked	Direct delivery		Many forms		Direct delivery and personal shelf management
Vlasic Pickles		Full line and aggresive promotion			Several competitors with small role		Provided full line
Polaroid	Synonymous	Instant				Response gives attention to 'up-start'	
Johnson & Johnson Tylenol	Synonymous	Non-aspirin			Several brands		
Perrier	Synonymous		Aggressive marketing and full line	Yes	Several forms and brands		Provided full line
BIC ball points	Synonymous		Heavy advertising		Several forms and brands	Disposables threaten established 'economics'	Provided full line

First signifi-cantly

Develop a new product form which is an improvement over existing products

A number of the successful cases we studied had introduced a new product form — disposable pens, light beer, etc. A new product form has an advantage in that it can make existing products look 'obsolete' to consumers. Further, new product forms may outdate the existing production systems of the dominant competitors, thus requiring considerable product and manufacturing research which is both expensive and time-consuming. At the very least, new product forms can undermine brand loyalties currently in existence.

Johnson and Johnson's *non-aspirin* Tylenol was such a product, as were Quaker Oats' Tender Chunks *soft-dry, complete meal* dog food and Polaroid's *instant* photography. Lorillard offered Kent Golden Lights as a cigarette with only *8 milligrams* of tar at a time when no other cigarette brands were being offered in the range of 5–10 milligrams of tar (see column 2 in Table 6.2.3).

Change the 'rules of the game' by introducing new and different competitive variables into the industry's traditional marketing mix

If a firm can make a significant and effective change in its marketing relative to the industry's traditional marketing, it may create a difference which competitors will not immediately duplicate because (a) they do not think it will succeed, (b) it is not easy to change 'traditional thinking' in a short time, and/or (c) they are unable to do so exept at great expense.

One of the most successful examples of this strategy was Hanes' marketing of hoisery (L'eggs) as a consumer package good on consignment with direct distribution through food and drug stores — the first time a major competitor made a serious attempt to do so. Once it became established in those channels, competitors found it difficult to duplicate L'eggs' strategy.

Traditionally, the beer industry concentrated on a product line consisting of a 'premium' brand and a 'price' brand. Miller Brewing 'changed the rules' by offering a product line consisting of a 'regular' tasting beer, a 'light' beer, and a European type of beer. Miller was so successful that soon every other large brewery was attempting to duplicate the strategy.

Heublein led the way in changing the nature of whiskey marketing from a 'price and distribution' orientation to a 'promotion' orientation. They were the first to use heavy advertising to create a brand awareness and a favourable brand image for their Smirnoff vodka which would permit the company to charge premium — rather than equivalent — prices. This strategy's success is evident from the fact that Smirnoff became the No. 1 brand among all alcoholic brands.

Others have also succeeded by changing the rules. Entermann's introduced new distribution; BIC significantly upped the advertising ante relative to industry tradition, changed packaging concepts to the multi-pack, and made frequent modifications to its packaging; and Vlasic both introduced a much broader product line and spent much more on advertising than the industry norm (see column 3 in Table 6.2.3).

MINIMIZE LIKELIHOOD OF COMPETITIVE RESPONSE

If a small-share firm can successfully employ one or more of the three foregoing strategies to create a noticeable and effective difference between itself and its competitors, it will have made a good start toward increasing its market share. However, the firm can further improve its position if it also takes steps to minimize the likelihood of a competitive response. There seem to be at least three ways this can be done.

Be first to vigorously enter a new growth segment

A firm has a better chance of capturing a sizeable share of a growth segment if it establishes itself in the segment while it is either unnoticed or too small to attract the attention of important competitors.

Heublein was one of the first to recognize the trend toward increased consumption of light and 'white' liquors, due in part to the changing demographics toward more young drinkers in the late 1960s and the 1970s. Heublein devoted considerable resources to its Smirnoff vodka, and exploited this light trend by promoting a number of drinks such as Bloody Marys and Screwdrivers.

Other successful examples of firms capitalizing on the trend to 'lightness' in beverages include Miller's Lite and Perrier. Lorillard's Kent Golden Lights was the first to exploit the trend toward low-tar cigarettes by aggressively going after that segment, and L'eggs' success was due in part to their recognition that there was a small but growing trend of sales of woman's hosiery through supermarkets (see column 4 in Table 6.2.3).

Compete against many product to avoid direct competitive counterattack

Probably one of the fortunes for Lorillard's Kents, Miller's Lite, and Heublein's Smirnoff was that their gains came at the expense of many competitors — each losing only a scarcely noticeable amount. The small-share firm that competes in this manner may be graced with a period of 'competitive peace' which will allow its brand to become established. One way a small-share firm can avoid a direct counterattack is to seek situations in which it can take sales away from a number of competitors who each market a number of different brands.

Successful examples of firms competing against many products include Hanes L'eggs (which competed against many small unadvertised, private brands of hosiery being sold in food and drug stores), Mr Coffee's coffee-maker (which competed against many producers of various types of coffee-makers), Vlasic's pickles (which expanded from a regional supplier to a national supplier by frequently displacing a small, local brand of pickle from the retailers' shelves), and Perrier (which essentially competed against many small, little-known brands of mineral water). Even Miller's Lite probably took sales away from the various brands of all brewers, rather than from only one or two brands (see column 5 in Table 6.2.3).

Compete where competitors fear their response might hurt them more than you

The strong, established competitors to BIC's stick pen, the Hanes' L'eggs, and to Quaker Oat's Tender Chunks had to be hoping that those new product forms would not attain market aceptance. Each was taking share, and profits, from a mature product form and from a different production and/or distribution system. If the established competitors aided in the market development of the new segment and form, they would cannibalize their own well-established products and be forced into costly new production and distribution efforts. Such inactivity on the part of big competitors can give the small-share firm time to consolidate its new production and distribution system and to establish its brand in the market place. For the market leaders, it is a heads-you-win, tails-I-lose situation—at least until they ultimately forge a significant, powerful response.

Two particular types of product concepts can create this dilemma for the established leader: *disposable* products and *'straddle'* products. The market leaders would prefer not to switch over to a disposable product because it is likely to require an entirely different production system while yielding a smaller per unit profit margin. BIC's disposable pen caused such a dilemma for Scripto, Paper Mate, and others. Quaker Oats' soft-dry, complete meal dog food (Tender Chunks) competed with canned dog food because of its lower price and with dry dog food because of its additional benefits. A new product form which successfuly 'straddles' to established product categories by offering the best of both in one product form (such as Tender Chunks) also creates the same dilemma for the established competitors. They must broaden their product line and develop a brand preference that will take more sales from their existing products than from the smaller competitor (see column 6 of Table 6.2.3). 'Straddling' also has the advantage of competing against several products or brands, as discussed earlier.

USE DISTRIBUTION TO SECURE AN EARLY ADVANTAGE

In a number of the cases studied, distribution became important to the long-term defense and exploitation of a growing market segment or differentiated product niche. Such distribution strength was developed in two ways (see column 7 of Table 6.2.3).

Provide distributors with a full, relatively broad product line

Independent distributors tend to want a full product line in order to maximize the returns from their efforts. From the firm's viewpoint, a full line helps a firm maintain distributors' loyalty due to the larger sales volume accruing from the line. Certainly a full line makes it more difficult for competitors to tag onto your distributors or to capture retailer shelf space left vacant due to an incomplete line.

Heublein provided its distributors with a line of vodka brands in addition to Smirnoff. Other examples where a small-share firm offered its distributors a more full line relative to competitors were Vlasic, BIC, and Miller Brewing.

Control your own distribution

Both Hanes and Entermann's developed their own direct distribution and in-store display management. Once established, competitors found it extremely difficult to overcome these distribution methods. As a result, these methods provided the small-share firms with a solid basis for defending their market gains.

CONCLUSIONS

Successful strategies for small-share competitors in established markets are not simple or accidental. The literature and our research suggest that such firms should address fast-growth segments and/or emphasize product differentation.

Our study further suggests that the following three 'refinements' may be as important as the two basic marketing strategies in the literature: (1) maximize the differences between the firm and the competitors; (2) minimize the likelihood of competitive response; and (3) secure the early advantages through relative distribution strengths.* Our findings show that each successful small-share firm used at least two of these 'refinements' and several firms, to some extent, made effective use of all three.

REFERENCES

Abell D. F., and J. S. Hammond, *Strategic Market Planning*. Prentice-Hall, Englewood Cliffs, N.J., 1979.

* In another paper in this volume — Urban (1984) — some of the advantages of being the first company to enter an emerging segment are discussed.

Boston Consulting Group, *Perspectives on Experience*. Boston Consulting Group, Boston, MA, 1968.

Buzzell, R. D., and F. D. Wiersema, 'Successful share building strategies', *Harvard Business Review*, Jan.-Feb. 1981, pp. 135–144.

Hall, W. K., 'Survival strategies in a hostile environment'. *Harvard Business Review*, Sept.–Oct. 1980, pp. 75–85.

Hammermesh, R. G., M. J. Anderson, and J. E. Harris, 'Strategies for low market share business'. *Harvard Business Review*, May–June 1978, pp. 95–102.

Hammermech, R. G., and S. B. Sills, 'How to compete in stagnant industries', *Harvard Business Review*, Sept.–Oct. 1979, pp. 161–168.

Hofer, C. W., and M. J. Davoust, *Successful Strategic Management*. A. T. Kearney, Chicago, IL., 1977.

Hofer, C. W., and Dan Schendel, *Strategy Formulation: Analytical Concepts*. West, St. Paul, MN, 1977.

Leavitt, T., 'Marketing success through differentation—of anything', *Harvard Business Review*, Jan.–Feb. 1980, pp. 83–91.

Rothschild, W. E., *Strategic Alternatives*. AMACOM, New York, NY, 1979.

Strategic Planning Institute, *Selected Findings from the PIMS Program*. Strategic Planning Institute, Cambridge, MA, 1979.

Urban, G. 'Market entry strategy: an empirical investigation of the effects of order of entry on market share'. Paper presented at the Strategic Marketing Conference, University of Illinois, May 1982.

Urban G. L., T. Carter and Z. Mucha, see paper on pp. 239–240 this volume

Ward, J. L., and S. F. Stasch, 'A conceptual framework for analyzing marketing strategy cases,' *Journal of Marketing Education*, April 1980(a), pp. 57–63.

Ward, J. L., and S. F. Stasch, 'Critical questions second tier firms should ask before becoming aggressive in mature markets'. *Proceedings*. American Marketing Association's Educators Conference. August 1980 (b), pp. 206–208.

Woo, C. Y. Y., and A. C. Cooper, 'Strategies of effective low market share businesses', Working Paper, Purdue University, Krannert School of Business, 1979.

Strategic Marketing and Management
Edited by H. Thomas and D. Gardner
© 1985 John Wiley & Sons Ltd

6.3
Corporate Settings of Effective Low-Share Businesses

CAROLYN Y. WOO and ARNOLD C. COOPER
Purdue University, W. Lafayette, IN 47906

INTRODUCTION

This paper is concerned with an exceptional group of businesses—those with low market shares and high performance. The limited research to date on these businesses has considered the ways in which they compete and the environments in which they locate. However, there has been no consideration of whether high-performing, low market share businesses are to be found in particular kinds of multi-business corporations. This is the focus of this paper.

LITERATURE OVERVIEW

The correlation between high market share and profitability has received both empirical and theoretical support (Boston Consulting Group, 1974; Gale, 1972; Imel and Helmberger, 1971; PIMS, 1977; Shepherd, 1972). On the basis of this correlation it has been generally concluded that low-share sellers occupy rather dismal positions. Accordingly, it has often been recommended that such businesses should be supported at a level which permits them to achieve leading market shares, be repositioned to dominate smaller market segments or, if neither of these is possible, be harvested or liquidated. However, a very large number, perhaps most, businesses have low market shares and these recommendations may be infeasible or unattractive for many corporations (Christensen *et al.*, 1981).

The gloomy prospects for low-share businesses were first challenged by Hamermesh *et al.* (1978). These authors disputed the invariably pessimistic projections for low market share businesses by identifying a pool of highly profitable businesses operating from low-share positions. Based upon detailed analysis of three companies, four strategies were advocated: (1) creative market segmentation, (2) good leadership, (3) controlled growth, and (4) efficient use of R&D resources.

465

In a subsequent study, Woo and Cooper (1981) examined the strategies of 40 effective low-share businesses in regard to the environments in which they were located and the ways in which they competed within these settings. These effective low-share businesses were found to locate in certain environments. These environments often involved manufacture of standardized industrial components and supplies, and were characterized by frequent purchase, slow real market growth, and infrequent product change. It appeared that these environments did not so much shield them from large-share competitors, as provide them with a high degree of stability. Within their individual product-market environments these businesses competed by selectively focusing upon particular competitive variables. They often followed strategies involving high-quality products and medium prices, complemented by conservative spending on marketing, R&D and vertical integration. By contrast, poor-performing low-share businesses tended to adopt broad-based, aggressive postures which mirrored the competitive strategies of successful high-share businesses.

Although the above studies have examined the external environment and competitive strategy of effective low-share businesses, there has been no consideration to date of whether these businesses are located in particular kinds of corporations. Drawing on the stream of research which relates *corporate* characteristics to *business-level* performance, we may expect a number of corporate characteristics to have a bearing. These include portfolio characteristics and degree of corporate diversity, extent of relatedness to other divisions of the corporation, and corporate financial strength. The impact of these factors on low-share performance will be considered in this study.

Portfolio characteristics

Portfolio theory involves classifying different businesses within a multi-business corporation, appraising the relative attractiveness of these businesses, and then allocating resources accordingly (Ansoff and Leontiades, 1976; Cox, 1977; Day, 1977; Kiechel, 1981; Hedley, 1977; Henderson, 1979; Hussey, 1978; Wind and Mahajan, 1981). Generally, high-share businesses ('cash cows' or 'stars') would be deemed more important to the future success of the corporation and would be assigned greater managerial attention, more generous financial support, and a more tolerant time horizon to build or reinforce the appropriate strategies. A few low-share businesses which demonstrate promising potential ('problem children') would also be supported. Other low-share businesses would normally be classified as 'dogs' or unpromising 'problem children' and would be managed for asset maintenance or liquidation. Hence, relative position within the corporate portfolio would determine the resources available to each business and the strategy alternatives within reach.

However, those low-share businesses which have demonstrated strong profit performance (as in the Hamermesh *et al.* (1979) and Woo and Cooper (1981) samples) may receive more corporate resources. Their level of support would presumably depend upon the nature of the other businesses within their corporations, including historic levels of performance, growth potential, and needs for funds. Accordingly, this study will examine the growth of effective low-share businesses, relative to the growth of their parents. We expect these successful low-share businesses to be located in corporations experiencing lower growth; this corporate environment may enable them to compete successfully for support, despite what might be viewed as weak competitive positions.

The diversity of parent portfolios may also influence the strategy and performance of low-share businesses. We would anticipate less diversified parents to be more familiar with the nature, problems, and opportunities of the individual businesses and to demonstrate greater involvement in their management and direction. On the other hand, diversified parents presumably would rely more heavily on formal planning and control systems and on financial performance criteria. We expect effective low-share businesses to be in less diversified corporations, where their individual strategies and needs might be better understood by corporate management. Accordingly, this research will examine the relationship between corporate diversity and performance for low-share businesses.

Relatedness

Another factor which might be expected to bear upon the performance of effective low-share businesses is the degree of relatedness to other businesses in the corporation. This might involve the sharing of facilities, customers, or marketing efforts. It might also involve purchasing from or selling to other businesses within the corporation.

The diversification literature, focusing primarily on corporate-level performance, suggests that related diversifiers do better than those which are unrelated (Rumelt, 1974; Christensen and Montgomery, 1981). These findings are, of course, consistent with the notion of synergy. Relatedness would foster more opportunities to cultivate synergistic benefits in operations, technology, marketing, and even administration. Relatedness also allows managers to operate within the scope of 'bounded rationality' (Williamson, 1974), hence increasing the likelihood of success. Moreover, findings by Christensen and Montgomery (1981) indicated that relatedness might reflect a more basic trait—i.e. more thoughtful and well-planned managerial practices resulting in location in concentrated growth markets. Interestingly, they found that relatedness was associated not only with higher profitability, but also with higher market shares. Extending these results to lower organizational levels, one might surmise that relatedness among subsidiaries would likewise have a favorable impact on business performance.

A direct examination of business-level performance for one class of businesses, however, led to different conclusions. Woo (1981) found that successful market leaders had lower degrees of sharing with other divisions, while the less successful leaders had higher degrees of sharing. Furthermore, the extent to which synergy actually develops in multi-business corporations was questioned by Kitching (1967). His sample of post-merger corporations failed to enjoy significant technological, operating, and marketing synergies. Financial synergy, in which the firm acted as a mini-capital market to redistribute cash, was the primary observable benefit in his acquisition sample. His subjects also ranked the non-financial synergies as most difficult to achieve.

If the presence of synergy is indeed more theoretical or elusive than actual, then closer relatedness among subsidiaries may not be associated with higher performance for low-share businesses. The question is whether relatedness would reduce the degrees of freedom needed for effective strategy selection and implementation more than it would reduce costs through divisional sharing. Previous research findings give some basis for both arguments. In this study we will consider whether relatedness to other divisions is associated with low-share success, although no direction of influence can be pre-specified.

Corporate financial strength

The final set of corporate characteristics considered in this study describes the financial strength of the parents. Though no empirical effort has addressed the possible correlation between healthy parents and healthy subsidiaries, expectation of this association can be based on two factors. First, financially healthy parents are more likely to have the resources to support businesses within their portfolios. Second, successful subsidiaries may simply mirror the health of well-managed parents. The systems, decision-making criteria, values, and attitudes which produce healthy parent performance may also characterize the management of subsidiaries. Existing corporate culture, role models, peer pressure, timely monitoring, and shared expertise serve to reinforce success at all organizational levels. These factors would lead us to expect a more frequent kinship between healthy subsidiary and healthy parent and vice versa.

RESEARCH FRAMEWORK AND SAMPLE SELECTION

The above overview suggests that, for divisions within multi-business corporations, strategy choices and subsequent performance are likely to be shaped by the nature of the parent corporation. The research reported here specifically examines high-performing, low-share businesses and considers the influence of the following: (1) the role of the business in the corporate portfolio and the degree of corporate diversity; (2) the relatedness of the business to other activities of the corporation; and (3) corporate financial strength. In turn, each factor is represented by the variables depicted in Table 6.3.1. Definitions of each variable are reported in the Appendix.

Table 6.3.1   Representation of corporate characteristics

---

1. *Portfolio characteristics*
   Corporate diversity
   Business growth/corporate growth
   Corporate growth
2. *Relatedness*
   Percentage of purchases from other internal divisions
   Percentage of sales to other internal divisions
   Extent of production facilities shared
   Percentage of sales to customers also served by other divisions
   Percentage of sales which went through the same sales force and promotional
      programs as other divisions
3. *Corporate financial strength*
   Corporate debt to equity
   Corporate return on equity
   Corporate payout

To highlight the findings pertaining to low-share businesses, and to provide a context for their interpretation, we contrasted effective low-share businesses with (1) ineffective low-share businesses and (2) effective high-share businesses. These were logical choices stemming from the expectations that the strategies of effective low-share businesses must differ from the former because of unequal performance outcomes and from the latter because of unequal resources.

The sample employed in the following analysis was selected from the PIMS (Profit Impact of Market Strategy) data base. It is made up of businesses, each defined as 'a division, product line, or other profit center within its parent company, selling a distinct set of products or services to an identifiable group or groups of customers, in competition with a well-defined set of competitors' (Buzzell *et al.*, 1975: 105). From this data base, foreign businesses and non-manufacturing operations were excluded. To generate a sample consistent with the earlier Woo and Cooper study (1981), the time period and sample selection criteria were not changed from this prior effort. The time period covered was from 1972 to 1975. For each variable in the data base, PIMS reported values for the beginning year 1972, the end year 1975 and the average value over these 4 years. The average value was used in this study.

Criteria for the categorization of effective low share businesses and the control groups were as shown in Table 6.3.2. The total sample obtained

Table 6.3.2 Classification of sample businesses

Businesses	Pre-tax ROI	Market share relative to combined share of three largest competitors	Number
Effective low-share	Greater than 20%	Less than 20%	35
Ineffective low-share	Less than 5%	Less than 20%	47
Effective high-share	Greater than 20%	Greater than 125%	55

consisted of 35 effective low-share businesses, 47 ineffective low-share businesses, and 55 effective high-share businesses.

Before proceeding further, some limitations of the PIMS data base and their implications for this research should be noted. Since the data base was constructed around business units and not corporations, only a small number of corporate variables was available. This limitation severely restricted the scope of this analysis and the adequate representation of the factors being studied. In addition, some of the data were ordinal-scaled, thus reducing numerical variation for statistical analysis. These limitations suggest that this should be viewed as a preliminary investigation. Since this is the first empirical examination of these relationships, even limited findings should suggest directions for future hypothesis formulation and validation.

METHODOLOGY

The influence of corporate characteristics will be understood in this study through a contrast of their differential impact on the three share-performance groups: effective low-share, ineffective low-share, and effective high-share businesses. Discriminant analysis was used for this purpose. Through discriminant analysis, linear combinations of the 11 organizational variables were formed to maximize the differences between the groups under comparison.

The discriminant functions provided in PIMS are known as log-odds functions. As the name indicates, these are logarithmic functions based on the ratios of the posterior odds of an observation belonging to one group versus another. The model accommodates two groups at one time and can be expressed as:

$$\log \frac{P(A/Xi)}{P(B/Xi)} = B_0 + B_1X_1 + B_2X_2 + \ldots B_{11}X_{11}$$

where: $P(A/Xi)$ = probability that the ith business unit belongs to group A given its vector of characteristics,

$P(B/Xi)$ = probability that the ith business unit belongs to
                       group B given its vector of characteristics,
X_1 = n observations of organizational characteristic 1,
X_2 = n observations of organizational characteristic 2,
$\vdots$
X_{11} = n observations of organizational characteristic 11.
$(B_0, B_1 \ldots B_{11})$ = log odds discriminant function coefficients.

The objective of the analysis is to identify the linear function $(B_0, B_1, \ldots B_{11})$ which provides the strongest discriminatory power. The latter is measured by the Separation value generated along with each pairwise comparison. The Separation value gives the probability that a group A member will be correctly classified into A and a group B member into B. Separation values range from zero to one. High separation values are associated with effective discriminant functions able to distinguish clearly between two groups. (For further reference, see Woo, 1979 and Schlaifer, 1978).

In our analysis, discriminant functions were generated for two comparisons: (1) effective low-share businesses versus ineffective low-share businesses, and (2) effective low-share businesses versus effective high-share businesses.

RESULTS

The means and standard deviations for the three share performance groups are reported in Table 6.3.3. Table 6.3.4 lists discriminant functions for each of the two comparisons. Separation values close to 0.70 were obtained, indicating moderately strong discriminatory power.

In view of the data limitations, high Separation values were definitely not expected. We believe the strength of the current results is adequate for identifying those corporate factors which have the most impact on low-share success. Our discussion will first focus on the contrast between effective and ineffective low-share businesses and then proceed to the remaining comparison with effective high-share businesses.

Effective low-share versus ineffective low-share businesses

Based on the five characteristics which contributed most to the differentiation between these two low-share groups (Table 6.3.4), we can see that effective low-share businesses:

(1)   were more likely to be the growth subsidiaries within parent corporations;
(2)   were associated with corporate parents which had lower payout ratios;

Table 6.3.3 Distribution of variables in target and control groups

	Effective low-share		Ineffective low-share		Effective high-share	
	$\bar{X}$	S	$\bar{X}$	S	$\bar{X}$	S
Percentage internal purchase	18.486	27.401	16.191	25.408	9.364	18.756
Percentage sales internal	7.371	13.875	3.000	7.290	4.582	10.130
Shared facilities	1.400	0.641	1.638	0.727	1.873	0.810
Shared customers	1.857	1.268	2.298	1.398	2.473	1.399
Shared marketing	1.771	0.897	1.894	0.856	1.927	0.891
Corporate payout	0.353	0.198	0.380	0.332	0.303	0.205
Corporate growth	10.657	4.329	11.182	5.391	11.473	5.877
Corporate diversity	1.450	0.615	1.523	0.652	1.234	0.575
Corporate debt to equity	0.436	0.224	0.577	0.372	0.437	0.331
Corporate return on equity	17.31	6.178	16.076	7.306	16.639	7.476
Business growth/corporate growth	2.637	1.811	1.603	1.721	1.634	1.696

Table 6.3.4   Standardized log-odds discriminant coefficients

		Ineffective low-share over effective low-share businesses		Effective high-share over effective low-share businesses	
1.	Constant	−1.800		1.028	
2.	Percentage internal purchase	0.1176	(11)	−0.2927	(5)
3.	Percentage sales internal	−0.3898	(5)	−0.1613	(8)
4.	Shared facilities	−0.3551	(7)	0.4950	(2)
5.	Shared customers	0.2203	(8)	0.3794	(4)
6.	Shared marketing	−0.1177	(10)	−0.1766	(7)
7.	Corporate payout	0.5553	(2)	0.0213	(11)
8.	Corporate growth	0.3753	(6)	−0.1243	(9)
9.	Corporate diversity	0.1628	(9)	−0.3851	(3)
10.	Corporate debt to equity	0.4794	(3)	0.1236	(10)
11.	Corporate return on equity	−0.4091	(4)	−0.2608	(6)
12.	Business growth/ corporate growth	−0.6096	(1)	−0.5238	(1)
	Separation value	0.69		0.68	

( ) Denotes order of importance to the discrimination.

(3)   were associated with corporate parents with lower debt-to-equity ratios;
(4)   had parents which demonstrated higher ROEs; and
(5)   enjoyed a higher level of internal sales.

The above list indicates that three of the variables portraying corporate financial strength played an important role in discriminating between the two groups. Only one of the five leading variables described relatedness to other corporate activities, and it ranked fifth in order of importance. These variables which seem to discriminate between effective and ineffective low-share businesses are discussed below in their order of importance in the discriminant analysis.

High relative growth

Effective low-share businesses were growing significantly faster than ineffective low-share businesses, their respective growth rates being 25.9 percent and 17.6 percent. However, the parent corporations of both groups had similar growth rates.* Presumably, both groups faced similar internal competitors for

* The coded parent growth rates of effective and ineffective low-share businesses were 10.7 percent and 11.2 percent respectively. These growth rates had been adjusted by a disguise factor to preserve client confidentiality. This variable would lend itself to straightforward comparison across sample businesses. However, its relationship to other variables, and particularly to growth rates which have not been disguised, must be interpreted with recognition of the different scales involved.

parent resources, at least in regard to growth. Yet, within these portfolios, effective low-share businesses were clearly the stronger and more prominent growth contributors.

Interestingly, an earlier study, utilizing a comparable sample (Woo and Cooper, 1981) found that a large proportion of low-share businesses located in low-growth markets. These markets kept pace with inflation, but unit growth was only about 1 percent or so. Thus, these findings suggest that effective low-share businesses were gaining share in their segments. Indeed, from 1972 to 1975 their relative market share gain was 1.08 percentage points, representing a statistically significant increase from their earlier position.

Because these businesses had low market shares, and because they were largely located in low-growth markets, they would be labeled as 'dogs' in the typical corporate portfolio. Yet they demonstrated both market share growth and good return on investment, achievements normally considered out of reach for 'dog' businesses.

It is clear from this analysis that effective low-share businesses would be considered as strong performers in their corporate portfolios. Whether effectiveness resulted, in part, from proper parental nurturing and appropriate support given in the first place is less clear without data on the patterns of internal resource allocation over time. Nevertheless, these effective low-share businesses differed from their ineffective counterparts in the extent to which they stood out as the growth subsidiaries within the parents.

Lower payout, lower debt to equity, higher return on equity

The findings indicated a clear association between high-performing subsidiaries and high-performing parents. The parent corporations of effective low-share businesses were financially stronger and more conservative in their use of debt and their retention policies.

Average corporate return on equity for effective low-share businesses was 17.3 percent compared to 16.1 percent for the less effective group. The debt to equity ratios for the two groups were 43.6 percent and 57.7 percent respectively. In addition, parents of the first group also tended to retain a slightly higher level of earnings (65 percent vs. 62 percent). Except for the leverage ratio, these comparisons were not statistically significant at the 5 percent level.

The association between high-performing subsidiaries and high-performing parents was not surprising. Indeed, we expected effective low-share businesses to be located in corporations with adequate resources and effective managerial systems and practices. Of course, the influence could work both ways, with profitable subsidiaries contributing to the earnings and overall performance of the parents. It is still interesting to note, however, that differences between high-performing and low-performing low-share businesses were accounted for more by the financial strength of their parents than by their relatedness to other corporate activities.

Higher percentage of internal sales

Another differentiating characteristic between effective and ineffective low-share businesses was the higher percentage of internal sales associated with the former. How would internal sales benefit low-share businesses? A significant level of internal sales would provide demand stability and reduce reliance on external markets. Profit margins and supply conditions would be less vulnerable to the bargaining leverage of external customers. Profitability of the business may also be protected through transfer pricing if adequate returns have been incorporated. An internal market also provides the 'proving ground' where feedback from mistakes or product changes can be received on a timely basis at less cost. This experience and familiarity with the characteristics of downstream users may serve to enhance market acceptance of the business' products.

Interestingly, other measures of relatedness, such as sharing of facilities, customers, or marketing, as well as internal purchasing within the corporation, did not play much of a role in differentiating between effective and ineffective low-share businesses.

Effective low-share versus effective high-share businesses

Again, we focused on the five characteristics which were most important in discriminating between effective low-share and high-share businesses. The results (Table 6.3.4) showed that, compared to effective high-share businesses, effective low-share businesses:

(1)   were more likely to be the growth subsidiaries;
(2)   did not share facilities as extensively;
(3)   located in more diversified parent corporations;
(4)   did not tend to sell to the customers of other divisions;
(5)   had a higher percentage of internal purchases.

Note that variables related to corporate financial position did not play a large role in differentiating between these two groups. Effective high-share businesses and effective low-share were similar in having parent corporations with strong financial positions.

The variables which seemed to be most important are discussed below, those dealing with relatedness being considered together.

High relative growth

As with the earlier comparison, effective low-share businesses demonstrated higher growth than the control group (25.9 percent versus 15.5 percent), while both were located within parents characterized by similar growth potential.* In addition, these high-share businesses, though profitable, were losing market share relative to their three largest competitors. The change in relative market share over 4 years for these businesses was −13.75 percentage points. As we might recall, the same statistic yielded a gain of 1.08 points† for effective low-share businesses. On the whole, effective high-share businesses were losing share position at a more rapid rate than the PIMS total sample of 609 domestic manufacturing businesses over the same period of time (−13.75 percent vs. −1.20 percent).

The benefits to low-share businesses from being high-growth subsidiaries within their corporate portfolios were discussed earlier. For successful high-share businesses questions can be raised as to whether they have been treated as cash cows and given less resource support in view of their lower growth rates and declining share positions. Lack of data on corporate resource allocation prevent our exploring these questions.

Low operating relatedness

Among these two groups of effective performers, noticeable differences existed in the degree of facilities and customer sharing. It appeared that while a high degree of sharing was appropriate for high-share businesses, a low degree of sharing worked out well for low-share businesses.

For low-share businesses, operating dependencies may reduce flexibility. As shown in an earlier study (Woo and Cooper, 1981), the competitive strategies of effective low-share businesses were characterized primarily by a concentrated focus attuned to the specific product-market environments in which they operated. Such focus would be more difficult to attain when the operations and marketing programs of other divisions were also involved.

The sharing of functions among divisions may also lead low-share businesses to support more activities and programs than prudent. Indeed, the earlier study (Woo and Cooper, 1981) suggested that it is important for low-share businesses to avoid the aggressive broadly-based strategies which high-share businesses can support better than they.

On the other hand, high-share businesses seemed to gain from more

---

* The coded parent growth rates of effective low- and high-share businesses were 10.7 percent and 11.5 percent respectively.

† *T*-tests show that the relative share loss for effective high-share businesses and the relative share gain for effective low-share businesses are both significant at the 0.001 level.

extensive sharing. This may occur because the operating facilities and marketing programs of sister divisions are structured around these high-share businesses. Such support may develop because of the greater perceived attractiveness of high-share businesses and their political and economic importance within the parent corporation. In this context, sharing with other divisions would contribute to sharing of costs at a minimal loss of control or flexibility. Sharing for high-share businesses in this sample would also be appropriate in view of the less diversified nature of the parent corporations.

More diversified parents

Contrary to expectations, effective low-share businesses were located more frequently in diversified companies; within these, as we have seen, they were not highly linked to other operating divisions except for internal sales and purchases. These businesses may be viewed as independent divisions within relatively diversified portfolios. On the other hand, effective high-share businesses were more often associated with less diversified parents. Interestingly, this latter finding is consistent with the correlation between high-share, high-profitability and relatedness demonstrated in the Christensen and Montgomery study (1981).

The current analysis yielded two corporate settings which were related to profitable businesses: one characterized by a higher degree of diversity and few operating linkages; the other by the inverse of these characteristics. The research by Vancil (1971) on corporate planning systems, and Pitts (1976) on organizational characteristics of corporations expanding through internal development or acquisition bear on our findings. Based on their conclusions we might infer greater autonomy, delegation, and reliance on financial controls in the first setting, and more centralized decision-making with emphasis on qualititative measures to describe the management style in the second context. Though markedly different, both settings supported successful performance, the first for low-share businesses and the second for high-share businesses.

High internal purchases

Effective low-share businesses, more than effective high-share businesses, had substantial internal purchases. This would provide greater control over material quality, cost, and availability. These advantages would partially compensate low-share businesses for the leverage they lack with external suppliers. To some degree high internal purchase also would enable these low-share businesses to enjoy some of the benefits of backward integration without shouldering the investment. Hence, the greater dependence of low-share, rather than high-share businesses, on internal supply sources would seem reasonable.

SUMMARY

The results demonstrate that effective low-share businesses in this sample were relatively high-growth subsidiaries within their firms. In addition they were also profitable and gaining share. These attributes all suggest relatively favorable positions within the parent firms. On the basis of portfolio theory, subsidiaries would be ranked differently for resource allocation. In this study the sample businesses, despite low market shares, exhibited those characteristics which would lead to greater corporate support.

The kinship between healthy parents and healthy subsidiaries was strongly supported. While successful businesses (both high- and low-share) were associated with financially strong parents, the reverse was true for ineffective low-share businesses. This relationship, though intuitively appealing, has not been the subject of much exploration. What explains this kinship? How do corporate culture, planning, control, and other managerial systems foster this observed symmetry? Our current findings reveal an interesting relationship, the cause of which, however, remains a question.

This study raised questions about the advantages of relatedness and internal synergies. Not all forms of synergy were helpful and not all businesses benefited equally. Effective low-share businesses appeared to gain relatively more from internal selling and purchasing than from sharing of facilities, customers, and marketing programs. High-share businesses, however, tended to gain from the latter. Ineffective low-share businesses were more closely related in the sense of sharing facilities, customers, and programs, but without realizing the same benefits as high-share businesses.

One contrast worth noting is the different degree of diversity associated with the parents of effective low-share and effective high-share businesses. Contrary to expectations the former were found more frequently in relatively diversified corporations. For high-share businesses, strong correlation existed between high-share effectiveness, high degrees of operating linkage, and low corporate diversity. These businesses appeared to be part of a related cluster of subsidiaries in focused corporations.

On the whole, this study supports the proposition that internal corporate characteristics influence low-share effectiveness. The restrictions of the data mentioned earlier, including the lack of data which might be used to judge causality, render these findings preliminary rather than conclusive. Hopefully, the corporate characteristics identified in this investigation will aid future research and lead to a better understanding of effective low-share businesses.

Appendix: Definition of research variables

Variable	Description
Sample selection criteria	
(1) Return on investment	Net income/average investment
(2) Relative market share	Share of this business/combined share of three largest competitors
Portfolio characteristics	
(1) Corporate Diversity	Qualitative evaluation of the corporate parent's degree of diversity by the PIMS staff 1 = low; 3 = high
(2) Business growth/corporate growth	The ratio of this business's sales growth to its parent's sales growth. Revenue of corporate parents adjusted by a disguise factor
(3) Corporate growth	Coded growth rate of corporate parent
Relatedness	
(1) Percentage internal purchases	Percentage of this business' purchase of materials from the other divisions of the same company
(2) Percentage internal sales	Percentage of total sales of this business made to other divisions of the same company
(3) Shared facilities	The extent to which this business shared its plant and equipment and production personnel with other divisions of the same company 1 = less than 10%; 2 = between 10% and 80%; 3 = 80% or more
(4) Shared customers	Percentage of sales to customers which are also served by other divisions of the same company 1 = less than 25%; 2 = between 25% and 49%; 3 = between 50% and 74%; 4 = 75% or more
(5) Shared marketing	The extent to which this business' products were handled by the same sales force and/or promoted through the same advertising and sales promotion programs of the other divisions of the same company 1 = less than 10%; 2 = between 10% and 80%; 3 = 80% or more
Corporate financial strength	
(1) Corporate debt to equity	Debt to equity ratio of the corporate parent of this business
(2) Corporate return on equity	Return on equity of the corporate parent of this business estimated by division of corporate growth by corporate retention
(3) Corporate payout	Payout ratio of the corporate parent of this business

REFERENCES

Ansoff, H. I., and J. C. Leontiades, 'Strategic portfolio management', *Journal of General Management*, Autumn 1976, pp. 13–29.

Boston Consulting Group, *Perspectives on Experience*. The Boston Consulting Group, Boston, 1974.

Buzzell, R. D., B. T. Gale, and R. G. M. Sultan, 'Market share—a key to profitability', *Harvard Business Review*, 53(1) (1975), 97–106.

Christensen, H. K., A. C. Cooper, and C. A. de Kluyver, 'The "dog" business: a re-examination', *Academy of Management Proceedings*, 1981, pp. 26–30.

Christensen, H. Kurt, and Cynthia A. Montgomery, 'Corporate economic performance: diversification strategy versus market structure', *Strategic Management Journal*, 2(4) (Oct.–Dec. 1981), 327–343.

Cox, W. E., Jr, 'Product portfolio strategy, market structure and performance', in H. B. Thorelli (ed.), *Strategy + Structure = Performance*. Indiana University Press, Bloomington, 1977, pp. 83–107.

Day, G. S., 'Diagnosing the product portfolio', *Journal of Marketing*, 41 (Apr. 1977), 29–38.

Gale, B. T., 'Market share and rate of return', *Review of Economics and Statistics*, 54(4) (1972), 412–423.

Hamermesh, R. G., M. J. Anderson Jr, and J. E. Harris, 'Strategies for low market share businesses', *Harvard Business Review*, 56(3) (1978), 95–102.

Hedley, B., 'Strategy and the business portfolio', *Long Range Planning*, 10(2) (Feb. 1977), 9–15.

Henderson, Bruce D., *Henderson On Corporate Strategy*. Abt Books, Cambridge, MA, 1979.

Hussey, D. E., 'Portfolio analysis: practical experience with the directional policy matrix', *Long Range Planning*, 11 (Aug. 1978), 2–8.

Imel, Blake, and Peter Helmberger, 'Estimation of structure–profit relationships with application to the food processing sector', *American Economic Review*, 61 (Sept. 1971), 614–627.

Kiechel, III, Walter, 'Oh, where, oh where has my little dog gone? Or my cash cow? Or my star?', *Fortune*, (Nov 2, 1981) 148–154.

Kitching, John, 'Why do mergers miscarry?' *Harvard Business Review*, 45(6), 84–101.

PIMS, *Selected Findings from the PIMS Program*. The Strategic Planning Institute, Cambridge, MA, 1977.

Pitts, R. A., 'Diversification strategies and organization policies of large diversified firms', *Journal of Economics and Business*, 28 (Spring-Summer 1976).

Rumelt, Richard P., *Strategy Structure and Economic Performance*. Harvard Graduate School of Business Administration, Boston, MA, 1974.

Schlaifer, Robert, *Users' Guide to AQD Collection*, 7th edn. Harvard Business School, Cambridge, MA, 1978.

Shepherd, W., 'The elements of market structure', *Review of Economics and Statistics*, 54(1) (1972), 25–37.

Vancil, R. F. (ed.) *Formal Planning Systems* Harvard University Press, Cambridge, Mass. 1971.

Williamson, Oliver E., 'Assessing the modern corporation: transaction cost considerations', *Large Corporations in a Changing Society*. New York University Press, N.Y., 1974.

Wind, Y. and Y. Mahajan, 'Designing product and business portfolios', *Harvard Business Review*, Jan.–Feb. 1981, pp. 155–165.

Woo, Carolyn Y., *Strategies of Effective Low Share Businesses*. Unpublished dissertation, Purdue University, 1979, pp. 161–174.

Woo, C. Y. Y., 'Market share leadership—does it always pay off?', *Academy of Management Proceedings*, 1981, pp. 7–11.

Woo, C. Y. Y., and A. C. Cooper, 'Strategies for effective low share businesses', *Strategic Management Journal*, **2**(3) (July–Sept. 1981), 301–318.

Strategic Marketing and Management
Edited by H. Thomas and D. Gardner
© 1985 John Wiley & Sons Ltd

CHAPTER 7

Conclusions and Future Research Directions

INTRODUCTION

It has been noted elsewhere in this volume that many of the strategic market planning approaches adopted by firms were developed by consulting organizations (BCG, Arthur D. Little, McKinsey, etc.) and by research institutes such as the Strategic Planning Institute (PIMS) sometimes in association with firms such as General Electric. Disenchantment and rejection of some of these approaches has been evident in recent years (Day, 1983; Kiechel, 1981; Wensley, 1982). However, this has been replaced lately by the argument that effective strategic analysis relies on finding that combination of planning approaches which improves management understanding and insight prior to debate about policy choice (Day, 1983; Mason and Mitroff, 1981; Lock and Thomas, 1983).

Wensley (1981), in a much-quoted review of the role of strategic marketing and modelling approaches, states that no one approach or model is the key to achieving the objective of identifying sustainable competitive advantage. Cunningham and Robertson (1983) also note that 'Marketing strategy stresses issues of gaining long run advantage at the level of the firm or strategic business unit and go on to say that "the focus of marketing strategy is on consumer and competitive analyses"' (Editorial to Spring 1983 issue of the *Journal of Marketing*). Larreche and Strong (1982) also concur with the competitive analysis and strategy focus for the marketing strategy discipline advanced by Wensley, Cunningham and Robertson and other marketing strategy researchers.

Wind and Robertson (1983) imply that the relatively recent emergence of the field of marketing strategy may be due in part to a number of limitations with the marketing concept which have been obvious to those active in the marketing field for some time.

Clearly, each of the aforementioned authors see marketing strategy as a stimulus and opportunity for development in the marketing field. Therefore, the aim of this review is to synthesize and predict some of these newer directions and contrast them with the predictions made for the strategic management field in general.

FUTURE DIRECTIONS IN MARKETING STRATEGY

From a review of such writers as Larreche and Strong (1982), Wensley (1981), and Wind and Robertson (1983) it is clear that they see similar needs for research in the strategy field. Larreche and Strong argue that with slackening growth and increasingly sophisticated competition, marketing must integrate and balance the objectives of satisfying customers with the needs to keep ahead of competitors and seek competitive advantage. Wensley believes that the basics must be addressed in marketing strategy. His implied thesis is that marketing problems are now more complex and difficult to formulate. Therefore, there is a need for greater understanding and insight about such factors as the dynamics of markets and theories of market evolution (e.g. how and why strategic segments shift through time). Thus, competitive analyses, along with findings from other planning models (e.g. BCG, PIMS), should be thoroughly reviewed in the strategy formulation process. In other words no single model is a panacea. Problems of marketing strategy will be more effectively handled through generating several views and analyses about those problems and then subjecting them to dialogue and debate by the marketing strategy team.

Wind and Robertson believe that marketing strategy heralds a major opportunity for the marketing field to broaden its perspective. They feel that future research should concentrate upon such areas as the development of better definitions and paradigms for marketing strategy, the formulation of research models and planning methods that are less narrowly based and more appropriate to the current marketing environment, and the construction of new marketing theory focused around a more strategic perspective. Among the limitations they perceive in current marketing theory which they feel the marketing strategy perspective may eliminate are the following (1983; 13):

a fixation with the brand as the unit of analysis;
the interdisciplinary isolation of marketing;
the failure to examine synergy in the design of the marketing program;
marketing's short-term orientation;
the lack of rigorous competitive analysis;
the lack of an international orientation; and
the lack of an integrated strategic framework.

Schendel's paper in this volume (Chapter 1.3) addresses aspects of narrowness, isolation, and rigidity in the marketing function. Schendel argues that organizational changes which have taken place over the last decade have changed the nature of the marketing function. Seeing it in a narrow vein leads some people to argue that strategy-making is a marketing function. Using Hofer and Schendel's (1978) levels of strategy concept as a framework, he postulates that marketing has much to say, through extensive environmental, competitive, and consumer analysis, about how to attain competitive advantage at the business level. However, it may have less to contribute than finance-based approaches at the corporate level.

In summary, it is apparent that the authors cited previously concur about the following points for future directions in the field:

(1) The need to broaden the nature and scope of the marketing function in the light of organizational and enviromental changes.
(2) The need to develop more integrated strategic marketing paradigms. Recent examples include those of Wind and Robertson (1983) and Larreche and Srinavasan (1981). A feature of both these papers was the incorporation of financial portfolio theory into strategic marketing perspective.
(3) The need to develop research methods and planning techniques for handling broader marketing strategy problems.
(4) The hope that marketing strategy perspective might lead to a recasting of some parts of marketing theory. Theory development can flow from current empirical research such as PIMS and be subject to rigorous deductive testing using some of the newer research approaches in (3).

STRATEGIC MARKETING RESEARCH AND STRATEGIC MANAGEMENT RESEARCH

It is fascinating to contrast the future research perceptions of those at the leading edge of the strategic marketing field with similar researchers in the emerging strategic management discipline.

The terms marketing strategy and strategic management are of relatively recent origin. Strategic management (Schendel and Hofer, 1979) is currently the accepted term for the field of business policy and planning. However, as a separate field of study it is still at a fairly young and relatively evolutionary stage.

Strategic management will be interpreted in relation to Schendel and Hofer's (1979) paradigm. This paradigm conceives of the management of strategy as consisting of the following steps and tasks: goal formulation, environmental analysis, strategy formulation, strategy evaluation, and strategy control.

Schendel and Cool (1983: 16) argue that despite the existence of the Schendel and Hofer (1979) paradigm, there is currently no central organizing paradigm for the strategic management field, which makes it very difficult to focus the research energies of the field. We believe, however, that Schendel and Hofer's paradigm is a practical and useful framework with which to consider the research literature in strategic management.

Leading policy academics certainly place different emphases on the relevant areas of research. Anshen and Guth (1973: 499) state that the policy area 'lags all others in the development of a body of theory and formal analytic techniques'. They argue that this lack of theory and formal analytic techniques requires that at least four basic alternative research strategies be adopted to improve research capital of the field. They suggest that these strategies should be as follows. First, the study of science and art in policy formulation. Second, the design and use of analytic concepts and operational approaches. Third, the study of historical relationships and implementation problems. Fourth, the examination of the interface of policy formulation with social problems and with other institutions.

Bower (1982: 632) argues that research in policy should concentrate upon the life-and-death issues of concern to the top management of firms. In the 1980s environment he believes that much greater attention must be directed towards corporate management of the boundaries and interfaces between business and government. In addition, many corporate problems now have a multinational focus involving competition and marketing on a global scale. Bower would like research in this field to be more exploratory and long-range, and seek to identify new problems, with albeit small case-study type samples, in painstaking but scholarly manner. His research strategy is to attack 'the elephants' and enrich the field rather than to pursue 'the ants' by looking at well-structured problems (and 'estimating R squared on relationships that have been recognized to be true since biblical times' (1982: 637). He also recognizes that this research strategy raises the questions of rewards for policy academics. Put another way, can policy researchers be promoted by doing case-studies and action research?

Jemison (1981: 601) states that 'strategic management has reached the point where integrative research approaches are necessary for continued progress in the field'. He advocates the development initially of mid-range theories which draw from, and attempt to integrate, disciplines such as marketing, administrative behaviour, and economics which contribute to our understanding of strategic management. Such mid-range theories then form the basis from which richer integrative, hypotheses-testing research will hopefully emerge. He suggests that opportunities for research cross-fertilization exist in the areas of joint evolution of industries, markets, and organizations; in content and process research integration; and in the domain of inter-organizational analysis.

Saunders and Thompson (1980) analyzed papers submitted for the 1979 Academy of Management meetings in Atlanta in terms of the Schendel/ Hofer classification of the field. They state (1980: 128) that 'As might be expected, smaller-scale investigative undertakings typify the mix of topics, since the narrower compass of "elements" research makes it simpler and more straighforward than "process" research.' This simplicity also makes it attractive for policy researchers aiming for a smooth promotion path. Further, in comparing conceptual with empirical research (1980: 129) they speculate that 'a turn away (in research) from feeble attempts at the insight type and toward hard examination of applicable data in an empirical framework is what is needed now'. They argue that important and valuable conceptual papers are few and far between.

Harrigan (1983) argues that contingency approaches to strategy require new hybrid research methods which combine the depth gained from field study approaches with the analytical rigor associated with significance testing of generalizable hypotheses about business strategy. She states (1983: 398) her position as follows:

> In much existing research, insights gained using 'fine-grained' (Hambrick, 1981) methodologies (such as case studies) lack generalisability and statistical rigor, but 'coarse-grained' methodologies such as the profit impact of market strategies (PIMS) studies, lose the nuances and insights concerning individual firm's strategies that a contingency approach seeks to capture.

Later in the article, citing her own innovative research on declining industries and vertical integration, she gives examples of hybrid designs incorporating attributes of 'fine-grained' and 'coarse-grained' methodologies.

Thomas (1984) advances future research directions for the field in the following terms:

> it would appear that there is a need to continually develop the theory base of the field (using alternative perspectives) and design straategic inquiry systems which adequately model the managerial processes of dialogue and debate prior to choice and action.

None of the authors previously cited believes that research in policy is impossible. However, authors differ in two respects. First, they use varying definitions of what policy research is. Second, they emphasize the importance of different aspects of the field. Bower would argue for the best possible field research involving case inquiry into the behaviour of practitioners followed by conceptualization of this behaviour. This would be carried out in a scholarly manner using carefully specified rules of evidence. The aim is to achieve a careful, accurate description of important issues, problems, and phenomena in the broad general management field, with particular emphasis on management is a 'boundary-spanning' role operating between the organizational, government, and multi-national environments. Saunders and Thompson believe that methodology and empirical research areas should be emphasized. They favor model-building, hypothesis-testing, and new models and techniques for strategy research. Anshen and Guth prescribe a mix of empirical testing and explanatory, conceptual research on a broader strategic canvas (nearer and closer to Andrews' holistic strategy definition) with a clear aim directed toward the promotion of richer theory-building and developing for the field. Jemison, Harrigan, and Thomas, in many respects, echo the position taken by Anshen and Guth but with strong emphasis on the need for integrative, multi-disciplinary and contingency-based research in the field.

Perhaps the strongest point of agreement between those authors would be their lack of interest in well-written but rather empty papers full of conjecture and plausible statements incapable of being tested or further researched. Such offerings typically emanate from practitioners, consultants, and less research-orientated academics. In addition, they might all agree that a mix of exploratory theory-building with scientific hypothesis-testing research would be worthwhile for theory development. They would certainly not agree on the 'weightings' which should be given to the various elements of the mix, and this is a reasonable expectation. As long as the conduct of research involves alternative perspectives and viewpoints, the future diet of researchable topics is likely to be much more extensive, well contructed, and valuable.

Researchers in both strategic marketing and strategic management appear to advance similar topics for future research. They all stress the need for new theory, better research methods and approaches, and more acceptable underlying paradigms emphasizing integration and breadth.

However, there is one major difference between strategic marketing research and strategic management research. Strategic marketing's focus should be directed mainly toward structuring and creating competative advantage mainly at the business unit level of strategy, whereas strategic management encompasses corporate as well as business and functional aspects of strategy.

CONCLUSION

Since strategy's fare is complex, ill-structured problems, it is useful to cast the strategic management process as involving elements of a complex inquiry system based upon the examination of alternative perspectives and a 'simulation' of entrepreneurial activity through institutionalizing the strategy-making process. Therefore a top manager needs first to build his strategic agenda through careful inquiry and examination of his problems in terms of alternative 'mixed scanning frameworks' (so-called 'theories'). Armed with an adequate strategic problem formulation, he can then determine the means of achieving and implementing strategic agendas by examining process aspects in terms of an organizing paradigm such as Schendel and Hofer's. That is, he should examine the degree to which his strategy choice would be consistent with the pressures of the external environment, the corporation's goals and resources including its marketing and competitive expertise, the risk-taking propensities of the corporation, and the culture and value systems embedded within the organization.

REFERENCES

Andrews, K. (1971). *The Concept of Corporate Strategy*. Irwin, Homewood, IL.

Anshen, M., and W. D. Guth (1973). 'Strategies for research in policy formulation', *Journal of Business*, Oct. 1973. pp. 499–511.

Bower, J. L. (1982) 'Business policy in the 1980's', *Academy of Management Review*, 7(4), 630–638.

Cunningham, W. H., and T. S. Robertson (1983). 'From the Editor', *Journal of Marketing*, 47 (Spring), 5–6.

Day, G. S. (1983). Gaining insights through strategy analysis', *Journal of Business Strategy*, 4(1), 51–59.

Hambrick, D. C. (1981). 'Toward an empirical typology of mature business enviroments'. Unpublished manuscript, Columbia University, May.

Harrigan, K. R. (1983). 'Research methodologies for contingency approaches to business statagy', *Academy of Management Review*, 8(3) (July), 398–406.

Hofer, C. W., and D. E. Schendel (1978) *Strategy Formulation: Analytical Concepts*, West Publishing Co., St. Paul, MN.

Jemison, D. B. (1981) 'The importance of an integrative approach to strategic management research', *Academy of Management Review*, 6(4), 601–608.

Kiechel III, W. (1981). 'Oh where, oh where has my little dog gone? or my cash cow? or my star?,' *Fortune*, 2 Nov. pp. 148–154.

Larreche, J. C., and V. Srinavasan (1981) 'STRATPORT: a decision support system for stategic planning', *Journal of Marketing*, 45 (Fall), 39–52.

Larreche, J. C., and E. C. Strong (eds.) (1982) *Readings in Marketing Strategy*. Scientific Press, Palo Alto. CA.

Lock, A. R., and H. Thomas (1983) 'Making policy analysis portable in organizations: the policy dialogue paradigm'. Working Paper, Department of Business Administration, University of Illinois at Urbana-Champaign.

Mason, R. O., and I. I. Mitroff (1981) *Challenging Strategic Planning Assumptions*. John Wiley & Sons, New York.

Saunders, C. B., and J. C. Thompson (1980). A survey of the current state of business policy research', *Strategic Management Journal*, 1 119–130.

Schendel, D. E., and K. Cool (1983). 'Research in strategic management: accomplishments and challenges'. Invited paper at Strategic Management/Business Policy International Symposium, University of Texas at Arlington, February.

Schendel, D. E., and C. W. Hofer (1979) *Strategic Management: A New View of Business Policy and Planning*. Little, Brown, Boston, Mass.

Thomas, H. (1984), 'Mapping strategic management research', *Journal of General Management*, (forthcoming, Summer Issue)

Wensley, J. R. C (1981). 'Strategic marketing: betas, boxes or basics', *Journal of Marketing*, 45 (Summer).

Wensley, J. R. C. (1982). 'PIMS and BCG: new horizons or false dawn', *Strategic management Journal*, 3, 147–158.

Wind, Y., and T. S. Robertson (1983). 'Marketing strategy: new directions for theory and research', *Journal of Marketing*, 47 (Spring), 12–25.

APPENDIX
Marketing strategy and strategic management workshop—participants

ALAN R. ANDREASEN
University of Illinois at
Urbana-Champaign and UCLA

DAVID L. APPEL.
University of Notre Dame

J. SCOTT ARMSTRONG
University of Pennsylvania,
Wharton School

ARNOLD BARBAN
University of Illinois
at Urbana-Champaign

PETER D. BENNETT
Pennsylvania State
University

ROGER BEST
University of Oregon

F. W. A. BLIEMEL
Queens University, Canada

HERBERT BLITZER
Eastman Kodak,
Rochester, N.Y.

SVEIN-ERIK BLOM
Norway

NORMAN R. BRUVOLD
University of Cincinnati

JOHN. F. CADY
Harvard Business School

THERESA CARTER
Sloan School of Management,
MIT

HENRY CLAYCAMP
International Harvester and Purdue
University

JAMES COOK
General Electric Company

ARNIE COOPER
Purdue University

DAVID W. CRAVENS
Texas Christian University

PAUL DAEMEN
Pioneer Hi-Bred

JACK DAVOUST
A. T. Kearney, Inc.

GEORGE S. DAY
University of Toronto

491

RAYMOND J. DEFILIPPO
Country Life Insurance

RONALD J. DORNOFF
University of Cincinnati

IRENE DUHAIME
University of Illinois at
Urbana-Champaign

F. ROBERT DWYER
University of Cincinnati

ROBERT C. EVANS

LIAM FAHEY
Northwestern University

CAROLYN FARQUHAR
The Conference Board of Canada

O. C. FERRELL
Illinois State University and
Texas A and M

PETER D. FITZROY
Monash University, Australia

GARY FRAZIER
University of Illinois at
Urbana-Champaign and USC

DAVID T. FRITZSCHE
Illinois State University

DAVID M. GARDNER
University of Illinois at
Urbana-Champaign

BETSY D. GELB
University of Houston

JIM GENTRY
University of Illinois at
Urbana-Champaign

GEORGE B. GLISAN
Illinois State University

PETER GOULET
University of Northern Iowa

JIM L. GRIMM
Illinois State University

KENNETH L. HATTEN
Boston University

MARY L. HATTEN
Boston College

DEL HAWKINS
University of Oregon

DAVID B. HERTZ
University of Miami at
Coral Gables

ROY HOWELL
University of Illinois at
Urbana-Champaign and Texas
Tech University

HIX HUEGY (Emeritus)
University of Illinois

SUSAN E. HUME
Office of Economic Planning and
Development

JEFFREY A. HUNKER
Boston Consulting Group

HENRIK KALLEN
DeLaval

INDER P. KHERA
Wright State University

CHARLES W. LAMB Jr.
Texas Christian University

KENT M. LANCASTER
University of Illinois at
Urbana-Champaign

DAVID J. LEMAK
USAF Academy

PHILIP KOTLER
Northwestern University

CHARLES LILLIS
General Electric Company

ANDREW R. LOCK
Kingston Polytechnic, England

M. CAROLE MACKLIN
University of Cincinnati

VIJAY MAHAJAN
Wharton School and Southern
Methodist University

JOHN MARTIN
Boston University

JOHN McGEE
London Business School, England

F. EMMETT MEYER
Wabco. Ltd.

BOB MITCHELL
Illinois Agriculture Assn.

DAVID B. MONTGOMERY
Stanford University

ZOFIA MUCHA
Sloan School of Management,
MIT

CHEM L. NARAYANA
University of Illinois at Chicago
Circle

ROBERT NELSON
University of Illinois at Urbana-
Champaign and Texas A and M

NORMAN H. NELSON.
Country Companies

FRANK T. ORTHOEFER
A. E. Staley Manufacturing Co.

EDGAR A. PESSEMIER
Purdue and Virginia

LOUIS R. PONDY
University of Illinois at
Urbana-Champaign

WALTER PRIMEAUX Jr.
University of Illinois at
Urbana–Champaign

DAVID REIBSTEIN
Wharton School, University of
Pennsylvania

WILLIAM T. ROBINSON
University of Michigan

KEN ROERING
University of Minnesota

WILLIAM RUDELIUS
University of Minnesota

ADRIAN RYANS
University of Western Ontario

DAN SCHENDEL
Purdue University

CHARLES SCHWENK
University of Illinois
at Urbana-Champaign

SUBRATA K. SEN
University of Rochester and Yale
University

ALLAN D. SHOCKER
Vanderbilt University

BRYCE SIDES
Country Companies

RAVI SINGH
University of Notre Dame

JAMES P. SPALDING
Spalding & Associates

ROBERT SPEKMAN
University of Maryland

STANLEY STASCH
Loyola University of Chicago

DEVANATHAN SUDHARSHAN
University of Illinois
at Urbana-Champaign

SEYMOUR SUDMAN
University of Illinois
at Urbana-Champaign

GARY L. SULLIVAN
University of Cincinnati

HOWARD THOMAS
University of Illinois
at Urbana-Champaign

DILLARD TINSLEY
Stephen F. Austin State University

GLEN L. URBAN
Sloan School of Management,
MIT

PAUL USELDING
University of Illinois at
Urbana-Champaign

TIMOTHY VANCIL
Indiana Farm Bureau Co-op
Assn.

JOHN L. WARD
Loyola University of
Chicago

PAUL WEINSTEIN
Indiana Farm Bureau Co-op
Assn.

BARTON WEITZ
UCLA and Wharton School,
University of Pennsylvania

ROBIN WENSLEY
London Business School,
England

JEFFREY WILLIAMS
Carnegie–Mellon
University

JERRY WIND
Wharton School,
University of Pennsylvania

RICK WINTER
University of Illinois
at Urbana-Champaign

DICK WITTINK
Cornell University

CAROLYN WOO
Purdue University

LARRY WOODSON
State Farm Insurance Companies

RICHARD WRIGHT
Illinois Agriculture Assn.

Author Index

Subject Index